The
Comprehensive Analysis
of the Bible

MOSES.

BY MICHAELANGELO BUONARROTI (1475-1564).

CHRIST.

BY BERTEL THORWALDSEN (1770-1844).

The
Comprehensive Analysis
of the Bible

BY

MONTGOMERY F. ESSIG

Being an Arrangement of the Topics, Persons, Places, and Things
Mentioned and Discussed in the Old and New Testaments, with
Descriptions, Comments, and the Principal Scriptural References
Thereto, Compiled in Handy Form for the Use of the Bible Reader
and Student; to the Whole Being Added Many New and Valuable
Tables Containing Information upon Biblical Subjects.

THE SOUTHWESTERN COMPANY
NASHVILLE, TENNESSEE

TO ALL MEN

WHO LOVE GOD AND READ HIS WORD

SEEKING BETTER UNDERSTANDING OF THE SAME

THIS BOOK IS DEDICATED

And now unto Thee, O Lord, and to Thy Son, our Saviour, and to the Holy Ghost, proceeding from the Father and the Son, Three Persons and One God, be all glory, laud, and honor, both now and evermore.   Amen.

TABLE OF CONTENTS

INTRODUCTION. By George A. Lofton, A.M., D.D., LL.D.....Page 21

AUTHOR'S FOREWORD......................................Page 23

THE COMPREHENSIVE ANALYSIS

13

TABLE OF CONTENTS

TABLE OF CONTENTS

TABLE OF CONTENTS

TABLE OF CONTENTS

TABLE OF CONTENTS

TABLE OF CONTENTS

TABLE OF CONTENTS

INTRODUCTION

BY GEORGE A. LOFTON, A.M., D.D., LL.D.

THE one indispensable book is the Bible. It is God's literature, and, as such, is essential to the salvation and civilization of the world. In this age, when the Holy Scriptures are obtainable at a price within the reach of the poorest, it is certainly a personal misfortune and almost a religious crime not to have read and diligently studied the divine work. Not only is the Bible the Christian's text-book, but it is a mine illuminated by God's Holy Spirit wherein may be found gems and jewels of untold spiritual and moral wealth, no matter how simple in mind or humble in station may be the person who delves in it. Again, it is a storehouse of religious sustenance, a vast granary to provide humanity with the true Bread of Life, and God has given the keys of it to every man. Again, it is a fountain of wisdom, ceaselessly sending forth its waters of knowledge. And to the philosopher, the poet, the statesman, the educator, and the citizen it is the guide to all goodness and virtue. Assuredly, whatever else man can do without in the way of literature he must have the Bible.

And yet, of all the books in the world, and despite its sacred nature and its richness, the Bible is the most carelessly read and the most inefficiently studied. Alas! that it should be said, it nevertheless is a fact that the great bulk of Bible reading is without system or seriousness; that it is haphazard; and that a vast amount of spiritual profit is lost or overlooked or let go to waste. Since we have the Bible, and it cannot be taken away from us, the matter of chief importance, then, is how to read and study it to the best advantage. These things we are commanded to do when we are told to search and understand its golden pages, and in this respect the *how* is next in importance to the *what*. True, many Christians read a chapter of the Bible every day. But simple reading is not all that is required. Thought, comparison, and close attention are quite as essential. The man or woman who reads but a verse daily and masters its outward and inward meanings, who finds its relation to other verses in the same book or in other books, who classifies it in its proper place with regard to the thought or topic it illumines or suggests, is doing a great deal more toward appreciating the Holy Book at its true value and toward becoming a good Bible scholar than the careless reader of a whole chapter. Indeed, the greater the amount of reading without study the greater the amount of spiritual loss. A very simple and homely illustration will prove this: It would be foolish and senseless to eat two breakfasts. The result would be a very bad case of indigestion, since the stomach was made to digest and assimilate but one meal at a time. On the same basis, the human mind cannot overload itself.

To be effective, Bible reading and study should be done with all the helps and aids the reader or student can secure. Many editions of the Book now printed contain such features in a more or less perfect shape, while nearly every Bible that comes from the press is accompanied by references and a concordance. Few of them, however, are in a form suited to the needs of the average person. It is true that ministers and advanced students are sufficiently familiar with the Scriptures and the use of references and concordances to handle them with advantage; but it is not so with the general reader or the person who has just come to a knowledge of what serious Bible study means. There is, therefore, a very great need for a first-class reference text-book on the Bible —a work that will give an arrangement of Scripture by topics and setting forth what God's Word says on any given subject. Such a book cannot be a concordance, a subject-index, a dictionary, or a cyclopedia as a whole; but it must partake of the nature of all of these and contain certain other analytical features as well.

With a view to filling this need and to the high and holy purpose of leading people to read, study, and understand the Word of God, the present volume, THE COMPREHENSIVE ANALYSIS OF THE BIBLE has been written. It combines the cyclopedia, the reference book, the dictionary, and the commentary all in one, conveniently arranged in alphabetical order and treating all the leading subjects of revelation in such a simple and lucid manner as to afford abundant help to the reader of Scripture, no matter whether he be pursuing a thorough study of the whole or simply seeking to inform himself upon any given subject or topic of the sacred canon. Although not intended to be exhaustive, the work is voluminous, diligently and carefully studied, and luminously presented. While not entirely agreeing with the author in some of his interpretations, he has given to the world a vast amount of Biblical knowledge in such compact and intelligible form as largely to enhance interest in the study of Holy Writ. One of the book's chief excellencies is its wealth of Scriptural references, and the setting-out in full of these references under each subject in support of the many definitions, comments, and topical discussions.

Geo. A. Loyton.

AUTHOR'S FOREWORD

Purposes of the Work. THE chief purpose of this work is to provide a ready reference book on the Bible, the need for which long has been manifest. While it is true that almost all Bibles are supplied with references, they are not in such shape as to be handled with ease and intelligence by all Bible readers. Very often they are arranged in such a way that none but a minister or an advanced Bible student can follow them to advantage and get from them just exactly what is wanted. Still more often they are not sufficiently full to meet the requirements of the person searching the Scriptures. A third difficulty is that, in going from one reference to another, the mind of the student becomes confused and the real end of research is lost in the maze of conflicting ideas and thoughts encountered by the searcher. This obstacle to the attainment of Biblical knowledge often confronts the trained intellect of the minister or the student. How much more of a barrier is it then to the untrained person seeking further and deeper acquaintance with the vast wealth of religious treasure and thought contained in the Holy Book?

To overcome this difficulty many methods have been devised at various times, but only a few of them have proved successful. The only perfect way is to set out all references in full. By this plan the reader has ever before the eye just exactly what the Bible has to say upon a subject, thus doing away with long and confusing searches from book to book, chapter to chapter, and verse to verse, a task which often results in the searcher losing the kernel of thought in the last reference read. This perfect way has been followed in the ensuing pages. Moreover, it has been the effort so to arrange all topics and references that finding a given topic and gathering the various allusions to it throughout the Bible will be a simple matter. Simplicity of arrangement and style has been observed from the first page to the last, both for the sake of making the work perfectly intelligible and for the saving of space.

So far as is possible, each person, place, or topic discussed has been explained before the references to it are given, and in these explanations the latest thought and comment upon the subject set down for the benefit of the reader. In many instances, subjects are treated upon which there are differences of thought according to differences in denominational belief and theology. But in no instance of this character has the author permitted himself to be influenced by any considerations of denominational doctrine whatever. It has been his sole aim to set forth plain facts of a nature that all persons, no matter what their shade of faith, can accept. THE COMPREHENSIVE ANALYSIS OF THE BIBLE is designed to be a work of reference for the Bible reader and the Bible student of all denominations, catering neither to the one nor to the other, and aiming simply to throw as much light upon the Scriptures as careful preparation and research will enable and the difficulties of the task will allow.

AUTHOR'S FOREWORD

Plan of the Work. It has been deemed best, throughout the body of the book, to adopt the alphabetical arrangement in the treatment of the subjects discussed. This eliminates the possibility of having to weigh questions of precedence or importance, besides greatly simplifying the work so that the reader can experience no difficulty in finding any given topic. In the handling of a subject a description or explanation is first given, and following this come the references to it, quoted in full and with book, chapter, and verse number attached. These references are arranged, so far as possible, in the order in which they appear in the Bible. In the case of a person, the references give an outline of his or her life. In the case of a topic, they are arranged under logical subdivisions, showing the various phases, attributes, or characteristics of it.

As it is manifestly impossible, by reason of the limitations of a single volume, to give every reference to a subject in full, care has been taken to give the more important ones in that fashion, and then, in the shape of additional ones, the book, chapter, and verse of those that are of less importance.

Cross references are given wherever it is possible so to do, in order that the reader may keep in complete touch with any given subject by referring to collateral and related subjects. Careful study of these cross references will be found to be very beneficial, throwing a vast amount of light, additional to the regular references, upon the subject under consideration. An instance of this may be found in the topic of Aaron. The reader, on beginning to investigate Aaron, will find that attention is also directed to Moses, Aaron's brother; to Miriam, his sister; and to the priesthood, of which Aaron was the first chief.

In still another respect an effort has been made to simplify reading and study. Bold face letters at the top of each column tell what is discussed in it, enabling the reader to turn over the leaves rapidly to the place or thing for which search is being made. Bold face letters are used as captions for each subject and subdivision, thus bringing each point sharply before the reader's eye.

In the matter of tables care has been taken to make the arrangement simple and easily understood. Tables very often are confusing to persons unaccustomed to their use; but when once the mind grasps the form in which they are arranged, they are one of the very best of mediums for conveying information in a terse and handy manner.

With regard to the plan for a year's Bible-reading, it is offered for the benefit of those who care to take advantage of it. No special merit is claimed for it so far as educational value is concerned. It is rather more of a series of daily mottoes or thoughts than anything else, put down as a sort of a spiritual food. The writer is firmly convinced that no method of Bible-reading which insists upon the perusal of a full chapter or more each day is of real educational value, so far as Biblical knowledge is concerned. No man can become a Bible scholar in a year by simply dividing the Scriptures into 365 parts for daily reading. The Scriptures need to be studied slowly and carefully if the reader aspires to real scholarship. M. F. E.

THE COMPREHENSIVE ANALYSIS OF THE BIBLE

AARON. (See Miriam, Moses, Priesthood.)

Aar'on (pronounced aron or airon). Name means "mountaineer" or "enlightener." Was the eldest son of Amram and Jochebed, direct descendants of Levi, and brother of Miriam and Moses. Born about 1725 B.C., three years before Moses. Divinely appointed to be Moses' interpreter and "mouth" because of his eloquence, Moses being "slow of speech." Married Elisheba, and had four sons, Nadab, Abihu, Eleazar and Ithamar. About 83 years old when first seen in the Bible. Aided his brother in bringing about the Exodus and worked miracles at the court of the Pharaoh. Yielded to idolatry when Moses went up on Mount Sinai to receive the law and made a golden calf for the worship of the Israelites. Repented, was forgiven, and was made high-priest, the first of the line. Filled the office for forty years. Was confirmed in it by several acts of God, notably that of the budding of his rod into a yielding almond tree. Fell under God's displeasure, when, with his brother Moses, he showed unbelief at the striking of the rock of Meribah. Punished like Moses by being barred from entering the Promised Land. Died (about 1602 B.C.) on Mount Hor, after turning over his robes and office to his son Eleazar, and thus founding in his family the succession to the high-priesthood.

Aaron's character was a strange one, although very human. He was impulsive and likely to yield to temptation and loneliness. He depended much on his brother and often made serious mistakes when not advised by him. He was devoted to God's work, however, and was capable of making great sacrifices for his faith. He sincerely loved his people and always wanted to aid them.

REFERENCES.

Chosen to Aid Moses.

And the anger of the Lord was kindled against Moses, and he said, Is not Aaron the Levite thy brother? I know that he can speak well. And also, behold, he cometh forth to meet thee: and when he seeth thee, he will be glad in his heart.

And thou shalt speak unto him, and put words in his mouth: and I will be with thy mouth, and with his mouth, and will teach you what ye shall do.

And he shall be thy spokesman unto the people: and he shall be, even he shall be to thee instead of a mouth, and thou shalt be to him instead of God. (Exodus 4: 14-16.)

And the Lord said to Aaron, Go into the wilderness to meet Moses. And he went, and met him in the mount of God, and kissed him.

And Moses told Aaron all the words of the Lord who had sent him, and all the signs which he had commanded him.

And Moses and Aaron went, and gathered together all the elders of the children of Israel. (Exodus 4: 27-29.)

And afterward Moses and Aaron went in, and told Pharaoh, Thus saith the Lord God of Israel, Let my people go, that they may hold a feast unto me in the wilderness. (Exodus 5: 1.)

Works Miracles.

And they did so as the Lord had commanded: and Aaron cast down his rod before Pharaoh, and before his servants, and it became a serpent. (Exodus 7: 10.)

25

And Moses and Aaron did so, as the Lord commanded; and he lifted up the rod and smote the waters that were in the river, in the sight of Pharaoh, and in the sight of his servants; and all the waters that were in the river were turned into blood. (Exodus 7: 20.)

And Aaron stretched out his hand over the waters of Egypt; and the frogs came up, and covered the land of Egypt. (Exodus 8: 6.)

And they did so; for Aaron stretched out his hand with his rod, and smote the dust of the earth, and it became lice in man and in beast: all the dust of the land became lice throughout all the land of Egypt. (Exodus 8: 17.)

And the Lord said unto Moses and unto Aaron, Take to you handfuls of ashes of the furnace, and let Moses sprinkle it toward the heaven in the sight of Pharaoh. (Exodus 9: 8.)

And they took ashes of the furnace, and stood before Pharaoh; and Moses sprinkled it up toward heaven: and it became a boil breaking forth with blains upon man, and upon beast. (Exodus 9: 10.)

Holds Moses' Hands.

Then came Amalek, and fought with Israel in Rephidim.

And Moses said unto Joshua, Choose us out men, and go out, fight with Amalek: to-morrow I will stand on the top of the hill with the rod of God in mine hand. (Exodus 17: 8, 9.)

And it came to pass, when Moses held up his hand, that Israel prevailed: and when he let down his hand, Amalek prevailed.

But Moses' hands were heavy; and they took a stone, and put it under him, and he sat thereon: and Aaron and Hur stayed up his hands, the one on the one side, and the other on the other side; and his hands were steady until the going down of the sun. (Exodus 17: 11, 12.)

Priesthood and Sins.

And take thou unto thee Aaron thy brother, and his sons with him, from among the children of Israel, that he may minister unto me in the priest's office, even Aaron, Nadab and Abihu, Eleazar and Ithamar, Aaron's sons. (Exodus 28: 1.)

And all the people brake off the golden ear-rings which were in their ears, and brought them unto Aaron.

And he received them at their hand, and fashioned it with a graving tool, after he had made it a molten calf: and they said, These be thy gods, O Israel, which brought thee up out of the land of Egypt. (Exodus 32: 3, 4.)

And Aaron said, Let not the anger of my lord wax hot: thou knowest the people, that they are set on mischief. (Exodus 32: 22.)

And Nadab and Abihu, the sons of Aaron, took either of them his censer, and put fire therein, and put incense thereon, and offered strange fire before the Lord, which he commanded them not.

And there went out fire from the Lord, and devoured them, and they died before the Lord. (Leviticus 10: 1, 2.)

And the Lord spake unto Aaron, saying,

Do not drink wine nor strong drink, thou, nor thy sons with thee, when ye go into the tabernacle of the congregation, lest ye die; it shall be a statute for ever throughout your generations. (Leviticus 10: 8, 9.)

And Miriam and Aaron spake against Moses because of the Ethiopian woman whom he had married: for he had married an Ethiopian woman.

And they said, Hath the Lord indeed spoken only by Moses? hath he not spoken also by us? And the Lord heard it. (Numbers 12: 1, 2.)

And the anger of the Lord was kindled against them; and he departed.

And the cloud departed from off the tabernacle; and behold, Miriam became leprous, white as snow: and Aaron looked upon Miriam, and behold, she was leprous.

And Aaron said unto Moses, Alas, my lord, I beseech thee, lay not the sin upon us, wherein we have done foolishly, and wherein we have sinned. (Numbers 12: 9-11.)

Stays Plague after Korah's Rebellion.

Now Korah, the son of Izhar, the son of Kohath, the son of Levi; and Dathan and Abiram, the sons of Eliab; and On, the son of Peleth, sons of Reuben, took men;

And they rose up before Moses, with certain of the children of Israel, two hundred and fifty princes of the assembly, famous in the congregation, men of renown:

And they gathered themselves together against Moses and against Aaron, and said unto them, Ye take too much upon you, seeing all the congregation are holy, every one of them, and the Lord is among them: wherefore then lift ye up yourselves above the congregation of the Lord? (Numbers 16: 1-3.)

And Moses said unto Aaron, Take a censer, and put fire therein from off the altar, and put on incense, and go quickly unto the congregation, and make an atonement for them: for there is wrath

gone out from the Lord; the plague is begun.

And Aaron took as Moses commanded, and ran into the midst of the congregation; and behold, the plague was begun among the people: and he put on incense, and made an atonement for the people.

And he stood between the dead and the living; and the plague was stayed. (Numbers 16: 46-48.)

Confirmed as High-Priest.

And it came to pass, that on the morrow Moses went into the tabernacle of witness; and behold, the rod of Aaron for the house of Levi was budded, and brought forth buds, and bloomed blossoms, and yielded almonds. (Numbers 17: 8.)

And the Lord said unto Aaron, Thou, and thy sons, and thy father's house with thee, shall bear the iniquity of the sanctuary: and thou and thy sons with thee shall bear the iniquity of your priesthood. (Numbers 18: 1.)

Final Sin and Punishment.

And the Lord spake unto Moses, saying,

Take the rod, and gather thou the assembly together, thou and Aaron thy brother, and speak ye unto the rock before their eyes; and it shall give forth his water, and thou shalt bring forth to them water out of the rock: so thou shalt give the congregation and their beasts drink.

And Moses took the rod from before the Lord, as he commanded him.

And Moses and Aaron gathered the congregation together before the rock, and he said unto them, Hear now, ye rebels; must we fetch you water out of this rock?

And Moses lifted up his hand, and with his rod he smote the rock twice: and the water came out abundantly, and the congregation drank, and their beasts also.

And the Lord spake unto Moses and Aaron, Because ye believed me not, to sanctify me in the eyes of the children of Israel, therefore ye shall not bring this congregation into the land which I have given them. (Numbers 20: 7-12.)

Death of Aaron.

And Moses did as the Lord commanded: and they went up into mount Hor in the sight of all the congregation.

And Moses stripped Aaron of his garments, and put them upon Eleazar his son; and Aaron died there in the top of the mount: and Moses and Eleazar came down from the mount. (Numbers 20: 27, 28.)

Additional References.—Exodus 14: 1-11; Exodus 29; Leviticus 8; Psalms 105: 26; 1 Chronicles 6: 49; Hebrews 5: 4.

AARONITES.

AA'RON-ITES—the Israelitish priesthood of the family of Aaron and the tribe of Levi; mostly those who served in the sanctuary and in David's time a most important family. They give him 3,700 fighting men at Hebron.

REFERENCES.

And when the camp setteth forward, Aaron shall come, and his sons, and they shall take down the covering vail, and cover the ark of testimony with it. (Numbers 4: 5.)

And Jehoiada was the leader of the Aaronites, and with him were three thousand and seven hundred. (1 Chronicles 12: 27.)

ABADDON. (See Hell.)

A-BAD'DON—a Hebrew word meaning "destruction" or "place of the dead." It was applied to the angel of the bottomless pit by John in Revelation. The Greek rendering of the word is Apollyon. In the Old Testament wherever the word occurs it is translated "destruction" or "place of the dead."

REFERENCES.

And the fifth angel sounded, and I saw a star fall from heaven unto the earth: and to him was given the key of the bottomless pit.

And he opened the bottomless pit; and there arose a smoke out of the pit, as the smoke of a great furnace; and the sun and the air were darkened by reason of the smoke of the pit.

And there came out of the smoke locusts upon the earth: and unto them was given power, as the scorpions of the earth have power. (Revelation 9: 1-3.)

And they had a king over them, which is the angel of the bottomless pit, whose name in the Hebrew tongue is Abaddon, but in the Greek tongue hath his name Apollyon. (Revelation 9: 11.)

ABARIM.

AB'A-RIM—a chain of high mountains east of the Dead Sea and the lower Jordan. From one of the highest of these, Mount Nebo, Moses caught a glimpse of the Promised Land. Pisgah is supposed to have been the pinnacle of Nebo rather than a separate peak. Modern research has identified a mountain of the Abarim range called Attarous as the probable Nebo. It is the highest of the chain, barren and stony, and gives a splendid view of the Promised Land.

REFERENCES.

And the Lord said unto Moses, Get thee up into this mount Abarim, and see the land which I have given unto the children of Israel. (Numbers 27: 12.)

And the Lord spake unto Moses that selfsame day, saying,

Get thee up into this mountain Abarim, unto mount Nebo, which is in the land of Moab, that is over against Jericho; and behold the land of Canaan which I give unto the children of Israel for a possession:

And die in the mount whither thou goest up, and be gathered unto thy people; as Aaron thy brother died in mount Hor, and was gathered unto his people. (Deuteronomy 32: 48-50.)

And Moses went up from the plains of Moab, unto the mountain of Nebo, to the top of Pisgah, that is over against Jericho: and the Lord shewed him all the land of Gilead. (Deuteronomy 34: 1.)

ABASE.

A-BASE'—to make low, to humble.

REFERENCES.

Cast abroad the rage of thy wrath: and behold every one that is proud, and abase him. (Job 40: 11.)

Thus saith the Lord God; Remove the diadem, and take off the crown: this shall not be the same: exalt him that is low, and abase him that is high. (Ezekiel 21: 26.)

Now I Nebuchadnezzar praise and extol and honor the King of heaven, all whose works are truth, and his ways judgment: and those that walk in pride he is able to abase. (Daniel 4: 37.)

And whosoever shall exalt himself, *shall be abased; and he that shall humble himself, shall be exalted.* (Matthew 23: 12.)

Additional References.—Luke 14: 11; Luke 18: 14; Philippians 4: 12; 2 Corinthians 11: 7.

ABBA.

AB'BA—a very ancient word meaning "father." In the Hebrew it is "awb," "abba" being the Chaldee form. Jesus used it to indicate the Father, and the New Testament writers in many instances used it also rather than the Greek form, equivalent to "papa," for the purpose of giving greater emphasis and dignity.

REFERENCES.

And he said, Abba, Father, all things are possible unto thee; take away this cup from me: nevertheless, not what I will, but what thou wilt. (Matthew 14: 36.)

For ye have not received the spirit of bondage again to fear; but ye have received the Spirit of adoption, whereby we cry, Abba, Father. (Romans 8: 15.)

And because ye are sons, God hath sent forth the Spirit of his Son into your hearts, crying, Abba, Father. (Galatians 4: 6.)

ABEDNEGO. (See Daniel, Shadrach, and Meshach.)

A-BED'NE-GO—meaning "the servant of Nego." The word is the Chaldee form of a name given to Azariah, one of the three companions of Daniel. With Shadrach and Meshach he was miraculously delivered from Nebuchadnezzar's fiery furnace, into which he had been cast for refusing to worship that king's great image. Some commentaries have erroneously supposed Azariah to have been the prophet Ezra. Ezra, however, was a Levite and priest, while Azariah was of royal or Judean blood.

REFERENCES.

Now, among these were of the children of Judah, Daniel, Hananiah, Mishael, and Azariah:

Unto whom the prince of the eunuchs gave names: for he gave unto Daniel the name of Belteshazzar; and to Hananiah, of Shadrach; and to Mishael, of Meshach; and to Azariah, of Abednego. (Daniel 1: 6, 7.)

Then Daniel requested of the king, and he set Shadrach, Meshach, and Abednego, over the affairs of the province of Babylon; but Daniel sat in the gate of the king. (Daniel 2: 49.)

And these three men, Shadrach, Meshach, and Abednego, fell down bound into the midst of the burning fiery furnace. (Daniel 3: 23.)

Then the king promoted Shadrach, Meshach, and Abednego, in the province of Babylon. (Daniel 3: 30.)

ABEL. (See Adam, Cain, Eve.)

A′BEL—a form of the Hebrew word Hebel, meaning "weakness" or "breath," and the name of Adam's second son. The story of the murder of Abel by Cain is told in Genesis 4. Much has been written by commentators on the mystical character of Abel and the meaning of his death. Chrysostom calls him "the lamb of Christ" because of the injuries he suffered. Augustine says he represents the new or spiritual man as opposed to the natural or corrupt man. The Jews long held a tradition that the plain of Damascus was the scene of the murder, but there is nothing to support it.

REFERENCES.

And Adam knew Eve his wife; and she conceived, and bare Cain, and said, I have gotten a man from the Lord.

And she again bare his brother Abel: and Abel was a keeper of sheep, but Cain was a tiller of the ground.

And in process of time it came to pass, that Cain brought of the fruit of the ground an offering unto the Lord.

And Abel, he also brought of the firstlings of his flock, and of the fat thereof. And the Lord had respect unto Abel, and to his offering.

But unto Cain, and to his offering, he had not respect: and Cain was very wroth, and his countenance fell.

And the Lord said unto Cain, Why art thou wroth? and why is thy countenance fallen?

If thou doest well, shalt thou not be accepted? and if thou doest not well, sin lieth at the door: and unto thee shall be his desire, and thou shalt rule over him.

And Cain talked with Abel his brother: and it came to pass when they were in the field, that Cain rose up against Abel his brother, and slew him. (Genesis 4: 1-8.)

That upon you may come all the righteous blood shed upon the earth, from the blood of righteous Abel, unto the blood of Zacharias, son of Barachias, whom ye slew between the temple and the altar. (Matthew 23: 35.)

By faith Abel offered unto God a more excellent sacrifice than Cain, by which he obtained witness that he was righteous, God testifying of his gifts: and by it he being dead yet speaketh. (Hebrews 11: 4.)

And to Jesus the Mediator of the new covenant, and to the blood of sprinkling, that speaketh better things than that of Abel. (Hebrews 12: 24.)

Not as Cain, who was of that wicked one, and slew his brother. And wherefore slew he him? Because his own works were evil, and his brother's righteous. (1 John 3: 12.)

ABEL.

A'BEL—a from of the Hebrew word "awb-ale," meaning "grassy place" or "meadow." It is found in many places in the Old Testament as a part of a compound name of a village or a place.

References.—Genesis 50: 11; Numbers 33: 49; Judges 7: 22; 1 Kings 4: 12; 19: 16; 1 Samuel 6: 18.

ABIATHAR.

A-BI'A-THAR—meaning "father of abundance." Was thirteenth high-priest of Israel and fourth in line from Eli. Escaped Saul's persecutions and fled to David. Was made joint high-priest with Zadok by David and was deposed by Solomon for taking part in the conspiracy to put Adonijah on the throne, thus sealing the doom of the house of Eli pronounced by Samuel.

REFERENCES.

And one of the sons of Ahimelech the son of Ahitub, named Abiathar, escaped, and fled after David. (1 Samuel 22: 20.)

And it came to pass, when Abiathar the son of Ahimelech fled to David to Keilah, that he came down with an ephod in his hand. (1 Samuel 23: 6.)

And Zadok the son of Ahitub, and Ahimelech the son of Abiathar, were the priests; and Seraiah was the scribe. (2 Samuel 8: 17.)

And king Solomon answered and said unto his mother, And why dost thou ask Abishag the Shunammite for Adonijah? ask for him the kingdom also; for he is mine elder brother; even for him, and for Abiathar the priest, and for Joab the son of Zeruiah. (1 Kings 2: 22.)

So Solomon thrust out Abiathar from being priest unto the Lord; that he might fulfil the word of the Lord, which he spake concerning the house of Eli in Shiloh. (1 Kings 2: 27.)

How he went into the house of God, in the days of Abiathar the high priest, and did eat the shew-bread, which is not lawful to eat, but for the priests, and gave also to them which were with him? (Mark 2: 26.)

ABIDE.

A-BIDE'—dwell, sit, settle, stay.

REFERENCES.

Lord, who shall abide in thy tabernacle? who shall dwell in thy holy hill? (Psalm 15: 1.)

I will abide in thy tabernacle for ever: I will trust in the covert of thy wings. Selah. (Psalm 61: 4.)

He that dwelleth in the secret place of the Most High shall abide under the shadow of the Almighty. (Psalm 91: 1.)

And when Jesus came to the place, he looked up, and saw him, and said unto him, *Zaccheus, make haste, and come down: for to-day I must abide at thy house.* (Mark 19: 5.)

I am come a light into the world, that whosoever believeth on me should not abide in darkness. (John 12: 46.)

ABIGAIL. (See David.)

AB'I-GAIL—a form of a Hebrew word meaning "father of joy," "delight," or "exultation." The Bible tells of two women named Abigail. The lesser of the two was David's sister. The more important was the wife of Nabal, who by her prudence in averting David's wrath from her husband won his regard and at Nabal's death became David's wife, sharing all his future fortunes. She is said to have been a woman of much beauty as well as discretion. She bore him one or two sons.

REFERENCES.

Now the name of the man was Nabal; and the name of his wife Abigail: and she was a woman of good understanding, and of a beautiful countenance: but the man was churlish and evil in his doings; and he was of the house of Caleb. (1 Samuel 25: 3.)

And when David heard that Nabal was dead, he said, Blessed be the Lord, that hath pleaded the cause of my reproach from the hand of Nabal, and hath kept his servant from evil: for the Lord hath returned the wickedness of Nabal upon his own head. And David sent and communed with Abigail, to take her to him to wife. (1 Samuel 25: 39.)

And David dwelt with Achish at Gath, he and his men, every man with his household, even David with his two wives, Ahinoam the Jezreelitess, and Abigail the Carmelitess, Nabal's wife. (1 Samuel 27: 3.)

Additional References.—1 Samuel 30: 5; 2 Samuel 2: 2; 2 Samuel 3: 3.

ABIHU.

A-BI'HU—a form of a Hebrew word meaning "to whom God is father." One of the two sons of Aaron consumed by fire from heaven for offering strange fire on the altar. It was the duty of Abihu and his brother Nadab to keep up the fire on the altar and to use it only in burning the incense. Failure to do this and the use of fire from elsewhere in the censers brought about the punishment. It is presumed they were drunk, as wine was forbidden the priesthood immediately after.

REFERENCES.

And Aaron took him Elisheba daughter of Amminadab, sister of Naashon to wife; and she bare him Nadab and Abihu, Eleazar and Ithamar. (Exodus 6: 23.)

And Nadab and Abihu, the sons of Aaron, took either of them his censer, and put fire therein, and put incense thereon, and offered strange fire before the Lord, which he commanded them not.

And there went out fire from the Lord, and devoured them, and they died before the Lord. (Leviticus 10: 1, 2.)

ABIMELECH.

A-BIM'E-LECH—a form of a Hebrew word meaning "father of the king." The name appears to have been chiefly given to a line of Philistine rulers much the same as Cæsar or Pharaoh was given to Roman and Egyptian rulers. Both Abraham and Isaac had trouble with Abimelechs, and from the same cause—the desire on the part of the Philistine to possess Sarah and Rebekah (Rebecca). The troubles were settled in the same way, amicably and with covenant. One or two other unimportant Abimelechs appear in the Old Testament.

References.—Genesis 20: 2; 21: 22; 26: 1-16; Judges 8: 31; 2 Samuel 11: 21; 1 Chronicles 18: 16.

ABINADAB.

A-BIN'A-DAB—a form of a Hebrew word meaning "father of generosity." The name is given to several Bible characters, the chief of them being the Levite of Kirjath-jearim, to whose house the Ark of the Covenant was brought after its return from the land of the Philistines, resting with him twenty years.

References.—1 Samuel 7: 1; 2 Samuel 6: 3.

ABISHAG. (See Adonijah, Bathsheba, David, Solomon.)

AB'I-SHAG—a form of a Hebrew word meaning "the father of error." The name of a beautiful young woman placed in the harem of David in his old age to minister specially to him. After David's death, Adonijah, his eldest son, wanted Abishag, and she became a part of the conspiracy against Solomon that resulted in Adonijah's death.

REFERENCES.

So they sought for a fair damsel throughout all the coasts of Israel, and found Abishag a Shunammite, and brought her to the king. (1 Kings 1: 3.)

And he said, Speak, I pray thee, unto Solomon the king, (for he will not say thee nay,) that he give me Abishag the Shunammite to wife. (1 Kings 1: 17.)

And she said, Let Abishag the Shunammite be given to Adonijah thy brother to wife.

And king Solomon answered and said unto his mother, And why dost thou ask Abishab the Shunammite for Adonijah? ask for him the kingdom also; for he is mine elder brother. (1 Kings 2: 21, 22.)

ABNER. (See David, Joab, Saul.)

AB'NER—a form of a Hebrew word meaning "father of light." The name of a well-known character who lived in the time of Saul and David, about 1000 B.C. He was a full cousin to Saul and commander of his army. After Saul's death at Gilboa he took advantage of his influence with the element adverse to David and made Saul's imbecile son, Ishbosheth, king and assumed the government for him. During the war that followed he slew Asahel, Joab's brother. Later he abandoned Ishbosheth's cause and went over to David, who received him with great honor. Joab, however, had sworn blood revenge against Abner, and at the first opportunity killed him. David paid him the honor of following his body to the grave.

REFERENCES.

And Kish was the father of Saul; and Ner the father of Abner was the son of Abiel. (1 Samuel 14: 51.)

And when Saul saw David go forth against the Philistine, he said unto Abner the captain of the host, Abner, whose son is this youth? And Abner said, As thy soul liveth, O King, I cannot tell. (1 Samuel 17: 55.)

So David and Abishai came to the people by night: and behold, Saul lay sleeping within the trench, and his spear stuck in the ground at his bolster: but Abner and the people lay round about him. (1 Samuel 26: 7.)

And David cried to the people, and to Abner the son of Ner, saying, Answerest thou not, Abner? Then Abner answered and said, Who art thou that criest to the king? (1 Samuel 26: 14.)

So Joab and Abishai his brother slew Abner, because he had slain their brother Asahel at Gibeon in the battle.

And David said to Joab, and to all the people that were with him, Rend your clothes, and gird you with sackcloth, and mourn before Abner. And king David himself followed the bier.

And they buried Abner in Hebron: and the king lifted up his voice and wept at the grave of Abner; and all the people wept. (2 Samuel 3: 30-32.)

ABOMINATION.

A-BOM'I-NA'TION—the feeling of extreme disgust and abhorrence; that which causes disgust and loathing. The term in the Bible is applied to objects of detestation, to impure or detestable actions, to things causing ceremonial pollution, and especially to idols and food of a forbidden nature. The Egyptians considered themselves defiled by eating with Jews, who ate the meat of cows, which animals were sacred to the Egyptians. To the Jew the flesh of swine was an abomination, although the Egyptians ate it. To the Jew the idols and sacred animals of the Egyptians, Assyrians, Babylonians, and the other idolatrous nations about them were abominations. "The abominations of desolation" to which Jesus and Daniel referred are believed to have been the idolatrous practices of the conquerors of Jerusalem, with special reference by

Jesus to the military standards of the Romans, upon which were images to which certain religious honors were paid.

REFERENCES.

Abomination of Desolation.

And he shall confirm the covenant with many for one week: and in the midst of the week he shall cause the sacrifice and the oblation to cease, and for the overspreading of abominations, he shall make it desolate, even until the consummation, and that determined shall be poured upon the desolate. (Daniel 9: 27.)

And from the time that the daily sacrifice shall be taken away, and the abomination that maketh desolate set up, there shall be a thousand two hundred and ninety days. (Daniel 12: 11.)

And arms shall stand on his part, and they shall pollute the sanctuary of strength, and shall take away the daily sacrifice, and they shall place the abomination that maketh desolate. (Daniel 11: 31.)

But when ye shall see the abomination of desolation spoken of by Daniel the Prophet, standing where it ought not (let him that readeth understand), then let them that be in Judea flee to the mountains. (Mark 13: 14.)

Abominations of National Character.

When thou art come into the land which the Lord thy God giveth thee, thou shalt not learn to do after the abominations of those nations. (Deuteronomy 18: 9.)

For all that do these things are an abomination unto the Lord: and because of these abominations the Lord thy God doth drive them out from before thee. (Deuteronomy 18: 12.)

Wherefore, as I live, saith the Lord God; Surely, because thou hast defiled my sanctuary with all thy detestable things, and with all thine abominations, therefore will I also diminish thee; neither shall mine eye spare, neither will I have any pity. (Ezekiel 5: 11.)

He said furthermore unto me, Son of man, seest thou what they do? even the great abominations that the house of Israel committeth here, that I should go far off from my sanctuary? but turn thee yet again, and thou shalt see greater abominations. (Ezekiel 8: 6.)

Abomination of Offerings.

Thou shalt not sacrifice unto the Lord thy God any bullock, or sheep, wherein is blemish, or any evil favouredness, for that is an abomination unto the Lord thy God. (Deuteronomy 17: 1.)

The sacrifice of the wicked is an abomination to the Lord; but the prayer of the upright is his delight.

The way of the wicked is an abomination unto the Lord; but he loveth him that followeth after righteousness. (Proverbs 15: 8, 9.)

Bring no more vain oblations: incense is an abomination unto me; the new-moons and sabbaths, the calling of assemblies, I cannot away with; it is iniquity, even the solemn meeting. (Isaiah 1: 13.)

Abomination of Prayer of Wicked.

He that turneth away his ear from hearing the law, even his prayer shall be abomination. (Proverbs 28: 9.)

Abomination of Defilement.

Her former husband which sent her away, may not take her again to be his wife, after that she is defiled; for that is abomination before the Lord: and thou shalt not cause the land to sin, which the Lord thy God giveth thee for an inheritance. (Deuteronomy 24: 4.)

It is an abomination to kings to commit wickedness: for the throne is established by righteousness. (Proverbs 16: 12.)

They that sanctify themselves, and purify themselves in the gardens behind one tree in the midst, eating swine's flesh, and the abomination, and the mouse, shall be consumed together, saith the Lord. (Isaiah 66: 17.)

And there shall in no wise enter into it any thing that defileth, neither whatsoever worketh abomination, or maketh a lie: but they which are written in the Lamb's book of life. (Revelation 21: 27.)

Abomination of Falsity.

A false balance is abomination to the Lord: but a just weight is his delight. (Proverbs 11: 1.)

He that justifieth the wicked, and he that condemneth the just, even they both are abomination to the Lord. (Proverbs 17: 15.)

Divers weights, and divers measures, both of them are alike abomination to the Lord. (Proverbs 20: 10.)

Divers weights are an abomination unto the Lord; and a false balance is not good. (Proverbs 20: 23.)

Abomination of Idolatry.

The graven images of their gods shall ye burn with fire: thou shalt not desire the silver or gold that is on them, nor take it unto thee, lest thou be snared therein: for it is an abomination to the Lord thy God.

Neither shalt thou bring an abomination into thine house, lest thou be a

cursed thing like it: but thou shalt utterly detest it, and thou shalt utterly abhor it: for it is a cursed thing. (Deuteronomy 7: 25, 26.)

Cursed be the man that maketh any graven or molten image, an abomination unto the Lord, the work of the hands of the craftsman, and putteth it in a secret place: and all the people shall answer and say, Amen. (Deuteronomy 27: 15.)

And I brought you into a plentiful country, to eat the fruit thereof and the goodness thereof; but when ye entered, ye defiled my land, and made mine heritage an abomination. (Jeremiah 2: 7.)

Hath oppressed the poor and needy, hath spoiled by violence, hath not restored the pledge, and hath lifted up his eyes to the idols, hath committed abomination. (Ezekiel 18: 12.)

And he said unto them, *Ye are they which justify yourselves before men, but God knoweth your hearts: for that which is highly esteemed amongst men, is abomination in the sight of God.* (Luke 16: 15.)

Additional References.—Genesis 43: 32; 46: 34; Exodus 8: 26; Psalm 88: 8; Proverbs 3: 32; 6: 16; 8: 17; 11: 20; 12: 22; 13: 19; 16: 5; 24: 9; 29: 27; Ezekiel 33: 26; 18: 24; 20: 4; 36: 31; 44: 6; Revelation 17: 4.

ABRAHAM. (See Isaac, Israelites, Lot, Sarah, etc.)

A'BRA-HAM—a form of a Hebrew word meaning "father of a multitude." The name, as it appears in the Bible, was given to the wonderful man who was the founder of the Hebrew nation. His original name was Abram, meaning "high father" or "father of elevation." He was a native of Chaldea, having been born in the very ancient city of Ur about 2333 B.C., as the most recent researches give it. He was a descendant in the ninth generation of Shem, the son of Noah. Unlike the

Chaldeans, who were an idolatrous people, he seems always to have been a worshiper of Jehovah. Led by a call from God, he left his native land and went to dwell elsewhere. Still led by God he wandered to Canaan, and to him there God made a promise that he should be the founder of a great nation. Driven by famine he went from Canaan to Egypt, where, after numerous adventures, he acquired considerable wealth. Returning to Canaan he led the life of a patriarch with his household and his nephew Lot, taking part with the inhabitants of the country in repelling and punishing foreign invaders. Even at this time his faith in God and his devotion to Him were strong characteristics of the man.

Soon after meeting with Melchizedek, God promised him a son and made a covenant with him. The birth of his first child, Ishmael, followed, and for a time this son was regarded as the heir to Abraham's estate as well as to God's promises. Later, however, God revealed that Ishmael was not to be so honored and that the real heir was to be a son by Sarah, Abraham's wife, then a woman of advanced years. At the same time God said Abraham was to be the father of not only one nation but of many nations. Thereupon his name was changed from Abram to Abraham, to show his altered condition. The birth of Isaac soon revealed God's intention to keep his promise. The tests the Almighty put upon His chosen man were many and severe—in the events surrounding the visit of angels, the destruction of Sodom, and more especially in the command that he make a living sacrifice of his beloved son Isaac, which occurred when Isaac had grown almost to manhood. In all these tests Abraham was not found wanting, and by various ways God confirmed his promises that this man should be the father of a chosen and blessed people. He died about 2158 B.C., at the age of 175 years, seeing many signs of the fulfillment of the divine pledges.

Abraham's character is one of the grandest in Scripture. Nothing ever shook his loyalty to God and he trusted Him with fullest confidence. Nor was his attitude toward mankind less noble, as is evidenced in his treatment of Lot and his refusal to share in the spoils of war, and his effort to avert the doom of Sodom and Gomorrah. He and his works and character are typical of many things in religion. His family life may be regarded as a type of the Church of God in all ages. The intentional offering-up of Isaac, an only son, seems a prophecy in facts of the sacrifice of the Redeemer by His Father, while the return of Isaac from the pile of fagots upon which he was to have been burned may be regarded as a forecast of the Resurrection. Indeed, beneath the whole incident, seems buried the mystery of the great sacrifice that was to take place two thousand years later on Calvary.

REFERENCES.

Abraham's Family.

Now these are the generations of Terah: Terah begat Abram, Nahor, and Haran: and Haran begat Lot.

And Haran died before his father Terah in the land of his nativity, in Ur of the Chaldees.

And Abram and Nahor took them wives: the name of Abram's wife was Sarai; and the name of Nahor's wife Milcah, the daughter of Haran, the father of Milcah, and the father of Iscah. (Genesis 11: 27-29.)

First Promise.

Now the Lord had said unto Abram, Get thee out of thy country, and from thy kindred, and from thy father's house, unto a land that I will shew thee:

And I will make of thee a great nation, and I will bless thee, and make thy name great; and thou shalt be a blessing:

And I will bless them that bless thee, and curse him that curseth thee: and in thee shall all families of the earth be blessed. (Genesis 12: 1-3.)

Wanderings and Adventures.

And Abram took Sarai his wife, and Lot his brother's son, and all their substance that they had gathered, and the souls that they had gotten in Haran; and they went forth to go into the land of Canaan; and into the land of Canaan they came. (Genesis 12: 5.)

And there was a famine in the land: and Abram went down into Egypt to sojourn there; for the famine was grievous in the land.

And it came to pass, when he was come near to enter into Egypt, that he said unto Sarai his wife, Behold now, I know that thou art a fair woman to look upon:

Therefore it shall come to pass, when the Egyptians shall see thee, that they shall say, This is his wife: and they will kill me, but they will save thee alive.

Say, I pray thee, thou art my sister: that it may be well with me for thy sake; and my soul shall live because of thee. (Genesis 12: 10-13.)

And Pharaoh called Abram, and said, What is this that thou hast done unto me? why didst thou not tell me that she was thy wife?

Why saidst thou, She is my sister? so I might have taken her to me to wife: now therefore behold thy wife, take her, and go thy way.

And Pharoah commanded his men concerning him: and they sent him away, and his wife, and all that he had. (Genesis 12: 18-20.)

And Abram went up out of Egypt, he, and his wife, and all that he had, and Lot with him, into the south.

And Abram was very rich in cattle, in silver, and in gold. (Genesis 13: 1, 2.)

And Abram said unto Lot, Let there be no strife, I pray thee, between me and thee, and between my herdmen and thy herdmen; for we be brethren. (Genesis 13: 8.)

And the Lord said unto Abram, after that Lot was separated from him, Lift up now thine eyes, and look from the place where thou art, northward, and southward, and eastward, and westward:

For all the land which thou seest, to thee will I give it, and to thy seed for ever.

And I will make thy seed as the dust of the earth: so that if a man can number the dust of the earth, then shall thy seed also be numbered. (Genesis 13: 14-16.)

And Abram said to the king of Sodom, I have lifted up my hand unto the Lord, the most high God, the possessor of heaven and earth,

That I will not take from a thread even to a shoe-latchet, and that I will not take any thing that is thine, lest thou shouldest say, I have made Abram rich. (Genesis 14: 22, 23.)

Promise of a Son.

After these things the word of the Lord came unto Abram in a vision, saying, Fear not, Abram, I am thy shield, and thy exceeding great reward.

And Abram said, Lord God, what wilt thou give me, seeing I go childless, and the steward of my house is this Eliezer of Damascus?

And Abram said, Behold, to me thou hast given no seed: and lo, one born in my house is mine heir.

And behold, the word of the Lord came unto him, saying, This shall not be thine heir; but he that shall come forth out of thine own bowels shall be thine heir. (Genesis 15: 1-4.)

And he said unto Abram, Know of a surety that thy seed shall be a stranger in a land that is not theirs, and shall serve them; and they shall afflict them four hundred years;

And also that nation whom they shall serve, will I judge: and afterward shall they come out with great substance.

And thou shalt go to thy fathers in peace; thou shalt be buried in a good old age. (Genesis 15: 13-15.)

In that same day the Lord made a covenant with Abram, saying, Unto thy seed have I given this land, from the river of Egypt unto the great river, the river Euphrates. (Genesis 15: 18.)

Now Sarai, Abram's wife, bare him no children: and she had an handmaid, an Egyptian, whose name was Hagar. (Genesis 16: 1.)

And Hagar bare Abram a son; and Abram called his son's name, which Hagar bare, Ishmael. (Genesis 16: 15.)

Covenant and Change of Name.

And Abram fell on his face: and God talked with him, saying,

As for me, behold, my covenant is with thee, and thou shalt be a father of many nations.

Neither shall thy name any more be called Abram; but thy name shall be Abraham: for a father of many nations have I made thee.

And I will make thee exceedingly fruitful, and I will make nations of thee; and kings shall come out of thee.

And I will establish my covenant between me and thee, and thy seed after thee, in their generations, for an everlasting covenant; to be a God unto thee, and to thy seed after thee. (Genesis 17: 3-7.)

And God said, Sarah thy wife shall bear thee a son indeed; and thou shalt call his name Isaac: and I will establish my covenant with him for an everlast-

ing covenant, and with his seed after him. (Genesis 17: 19.)

Birth of Isaac.

And Abraham called the name of his son that was born unto him, whom Sarah bare to him, Isaac. (Genesis 21: 3.)

Abraham's Temptation.

And it came to pass after these things, that God did tempt Abraham, and said unto him, Abraham: and he said, Behold, here I am.

And he said, Take now thy son, thine only son Isaac, whom thou lovest, and get thee into the land of Moriah; and offer him there for a burnt-offering upon one of the mountains which I will tell thee of. (Genesis 22: 1, 2.)

And Abraham lifted up his eyes, and looked, and behold behind him a ram caught in a thicket by his horns: and Abraham went and took the ram, and offered him up for a burnt-offering in the stead of his son. (Genesis 22: 13.)

Abraham's Death.

And these are the days of the years of Abraham's life which he lived, an hundred threescore and fifteen years.

Then Abraham gave up the ghost, and died in a good old age, an old man, and full of years; and was gathered to his people.

And his sons Isaac and Ishmael buried him in the cave of Machpelah, in the field of Ephron the son of Zohar the Hittite, which is before Mamre. (Genesis 25: 7-9.)

Additional References.—Isaiah 41: 8; Jeremiah 33: 26; Micah 7: 20; Luke 1: 55, 73; John 8: 39; Acts 7: 2-5; Romans 4: 1-13; Galatians 3: 6, 16; Hebrews 11: 8-10; James 2: 21; Matthew 3: 9; 8: 11; Luke 3: 8; 16: 22; Romans 9: 7; John 8: 56.

ABSALOM. (See David, Joab, Tamar.)

AB'SA-LOM—a form of a Hebrew word meaning "father of peace." The name of the third son of David, and his only son by Maacah, daughter of Talmai, king of Geshur. He was born about the year 1060 B.C. and grew up to be accounted the handsomest man in the kingdom, noted particularly for the remarkable beauty of his hair. His life was full of troubles and his death was a tragedy from which his aged father never quite recovered. We hear little about him until he took it upon himself to avenge the wrongs his sister, Tamar, had suffered at the hands of her half-brother Amnon, David's eldest son. Absalom bided his time and when an opportunity offered, two years later, caused Amnon to be slain. At the great outcry raised over the killing, Absalom fled to the court of his grandfather, remaining three years. David, who loved his handsome son most fondly, was anxious for his return, which was brought about somewhat cleverly by Joab.

Shortly after his return, Absalom seems to have begun plotting to succeed his father on the throne. He was at this time David's eldest surviving son, and the only one of truly royal descent on the maternal side. He thus felt that his rights were superior to those of Solomon, then a child. Absalom's beauty and popularity soon rallied around him a strong party, and he is said to have "stolen the hearts of the men of Israel." A revolt was proclaimed and David was forced to flee from his capital, even David's most gracious counsellor, Ahithophel, going over to the rebel son. Ahithophel advised Absalom to kill David, but while he hesitated Joab succeeded in organizing a force sufficient for Absalom's overthrow. Absalom's army was defeated in the forest of Ephraim, and he was killed as he fled, his beautiful hair catching in the limbs of a tree and holding him until Joab pierced him with darts. David's grief was intense.

Absalom's character seems to have been an impetuous, impulsive, and wayward one. Adulation and flattery seem to have spoiled him after his return from exile, although the tragedy of Tamar doubtless had something to do with the wrecking of his life. That he could inspire great love, however, is shown by the fact that even though he sought to dethrone his father David, the old king would have been glad to have died for his erring son.

REFERENCES.

Birth and Early History.

And unto David were sons born in Hebron: and his first-born was Amnon, of Ahinoam the Jezreelitess;

And his second, Chileab, of Abigail the wife of Nabal the Carmelite; and the third, Absalom the son of Maacah, the daughter of Talmai king of Geshur. (2 Samuel 3: 2, 3.)

And it came to pass after this, that Absalom the son of David had a fair sister, whose name was Tamar; and Amnon the son of David loved her. (2 Samuel 13: 1.)

And Absalom spake unto his brother Amnon neither good nor bad: for Absalom hated Amnon, because he had forced his sister Tamar.

And it came to pass after two full years, that Absalom had sheep-shearers in Baal-hazor, which is beside Ephraim: and Absalom invited all the king's sons. (2 Samuel 13: 22, 23.)

Now Absalom had commanded his servants, saying, Mark ye now when Amnon's heart is merry with wine, and when I say unto you, Smite Amnon; then kill him, fear not; have not I commanded you? be courageous, and be valiant.

And the servants of Absalom did unto Amnon as Absalom had commanded. Then all the king's sons arose, and every man gat him up upon his mule, and fled. (2 Samuel 13: 28, 29.)

But Absalom fled, and went to Talmai, the son of Ammihud, king of Geshur. And David mourned for his son every day.

So Absalom fled, and went to Geshur, and was there three years.

And the soul of King David longed to go forth unto Absalom: for he was comforted concerning Amnon, seeing he was dead. (2 Samuel 13: 37-39.)

Now Joab the son of Zeruiah perceived that the king's heart was toward Absalom. (2 Samuel 14: 1.)

So Joab arose and went to Geshur, and brought Absalom to Jerusalem.

And the king said, Let him turn to his own house, and let him not see my face. So Absalom returned to his own house, and saw not the king's face.

But in all Israel there was none to be so much praised as Absalom for his beauty: from the sole of his foot even to the crown of his head there was no blemish in him.

And when he polled his head, (for it was at every year's end that he polled it; because the hair was heavy on him, therefore he polled it;) he weighed the hair of his head at two hundred shekels after the king's weight. (2 Samuel 14: 23-26.)

Plots against David.

Absalom said moreover, Oh that I were made judge in the land, that every man which hath any suit or cause might come unto me, and I would do him justice!

And it was so, that when any man came nigh to him to do him obeisance, he put forth his hand, and took him, and kissed him.

And on this manner did Absalom to all Israel that came to the king for judgment: so Absalom stole the hearts of the men of Israel. (2 Samuel 15: 4-6.)

But Absalom sent spies throughout all the tribes of Israel, saying, As soon as ye hear the sound of the trumpet, then ye shall say, Absalom reigneth in Hebron. (2 Samuel 15: 10.)

And David said unto all his servants that were with him at Jerusalem, Arise, and let us flee; for we shall not else escape from Absalom: make speed to depart, lest he overtake us suddenly, and bring evil upon us, and smite the city with the edge of the sword. (2 Samuel 15: 14.)

Revolt and Death.

Moreover, Ahithophel said unto Absalom, Let me now choose out twelve thousand men, and I will arise and pursue after David this night:

And I will come upon him while he is weary and weak-handed, and will make him afraid: and all the people that are with him shall flee; and I will smite the king only. (2 Samuel 17: 1, 2.)

And Absalom and all the men of Israel said, The counsel of Hushai the Archite is better than the counsel of Ahithophel. For the Lord had appointed to defeat the good counsel of Ahithophel, to the intent that the Lord might bring evil upon Absalom. (2 Samuel 17: 14.)

And the king commanded Joab and Abishai and Ittai, saying, Deal gently for my sake with the young man, even with Absalom. And all the people heard when the king gave all the captains charge concerning Absalom.

So the people went out into the field against Israel; and the battle was in the wood of Ephraim. (2 Samuel 18: 5, 6.)

And Absalom met the servants of David. And Absalom rode upon a mule, and the mule went under the thick boughs of a great oak, and his head caught hold of the oak, and he was taken up between the heaven and the earth; and the mule that was under him went away. (2 Samuel 18: 9.)

Then said Joab, I may not tarry thus with thee. And he took three darts in his hand, and thrust them through the heart of Absalom, while he was yet alive in the midst of the oak. (2 Samuel 18: 14.)

And the king was much moved, and went up to the chamber over the gate, and wept: and as he wept, thus he said, O my son Absalom! my son, my son Absalom! would God I had died for thee, O Absalom, my son, my son! (2 Samuel 18: 33.)

ABSTINENCE. (See Fasting, Temperance.)

AB'STI-NENCE—refraining from the use of certain things, such as forbidden luxuries, foods, drinks, or acts. It is distinguished from temperance, which is a moderate use of things, and from fasting, which is abstinence for a time only from a religious motive.

REFERENCES.

Jewish Abstinence.

But flesh with the life thereof, which is the blood thereof, shall ye not eat. (Genesis 9: 4.)

Therefore the children of Israel eat not of the sinew which shrank, which is upon the hollow of the thigh, unto this day; because he touched the hollow of Jacob's thigh in the sinew that shrank. (Genesis 32: 32.)

And ye shall be holy men unto me: neither shall ye eat any flesh that is torn of beasts in the field; ye shall cast it to the dogs. (Exodus 22: 31.)

Ye shall not eat of any thing that dieth of itself: thou shalt give it unto the stranger that is in thy gates, that he may eat it; or thou mayest sell it unto an alien: for thou art an holy people unto the Lord thy God. Thou shalt not seethe a kid in his mother's milk. (Deuteronomy 14: 21.)

(See Leviticus 11 for flesh and meat forbidden to the Jews.)

Christian Abstinence.

Wherefore, if meat make my brother to offend, I will eat no flesh while the world standeth, lest I make my brother to offend. (1 Corinthians 8: 13.)

That ye abstain from meats offered to idols, and from blood, and from things strangled, and from fornication: from which if ye keep yourselves, ye shall do well. Fare ye well. (Acts 15: 29.)

Abstain from all appearance of evil. (1 Thessalonians 5: 22.)

Forbidding to marry, and commanding to abstain from meats, which God hath created to be received with thanksgiving of them which believe and know the truth.

For every creature of God is good, and nothing to be refused, if it be received with thanksgiving. (1 Timothy 4: 3, 4.)

Dearly beloved, I beseech you, as strangers and pilgrims, abstain from fleshly lusts, which war against the soul. (1 Peter 2: 11.)

ACCEPTABLE.

AC-CEPT'A-BLE—pleasing, receivable, good in the sight of, well-pleasing.

REFERENCES.

And of Asher he said, Let Asher be blessed with children; let him be acceptable to his brethren, and let him dip his foot in oil. (Deuteronomy 33: 24.)

Let the words of my mouth, and the

meditation of my heart, be acceptable in thy sight, O Lord, my strength, and my redeemer. (Psalm 19: 14.)

The lips of the righteous know what is acceptable: but the mouth of the wicked speaketh frowardness. (Proverbs 10: 32.)

To do justice and judgment is more acceptable to the Lord than sacrifice. (Proverbs 21: 3.)

The Preacher sought to find out acceptable words: and that which was written was upright, even words of truth. (Ecclesiastes 12: 10.)

To proclaim the acceptable year of the Lord, and the day of vengeance of our God; to comfort all that mourn. (Isaiah 61: 2.)

Wherefore, O king, let my counsel be acceptable unto thee, and break off thy sins by righteousness, and thine iniqities by shewing mercy to the poor; if it may be a lengthening of thy tranquility. (Daniel 4: 27.)

I beseech you therefore, brethren, by the mercies of God, that ye present your bodies a living sacrifice, holy, acceptable unto God, which is your reasonable service.

And be not conformed to this world: but be ye transformed by the renewing of your mind, that ye may prove what is that good, and acceptable, and perfect will of God. (Romans 12: 1, 2.)

For he that in these things serveth Christ, is acceptable to God, and approved of men. (Romans 14: 18.)

Proving what is acceptable unto the Lord. (Ephesians 5: 10.)

For this is good and acceptable in the sight of God our Saviour. (1 Timothy 2: 3.)

But if any widow have children or nephews, let them learn first to shew piety at home, and to requite their par-

ents; for that is good and acceptable before God. (1 Timothy 5: 4.)

Ye also, as lively stones, are built up a spiritual house, an holy priesthood, to offer up spiritual sacrifices, acceptable to God by Jesus Christ. (1 Peter 2: 5.)

For what glory is it, if, when ye be buffeted for your faults, ye shall take it patiently? but if, when ye do well, and suffer for it, ye take it patiently, this is acceptable with God. (1 Peter 2: 20.)

ACCEPTATION.

Ac'cep-ta'tion—the act of receiving; full reception.

REFERENCE.

This is a faithful saying, and worthy of all acceptation, that Christ Jesus came into the world to save sinners; of whom I am chief. (1 Timothy 1: 15.)

ACCEPTED.

Ac-cept'ed—received, found good, well-pleasing.

REFERENCES.

If thou doest well, shalt thou not be accepted? and if thou doest not well, sin lieth at the door: and unto thee shall be his desire, and thou shalt rule over him. (Genesis 4: 7.)

Even them will I bring to my holy mountain, and make them joyful in my house of prayer: their burnt-offerings and their sacrifices shall be accepted upon mine altar; for mine house shall be called an house of prayer for all people. (Isaiah 56: 7.)

And he said, *Verily I say unto you, no Prophet is accepted in his own country.* (Luke 4: 24.)

But in every nation, he that feareth him, and worketh righteousness, is accepted with him. (Acts 10: 35.)

Wherefore we labour, that, whether present or absent, we may be accepted of him. (2 Corinthians 5: 9.)

For he saith, I have heard thee in a time accepted, and in the day of salvation have I succoured thee: behold, now is the accepted time, behold, now is the day of salvation. (2 Corinthians 6: 2.)

For if there be first a willing mind, it is accepted according to that a man hath, and not according to that he hath not. (2 Corinthians 8: 12.)

ACCESS. (See God, Christ, Holy Spirit.)

Ac′cess—a coming to, a near approach, admission. Used in the Bible chiefly with reference to the approach by faith of one of God's children to Him.

REFERENCES.

By whom also we have access by faith into this grace wherein we stand, and rejoice in hope of the glory of God. (Romans 5: 2.)

For through him we both have an access by one Spirit unto the Father. (Ephesians 2: 18.)

In whom we have boldness and access, with confidence, by the faith of him. (Ephesians 3: 12.)

Additional and Collateral References.—Hebrews 7: 19; 10: 19; Isaiah 55: 6; Hosea 14: 2; Joel 2: 12; John 14: 6; James 4: 8; Psalms 65: 4; 73: 28; Isaiah 2: 3; Jeremiah 31: 6.

ACCURSED. (See Achan.)

Ac-curs′ed—under a curse; doomed to destruction or misery; sentenced to be turned over to the powers of evil; under the divine wrath.

REFERENCES.

His body shall not remain all night upon the tree, but thou shalt in any wise bury him that day; (for he that is hanged is accursed of God); that thy land be not defiled, which the Lord thy God giveth thee for an inheritance. (Deuteronomy 21: 23.)

And the city shall be accursed, even it, and all that are therein, to the Lord: only Rahab the harlot shall live, she and all that are with her in the house, because she hid the messengers that we sent. (Joshua 6: 17.)

And ye, in any wise keep yourselves from the accursed thing, lest ye make yourselves accursed, when ye take of the accursed thing, and make the camp of Israel a curse, and trouble it. (Joshua 6: 18.)

But the children of Israel committed a trespass in the accursed thing: for Achan, the son of Carmi, the son of Zabdi, the son of Zerah, of the tribe of Judah, took of the accursed thing: and the anger of the Lord was kindled against the children of Israel. (Joshua 7: 1.)

Israel hath sinned, and they have also transgressed my covenant which I commanded them: for they have even taken of the accursed thing, and have also stolen, and dissembled also, and they have put it even among their own stuff.

Therefore the children of Israel could not stand before their enemies, but turned their backs before their enemies, because they were accursed: neither will I be with you any more, except ye destroy the accursed from among you. (Joshua 7: 11, 12.)

And it shall be, that he that is taken with the accursed thing shall be burnt with fire, he and all that he hath: because he hath transgressed the covenant of the Lord, and because he hath wrought folly in Israel. (Joshua 7: 15.)

For I could wish that myself were accursed from Christ, for my brethren, my kinsmen according to the flesh. (Romans 9: 3.)

Wherefore I give you to understand, that no man speaking by the Spirit of God, calleth Jesus accursed: and that no man can say that Jesus is the Lord, but by the Holy Ghost. (1 Corinthians 12: 3.)

But though we, or an angel from heaven, preach any other gospel unto you than that which we have preached unto you, let him be accursed. (Galatians 1: 8.)

ACELDAMA.

A-CEL′DA-MA—meaning "the field of blood." This is a name of Syro-Chaldaic origin applied to the field purchased with the money for which Judas betrayed Christ, and used as a burial-place for strangers. A field on the slope of the hills beyond the valley of Hinnom, south of Mount Zion, near Jerusalem, is pointed out as the original Aceldama. A ruined charnel-house occupies a part of it. There are no marks to point out its exact bounds.

REFERENCES.

And the chief priests took the silver pieces, and said, It is not lawful for to put them into the treasury, because it is the price of blood.

And they took counsel, and bought with them the potter's field, to bury strangers in.

Wherefore that field was called, The field of blood, unto this day. (Matthew 27: 6-8.)

And it was known unto all the dwellers at Jerusalem; insomuch as that field is called in their proper tongue, Aceldama, that is to say, The field of blood. (Acts 1: 19.)

ACHAN.

A′CHAN—a form of a Hebrew word meaning "trouble" or "troublesome." The name of a Judahite who, at the siege of Jericho, could not resist the temptation to take certain valuable things from the loot of the city which had been declared accursed, a deed which he later confessed. He was stoned, along with his family and his possessions.

REFERENCES.

But the children of Israel committed a trespass in the accursed thing: for Achan, the son of Carmi, the son of Zabdi, the son of Zerah, of the tribe of Judah, took of the accursed thing: and the anger of the Lord was kindled against the children of Israel. (Joshua 7: 1.)

And he brought his household man by man; and Achan, the son of Carmi, the son of Zabdi, the son of Zerah, of the tribe of Judah, was taken.

And Joshua said unto Achan, My son, give, I pray thee, glory to the Lord God of Israel, and make confession unto him; and tell me now what thou hast done; hide it not from me.

And Achan answered Joshua, and said, Indeed I have sinned against the Lord God of Israel, and thus and thus have I done:

When I saw among the spoils a goodly Babylonish garment, and two hundred shekels of silver, and a wedge of gold of fifty shekels weight, then I coveted them, and took them; and, behold, they are hid in the earth in the midst of my tent, and the silver under it.

So Joshua sent messengers, and they ran unto the tent; and, behold, it was hid in his tent, and the silver under it.

And they took them out of the midst of the tent, and brought them unto Joshua, and unto all the children of

Israel, and laid them out before the Lord.

And Joshua, and all Israel with him, took Achan the son of Zerah, and the silver, and the garment, and the wedge of gold, and his sons, and his daughters, and his oxen, and his asses, and his sheep, and his tent, and all that he had: and they brought them unto the valley of Achor.

And Joshua said, Why hast thou troubled us? the Lord shall trouble thee this day. And all Israel stoned him with stones, and burned them with fire, after they had stoned them with stones. (Joshua 7: 18-25.)

Did not Achan the son of Zerah commit a trespass in the accursed thing, and wrath fell on all the congregation of Israel? and that man perished not alone in his iniquity. (Joshua 22: 20.)

ADAM. (See Creation, Christ, Eden, Eve, Fall.)

AD'AM—a form of a very ancient Hebrew word meaning "red" or "red earth." It is the name given to the first created man. It also seems to have been used as a word expressive of the human race in general, and when used in this way was translated "man." According to the Bible Adam was created by God "in his own image" out "of the dust of the ground." This indicates that the first man was created in maturity. The creation of woman followed, according to the narrative of Genesis 1 and 2. Subsequently came the sin and fall of Adam and Eve, with their expulsion from the Garden of Eden, with the curse upon their heads that entailed sin and suffering for the entire human race, their descendants. Figuratively, Adam is represented in the Bible as a breaker of covenants, as a coverer of transgressions, as the source of death and death to his posterity, and also as a figure of the promised Messiah, in that he is a son of God. Jesus Christ, the second Adam, was so-called because of a certain similitude to the first Adam, being peculiarly the Son of God; the express image of His person, a new thing created in the earth, and the ornament and center of His works; the head of mankind in a new and better covenant, and all things are subjected to Him, as were all created things subjected to the first Adam before the Fall.

REFERENCES.

Adam as Mankind.

And God said, Let us make man in our image, after our likeness: and let them have dominion over the fish of the sea, and over the fowl of the air, and over the cattle, and over all the earth, and over every creeping thing that creepeth upon the earth.

So God created man in his own image, in the image of God created he him; male and female created he them. (Genesis 1: 26, 27.)

This is the book of the generations of Adam: In the day that God created man, in the likeness of God made he him:

Male and female created he them; and blessed them, and called their name Adam, in the day when they were created. (Genesis 5: 1, 2.)

Adam the First Man.

And the Lord God formed man of the dust of the ground, and breathed into his nostrils the breath of life; and man became a living soul.

And the Lord God planted a garden eastward in Eden; and there he put the man whom he had formed. (Genesis 2: 7, 8.)

And out of the ground the Lord God formed every beast of the field, and every fowl of the air, and brought them unto Adam to see what he would call them; and whatsoever Adam called every living creature, that was the name thereof.

And Adam gave names to all cattle, and to the fowl of the air, and to every beast of the field: but for Adam there was not found an help meet for him.

And the Lord God caused a deep sleep to fall upon Adam, and he slept; and he took one of his ribs, and closed up the flesh instead thereof. (Genesis 2: 19-21.)

And Adam called his wife's name Eve, because she was the mother of all living. (Genesis 3: 20.)

And Adam lived an hundred and thirty years, and begat a son in his own likeness, after his image; and called his name Seth:

And the days of Adam after he had begotten Seth were eight hundred years: and he begat sons and daughters. (Genesis 5: 3, 4.)

And all the days that Adam lived were nine hundred and thirty years: and he died. (Genesis 5: 5.)

Adam's Transgression.

And unto Adam he said, Because thou hast hearkened unto the voice of thy wife, and hast eaten of the tree of which I commanded thee, saying, Thou shalt not eat of it: cursed is the ground for thy sake; in sorrow shalt thou eat of it all the days of thy life. (Genesis 3: 17.)

If I covered my transgressions as Adam, hiding mine iniquity in my bosom. (Job 31: 33.)

Nevertheless, death reigned from Adam to Moses, even over them that had not sinned after the similitude of Adam's transgression, who is the figure of him that was to come. (Romans 5: 14.)

Relation to Second Adam.

Which was the son of Enos, which was the son of Seth, which was the son of Adam, which was the son of God. (Luke 3: 38.)

For as in Adam all die, even so in Christ shall all be made alive. (1 Corinthians 15: 22.)

And so it is written, The first man Adam was made a living soul, the last Adam was made a quickening spirit. (1 Corinthians 15: 45.)

Additional References.—Genesis 1: 2, 3; 1 Timothy 2: 13, 14; Jude 1: 14.

ADONIJAH.

AD-O-NI'JAH—a form of a Hebrew word meaning "my lord is Jehovah." The name of the fourth son of David. After Absalom's death Adonijah set up pretensions to the throne and was supported by Joab and some of the important officers of the realm. David, in obedience to the Divine command, had Solomon proclaimed and crowned, thus shutting off Adonijah's claim. He was granted pardon; but after David's death he again began plotting, and was put to death by Solomon's order.

REFERENCES.

And the fourth, Adonijah the son of Haggith; and the fifth, Shephatiah the son of Abital. (2 Samuel 3: 4.)

Then Adonijah the son of Haggith exalted himself, saying, I will be king: and he prepared him chariots and horsemen, and fifty men to run before him. (1 Kings 1: 5.)

And he conferred with Joab the son of Zeruiah, and with Abiathar the priest: and they, following Adonijah, helped him. (1 Kings 1: 7.)

And Nathan said, My lord, O king, hast thou said, Adonijah shall reign after me, and he shall sit upon my throne?

For he is gone down this day, and hath slain oxen, and fat cattle, and sheep in abundance, and hath called all the king's sons, and the captains of the host, and Abiathar the priest; and behold, they eat and drink before him, and say, God save king Adonijah. (1 Kings 1: 24, 25.)

And Adonijah feared because of Solomon, and arose, and went, and caught hold on the horns of the altar.

And it was told Solomon, saying, Behold, Adonijah feareth king Solomon: for lo, he hath caught hold on the horns of the altar, saying, Let king Solomon swear unto me to-day that he will not slay his servant with the sword.

And Solomon said, If he will shew himself a worthy man, there shall not an hair of him fall to the earth: but if wickedness shall be found in him, he shall die.

So king Solomon sent, and they brought him down from the altar. And he came and bowed himself to king Solomon: and Solomon said unto him, Go to thine house. (1 Kings 1: 50-53.)

And king Solomon sent by the hand of Benaiah the son of Jehoiada; and he fell upon him that he died. (1 Kings 2: 25.)

ADOPTION.

A-DOP'TION—the act of taking the child of other parents to be one's own child. In the Bible, instances of adoption are exceedingly rare, Mosaic law having so regulated families that even if a man died without children some sort of a representative posterity was secured to him. In almost all of the cases the adoption was through the female side, wives taking the children of servants by their husbands as their own. The word or thought is more often used in the Bible to indicate the benign purpose of God in accepting as His children those of mankind that accept Him.

REFERENCES.

Adoption by God the Father.

But as many as received him, to them gave he power to become the sons of God, even to them that believe on his name. (John 1: 12.)

Jesus saith unto her, *Touch me not: for I am not yet ascended to my Father: but go to my brethren, and say unto them, I ascend unto my Father and your Father, and to my God and your God.* (John 20: 17.)

For as many as are led by the Spirit of God, they are the sons of God. (Romans 8: 14.)

And will be a Father unto you, and ye shall be my sons and daughters, saith the Lord Almighty. (2 Corinthians 6: 18.)

Having predestinated us unto the adoption of children by Jesus Christ to himself, according to the good pleasure of his will. (Ephesians 1: 5.)

To redeem them that were under the law, that we might receive the adoption of sons. (Galatians 4: 5.)

Of his own will begat he us with the word of truth, that we should be a kind of first-fruits of his creatures. (James 1: 18.

Behold what manner of love the Father hath bestowed upon us, that we should be called the sons of God! therefore the world knoweth us not, because it knew him not. (1 John 3: 1.)

Adoption of the Gentiles.

And I will set a sign among them, and I will send those that escape of them unto the nations, to Tarshish, Pul, and Lud, that draw the bow, to Tubal, and Javan, to the isles afar off, that have not heard my fame, neither have seen my glory; and they shall declare my glory among the Gentiles. (Isaiah 66: 19.)

And I will sow her unto me in the earth; and I will have mercy upon her that had not obtained mercy; and I will

say to them which were not my people,
Thou art my people; and they shall say,
Thou art my God. (Hosea 2:23.)

And not only they, but ourselves also,
which have the first-fruits of the Spirit,
even we ourselves groan within ourselves, waiting for the adoption, to wit,
the redemption of our body. (Romans
8:23.)

ADULLAM.

A-DUL'LAM—a form of a Hebrew word
meaning "people's justice." The name was
applied to a cave wherein David took refuge
and which he used as a stronghold during the
Saulian persecutions. The exact location of
it is in doubt, but it seems to have been one
of a number of large caves in the vicinity of
Bethlehem or in the mountainous regions west
of Judah toward the Dead Sea. There is evidence to support both contentions, although
the weight of it inclines to the Bethlehem
location.

REFERENCES.

David therefore departed thence, and
escaped to the cave Adullam: and when
his brethren and all his father's house
heard it, they went down thither to him.
(1 Samuel 22:1.)

And three of the thirty chief went
down, and came to David in the harvest-time unto the cave of Adullam:
and the troop of the Philistines pitched
in the valley of Rephaim. (2 Samuel
23:13.)

ADVENT, SECOND. (See Millennium.)

ADVERSARY. (See Devil, Satan.)

AD'VER-SA-RY—an enemy; an antagonist;
one who is opposed to you more or less bitterly; also used as a synonym for Satan as the
great antagonist of the human race and an
enemy of good.

REFERENCES.

But if thou shalt indeed obey his
voice, and do all that I speak; then I
will be an enemy unto thine enemies,
and an adversary unto thine adversaries. (Exodus 23:22.)

And Esther said, The adversary and
enemy is this wicked Haman. Then
Haman was afraid before the king and
the queen. (Esther 7:6.)

Therefore saith the Lord, the Lord
of hosts, the mighty One of Israel, Ah,
I will ease me of mine adversaries, and
avenge me of mine enemies. (Isaiah
1:24.)

And he shewed me Joshua the high
priest standing before the angel of the
Lord, and Satan standing at his right
hand to resist him. (Zechariah 3:1.)

Be sober, be vigilant; because your
adversary the devil, as a roaring lion,
walketh about, seeking whom he may
devour. (1 Peter 5:8.)

Additional References.—Numbers 22:22;
1 Samuel 1:6; 1 Samuel 29:4; 1 Kings 5:
4; 1 Kings 11:14; Job 31:35; Psalms 74:
10; Isaiah 50:8; Lamentations 1:10; Luke
18:3; 1 Timothy 5:14; Hebrews 10:27;
Philippians 1:28; 1 Corinthians 16:9; Luke
3:17; 21:15; Lamentations 2:17; Psalm
109:20, 29.

ADVOCATE. (See Christ, Comforter, God, Holy Ghost, Mediator, Propitiation.)

AD'VO-CATE—one who pleads the cause of
another. One who exhorts, defends, comforts, or prays for another. Christ called the
Holy Spirit the Advocate and John gives the
same appellation to Christ Himself. The
Greek word so translated, *paraclaytos* (paraclete) is also translated "comforter."

REFERENCES.

*And I will pray the Father, and he
shall give you another Comforter, that
he may abide with you for ever.* (John
14:16.)

But when the Comforter is come, whom I will send unto you from the Father, even the Spirit of truth, which proceedeth from the Father, he shall testify of me. (John 15: 26.)

Nevertheless, I tell you the truth: It is expedient for you that I go away: for if I go not away, the Comforter will not come unto you; but if I depart, I will send him unto you. (John 16: 7.)

Who is he that condemneth? It is Christ that died, yea rather, that is risen again, who is even at the right hand of God, who also maketh intercession for us. (Romans 8: 34.)

Wherefore he is able also to save them to the uttermost that come unto God by him, seeing he ever liveth to make intercession for them. (Hebrews 7: 25.)

My little children, these things write I unto you, that ye sin not. And if any man sin we have an advocate with the Father, Jesus Christ the righteous. (1 John 2: 1.)

AFFLICTION. (See Repentance, Persecution, Trouble, Tribulation.)

Af-flic'tion—the cause of continued pain of body or mind; the state of being in continuous pain of body or mind; all manner of distress, persecution, oppression, pain, or sorrow; anything that causes sorrow.

REFERENCES.

Affliction as the Result of Sin.

Howbeit, because by this deed thou hast given great occasion to the enemies of the Lord to blaspheme, the child also that is born unto thee shall surely die. (2 Samuel 12: 14.)

For we are consumed by thine anger, and by thy wrath are we troubled. (Psalm 90: 7.)

Although affliction cometh not forth of the dust, neither doth trouble spring out of the ground;

Yet man is born unto trouble, as the sparks fly upward. (Job 5: 6, 7.)

Affliction Comes from God.

And he said unto Abram, Know of a surety that thy seed shall be a stranger in a land that is not theirs, and shall serve them; and they shall afflict them four hundred years. (Genesis 15: 13.)

And while he yet talked with them, behold, the messenger came down unto him: and he said, Behold, this evil is of the Lord; what should I wait for the Lord any longer? (2 Kings 6: 33.)

If I be wicked, woe unto me; and if I be righteous, yea will I not lift up my head. I am full of confusion; therefore see thou mine affliction. (Job 10: 15.)

Thou broughtest us into the net; thou laidest affliction upon our loins. (Psalm 66: 11.)

Afflictions Sent in Love and Mercy.

But as for you, ye thought evil against me; but God meant it unto good, to bring to pass, as it is this day, to save much people alive. (Genesis 50: 20.)

Who fed thee in the wilderness with manna, which thy fathers knew not, that he might humble thee, and that he might prove thee, to do thee good at thy latter end. (Deuteronomy 8: 16.)

I know, O Lord, that thy judgments are right, and that thou in faithfulness hast afflicted me. (Psalm 119: 75.)

And I will cause you to pass under the rod, and I will bring you into the bond of the covenant. (Ezekiel 20: 37.)

Then shall they deliver you up to be afflicted, and shall kill you: and ye shall be hated of all nations for my name's sake. (Matthew 24: 9.)

Save that the Holy Ghost witnesseth in every city, saying, that bonds and afflictions abide me. (Acts 20: 23.)

For I reckon, that the sufferings of this present time are not worthy to be compared with the glory which shall be revealed in us. (Romans 8: 18.)

For whom the Lord loveth he chasteneth, and scourgeth every son whom he receiveth. (Hebrews 12: 6.)

Take, my brethren, the prophets, who have spoken in the name of the Lord, for an example of suffering affliction, and of patience. (James 5: 10.)

Support under Affliction.

When thou passest through the waters, I will be with thee; and through the rivers, they shall not overflow thee: when thou walkest through the fire, thou shalt not be burned; neither shall the flame kindle upon thee. (Isaiah 43: 2.)

O Lord, my strength and my fortress, and my refuge in the day of affliction, the Gentiles shall come unto thee from the ends of the earth, and shall say, Surely our fathers have inherited lies, vanity, and things wherein there is no profit. (Jeremiah 16: 19.)

But I will deliver thee in that day, saith the Lord: and thou shalt not be given into the hand of the men of whom thou art afraid. (Jeremiah 39: 17.)

The Lord is good, a strong hold in the day of trouble; and he knoweth them that trust in him. (Nahum 1: 7.)

Come unto me, all ye that labour, and are heavy laden, and I will give you rest. (Matthew 11: 28.)

Peace I leave with you, my peace I give unto you: not as the world giveth, *give I unto you. Let not your heart be troubled, neither let it be afraid.* (John 14: 27.)

For in that he himself hath suffered, being tempted, he is able to succour them that are tempted. (Hebrews 2: 18.)

Comfort under Affliction.

For in the time of trouble he shall hide me in his pavilion: in the secret of his tabernacle shall he hide me; he shall set me up upon a rock. (Psalm 27: 5.)

Sing, O heavens; and be joyful, O earth; and break forth into singing, O mountains: for the Lord hath comforted his people, and will have mercy upon his afflicted. (Isaiah 49: 13.)

Then shall the virgin rejoice in the dance, both young men and old together: for I will turn their mourning into joy, and will comfort them, and make them rejoice from their sorrow. (Jeremiah 31: 13.)

Blessed are they that mourn: for they shall be comforted. (Matthew 5: 4.)

And when the Lord saw her, he had compassion on her, and said unto her, *Weep not.* (Luke 7: 13.)

Verily, verily, I say unto you, that ye shall weep and lament, but the world shall rejoice: and ye shall be sorrowful, but your sorrow shall be turned into joy. (John 16: 20.)

These things I have spoken unto you, that in me ye might have peace. In the world ye shall have tribulation, but be of good cheer: I have overcome the world. (John 16: 33.)

Who comforteth us in all our tribulation, that we may be able to comfort them which are in any trouble by the comfort wherewith we ourselves are comforted of God. (2 Corinthians 1: 4.)

Objects and Effects.

But when we are judged, we are chastened of the Lord, that we should not be condemned with the world. (1 Corinthians 11: 32.)

For our light affliction, which is but for a moment, worketh for us a far more exceeding and eternal weight of glory. (2 Corinthians 4: 17.)

But the God of all grace, who hath called us unto his eternal glory by Christ Jesus, after that ye have suffered a while, make you perfect, stablish, strengthen, settle you. (1 Peter 5: 10.)

Endurance of Affliction.

The Lord gave, and the Lord hath taken away; blessed be the name of the Lord. (Job 1: 21.)

But he said unto her, Thou speakest as one of the foolish women speaketh. What! shall we receive good at the hand of God, and shall we not receive evil? In all this did not Job sin with his lips. (Job 2: 10.)

Behold, happy is the man whom God correcteth: therefore despise not thou the chastening of the Almighty. (Job 5: 17.)

Though he slay me, yet will I trust in him: but I will maintain mine own ways before him. (Job 13: 15.)

I was dumb, I opened not my mouth; because thou didst it. (Psalm 39: 9.)

In your patience possess ye your souls. (Luke 21: 19.)

Rejoicing in hope; patient in tribulation; continuing instant in prayer. (Romans 12: 12.)

So that we ourselves glory in you in the churches of God, for your patience and faith in all your persecutions and tribulations that ye endure. (2 Thessalonians 1: 4.)

Supplication under Affliction.

In those days was Hezekiah sick unto death. And the prophet Isaiah the son of Amoz came to him, and said unto him, Thus saith the Lord, Set thine house in order; for thou shalt die, and not live.

Then he turned his face to the wall, and prayed unto the Lord. (2 Kings 20: 1, 2.)

And Asa cried unto the Lord his God, and said, Lord, it is nothing with thee to help, whether with many, or with them that have no power: help us, O Lord our God; for we rest on thee, and in thy name we go against this multitude. O Lord, thou art our God; let not man prevail against thee. (2 Chronicles 14: 11.)

I have surely heard Ephraim bemoaning himself thus; Thou hast chastised me, and I was chastised, as a bullock unaccustomed to the yoke: turn thou me, and I shall be turned; for thou art the Lord my God. (Jeremiah 31: 18.)

Remember, O Lord, what is come upon us: consider, and behold our reproach. (Lamentations 5: 1.)

And I set my face unto the Lord God, to seek by prayer and supplications, with fasting, and sackcloth, and ashes. (Daniel 9: 3.)

And he went a little further, and fell on his face, and prayed, saying, *O my Father, if it be possible, let this cup pass from me: nevertheless, not as I will, but as thou wilt.* (Matthew 26: 39.)

And lest I should be exalted above measure through the abundance of the revelations, there was given to me a thorn in the flesh, the messenger of Satan to buffet me, lest I should be exalted above measure.

For this thing I besought the Lord thrice, that it might depart from me. (2 Corinthians 12: 7, 8.)

Is any among you afflicted? let him pray. Is any merry? let him sing psalms. (James 5: 13.)

Brings Confession and Repentance.

Therefore the people came to Moses, and said, We have sinned, for we have spoken against the Lord, and against thee; pray unto the Lord, that he take away the serpents from us. And Moses prayed for the people. (Numbers 21: 7.)

I have sinned; what shall I do unto thee, O thou preserver of men? why hast thou set me as a mark against thee, so that I am a burden to myself? (Job 7: 20.)

I acknowledged my sin unto thee, and mine iniquity have I not hid. I said, I will confess my transgressions unto the Lord; and thou forgavest the iniquity of my sin. Selah. (Psalm 32: 5.)

Come, and let us return unto the Lord: for he hath torn, and he will heal us; he hath smitten, and he will bind us up. (Hosea 6: 1.)

I will bear the indignation of the Lord, because I have sinned against him, until he plead my cause, and execute judgment for me: he will bring me forth to the light, and I shall behold his righteousness. (Micah 7: 9.)

I will arise and go to my father, and will say unto him, Father, I have sinned against heaven and before thee. (Luke 15: 18.)

Deliverances from Affliction.

I sought the Lord, and he heard me, and delivered me from all my fears. (Psalm 34: 4.)

Many are the afflictions of the righteous: but the Lord delivereth him out of them all. (Psalm 34: 19.)

He brought me up also out of an horrible pit, out of the miry clay, and set my feet upon a rock, and established my goings. (Psalm 40: 2.)

In all their affliction he was afflicted, and the angel of his presence saved them: in his love and in his pity he redeemed them; and he bare them, and carried them all the days of old. (Isaiah 63: 9.)

Then Jonah prayed unto the Lord his God out of the fish's belly,

And said, I cried by reason of mine affliction unto the Lord, and he heard me; out of the belly of hell cried I, and thou heardest my voice. (Jonah 2: 1, 2.)

Persecutions, afflictions, which came unto me at Antioch, at Iconium, at Lystra; what persecutions I endured: but out of them all the Lord delivered me. (2 Timothy 3: 11.)

Notwithstanding, the Lord stood with me, and strengthened me; that by me the preaching might be fully known, and that all the Gentiles might hear; and I was delivered out of the mouth of the lion.

And the Lord shall deliver me from every evil work, and will preserve me unto his heavenly kingdom; to whom be glory for ever and ever. Amen. (2 Timothy 4: 17, 18.)

Benefits of Affliction.

But he knoweth the way that I take: when he hath tried me, I shall come forth as gold. (Job 23: 10.)

And if they be bound in fetters, and be holden in cords of affliction,

Then he sheweth them their work,

and their transgressions that they have exceeded. (Job 36: 8, 9.)

Before I was afflicted I went astray: but now have I kept thy word. (Psalm 119: 67.)

It is good for me that I have been afflicted; that I might learn thy statutes. (Psalm 119: 71.)

It is better to go to the house of mourning, than to go to the house of feasting: for that is the end of all men; and the living will lay it to his heart. (Ecclesiastes 7: 2.)

Behold, I have refined thee, but not with silver; I have chosen thee in the furnace of affliction. (Isaiah 48: 10.)

I will go and return to my place, till they acknowledge their offense, and seek my face: in their affliction they will seek me early. (Hosea 5: 15.)

And not only so, but we glory in tribulations also; knowing that tribulation worketh patience. (Romans 5: 3.)

AGABUS.

Ag′a-bus—the name of a man who is supposed to have been one of the seventy later disciples of Christ. He is chiefly noted for two prophecies made about the time Paul and Barnabas were at Antioch (about A.D. 43) and about fourteen years later, to the effect that there was to be a great famine and that Paul would be persecuted in Jerusalem. Little is known of him save that the prophecies were fulfilled.

REFERENCES.

And in these days came prophets from Jerusalem unto Antioch.

And there stood up one of them named Agabus, and signified by the Spirit, that there should be great dearth throughout all the world: which came to pass in the days of Claudius Cesar.

Then the disciples, every man according to his ability, determined to send relief unto the brethren which dwelt in Judea.

Which also they did, and sent it to the elders by the hands of Barnabas and Saul. (Acts 11: 27-30.)

And as we tarried there many days, there came down from Judea a certain prophet, named Agabus.

And when he was come unto us, he took Paul's girdle, and bound his own hands and feet, and said, Thus saith the Holy Ghost, So shall the Jews at Jerusalem bind the man that owneth this girdle, and shall deliver him into the hands of the Gentiles. (Acts 21: 10, 11.)

AGE.

Age—that period of life wherein youth and prime have been left behind—commonly called old age. Almost all nations from the beginning of the human race have paid respect to age. In the Scripture especially we find many instances of this veneration.

REFERENCES.

The young men saw me, and hid themselves: and the aged arose, and stood up. (Job 29: 8.)

Thou shalt come to thy grave in a full age, like as a shock of corn cometh in in his season. (Job 5: 26.)

With us are both the gray-headed and very aged men, much elder than thy father. (Job 15: 10.)

Thou shalt rise up before the hoary head, and honour the face of the old man, and fear thy God: I am the Lord. (Leviticus 19: 32.)

And thou shalt go to thy fathers in peace; thou shalt be buried in a good old age. (Genesis 15: 15.)

Thus saith the Lord of hosts; There shall yet old men and old women dwell in the streets of Jerusalem, and every man with his staff in his hand for very age. (Zechariah 8: 4.)

AGRIPPA. (See Herod.)

AHAB. (See Jezebel, Elijah.)

A'HAB—a form of a Hebrew word meaning "father's brother." The name of the seventh king of Israel, who reigned from about 918 to 897 B.C. He was entirely under the influence of his Tyrian wife, Jezebel, who introduced into Israel the worship of Baal and Astarte, idolatries that were accompanied by rites of the most vile and disgusting character. The prophet Elijah opposed Ahab and his evil doings. The seizure of Naboth's vineyard and Naboth's murder, both deeds done at the instigation of Jezebel, was the real culmination of Ahab's career. Elijah assured him of the divine vengeance for these deeds, and for a time Ahab was repentant, his contrition staving off the promised punishment until the reign of his son, Jehoram, when all Ahab's house was wiped out. He died of wounds received in battle.

Ahab's character is one of the most notorious in the Old Testament. He had many weaknesses, and yet he seems to have governed firmly. It is probable that he would have been a much better man had it not been for his detestable wife, who seems to have led him into most of his wickedness.

REFERENCES.

And in the thirty and eighth year of Asa king of Judah began Ahab the son of Omri to reign over Israel: and Ahab the son of Omri reigned over Israel in Samaria twenty and two years.

And Ahab the son of Omri did evil in the sight of the Lord above all that were before him.

And it came to pass, as if it had been a light thing for him to walk in the sins of Jeroboam the son of Nebat, that he took to wife Jezebel the daughter of Ethbaal king of the Zidonians, and went and served Baal, and worshiped him.

And he reared up an altar for Baal in the house of Baal, which he had built in Samaria.

And Ahab made a grove; and Ahab did more to provoke the Lord God of Israel to anger than all the kings of Israel that were before him. (1 Kings 16: 29-33.)

And Elijah the Tishbite, who was of the inhabitants of Gilead, said unto Ahab, As the Lord God of Israel liveth, before whom I stand, there shall not be dew nor rain these years, but according to my word. (1 Kings 17: 1.)

And it came to pass when Ahab saw Elijah, that Ahab said unto him, Art thou he that troubleth Israel? (1 Kings 18: 17.)

And Ahab told Jezebel all that Elijah had done, and withal how he had slain all the prophets with the sword. (1 Kings 19: 1.)

And Ahab spake unto Naboth, saying, Give me thy vineyard, that I may have it for a garden of herbs, because it is near unto my house: and I will give thee for it a better vineyard than it; or if it seem good to thee, I will give thee the worth of it in money.

And Naboth said to Ahab, The Lord forbid it me, that I should give the inheritance of my fathers unto thee.

And Ahab came into his house heavy and displeased, because of the word which Naboth the Jezreelite had spoken to him: for he had said, I will not give thee the inheritance of my fathers. And he laid him down upon his bed, and turned away his face, and would eat no bread. (1 Kings 21: 2-4.)

And it came to pass, when Jezebel heard that Naboth was stoned, and was dead, that Jezebel said to Ahab, Arise, take possession of the vineyard of Naboth the Jezreelite, which he refused to give thee for money: for Naboth is not alive, but dead.

And it came to pass, when Ahab heard that Naboth was dead, that Ahab rose up to go down to the vineyard of Naboth the Jezreelite, to take possession of it.

And the word of the Lord came to Elijah the Tishbite, saying,

Arise, go down to meet Ahab king of Israel, which is in Samaria: behold, he is in the vineyard of Naboth, whither he is gone down to possess it.

And thou shalt speak unto him, saying, Thus saith the Lord, Hast thou killed, and also taken possession? And thou shalt speak unto him, saying, Thus saith the Lord, In the place where dogs licked the blood of Naboth shall dogs lick thy blood, even thine.

And Ahab said to Elijah, Hast thou found me, O mine enemy? And he answered, I have found thee: because thou hast sold thyself to work evil in the sight of the Lord. (1 Kings 21: 14-20.)

And it came to pass, when Ahab heard those words, that he rent his clothes, and put sackcloth upon his flesh, and fasted, and lay in sackcloth, and went softly.

And the word of the Lord came to Elijah the Tishbite, saying,

Seest thou how Ahab humbleth himself before me? because he humbleth himself before me, I will not bring the evil in his days: but in his son's days will I bring the evil upon his house. (1 Kings 21: 27-29.)

And a certain man drew a bow at a venture, and smote the king of Israel between the joints of the harness: wherefore he said unto the driver of his chariot, Turn thine hand, and carry me out of the host: for I am wounded. (1 Kings 22: 34.)

So the king died, and was brought to Samaria; and they buried the king in Samaria.

And one washed the chariot in the pool of Samaria; and the dogs licked up his blood; and they washed his armour; according unto the word of the Lord which he spake. (1 Kings 22: 37, 38.)

And thou shalt smite the house of Ahab thy master, that I may avenge the blood of my servants the prophets, and the blood of all the servants of the Lord, at the hand of Jezebel. (2 Kings 9: 7.)

So Jehu slew all that remained of the house of Ahab in Jezreel, and all his great men, and his kinsfolks, and his priests, until he left him none remaining. (2 Kings 10: 11.)

AHASUERUS. (See Esther, Haman, Mordecai, Vashti.)

A-HAS'U-E'RUS—pronounced a-haz-u-e-rus. The name of at least four Persian kings mentioned in the Bible, the most important being the one who took Esther to wife. He has been identified as the celebrated Xerxes I., who was so disastrously defeated by the Greeks at Salamis in the year 480 B.C. His first chief wife, Vashti, he divorced because she refused to display her beauty to the people at his order. He wedded Esther the year of his defeat by the Greeks after his return to his kingdom. Five years later the Mordecai-Haman incident arose. Haman offered his master the enormous sum of 10,000 talents of silver ($250,000) if he would permit a massacre of the Jews. The money was refused, but the consent given. Before the slaughter could take place Esther and Mordecai influenced the king to favor the Jews, as is told in the book of Esther, to which the reader is referred.

AHAZ.

A'HAZ—a form of a Hebrew word meaning "possessor." The name of the twelfth king of Judah and one of the worst of the Hebrew princes. He abandoned himself to all kinds of idolatries, sacrificed one of his sons to Moloch, and desecrated the temple. Judah, in his reign, became dependent upon Assyria. So bad was he that when he died, after reigning sixteen years, his body was not permitted burial in the tombs of the kings.

References.—2 Kings 16: 2, 11, 17; 20: 11; 23: 12, 17; 2 Chronicles 28: 2, 5; Isaiah 7.

AHAZIAH.

A-HA-ZI'AH—a form of a Hebrew word meaning "whom Jehovah possesses." The name of the son and successor of Ahab and eighth king of Israel. He was almost as bad as his father and reigned but two years. He received mortal injuries in a fall and sent to idolatrous priests for comfort. Elijah then warned him that he should die in a short time, which prophesy came to pass. Also the name of the nephew of the above and the son of Jehoram, who likewise perished in the consummation of the divine wrath against the house of Ahab.

References.—1 Kings 22: 40, 49; 2 Kings 1: 2, 4, 17; 2 Kings 8: 25; 2 Kings 9: 21; 2 Chronicles 8: 25; 2 Chronicles 22: 9.

ALABASTER.

AL'A-BAS'TER—a fine, light-colored, marble-like stone; very much prized by the ancients for the manufacture of vessels to hold pomades, ointments, and perfumes. Such vessels were often called alabasters even while made of some other material.

References.—Matthew 26: 6, 7; Mark 14: 3; Luke 7: 37; John 12: 3.

ALPHA AND OMEGA.

AL'PHA AND O-ME'GA—the first and the last letters of the Greek alphabet. The phrase was used by our Lord to indicate his position—the first and the last, the beginning and the ending. Greek was the language of polite society, and the expression doubtless was thoroughly understood as given to Christians of that day.

REFERENCES.

I am Alpha and Omega, the beginning and the ending, saith the Lord, which is, and which was, and which is to come, the Almighty. (Revelation 1: 8.)

Saying, I am Alpha and Omega, the first and the last: and, What thou seest write in a book, and send it unto the seven churches which are in Asia; unto Ephesus, and unto Smyrna, and unto Pergamos, and unto Thyatira, and unto Sardis, and unto Philadelphia, and unto Laodicea. (Revelation 1: 11.)

And he said unto me, It is done. I am Alpha and Omega, the beginning and the end. I will give unto him that is athirst of the fountain of the water of life freely. (Revelation 21: 6.)

AMBITION.

AM-BI'TION—an eager, often inordinate desire for place, power, preferment, superiority; the desire to attain something.

REFERENCES.

Reproof and Punishment of.

He loveth transgression that loveth strife: and he that exalteth his gate seeketh destruction. (Proverbs 17: 19.)

How art thou fallen from heaven, O Lucifer, son of the morning! how art thou cut down to the ground, which didst weaken the nations! (Isaiah 14: 12.)

At the same time came the disciples unto Jesus, saying, Who is the greatest in the kingdom of heaven?

And Jesus called a little child unto him, and set him in the midst of them,

And said, *Verily I say unto you, Except ye be converted, and become as little children, ye shall not enter into the kingdom of heaven.* (Matthew 18: 1-3.)

But Jesus called them unto him, and said, *Ye know that the princes of the Gentiles exercise dominion over them, and they that are great exercise author-ity upon them.*

But it shall not be so among you: but whosoever will be great among you, let him be your minister. (Matthew 20: 25, 26.)

But be not ye called Rabbi: for one is your Master, even Christ; and all ye are brethren. (Matthew 23: 8.)

And there was also a strife among them, which of them should be account-ed the greatest. (Luke 22: 24.)

Additional References.—Genesis 11: 4; Numbers 12: 10; Numbers 16: 3; 2 Samuel 18: 9; 1 Kings 1: 5; Jeremiah 51: 53; 2 Thes-salonians 2: 4.

AMEN.

A'MEN—also pronounced ah-men. The word comes originally from the Hebrew. In its purest form it was an adjective and meant firm or faithful. We find some instances of its use thus in the Bible. It is now mostly heard of in its form as an adverb meaning certainly, surely, truly. There are passages in John's gospel where it is translated verily. Its repetition at the end of a statement was like an oath or affirmation of the person mak-ing it to the statement which it followed.

REFERENCES.

And this water that causeth the curse shall go into thy bowels, to make thy belly to swell, and thy thigh to rot. And the woman shall say, Amen, amen. (Numbers 5: 22.)

Cursed be the man that maketh any graven or molten image, an abomina-tion unto the Lord, the work of the hand of the craftsman, and putteth it in a secret place: and all the people shall answer and say, Amen. (Deuterono-my 27: 15.)

And Benaiah the son of Jehoiada an-swered the king, and said, Amen: the Lord God of my lord the king say so too. (1 Kings 1: 36.)

Blessed be the Lord God of Israel for ever and ever. And all the people said, Amen, and praised the Lord. (2 Chron-icles 16: 36.)

Blessed be the Lord God of Israel from everlasting, and to everlasting. Amen, and Amen. (Psalm 41: 13.)

And blessed be his glorious name for ever: and let the whole earth be filled with his glory; Amen, and Amen. (Psalm 72: 19.)

Blessed be the Lord for evermore. Amen, and Amen. (Psalm 89: 52.)

Even the prophet Jeremiah said, Amen: the Lord do so: the Lord per-form thy words which thou hast proph-esied, to bring again the vessels of the Lord's house, and all that is carried away captive from Babylon into this place. (Jeremiah 28: 6.)

And lead us not into temptation, but deliver us from evil. For thine is the kingdom, and the power, and the glory, for ever. Amen. (Matthew 6: 13.)

Jesus answered and said unto him, *Verily, verily, I say unto thee, Except a man be born again, he cannot see the kingdom of God.* (John 3: 3.)

For all the promises of God in him are yea, and in him Amen, unto the glory of God by us. (2 Corinthians 1: 20.)

I am he that liveth, and was dead; and behold, I am alive for evermore, Amen; and have the keys of hell and of death. (Revelation 1: 18.)

And the four beasts said, Amen. And the four and twenty elders fell down and worshiped him that liveth for ever and ever. (Revelation 5: 14.)

He which testifieth these things saith, Surely I come quickly: Amen. Even so, come. Lord Jesus. (Revelation 22: 20.)

AMMONITES.

Am'mon-ites—a tribe descended from the younger son of Lot. In the early days of the Hebrew nation there was little trouble between it and the Ammonites, but in later times the warfare was almost continual and very bitter. They were idolatrous. Solomon had some of their women in his palace.

References.—Genesis 19: 38; Deuteronomy 2: 19; 23: 3; Judges 11: 4, 33; 1 Samuel 11: 11; 2 Samuel 12: 26; Jeremiah 25: 21; Jeremiah 49: 1; Ezekiel 21: 28; Ezekiel 25: 2, 3; Amos 1: 13; Zephaniah 2: 8.

AMOS.

A'mos—a form of a Hebrew word meaning "a burden." The name of one of the twelve minor prophets, who lived about 800 to 730 B.C. He was a contemporary of Isaiah and Hosea. He seems to have been born in the vicinity of Bethlehem and to have been a shepherd and tree-dresser. His denunciation and prophecy are directed against the licentiousness not only of the Jews but the world as it then existed.

ANDREW. (See Apostles.)

An'drew—a form of a Greek word meaning "manly." The name of one of the twelve apostles. He was a fisherman of Galilee, the brother of Simon Peter, and originally a disciple of John the Baptist, accepting and following Jesus when John pointed Him out as the Lamb of God. His first work as a Christian was to bring his brother to the Lord. Not much is related of his subsequent labors, although tradition states that he ministered in Scythia, Greece and Thrace. He is said to have been crucified on a cross formed like the letter X, which has since been called St. Andrew's cross.

REFERENCES.

And Jesus, walking by the sea of Galilee, saw two brethren, Simon called Peter, and Andrew his brother, casting a net into the sea; for they were fishers. (Matthew 4: 18.)

Now the names of the twelve apostles are these; The first, Simon, who is called Peter, and Andrew his brother; James the son of Zebedee, and John his brother. (Matthew 10: 2.)

Now as he walked by the sea of Galilee, he saw Simon, and Andrew his brother, casting a net into the sea: for they were fishers. (Mark 1: 16.)

And forthwith, when they were come out of the synagogue, they entered into the house of Simon and Andrew, with James and John. (Mark 1: 29.)

One of the two which heard John speak, and followed him, was Andrew, Simon Peter's brother.

He first findeth his own brother Simon, and saith unto him, We have found the Messias; which is, being interpreted, the Christ. (John 1: 40, 41.)

ANGEL. (See Heaven, Hell.)

An'gel—a form of a Greek word meaning "messenger." A name given to the spiritual beings by whom God is surrounded and who do His bidding and manifest His will or power. We are told that they are very numerous, that their intelligence is superhuman, that they neither marry nor are given in marriage, and that there is no distinction of sex among them. The Jews believed and taught that the angels formed a vast hierarchy, or order, with regular gradations of rank, each having its special powers and functions, and ascending from man up to God, only a few being chosen to stand before the Almighty. The Bible is full of allusions to this heavenly host, and many instances are given of their visitations to earth and to men, carrying messages from God and doing His will. This ministry is very clearly taught in all Scripture. It was a favorite thought with the fathers of the Church that every mortal had his or her guardian angel. To a certain extent this view is still held in some quarters. Scripture also teaches that Satan is also the possessor of angels, who do his bidding. The Bible is very clear as to this. Satan himself was once one of the angelic host. He as Lucifer rebelled against God because of excessive ambition and pride and was expelled from Heaven. Revelation tells of the war, relating that Michael and his host fought against Satan and his host, and conquered them.

REFERENCES.

Nature, Office, Duties, Etc., of Angels.

And as he lay and slept under a juniper-tree, behold, then an angel touched him, and said unto him, Arise and eat. (1 Kings 19: 5.)

Thou, even thou, art Lord alone; thou hast made heaven, the heaven of heavens, with all their host, the earth, and all things that are therein, the seas, and all that is therein, and thou preservest them all; and the host of heaven worshippeth thee. (Nehemiah 9: 6.)

And when the angel stretched out his hand upon Jerusalem to destroy it, the Lord repented him of the evil, and said to the angel that destroyed the people, It is enough: stay now thine hand. And the angel of the Lord was by the threshingplace of Araunah the Jebusite. (2 Samuel 24: 16.)

When the morning stars sang together, and all the sons of God shouted for joy. (Job 38: 7.)

The chariots of God are twenty thousand, even thousands of angels: the Lord is among them, as in Sinai, in the holy place. (Psalm 68: 17.)

For he shall give his angels charge over thee, to keep thee in all thy ways. (Psalm 91: 11.)

Bless the Lord, ye his angels, that excel in strength, that do his commandments, hearkening unto the voice of his word.

Bless ye the Lord, all ye his hosts; ye ministers of his, that do his pleasure. (Psalm 103: 20, 21.)

In the year that king Uzziah died I saw also the Lord sitting upon a throne, high and lifted up, and his train filled the temple.

Above it stood the seraphims: each one had six wings; with twain he covered his face, and with twain he covered his feet, and with twain he did fly.

And one cried unto another, and said, Holy, holy, holy, is the Lord of hosts: the whole earth is full of his glory. (Isaiah 6: 1-3.)

The enemy that sowed them is the devil; the harvest is the end of the world; and the reapers are the angels. (Matthew 13: 39.)

When the Son of man shall come in his glory, and all the holy angels with him, then shall he sit upon the throne of his glory. (Matthew 25: 31.)

For the son of man shall come in the glory of his Father, with his angels; and then he shall reward every man according to his works. (Matthew 16: 27.)

Take heed that ye despise not one of these little ones: for I say unto you, That in heaven their angels do always behold the face of my Father which is in heaven. (Matthew 18: 10.)

And he shall send his Angels with a great sound of a trumpet, and they shall gather together his Elect from the four winds, from one end of heaven to the other. (Matthew 24: 31.)

When the Son of man shall come in his glory, and all the holy angels with him, then shall he sit upon the throne of his glory. (Matthew 25: 31.)

Whosoever therefore shall be ashamed of me, and of my words, in this adulterous and sinful generation; of him also shall the Son of man be ashamed, when he cometh in the glory of his Father with the holy angels. (Mark 8: 38.)

And it came to pass, that the beggar died, and was carried by the angels into

Abraham's bosom. The rich man also died, and was buried. (Luke 16: 22.)

For there stood by me this night the angel of God, whose I am, and whom I serve. (Acts 27: 23.)

Know ye not that we shall judge angels? how much more, things that pertain to this life? (1 Corinthians 6: 3.)

For the Lord himself shall descend from heaven with a shout, with the voice of the archangel, and with the trump of God: and the dead in Christ shall rise first. (Colossians 1: 16.)

Let no man beguile you of your reward in a voluntary humility and worshipping of angels, intruding into those things which he hath not seen, vainly puffed up by his fleshly mind. (Colossians 2: 18.)

And to you, who are troubled, rest with us, when the Lord Jesus shall be revealed from heaven with his mighty angels,

In flaming fire taking vengeance on them that know not God, and that obey not the gospel of our Lord Jesus Christ. (2 Thessalonians 1: 7, 8.)

I charge thee before God, and the Lord Jesus Christ, and the elect angels, that thou observe these things without preferring one before another, doing nothing by partiality. (Ephesians 1: 21.)

Being made so much better than the angels, as he hath by inheritance obtained a more excellent name than they.

For unto which of the angels said he at any time, Thou art my Son, this day have I begotten thee? And again, I will be to him a Father, and he shall be to me a Son?

And again, when he bringeth in the first-begotten into the world, he saith, And let all the angels of God worship him.

And of the angels he saith, Who maketh his angels spirits, and his ministers a flame of fire. (Hebrews 1: 4-7.)

But ye are come unto mount Sion, and unto the city of the living God, the heavenly Jerusalem, and to an innumerable company of angels. (Hebrews 12: 22.)

Unto whom it was revealed, that not unto themselves, but unto us they did minister the things which are now reported unto you by them that have preached the gospel unto you, with the Holy Ghost sent down from heaven; which things the angels desire to look into. (1 Peter 1: 12.)

Yet Michael the archangel, when contending with the devil, he disputed about the body of Moses, durst not bring against him a railing accusation, but said, The Lord rebuke thee. (Jude 1: 9.)

And I saw a strong angel proclaiming with a loud voice, Who is worthy to open the book, and to loose the seals thereof? (Revelation 5: 2.)

And after these things, I saw four Angels standing on the four corners of the Earth, holding the four winds of the earth, that the wind should not blow on the earth, nor on the sea, nor on any tree.

And I saw another angel ascending from the east, having the seal of the living God: and he cried with a loud voice to the four angels, to whom it was given to hurt the earth and the sea,

Saying, Hurt not the earth, neither the sea, nor the trees, till we have sealed the servants of our God in their foreheads. (Revelation 7: 1-3.)

And I fell at his feet to worship him. And he said unto me. See thou do it not: I am thy fellow-servant, and of thy brethren that have the testimony of Jesus: worship God: for the testimony of Jesus is the spirit of prophecy. (Revelation 19: 10.)

And I John saw these things, and heard them. And when I had heard and seen, I fell down to worship before the feet of the angel which shewed me these things.

Then saith he unto me, See thou do it not: for I am thy fellow-servant, and of thy brethren the prophets, and of them which keep the sayings of this book: worship God. (Revelation 22: 8, 9.)

Rebellion of the Angels.

And there was war in heaven: Michael and his angels fought against the dragon; and the dragon fought and his angels,

And prevailed not; neither was their place found any more in heaven. (Revelation 12: 7, 8.)

For if God spared not the angels that sinned, but cast them down to hell, and delivered them into chains of darkness, to be reserved unto judgment. (2 Peter 2: 4.)

And the angels which kept not their first estate, but left their own habitation, he hath reserved in everlasting chains under darkness unto the judgment of the great day. (Jude 1: 6.)

Then shall he say also unto them on the left hand, Depart from me, ye cursed, into everlasting fire, prepared for the devil and his angels. (Matthew 25: 41.)

Visitations of Angels.

To Hagar:

And the Angel of the Lord found her by a fountain of water in the wil-derness, by the fountain in the way to Shur. (Genesis 16: 7.)

And God heard the voice of the lad; and the angel of God called to Hagar out of heaven, and said unto her, What aileth thee, Hagar? Fear not; for God hath heard the voice of the lad where he is. (Genesis 21: 17.)

To Abraham:

And the Lord appeared unto him in the plains of Mamre: and he sat in the tent door in the heat of the day;

And he lift up his eyes and looked, and, lo, three men stood by him: and when he saw them, he ran to meet them from the tent door, and bowed himself toward the ground. (Genesis 18: 1, 2.)

And the angel of the Lord called unto him out of heaven, and said, Abraham, Abraham: and he said, Here am I. (Genesis 22: 11.)

To Lot:

And there came two angels to Sodom at even; and Lot sat in the gate of Sodom; and Lot, seeing them, rose up to meet them; and he bowed himself with his face toward the ground. (Genesis 19: 1.)

To Balaam:

Then the Lord opened the eyes of Balaam, and he saw the angel of the Lord standing in the way, and his sword drawn in his hand: and he bowed down his head, and fell flat on his face. (Numbers 22: 31.)

To the Israelites:

And an angel of the Lord came up from Gilgal to Bochim, and said, I made you to go up out of Egypt, and have brought you unto the land which I sware unto your fathers; and I said, I will never break my covenant with you. (Judges 2: 1.)

To Gideon:

And there came an angel of the Lord, and sat under an oak which was in Ophrah, that pertained unto Joash the Abi-ezrite: and his son Gideon threshed wheat by the wine-press, to hide it from the Midianites.

And the angel of the Lord appeared unto him, and said unto him, The Lord is with thee, thou mighty man of valour. (Judges 6: 11, 12.)

To Manoah's wife:

And there was a certain man of Zorah, of the family of the Danites, whose name was Manoah; and his wife was barren, and bare not.

And the angel of the Lord appeared unto the woman, and said unto her, Behold, now, thou art barren, and bearest not: but thou shalt conceive, and bear a son. (Judges 13: 2, 3.)

To David:

And God sent an angel unto Jerusalem to destroy it: and as he was destroying, the Lord beheld, and he repented him of the evil, and said to the angel that destroyed, It is enough, stay now thine hand. And the angel of the Lord stood by the threshingfloor of Ornan the Jebusite.

And David lifted up his eyes, and saw the angel of the Lord stand between the earth and the heaven, having a drawn sword in his hand stretched out over Jerusalem. Then David and the elders of Israel, who were clothed in sackcloth, fell upon their faces. (1 Chronicles 21: 15, 16.)

To Elijah:

And as he lay and slept under a juniper-tree, behold, then an angel touched him, and said unto him, Arise and eat.

And he looked, and behold, there was a cake baken on the coals, and a cruse of water at his head: and he did eat and drink, and laid him down again.

And the angel of the Lord came again the second time, and touched him, and said, Arise and eat, because the journey is too great for thee. (1 Kings 19: 5-7.)

To Daniel:

And I heard a man's voice between the banks of Ulai, which called, and said, Gabriel, make this man to understand the vision.

So he came near where I stood: and when he came, I was afraid, and fell upon my face: but he said unto me, Understand, O son of man: for at the time of the end shall be the vision. (Daniel 8: 16, 17.)

Yea, while I was speaking in prayer, even the man Gabriel, whom I had seen in the vision at the beginning, being caused to fly swiftly, touched me about the time of the evening oblation. (Daniel 9: 21.)

And behold, one like the similitude of the sons of men touched my lips: then I opened my mouth, and spake, and said unto him that stood before me, O my lord, by the vision my sorrows are turned upon me, and I have retained no strength. (Daniel 10: 16.)

To Nebuchadnezzar:

Then Nebuchadnezzar the king was astonied, and rose up in haste, and spake, and said unto his counsellors, Did not we cast three men bound into the midst of the fire? They answered and said unto the king, True, O king.

He answered and said, Lo, I see four men loose, walking in the midst of the fire, and they have no hurt: and the form of the fourth is like the Son of God. (Daniel 3: 24, 25.)

To Jesus:

Then the devil leaveth him, and behold, Angels came and ministered unto him. (Matthew 4: 11.)

And there appeared an Angel unto him from heaven, strengthening him. (Luke 22: 43.)

To Joseph:

But while he thought on these things, behold, the Angel of the Lord appeared unto him in a dream, saying, Joseph, thou son of David, fear not to take unto thee Mary thy wife; for that which is conceived in her is of the holy Ghost. (Matthew 1: 20.)

To Mary Magdalene:

In the end of the sabbath, as it began to dawn toward the first day of the week, came Mary Magdalene and the other Mary to see the sepulchre.

And behold, there was a great earthquake: for the angel of the Lord descended from heaven, and came and rolled back the stone from the door, and sat upon it. (Matthew 28: 1, 2.)

To Zacharias:

And there appeared unto him an angel of the Lord, standing on the right side of the altar of incense.

And when Zacharias saw him, he was troubled, and fear fell upon him. (Luke 1: 11, 12.)

To the Virgin Mary:

And in the sixth month the angel Gabriel was sent from God unto a city of Galilee, named Nazareth,

To a virgin espoused to a man whose name was Joseph, of the house of David; and the virgin's name was Mary. (Luke 1: 26, 27.)

To the Shepherds:

And there were in the same country shepherds abiding in the field, keeping watch over their flock by night.

And lo, the angel of the Lord came upon them, and the glory of the Lord shone round about them; and they were sore afraid. (Luke 2: 8, 9.)

And suddenly there was with the angel a multitude of the heavenly host praising God, and saying,

Glory to God in the highest, and on earth peace, good will toward men. (Luke 2: 13, 14.)

To Peter and others:

But the angel of the Lord by night opened the prison-doors, and brought them forth, and said,

Go, stand and speak in the temple to the people all the words of this life. (Acts 5: 19, 20.)

And behold, the angel of the Lord came upon him, and a light shined in the prison; and he smote Peter on the side, and raised him up, saying, Arise up quickly. And his chains fell off from his hands. (Acts 12: 7.)

To Philip:

And the angel of the Lord spake unto Philip, saying, Arise, and go toward the south, unto the way that goeth down from Jerusalem unto Gaza, which is desert. (Acts 8: 26.)

To Cornelius:

He saw in a vision evidently, about the ninth hour of the day, an angel of God coming in to him, and saying unto him, Cornelius. (Acts 10: 3.)

To Paul:

For there stood by me this night the Angel of God, whose I am, and whom I serve,

Saying, Fear not, Paul, thou must be

brought before Cæsar, and lo, God hath given thee all them that sail with thee. (Acts 27: 23, 24.)

ANGER.

AN'GER—a strong passion or emotion of displeasure, antagonism or indignation roused by real or supposed injury, insult or wrong. It is sinful or wise according to its motive. Displeasure at sin, especially the divine displeasure, is just and holy. When ascribed to God anger is not to be understood to be a wild, tumultuous passion such as men feel, but a righteous aversion to sin and wrong-doing. Sinful anger often exists in man, as a work of the flesh or as a fruit of pride. It often also leads to the commission of even greater sins.

REFERENCES.

Human Anger: Nature and Effects.

But unto Cain and to his offering he had not respect. And Cain was very wroth, and his countenance fell. (Genesis 4: 5.)

And Cain talked with Abel his brother: and it came to pass, when they were in the field, that Cain rose up against Abel his brother, and slew him. (Genesis 4: 8.)

Then Judah came near unto him, and said, O my lord, let thy servant, I pray thee, speak a word in my lord's ears, and let not thine anger burn against thy servant: for thou art even as Pharaoh. (Genesis 44: 18.)

Cursed be their anger, for it was fierce: and their wrath, for it was cruel: I will divide them in Jacob, and scatter them in Israel. (Genesis 49: 7.)

And it came to pass as soon as he came nigh unto the camp, that he saw the calf, and the dancing: and Moses' anger waxed hot, and he cast the tables out of his hands, and brake them beneath the mount. (Exodus 32: 19.)

A wrathful man stirreth up strife: but he that is slow to anger appeaseth strife. (Proverbs 15: 18.)

He that is slow to anger is better than the mighty; and he that ruleth his spirit, than he that taketh a city. (Proverbs 16: 32.)

The discretion of a man deferreth his anger; and it is his glory to pass over a transgression. (Proverbs 19: 11.)

It is better to dwell in the wilderness, than with a contentious and an angry woman. (Proverbs 21: 19.)

An angry man stirreth up strife, and a furious man aboundeth in transgression. (Proverbs 29: 22.)

Be not hasty in thy spirit to be angry: for anger resteth in the bosom of fools. (Ecclesiastes 7: 9.)

But I say unto you, That whosoever is angry with his brother without a cause, shall be in danger of the judgment: and whosoever shall say to his brother, Raca, shall be in danger of the council: but whosoever shall say, Thou fool, shall be in danger of hell-fire. (Matthew 5: 22.)

Human Anger: Remedies and Warnings.

Cease from anger, and forsake wrath: fret not thyself in any wise to do evil. (Psalm 37: 8.)

A soft answer turneth away wrath: but grievous words stir up anger. (Proverbs 15: 1.)

A gift in secret pacifieth anger: and a reward in the bosom, strong wrath. (Proverbs 21: 14.)

Be ye angry, and sin not: let not the sun go down upon your wrath. (Ephesians 4: 26.)

Let all bitterness, and wrath, and anger, and clamour, and evil-speaking, be put away from you, with all malice. (Ephesians 4: 31.)

But now ye also put off all these; anger, wrath, malice, blasphemy, filthy communication out of your mouth. (Colossians 3: 8.)

Divine Anger: Existence, Etc.

And the Lord God said unto the serpent, Because thou hast done this, thou art cursed above all cattle, and above every beast of the field: upon thy belly shalt thou go, and dust shalt thou eat all the days of thy life. (Genesis 3: 14.)

Unto the woman he said, I will greatly multiply thy sorrow and thy conception; in sorrow thou shalt bring forth children; and thy desire shall be to thy husband, and he shall rule over thee.

And unto Adam he said, Because thou hast hearkened unto the voice of thy wife, and hast eaten of the tree, of which I commanded thee, saying, Thou shalt not eat of it: cursed is the ground for thy sake; in sorrow shalt thou eat of it all the days of thy life. (Genesis 3: 16, 17.)

And he said, What hast thou done? the voice of thy brother's blood crieth unto me from the ground.

And now art thou cursed from the earth, which hath opened her mouth to receive thy brother's blood from thy hand. (Genesis 4: 10, 11.)

The Lord will not spare him, but then the anger of the Lord and his jealousy shall smoke against that man, and all the curses that are written in this book shall lie upon him, and the Lord shall blot out his name from under heaven. (Deuteronomy 29: 20.)

They provoked him to jealousy with strange gods, with abominations provoked they him to anger. (Deuteronomy 32: 16.)

When ye have transgressed the covenant of the Lord your God, which he commanded you, and have gone and served other gods, and bowed yourselves to them; then shall the anger of the Lord be kindled against you, and ye shall perish quickly from off the good land which he hath given unto you. (Joshua 23: 16.)

If God will not withdraw his anger, the proud helpers do stoop under him. (Job 9: 13.)

God judgeth the righteous, and God is angry with the wicked every day. (Psalm 7: 11.)

Thou shalt make them as a fiery oven in the time of thine anger: the Lord shall swallow them up in his wrath, and the fire shall devour them. (Psalm 21: 9.)

Pour out thine indignation upon them, and let thy wrathful anger take hold of them. (Psalm 69: 24.)

Therefore the Lord heard this, and was wroth: so a fire was kindled against Jacob, and anger also came up against Israel. (Psalm 78: 21.)

For they provoked him to anger with their high places, and moved him to jealousy with their graven images. (Psalm 78: 58.)

Who knoweth the power of thine anger? even according to thy fear so is thy wrath. (Psalm 90: 11.)

Behold, the name of the Lord cometh from far, burning with his anger, and the burden thereof is heavy: his lips are full of indignation, and his tongue as a devouring fire. (Isaiah 30: 27.)

Will he reserve his anger for ever? will he keep it to the end? Behold, thou hast spoken and done evil things as thou couldest. (Jeremiah 3: 5.)

Do they provoke me to anger? saith the Lord: do they not provoke themselves to the confusion of their own faces? (Jeremiah 7: 19.)

Because of their wickedness which they have committed to provoke me to anger, in that they went to burn incense, and to serve other gods, whom they knew not, neither they, ye, nor your fathers. (Jeremiah 44: 3.)

And when he had looked round about on them with anger, being grieved for the hardness of their hearts, he saith unto the man, *Stretch forth thine hand.* And he stretched it out: and his hand was restored whole as the other. (Mark 3: 5.)

Divine Anger: Kindled.

And when the people complained, it displeased the Lord: and the Lord heard it: and his anger was kindled; and the fire of the Lord burnt among them, and consumed them that were in the uttermost parts of the camp. (Numbers 11: 1.)

But the children of Israel committed a trespass in the accursed thing: for Achan, the son of Carmi, the son of Zabdi, the son of Zerah, of the tribe of Judah, took of the accursed thing: and the anger of the Lord was kindled against the children of Israel. (Joshua 7: 1.)

And the anger of the Lord was kindled against Uzzah, and God smote him there for his error; and there he died by the ark of God. (2 Samuel 6: 7.)

And again the anger of the Lord was kindled against Israel, and he moved David against them to say, Go, number Israel and Judah. (2 Samuel 24: 1.)

Kiss the Son, lest he be angry, and ye perish from the way, when his wrath is kindled but a little. Blessed are all they that put their trust in him. (Psalm 2: 12.)

And thou, even thyself, shalt discontinue from thine heritage that I gave thee; and I will cause thee to serve thine enemies in the land which thou knowest not: for ye have kindled a fire in mine anger, which shall burn forever. (Jeremiah 17: 4.)

Thy calf, O Samaria, hath cast thee off; mine anger is kindled against them: how long will it be ere they attain to innocency? (Hosea 8: 5.)

Mine anger was kindled against the shepherds, and I punished the goats: for the Lord of hosts hath visited his flock the house of Judah, and hath made them as his goodly horse in the battle. (Zechariah 10: 3.)

Divine Anger: Slow or Deferred.

The Lord is merciful and gracious, slow to anger, and plenteous in mercy.

He will not always chide; neither will he keep his anger for ever. (Psalm 103: 8, 9.)

For my name's sake will I defer mine anger, and for my praise will I refrain for thee, that I cut thee not off. (Isaiah 48: 9.)

I will heal their backsliding, I will love them freely: for mine anger is turned away from him. (Hosea 14: 4.)

Divine Anger: Laid Up for Wicked.

But after thy hardness and impenitent heart, treasurest up unto thyself wrath against the day of wrath, and revelation of the righteous judgment of God;

Who will render to every man according to his deeds. (Romans 2: 5, 6.)

But the heavens and the earth, which

are now, by the same word are kept in store, reserved unto fire against the day of judgment and perdition of ungodly men. (2 Peter 3: 7.)

Divine Anger: Prayer against.

And Moses besought the Lord, his God, and said, Lord, why doth thy wrath wax hot against thy people, which thou hast brought forth out of the land of Egypt, with great power, and with a mighty hand? (Exodus 32: 11.)

And David spake unto the Lord when he saw the angel that smote the people, and said, Lo, I have sinned, and I have done wickedly: but these sheep, what have they done? Let thine hand, I pray thee, be against me, and against my father's house. (2 Samuel 24: 17.)

O Lord, rebuke me not in thine anger, neither chasten me in thy hot displeasure. (Psalm 6: 1.)

Hide not thy face far from me; put not thy servant away in anger: thou hast been my help; leave me not, neither forsake me, O God of my salvation. (Psalm 27: 9.)

Remove thy stroke away from me: I am consumed by the blow of thine hand. (Psalm 39: 10.)

O God, why hast thou cast us off for ever? why doth thine anger smoke against the sheep of thy pasture? (Psalm 74: 1.)

How long, Lord? wilt thou be angry for ever? shall thy jealousy burn like fire?

Pour out thy wrath upon the heathen that have not known thee, and upon the kingdoms that have not called upon thy name. (Psalm 79: 5, 6.)

O Lord God of hosts, how long wilt thou be angry against the prayer of thy people? (Psalm 80: 4.)

Turn us, O God of our salvation, and cause thine anger toward us to cease.

Wilt thou be angry with us for ever? wilt thou draw out thine anger to all generations? (Psalm 85: 4, 5.)

Be not wroth very sore, O Lord, neither remember iniquity for ever: behold, see, we beseech thee, we are all thy people. (Isaiah 64: 9.)

O Lord, according to all thy righteousness, I beseech thee, let thine anger and thy fury be turned away from thy city Jerusalem, thy holy mountain: because for our sins, and for the iniquities of our fathers, Jerusalem and thy people are become a reproach to all that are about us. (Daniel 9: 16.)

O Lord, I have heard thy speech and was afraid: O Lord, revive thy work in the midst of the years, in the midst of the years make known; in wrath remember mercy. (Habakkuk 3: 2.)

And the publican, standing afar off, would not lift up so much as his eyes unto heaven, but smote upon his breast, saying, God be merciful to me a sinner. (Luke 18: 13.)

Divine Anger: Christ's Propitiation.

Whom God hath set forth to be a propitiation, through faith in his blood, to declare his righteousness for the remission of sins that are past, through the forbearance of God. (Romans 3: 25.)

Much more then, being now justified by his blood, we shall be saved from wrath through him. (Romans 5: 9.)

And all things are of God, who hath reconciled us to himself by Jesus Christ, and hath given to us the ministry of reconciliation. (2 Corinthians 5: 18.)

And, having made peace through the blood of his cross, by him to reconcile all things unto himself; by him, I say, whether they be things in earth, or things in heaven. (Colossians 1: 20.)

And to wait for his Son from heaven, whom he raised from the dead, even Jesus, which delivered us from the wrath to come. (1 Thessalonians 1: 10.)

And he is the propitiation for our sins: and not for ours only, but also for the sins of the whole world. (1 John 2: 2.)

Divine Anger: Turned by Repentance.

Seest thou how Ahab humbleth himself before me? because he humbleth himself before me, I will not bring the evil in his days: but in his son's days will I bring the evil upon his house. (1 Kings 21: 29.)

Go and proclaim these words toward the north, and say, Return, thou backsliding Israel, saith the Lord; and I will not cause mine anger to fall upon you: for I am merciful, saith the Lord, and I will not keep anger for ever. (Jeremiah 3: 12.)

Who knoweth if he will return and repent, and leave a blessing behind him; even a meat-offering and a drink-offering unto the Lord your God? (Joel 2: 14.)

ANNAS.

AN'NAS—a high-priest of the Jews about the time of Christ. He ruled from A.D. 7 to A.D. 23, and was succeeded by Caiaphas, his son-in-law. Luke says he was high-priest along with Caiaphas; but this is taken generally to mean that by reason of his rank he had great influence. He interviewed and questioned Jesus after His arrest, and then sent Him bound to Caiaphas and the Sanhedrin for formal trial.

References.—Luke 3: 2; John 18: 13-24; Acts 4: 6.

ANOINTING.

A-NOINT'ING—a practice of putting perfumed oils or ointments upon the heads or bodies or limbs indulged in by the ancients, especially the Egyptians and Hebrews. It was done for three reasons: consecration or inauguration, as a mark of esteem for guests and strangers, and for sanative purposes. Kings and high-priests were so treated. The first instance in the Bible is that of Aaron.

REFERENCES.
Aaron.

And he poured of the anointing oil upon Aaron's head, and anointed him, to sanctify him. (Leviticus 8: 12.)

Saul.

Then Samuel took a vial of oil, and poured it upon his head, and kissed him, and said, Is it not because the Lord hath anointed thee to be captain over his inheritance? (1 Samuel 10: 1.)

David.

Then Samuel took the horn of oil, and anointed him in the midst of his brethren: and the Spirit of the Lord came upon David from that day forward. So Samuel rose up, and went to Ramah. (1 Samuel 16: 13.)

Solomon.

And Zadok the priest took an horn of oil out of the tabernacle, and anointed Solomon. And they blew the trumpet; and all the people said, God save king Solomon. (1 Kings 1: 39.)

Elisha and Jehu.

And Jehu the son of Nimshi shalt thou anoint to be king over Israel: and Elisha the son of Shaphat of Abelmeholah shalt thou anoint to be prophet in thy room. (1 Kings 19: 16.)

Jehu.

And he arose, and went into the house; and he poured the oil on his head, and said unto him, Thus saith the Lord God of Israel, I have anointed thee king over the people of the Lord, even over Israel. (2 Kings 9: 6.)

Joash.

And he brought forth the king's son, and put the crown upon him, and gave him the testimony; and they made him king, and anointed him; and they clapped their hands, and said, God save the king. (2 Kings 11: 12.)

Jesus.

There came unto him a woman having an alabaster-box of very precious ointment, and poured it on his head as he sat at meat. (Matthew 26: 7.)

And being in Bethany, in the house of Simon the leper, as he sat at meat, there came a woman having an alabaster-box of ointment of spikenard, very precious; and she brake the box, and poured it on his head. (Mark 14: 3.)

Then took Mary a pound of ointment of spikenard, very costly, and anointed the feet of Jesus, and wiped his feet with her hair: and the house was filled with the odour of the ointment. (John 12: 3.)

And behold, a woman in the city, which was a sinner, when she knew that Jesus sat at meat in the Pharisee's house, brought an alabaster-box of ointment,

And stood at his feet behind him weeping, and began to wash his feet with tears, and did wipe them with the hairs of her head, and kissed his feet, and anointed them with the ointment. (Luke 7: 37, 38.)

Additional References.—1 Samuel 2: 35; 1 Samuel 24: 10; 1 Samuel 28: 9; 1 Chronicles 16: 22; Psalm 132: 10; Isaiah 61: 1: Luke 4: 18; Acts 4: 27; Acts 10: 38; 2 Corinthians 1: 21; 1 John 2: 20.

ANTICHRIST.

AN'TI-CHRIST—some one who is the opponent of Christ; Christ's antagonist. This is an expression used in the Bible only by John, and the subject of much contention among commentators. By the word John most probably meant the ruling spirit of error and the natural personification of this is Satan. It is also told us that there are many antichrists, and thus the term seems to be used in a general and broad sense. Paul's "man of sin" is almost synonymous with the word. Some commentators have seen fit to suggest Nero as the antichrist meant by John. Excluding Satan, Nero seems to have the best claim to the title.

REFERENCES.

Little children, it is the last time: and as ye have heard that antichrist shall come, even now are there many antichrists; whereby we know that it is the last time. (1 John 2: 18.)

Who is a liar but he that denieth that Jesus is the Christ? He is antichrist, that denieth the Father and the Son. (1 John 2: 22.)

And every spirit that confesseth not that Jesus Christ is come in the flesh, is not of God. And this is that spirit of antichrist, whereof ye have heard that it should come; and even now already is it in the world. (1 John 4: 3.)

For many deceivers are entered into the world, who confess not that Jesus Christ is come in the flesh. This is a deceiver and an antichrist. (2 John 1: 7.)

The Man of Sin.

That ye be not soon shaken in mind, or be troubled, neither by spirit, nor by word, nor by letter as from us, as that the day of Christ is at hand.

Let no man deceive you by any means: for that day shall not come, except there come a falling away first, and that man of sin be revealed, the son of perdition. (2 Thessalonians 2: 3, 4.)

ANTIOCH.

AN'TI-OCH. The Bible mentions two cities of this name—Antioch in Syria and Antioch in Pisidia. Of the two, the former was by far the greater and more important. It is situated on the river Orontes, 300 miles north of Jerusalem. It was founded in 300 B.C., and was long the residence of the Syrian kings as well as the metropolis of Syria. After the Roman occupation it continued to be the seat of government. In Christian history it holds an important place. Within it Paul founded the first Gentile church, the members of which were the first to be distinguished by the name of Christians. In the early days of the Church it gave many great scholars, teachers, and preachers to the faith. During the Crusades it was the scene of many battles between the Christians and the Moslems. It is now nothing like it was in the days of its splendor, although it has many ruins which show traces of its former greatness.

References.—Acts 11: 25, 26; Acts 13: 1, 2; Galatians 2: 11.

APOLLOS.

A-POL'LOS—a form of a Greek word meaning "belonging to Apollo." The name of a fellow-laborer of Paul's, mentioned a number of times in the New Testament. He was an Alexandrian Jew and began his work about A.D. 56 at Ephesus, first teaching the doctrine of the Messiah without reference to Jesus. Paul's aids, Aquila and Priscilla, soon taught him the "way of God more perfectly," and he went to Greece to aid Paul. He must have been a man of strong personality as well as great knowledge, for he soon became the center of a church party. Paul, with the consent and approval and probably at the instigation of Apollos, took the Corinthians to task for this. They labored together quite a long time, and tradition says that Apollos rose to considerable eminence in the Church. He probably was pastor of the Church at Corinth at his death.

REFERENCES.

And a certain Jew, named Apollos, born at Alexandria, an eloquent man, and mighty in the scriptures, came to Ephesus. (Acts 18: 24.)

Now this I say, that every one of you saith, I am of Paul; and I of Apollos; and I of Cephas; and I of Christ. (1 Corinthians 1: 12.)

For while one saith, I am of Paul; and another, I am of Apollos; are ye not carnal?

Who then is Paul, and who is Apollos, but ministers by whom ye believed, even as the Lord gave to every man?

I have planted, Apollos watered: but God gave the increase. (1 Corinthians 3: 4-6.)

And these things, brethren, I have in a figure transferred to myself and to Apollos for your sakes; that ye might learn in us not to think of men above that which is written, that no one of you be puffed up for one against another. (1 Corinthians 4: 6.)

Bring Zenas the lawyer and Apollos on their journey diligently, that nothing be wanting unto them. (Titus 3: 13.)

APOSTLE.

A-POS'TLE—a form of a Greek word meaning "one who is sent." Research shows that the Jews, even before the time of Christ, called apostles such men as were sent by their rulers to the people with letters or proclamations or to collect the yearly temple tax. In the New Testament the term was applied to the chosen band of men that surrounded the Master, to whom after His death was to be given the organization of His Church and the dissemination of His faith. These men were Peter, Andrew, John, Philip, James the greater,

Bartholomew, Thomas, Matthew (Levi), Simon, Jude, James the lesser, Judas Iscariot, and, after the latter's apostasy, Matthias. Later, to these was added by special call the great Paul, the apostle to the Gentiles. Christ gave them special powers during His life and promised them special gifts after His death. While there were no absolute distinctions of rank among them, temperament, devotion, and natural ability soon brought out leadership. Peter seems always to have been a sort of a spokesman for his fellows during the ministry of his Master. All of them were men of the people and all in humble walks of life when called to their work. The call of Paul was from a higher sphere. He was from a better class and was more deeply learned. Some writers take exception to the giving of the title of apostle to any others than the men above-named, although others call apostles all the leaders in the early Church down to the death of John, between the years 90 and 100 A.D., which event has been termed the end of the apostolic age. The statement of faith known as the Apostles' Creed was not formulated by any of the men delegated by Christ, but is a product of the fifth century, some evidence tending to show that its author was Augustine. It is only the Apostles' Creed in that it is concentrated expression of the doctrine that they taught.

REFERENCES.

Calling of the Apostles.

And Jesus walking by the sea of Galilee, saw two brethren, Simon, called Peter, and Andrew his brother, casting a net into the Sea (for they were fishers.)

And he saith unto them, *Follow me: and I will make you fishers of men.*

And they straightway left their nets, and followed him.

And going on from thence, he saw other two brethren, James the son of Zebedee, and John his brother, in a ship with Zebedee their father, mending their nets: and he called them. (Matthew 4: 18-21.)

And as Jesus passed forth from thence, he saw a man named Matthew, sitting at the receipt of custom: and he saith unto him, *Follow me.* And he arose, and followed him. (Matthew 9: 9.)

The day following, Jesus would go forth into Galilee, and findeth Philip, and saith unto him, *Follow me.*

Now Philip was of Bethsaida, the city of Andrew and Peter.

Philip findeth Nathanael, and saith unto him, We have found him of whom Moses in the Law, and the Prophets did write, Jesus of Nazareth the son of Joseph. (John 1: 43-45.)

And he fell to the earth, and heard a voice saying unto him, *Saul, Saul, why persecutest thou me?*

And he said, Who art thou, Lord? And the Lord said, *I am Jesus whom thou persecutest. It is hard for thee to kick against the pricks.*

And he trembling, and astonished, said, Lord, what wilt thou have me to do? And the Lord said unto him, *Arise, and go into the city, and it shall be told thee what thou must do.* (Acts 9: 4-6.)

But the Lord said unto him, *Go thy way: for he is a chosen vessel unto me, to bear my name before the Gentiles, and kings, and the children of Israel.*

For I will shew him how great things he must suffer for my name's sake.

Now the names of the twelve apostles are these; The first, Simon, who is called Peter, and Andrew his brother; James the son of Zebedee, and John his brother;

Philip, and Bartholomew; Thomas, and Matthew the publican; James the son of Alpheus, and Lebbeus, whose surname was Thaddeus;

Simon the Canaanite, and Judas Iscariot, who also betrayed him. (Matthew 10: 2-4.)

Instructions and Powers.

And when he had called unto him his twelve disciples, he gave them power against unclean spirits, to cast them out, and to heal all manner of sickness and all manner of disease. (Matthew 10: 1.)

And as ye go, preach, saying, The kingdom of heaven is at hand:

Heal the sick, cleanse the lepers, raise the dead, cast out devils: freely ye have received, freely give. (Matthew 10: 7, 8.)

Behold, I send you forth as sheep in the midst of wolves: be ye therefore wise as serpents, and harmless as doves. (Matthew 10: 16.)

But when they deliver you up, take no thought how or what ye shall speak, for it shall be given you in that same hour what ye shall speak.

For it is not ye that speak, but the Spirit of your Father, which speaketh in you. (Matthew 10: 19, 20.)

And ye shall be hated of all men for my Name's sake: but he that endureth to the end, shall be saved. (Matthew 10: 22.)

And I will give unto thee the keys of the kingdom of heaven: and whatsoever thou shalt bind on earth, shall be bound in heaven: and whatsoever thou shalt loose on earth, shall be loosed in heaven. (Matthew 16: 19.)

Go ye therefore and teach all nations, baptizing them in the name of the Father, and of the Son, and of the Holy Ghost;

Teaching them to observe all things whatsoever I have commanded you: and lo, I am with you alway, even unto the end of the world. Amen. (Matthew 28: 19.)

Whosoever sins ye remit, they are remitted unto them; and whosoever sins ye retain, they are retained. (John 20: 23.)

But none of these things move me, neither count I my life dear unto myself, so that I might finish my course with joy, and the ministry which I have received of the Lord Jesus, to testify the gospel of the grace of God. (Acts 20: 24.)

And the wall of the city had twelve foundations, and in them the names of the twelve apostles of the Lamb. (Revelation 21: 14.)

Witnesses of Christ.

Even as they delivered them unto us, which from the beginning were eyewitnesses, and ministers of the word. (Luke 1: 2.)

And ye are witnesses of these things. (Luke 24: 48.)

To whom also he shewed himself alive after his passion, by many infallible proofs, being seen of them forty days, and speaking of the things pertaining to the kingdom of God. (Acts 1: 3.)

Beginning from the baptism of John, unto that same day that he was taken up from us, must one be ordained to be a witness with us of his resurrection. (Acts 1: 22.)

Not to all the people, but unto witnesses chosen before of God, even to us, who did eat and drink with him after he rose from the dead. (Acts 10: 41.)

Am I not an apostle? am I not free? have I not seen Jesus Christ our Lord? are not ye my work in the Lord? (1 Corinthians 9: 1.)

And that he was seen of Cephas, then of the twelve. (1 Corinthians 15: 5.)

For we have not followed cunningly devised fables, when we made known unto you the power and coming of our Lord Jesus Christ, but were eyewitnesses of his majesty. (2 Peter 1: 16.)

That which was from the beginning, which we have heard, which we have seen with our eyes, which we have looked upon, and our hands have handled, of the Word of Life. (1 John 1: 1.)

Apostles' Sufferings.

And ye shall be betrayed both by parents, and brethren, and kinsfolks, and friends; and some of you shall they cause to be put to death. (Luke 21: 16.)

Remember the word that I said unto you, The servant is not greater than the Lord: if they have persecuted me, they will also persecute you: if they have kept my saying, they will keep yours also. (John 15: 20.)

They shall put you out of the synagogues: yea, the time cometh, that whosoever killeth you, will think that he doeth God service. (John 16: 2.)

These things I have spoken unto you, that in me ye might have peace, in the world ye shall have tribulation: but be of good cheer, I have overcome the world. (John 16: 33.)

For I think that God hath set forth us the apostles last, as it were appointed to death: for we are made a spectacle unto the world, and to angels, and to men. (1 Corinthians 4: 9.)

Who comforteth us in all our tribulation, that we may be able to comfort them which are in any trouble, by the comfort wherewith we ourselves are comforted of God. (2 Corinthians 1: 4.)

We are troubled on every side, yet not distressed; we are perplexed, but not in despair;

Persecuted, but not forsaken; cast down, but not destroyed. (2 Corinthians 4: 8, 9.)

Are they ministers of Christ? I speak as a fool, I am more: in labours more abundant: in stripes above measure: in prisons more frequent: in deaths oft. (2 Corinthians 11: 23.)

I John, who also am your brother, and companion in tribulation, and in the kingdom and patience of Jesus Christ, was in the Isle that is called Patmos, for the word of God, and for the testimony of Jesus Christ. (Revelation 1: 9.)

AQUILA.

Aq'ui-la—a Latinized form of a Greek word meaning "eagle." The name of one of Paul's fellow-workers at Corinth and Ephesus. He was a Jew from Asia Minor and had been driven from Rome during the persecutions by the Emperor Claudius. Paul doubtless taught him the Christian faith. He is mentioned as one of the zealous workers, and aided in the higher instruction of Apollos. He seems to have been a tent-maker by trade and employed a number of men, which fact explains the reference to the church that was in his house.

References.—Acts 18: 2, 18, 26; Romans 16: 3; 1 Corinthians 16: 19; 2 Timothy 4: 19.

ARARAT.

Ar'a-rat—a form of a Hebrew word meaning "wilderness." The Biblical name of the country upon the mountains of which the Ark rested. It has been impossible to modern research to fix the exact location of the peak. A number of mountains have been selected, but none with certainty. Mount Ararat, the height to which the greatest amount of evidence leans, is a peak in Armenia, in Asia, about 16,250 feet above sea level. It is a most magnificent mountain of the twin-peak variety. Its summit is covered with eternal snow and ice.

References.—Genesis 8: 4; 2 Kings 19: 37; Jeremiah 51: 27.

ARIMATHEA.

AR-I-MA-THE'A—a form of a Greek word meaning "a height." The name of the birthplace of the wealthy Joseph, in whose new tomb the body of the crucified Christ was laid. There is some doubt as to the exact location of Arimathea. The weight of evidence tends to locate it at what is now the village of Ramleh, about 24 miles northwest of Jerusalem.

References.—Matthew 27: 57; Mark 15: 43; Luke 23: 51; John 19: 38.

ARK. (See Flood, Covenant, Moses.)

The Bible mentions three different sorts of arks: (1) that in which Noah, his family, and specimens of every sort of animal survived the Flood; (2) the small vessel in which Moses was set adrift; (3) the ark of the covenant.

1. Genesis does not throw much light upon the actual structure of Noah's ark, save that it was of gopher wood (probably cypress or pine), and that it was 300 cubits long, 50 broad, and 30 high. It probably was merely a huge raft with a house upon it, since it was built to float only and not to sail. Its passengers were Noah, his wife, his three sons and their wives—eight persons in all—and one pair of every "unclean animal" and seven pairs of all that were "clean."

2. The ark in which Moses was set adrift was probably a small basket-like boat made of papyrus, a fabric like heavy parchment or paper made from bulrushes by the Egyptians, and plentifully daubed with pitch or bitumen to make it waterproof.

3. The ark of the covenant was a large chest or coffer, two and a half cubits long, and a cubit and a half broad and high. It was made of shittim (acacia) wood and covered with plates of pure gold. It had a border ornamentation of gold and gold-covered poles by which to carry it. On the upper surface or lid it had two cherubim with their faces turned toward each other. Their wings, spread out over the top, formed the throne of God. This object was the most sacred thing possessed by the Israelites, and it was kept in the holy of holies of the tabernacle and temple. In it were kept the tables of the law. While the nation was on the march it was borne by priests in advance of the host. What became of it never has been known definitely. It is supposed to have fallen into the hands of the Babylonians at the plunder and destruction of the Temple, and probably was destroyed by them for the sake of its precious metal. The Jews, however, still believe that it was concealed from the Babylonians and that the Messiah will eventually reveal its whereabouts. That it was not in the second Temple is quite certain.

REFERENCES.

Noah's Ark.

Make thee an ark of gopher-wood: rooms shalt thou make in the ark, and shalt pitch it within and without with pitch.

And this is the fashion which thou shalt make it of: The length of the ark shall be three hundred cubits, the breadth of it fifty cubits, and the height of it thirty cubits.

A window shalt thou make to the ark, and in a cubit shalt thou finish it above; and the door of the ark shalt thou set in the side thereof: with lower, second, and third stories shalt thou make it.

And behold, I, even I, do bring a flood of waters upon the earth, to destroy all flesh, wherein is the breath of life, from under heaven: and every thing that is in the earth shall die.

But with thee will I establish my covenant: and thou shalt come into the ark, thou, and thy sons, and thy wife, and thy sons' wives with thee. (Genesis 6: 14-18.)

Of every clean beast thou shalt take to thee by sevens, the male and his female: and of beasts that are not clean by two, the male and his female. (Genesis 7: 2.)

By faith Noah, being warned of God of things not seen as yet, moved with fear, prepared an ark to the saving of his house; by the which he condemned the world, and became heir of the righteousness which is by faith. (Hebrews 11: 7.)

Which sometime were disobedient, when once the long-suffering of God waited in the days of Noah, while the ark was a preparing, wherein few, that is, eight souls, were saved by water. (1 Peter 3: 20.)

Moses' Ark.

And when she could not longer hide him, she took for him an ark of bulrushes, and daubed it with slime and with pitch, and put the child therein; and she laid it on the flags by the river's brink. (Exodus 2: 3.)

Ark of the Covenant.

And they shall make an ark of shittim-wood: two cubits and a half shall be the length thereof, and a cubit and a half the breadth thereof, and a cubit and a half the height thereof.

And thou shalt overlay it with pure gold, within and without shalt thou overlay it; and shalt make upon it a crown of gold round about.

And thou shalt cast four rings of gold for it, and put them in the four corners thereof; and two rings shall be in the one side of it, and two rings in the other side of it.

And thou shalt make staves of shittim-wood, and overlay them with gold.

And thou shalt put the staves into the rings by the sides of the ark, that the ark may be borne with them.

The staves shall be in the rings of the ark: they shall not be taken from it.

And thou shalt put into the ark the testimony which I shall give thee.

And thou shalt make a mercy-seat of pure gold: two cubits and a half shall be the length thereof, and a cubit and a half the breadth thereof.

And thou shalt make two cherubims of gold, of beaten work shalt thou make them, in the two ends of the mercy-seat.

And make one cherub on the one end, and the other cherub on the other end: even of the mercy-seat shall ye make the cherubims on the two ends thereof.

And the cherubims shall stretch forth their wings on high, covering the mercy-seat with their wings, and their faces shall look one to another; toward the mercy-seat shall the faces of the cherubims be.

And thou shalt put the mercy-seat above upon the ark; and in the ark thou shalt put the testimony that I shall give thee.

And there I will meet with thee, and I will commune with thee from above the mercy-seat, from between the two cherubims which are upon the ark of the testimony, of all things which I will give thee in commandment unto the children of Israel. (Exodus 25: 10-22.)

And Bezaleel made the ark of shittim-wood: two cubits and a half was the length of it, and a cubit and a half the breadth of it, and a cubit and a half the height of it. (Exodus 37: 1.)

And it came to pass, when the people removed from their tents to pass over Jordan, and the priests bearing the ark of the covenant before the people;

And as they that bare the ark were come unto Jordan, and the feet of the priests that bare the ark were dipped in the brim of the water, (for Jordan overfloweth all his banks all the time of harvest,)

That the waters which came down from above stood and rose up upon an heap very far from the city Adam, that is beside Zaretan; and those that came down toward the sea of the plain, even the salt sea, failed, and were cut off: and the people passed over right against Jericho.

And the priests that bare the ark of the covenant of the Lord stood firm on dry ground in the midst of Jordan, and all the Israelites passed over on dry ground, until all the people were passed clean over Jordan. (Joshua 3: 14-17.)

And the Lord said unto Joshua, See, I have given into thine hand Jericho, and the king thereof, and the mighty men of valour.

And ye shall compass the city, all ye men of war, and go round about the city once: thus shalt thou do six days.

And seven priests shall bear before the ark seven trumpets of ram's horns: and the seventh day ye shall compass the city seven times, and the priests shall blow with the trumpets.

And it shall come to pass, that when they make a long blast with the ram's horn, and when ye hear the sound of the trumpet, all the people shall shout with a great shout: and the wall of the city shall fall down flat, and the people shall ascend up every man straight before him. (Joshua 6: 2-5.)

And the Philistines fought, and Israel was smitten, and they fled every man into his tent: and there was a very great slaughter, for there fell of Israel thirty thousand footmen.

And the ark of God was taken; and the two sons of Eli, Hophni and Phinehas, were slain. (1 Samuel 4: 10, 11.)

And the Philistines took the ark of God, and brought it from Eben-ezer unto Ashdod.

When the Philistines took the ark of God, they brought it into the house of Dagon, and set it by Dagon.

And when they of Ashdod arose early on the morrow, behold, Dagon was fallen upon his face to the earth before the ark of the Lord. And they took Dagon, and set him in his place again.

And when they arose early on the morrow morning, behold, Dagon was fallen upon his face to the ground before the ark of the Lord: and the head of Dagon, and both the palms of his hands were cut off upon the threshold; only the stump of Dagon was left to him. (1 Samuel 5: 1-4.)

And the ark of the Lord was in the country of the Philistines seven months. (1 Samuel 6: 1.)

And the men of Kirjath-jearim came, and fetched up the ark of the Lord, and brought it into the house of Abinadab in the hill, and sanctified Eleazar his son to keep the ark of the Lord.

And it came to pass, while the ark abode in Kirjath-jearim, that the time was long; for it was twenty years: and all the house of Israel lamented after the Lord. (1 Samuel 7: 1, 2.)

And David was afraid of the Lord that day, and said, How shall the ark of the Lord come to me?

So David would not remove the ark of the Lord unto him into the city of David: but David carried it aside into the house of Obed-edom the Gittite.

And the ark of the Lord continued in the house of Obed-edom the Gittite three months: and the Lord blessed Obed-edom and all his household.

And it was told king David, saying, The Lord hath blessed the house of

Obed-edom, and all that pertaineth unto him, because of the ark of God. So David went and brought up the ark of God from the house of Obed-edom into the city of David with gladness. (2 Samuel 6: 9-12.)

Thus all the work that Solomon made for the house of the Lord was finished: and Solomon brought in all the things that David his father had dedicated; and the silver, and the gold, and all the instruments, put he among the treasures of the house of God.

Then Solomon assembled the elders of Israel, and all the heads of the tribes, the chief of the fathers of the children of Israel, unto Jerusalem, to bring up the ark of the covenant of the Lord out of the city of David, which is Zion. (2 Chronicles 5: 1, 2.)

And the priests brought in the ark of the covenant of the Lord unto his place, to the oracle of the house, into the most holy place, even under the wings of the cherubims. (2 Chronicles 5: 7.)

ARM.

ARM. Special reference is made in a number of places in the Bible to the power of God and the figurative use of the word "arm" employed to indicate it.

REFERENCES.

Fear and dread shall fall upon them; by the greatness of thine arm they shall be as still as a stone; till thy people pass over, O Lord, till the people pass over, which thou hast purchased. (Exodus 15: 16.)

The eternal God is thy refuge, and underneath are the everlasting arms: and he shall thrust out the enemy from before thee; and shall say, Destroy them. (Deuteronomy 33: 27.)

Thou hast with thine arm redeemed thy people, the sons of Jacob and Joseph. Selah. (Psalm 77: 15.)

Thou hast a mighty arm: strong is thy hand, and high is thy right hand. (Psalm 89: 13.)

O sing unto the Lord a new song: for he hath done marvelous things: his right hand, and his holy arm, hath gotten him the victory. (Psalm 98: 1.)

O Lord, be gracious unto us; we have waited for thee: be thou their arm every morning, our salvation also in the time of trouble. (Isaiah 33: 2.)

Who hath believed our report? and to whom is the arm of the Lord revealed? (Isaiah 53: 1.)

I have made the earth, the man and the beast that are upon the ground, by my great power and by my outstretched arm, and have given it unto whom it seemed meet unto me. (Jeremiah 27: 5.)

He hath shewed strength with his arm; he hath scattered the proud in the imagination of their hearts. (Luke 1: 51.)

The God of this people of Israel chose our fathers, and exalted the people when they dwelt as strangers in the land of Egypt, and with an high arm brought he them out of it. (Acts 13: 17.)

ARMOR. (Spelled "armour" throughout the Bible.)

AR'MOR. From the earliest times up to the invention of firearms mankind wore and used devices for the protection of the body in battle. These devices were of different types and made of different material from heavy leather to hardened steel. Usually they consisted of a shield carried on one arm, a coat or breastplate, leather or iron casings for the lower limbs, and a helmet for the head. All through the Bible there are frequent references to armor. Very often the word is used in a figurative sense, chiefly with reference to righteousness as a protection to the follower of God against the assaults of evil or temptation. The Pauline references are the most notable and important.

REFERENCES.

The night is far spent, the day is at hand: let us therefore cast off the works of darkness, and let us put on the armour of light. (Romans 13: 12.)

By the word of truth, by the power of God, by the armour of righteousness on the right hand and on the left. (2 Corinthians 6: 7.)

Wherefore take unto you the whole armour of God, that ye may be able to withstand in the evil day, and having done all, to stand.

Stand therefore, having your loins girt about with truth, and having on the breast-plate of righteousness;

And your feet shod with the preparation of the gospel of peace.

Above all, taking the shield of faith, wherewith ye shall be able to quench all the fiery darts of the wicked.

And take the helmet of salvation, and the sword of the Spirit, which is the word of God. (Ephesians 6: 13-17.)

But let us, who are of the day, be sober, putting on the breast-plate of faith and love; and for an helmet, the hope of salvation. (1 Thessalonians 5: 8.)

ASA.

A′sa—a form of a Hebrew word meaning "a physician" or "healing." The name of the third king of Judah, who reigned forty-one years, from 955 to 914 B.C. He was noted as a very good monarch. He rooted out the various idolatries and placed his kingdom on a first-class military basis. He waged many successful wars and won the love of his people. Toward the latter part of his reign he met with some reverses.

REFERENCES.

And Abijam slept with his fathers; and they buried him in the city of David: and Asa his son reigned in his stead. (1 Kings 15: 8.)

And Asa did that which was right in the eyes of the Lord, as did David his father. (1 Kings 15: 11.)

And there was war between Asa and Baasha king of Israel all their days. (1 Kings 15: 16.)

And Asa did that which was good and right in the eyes of the Lord his God:

For he took away the altars of the strange gods, and the high places, and brake down the images, and cut down the groves. (2 Chronicles 14: 2, 3.)

And Asa in the thirty and ninth year of his reign was diseased in his feet, until his disease was exceeding great: yet in his disease he sought not to the Lord, but to the physicians.

And Asa slept with his fathers, and died in the one and fortieth year of his reign. (2 Chronicles 16: 12, 13.)

ASAPH. (See Psalms.)

A′saph—a form of a Hebrew word meaning "gatherer" or "assembler." The name of several persons mentioned in the Bible, the most important of whom was the leader and director of the Temple choir in the time of David. He is supposed to have been a musician of much ability, as well as a prophet and writer. No less than twelve of the Psalms are ascribed to his authorship. They are Nos. 50 and 73 to 83.

References.—1 Chronicles 6: 39; 2 Chronicles 5: 12; 29: 30; 33: 15; Nehemiah 12: 46.

ASCENSION. (See Christ, Jesus.)

As-cen′sion. To the Christian the ascension of Jesus Christ will always be an event to be contemplated with awe, reverence, and satisfaction. Not only was it the final and irrevocable proof of His divinity, but it was the logical sequence of His glorious resurrection and the final triumph of His mortal ministry. Besides, it fulfilled the ancient prophecies. It occurred forty days after He rose from the dead. The scene of it was Mount Olivet. The evidences were many and complete.

REFERENCES.

Prophecies.

Thou wilt shew me the path of life: in thy presence is fulness of joy; at thy right hand there are pleasures for evermore. (Psalm 16: 11.)

Lift up your heads, O ye gates; and be ye lift up, ye everlasting doors; and the King of glory shall come in. (Psalm 24: 7.)

Thou hast ascended on high, thou hast led captivity captive: thou hast received gifts for men; yea, for the rebellious also, that the Lord God might dwell among them. (Psalm 68: 18.)

The Lord said unto my Lord, Sit thou at my right hand, until I make thine enemies thy footstool. (Psalm 110: 1.)

Typifications: General.

Which hope we have as an anchor of the soul, both sure and steadfast, and which entereth into that within the vail;

Whither the forerunner is for us entered, even Jesus, made an high priest for ever after the order of Melchisedec. (Hebrews 6: 19, 20.)

But Christ being come an high priest of good things to come, by a greater and more perfect tabernacle, not made with hands, that is to say, not of this building;

Neither by the blood of goats and calves, but by his own blood, he entered in once into the holy place, having obtained eternal redemption for us. (Hebrews 9: 11, 12.)

By Enoch:

And Enoch walked with God, and he was not: for God took him. (Genesis 5: 24.)

By Elijah:

And it came to pass, as they still went on, and talked, that behold, there appeared a chariot of fire, and horses of fire, and parted them both asunder; and Elijah went up by a whirlwind into heaven. (2 Kings 2: 11.)

The Ascension.

So then after the Lord had spoken unto them, he was received up into heaven, and sat on the right hand of God. (Mark 16: 19.)

And he led them out as far as to Bethany: and he lifted up his hands, and blessed them.

And it came to pass, while he blessed them, he was parted from them, and carried up into heaven. (Luke 24: 50, 51.)

In my Father's house are many mansions: if it were not so, I would have told you. I go to prepare a place for you. (John 14: 2.)

Nevertheless, I tell you the truth, it is expedient for you that I go away: for if I go not away, the Comforter will not come unto you: but if I depart, I will send him unto you. (John 16: 7.)

And when he had spoken these things, while they beheld, he was taken up; and a cloud received him out of their sight.

And while they looked steadfastly toward heaven as he went up, behold, two men stood by them in white apparel;

Which also said, Ye men of Galilee, why stand ye gazing up into heaven? this same Jesus which is taken up from you into heaven, shall so come in like manner as ye have seen him go into heaven. (Acts 1: 9-11.)

Who is gone into heaven, and is on the right hand of God; angels, and authorities, and powers being made subject unto him. (1 Peter 3: 22.)

ASHES. (See Repentance.)

Ash'es. In the symbolism with which the Scriptures are full ashes have a deep and significant meaning, denoting the frailty of humankind, humiliation of the deepest order, and grief and sorrow.

REFERENCES.

And Abraham answered and said, Behold now, I have taken upon me to speak unto the Lord, which am but dust and ashes. (Genesis 18: 27.)

And Tamar put ashes on her head, and rent her garment of divers colours that was on her, and laid her hand on her head, and went on crying. (2 Samuel 13: 19.)

When Mordecai perceived all that was done, Mordecai rent his clothes, and put on sackcloth with ashes, and went out into the midst of the city, and cried with a loud and a bitter cry. (Esther 4: 1.)

He hath cast me into the mire, and I am become like dust and ashes. (Job 30: 19.)

Wherefore I abhor myself, and repent in dust and ashes. (Job 42: 6.)

For I have eaten ashes like bread, and mingled my drink with weeping. (Psalm 102: 9.)

He feedeth on ashes: a deceived heart hath turned him aside, that he cannot deliver his soul, nor say, Is there not a lie in my right hand? (Isaiah 44: 20.)

Is it such a fast that I have chosen? a day for a man to afflict his soul? is it to bow down his head as a bulrush, and to spread sackcloth and ashes under him? wilt thou call this a fast, and an acceptable day to the Lord? (Isaiah 58: 5.)

O daughter of my people, gird thee with sackcloth, and wallow thyself in ashes: make thee mourning, as for an only son, most bitter lamentation: for the spoiler shall suddenly come upon us. (Jeremiah 6: 26.)

For word came unto the king of Nineveh, and he arose from his throne, and he laid his robe from him, and covered him with sackcloth, and sat in ashes. (Jonah 3: 6.)

Wo unto thee, Chorazin! wo unto thee, Bethsaida! for if the mighty works had been done in Tyre and Sidon, which have been done in you, they had a great while ago repented, sitting in sackcloth and ashes. (Luke 10: 13.)

ASHTORETH. (See Baal.)

Ash'to-reth—one of the Hebrew forms of the name of Astarte, the celebrated goddess of the Sidonians and the Philistines. Her worship was by no means confined to these people, but spread all over Asia Minor, into Mesopotamia, to Egypt, and even crossed the seas into Greece and Italy. It was one of the chief idolatries into which the Israelites fell, even Solomon having been guilty of it. Like most of the paganisms of the period, the worship of the goddess was to a great extent a worship of certain forces of nature. Her rites were of the most demoralizing character. She had many great temples where she was venerated in conjunction with Baal, as well as many groves and gardens specially dedicated to her.

References.—Judges 2: 13; 1 Samuel 12: 10; 1 Kings 11: 5, 33.

ASSYRIA. (See Nineveh.)

As'syr'i-a. Assyria received its name from Assur, son of Shem, who founded the city of Assur, from which the nation developed. At first it seems to have been only a weak dependency of Babylon. It gradually grew in strength until its capital, Nineveh, became greater than Babylon itself. A long line of able and warlike kings raised it from a small nation to a great empire, which subdued Babylon, Palestine, Egypt, and might have extended its conquests further had not it fallen into luxury and degeneracy. In the reign of Sargon, one of its later monarchs, Jerusalem and the larger Hebrew cities were taken, the Israelites thus being punished for their sins. Sargon's successor, Sennacherib, besieged Jerusalem, but the larger part of his army was miraculously destroyed.

REFERENCES.

Assyria and the Jews.

In the days of Pekah king of Israel came Tiglath-pileser king of Assyria, and took Ijon, and Abel-beth-maachah, and Janoah, and Kedesh, and Hazor, and Gilead, and Galilee, all the land of Naphtali, and carried them captive to Assyria. (1 Kings 15: 29.)

In the ninth year of Hoshea the king of Assyria took Samaria, and carried Israel away into Assyria, and placed them in Halah and in Habor by the river of Gozan, and in the cities of the Medes. (1 Kings 17: 6.)

For the children of Israel walked in all the sins of Jeroboam which he did; they departed not from them;

Until the Lord removed Israel out of his sight, as he had said by all his servants the prophets. So was Israel carried away out of their own land to Assyria unto this day.

And the king of Assyria brought men from Babylon, and from Cuthah, and from Ava, and from Hamath, and from Sepharvaim, and placed them in the cities of Samaria instead of the children of Israel: and they possessed Samaria, and dwelt in the cities thereof. (1 Kings 17: 22-24.)

And it came to pass that night, that the angel of the Lord went out, and smote in the camp of the Assyrians an hundred fourscore and five thousand: and when they arose early in the morning, behold, they were all dead corpses.

So Sennacherib king of Assyria departed, and went and returned, and dwelt at Nineveh. (2 Kings 19: 35, 36.)

Prophecies Concerning Assyria.

For before the child shall have knowledge to cry, My father, and my mother, the riches of Damascus and the spoil of Samaria shall be taken away before the king of Assyria. (Isaiah 8: 4.)

O Assyrian, the rod of mine anger, and the staff in their hand is mine indignation.

I will send him against an hypocritical nation, and against the people of my wrath will I give him a charge, to take the spoil, and to take the prey, and to tread them down like the mire of the streets. (Isaiah 10: 5, 6.)

That I will break the Assyrian in my land, and upon my mountains tread him under foot: then shall his yoke depart from off them, and his burden depart from off their shoulders. (Isaiah 14: 25.)

Then shall the Assyrian fall with the sword, not of a mighty man; and the sword, not of a mean man, shall devour him: but he shall flee from the sword, and his young men shall be discomfited. (Isaiah 31: 8.)

And they shall waste the land of Assyria with the sword, and the land of Nimrod in the entrances thereof: thus shall he deliver us from the Assyrian, when he cometh into our land, and when he treadeth within our borders. (Micah 5: 6.)

ATHALIAH.

ATH'A-LI'AH—a form of a Hebrew word meaning "afflicted by Jehovah." The name of the notorious wife of Jehoram, son of Jehoshaphat. She was the daughter of Ahab, against whose house divine doom had been pronounced. After the death of her husband and son she sought to seize the throne for herself and caused the male line of the royal family to be murdered. One grandson, Joash, escaped and was secretly brought up in the Temple, and in the seventh year of her reign he was suddenly proclaimed king, while his evil grandmother was put to death.

References.—2 Kings 8: 26; 2 Kings 11: 1; 2 Chronicles 22: 10; 2 Chronicles 11: 16; 2 Chronicles 23.

ATONEMENT. (See Redemption.)

A-TONE'MENT—satisfaction or reparation for an injury or a misdeed by giving an equivalent or by doing something that will be received in satisfaction; also a reconciliation not only of man to man but more specifically man to God. Atonement and redemption are terms very often coupled in religious matters, but they are in no sense synonymous or interchangeable. Atonement is offered to God, while redemption comes from God. Thus, the Great Atonement made by Jesus, once and for all for the sins of mankind by death on the cross, brings from God the Father the redemption promised to all who believe. Under the old, or Mosaic, dispensation the doctrine of atonement was a strong feature of the Jewish faith, atonement being made by sacrifices and offerings. Under the Christian dispensation atonement and propitiation was made for all men by the incarnation, life, suffering, and death of Jesus.

REFERENCES.

Hebrew Phase of Atonement.

And thou shalt offer every day a bullock for a sin-offering for atonement; and thou shalt cleanse the altar, when thou hast made an atonement for it, and thou shalt anoint it, to sanctify it.

Seven days thou shalt make an atonement for the altar, and sanctify it; and it shall be an altar most holy: whatsoever toucheth the altar shall be holy. (Exodus 29: 36, 37.)

And Aaron shall make an atonement upon the horns of it once in a year, with the blood of the sin-offering of atonements: once in the year shall he make atonement upon it throughout your generations: it is most holy unto the Lord.

And the Lord spake unto Moses, saying,

When thou takest the sum of the children of Israel after their number, then shall they give every man a ransom for his soul unto the Lord, when thou numberest them: that there be no plague among them when thou numberest them. (Exodus 30: 10-12.)

And this shall be a statute for ever unto you: that in the seventh month, on the tenth day of the month, ye shall afflict your souls, and do no work at all, whether it be one of your own country, or a stranger that sojourneth among you:

For on that day shall the priest make an atonement for you, to cleanse you, that ye may be clean from all your sins before the Lord. (Leviticus 16: 29, 30.)

Prophecies Concerning Christ's Atonement.

Surely he hath borne our griefs, and carried our sorrows: yet we did esteem him stricken, smitten of God, and afflicted.

But he was wounded for our transgressions, he was bruised for our iniquities; the chastisement of our peace was upon him; and with his stripes we are healed.

All we like sheep have gone astray; we have turned every one to his own way; and the Lord hath laid on him the iniquity of us all. (Isaiah 53: 4-6.)

And after threescore and two weeks shall Messiah be cut off, but not for himself: and the people of the prince that shall come shall destroy the city and the sanctuary; and the end thereof shall be with a flood, and unto the end of the war desolations are determined. (Daniel 9: 26.)

In that day there shall be a fountain opened to the house of David and to the inhabitants of Jerusalem for sin and for uncleanness. (Zechariah 13: 1.)

And one of them, named Caiaphas, being the high priest that same year, said unto them, Ye know nothing at all,

Nor consider that it is expedient for us, that one man should die for the people, and that the whole nation perish not.

And this spake he not of himself: but being high priest that year, he prophesied that Jesus should die for that nation;

And not for that nation only, but that also he should gather together in one the children of God that were scattered abroad. (John 11: 49-52.)

Benefits of Christ's Atonement.

Being justified freely by his grace, through the redemption that is in Christ Jesus. (Romans 3: 24.)

For when we were yet without strength, in due time Christ died for the ungodly. (Romans 5: 6.)

And all things are of God, who hath reconciled us to himself by Jesus Christ, and hath given to us the ministry of reconciliation. (2 Corinthians 5: 18.)

Who gave himself for our sins, that he might deliver us from this present evil world, according to the will of God and our Father. (Galatians 1: 4.)

Christ hath redeemed us from the curse of the law, being made a curse for us: for it is written, Cursed is every one that hangeth on a tree. (Galatians 3: 13.)

Who gave himself for us, that he might redeem us from all iniquity, and purify unto himself a peculiar people, zealous of good works. (Titus 2: 14.)

So Christ was once offered to bear the sins of many; and unto them that look for him shall he appear the second time without sin unto salvation. (Hebrews 9: 28.)

But with the precious blood of Christ, as of a lamb without blemish and without spot. (1 Peter 1: 19.)

Who his own self bare our sins in his own body on the tree, that we, being dead to sins, should live unto righteousness: by whose stripes ye were healed. (1 Peter 2: 24.)

For Christ also hath once suffered for sins, the just for the unjust, that he might bring us to God, being put to death in the flesh, but quickened by the Spirit. (1 Peter 3: 18.)

And he is the propitiation for our sins: and not for ours only, but also for the sins of the whole world. (2 John 2: 2.)

Commemorated by Lord's Supper.

And as they were eating, Jesus took bread, and blessed it, and brake it, and gave it to the disciples, and said, *Take, eat; this is my body.*

And he took the cup, and gave thanks, and gave it to them, saying, *Drink ye all of it;*

For this is my blood of the new testament, which is shed for many for the remission of sins. (Matthew 26: 26-28.)

BAAL. (See Ashtoreth.)

BA'AL—the generic term for "god" in many of the languages of the nations that surrounded the Israelites. The name, however, was chiefly given to the leading male divinity of the Phœnicians. The original seat of his worship was at Tyre, but it spread in every direction. The Israelites fell under its influence and for a long time worshiped him to the exclusion of the true God. In almost every instance with adoration of Baal was coupled veneration of Astarte, his female companion goddess. There is much internal evidence to show that Baal originally represented the sun and Astarte the moon. The theology of almost all pagan nations is based upon worship of the forces of nature, and it is therefore easy to see how, in the development of such a theology, sun, moon, fire, etc., became primitive bases of a faith leading eventually to the deification of other natural forces, as well as to understand that in the evolution of such a faith the rites of such gods must become gross, vicious, and licentious. The worship of Baal can be traced to very ancient times, and many modifications of it can be found, such as Baal-peor (the Jews' form), Baal-berith, and Baal-zebub.

REFERENCES.

And they forsook the Lord, and served Baal and Ashtaroth. (Judges 2: 13.)

And they left all the commandments of the Lord their God, and made them molten images, even two calves, and made a grove, and worshipped all the host of heaven, and served Baal. (2 Kings 17: 16.)

They have built also the high places of Baal, to burn their sons with fire for burnt-offerings unto Baal, which I commanded not, nor spake it, neither came it into my mind. (Jeremiah 19: 5.)

And Elijah said unto them, Take the prophets of Baal; let not one of them escape. And they took them; and Elijah brought them down to the brook Kishon, and slew them there. (1 Kings 18: 40.)

And they brought forth the images out of the house of Baal, and burned them.

And they brake down the image of Baal, and brake down the house of Baal, and made it a draught-house unto this day.

Thus Jehu destroyed Baal out of Israel. (2 Kings 10: 26-28.)

Your eyes have seen what the Lord did because of Baal-peor: for all the men that followed Baal-peor, the Lord thy God hath destroyed them from among you. (Deuteronomy 4: 3.)

BABEL. (See Babylon.)

BA'BEL—a form of a very ancient Hebrew word meaning "gate of god." The word was given to the immense tower-like structure whose top should reach to Heaven, which was built in the land of Shinar, resulting in the confusion of tongues and the dispersion of the races. An account of it is found in the 11th chapter of Genesis.

BABYLON. (See Assyria.)

BAB'Y-LON. The word Babylon is derived from a Hebrew word meaning "confusion of tongues," and it, therefore, is very likely that the city which took it for a name was built on the site of the tower of Babel. Tradition and research show that it probably was founded by the monarch known as Nimrod, but the date of its founding is lost in the mists of antiquity. It rapidly became the greatest city of the then-known world. Its kings conquered the surrounding towns and peoples and built up a great and powerful empire. Babylon, which was built on both banks of the Euphrates, unquestionably was one of the largest and most magnificent cities ever built. Its buildings and walls were huge and beautiful, and the vast wealth that constantly poured into it was lavishly spent in increasing its splendor. The walls are said to have been 56 miles in circumference, the entire town taking up about 200 square miles of space. For centuries its people were hardy and warlike, but much luxury and the corruption of morals which so often occurs within a rich and conquering nation reduced the power of Babylon to a mere shell. It fell an easy victim to Cyrus the Great in 539 B.C., and later to Alexander. Now nothing remains of it save vast heaps of ruins, over which the desert sands have accumulated so that scientific expeditions are forced to dig deep into the mounds in order to unearth any traces of the city's former greatness. The city is mentioned more than 250 times in the Bible, because it was intimately connected with the history of the Israelites. They knew its wealth, power, cruelty, splendor, and licentiousness; but they were always warned by the prophets that the city eventually must be wiped out. None of the great cities of antiquity was so great, and yet none has been so completely destroyed.

REFERENCES.

General.

And Cush begat Nimrod: he began to be a mighty one in the earth.

He was a mighty hunter before the Lord: wherefore it is said, Even as Nimrod the mighty hunter before the Lord.

And the beginning of his kingdom was Babel, and Erech, and Accad, and Calneh, in the land of Shinar. (Genesis 10: 8-10.)

The king spake, and said, Is not this great Babylon, that I have built for the house of the kingdom by the might of my power, and for the honour of my majesty? (Daniel 4: 30.)

Babylonian Captivity Foretold.

And Isaiah said unto Hezekiah, Hear the word of the Lord.

Behold, the days come, that all that is in thine house, and that which thy fathers have laid up in store unto this day, shall be carried into Babylon: nothing shall be left, saith the Lord. (2 Kings 20: 16, 17.)

Babylonian Captivity.

And in the fifth month, on the seventh day of the month, (which is the nineteenth year of king Nebuchadnezzar king of Babylon,) came Nebuzaradan, captain of the guard, a servant of the king of Babylon, unto Jerusalem:

And he burnt the house of the Lord, and the king's house, and all the houses of Jerusalem, and every great man's house burnt he with fire.

And all the army of the Chaldees, that were with the captain of the guard, brake down the walls of Jerusalem round about.

Now the rest of the people that were left in the city, and the fugitives that fell away to the king of Babylon, with the remnant of the multitude, did Nebuzar-adan the captain of the guard carry away. (2 Kings 25: 8-11.)

Fall of Babylon.

And Babylon, the glory of kingdoms, the beauty of the Chaldees' excellency, shall be as when God overthrew Sodom and Gomorrah.

It shall never be inhabited, neither shall it be dwelt in from generation to generation: neither shall the Arabian pitch tent there; neither shall the shepherds make their fold there. (Isaiah 13: 19, 20.)

Come down, and sit in the dust, O virgin daughter of Babylon, sit on the ground: there is no throne, O daughter of the Chaldeans: for thou shalt no more be called tender and delicate. (Isaiah 47: 1.)

And it shall come to pass, when seventy years are accomplished, that I will punish the king of Babylon, and that nation, saith the Lord, for their iniquity, and the land of the Chaldeans, and will make it perpetual desolations. (Jeremiah 25: 12.)

Declare ye among the nations, and publish, and set up a standard; publish, and conceal not: say, Babylon is taken, Bel is confounded, Merodach is broken in pieces; her idols are confounded, her images are broken in pieces.

For out of the north there cometh up a nation against her, which shall make her land desolate, and none shall dwell therein: they shall remove, they shall depart, both man and beast. (Jeremiah 50: 2, 3.)

In that night was Belshazzar the king of the Chaldeans slain.

And Darius the Median took the kingdom, being about threescore and two years old. (Daniel 5: 30, 31.)

BACKBITE.

BACK'BITE—to slander or speak evil of an absent person. The Bible, in various places, cautions against this sin.

REFERENCES.

He that backbiteth not with his tongue, nor doeth evil to his neighbour, nor taketh up a reproach against his neighbor. (Psalm 15: 3.)

The north wind driveth away rain: so doth an angry countenance a backbiting tongue. (Proverbs 25: 23.)

Backbiters, haters of God, despiteful, proud, boasters, inventors of evil things, disobedient to parents. (Romans 1: 30.)

For I fear, lest, when I come, I shall not find you such as I would, and that I shall be found unto you such as ye would not: lest there be debates, envyings, wraths, strifes, backbitings, whisperings, swellings, tumults. (2 Corinthians 12: 20.)

BACKSLIDE.

BACK'SLIDE—to turn gradually, voluntarily, or insensibly from the knowledge, faith, love, and profession of God, after having once solemnly become His.

REFERENCES.
General.

And the Lord was angry with Solomon, because his heart was turned from the Lord God of Israel, which had appeared unto him twice. (1 Kings 11: 9.)

But I fear, lest by any means, as the serpent beguiled Eve through his subtilty, so your minds should be corrupted from the simplicity that is in Christ. (2 Corinthians 11: 3.)

O foolish Galatians, who hath bewitched you, that ye should not obey the truth, before whose eyes Jesus Christ hath been evidently set forth, crucified among you? (Galatians 3: 1.)

Christ is become of no effect unto you, whosoever of you are justified by the law; ye are fallen from grace. (Galatians 5: 4.)

Israel's Backsliding.

And when the people saw that Moses delayed to come down out of the mount, the people gathered themselves together unto Aaron, and said unto him, Up, make us gods which shall go before us: for as for this Moses, the man that brought us up out of the land of Egypt, we wot not what is become of him. (Exodus 32: 1.)

Thine own wickedness shall correct thee, and thy backslidings shall reprove thee: know therefore and see that it is an evil thing and bitter, that thou hast forsaken the Lord thy God, and that my fear is not in thee, saith the Lord God of hosts. (Jeremiah 2: 19.)

The Lord said also unto me in the days of Josiah the king, Hast thou seen that which backsliding Israel hath done? (Jeremiah 3: 6.)

For Israel slideth back as a backsliding heifer: now the Lord will feed them as a lamb in a large place. (Hosea 4: 16.)

And my people are bent to backsliding from me: though they called them to the Most High, none at all would exalt him. (Hosea 11: 7.)

Saul's Backsliding.

It repenteth me that I have set up Saul to be king: for he is turned back from following me, and hath not performed my commandments. And it grieved Samuel; and he cried unto the Lord all night. (1 Samuel 15: 11.)

Solomon's Backsliding.

And he had seven hundred wives, princesses, and three hundred concubines: and his wives turned away his heart.

For it came to pass, when Solomon was old, that his wives turned away his heart after other gods: and his heart was not perfect with the Lord his God, as was the heart of David his father. (1 Kings 11: 3, 4.)

Peter's Backsliding.

Now Peter sat without in the palace: and a damsel came unto him, saying, Thou also wast with Jesus of Galilee.

But he denied before them all, saying, I know not what thou sayest.

And when he was gone out into the porch, another maid saw him, and said unto them that were there, This fellow was also with Jesus of Nazareth.

And again he denied with an oath, I do not know the man.

And after a while came unto him they that stood by, and said to Peter, Surely thou also art one of them; for thy speech bewrayeth thee.

Then began he to curse and to swear, saying, I know not the man. And immediately the cock crew. (Matthew 26: 69-74.)

Displeasure and Punishment.

Yet they tempted and provoked the most high God, and kept not his testimonies:

But turned back, and dealt unfaithfully like their fathers: they were turned aside like a deceitful bow.

For they provoked him to anger with their high places, and moved him to jealousy with their graven images.

When God heard this, he was wroth, and greatly abhorred Israel. (Psalm 58: 56-59.)

The backslider in heart shall be filled with his own ways: and a good man shall be satisfied from himself. (Proverbs 14: 14.)

Pardon for Backsliding.

If my people, which are called by my name, shall humble themselves, and pray, and seek my face, and turn from their wicked ways; then will I hear from heaven, and will forgive their sin, and will heal their land. (2 Chronicles 7: 14.)

Go and proclaim these words toward the north, and say, Return, thou backsliding Israel, saith the Lord; and I will not cause mine anger to fall upon you: for I am merciful, saith the Lord, and I will not keep anger for ever. (Jeremiah 3: 12.)

Turn us again, O God, and cause thy face to shine: and we shall be saved. (Psalm 80: 3.)

Turn thou us unto thee, O Lord, and we shall be turned; renew our days as of old.

But thou hast utterly rejected us, thou art very wroth against us. (Lamentations 5: 21, 22.)

Return, ye backsliding children, and I will heal your backslidings. Behold, we come unto thee; for thou art the Lord our God. (Jeremiah 3: 22.)

BALAAM.

Ba'laam—a form of a Hebrew word meaning "foreigner." Balaam was the name of one of the most remarkable characters in the Old Testament. It is unquestioned that he practiced the forbidden arts of soothsaying and divination, and it is equally unquestioned that he was a worshiper of Jehovah and a prophet. In the latter case, some of his prophecies are equal in dignity and fervor to the greatest to be found in the Old Testament. He refused to call down curses on Israel and asked a blessing instead; but later gave Israel's enemies advice which resulted in vast trouble for the Jews, and in the loss of his own life. The incident of his rebuke by the ass he rode is one of the best-known in the Bible.

REFERENCES.

And Balaam said unto God, Balak the son of Zippor, king of Moab, hath sent unto me, saying,

Behold, there is a people come out of Egypt, which covereth the face of the earth: come now, curse me them; peradventure I shall be able to overcome them, and drive them out.

And God said unto Balaam, Thou shalt not go with them; thou shalt not curse the people: for they are blessed. (Numbers 22: 10-12.)

And the Lord opened the mouth of the ass, and she said unto Balaam, What have I done unto thee, that thou hast smitten me these three times?

And Balaam said unto the ass, Because thou hast mocked me: I would there were a sword in mine hand, for now would I kill thee.

And the ass said unto Balaam, Am not I thine ass, upon which thou hast ridden ever since I was thine unto this day? was I ever wont to do so unto thee? And he said, Nay.

Then the Lord opened the eyes of Balaam, and he saw the angel of the Lord standing in the way, and his sword drawn in his hand: and he bowed down his head, and fell flat on his face. (Numbers 22: 28-31.)

And Balaam said unto Balak, Spake I not also to thy messengers which thou sentest unto me, saying,

If Balak would give me his house full of silver and gold, I cannot go beyond the commandment of the Lord, to do either good or bad of mine own mind; but what the Lord saith, that will I speak? (Numbers 24: 12, 13.)

Behold, these caused the children of Israel, through the counsel of Balaam, to commit trespass against the Lord in the matter of Peor, and there was a plague among the congregation of the Lord. (Numbers 31: 16.)

And they slew the kings of Midian, beside the rest of them that were slain; *namely,* Evi, and Rekem, and Zur, and Hur, and Reba, five kings of Midian: Balaam also the son of Beor they slew with the sword. (Numbers 31: 8.)

BAPTISM. (See Ordinances.)

Bap'tism—the initiatory rite of the Christian religion as instituted by the Lord Jesus Christ. Prior to the time of Christ it was a custom among almost all the ancients, even those addicted to idolatry, to wash before engaging in prayer or worship, in order to set forth their spiritual fitness in physical cleanness. John the Baptist was the first to baptize with any relation between the baptism itself and the future state, preaching "the baptism of repentance for the remission of sins." Jesus Himself did not baptize with water but with the Spirit, although the rite was administered to Him and He preached it as essential in connection with the baptism of the Spirit, ordering His followers to baptize "in the name of the Father, and of the Son, and of the Holy Ghost." Baptism thus became an ordinance obligatory upon all Christians.

It is but natural that a rite of this character should be viewed in many different lights with regard to its nature and efficacy. While it is not in the providence of this discussion to go into the doctrinal difficulties of these views they may be summarized as follows: (1) That it is a direct act of grace, and, when applied by a person properly qualified, gives to the soul positive goodness. (2) That it is a direct act of grace giving only the capacity for goodness, which, if fostered, will lead to salvation. (3) That it is a seal of grace, thereby confirming divine blessings to the soul. (4) That it is only a sign of initiation into the religion of the Lord Jesus Christ. (5) That it is a symbol or token of regeneration, to be given or received only by those who exhibit true signs of regeneration. (6) That it is a symbol of purification only. The mode of baptism differs, both immersion and affusion, or sprinkling, being practiced.

REFERENCES.

General.

And were baptized of him in Jordan, confessing their sins. (Matthew 3: 6.)

John did baptize in the wilderness, and preach the baptism of repentance, for the remission of sins. (Mark 1: 4.)

John answered, saying unto them all, I indeed baptize you with water; but one mightier than I cometh, the latchet of whose shoes I am not worthy to unloose: he shall baptize you with the Holy Ghost, and with fire. (Luke 3: 16.)

Then said Paul, John verily baptized

with the baptism of repentance, saying unto the people, that they should believe on him which should come after him, that is, on Christ Jesus.

When they heard this, they were baptized in the name of the Lord Jesus. (Acts 19: 4, 5.)

(Though Jesus himself baptized not, but his disciples.) (John 4: 2.)

Baptism Appointed by Christ.

Go ye therefore, and teach all nations, baptizing them in the Name of the Father, and of the Son, and of the Holy Ghost. (Matthew 28: 19.)

And he said unto them, *Go ye into all the world, and preach the gospel to every creature.*

He that believeth and is baptized, shall be saved; but he that believeth not, shall be damned. (Mark 16: 15, 16.)

After these things came Jesus and his disciples into the land of Judea; and there he tarried with them, and baptized. (John 3: 22.)

Baptism's Significance.

Then Peter said unto them, Repent, and be baptized every one of you in the name of Jesus Christ, for the remission of sins, and ye shall receive the gift of the Holy Ghost. (Acts 2: 38.)

And now why tarriest thou? arise, and be baptized, and wash away thy sins, calling on the name of the Lord. (Acts 22: 16.)

Know ye not that so many of us as were baptized into Jesus Christ, were baptized into his death?

Therefore we are buried with him by baptism into death: that like as Christ was raised up from the dead by the glory of the Father, even so we also should walk in newness of life. (Romans 6: 3, 4.)

For by one Spirit are we all baptized into one body, whether we be Jews or Gentiles, whether we be bond or free; and have been all made to drink into one Spirit. (1 Corinthians 12: 13.)

Else what shall they do, which are baptized for the dead, if the dead rise not at all? why are they then baptized for the dead? (1 Corinthians 15: 29.)

For as many of you as have been baptized into Christ, have put on Christ. (Galatians 3: 27.)

Buried with him in baptism, wherein also ye are risen with him through the faith of the operation of God, who hath raised him from the dead. (Colossians 2: 12.)

Not by works of righteousness which we have done, but according to his mercy he saved us, by the washing of regeneration, and renewing of the Holy Ghost. (Titus 3: 5.)

The like figure whereunto, even Baptism, doth also now save us, (not the putting away of the filth of the flesh, but the answer of a good conscience toward God,) by the resurrection of Jesus Christ. (1 Peter 3: 21.)

One Lord, one faith, one baptism. (Ephesians 4: 5.)

Instances of Baptism:

Jesus:

Then cometh Jesus from Galilee to Jordan unto John, to be baptized of him.

But John forbade him, saying, I have need to be baptized of thee, and comest thou to me?

And Jesus answering said unto him, *Suffer it to be so now: for thus it becometh us to fulfil all righteousness.* Then he suffered him. (Matthew 3: 13-15.)

Simon:

But when they believed Philip, preaching the things concerning the kingdom of God, and the name of Jesus Christ, they were baptized both men and women.

Then Simon himself believed also: and when he was baptized, he continued with Philip, and wondered, beholding the miracles and signs which were done. (Acts 8: 12, 13.)

The Eunuch:

And he commanded the chariot to stand still: and they went down both into the water, both Philip and the eunuch; and he baptized him. (Acts 8: 38.)

Paul:

And Ananias went his way, and entered into the house: and putting his hands on him, said, Brother Saul, the Lord (even Jesus that appeared unto thee in the way as thou camest) hath sent me, that thou mightest receive thy sight, and be filled with the Holy Ghost.

And immediately there fell from his eyes as it had been scales: and he received sight forthwith, and arose, and was baptized. (Acts 9: 18.)

Cornelius:

Can any man forbid water, that these should not be baptized, which have received the Holy Ghost as well as we?

And he commanded them to be baptized in the name of the Lord. Then prayed they him to tarry certain days. (Acts 10: 47, 48.)

Lydia:

And a certain woman named Lydia, a seller of purple, of the city of Thyatira, which worshipped God, heard us: whose heart the Lord opened, that she attended unto the things which were spoken of Paul.

And when she was baptized, and her household, she besought us, saying, If ye have judged me to be faithful to the Lord, come into my house, and abide there. And she constrained us. (Acts 16: 14, 15.)

BARABBAS.

Bar-ab′bas—a form of a Hebrew word meaning "the son of Abba." The name of a notorious robber, rebel, and murderer, who was in prison in Jerusalem at the time of the trial of Jesus and under sentence of death. The Jews, however, were so determined to kill Jesus that when offered the pardon of one or the other, they chose Barabbas.

References.—Matthew 27: 16; Mark 15: 6; Luke 23: 18; John 18: 40.

BARNABAS.

Bar′na-bas—a form of a Syro-Chaldaic word meaning "the son of prophecy;" but which has also been translated "the son of exhortation" and "the son of consolation." Barnabas is a very familiar figure in the New Testament. He seems to have been a wealthy Jew of Cyprus, and originally named Joses or Joseph. Evidence shows that he was a convert of the stirring days that immediately followed Pentecost. His devotion was such that he sold his property and gave the proceeds to the cause. He soon became associated with Paul and was with him in the missionary campaign at Antioch. Later a dispute seems to have arisen, after which Paul went in one direction and Barnabas in another, but there is evidence to show that this disagreement was settled finally and a reconciliation effected. He is said to have been a man of dignified and commanding appearance, and it is quite certain that he was wise, scholarly, and jealous. He is believed to have died about the year 63 or 64 A.D.

REFERENCES.

And Joses, who by the apostles was surnamed Barnabas, (which is, being interpreted, The son of consolation,) a Levite, and of the country of Cyprus,

Having land, sold it, and brought the money, and laid it at the apostles' feet. (Acts 4: 36, 37.)

Then tidings of these things came unto the ears of the church which was in Jerusalem: and they sent forth Barnabas, that he should go as far as Antioch.

Who, when he came, and had seen the grace of God, was glad, and exhorted them all, that with purpose of heart they would cleave unto the Lord.

For he was a good man, and full of the Holy Ghost, and of faith: and much people was added unto the Lord.

Then departed Barnabas to Tarsus, for to seek Saul.

And when he had found him, he brought him unto Antioch. And it came to pass, that a whole year they assembled themselves with the Church, and taught much people, and the disciples were called Christians first in Antioch. (Acts 11: 22-26.)

And Barnabas and Saul returned from Jerusalem, when they had fulfilled their ministry, and took with them John, whose surname was Mark. (Acts 12: 25.)

Then all the multitude kept silence, and gave audience to Barnabas and Paul, declaring what miracles and wonders God had wrought among the Gentiles by them. (Acts 15: 12.)

And some days after, Paul said unto Barnabas, Let us go again and visit our brethren, in every city where we have preached the word of the Lord, and see how they do.

And Barnabas determined to take with them John, whose surname was Mark.

But Paul thought not good to take

him with them, who departed from them from Pamphylia, and went not with them to the work.

And the contention was so sharp between them, that they departed asunder one from the other: and so Barnabas took Mark, and sailed unto Cyprus. (Acts 15: 36-39.)

For before that certain came from James, he did eat with the Gentiles: but when they were come, he withdrew, and separated himself, fearing them which were of the circumcision.

And the other Jews dissembled likewise with him, insomuch that Barnabas also was carried away with their dissimulation. (Galatians 2: 12, 13.)

BARTHOLOMEW.

Bar-thol'o-mew—meaning "the son of Tolmai." Bartholomew was one of the original twelve apostles. Certain internal evidences indicate that his name was really Nathaniel. He was a native of Cana. He was one of those to whom Jesus appeared after His resurrection. He also witnessed the ascension. He worked as a missionary afterwards, although the exact scene of his labors is not known. He is believed to have suffered martyrdom by crucifixion.

References.—Matthew 10: 3; Mark 3: 18; Luke 6: 14; Acts 1: 13.

BARUCH.

Ba'ruch—a form of a Hebrew word meaning "blessed." There are several persons named Baruch mentioned by the Bible, the most important being Baruch, the friend and amanuensis of the prophet Jeremiah. This man lived about B.C. 600. He wrote Jeremiah's prophecies at the latter's dictation, and after they were destroyed by the wicked Jewish king Jehoiachim re-wrote them in their present form. He shared Jeremiah's imprisonment and exile.

References.—Jeremiah 32: 13; Jeremiah 36; Jeremiah 43: 6; Jeremiah 45.

BATH.

Bath—a Hebrew prefix meaning "daughter."

BATH-SHEBA. (See David, Solomon, Uriah.)

Bath-she'ba—a form of a Hebrew word meaning "daughter of the oath;" also written Bath-shua. Bath-sheba was the wife of Uriah, the Hittite. She and David committed sin, and later David, in order that she might become his wife, procured the assassination of Uriah. After having been wedded to David she became the mother of Solomon. In later years, when her son had succeeded his father on the throne, she is mentioned as interceding for the rebellious Adonijah.

References.—2 Samuel 11; 2 Samuel 12; 1 Kings 1: 15; 1 Kings 2: 19.

BEATITUDE.

Be-at'i-tude. This word does not appear in the Bible. It means (1) felicity of the highest kind, and (2) any one of the declarations (collectively called The Beatitudes) made by the Master in the opening of His Sermon on the Mount. They are as follows:

Blessed are the poor in spirit: for theirs is the kingdom of heaven.

Blessed are they that mourn: for they shall be comforted.

Blessed are the meek: for they shall inherit the earth.

Blessed are they which do hunger and thirst after righteousness: for they shall be filled.

Blessed are the merciful: for they shall obtain mercy.

Blessed are the pure in heart: for they shall see God.

Blessed are the peacemakers: for they shall be called the children of God.

Blessed are they which are persecuted for righteousness' sake: for theirs is the kingdom of heaven.

Blessed are ye, when men shall re-

vile you, and persecute you, and shall say all manner of evil against you falsely for my sake. (Matthew 5: 3-11.)

BEAUTY.

BEAU'TY—such graces and properties as are pleasing to the eye, the ear, the mind, the esthetic faculties, or the moral sense. The Bible is full of references to these various sorts of beauties, pointing out the vanity, danger, and temporary quality of mere personal attractions and calling attention to the higher and more permanent quality of the beauties of. mind, character, and temperament.

REFERENCES.

Vanity of Beauty.

When thou with rebukes dost correct man for iniquity, thou makest his beauty to consume away like a moth: surely every man is vanity. Selah. (Psalm 39: 11.)

Lust not after her beauty in thine heart; neither let her take thee with her eye-lids. (Proverbs 6: 25.)

Favour is deceitful, and beauty is vain: but a woman that feareth the Lord, she shall be praised. (Proverbs 31: 30.)

Like sheep they are laid in the grave; death shall feed on them; and the upright shall have dominion over them in the morning; and their beauty shall consume in the grave from their dwelling. (Psalm 49: 14.)

Danger of Beauty.

And it came to pass, that, when Abram was come into Egypt, the Egyptians beheld the woman that she was very fair.

The princes also of Pharaoh saw her, and commended her before Pharaoh: and the woman was taken into Pharaoh's house. (Genesis 12: 14, 15.)

And the men of the place asked him of his wife; and he said, She is my sister: for he feared to say, She is my wife; lest, said he, the men of the place should kill me for Rebekah; because she was fair to look upon. (Genesis 26: 7.)

Now therefore the sword shall never depart from thine house; because thou hast despised me, and hast taken the wife of Uriah the Hittite to be thy wife. (2 Samuel 12: 10.)

Beauty of Holiness.

Give unto the Lord the glory due unto his name: bring an offering, and come before him: worship the Lord in the beauty of holiness. (1 Chronicles 16: 29.)

And when he had consulted with the people, he appointed singers unto the Lord, and that should praise the beauty of holiness, as they went out before the army, and to say, Praise the Lord; for his mercy endureth for ever. (2 Chronicles 20: 21.)

Thy people shall be willing in the day of thy power, in the beauties of holiness from the womb of the morning: thou hast the dew of thy youth. (Psalm 110: 3.)

BEELZEBUB. (See Devil, Satan.)

BE-EL'ZE-BUB—a form of a Greek word, given as the name of a heathen god, supposed to be the prince or leader of all devils. The name should properly be Beelzebul; but early commentators confused it with the Philistine god Baalzebub, and except among scholars it has continued to be written Beelzebub. The name is often used as a synonym for Satan.

References.—Matthew 12: 24; Mark 3: 22; Luke 11: 15.

BEER.

BE'ER—a Hebrew prefix meaning "well," "spring," or "fountain."

BEER=SHEBA.

BE'ER-SHE'BA—a form of a Hebrew word meaning "the well of the oath." Beer-sheba was on the southern border of Judah. It took its name from the wells dug there by Abraham when covenanting with Abimelech. It became a favorite halting-place for travelers, and the town of Beer-sheba grew up in the vicinity. Seven wells exist to this day at the spot. The phrase "from Dan to Beer-sheba" has reference to the fact that Dan is on the northern border of the land and Beer-sheba is on the southern, thus indicating the long stretch of territory between.

References.—Genesis 21: 31; Genesis 22: 19; Genesis 28: 10; Genesis 21: 14; Genesis 46: 1; 1 Kings 19: 3.

BELSHAZZAR.

BEL-SHAZ'ZAR—a form of a Hebrew and Syro-Chaldaic word meaning "Bel's prince." Belshazzar is the name given in the book of Daniel to the last king of Babylon, to whom came, during a great feast, the handwriting on the wall, which was translated by Daniel. Recent researches show that Belshazzar was the son of Nabonidus and that Nabonidus was still on the throne at the fall of Babylon, Belshazzar being the master of the army and not the actual king, although it is highly probable he was associated in the government with his father. It is supposed that Nabonidus was not in Babylon at the time.

Reference.—Daniel 5.

BEN.

BEN—a Hebrew prefix meaning "son."

BENEDICTION.

BEN-E-DIC'TION—a blessing, or an expression of a blessing; a calling down upon the people of God's goodness. In Numbers 6: 24-26 the following form of the priestly benediction is given: "The Lord bless and keep thee: the Lord make his face shine upon thee and be gracious unto thee; the Lord lift up his countenance upon thee and give thee peace." This blessing was pronounced with uplifted hands, and the people responded by saying "Amen."

In Mark 10: 16 and Luke 24: 50 Jesus is spoken of as having blessed little children, and in Matthew 26: 26 He delivered a blessing on the occasion of the institution of the Lord's Supper.

The apostolic benediction is the universal Christian benediction. It is found in 2 Corinthians 13: 14: "The grace of our Lord Jesus Christ, and the love of God, and the communion of the Holy Ghost, be with you all. Amen."

BENJAMIN. (See Jacob, Joseph, Rachel.)

BEN'JA-MIN—a form of a Hebrew word meaning "son of my right hand." The name of the youngest son of Jacob by Rachel, named by his dying mother Benoni, or "son of my sorrow," a name later changed by his father, because of the support and protection he expected to get from this child of his old age. Benjamin was born about B.C. 1729, near Bethlehem. He was a man of quiet, gentle, and retiring temperament, and made little important history for himself. The tribe of Israelites that took his name was always the least important of the twelve, although it gave the Jews some great men. Saul was a Benjamite, and Paul the apostle was proud of his Benjamite lineage.

REFERENCES.

And it came to pass, as her soul was in departing, (for she died,) that she called his name Benoni: but his father called him Benjamin. (Genesis 35: 18.)

And the men took that present, and they took double money in their hand, and Benjamin; and rose up, and went down to Egypt, and stood before Joseph. (Genesis 43: 15.)

And the sons of Benjamin were Belah, and Becher, and Ashbel, Gera, and Naaman, Ehi, and Rosh, Muppim, and Huppim, and Ard. (Genesis 46: 21.)

Of the children of Benjamin, by their generations, after their families, by the house of their fathers, according to the number of the names, from twenty years old and upward, all that were able to go forth to war;

Those that were numbered of them, even of the tribe of Benjamin, were thirty and five thousand and four hundred. (Numbers 1: 36, 37.)

And of Benjamin he said, The beloved of the Lord shall dwell in safety by him; and the Lord shall cover him all the day long, and he shall dwell between his shoulders. (Deuteronomy 33: 12.)

Now there was a man of Benjamin whose name was Kish, the son of Abiel, the son of Zeror, the son of Bechorath, the son of Aphiah, a Benjamite, a mighty man of power.

And he had a son, whose name was Saul, a choice young man, and a goodly: and there was not among the children of Israel a goodlier person than he: from his shoulders and upward he was higher than any of the people. (1 Samuel 9: 1, 2.)

Circumcised the eighth day, of the stock of Israel, of the tribe of Benjamin, an Hebrew of the Hebrews; as touching the law, a Pharisee. (Philippians 3: 5.)

BETH.

BETH—a Hebrew prefix meaning "house."

BETHABARA.

BETH'AB'A-RA—meaning "the house of the ford." Given to the spot where John baptized.

Reference.—John 1: 28.

BETHANY.

BETH'A-NY—meaning "the house of dates." The name of one of the most interesting places mentioned in the Bible. It was a few miles outside of Jerusalem, on one of the slopes of the Mount of Olives. Lazarus, who was raised from the dead, lived there; Jesus very often sojourned there, and began his triumphal entry to Jerusalem from there. Likewise it was the scene of the ascension. It is now called El Azariyeh, or the city of Lazarus. It is almost a heap of ruins. A very old tower is pointed out as the house of Lazarus. In Christ's time it doubtless was a thriving and populous village.

REFERENCES.

And he left them, and went out of the city into Bethany, and he lodged there. (Matthew 21: 17.)

Now when Jesus was in Bethany, in the house of Simon the leper. (Matthew 26: 6.)

And when they came nigh to Jerusalem, unto Bethphage, and Bethany, at the mount of Olives, he sendeth forth two of his disciples,

And saith unto them, *Go your way into the village over against you: and as soon as ye be entered into it, ye shall find a colt tied, whereon never man sat; loose him, and bring him.* (Mark 11: 1, 2.)

Then Jesus, six days before the passover, came to Bethany, where Lazarus was which had been dead, whom he raised from the dead.

There they made him a supper; and Martha served: but Lazarus was one of them that sat at the table with him. (John 12: 1, 2.)

And he led them out as far as to Bethany, and he lift up his hands, and blessed them.

And it came to pass, while he blessed them, he was parted from them, and carried up into heaven. (Luke 24: 50 51.)

BETHEL.

BETH'EL—meaning "the house of God." A place about ten miles north of Jerusalem originally known as Luz. There Jacob stopped to rest and had his dream of the heaven-reaching ladder. He built an altar and changed the name to Bethel. A cluster of ruins still marks the site of the town.

References.—Genesis 28: 19; Genesis 31: 13; Genesis 35: 1; Judges 1: 22; 1 Kings 12: 28; 2 Kings 23: 15.

BETHESDA.

BE-THES'DA—meaning "house of mercy." The name of a noted pool at Jerusalem, the resort of persons for the purpose of bathing in its healing waters. The exact site is lost, but it is supposed to have been what is now a great excavation near St. Stephen's gate, having all the appearance of an ancient pool.

Reference.—John 5: 2.

BETHLEHEM.

BETH'LE-HEM—meaning "the place of bread." The name of one of the most famous and sanctified spots in the world—the birthplace of the Lord Jesus Christ. It is a small town about four-and-a-half miles south of Jerusalem. One of the most ancient towns in Palestine, it originally was called Ephrath (fruitful), and sometimes spelled Ephratah. Ruth and Boaz dwelt there, as also did Saul, and David first saw the light there. The little place has been the goal of many pious pilgrimages and many Christians have visited it. The modern town is a beautiful place, built upon the brow of a hill. Its population is about 3,000. There are some handsome old church and convent buildings in it. A field half a mile to the east of the place is pointed out as the spot where the angels appeared to the shepherds.

REFERENCES.

David and Bethlehem.

And the Lord said unto Samuel, How long wilt thou mourn for Saul, seeing I have rejected him from reigning over Israel? fill thy horn with oil, and go, I will send thee to Jesse the Beth-lehemite: for I have provided me a king among his sons. (1 Samuel 16: 1.)

And Samuel did that which the Lord spake, and came to Beth-lehem. And the elders of the town trembled at his coming, and said, Comest thou peaceably? (1 Samuel 16: 4.)

And David longed, and said, Oh that one would give me drink of the water of the well of Beth-lehem, which is by the gate! (2 Samuel 23: 15.)

Jesus' Birth at Bethlehem.

Now when Jesus was born in Bethlehem of Judea in the days of Herod the king, behold, there came wise men from the east to Jerusalem. (Matthew 2: 1.)

And Joseph also went up from Galilee, out of the city of Nazareth, into Judea, unto the city of David, which is called Bethlehem, (because he was of the house and lineage of David.) (Luke 2: 4.)

Hath not the scripture said, That Christ cometh of the seed of David, and out of the town of Bethlehem, where David was? (John 7: 42.)

Jesus' Birth There Foretold.

Until I find out a place for the Lord, an habitation for the mighty God of Jacob.

Lo, we heard of it at Ephratah: we found it in the fields of the wood. (Psalm 132: 5, 6.)

But thou, Beth-lehem Ephratah, though thou be little among the thousands of Judah, yet out of thee shall he come forth unto me that is to be Ruler in Israel; whose goings forth have been from of old, from everlasting. (Micah 5: 2.)

BETHSAIDA.

BETH'SA'IDA—meaning "the house of fish." Bethsaida was the name of two places on the Sea of Galilee, one on the west side and the other on the east. The former was the native place of Peter, Andrew, and Philip, and the frequent stopping-place of Jesus. At the latter place the 5,000 were fed.

References.—Matthew 11: 21; Mark 6: 45; Mark 8: 22; Luke 9: 10-17; John 1: 44; John 12: 21.

BEZALEEL.

BE-ZAL'E-EL—meaning "in the protection of God." The name of the artisan to whom God trusted the building of the ark of the covenant.

References.—Exodus 31: 16; 35: 30.

BIRTHRIGHT.

BIRTH'RIGHT'—the old Hebrew privilege of the firstborn son to a double share of any inheritance from his father and the descent of the priesthood as well if the family were of the priestly tribe.

REFERENCES.

If a man have two wives, one beloved, and another hated, and they have borne him children, both the beloved and the hated; and if the first-born son be hers that was hated:

Then it shall be, when he maketh his sons to inherit that which he hath, that he may not make the son of the beloved first-born before the son of the hated, which is indeed the first-born:

But he shall acknowledge the son of the hated for the first-born, by giving him a double portion of all that he hath: for he is the beginning of his strength; the right of the first-born is his. (Deuteronomy 21: 15.)

And Jacob said, Sell me this day thy birthright.

And Esau said, Behold, I am at the point to die: and what profit shall this birthright do to me?

And Jacob said, Swear to me this day; and he sware unto him: and he sold his birthright unto Jacob.

Then Jacob gave Esau bread and pottage of lentiles; and he did eat and drink, and rose up, and went his way: thus Esau despised his birthright. (Genesis 25: 31-34.)

BLASPHEMY.

BLAS'PHE-MY—speaking or uttering evil things concerning God; an indignity offered to God either in words, writing, or signs. The sin of blasphemy has always been a most serious one. Among the Jews it was punishable with death. The Scriptures at various places speak of the magnitude of the crime, and blasphemy against the Holy Ghost is mentioned as a sin forever unpardonable. The specific nature of this phase of blasphemy has not been definitely settled, some commentators holding that it is attributing the miracles of Jesus to Satan, while others incline to the belief that it is constant and unalterable opposition to the benign workings of the Holy Spirit.

REFERENCES.

General.

Thou shalt not take the name of the Lord thy God in vain: for the Lord will not hold him guiltless that taketh his name in vain. (Exodus 20: 7.)

And he that blasphemeth the name of the Lord, he shall surely be put to death, and all the congregation shall certainly stone him: as well the stranger, as he that is born in the land, when he blasphemeth the name of the Lord, shall be put to death. (Leviticus 24: 16.)

And David said unto Nathan, I have sinned against the Lord. And Nathan said unto David, The Lord also hath put away thy sin; thou shalt not die.

Howbeit, because by this deed thou hast given great occasion to the enemies of the Lord to blaspheme, the child also that is born unto thee shall surely die. (2 Samuel 12: 13, 14.)

Remember this, that the enemy hath reproached, O Lord, and that the foolish people have blasphemed thy name. (Psalm 74: 18.)

For out of the heart proceed evil thoughts, murders, adulteries, fornications, thefts, false witness, blasphemies. (Matthew 15: 19.)

But now you also put off all these, anger, wrath, malice, blasphemy, filthy communication out of your mouth. (Colossians 3: 8.)

Who was before a blasphemer, and a persecutor, and injurious: but I obtained mercy, because I did it ignorantly in unbelief. (1 Timothy 1: 13.)

False Accusations of Blasphemy.

And there came in two men, children of Belial, and sat before him: and the men of Belial witnessed against him, even against Naboth, in the presence of the people, saying, Naboth did blaspheme God and the king. Then they carried him forth out of the city, and stoned him with stones, that he died. (1 Kings 21: 13.)

And behold, they brought to him a man sick of the palsy, lying on a bed: and Jesus, seeing their faith, said unto the sick of the palsy, *Son, be of good cheer; thy sins be forgiven thee.*

And behold, certain of the scribes said within themselves, This man blasphemeth. (Matthew 9: 2, 3.)

Then the high priest rent his clothes, saying, He hath spoken blasphemy; what further need have we of witnesses? behold, now ye have heard his blasphemy. (Matthew 26: 65.)

The Jews answered him, saying, For a good work we stone thee not; but for blasphemy, and because that thou, being a man, makest thyself God.

Jesus answered them, *Is it not written in your law, I said, Ye are gods?*

If he called them gods, unto whom the word of God came, and the scripture cannot be broken;

Say ye of him whom the Father hath sanctified, and sent into the world, Thou blasphemest; because I said, I am the Son of God? (John 10: 33-36.)

And Stephen, full of faith and power, did great wonders and miracles among the people.

Then there arose certain of the synagogue, which is called the synagogue of the Libertines, and Cyrenians, and Alexandrians, and of them of Cilicia, and of Asia, disputing with Stephen.

And they were not able to resist the wisdom and the spirit by which he spake.

Then they suborned men, which said, We have heard him speak blasphemous words against Moses, and against God. (Acts 6: 8-11.)

Blasphemy against the Holy Ghost.

Wherefore I say unto you, All manner of sin and blasphemy shall be forgiven unto men: but the blasphemy against the Holy Ghost shall not be forgiven unto me. (Matthew 12: 31.)

Verily I say unto you, All sins shall be forgiven unto the sons of men, and blasphemies wherewith soever they shall blaspheme:

But he that shall blaspheme against the Holy Ghost hath never forgiveness, but is in danger of eternal damnation. (Mark 3: 28.)

And whosoever shall speak a word against the Son of man, it shall be forgiven him: but unto him that blasphemeth against the Holy Ghost, it shall not be forgiven. (Luke 12: 10.)

BLESS AND BLESSED. (See Beatitude.)

BLESS—a word used in the Bible a great number of times and with many different meanings. The more important of them are: (1) to make holy; (2) to confer happiness upon; (3) to grant divine favor to; (4) to express a wish for happiness for some other person; (5) to invoke special attributes upon; (6) to praise or glorify.

BLESS'ED—hallowed, consecrated, or holy; enjoying blessings or highly favored; blissful or joyful; enjoying spiritual happiness or heavenly felicity.

REFERENCES.

General.

And I will bless them that bless thee, and curse him that curseth thee: and in thee shall all families of the earth be blessed. (Genesis 12: 3.)

And therefore will the Lord wait, that he may be gracious unto you, and therefore will he be exalted, that he may have mercy upon you: for the Lord is a God of judgment: blessed are all they that wait for him. (Isaiah 30: 18.)

Then shall the King say unto them on his right hand, Come, ye blessed of my Father, inherit the kingdom prepared for you from the foundation of the world. (Matthew 25: 34.)

And thou shalt be blessed: for they cannot recompense thee: for thou shalt be recompensed at the resurrection of the just.

And when one of them that sat at meat with him, heard these things, he said unto him, Blessed is he that shall eat bread in the kingdom of God. (Luke 14: 14, 15.)

Even as David also describeth the blessedness of the man unto whom God imputeth righteousness without works,

Saying, Blessed are they whose iniquities are forgiven, and whose sins are covered.

Blessed is the man to whom the Lord will not impute sin.

Cometh this blessedness then upon the circumcision only, or upon the uncircumcision also? For we say that faith was reckoned to Abraham for righteousness. (Romans 4: 6-9.)

Those Chosen, Called or Chastened by God.

Blessed is the man whom thou choosest, and causest to approach unto thee, that he may dwell in thy courts: we shall be satisfied with the goodness of thy house, even of thy holy temple. (Psalm 65: 4.)

Blessed be the God and Father of our Lord Jesus Christ, who hath blessed us with all spiritual blessings in heavenly places in Christ:

According as he hath chosen us in him, before the foundation of the world, that we should be holy and without blame before him in love. (Ephesians 1: 3, 4.)

Look unto Abraham your father, and unto Sarah that bare you: for I called him alone, and blessed him, and increased him. (Isaiah 51: 2.)

And he saith unto me, Write, Blessed are they which are called unto the marriage-supper of the Lamb. And he saith unto me, These are the true sayings of God. (Revelation 19: 9.)

Blessed is the man whom thou chastenest, O Lord, and teachest him out of thy law. (Psalm 94: 12.)

Those Who Trust, Fear, and Delight in the Lord.

Kiss the Son, lest he be angry, and ye perish from the way, when his wrath is kindled but a little. Blessed are all they that put their trust in him. (Psalm 2: 12.)

O taste and see that the Lord is good: blessed is the man that trusteth in him. (Psalm 34: 8.)

Blessed is that man that maketh the Lord his trust, and respecteth not the proud, nor such as turn aside to lies. (Psalm 40: 4.)

O Lord of hosts, blessed is the man that trusteth in thee. (Psalm 84: 12.)

Blessed is the man that trusteth in the Lord, and whose hope the Lord is. (Jeremiah 17: 7.)

Behold, that thus shall the man be blessed that feareth the Lord. (Psalm 128: 4.)

Praise ye the Lord. Blessed is the man that feareth the Lord, that delight-eth greatly in his commandments. (Psalm 112: 1.)

Those Who Hear and Obey.

Blessed are they that keep his testi-monies, and that seek him with the whole heart. (Psalm 119: 2.)

But blessed are your eyes, for they see: and your ears, for they hear. (Matthew 13: 16.)

But he said, *Yea, rather blessed are they that hear the word of God, and keep it.* (Luke 11: 28.)

But whoso looketh into the perfect law of liberty, and continueth therein, he being not a forgetful hearer, but a doer of the work, this man shall be blessed in his deed. (James 1: 25.)

Blessed is he that readeth, and they that hear the words of this prophecy, and keep those things which are writ-ten therein: for the time is at hand. (Revelation 1: 3.)

Blessed are they that do his com-mandments, that they may have right to the tree of life, and may enter in through the gates into the city. (Rev-elation 22: 14.)

Those Who Know, Believe in, and Suffer for Christ.

And Jesus answered and said unto him, *Blessed art thou, Simon Bar-jona: for flesh and blood hath not revealed it unto thee, but my Father which is in heaven.* (Matthew 16: 17.)

And blessed is she that believed: for there shall be a performance of those things which were told her from the Lord. (Luke 1: 45.)

So then they which be of faith are blessed with faithful Abraham. (Gala-tians 3: 9.)

Blessed are ye when men shall hate you, and when they shall separate you from their company, and shall reproach you, and cast out your name as evil, for the Son of man's sake. (Luke 6: 22.)

Blessed are they which are persecu-ted for righteousness' sake: for theirs is the kingdom of heaven.

Blessed are ye, when men shall revile you, and persecute you, and shall say all manner of evil against you falsely, for my sake. (Matthew 5: 10, 11.)

Other Special Blessings. (See Beatitudes.)

Blessed is the man that walketh not in the counsel of the ungodly, nor standeth in the way of sinners, nor sit-teth in the seat of the scornful. (Psalm 1: 1.)

Blessed are they that dwell in thy house: they will be still praising thee. Selah.

Blessed is the man whose strength is in thee; in whose heart are the ways of them. (Psalm 84: 4, 5.)

Blessed is the man that endureth temptation: for when he is tried, he shall receive the crown of life, which the Lord hath promised to them that love him. (James 1: 12.)

Blessed are the undefiled in the way,

who walk in the law of the Lord. (Psalm 119: 1.)

Blessed are they that keep judgment, and he that doeth righteousness at all times. (Psalm 106: 3.)

Blessings are upon the head of the just: but violence covereth the mouth of the wicked. (Proverbs 10: 6.)

The just man walketh in his integrity: his children are blessed after him. (Proverbs 20: 7.)

For thou, Lord, wilt bless the righteous; with favour wilt thou compass him as with a shield. (Psalm 5: 12.)

His seed shall be mighty upon earth: the generation of the upright shall be blessed. (Psalm 112: 2.)

A faithful man shall abound with blessings: but he that maketh haste to be rich shall not be innocent. (Proverbs 28: 20.)

Thou shalt surely give him, and thine heart shall not be grieved when thou givest unto him: because that for this thing the Lord thy God shall bless thee in all thy works, and in all that thou puttest thine hand unto. (Deuteronomy 15: 10.)

Blessed is he that considereth the poor: the Lord will deliver him in time of trouble.

The Lord will preserve him, and keep him alive; and he shall be blessed upon the earth: and thou wilt not deliver him unto the will of his enemies. (Psalm 41: 1, 2.)

He that hath a bountiful eye shall be blessed; for he giveth of his bread to the poor. (Proverbs 22: 9.)

Blessed are they which do hunger and thirst after righteousness: for they shall be filled. (Matthew 5: 6.)

And he lifted up his eyes on his disciples, and said, *Blessed be ye poor; for yours is the kingdom of God.*

Blessed are ye that hunger now: for ye shall be filled. Blessed are ye that weep now: for ye shall laugh. (Luke 6: 20, 21.)

Blessed is he whose transgression is forgiven, whose sin is covered.

Blessed is the man unto whom the Lord imputeth not iniquity, and in whose spirit there is no guile. (Psalm 32: 1, 2.)

And I heard a voice from heaven, saying unto me, Write, Blessed are the dead which die in the Lord from henceforth: Yea, saith the Spirit, that they may rest from their labours; and their works do follow them. (Revelation 14: 13.)

BLIND AND BLINDNESS.

BLIND AND BLIND'NESS. Blindness is very common in Oriental countries, and has been so from the earliest times. This is due to a disease of the eyes which is very contagious, and to the ravages of smallpox. Mosaic law and custom taught that persons suffering from loss of sight should be treated with great humanity; Christ's example and doctrine do the same. Blindness is often used in the Bible as a figurative term for ignorance, either in spiritual or general knowledge, or from obstinate purpose not to understand. There are also a number of places wherein blindness is mentioned as having been inflicted by divine agency as a punishment, or as a means to accomplish a purpose of God, as in the case of Paul.

REFERENCES.

Physical Blindness.

Laws Concerning the Blind:

Thou shalt not curse the deaf, nor put a stumbling-block before the blind, but shalt fear thy God: I am the Lord. (Leviticus 19: 14.)

Cursed be he that maketh the blind to wander out of the way: and all the people shall say, Amen. (Deuteronomy 28: 18.)

Blindness Inflicted.

Upon Syrians:

And when they came down to him, Elisha prayed unto the Lord, and said, Smite this people, I pray thee, with blindness. And he smote them with blindness, according to the word of Elisha. (2 Kings 6: 18.)

Upon Paul:

And Saul arose from the earth; and when his eyes were opened, he saw no man: but they led him by the hand, and brought him into Damascus.

And he was three days without sight, and neither did eat nor drink. (Acts 9: 8, 9.)

Upon Elymas:

And now behold, the hand of the Lord is upon thee, and thou shalt be blind, not seeing the sun for a season. And immediately there fell on him a mist and a darkness, and he went about, seeking some to lead him by the hand. (Acts 13: 11.)

Healed by Christ.

And when Jesus departed thence, two blind men followed him, crying, and saying, Thou son of David, have mercy on us.

And when he was come into the house, the blind men came to him: and Jesus saith unto them, *Believe ye that I am able to do this?* They said unto him, Yea, Lord.

Then touched he their eyes, saying, *According to your faith, be it unto you.* (Matthew 9: 27-29.)

Then was brought unto him one possessed with a devil, blind, and dumb: and he healed him, insomuch that the blind and dumb both spake and saw. (Matthew 12: 22.)

So Jesus had compassion on them, and touched their eyes: and immediately their eyes received sight, and they followed him. (Matthew 20: 34.)

And he cometh to Bethsaida; and they bring a blind man unto him, and besought him to touch him.

And he took the blind man by the hand, and led him out of the town; and when he had spit on his eyes, and put his hands upon him, he asked him if he saw aught. (Mark 8: 22, 23.)

And they came to Jericho: and as he went out of Jericho with his disciples, and a great number of people, blind Bartimeus, the son of Timeus, sat by the highway side begging.

And Jesus said unto him, *Go thy way; thy faith hath made thee whole.* And immediately he received his sight, and followed Jesus in the way. (Mark 10: 46 and 52.)

And in that same hour he cured many of their infirmities, and plagues, and of evil spirits; and unto many that were blind he gave sight. (Luke 7: 21.)

He answered and said, A man that is called Jesus, made clay, and anointed mine eyes, and said unto me, Go to the pool of Siloam, and wash: and I went and washed, and I received sight. (John 9: 11.)

Spiritual Blindness.

They know not, neither will they understand: they walk on in darkness: all the foundations of the earth are out of course. (Psalm 82: 5.)

His watchmen are blind: they are all ignorant, they are all dumb dogs, they cannot bark; sleeping, lying down, loving to slumber. (Isaiah 56: 10.)

Therefore is judgment far from us, neither doth justice overtake us: we wait for light, but behold obscurity; for brightness, but we walk in darkness.

We grope for the wall like the blind, and we grope as if we had no eyes: we stumble at noon-day. (Isaiah 59: 9, 10.)

BLOOD. (See Christ, Lamb, Sacrifice.)

BLOOD—the fluid which circulates in the veins of animals, from the lowest orders to the highest, man, carrying nourishment to the various parts of the body and removing waste products. It is mentioned in the Bible in many ways, chiefly with reference to its prohibition as an article of food and its appointment, use, and significance in sacrifice. The Jews were forbidden to use it for food, as some of the nations that were their neighbors used it, and it was required to be "poured out" before the carcass of the slaughtered animal was fit for use. This shedding of blood being particularly bound up in the religious side of the Jewish life, the life-fluid of beasts was regarded as being a sacrifice to God. The old Jewish sacrificial system of offering the blood of beasts came to an end with the death of Jesus. His blood was shed as a perpetual sacrifice, and what is known in theology as the sacramental system took the place of the sacrificial system. To Christians, therefore, the prohibition of the use of blood as food was removed inferentially. Many references are to be found showing the nature of the sacrifice of Christ's blood. The shedding of human blood is expressly forbidden by divine command, both in the Ten Commandments and in the teachings of Jesus.

REFERENCES.

General: Blood as Food Forbidden.

But flesh with the life thereof, which is the blood thereof, shall ye not eat. (Genesis 9: 4.)

It shall be a perpetual statute for your generations throughout all your dwellings, that ye eat neither fat nor blood. (Leviticus 3: 17.)

Only ye shall not eat the blood; ye shall pour it upon the earth as water. (Deuteronomy 12: 16.)

Human Bloodshedding Forbidden.

And surely your blood of your lives will I require: at the hand of every beast will I require it, and at the hand of man; at the hand of every man's brother will I require the life of man.

Whoso sheddeth man's blood, by man shall his blood be shed: for in the image of God made he man. (Genesis 9: 5, 6.)

These six things doth the Lord hate; yea, seven are an abomination unto him:

A proud look, a lying tongue, and hands that shed innocent blood. (Proverbs 6: 16, 17.)

And the chief Priests took the silver pieces, and said, It is not lawful for to put them into the treasury, because it is the price of blood. (Matthew 27: 6.)

Sacrifice of Blood.

And thou shalt take of the blood of the bullock, and put it upon the horns of the altar with thy finger, and pour all the blood beside the bottom of the altar. (Exodus 29: 12.)

For the life of the flesh is in the blood; and I have given it to you upon the altar, to make an atonement for your souls: for it is the blood that maketh an atonement for the soul. (Leviticus 17: 11.)

For if the blood of bulls and of goats, and the ashes of an heifer sprinkling the unclean, sanctifieth to the purifying of the flesh:

How much more shall the blood of Christ, who through the eternal Spirit offered himself without spot to God, purge your conscience from dead works to serve the living God? (Hebrews 9: 13, 14.)

Christ's Sacrifice of Blood.

The cup of blessing which we bless, is it not the communion of the blood of Christ? The bread which we break, is it not the communion of the body of Christ? (1 Corinthians 10: 16.)

But now in Christ Jesus, ye who sometimes were far off are made nigh by the blood of Christ. (Ephesians 2: 13.)

But with the precious blood of Christ, as of a Lamb without blemish and without spot. (1 Peter 1: 19.)

But if we walk in the light, as he is in the light, we have fellowship one with another, and the blood of Jesus Christ his Son cleanseth us from all sin. (1 John 1: 7.)

Salvation by Blood.

Neither by the blood of goats and calves, but by his own blood he entered in once into the Holy place, having obtained eternal redemption for us. (Hebrews 9: 12.)

Wherefore Jesus also, that he might sanctify the people with his own blood, suffered without the gate. (Hebrews 13: 12.)

And almost all things are by the law purged with blood: and without shedding of blood is no remission. (Hebrews 9: 22.)

And from Jesus Christ, who is the faithful witness, and the first begotten of the dead, and the Prince of the kings of the earth: unto him that loved us, and washed us from our sins in his own blood. (Revelation 1: 5.)

Blood at the Lord's Supper.

For this is my blood of the new testament, which is shed for many for the remission of sins. (Matthew 26: 28.)

And he said unto them, *This is my blood of the new testament, which is shed for many.* (Mark 14: 24.)

Likewise also the cup after supper, saying, *This cup is the new testament in my blood, which is shed for you.* (Luke 22: 20.)

After the same manner also he took the cup when he had supped, saying, *This cup is the new testament in my blood: this do ye, as oft as ye drink it, in remembrance of me.* (1 Corinthians 11: 25.)

Redemption by Blood.

In whom we have redemption through his blood, the forgiveness of sins, according to the riches of his grace. (Ephesians 1: 7.)

And, having made peace through the blood of his cross, by him to reconcile all things unto himself; by him, I say, whether they be things in earth, or things in heaven. (Colossians 1: 20.)

And to Jesus the mediator of the new covenant, and to the blood of sprinkling, that speaketh better things than that of Abel. (Hebrews 12: 24.)

But if we walk in the light, as he is in the light, we have fellowship one with another, and the blood of Jesus Christ his Son cleanseth us from all sin. (1 John 1: 7.)

And they sung a new song, saying, Thou art worthy to take the book, and to open the seals thereof: for thou wast slain, and hast redeemed us to God by thy blood out of every kindred, and tongue, and people, and nation. (Revelation 5: 9.)

Redemption by Blood Typified.

And the blood shall be to you for a token upon the houses where ye are: and when I see the blood, I will pass over you, and the plague shall not be upon you to destroy you, when I smite the land of Egypt. (Exodus 12: 13.)

BOASTING.

Boast'ing—vaunting one's self; saying or telling things calculated to give others a high opinion of one's self. The Bible, in a number of places, teaches that boasting is to be shunned.

REFERENCES.

They that trust in their wealth, and boast themselves in the multitude of their riches;

None of them can by any means redeem his brother, nor give to God a ransom for him. (Psalm 49: 6, 7.)

Why boastest thou thyself in mischief, O mighty man? the goodness of God endureth continually. (Psalm 52: 1.)

How long shall they utter and speak hard things? and all the workers of iniquity boast themselves? (Psalm 94: 4.)

It is naught, it is naught, saith the buyer: but when he is gone his way, then he boasteth. (Proverbs 20: 14.)

Boast not thyself of to-morrow; for thou knowest not what a day may bring forth. (Proverbs 27: 1.)

Shall the axe boast itself against him that heweth therewith? or shall the saw magnify itself against him that shaketh it? as if the rod should shake itself against them that lift it up, or as if the staff should lift up itself, as if it were no wood. (Isaiah 10: 15.)

Boast not against the branches. But if thou boast, thou bearest not the root, but the root thee. (Romans 11: 18.)

Even so the tongue is a little member, and boasteth great things. Behold, how great a matter a little fire kindleth! (James 3: 5.)

But now ye rejoice in your boastings:

all such rejoicing is evil. (James 4: 10.)

For by grace are ye saved, through faith; and that not of yourselves: it is the gift of God:

Not of works, lest any man should boast. (Ephesians 2: 8, 9.)

Where is boasting then? It is excluded by what law? of works? Nay; but by the law of faith. (Romans 3: 27.)

BOAZ.

Bo'az—a Hebrew word meaning "alacrity." It was the name of a wealthy Bethlehemite and near kinsman of the first husband of Ruth, whom he married in conformity with the law upon the death of her husband. A son of this marriage was the father of Jesse, the father of David. Thus was Boaz one of the remote ancestors of Jesus. His fine spirit, piety, and manly character make him one of the most interesting and admired personages in the Bible.

References.—See Ruth, chapters 2, 3, and 4.

BODY.

Bod'y—the human frame. The Scriptures allude to the body in many different ways, both directly and with figurative meaning. It speaks of natural, spiritual, and mystical bodies, the latter being a figurative use of the word to show the unity of the entire Church of Christ.

REFERENCES.

Human Body.

To be kept pure and holy:

I beseech you therefore, brethren, by the mercies of God, that ye present your bodies a living sacrifice, holy, acceptable unto God, which is your reasonable service. (Romans 12: 1.)

That every one of you should know how to possess his vessel in sanctification and honour. (1 Thessalonians 4: 4.)

Holy Ghost's temple:

Know ye not that ye are the temple of God, and that the Spirit of God dwelleth in you?

If any man defile the temple of God, him shall God destroy: for the temple of God is holy, which temple ye are. (1 Corinthians 3: 16, 17.)

What! know ye not that your body is the temple of the Holy Ghost which is in you, which ye have of God, and ye are not your own?

For ye are bought with a price; therefore glorify God in your body, and in your spirit, which are God's. (1 Corinthians 6: 19, 20.)

And what agreement hath the temple of God with idols? for ye are the temple of the living God; as God hath said, I will dwell in them, and walk in them; and I will be their God, and they shall be my people. (2 Corinthians 6: 16.)

Law on dead bodies:

Command the children of Israel, that they put out of the camp every leper, and every one that hath an issue, and whosoever is defiled by the dead. (Numbers 5: 2.)

He that toucheth the dead body of any man shall be unclean seven days. (Numbers 19: 11.)

Will be raised again:

For in the resurrection they neither marry, nor are given in marriage, but are as the angels of God in heaven. (Matthew 22: 30.)

Now if Christ be preached that he rose from the dead, how say some among you that there is no resurrection of the dead?

But if there be no resurrection of the dead, then is Christ not risen. (1 Corinthians 15: 12, 13.)

Who shall change our vile body, that it may be fashioned like unto his glorious body, according to the working whereby he is able even to subdue all things unto himself. (Philippians 3: 21.)

Christ's Body.

General:

Wherefore when he cometh into the world, he saith, Sacrifice and offering thou wouldest not, but a body hast thou prepared me. (Hebrews 10: 5.)

By the which will we are sanctified through the offering of the body of Jesus Christ once for all. (Hebrews 10: 10.)

He went to Pilate, and begged the body of Jesus. Then Pilate commanded the body to be delivered.

And when Joseph had taken the body, he wrapped it in a clean linen cloth. (Matthew 27: 58, 59.)

The Church so-called:

For as we have many members in one body, and all members have not the same office:

So we, being many, are one body in Christ, and every one members one of another. (Romans 12: 4, 5.)

The cup of blessing which we bless, is it not the communion of the blood of Christ? The bread which we break, is it not the communion of the body of Christ?

For we being many are one bread, and one body: for we are all partakers of that one bread. (1 Corinthians 10: 16, 17.)

For as the body is one, and hath many members, and all the members of that one body, being many, are one body: so also is Christ. (1 Corinthians 12: 12.)

And hath put all things under his

feet, and gave him to be the head over all things to the church,

Which is his body, the fulness of him that filleth all in all. (Ephesians 1: 22, 23.)

For the perfecting of the saints, for the work of the ministry, for the edifying of the body of Christ. (Ephesians 4: 12.)

For the husband is the head of the wife, even as Christ is the head of the church: and he is the Saviour of the body. (Ephesians 5: 23.)

And he is the head of the body, the church: who is the beginning, the firstborn from the dead; that in all things he might have the pre-eminence. (Colossians 1: 18.)

BOLDNESS.

BOLD'NESS—the state of being bold, bravery of a certain type, hardihood; dauntlessness.

REFERENCES.

Boldness through Faith.

The wicked flee when no man pursueth: but the righteous are bold as a lion. (Proverbs 28: 1.)

For the Lord God will help me: therefore shall I not be confounded: therefore have I set my face like a flint, and I know that I shall not be ashamed. (Isaiah 50: 7.)

According to the eternal purpose which he purposed in Christ Jesus our Lord:

In whom we have boldness and access with confidence by the faith of him. (Ephesians 3: 11, 12.)

Herein is our love made perfect, that we may have boldness in the day of judgment: because as he is, so are we in this world.

There is no fear in love; but perfect love casteth out fear: because fear hath

torment. He that feareth, is not made perfect in love. (1 John 4: 17, 18.)

Now when they saw the boldness of Peter and John, and perceived that they were unlearned and ignorant men, they marvelled; and they took knowledge of them, that they had been with Jesus. (Acts 4: 13.)

BONDAGE. (See Captivity.)

BOND'AGE—a condition similar to slavery. The Israelites were in bondage to the Egyptians and to the Babylonians and their successors. Under Roman rule they occupied the position merely of a conquered race. Thus, there was no complete condition of servitude. Bondage is mentioned a number of times in the Bible in its literal significance, as outlined above, and in its figurative meaning with relation to the bondage of man to sin, etc.

REFERENCES.

Israel's Bondage in Egypt.

And the Egyptians made the children of Israel to serve with rigour.

And they made their lives bitter with hard bondage, in mortar, and in brick, and in all manner of service in the field: all their service wherein they made them serve was with rigour. (Exodus 1: 13, 14.)

And the Lord said, I have surely seen the affliction of my people which are in Egypt, and have heard their cry by reason of their taskmasters; for I know their sorrows. (Exodus 3: 7.)

And God spake on this wise, That his seed should sojourn in a strange land; and that they should bring them into bondage, and entreat them evil four hundred years. (Acts 7: 6.)

Israel's Bondage to Babylon.

Now the rest of the people that were left in the city, and the fugitives that fell away to the king of Babylon, with the remnant of the multitude, did Neb-uzar-adan the captain of the guard carry away. (2 Kings 25: 11.)

Since the days of our fathers have we been in a great trespass unto this day; and for our iniquities have we, our kings, and our priests, been delivered into the hand of the kings of the lands, to the sword, to captivity, and to a spoil, and to confusion of face, as it is this day. (Ezra 9: 7.)

Spiritual Bondage.

Jesus answered them, *Verily, verily, I say unto you, Whosoever committeth sin is the servant of sin.* (John 8: 34.)

For I perceive that thou art in the gall of bitterness, and in the bond of iniquity. (Acts 8: 23.)

Know ye not, that to whom ye yield yourselves servants to obey, his servants ye are to whom ye obey; whether of sin unto death, or of obedience unto righteousness? (Romans 6: 16.)

But I see another law in my members, warring against the law of my mind, and bringing me into captivity to the law of sin which is in my members. (Romans 7: 23.)

And that because of false brethren unawares brought in, who came in privily to spy out our liberty which we have in Christ Jesus, that they might bring us into bondage. (Galatians 2: 4.)

Even so we, when we were children, were in bondage under the elements of the world. (Galatians 4: 3.)

While they promise them liberty, they themselves are the servants of corruption: for of whom a man is overcome, of the same is he brought in bondage. (2 Peter 2: 19.)

Deliverance by Christ.

The Spirit of the Lord God is upon me; because the Lord hath anointed me

to preach good tidings unto the meek; he hath sent me to bind up the broken-hearted, to proclaim liberty to the captives, and the opening of the prison to them that are bound. (Isaiah 61: 1.)

The Spirit of the Lord is upon me, because he hath anointed me to preach the gospel to the poor; he hath sent me to heal the broken-hearted, to preach deliverance to the captives, and recovering of sight to the blind, to set at liberty them that are bruised. (Luke 4: 18.)

BOOK.

BOOK. Books are mentioned in the Bible in a number of places, both in a direct manner and in a figurative sense. The ancient book was in no sense like the book of the present. It was a written scroll or a large number of loose leaves covered with writing and held together by cords. To the Jews what was known as the Books of the Law were exceedingly sacred. They are contained in the modern Bible in the form of the books of Moses. The Book of Life is a figurative expression for the company of heaven and those who shall partake of its glories after the judgment.

REFERENCES.

Book of the Law.

Also every sickness, and every plague which is not written in the book of this law, them will the Lord bring upon thee, until thou be destroyed. (Deuteronomy 28: 61.)

And Hilkiah the high priest said unto Shaphan the scribe, I have found the book of the law in the house of the Lord. And Hilkiah gave the book to Shaphan, and he read it. (2 Kings 22: 8.)

For as many as are of the works of the law, are under the curse: for it is written, Cursed is every one that continueth not in all things which are written in the book of the law to do them. (Galatians 3: 10.)

Book of Life.

And the Lord said unto Moses, Whosoever hath sinned against me, him will I blot out of my book. (Exodus 32: 33.)

Let them be blotted out of the book of the living, and not be written with the righteous. (Psalm 69: 28.)

And I entreat thee also, true yokefellow, help those women which laboured with me in the gospel, with Clement also, and with other my fellowlabourers, whose names are in the book of life. (Philippians 4: 3.)

He that overcometh, the same shall be clothed in white raiment, and I will not blot out his name out of the book of life, but I will confess his name before my Father, and before his Angels. (Revelation 3: 5.)

And all that dwell upon the earth, shall worship him, whose names are not written in the book of life of the Lamb slain from the foundation of the world. (Revelation 13: 8.)

And there shall in no wise enter into it any thing that defileth, neither whatsoever worketh abomination, or maketh a lie; but they which are written in the Lamb's book of life. (Revelation 21: 27.)

And if any man shall take away from the words of the book of this prophecy, God shall take away his part out of the book of life, and out of the holy city, and from the things which are written in this book. (Revelation 22: 19.)

BRAZEN SEA.

Bra'zen Sea—the name applied to a huge dish or basin made of brass and placed in the priest's court of Solomon's Temple for the accommodation of the priests in performing certain cleansing rites before and after worship. It rested upon twelve brazen oxen. It was destroyed in the destruction of the Temple by the Babylonians.

References.—1 Kings 7: 23-26; 2 Chronicles 4: 2-6; 1 Kings 25: 13; Jeremiah 52: 17.

BREAD.

Bread. To the Hebrew the word "bread" had a very broad and significant meaning. It meant not only the article of diet now known by the term, but almost every other foodstuff as well. Naturally it came to be used very often in a figurative sense. The method of making bread was much the same in Biblical times as it is now, and all the ancient nations seem to have used it as a staple article of food. At certain seasons of the year the Jews used it without leavening for the observance of certain religious forms. This custom is still observed in the Passover bread. Figuratively there were many kinds of bread—of suffering, of adversity and tears, of heaven, of wickedness, deceit, idleness, etc.

REFERENCES.

General.

In the sweat of thy face shalt thou eat bread, till thou return unto the ground; for out of it wast thou taken: for dust thou art, and unto dust shalt thou return. (Genesis 3: 19.)

Then said the Lord unto Moses, Behold, I will rain bread from heaven for you; and the people shall go out and gather a certain rate every day, that I may prove them, whether they will walk in my law, or no. (Exodus 16: 4.)

Bread Miraculously Supplied.

And his servitor said, What! should I set this before an hundred men? He said again, Give the people, that they may eat: for thus saith the Lord, They shall eat, and shall leave thereof.

So he set it before them, and they

did eat, and left thereof, according to the word of the Lord. (2 Kings 4: 43, 44.)

And Jesus took the loaves; and when he had given thanks, he distributed to the disciples, and the disciples to them that were set down; and likewise of the fishes, as much as they would.

When they were filled, he said unto his disciples, *Gather up the fragments that remain, that nothing be lost.*

Therefore they gathered them together, and filled twelve baskets with the fragments of the five barley loaves, which remained over and above unto them that had eaten. (John 6: 11-13.)

Figurative and as Christ.

Then Jesus said unto them, *Verily, verily, I say unto you, Moses gave you not that bread from heaven; but my Father giveth you the true bread from heaven.*

For the bread of God is he which cometh down from heaven, and giveth life unto the world.

Then said they unto him, Lord, evermore give us this bread.

And Jesus said unto them, *I am the bread of life: he that cometh to me, shall never hunger; and he that believeth on me, shall never thirst.* (John 6: 32-35.)

This is the bread which cometh down from heaven, that a man may eat thereof, and not die.

I am the living bread which came down from heaven: if any man eat of this bread, he shall live for ever: and the bread that I will give is my flesh, which I will give for the life of the world. (John 6: 50, 51.)

Therefore let us keep the feast, not with old leaven, neither with the leaven of malice and wickedness; but with the

unleavened bread of sincerity and truth. (1 Corinthians 5: 8.)

The cup of blessing which we bless, is it not the communion of the blood of Christ? The bread which we break, is it not the communion of the body of Christ?

For we being many are one bread, and one body; for we are all partakers of that one bread. (1 Corinthians 10: 16, 17.)

Used in Lord's Supper.

And he took bread, and gave thanks, and brake it, and gave unto them, saying, *This is my body which is given for you: this do in remembrance of me.* (Luke 22: 19.)

And upon the first day of the week, when the disciples came together to break bread, Paul preached unto them, ready to depart on the morrow, and continued his speech until midnight. (Acts 20: 7.)

For I have received of the Lord, that which also I delivered unto you, That the Lord Jesus, the same night in which he was betrayed, took bread:

And when he had given thanks, he brake it, and said, Take, eat: this is my body, which is broken for you: this do in remembrance of me. (Acts 11: 23, 24.)

BRETHREN.

BRETH'REN—literally brothers. This word is used in many places in the Bible. In the New Testament particularly it is often employed to express the family unity that should exist between all kinds of professing Christians, either with reference to strict denominational lines or to the whole body of the Church.

Regarding the allusions to the brethren of Jesus, and the question as to wheher He had brothers, in Matthew 13: 55 James, Joses,

Simon, and Judas are mentioned as the brothers of Jesus, and in the following verse sisters are also mentioned. There always has been a great amount of discussion about the matter. The Roman Catholics deny that Jesus had any brothers or sisters; but the Protestant writers and commentators have held to the other view, preferring to take Matthew's meaning literally.

REFERENCES.

Duties of Brethren.

And Abram said unto Lot, Let there be no strife, I pray thee, between me and thee, and between my herdmen and thy herdmen; for we be brethren. (Genesis 13: 8.)

If there be among you a poor man of one of thy brethren within any of thy gates in thy land which the Lord thy God giveth thee, thou shalt not harden thy heart, nor shut thine hand from thy poor brother. (Deuteronomy 15: 7.)

Thou shalt not oppress an hired servant that is poor and needy, whether he be of thy brethren, or of thy strangers that are in thy land within thy gates. (Deuteronomy 24: 14.)

Behold, how good and how pleasant it is for brethren to dwell together in unity! (Psalm 133: 1.)

But I say unto you, that whosoever is angry with his brother without a cause, shall be in danger of the Judgment: and whosoever shall say to his brother, Raca, shall be in danger of the council: but whosoever shall say, Thou fool, shall be in danger of hell fire. (Matthew 5: 22.)

Moreover, if thy brother shall trespass against thee, go and tell him his fault between thee and him alone: if he shall hear thee, thou hast gained thy brother. (Matthew 18: 15.)

Then came Peter to him, and said, Lord, how oft shall my brother sin against me, and I forgive him? till seven times?

Jesus saith unto him, *I say not unto thee, Until seven times: but, Until seventy times seven.* (Matthew 18: 21, 22.)

And the King shall answer and say unto them, Verily I say unto you, Inasmuch as ye have done it unto one of the least of these my brethren, ye have done it unto me. (Matthew 25: 40.)

A new commandment I give unto you, That ye love one another; as I have loved you, that ye also love one another. (John 13: 34.)

Be kindly affectioned one to another with brotherly love; in honour preferring one another. (Romans 12: 10.)

I speak to your shame. Is it so, that there is not a wise man among you? no, not one that shall be able to judge between his brethren?

But brother goeth to law with brother, and that before the unbelievers.

Now therefore there is utterly a fault among you, because ye go to law one with another. Why do ye not rather take wrong? why do ye not rather suffer yourselves to be defrauded?

Nay, ye do wrong, and defraud, and that your brethren. (1 Corinthians 6: 5-8.)

Wherefore if meat make my brother to offend, I will eat no flesh while the world standeth, lest I make my brother to offend. (1 Corinthians 8: 13.)

Brethren, if a man be overtaken in a fault, ye which are spiritual, restore such an one in the spirit of meekness; considering thyself, lest thou also be tempted. (Galatians 6: 1.)

But as touching brotherly love ye need not that I write unto you: for ye yourselves are taught of God to love one another. (1 Thessalonians 4: 9.)

Let brotherly love continue. (Hebrews 13: 1.)

He that saith he is in the light, and hateth his brother, is in darkness even until now. (1 John 2: 9.)

But whoso hath this world's good, and seeth his brother have need, and shutteth up his bowels of compassion from him, how dwelleth the love of God in him? (1 John 3: 17.)

BRIBERY.

BRIB'ER-Y—the act of giving or taking bribes; the influencing of the actions of another by corrupt gifts. Bribery is denounced in the Scriptures.

REFERENCES.

And thou shalt take no gift; for the gift blindeth the wise, and perverteth the words of the righteous. (Exodus 23: 8.)

A wicked man taketh a gift out of the bosom to pervert the ways of judgment. (Proverbs 17: 23.)

The king by judgment establisheth the land: but he that receiveth gifts overthroweth it. (Proverbs 29: 4.)

For the congregation of hypocrites shall be desolate, and fire shall consume the tabernacles of bribery. (Job 15: 34.)

BRIDE AND BRIDEGROOM.

BRIDE AND BRIDE'GROOM'. In the New Testament John refers to the Church as the bride of Christ, thus showing the loving and close relationship existing between the divine Son and His people on earth. Matthew calls him the Bridegroom, quoting His own words.

REFERENCES.

And Jesus said unto them, *Can the children of the bridechamber mourn, as long as the bridegroom is with them? But the days will come when the bridegroom shall be taken from them, and then shall they fast.* (Matthew 9: 15.)

Then shall the kingdom of heaven be likened unto ten virgins, which took their lamps, and went forth to meet the bridegroom. (Matthew 25: 1.)

He that hath the bride, is the bridegroom: but the friend of the bridegroom, which standeth and heareth him, rejoiceth greatly, because of the bridegroom's voice: this my joy therefore is fulfilled. (John 3: 29.)

And I John saw the holy city, new Jerusalem, coming down from God out of heaven, prepared as a bride adorned for her husband. (John 21: 2.)

And the Spirit and the Bride say, Come. And let him that heareth, say, Come. And let him that is athirst, come. And whosoever will, let him take the water of life freely. (Revelation 22: 17.)

BRIMSTONE.

BRIM'STONE—the Jewish name for sulphur, probably given to it for the reason that it was found on the shores or brim of the Dead Sea. It is a favorite symbol for torment and punishment, particularly in the future state.

REFERENCES.

For Tophet is ordained of old; yea, for the king it is prepared; he hath made it deep and large: the pile thereof is fire and much wood; the breath of the Lord, like a stream of brimstone, doth kindle it. (Isaiah 30: 33.)

By these three was the third part of men killed, by the fire, and by the smoke, and by the brimstone, which issued out of their mouths. (Revelation 9: 18.)

The same shall drink of the wine of the wrath of God, which is poured out without mixture into the cup of his indignation; and he shall be tormented with fire and brimstone in the presence of the holy angels, and in the presence of the Lamb. (Revelation 14: 10.)

And the beast was taken, and with him the false prophet, that wrought miracles before him, with which he deceived them that had received the mark of the beast, and them that worshipped his image. These both were cast alive into a lake of fire burning with brimstone. (Revelation 19: 10.)

But the fearful, and unbelieving, and the abominable, and murderers, and whoremongers, and sorcerers, and idolaters, and all liars, shall have their part in the lake which burneth with fire and brimstone: which is the second death. (Revelation 21: 8.)

BUSYBODIES.

BUS'Y-BOD'Y—those who meddle in the affairs of other persons; those who meddle in affairs in which they have no concern. Various passages in the Bible censure busybodies.

REFERENCES.

It is an honour for a man to cease from strife: but every fool will be meddling. (Proverbs 20: 3.)

He that passeth by, and meddleth with strife belonging not to him, is like one that taketh a dog by the ears. (Proverbs 20: 17.)

And that ye study to be quiet, and to do your own business, and to work with your own hands, as we commanded you. (1 Thessalonians 4: 11.)

For we hear that there are some which walk among you disorderly, working not at all, but are busybodies.

Now them that are such, we command, and exhort by our Lord Jesus Christ, that with quietness they work, and eat their own bread. (2 Thessalonians 3: 11, 12.)

And withal they learn to be idle, wandering about from house to house; and not only idle, but tattlers also, and busybodies, speaking things which they ought not. (1 Timothy 5: 13.)

But let none of you suffer as a murderer, or as a thief, or as an evil-doer, or as a busybody in other men's matters. (1 Peter 4: 15.)

CÆSAR.

CÆ'SAR—a name adopted or conferred upon all the Roman emperors after the death of Julius Cæsar, part of whose name it was. It thus became a title like emperor, king, pharaoh. After the third century it became more common, the emperor taking the title of augustus for his special distinction, and sharing cæsar with such as were associated with him in royalty. The New Testament is full of references to Cæsar, although not always to the same one. The following fall within New Testament times:

Augustus ......B.C. 31 to A.D. 14
Tiberius ...............A.D. 14-37
Caius (Caligula).......A.D. 37-41
Claudius ..............A.D. 41-54
Nero ..................A.D. 54-68
Galba .................A.D. 68-69
Otho ..................A.D. 69
Vitellius ..............A.D. 69
Vespasian .............A.D. 69-79
Titus .................A.D. 79-81
Domitian ..............A.D. 81-96

References.—Augustus, Luke 2: 1; Tiberius, Luke 3: 1; Luke 20: 22; Claudius, Acts 11: 28; Nero, Acts 25: 8.

CÆSAREA.

CÆS-A-RE'A—the name of two towns in the Holy Land—Cæsarea Palestina, on the Mediterranean, 70 miles west of Jerusalem, and Cæsarea Philippi, near the sources of the Jordan. Both were named in honor of the Roman Cæsar. The former is the more important because of the events in Paul's life which occurred there.

CAIAPHAS.

CAI'A-PHAS—the high-priest before whom Jesus was taken and who pronounced Him guilty of blasphemy. Caiaphas was high-priest for about twelve years, a long term of office, which suggests that he was a man of great power. He was deposed about A.D. 37 or 38. He unconsciously uttered a prophecy concerning Jesus, which is to be found in John 11: 49-52.

References.—Matthew 26: 3; Matthew 26: 65; Mark 14: 63; Luke 22: 71; John 11: 49-52.

CAIN. (See Adam, Abel, Creation, Eve.)

CAIN—a form of a Hebrew word meaning "a lance." Cain is the name given in the Bible to the eldest son of Adam and Eve. The story of his crime, in the murder of his brother, Abel, to be found in Genesis 4, is too well-known to need repetition. It may be said, however, that there is a mystical quality in it not so widely appreciated. The narrative shows Cain as a type of the proud and confirmed sinner, denying God's right to condemn him and rejecting the proffered means of grace, a type of which the world always has been full and always will be so.

REFERENCES.

And Cain talked with Abel his brother: and it came to pass, when they were in the field, that Cain rose up against Abel his brother, and slew him.

And the Lord said unto Cain, Where is Abel thy brother? And he said, I know not: Am I my brother's keeper?

And he said, What hast thou done? the voice of thy brother's blood crieth unto me from the ground.

And now art thou cursed from the earth, which hath opened her mouth to receive thy brother's blood from thy hand.

When thou tillest the ground, it shall not henceforth yield unto thee her strength; a fugitive and a vagabond shalt thou be in the earth.

And Cain said unto the Lord, My punishment is greater than I can bear.

Behold, thou hast driven me out this day from the face of the earth; and

from thy face shall I be hid; and I shall be a fugitive and a vagabond in the earth; and it shall come to pass, that every one that findeth me shall slay me.

And the Lord said unto him, Therefore whosoever slayeth Cain, vengeance shall be taken on him sevenfold. And the Lord set a mark upon Cain, lest any finding him should kill him. (Genesis 4: 8-15.)

Not as Cain, who was of that wicked one, and slew his brother. And wherefore slew he him? Because his own works were evil, and his brother's righteous. (1 John 3: 12.)

CALEB.

CA'LEB—a form of a Hebrew word meaning "dog." He was one of the twelve sent by Moses to spy out the land of Canaan, and with Joshua gave a good report, while the others gave bad ones. For this he and Joshua were the only adults born in Egypt permitted to enter the promised land as conquerors.

References.—Numbers 13: 30; Numbers 14: 6; Numbers 26: 65; Numbers 32: 12; Deuteronomy 1: 36; Joshua 14: 6; Joshua 15: 13; Judges 1: 13.

CALL. (See Ministry.)

CALL—to invite or request, to appoint or charge, as for an office or duty. There are various other meanings to the word, but the preceding ones are the chief uses of the word when it is found in the Bible.

REFERENCES.
Call to Repentance and Salvation.

He shall call to the heavens from above, and to the earth, that he may judge his people. (Psalm 50: 4.)

Come now, and let us reason together, saith the Lord: though your sins be as scarlet, they shall be as white as snow; though they be red like crimson, they shall be as wool. (Isaiah 1: 18.)

Look unto me, and be ye saved, all

the ends of the earth: for I am God, and there is none else. (Isaiah 45: 22.)

Ho, every one that thirsteth, come ye to the waters, and he that hath no money; come ye, buy, and eat; yea, come, buy wine and milk without money and without price.

Wherefore do ye spend money for that which is not bread? and your labour for that which satisfieth not? hearken diligently unto me, and eat ye that which is good, and let your soul delight itself in fatness.

Incline your ear, and come unto me: hear, and your soul shall live; and I will make an everlasting covenant with you, even the sure mercies of David. (Isaiah 55: 1-3.)

Therefore also now, saith the Lord, Turn ye even to me with all your heart, and with fasting, and with weeping, and with mourning:

And rend your heart, and not your garments, and turn unto the Lord your God: for he is gracious and merciful, slow to anger, and of great kindness, and repenteth him of the evil. (Joel 2: 12, 13.)

And saying, Repent ye; for the kingdom of heaven is at hand. (Matthew 3: 2.)

Come unto me, all ye that labour and are heavy laden, and I will give you rest.

Take my yoke upon you, and learn of me; for I am meek and lowly in heart: and ye shall find rest unto your souls.

For my yoke is easy, and my burden is light. (Matthew 11: 28-30.)

In the last day, that great day of the feast, Jesus stood, and cried, saying, *If any man thirst, let him come unto me, and drink.*

He that believeth on me, as the Scrip-

ture hath said, out of his belly shall flow rivers of living water. (John 7: 37, 38.)

Jesus cried, and said, *He that believeth on me, believeth not on me, but on him that sent me.*

And he that seeth me. seeth him that sent me.

I am come a light into the world, that whosoever believeth on me. should not abide in darkness.

And if any man hear my words, and believe not, I judge him not; For I came not to judge the world, but to save the world. (John 12: 44-47.)

And we know that all things work together for good, to them that love God, to them who are the called according to his purpose.

For whom he did foreknow, he also did predestinate to be conformed to the image of his son, that he might be the firstborn amongst many brethren.

Moreover, whom he did predestinate, them he also called: and whom he called, them he also justified: and whom he justified, them he also glorified. (Romans 8: 28-30.)

Now then we are ambassadors for Christ, as though God did beseech you by us: we pray you in Christ's stead, be ye reconciled to God. (2 Corinthians 5: 20.)

And the Spirit and. the Bride say, Come. And let him that heareth say, Come. And let him that is athirst come. And whosoever will, let him take the water of life freely. (Revelation 22: 17.)

Danger of Declining Call.

Then shall they call upon me, but I will not answer; they shall seek me early, but they shall not find me. (Proverbs 1: 28.)

He that, being often reproved, hardeneth his neck, shall suddenly be destroyed, and that without remedy. (Proverbs 29: 1.)

I also will choose their delusions, and will bring their fears upon them; because when I called, none did answer; when I spake, they did not hear; but they did evil before mine eyes, and chose that in which I delighted not. (Isaiah 66: 4.)

Hear, O earth: Behold, I will bring evil upon this people, even the fruit of their thoughts, because they have not hearkened unto my words, nor to my law, but rejected it. (Jeremiah 6: 19.)

Therefore thus saith the Lord God of hosts, the God of Israel; Behold, I will bring upon Judah and upon all the inhabitants of Jerusalem all the evil that I have pronounced against them; because I have spoken unto them, but they have not heard; and I have called unto them, but they have not answered. (Jeremiah 35: 17.)

Then saith he to his servants, The wedding is ready, but they which were bidden, were not worthy.

Go ye therefore into the highways, and as many as ye shall find, bid to the marriage. (Matthew 22: 8, 9.)

He that rejecteth me, and receiveth not my words, hath one that judgeth him: the word that I have spoken, the same shall judge him in the last day. (John 12: 48.)

Then Paul and Barnabas waxed bold, and said, It was necessary that the word of God should first have been spoken to you: but seeing you put it from you, and judge yourselves unworthy of everlasting life, lo, we turn to the Gentiles. (Acts 13: 46.)

And with all deceivableness of un-righteousness in them that perish; because they received not the love of the truth, that they might be saved. (2 Thessalonians 2: 10.)

Call to the Ministry.

Now therefore go, and I will be with thy mouth, and teach thee what thou shalt say.

And he said, O my Lord, send, I pray thee, by the hand of him whom thou wilt send. (Exodus 4: 12, 13.)

The Lord gave the word: great was the company of those that published it. (Psalm 68: 11.)

Paul, a servant of Jesus Christ, called to be an apostle, separated unto the gospel of God. (Romans 1: 1.)

Now he which stablisheth us with you in Christ, and hath anointed us, is God. (2 Corinthians 1: 24.)

For we are unto God a sweet savour of Christ, in them that are saved, and in them that perish.

To the one we are the savour of death unto death; and to the other the savour of life unto life. And who is sufficient for these things?

For we are not as many, which corrupt the word of God: but as of sincerity, but as of God, in the sight of God speak we in Christ. (2 Corinthians 2: 15-17.)

Do we begin again to commend ourselves? or need we, as some others, epistles of commendation to you, or letters of commendation from you? (2 Corinthians 3: 1.)

Now then we are ambassadors for Christ, as though God did beseech you by us: we pray you in Christ's stead, be ye reconciled to God. (2 Corinthians 5: 20.)

Paul, an apostle, (not of men, neither by man, but by Jesus Christ, and God the Father, who raised him from the dead.) (Galatians 1: 1.)

From henceforth let no man trouble me: for I bear in my body the marks of the Lord Jesus. (Galatians 6: 17.)

The eyes of your understanding being enlightened; that ye may know what is the hope of his calling, and what the riches of the glory of his inheritance in the saints. (Ephesians 1: 18.)

I therefore, the prisoner of the Lord, beseech you that ye walk worthy of the vocation wherewith ye are called. (Ephesians 4: 1.)

I press toward the mark for the prize of the high calling of God in Christ Jesus. (Philippians 3: 14.)

Wherefore also we pray always for you, that our God would count you worthy of this calling, and fulfil all the good pleasure of his goodness, and the work of faith with power;

That the name of our Lord Jesus Christ may be glorified in you, and ye in him, according to the grace of our God, and the Lord Jesus Christ. (2 Thessalonians 1: 11, 12.)

Neglect not the gift that is in thee, which was given thee by prophecy, with the laying on of the hands of the presbytery. (1 Timothy 4: 14.)

Who hath saved us, and called us with an holy calling, not according to our works, but according to his own purpose and grace, which was given us in Christ Jesus, before the world began. (2 Timothy 1: 9.)

See that ye refuse not him that speaketh. For if they escaped not who refused him that spake on earth, much more shall not we escape, if we turn away from him that speaketh from heaven. (Hebrews 12: 25.)

But ye are a chosen generation, a royal priesthood, an holy nation, a peculiar people; that ye should shew forth the praises of him who hath called you out of darkness into his marvellous light. (1 Peter 2: 9.)

But the anointing which ye have received of him abideth in you, and ye need not that any man teach you: but as the same anointing teacheth you of all things, and is truth, and is no lie, and even as it hath taught you, ye shall abide in him. (1 John 2: 27.)

We are of God: he that knoweth God heareth us; he that is not of God heareth not us. Hereby know we the spirit of truth, and the spirit of error. (1 John 4: 6.)

Special Calls to Individuals.

To Abraham:

Now the Lord had said unto Abram, Get thee out of thy country and from thy kindred, and from thy father's house, unto a land that I will shew thee:

And I will make of thee a great nation, and I will bless thee, and make thy name great; and thou shalt be a blessing:

And I will bless them that bless thee, and curse him that curseth thee: and in thee shall all families of the earth be blessed. (Genesis 12: 1-3.)

To Jacob:

And, behold, the Lord stood above it, and said, I am the Lord God of Abraham thy father, and the God of Isaac: the land whereon thou liest, to thee will I give it, and to thy seed. (Genesis 28: 13.)

To Moses:

Come now therefore, and I will send thee unto Pharaoh, that thou mayest bring forth my people, the children of Israel, out of Egypt. (Exodus 3: 10.)

To Gideon:

And there came an angel of the Lord, and sat under an oak which was in Ophrah, that pertained unto Joash the Abi-ezrite: and his son Gideon threshed wheat by the wine-press, to hide it from the Midianites.

And the angel of the Lord appeared unto him, and said unto him, The Lord is with thee, thou mighty man of valour. (Judges 6: 11, 12.)

To Samuel:

And the Lord came, and stood and called as at other times, Samuel, Samuel. Then Samuel answered, Speak; for thy servant heareth. (1 Samuel 3: 10.)

To Elijah:

And the word of the Lord came unto him, saying,

Get thee hence, and turn thee eastward, and hide thyself by the brook Cherith, that is before Jordan.

And it shall be, that thou shalt drink of the brook; and I have commanded the ravens to feed thee there. (1 Kings 17: 2-4.)

To Elisha:

So he departed thence, and found Elisha the son of Shaphat, who was ploughing with twelve yoke of oxen before him, and he with the twelfth: and Elijah passed by him, and cast his mantle upon him. (1 Kings 19: 19.)

To Isaiah:

Also I heard the voice of the Lord, saying, Whom shall I send, and who will go for us? Then said I, Here am I; send me. (Isaiah 6: 8.)

To Jonah:

Now the word of the Lord came unto Jonah the son of Amittai, saying,

Arise, go to Nineveh, that great city, and cry against it; for their wickedness is come up before me. (Jonah 1: 1, 2.)

To Peter and Andrew:

And Jesus, walking by the sea of Galilee, saw two brethren, Simon called Peter, and Andrew his brother, casting a net into the sea: for they were fishers.

And he saith unto them, *Follow me, and I will make you fishers of men.* (Matthew 4: 18, 19.)

To Paul:

And he trembling and astonished, said, Lord, what wilt thou have me to do? And the Lord said unto him, *Arise, and go into the city, and it shall be told thee what thou must do.* (Acts 9: 6.)

CALVARY. (See Crucifixion, Golgotha, Jesus, etc.)

CAL'VA-RY—an Englished form of the Latin word Calvaria, which was a translation of the Hebrew word Golgotha and the Greek word Cranion, by which was known the hill upon which Christ was crucified. It occurs in the Bible only in the gospel of Luke (ch. 23, v. 33), although it is more commonly used by writers and speakers than either of the other two names.

CANA.

CA'NA—a town of Galilee, a few miles north of Nazareth, noted in the Scriptures as the place where Jesus performed his first miracle—that of turning water into wine during a marriage feast.

References.—John 2; John 4: 47.

CANAAN.

CA'NAAN—a form of a Hebrew word meaning "flat" or "low." The name of the land promised to the Israelites, and inhabited by the descendants of Canaan, the son of Ham and the grandson of Noah. It lay to the westward of the Jordan. It included the country of the Philistines and the Phœnicians and was fruitful and beautiful. The Israelites did not succeed in occupying it until after long and bitter warfare with its idolatrous inhabitants.

References.—Genesis 12: 7; Genesis 13: 14; Genesis 13: 8; Exodus 15: 15; Joshua 14; Numbers 13; Numbers 27: 12; Deuteronomy 3: 27; Deuteronomy 34: 1.

CAPERNAUM.

CA-PER'NA-UM—a city on the northwestern shore of the Sea of Galilee, where Jesus lived for a considerable time and where many of his important works were done. It is now little more than a heap of ruins, fulfilling the doom pronounced against it for its impenitence. Matthew was chosen there, and Simon Peter and Andrew were natives of the neighborhood.

References.—Matthew 4: 13-18; Matthew 8: 5; Matthew 13: 18-24; Matthew 17: 24; Mark 1: 21; Mark 4; Luke 10: 15; John 2: 12; John 4: 46; John 6: 17.

CAPTIVITY. (See Bondage.)

CAP-TIV'I-TY. In the Bible this word is chiefly used to indicate the periods when the Israelites were in bonds to a conquering nation. The Jews recognize four such captivities—Babylonian, Median, Grecian, and Roman, although the word is applicable only in two instances. In the first the flower of the nation was carried captive to Assyria. This bondage lasted 150 years, ending about B.C. 588. About the year 613 B.C. the tribe of Judah was carried away captive by Nebuchadnezzar. In 535 B.C. a part of the people started to return, permission having been granted by Cyrus, who had conquered the Babylonians. Streams of Jews, varying in number, flowed back to their native land for the next 145 years, but the majority remained away. The general result of these moves was to disperse the entire Hebrew nation. It soon lost its character as a nation, and the old tribal barriers fell down. They never have been restored completely.

REFERENCES.

Israel's Captivity Foretold.

And I will scatter you among the heathen, and will draw out a sword after you: and your land shall be desolate and your cities waste. (Leviticus 26: 33.)

The Lord shall bring thee, and thy king which thou shalt set over thee, unto a nation which neither thou nor thy fathers have known; and there shalt thou serve other gods, wood and stone.

And thou shalt become an astonishment, a proverb, and a by-word, among all nations whither the Lord shall lead thee. (Deuteronomy 28: 36, 37.)

Israel's Captivity Fulfilled.

In the ninth year of Hoshea the king of Assyria took Samaria, and carried Israel away into Assyria, and placed them in Halah and in Habor by the river of Gozan, and in the cities of the Medes. (2 Kings 17: 6.)

And the God of Israel stirred up the spirit of Pul king of Assyria, and the spirit of Tilgath-pilneser king of Assyria, and he carried them away, even the Reubenites, and the Gadites, and the half-tribe of Manasseh, and brought them unto Halah, and Habor, and Hara, and to the river Gozan, unto this day. (1 Chronicles 5: 26.)

Judah's Captivity Foretold.

Behold, the days come, that all that is in thine house, and that which thy fathers have laid up in store until this day, shall be carried to Babylon: nothing shall be left, saith the Lord. (Isaiah 39: 6.)

The cities of the south shall be shut up, and none shall open them: Judah shall be carried away captive all of it, it shall be wholly carried away captive. (Jeremiah 13: 19.)

And them that had escaped from the sword carried he away to Babylon; where they were servants to him and his sons until the reign of the kingdom of Persia. (2 Chronicles 36: 20.)

CARE.

CARE. This word is used in the Bible in almost all of its meanings. The more important of them are (1) burdensome sense of responsibility, anxiety, concern, solicitude; and (2) charge, oversight, management.

With relation to care itself Scripture condemns that sort which is the result of worldliness, while approving that which comes from good thoughts or motives and is directed toward a proper end.

REFERENCES.

Therefore I say unto you, Take no thought for your life, what ye shall eat, or what ye shall drink, nor yet for your body, what ye shall put on: Is not the life more than meat? and the body than raiment? (Matthew 6: 25.)

Take therefore no thought for the morrow: for the morrow shall take thought for the things of itself: sufficient unto the day is the evil thereof. (Matthew 6: 34.)

And that which fell among thorns, are they, which, when they have heard, go forth, and are choked with cares, and riches, and pleasures of this life, and bring no fruit to perfection. (Luke 8: 14.)

Labour not for the meat which perisheth, but for that meat which endureth unto everlasting life, which the Son of man shall give unto you: for him hath God the Father sealed. (John 6: 27.)

Be careful for nothing; but in every thing by prayer and supplication with thanksgiving let your requests be made known unto God. (Philippians 4: 6.)

Humble yourselves therefore under the mighty hand of God, that he may exalt you in due time,

Casting all your care upon him, for he careth for you. (1 Peter 5: 6, 7.)

CHARITY. (See Love.)

CHAR'I-TY. This word has quite a number of definite and distinct meanings, almost all of which appear in translation at some point or other in the Bible. The more important of them are (1) love, universal benevolence, good will, especially to our neighbor; (2) the disposition which inclines mankind to put the best construction upon the acts of others; (3) liberality and generosity to the poor and suffering, otherwise known as almsgiving.

REFERENCES.

Charity as Love to Neighbors.

And to love him with all the heart, and with all the understanding, and with all the soul, and with all the strength, and to love his neighbour as himself, is more than all whole burnt offerings and sacrifices. (Mark 12: 33.)

And now abideth faith, hope, charity, these three; but the greatest of these is charity. (1 Corinthians 13: 13.)

But now when Timotheus came from you unto us, and brought us good tidings of your faith and charity, and that ye have good remembrance of us always, desiring greatly to see us, as we also to see you. (1 Thessalonians 3: 6.)

But as touching brotherly love, ye need not that I write unto you: for ye yourselves are taught of God to love one another. (1 Thessalonians 4: 9.)

Now the end of the commandment is charity out of a pure heart, and of a good conscience, and of faith unfeigned. (1 Timothy 1: 5.)

Let no man despise thy youth, but be thou an example of the believers, in word, in conversation, in charity, in spirit, in faith, in purity. (1 Timothy 4: 12.)

But thou hast fully known my doctrine, manner of life, purpose, faith, long-suffering, charity, patience. (2 Timothy 3: 10.)

For God is not unrighteous to forget your work and labour of love, which ye have shewed toward his name, in that ye have ministered to the saints, and do minister. (Hebrews 6: 10.)

If ye fulfil the royal law according to the scripture, Thou shalt love thy neighbour as thyself, ye do well. (James 2: 8.)

If a man say, I love God, and hateth his brother, he is a liar. For he that loveth not his brother whom he hath seen, how can he love God whom he hath not seen?

And this commandment have we from him, that he who loveth God, love his brother also. (1 John 4: 20, 21.)

I know thy works, and charity, and service, and faith, and thy patience, and thy works; and the last to be more than the first. (Revelation 2: 19.)

Charity as Almsgiving.

And if thy brother be waxen poor, and fallen in decay with thee; then thou shalt relieve him: yea, though he be a stranger, or a sojourner; that he may live with thee. (Leviticus 25: 35.)

He that hath pity upon the poor, lendeth unto the Lord; and that which he hath given will he pay him again. (Proverbs 19: 17.)

Jesus said unto him, *If thou wilt be perfect, go and sell that thou hast, and give to the poor, and thou shalt have treasure in heaven: and come and follow me.* (Matthew 19: 21.)

But rather give alms of such things as ye have; and behold, all things are clean unto you. (Luke 11: 41.)

Sell that ye have, and give alms; pro-vide yourselves bags which wax not old, a treasure in the heavens that faileth not, where no thief approacheth, neither moth corrupteth. (Luke 12: 33.)

And when he looked on him, he was afraid, and said, What is it, Lord? And he said unto him, Thy prayers and thine alms are come up for a memorial before God. (Acts 10: 4.)

Every man according as he purposeth in his heart, so let him give; not grudgingly, or of necessity: for God loveth a cheerful giver.

And God is able to make all grace abound toward you; that ye, always having all sufficiency in all things, may abound to every good work. (2 Corinthians 9: 7, 8.)

Charity Commanded.

Thou shalt not avenge, nor bear any grudge against the children of thy people, but thou shalt love thy neighbour as thyself: I am the Lord. (Leviticus 19: 18.)

But I say unto you, Love your enemies, bless them that curse you, do good to them that hate you, and pray for them which despitefully use you, and persecute you. (Matthew 5: 44.)

And the second is like unto it, Thou shalt love thy neighbour as thyself. (Matthew 22: 39.)

A new commandment I give unto you, That ye love one another, as I have loved you, that ye also love one another. (John 13: 34.)

Signs and Effects of Charity.

Now as touching things offered unto idols, we know that we all have knowledge. Knowledge puffeth up: but Charity edifieth. (1 Corinthians 8: 1.)

Though I speak with the tongues of

men and of Angels, and have not charity, I am become as sounding brass or a tinkling cymbal.

And though I have the gift of prophecy, and understand all mysteries and all knowledge: and though I have all faith, so that I could remove mountains, and have not charity, I am nothing.

And though I bestow all my goods to feed the poor, and though I give my body to be burned, and have not charity, it profiteth me nothing.

Charity suffereth long, and is kind: charity envieth not: charity vaunteth not itself, is not puffed up,

Doth not behave itself unseemly, seeketh not her own, is not easily provoked, thinketh no evil,

Rejoiceth not in iniquity, but rejoiceth in the truth:

Beareth all things, believeth all things, hopeth all things, endureth all things.

Charity never faileth: but whether there be prophecies, they shall fail; whether there be tongues, they shall cease; whether there be knowledge, it shall vanish away. (1 Corinthians 13: 1-8.)

And above all these things put on charity, which is the bond of perfectness. (Colossians 3: 14.)

And above all things have fervent charity among yourselves: for charity shall cover the multitude of sins. (1 Peter 4: 8.)

Evidences of Charity.

Is it not to deal thy bread to the hungry, and that thou bring the poor that are cast out to thy house? when thou seest the naked, that thou cover him; and that thou hide not thyself from thine own flesh? (Isaiah 58: 7.)

For I was an hungred, and ye gave me meat: I was thirsty, and ye gave me drink: I was a stranger, and ye took me in:

Naked, and ye clothed me: I was sick, and ye visited me: I was in prison, and ye came unto me. (Matthew 25: 35, 36.)

By this shall all men know that ye are my disciples, if ye have love one to another. (John 13: 35.)

CHILDREN.

CHIL'DREN. Children are mentioned in the Bible in very many ways, both literal and figurative. Scripture teaches that they are the gift of God and that parents are blessed with them. They, on their part, are required to be obedient, and their duties to parents are plainly taught. Figuratively, the human race, especially that part which is good, is made up of the children of God.

REFERENCES.

Children the Gift of God.

And he lifted up his eyes, and saw the women and the children; and said, Who are those with thee? And he said, The children which God hath graciously given thy servant. (Genesis 33: 5.)

Lo, children are an heritage of the Lord. (Psalm 127: 3.)

Thy wife shall be as a fruitful vine by the sides of thine house: thy children like olive-plants round about thy table. (Psalm 128: 3.)

Children a Blessing.

The proverbs of Solomon. A wise son maketh a glad father; but a foolish son is the heaviness of his mother. (Proverbs 10: 1.)

Children's children are the crown of old men; and the glory of children are their fathers. (Proverbs 17: 6.)

The father of the righteous shall

greatly rejoice: and he that begetteth a wise child shall have joy of him. (Proverbs 23: 24.)

My son, be wise, and make my heart glad, that I may answer him that reproacheth me. (Proverbs 27: 11.)

Duty of Children.

Honour thy father and thy mother; that thy days may be long upon the land which the Lord thy God giveth thee. (Exodus 20: 12.)

Ye shall fear every man his mother and his father, and keep my sabbaths: I am the Lord your God. (Leviticus 19: 3.)

Honour thy father and thy mother, as the Lord thy God hath commanded thee; that thy days may be prolonged, and that it may go well with thee, in the land which the Lord thy God giveth thee. (Deuteronomy 5: 16.)

My son, hear the instruction of thy father, and forsake not the law of thy mother. (Proverbs 1: 8.)

A wise son heareth his father's instruction: but a scorner heareth not rebuke. (Proverbs 13: 1.)

A fool despiseth his father's instruction: but he that regardeth reproof is prudent. (Proverbs 15: 5.)

My son, fear thou the Lord and the king: and meddle not with them that are given to change. (Proverbs 24: 21.)

Remember now thy Creator in the days of thy youth, while the evil days come not, nor the years draw nigh, when thou shalt say, I have no pleasure in them. (Ecclesiastes 12: 1.)

Children, obey your parents in the Lord: for this is right.

Honour thy father and mother, (which is the first commandment with promise,)

That it may be well with thee, and thou mayest live long on the earth. (Ephesians 6: 1-3.)

Children, obey your parents in all things: for this is well-pleasing unto the Lord. (Colossians 3: 20.)

But if any widow have children or nephews, let them learn first to shew piety at home, and to requite their parents: for that is good and acceptable before God. (1 Timothy 5: 4.)

Blessed by Christ.

Then were there brought unto him little children, that he should put his hands on them, and pray: and the disciples rebuked them.

But Jesus said, *Suffer little children, and forbid them not, to come unto me: for of such is the kingdom of heaven.* (Matthew 19: 13, 14.)

Children of God and Light.

And ye have forgotten the exhortation which speaketh unto you as unto children, My son, despise not thou the chastening of the Lord, nor faint when thou art rebuked of him. (Hebrews 12: 5.)

Be ye therefore followers of God, as dear children. (Ephesians 5: 1.)

And the Lord commended the unjust Steward, because he had done wisely: for the children of this world are in their generation wiser than the children of light. (Luke 16: 8.)

While ye have light, believe in the light, that ye may be the children of light. These things spake Jesus, and departed, and did hide himself from them. (John 12: 36.)

For ye were sometimes darkness, but now are ye light in the Lord: walk as children of light. (Ephesians 5: 8.)

Ye are all the children of light, and

the children of the day: we are not of the night, nor of darkness. (1 Thessalonians 5: 5.)

Wicked Children.

He that begetteth a fool doeth it to his sorrow: and the father of a fool hath no joy. (Proverbs 17: 21.)

He that wasteth his father, and chaseth away his mother, is a son that causeth shame, and bringeth reproach. (Proverbs 19: 26.)

Whoso keepeth the law is a wise son: but he that is a companion of riotous men shameth his father. (Proverbs 28: 7.)

Whoso robbeth his father or his mother, and saith, It is no transgression; the same is the companion of a destroyer. (Proverbs 28: 24.)

Wicked Children's Punishment.

And he that smiteth his father, or his mother, shall be surely put to death. (Exodus 21: 15.)

If a man have a stubborn and rebellious son, which will not obey the voice of his father, or the voice of his mother, and that, when they have chastened him, will not hearken unto them:

Then shall his father and his mother lay hold on him, and bring him out unto the elders of his city, and unto the gate of his place;

And they shall say unto the elders of his city, This our son is stubborn and rebellious, he will not obey our voice; he is a glutton, and a drunkard.

And all the men of his city shall stone him with stones, that he die: so shalt thou put evil away from among you, and all Israel shall hear, and fear. (Deuteronomy 21: 18-21.)

Cursed be he that setteth light by his father or his mother. And all the people shall say, Amen. (Deuteronomy 27: 16.)

And he went up from thence unto Beth-el: and as he was going up by the way, there came forth little children out of the city, and mocked him, and said unto him, Go up, thou bald-head; go up, thou bald-head.

And he turned back, and looked on them, and cursed them in the name of the Lord. And there came forth two she-bears out of the wood, and tare forty and two children of them. (2 Kings 2: 23, 24.)

CHRIST. (See God, Jesus, Redeemer, Saviour, etc.)

CHRIST—an English version of the official name of Jesus of Nazareth, a Greek word meaning "the anointed one," and sympathetic with the Hebrew word "Messiah."

In handling such a vast subject as the life, works, character, and teachings of our Saviour it has been found advisable to treat each phase of it under its proper and separate head. This arrangement will do away with any confusion that might arise in considering the various relationships of the Master to God and man, and much simplify the whole matter. The present article will deal, then, with Him as Jesus Christ, the Son of God sent to earth for the salvation of mankind through suffering as a man, and will show him as a being with two natures, the one divine and the other human. Under the article God will be found His relationship to the Father and the Holy Spirit and the Trinity as a whole. Under Jesus will be found the story of his life on earth and his teachings, and under other special heads other special attributes.

The coming to earth of a Christ, or Messiah, as the Jews expressed it, was heralded by the prophets centuries before Jesus was born. His miraculous birth, the nature of his mission, his rejection by his own people, his suffering, his sacrifice of himself for the sins of all mankind, his glory, and the establishment of his kingdom and its everlasting dominion—all—were foretold by the prophets. The fulfillment came in the birth, life, and works of Jesus of Nazareth, divinely appointed to be the Messiah from everlasting, before the foundation of the world. Summed up the prophecies were that the Messiah should belong to the highest order of being, since the name of the Eternal One is His; and he should also be called Wonderful, Counselor, the Mighty God, the Everlasting Father; that he should assume human nature and be born of a virgin of the family of David (Isaiah 11: 1), in Bethlehem of Judæa (Micah 5: 2), and his mission should be the salvation of his people and all mankind (Isaiah 49: 6); that He should be despised and rejected of his people; be cut off, but not for himself; be wounded for men's transgressions, bruised for their iniquities; by His stripes men should be healed (Isaiah 53: 5); the Lord should lay on Him the iniquity of men; He should make his soul an offering for sin; and should be exalted and made very high; should see of the travail of his soul and be satisfied, and by his knowledge justify many; and Jehovah say to Him, "Sit thou at my right hand, until I make thine enemies thy footstool" (Psalm 105: 1); to Him should be given dominion, glory, and a kingdom, and all people should serve Him,—an everlasting dominion which shall not pass away (Daniel 7: 13, 14); all this was by divine will from everlasting (1 Peter 1: 20; Luke 2: 10).

REFERENCES.

The Lord Jesus Christ.

For unto you is born this day, in the city of David, a Saviour, which is Christ the Lord. (Luke 2: 11.)

He first findeth his own brother Simon, and saith unto him, We have found the Messias, which is, being interpreted, the Christ. (John 1: 41.)

And said unto the woman, Now we believe, not because of thy saying: for we have heard him ourselves, and know that this is indeed the Christ, the Saviour of the world. (John 4: 42.)

Forasmuch then as God gave them the like gift as he did unto us, who believed on the Lord Jesus Christ, what was I, that I could withstand God? (Acts 11: 17.)

But we believe that through the grace of the Lord Jesus Christ we shall be saved even as they. (Acts 15: 11.)

And they said, Believe on the Lord Jesus Christ, and thou shalt be saved, and thy house. (Acts 16: 31.)

Testifying both to the Jews, and also to the Greeks, repentance toward God, and faith toward our Lord Jesus Christ. (Acts 20: 21.)

Therefore being justified by faith, we have peace with God, through our Lord Jesus Christ. (Romans 5: 1.)

And not only so, but we also joy in God, through our Lord Jesus Christ, by whom we have now received the atonement. (Romans 5: 11.)

For the wages of sin is death: but the gift of God is eternal life, through Jesus Christ our Lord. (Romans 6: 23.)

I thank God through Jesus Christ our Lord. So then, with the mind I myself serve the law of God: but with the flesh the law of sin. (Romans 7: 25.)

But put ye on the Lord Jesus Christ, and make not provision for the flesh, to fulfil the lusts thereof. (Romans 13: 14.)

That ye may with one mind and one mouth glorify God, even the Father of our Lord Jesus Christ. (Romans 15: 6.)

Now I beseech you, brethren, for the Lord Jesus Christ's sake, and for the love of the Spirit, that ye strive together with me in your prayers to God for me. (Romans 15: 30.)

Grace be unto you, and peace from God our Father, and from the Lord Jesus Christ.

I thank my God always on your behalf, for the grace of God which is given you by Jesus Christ;

That in every thing ye are enriched by him, in all utterance, and in all knowledge;

Even as the testimony of Christ was confirmed in you:

So that ye come behind in no gift; waiting for the coming of our Lord Jesus Christ:

Who shall also confirm you unto the end, that ye may be blameless in the day of our Lord Jesus Christ.

God is faithful, by whom ye were called unto the fellowship of his Son Jesus Christ our Lord. (1 Corinthians 1: 3-9.)

Giving thanks always for all things unto God, and the Father, in the Name of our Lord Jesus Christ. (Ephesians 5: 20.)

For our conversation is in heaven, from whence also we look for the Saviour, the Lord Jesus Christ. (Philippians 3: 20.)

I charge thee before God, and the Lord Jesus Christ, and the elect Angels, that thou observe these things without preferring one before another, doing nothing by partiality. (1 Timothy 5: 21.)

But is now made manifest by the appearing of our Saviour Jesus Christ, who hath abolished death, and hath brought life and immortality to light, through the Gospel. (2 Timothy 1: 10.)

Grace to you, and peace from God our Father, and the Lord Jesus Christ. (Philemon 1: 3.)

Jesus Christ the same yesterday, and to-day, and for ever. (Hebrews 13: 8.)

Now the God of peace, that brought again from the dead our Lord Jesus, that great Shepherd of the sheep, through the blood of the everlasting covenant,

Make you perfect in every good work, to do his will, working in you that which is well-pleasing in his sight, through Jesus Christ; to whom be glory for ever and ever. Amen. (Hebrews 13: 20, 21.)

Blessed be the God and Father of our Lord Jesus Christ, which, according to his abundant mercy, hath begotten us again unto a lively hope by the resurrection of Jesus Christ from the dead. (1 Peter 1: 3.)

For so an entrance shall be ministered unto you abundantly into the everlasting kingdom of our Lord and Saviour Jesus Christ. (2 Peter 1: 11.)

Keep yourselves in the love of God, looking for the mercy of our Lord Jesus Christ unto eternal life. (Jude 1: 21.)

Jesus Christ, the Son of God.

And was there until the death of Herod, that it might be fulfilled which was spoken of the Lord by the Prophet, saying, Out of Egypt have I called my son. (Matthew 2: 15.)

And lo, a voice from heaven, saying, This is my beloved Son, in whom I am well pleased. (Matthew 3: 17.)

But Jesus held his peace. And the high priest answered and said unto him, I adjure thee by the living God, that thou tell us whether thou be the Christ, the Son of God.

Jesus saith unto him, *Thou hast said: nevertheless, I say unto you, Hereafter shall ye see the Son of man sitting on the right hand of power, and coming in the clouds of heaven.* (Matthew 26: 63, 64.)

He shall be great, and shall be called the Son of the Highest; and the Lord

God shall give unto him the throne of his father David. (Luke 1: 32.)

And the angel answered and said unto her, The Holy Ghost shall come upon thee, and the power of the Highest shall overshadow thee: therefore also that holy thing which shall be born of thee, shall be called the Son of God. (Luke 1: 35.)

And the Holy Ghost descended in a bodily shape like a dove upon him, and a voice came from heaven, which said, Thou art my beloved Son; in thee I am well pleased. (Luke 3: 22.)

And devils also came out of many, crying out, and saying, Thou art Christ the Son of God. And he rebuking them, suffered them not to speak: for they knew that he was Christ. (Luke 4: 41.)

And I saw and bare record, that this is the Son of God. (John 1: 34.)

Nathanael answered and saith unto him, Rabbi, thou art the Son of God; thou art the King of Israel. (John 1: 49.)

For God so loved the world, that he gave his only begotten Son, that whosoever believeth in him should not perish, but have everlasting life.

For God sent not his Son into the world to condemn the world, but that the world through him might be saved.

He that believeth on him, is not condemned: but he that believeth not, is condemned already, because he hath not believed in the name of the only begotten Son of God.   (John 3: 16-18.)

The Father loveth the Son, and hath given all things into his hand.

He that believeth on the Son hath everlasting life: and he that believeth not the Son, shall not see life; but the wrath of God abideth on him. (John 3: 35, 36.)

For the Father judgeth no man: but hath committed all judgment unto the Son:

That all men should honour the Son, even as they honour the Father. He that honoureth not the Son, honoureth not the Father which hath sent him. (John 5: 22, 23.)

Verily, verily, I say unto you, The hour is coming, and now is, when the dead shall hear the voice of the Son of God: and they that hear shall live.

For as the Father hath life in himself so hath he given to the Son to have life in himself. (John 5: 25, 26.)

And this is the will of him that sent me, that every one which seeth the Son, and believeth on him, may have everlasting life: and I will raise him up at the last day. (John 6: 40.)

And we believe and are sure that thou art that Christ, the Son of the living God. (John 6: 69.)

If any man serve me, let him follow me; and where I am, there shall also my servant be: if any man serve me, him will my Father honour. (John 12: 26.)

And whatsoever ye shall ask in my name, that will I do, that the Father may be glorified in the Son. (John 14: 13.)

He that hateth me, hateth my Father also. (John 15: 23.)

I came forth from the Father, and am come into the world: again, I leave the world, and go to the Father. (John 16: 28.)

These words spake Jesus, and lifted up his eyes to heaven, and said, *Father, the hour is come; glorify thy Son, that thy Son also may glorify thee.* (John 17: 1.)

For if when we were enemies, we were reconciled to God, by the death of his Son, much more, being reconciled, we shall be saved by his life. (Romans 5: 10.)

For what the law could not do, in that it was weak through the flesh, God sending his own Son in the likeness of sinful flesh, and for sin, condemned sin in the flesh. (Romans 8: 3.)

For whom he did foreknow, he also did predestinate to be conformed to the image of his Son, that he might be the first-born among many brethren. (Romans 8: 29.)

He that spared not his own Son, but delivered him up for us all, how shall he not with him also freely give us all things? (Romans 8: 32.)

God is faithful by whom ye were called unto the fellowship of his Son Jesus Christ our Lord. (1 Corinthians 1: 9.)

But when the fulness of the time was come, God sent forth his Son made of a woman, made under the law,

To redeem them that were under the law, that we might receive the adoption of sons.

And because ye are sons, God hath sent forth the spirit of his Son into your hearts, crying, Abba, Father. (Galatians 4: 4-6.)

And to wait for his Son from heaven, whom he raised from the dead, even Jesus which delivered us from the wrath to come. (1 Thessalonians 1: 10.)

God who at sundry times, and in divers manners, spake in time past unto the Fathers by the Prophets,

Hath in these last days spoken unto us by his Son, whom he hath appointed heir of all things, by whom also he made the worlds,

Who being the brightness of his glory, and the express image of his person, and upholding all things by the word of his power, when he had by himself purged our sins, sat down on the right hand of the Majesty on high,

Being made so much better than the Angels, as he hath by inheritance obtained a more excellent Name than they.

For unto which of the Angels said he at any time, Thou art my son, this day have I begotten thee? (Hebrews 1: 1-5.)

Seeing then that we have a great High Priest, that is passed into the heavens, Jesus the Son of God, let us hold fast our profession. (Hebrews 4: 14.)

Though he were a Son, yet learned he obedience by the things which he suffered. (Hebrews 5: 8.)

That which we have seen and heard, declare we unto you, that ye also may have fellowship with us; and truly our fellowship is with the Father, and with his Son Jesus Christ. (1 John 1: 3.)

But if we walk in the light, as he is in the light, we have fellowship one with another, and the blood of Jesus Christ his Son cleanseth us from all sin. (1 John 1: 7.)

In this was manifested the love of God towards us, because that God sent his only begotten Son into the world, that we might live through him.

Herein is love, not that we loved God, but that he loved us, and sent his Son to be the propitiation for our sins. (1 John 4: 9, 10.)

And we know that the Son of God is come, and hath given us an understanding that we may know him that is true: and we are in him that is true, even in his Son Jesus Christ. This is the true God, and eternal life. (1 John 5: 20.)

Jesus Christ as Son of Man.

And Jesus saith unto him, *The foxes have holes, and the birds of the air have nests: but the Son of man hath not where to lay his head.* (Matthew 8: 20.)

But that ye may know that the Son of man hath power on earth to forgive sins, (then saith he to the sick of the palsy,) *Arise, take up thy bed, and go unto thine house.* (Matthew 9: 6.)

But when they persecute you in this city, flee ye into another: for verily I say unto you, Ye shall not have gone over the cities of Israel till the Son of man be come. (Matthew 10: 23.)

The Son of man came eating and drinking, and they say, Behold, a man gluttonous, and a winebibber, a friend of publicans and sinners. But wisdom is justified of her children. (Matthew 11: 19.)

For the Son of man is Lord even of the sabbath-day. (Matthew 12: 8.)

And whosoever speaketh a word against the Son of man, it shall be forgiven him: but whosoever speaketh against the Holy Ghost, it shall not be forgiven him, neither in this world, neither in the world to come. (Matthew 12: 32.)

For as Jonas was three days and three nights in the whale's belly: so shall the Son of man be three days and three nights in the heart of the earth. (Matthew 12: 40.)

The Son of man shall send forth his Angels, and they shall gather out of his kingdom all things that offend, and them which do iniquity. (Matthew 13: 41.)

When Jesus came unto the coasts of Cesarea Philippi, he asked his disciples, saying, *Whom do men say that I, the Son of man, am?* (Matthew 16: 13.)

And as they came down from the mountain, Jesus charged them, saying, *Tell the vision to no man, until the Son of man be risen again from the dead.* (Matthew 17: 9.)

And while they abode in Galilee, Jesus said unto them, *The Son of man shall be betrayed into the hands of men.* (Matthew 17: 22.)

For as the lightning cometh out of the East, and shineth even unto the West: so shall also the coming of the Son of man be. (Matthew 24: 27.)

And then shall appear the sign of the Son of man in heaven: and then shall all the Tribes of the earth mourn, and they shall see the Son of man coming in the clouds of heaven, with power and great glory. (Matthew 24: 30.)

Therefore be ye also ready: for in such an hour as ye think not, the Son of man cometh. (Matthew 24: 44.)

When the Son of man shall come in his glory, and all the holy Angels with him, then shall he sit upon the throne of his glory. (Matthew 25: 31.)

The Son of man goeth, as it is written of him: but wo unto that man by whom the Son of man is betrayed! it had been good for that man if he had not been born. (Matthew 26: 24.)

Then cometh he to his disciples, and saith unto them, *Sleep on now, and take your rest: behold, the hour is at hand, and the Son of man is betrayed into the hands of sinners.* (Matthew 26: 45.)

Whosoever therefore shall be ashamed of me, and of my words, in this adulterous and sinful generation, of him also shall the Son of man be ashamed, when he cometh in the glory of his Father, with the holy Angels. (Mark 8: 38.)

And he answered and told them, *Elias verily cometh first, and restoreth all things; and how it is written of the Son of man, that he must suffer many things, and be set at nought.* (Mark 9: 12.)

Blessed are ye when men shall hate you, and when they shall separate you from their company, and shall reproach you, and cast out your name as evil, for the Son of man's sake. (Luke 6: 22.)

Saying, *The Son of man must suffer many things, and be rejected of the elders, and chief priests, and scribes, and be slain, and be raised the third day.* (Luke 9: 22.)

For the Son of man is not come to destroy men's lives, but to save them. (Luke 9: 56.)

Also I say unto you, Whosoever shall confess me before men, him shall the Son of man also confess before the Angels of God. (Luke 12: 8.)

For the Son of man is come to seek and to save that which was lost. Luke 19: 10.)

Watch ye therefore, and pray always, that ye may be accounted worthy to escape all these things that shall come to pass, and to stand before the Son of man. (Luke 21: 36.)

But Jesus said unto him, *Judas, betrayest thou the Son of man with a kiss?* (Luke 22: 48.)

And he saith unto him, *Verily, verily, I say unto you, Hereafter ye shall see heaven open, and the angels of God ascending and descending upon the Son of man.* (John 1: 51.)

And hath given him authority to execute judgment also, because he is the Son of man. (John 5: 27.)

Labour not for the meat which perisheth, but for that meat which endureth unto everlasting life, which the Son of man shall give unto you: for him hath God the Father sealed. (John 6: 27.)

Then Jesus said unto them, *Verily, verily I say unto you, Except ye eat the flesh of the Son of man, and drink his blood, ye have no life in you.* (John 6: 53.)

What and if ye shall see the Son of man ascend up where he was before? (John 6: 62.)

Then said Jesus unto them, *When ye have lifted up the Son of man, then shall ye know that I am. he, and that I do nothing of myself; but as my Father hath taught me, I speak these things.* (John 8: 28.)

Therefore, when he was gone out, Jesus said, *Now is the Son of man glorified, and God is glorified in him.* (John 13: 31.)

And said, Behold, I see the heavens opened, and the Son of man standing on the right hand of God. (Acts 7: 56.)

And in the midst of the seven candlesticks, one like unto the Son of man, clothed with a garment down to the foot, and girt about the paps with a golden girdle. (Revelation 1: 13.)

Christ as Emmanuel.

Therefore the Lord himself shall give you a sign; Behold, a virgin shall conceive, and bear a son, and shall call his name Immanuel. (Isaiah 7: 14.)

And he shall pass through Judah; he shall overflow and go over, he shall reach even to the neck; and the stretching out of his wings shall fill the breadth of thy land, O Immanuel. (Isaiah 8: 8.)

Behold, a virgin shall be with child, and shall bring forth a son, and they shall call his name Emmanuel, which being interpreted is, God with us. (Matthew 1: 23.)

Christ as the Word.

In the beginning was the Word, and the Word was with God, and the Word was God. (John 1: 1.)

And the Word was made flesh, and dwelt among us (and we beheld his glory, the glory as of the only begotten of the Father,) full of grace and truth. (John 1: 14.)

For there are three that bear record in heaven, the Father, the Word, and the Holy Ghost: and these three are one. (1 John 5: 7.)

And he was clothed with a vesture dipped in blood: and his name is called The Word of God. (Revelation 19: 13.)

Christ as the Lamb.

The next day, John seeth Jesus coming unto him, and saith, Behold the Lamb of God, which taketh away the sin of the world. (John 1: 29.)

And every creature which is in heaven, and on the earth, and under the earth, and such as are in the sea, and all that are in them, heard I, saying, Blessing, honour, glory, and power be unto him that sitteth upon the Throne, and unto the Lamb for ever and ever. (Revelation 5: 13.)

And I saw when the Lamb opened one of the seals, and I heard as it were the noise of thunder, one of the four beasts, saying, Come and see. (Revelation 6: 1.)

And said to the mountains and rocks, Fall on us, and hide us from the face of him that sitteth on the throne, and from the wrath of the Lamb. (Revelation 6: 16.)

And they overcame him by the blood of the Lamb, and by the word of their testimony; and they loved not their lives unto the death. (Revelation 12: 11.)

And all that dwell upon the earth shall worship him, whose names are not written in the book of life of the Lamb slain from the foundation of the world. (Revelation 13: 8.)

Let us be glad and rejoice, and give honour to him: for the marriage of the Lamb is come, and his wife hath made herself ready. (Revelation 19: 7.)

And I saw no Temple therein: For the Lord God Almighty, and the Lamb, are the Temple of it.

And the city had no need of the sun, neither of the moon to shine in it: for the glory of God did lighten it, and the Lamb is the light thereof. (Revelation 21: 22, 23.)

And he shewed me a pure river of water of life, clear as crystal, proceeding out of the throne of God, and of the Lamb. (Revelation 22: 1.)

Christ the Mediator.

For there is one God, and one Mediator between God and men, the man Christ Jesus. (1 Timothy 2: 5.)

Wherefore he is able also to save them to the uttermost, that come unto God by him, seeing he ever liveth to make intercession for them. (Hebrews 7: 25.)

But now hath he obtained a more excellent ministry, by how much also he is the Mediator of a better covenant, which was established upon better promises. (Hebrews 8: 6.)

And for this cause he is the mediator of the new testament, that by means of death, for the redemption of the transgressions that were under the first testament, they which are called might receive the promise of eternal inheritance. (Hebrews 9: 15.)

And to Jesus the mediator of the new Covenant, and to the blood of sprinkling, that speaketh better things than that of Abel. (Hebrews 12: 24.)

By him therefore let us offer the sacrifice of praise to God continually, that is, the fruit of our lips, giving thanks to his name. (Hebrews 13: 15.)

Christ Our Righteousness.

Behold, the days come, saith the Lord, that I will raise unto David a righteous Branch, and a King shall reign and prosper, and shall execute judgment and justice in the earth.

In his days Judah shall be saved, and Israel shall dwell safely: and this is his name whereby he shall be called, THE LORD OUR RIGHTEOUSNESS. (Jeremiah 23: 5, 6.)

But unto you that fear my name, shall the Sun of righteousness arise with healing in his wings; and ye shall go forth, and grow up as calves of the stall. (Malachi 4: 2.)

Because he hath appointed a day, in the which he will judge the world in righteousness, by that man whom he hath ordained: whereof he hath given assurance unto all men, in that he hath raised him from the dead. (Acts 17: 31.)

For if by one man's offence death reigned by one; much more they which receive abundance of grace, and of the gift of righteousness, shall reign in life by one, Jesus Christ.

Therefore, as by the offence of one judgment came upon all men to condemnation, even so by the righteousness of one the free gift came upon all men unto justification of life. (Romans 5: 17, 18.)

Christ as Prophet and Priest.

The Lord thy God will raise up unto thee a Prophet from the midst of thee, of thy brethren, like unto me; unto him ye shall hearken. (Deuteronomy 18: 15.)

How beautiful upon the mountains are the feet of him that bringeth good tidings, that publisheth peace; that bringeth good tidings of good, that publisheth salvation; that saith unto Zion, Thy God reigneth! (Isaiah 52: 7.)

And there was delivered unto him the book of the Prophet Esaias, and when he had opened the book, he found the place where it was written,

The Spirit of the Lord is upon me, because he hath anointed me to preach the Gospel to the poor, he hath sent me to heal the brokenhearted, to preach deliverance to the captives, and recovering of sight to the blind, to set at liberty them that are bruised,

To preach the acceptable year of the Lord. (Luke 4: 17-19.)

Christ as Lord and King.

Saying, Where is he that is born King of the Jews? for we have seen his star in the east, and are come to worship him. (Matthew 2: 2.)

Then shall the King say unto them on his right hand, Come ye blessed of my Father, inherit the kingdom prepared for you from the foundation of the world. (Matthew 25: 34.)

And it was the preparation of the passover, and about the sixth hour: and he saith unto the Jews, Behold your King! (John 19: 14.)

And Pilate wrote a title, and put it on the cross. And the writing was, JESUS OF NAZARETH, THE

KING OF THE JEWS. (John 19: 19.)

The word which God sent unto the children of Israel, preaching peace by Jesus Christ: (he is Lord of all). (Acts 10: 36.)

Which none of the princes of this world knew: for had they known it, they would not have crucified the Lord of glory. (1 Corinthians 2: 8.)

My brethren, have not the faith of our Lord Jesus Christ, the Lord of glory, with respect of persons. (James 2: 1.)

And he hath on his vesture and on his thigh a name written, KING OF KINGS, AND LORD OF LORDS. (Revelation 19: 16.)

Christ's Glory Manifested:

As Divine:

In the beginning was the Word, and the Word was with God, and the Word was God.

The same was in the beginning with God.

All things were made by him; and without him was not any thing made that was made.

In him was life; and the life was the light of men.

And the light shineth in darkness; and the darkness comprehended it not. (John 1: 1-5.)

Wherefore God also hath highly exalted him, and given him a Name which is above every name:

That at the Name of Jesus every knee should bow, of things in heaven, and things in earth, and things under the earth:

And that every tongue should confess, that Jesus Christ is Lord, to the glory of God the Father. (Philippians 2: 9-11.)

As God the Son:

And there came a voice from heaven, saying, Thou art my beloved Son, in whom I am well pleased. (Mark 1: 11.)

Who is the image of the invisible God, the firstborn of every creature. (Colossians 1: 15.)

And again, when he bringeth in the firstbegotten into the world, he saith, And let all the Angels of God worship him. (Hebrews 1: 6.)

As Equal to the Father:

I and my Father are one. (John 10: 30.)

But if I do, though ye believe not me, believe the works: that ye may know, and believe, that the Father is in me, and I in him. (John 10: 38.)

As Creator:

For by him were all things created that are in heaven, and that are in earth, visible and invisible, whether they be thrones, or dominions, or principalities, or powers: all things were created by him, and for him. (Colossians 1: 16.)

As Blessed of God:

Thou art fairer than the children of men: grace is poured into thy lips: therefore God hath blessed thee for ever. (Psalm 45: 2.)

As Mediator:

For there is one God, and one mediator between God and men, the man Christ Jesus. (1 Timothy 2: 5.)

As Prophet:

The Lord thy God will raise up unto thee a Prophet from the midst of thee, of thy brethren, like unto me; unto him ye shall hearken. (Deuteronomy 18: 15.)

For Moses truly said unto the fathers, A Prophet shall the Lord your God raise up unto you, of your brethren, like unto me; him shall ye hear in all things, whatsoever he shall say unto you. (Acts 3: 22.)

As Priest:

Unto you first, God, having raised up his Son Jesus, sent him to bless you, in turning away every one of you from his iniquities. (Acts 3: 26.)

For we have not an high priest which cannot be touched with the feeling of our infirmities: but was in all points tempted like as we are, yet without sin. (Hebrews 4: 15.)

As King:

These shall make war with the Lamb, and the Lamb shall overcome them: For he is Lord of lords, and King of kings; and they that are with him, are called, and chosen, and faithful. (Revelation 17: 14.)

As Judge:

For the Son of man shall come in the glory of his Father, with his Angels: and then he shall reward every man according to his works. (Matthew 16: 27.)

As Shepherd:

He shall feed his flock like a shepherd: he shall gather the lambs with his arm, and carry them in his bosom, and shall gently lead those that are with young. (Isaiah 40: 11.)

And I will set up one Shepherd over them, and he shall feed them, even my servant David; he shall feed them, and he shall be their shepherd. (Ezekiel 34: 23.)

I am the good shepherd, and know my sheep, and am known of mine.

As the Father knoweth me, even so

know I the Father: and I lay down my life for the sheep. (John 10: 14, 15.)

As Foundation and Head of the Church:

Therefore thus saith the Lord God, Behold, I lay in Zion for a foundation a stone, a tried stone, a precious corner stone, a sure foundation. (Isaiah 28: 16.)

And hath put all things under his feet, and gave him to be the head over all things to the Church. (Ephesians 1: 22.)

As the True Light:

Through the tender mercy of our God; whereby the day-spring from on high hath visited us,

To give light to them that sit in darkness and in the shadow of death, to guide our feet into the way of peace. (Luke 1: 78, 79.)

In him was life; and the life was the light of men.

And the light shineth in darkness; and the darkness comprehended it not. (John 1: 4, 5.)

That was the true Light, which lighteth every man that cometh into the world. (John 1: 9.)

Then spake Jesus again unto them, saying, *I am the light of the world: he that followeth me shall not walk in darkness, but shall have the light of life.* (John 8: 12.)

As the Way, Truth, and Life:

Jesus saith unto him, *I am the Way, the Truth, and the Life: no man cometh unto the Father but by me.* (John 14: 6.)

And we know that the Son of God is come, and hath given us an understanding, that we may know him that is true; and we are in him that is true, even in his Son Jesus Christ. This is the true God, and eternal life. (1 John 5: 20.)

And to the angel of the church in Philadelphia write; These things saith he that is holy, he that is true, he that hath the key of David, he that openeth, and no man shutteth; and shutteth, and no man openeth. (Revelation 3: 7.)

Jesus said unto her, *I am the resurrection, and the life: he that believeth in me, though he were dead, yet shall he live.* (John 11: 25.)

When Christ, who is our life, shall appear, then shall ye also appear with him in glory. (Colossians 3: 4.)

And this is the record, that God hath given to us eternal life: and this life is in his Son. (1 John 5: 11.)

In Christ's Words and Works:

And all bare him witness, and wondered at the gracious words which proceeded out of his mouth. And they said, Is not this Joseph's son? (Luke 4: 22.)

And when he was come into his own country, he taught them in their synagogue, insomuch that they were astonished, and said, Whence hath this man this wisdom, and these mighty works? (Matthew 13: 54.)

This beginning of miracles did Jesus in Cana of Galilee, and manifested forth his glory, and his disciples believed on him. (John 2: 11.)

In Sinless Perfection:

For such an high priest became us, who is holy, harmless, undefiled, separate from sinners, and made higher than the heavens;

Who needeth not daily, as those high priests, to offer up sacrifice, first for his own sins, and then for the people's: for this he did once, when he offered up himself.

For the law maketh men high priests which have infirmity; but the word of the oath, which was since the law, maketh the Son, who is consecrated for evermore. (Hebrews 7: 26-28.)

In Transfiguration and Exaltation:

And was transfigured before them: and his face did shine as the sun, and his raiment was white as the light. (Matthew 17: 2.)

And said, Behold, I see the heavens opened, and the Son of man standing on the right hand of God. (Acts 7: 56.)

Which he wrought in Christ when he raised him from the dead, and set him at his own right hand in the heavenly places,

Far above all principality, and power, and might, and dominion, and every name that is named, not only in this world, but also in that which is to come. (Ephesians 1: 20, 21.)

Christ's Divine Nature Proved.

As Jehovah:

For by him were all things created, that are in heaven, and that are in earth, visible and invisible, whether they be thrones, or dominions, or principalities, or powers: all things were created by him, and for him. (Colossians 1: 16.)

Behold the Lord God will come with strong hand, and his arm shall rule for him: behold, his reward is with him, and his work before him. (Isaiah 40: 10.)

Thus saith the Lord the King of Israel, and his Redeemer the Lord of hosts; I am the first, and I am the last; and besides me there is no God. (Isaiah 44: 6.)

And when I saw him, I fell at his

feet as dead: and he laid his right hand upon me, saying unto me, Fear not, I am the first, and the last. (Revelation 1: 17.)

Eternal God, Creator, Judge, Saviour:

Thy throne, O God, is for ever and ever: the sceptre of thy kingdom is a right sceptre. (Psalm 45: 6.)

Of old hast thou laid the foundation of the earth: and the heavens are the work of thy hands.

They shall perish, but thou shalt endure: yea, all of them shall wax old like a garment; as a vesture shalt thou change them, and they shall be changed:

But thou art the same, and thy years shall have no end. (Psalm 102: 25-27.)

For unto us a child is born, unto us a son is given: and the government shall be upon his shoulder: and his name shall be called Wonderful, Counsellor, The Mighty God, The Everlasting Father, The Prince of Peace. (Isaiah 9: 6.)

For God shall bring every work into judgment, with every secret thing, whether it be good, or whether it be evil. (Ecclesiastes 12: 14.)

For I know nothing by myself, yet am I not hereby justified: but he that judgeth me is the Lord.

Therefore judge nothing before the time, until the Lord come, who both will bring to light the hidden things of darkness, and will make manifest the counsels of the hearts: and then shall every man have praise of God. (1 Corinthians 4: 4, 5.)

In the beginning was the Word, and the Word was with God, and the Word was God. (John 1: 1.)

I charge thee therefore before God, and the Lord Jesus Christ, who shall judge the quick and the dead at his appearing, and his kingdom. (2 Timothy 4: 1.)

Equal with God:

That all men should honour the Son, even as they honour the Father. He that honoureth not the Son honoureth not the Father which hath sent him. (John 5: 23.)

All things that the Father hath, are mine: therefore said I that he shall take of mine, and shall shew it unto you. (John 16: 15.)

Let this mind be in you, which was also in Christ Jesus:

Who, being in the form of God, thought it not robbery to be equal with God. (Philippians 2: 5, 6.)

Son of God:

But Jesus held his peace. And the high Priest answered, and said unto him, I adjure thee by the living God, that thou tell us, whether thou be the Christ the Son of God.

Jesus saith unto him, *Thou hast said: Nevertheless I say unto you, Hereafter shall ye see the Son of man sitting on the right hand of power, and coming in the clouds of heaven.* (Matthew 26: 63, 64.)

For God so loved the world, that he gave his only begotten Son: that whosoever believeth in him, should not perish, but have everlasting life. (John 3: 16.)

One with the Father:

I and my Father are one. (John 10: 30.)

But if I do, though ye believe not me, believe the works: that ye may know and believe that the Father is in me, and I in him. (John 10: 38.)

And he that seeth me seeth him that sent me. (John 12: 45.)

If ye had known me, ye should have known my Father also: and from henceforth ye know him, and have seen him.

Philip saith unto him, Lord, shew us the Father, and it sufficeth us.

Jesus saith unto him, *Have I been so long time with you, and yet hast thou not known me, Philip? he that hath seen me hath seen the Father, and how sayest thou then, Shew us the Father?*

Believest thou not that I am in the Father, and the Father in me? The words that I speak unto you, I speak not of myself: but the Father that dwelleth in me, he doeth the works.

Believe me that I am in the Father, and the Father in me: or else believe me for the very works' sake. (John 14: 7-11.)

In Raising the Dead:

Jesus answered, and said unto them, *Destroy this temple, and in three days I will raise it up.*

Then said the Jews, Forty and six years was this Temple in building, and wilt thou rear it up in three days?

But he spake of the temple of his body. (John 2: 19-21.)

Therefore doth my Father love me, because I lay down my life that I might take it again.

No man taketh it from me, but I lay it down of myself: I have power to lay it down, and I have power to take it again. This commandment have I received of my Father. (John 10: 17, 18.)

Other Divine Properties:

For unto us a child is born, unto us a son is given: and the government shall be upon his shoulder: and his name shall be called Wonderful, Counsellor, The mighty God, The everlasting Father, The Prince of Peace. (Isaiah 9: 6.)

But thou, Beth-lehem Ephratah, though thou be little among the thousands of Judah, yet out of thee shall he come forth unto me that is to be Ruler in Israel; whose goings forth have been from of old, from everlasting. (Micah 5: 2.)

Teaching them to observe all things whatsoever I have commanded you: and, lo, I am with you alway, even unto the end of the world. Amen. (John 28: 20.)

Now are we sure that thou knowest all things, and needest not that any man should ask thee: by this we believe that thou camest forth from God. (John 16: 30.)

Who shall change our vile body, that it may be fashioned like unto his glorious body, according to the working whereby he is able even to subdue all things unto himself. (Philippians 3: 21.)

Christ's Human Nature Proved.

By Birth:

And Jacob begat Joseph the husband of Mary, of whom was born Jesus, who is called Christ. (Matthew 1: 16.)

And she brought forth her firstborn son, and wrapped him in swaddling clothes, and laid him in a manger, because there was no room for them in the Inn. (Luke 2: 7.)

By Human Soul:

Then saith he unto them, *My soul is exceeding sorrowful, even unto death: tarry ye here, and watch with me.*

And he went a little further, and fell on his face, and prayed, saying, *O my Father, if it be possible, let this cup pass from me: nevertheless, not as I will, but as thou wilt.* (Matthew 26: 38, 39.)

And when Jesus had cried with a loud voice, he said, *Father, into thy hands I commend my spirit:* And having said thus, he gave up the ghost. (Luke 23: 46.)

By Natural Means:

Then was Jesus led up of the Spirit into the wilderness, to be tempted of the devil.

And when he had fasted forty days and forty nights, he was afterward an hungred. (Matthew 4: 1, 2.)

There cometh a woman of Samaria to draw water: Jesus saith unto her, *Give me to drink.* (John 4: 7.)

And behold, there arose a great tempest in the Sea, insomuch that the ship was covered with the waves: but he was asleep. (Matthew 8: 24.)

By Death:

When Jesus therefore had received the vinegar, he said, *It is finished,* and he bowed his head, and gave up the ghost. (John 19: 30.)

By Likeness to Humanity:

But made himself of no reputation, and took upon him the form of a servant, and was made in the likeness of men:

And being found in fashion as a man, he humbled himself, and became obedient unto death, even the death of the cross. (Philippians 2: 7, 8.)

Wherefore in all things it behoved him to be made like unto his brethren, that he might be a merciful and faithful high Priest, in things pertaining to God, to make reconciliation for the sins of the people. (Hebrews 2: 17.)

Christ's Titles.

And so it is written: The first man Adam was made a living soul, the last

Adam was made a quickening spirit. (1 Corinthians 15: 45.)

My little children, these things write I unto you, that ye sin not. And if any man sin, we have an Advocate with the Father, Jesus Christ the righteous. (1 John 2: 1.)

I am Alpha and Omega, the beginning and the ending, saith the Lord, which is, and which was, and which is to come, the Almighty. (Revelation 1: 8.)

And unto the Angel of the Church of the Laodiceans, write, These things saith the Amen, the faithful and true witness, the beginning of the creation of God. (Revelation 3: 14.)

Wherefore holy brethren, partakers of the heavenly calling, consider the Apostle and high Priest of our profession Christ Jesus. (Hebrews 3: 1.)

Looking unto Jesus the Author and finisher of our faith, who for the joy that was set before him, endured the cross, despising the shame, and is set down at the right hand of the throne of God. (Hebrews 12: 2.)

Which in his times he shall shew, who is the blessed, and only Potentate, the King of kings, and Lord of lords. (1 Timothy 6: 15.)

For it became him, for whom are all things, and by whom are all things, in bringing many sons unto glory, to make the Captain of their salvation perfect through sufferings. (Hebrews 2: 10.)

And are built upon the foundation of the Apostles and Prophets, Jesus Christ himself being the chief corner stone. (Ephesians 2: 20.)

And when the chief shepherd shall appear, ye shall receive a crown of glory that fadeth not away. (1 Peter 5: 4.)

Through the tender mercy of our

God, whereby the dayspring from on high hath visited us. (Luke 1: 78.)

And I will shake all nations, and the Desire of all nations shall come: and I will fill this house with glory, saith the Lord of hosts. (Haggai 2: 7.)

Behold, a Virgin shall be with child, and shall bring forth a son, and they shall call his name Emmanual, which, being interpreted is, God with us. (Matthew 1: 23.)

For unto us a child is born, unto us a son is given: and the government shall be upon his shoulder: and his name shall be called Wonderful, Counsellor, The mighty God, The everlasting Father, The Prince of Peace. (Isaiah 9: 6.)

And he is the head of the body, the church: who is the beginning, the firstborn from the dead; that in all things he might have the preëminence. (Colossians 1: 18.)

Hath in these last days spoken unto us by his Son, whom he hath appointed heir of all things, by whom also he made the worlds. (Hebrews 1: 2.)

Saying, Let us alone, what have we to do with thee, thou Jesus of Nazareth? Art thou come to destroy us? I know thee who thou art, the holy One of God. (Mark 1: 24.)

And hath raised up an horn of salvation for us, in the house of his servant David. (Luke 1: 69.)

Jesus said unto them, *Verily, verily, I say unto you, Before Abraham was, I am.* (John 8: 58.)

And she shall bring forth a son, and thou shalt call his Name Jesus: for he shall save his people from their sins. (Matthew 1: 21.)

Which of the Prophets have not your fathers persecuted? And they have slain them which shewed before of the coming of the Just one, of whom ye have been now the betrayers and murderers. (Acts 7: 52.)

Saying, Where is he that is born King of the Jews? for we have seen his Star in the East, and are come to worship him. (Matthew 2: 2.)

The next day John seeth Jesus coming unto him, and saith, Behold the Lamb of God, which taketh away the sin of the world! (John 1: 29.)

And one of the elders saith unto me, Weep not: behold, the Lion of the tribe of Juda, the Root of David, hath prevailed to open the book, and to loose the seven seals thereof. (Revelation 5: 5.)

Which none of the princes of this world knew: for had they known it, they would not have crucified the Lord of glory. (1 Corinthians 2: 8.)

And they sing the song of Moses the servant of God, and the song of the Lamb, saying, Great and marvellous are thy works, Lord God Almighty; just and true are thy ways, thou King of saints. (Revelation 15: 3.)

In his days Judah shall be saved, and Israel shall dwell safely: and this is his name whereby he shall be called, THE LORD OUR RIGHTEOUSNESS. (Jeremiah 23: 6.)

For there is one God, and one mediator between God and man, the man Christ Jesus. (1 Timothy 2: 5.)

Behold, I will send my messenger, and he shall prepare the way before me: and the Lord, whom ye seek, shall suddenly come to his temple, even the messenger of the covenant, whom ye delight in: behold, he shall come, saith the Lord of hosts. (Malachi 3: 1.)

He first findeth his own brother Simon, and saith unto him, We have found the Messias, which is, being interpreted, the Christ. (John 1: 41.)

Thou shalt also suck the milk of the Gentiles, and shalt suck the breast of kings: and thou shalt know that I the Lord am thy Saviour and thy Redeemer, the mighty One of Jacob. (Isaiah 60: 16.)

I Jesus have sent mine Angel, to testify unto you these things in the Churches. I am the root and the offspring of David, and the bright and morning star. (Revelation 22: 16.)

And he came and dwelt in a city called Nazareth, that it might be fulfilled which was spoken by the Prophets, He shall be called a Nazarene. (Matthew 2: 23.)

And killed the Prince of life, whom God hath raised from the dead, whereof we are witnesses. (Acts 3: 15.)

And he said unto them, *What things?* And they said unto him, Concerning Jesus of Nazareth, which was a Prophet, mighty in deed and word before God, and all the people. (Luke 24: 19.)

Jesus said unto her, *I am the resurrection, and the life: he that believeth in me, though he were dead, yet shall he live.* (John 11: 25.)

For if after they have escaped the pollutions of the world through the knowledge of the Lord and Saviour Jesus Christ, they are again entangled therein, and overcome, the latter end is worse with them than the beginning. (2 Peter 2: 20.)

Jesus saith unto him, *I am the Way, the Truth, and the Life: no man cometh unto the Father, but by me.* (John 14: 6.)

In the beginning was the Word, and the Word was with God, and the Word was God. (John 1: 1.)

False Christs.

And Jesus answered, and said unto them, *Take heed that no man deceive you.*

For many shall come in my name, saying, I am Christ: and shall deceive many. (Matthew 24: 4, 5.)

For there shall arise false Christs, and false prophets, and shall shew great signs and wonders: insomuch that (if it were possible,) they shall deceive the very elect. (Matthew 24: 24.)

And then shall that Wicked be revealed, whom the Lord shall consume with the spirit of his mouth, and shall destroy with the brightness of his coming:

Even him, whose coming is after the working of Satan with all power and signs and lying wonders. (2 Thessalonians 2: 8, 9.)

CHURCH.

CHURCH: The derivation of the word Church is uncertain, but it is generally said to be derived from a Greek word meaning "the called out." In the Bible the word Church has three different and distinct meanings: (1) the entire number of people, all over the world, who believe in Christ and follow His teachings; (2) a local congregation, as "The church at Philippi," or "The church at Corinth;" (3) a local congregation of believers who worship as an assembled group.

REFERENCES.

The Church of God.

Take heed therefore unto yourselves, and to all the flock, over the which the holy Ghost hath made you overseers, to feed the Church of God, which he hath purchased with his own blood. (Acts 20: 28.)

Unto the Church of God which is at

Corinth, to them that are sanctified in Christ Jesus, called to be Saints, with all that in every place call upon the Name of Jesus Christ our Lord, both theirs and ours. (1 Corinthians 1: 2.)

For if a man know not how to rule his own house, how shall he take care of the Church of God? (1 Timothy 3: 5.)

Foundation and Increase.

And Simon Peter answered, and said, Thou art Christ the Son of the living God.

And Jesus answered, and said unto him, *Blessed art thou Simon Bar-jona: for flesh and blood hath not revealed it unto thee, but my Father which is in heaven.*

And I say also unto thee, that thou art Peter, and upon this rock I will build my Church: and the gates of hell shall not prevail against it. (Matthew 16: 16-18.)

Praising God, and having favour with all the people. And the Lord added to the Church daily such as should be saved. (Acts 2: 47.)

Authority and Teaching.

And if he shall neglect to hear them, tell it unto the Church: But if he neglect to hear the Church, let him be unto thee as an heathen man, and a Publican. (Matthew 18: 17.)

And God hath set some in the Church, first Apostles, secondarily Prophets, thirdly Teachers, after that miracles, then gifts of healings, helps in governments, diversities of tongues. (1 Corinthians 12: 28.)

CLOUD.

CLOUD. References to clouds are quite frequent in the Bible. When it is remem-bered that climatic conditions in the Holy Land and neighboring countries are such that clouds are rarely seen such references assume a larger importance than ordinarily they would to Americans and American readers, who are used to seeing clouds in the sky. The chief references are to the cloud that guided the Israelites and the appearance of the Lord at various times in clouds.

REFERENCES.

And the Lord went before them by day in a pillar of a cloud, to lead them the way; and by night in a pillar of fire, to give them light: to go by day and night.

He took not away the pillar of the cloud by day, nor the pillar of fire by night, from before the people. (Exodus 13: 21, 22.)

And the glory of the Lord abode upon mount Sinai, and the cloud covered it six days: and the seventh day he called unto Moses out of the midst of the cloud. (Exodus 24: 16.)

And it came to pass, as Moses entered into the tabernacle, the cloudy pillar descended, and stood at the door of the tabernacle, and the Lord talked with Moses. (Exodus 33: 9.)

And the Lord said unto Moses, Speak unto Aaron thy brother, that he come not at all times into the holy place within the vail, before the mercy-seat which is upon the ark; that he die not: for I will appear in the cloud upon the mercy-seat. (Leviticus 16: 2.)

And the Lord came down in a cloud, and spake unto him, and took of the spirit that was upon him, and gave it unto the seventy elders: and it came to pass, that when the spirit rested upon them, they prophesied, and did not cease. (Numbers 11: 25.)

And the Lord came down in the pillar of the cloud, and stood in the door of the tabernacle, and called Aaron and Miriam: and they both came forth. (Numbers 12: 5.)

While he yet spake, behold, a bright cloud overshadowed them: and behold a voice out of the cloud, which said, This is my beloved Son, in whom I am well pleased: hear ye him. (Matthew 17: 5.)

And then shall they see the Son of man coming in a cloud with power and great glory. (Luke 21: 27.)

COLOSSÆ.

Co-los'sæ—a city in Asia Minor, sometimes spelled Colosse. A church was established there by Paul while on his third missionary journey. To the members of it Paul wrote his Epistle to the Colossians.

COMFORTER. (See Holy Ghost.)

Com'fort-er—one of the names given to the Holy Spirit.

COMMANDMENTS. (See Decalogue.)

Com-mand'ments. The Ten Commandments, also known as the Law and the Decalogue, are the ten laws written by God on tablets of stone and given to Moses on Mount Sinai. They comprise commands against the commission of certain great sins, and are the base of all religious and civil law.

REFERENCES.

And God spake all these words, saying,

I am the Lord thy God, which have brought thee out of the land of Egypt, out of the house of bondage.

Thou shalt have no other gods before me.

Thou shalt not make unto thee any graven image, or any likeness of any thing that is in heaven above, or that is in the earth beneath, or that is in the water under the earth: Thou shalt not bow down thyself to them, nor serve

them: For I the Lord thy God am a jealous God, visiting the iniquity of the fathers upon the children unto the third and fourth generation of them that hate me; and showing mercy unto thousands of them that love me, and keep my commandments.

Thou shalt not take the name of the Lord thy God in vain: for the Lord will not hold him guiltless that taketh his name in vain.

Remember the sabbath-day to keep it holy. Six days shalt thou labour, and do all thy work: but the seventh day is the sabbath of the Lord thy God: in it thou shalt not do any work, thou, nor thy son, nor thy daughter, thy man-servant, nor thy maid-servant, nor thy cattle, nor thy stranger that is within thy gates: for in six days the Lord made heaven and earth, the sea and all that in them is, and rested the seventh day: wherefore the Lord blessed the sabbath-day and hallowed it.

Honour thy father and thy mother; that thy days may be long upon the land which the Lord thy God giveth thee.

Thou shalt not kill.

Thou shalt not commit adultery.

Thou shalt not steal.

Thou shalt not bear false witness against thy neighbour.

Thou shalt not covet thy neighbour's house, thou shalt not covet thy neighbour's wife, nor his man-servant, nor his maid-servant, nor his ox, nor his ass, nor any thing that is thy neighbour's. (Exodus 20: 1-17.)

And he gave unto Moses, when he had made an end of communing with him upon mount Sinai, two tables of testimony, tables of stone, written with the finger of God. (Exodus 31: 18.)

And it came to pass as soon as he came nigh unto the camp, that he saw the calf, and the dancing: and Moses' anger waxed hot, and he cast the tables out of his hands, and brake them beneath the mount. (Exodus 33: 19.)

And the Lord said unto Moses, Hew thee two tables of stone like unto the first: and I will write upon these tables the words that were in the first tables, which thou brakest. (Exodus 34: 1.)

Whosoever therefore shall break one of these least commandments, and shall teach men so, he shall be called the least in the kingdom of heaven: but whosoever shall do, and teach them, the same shall be called great in the kingdom of heaven. (Matthew 5: 19.)

And he said unto him, *Why callest thou me good? there is none good but one, that is God: but if thou wilt enter into life, keep the commandments.* (Matthew 19: 17.)

Jesus said unto him, *Thou shalt love the Lord thy God with all thy heart, and with all thy soul, and with all thy mind.*

This is the first and great Commandment.

And the second is like unto it, Thou shalt love thy neighbour as thyself.

On these two Commandments hang all the Law and the Prophets. (Matthew 22: 37-40.)

COMMUNION. (See Fellowship, Sacrament, Supper.)

Com-mun'ion—the name widely given to the ordinance originally and properly known as the Lord's Supper. The word means a fellowship or agreement when several persons join and partake of a thing. The ordinance was instituted by Jesus at the meal with his disciples just before his betrayal. It has continued to be one of the most solemn of the Church's rites, tending to the unity of the people and to the spiritual uplift of all those who worthily partake. The word communion is also used in the expression "communion of

saints," to express fellowship. This subject will be found treated under its appropriate heading.

REFERENCES.

Communion of the Body and Blood.

The cup of blessing which we bless, is it not the communion of the blood of Christ? The bread which we break, is it not the communion of the body of Christ? (1 Corinthians 10: 16.)

Its Institution or Beginning.

And as they were eating, Jesus took bread, and blessed it, and brake it, and gave it to the Disciples, and said, *Take, eat, this is my body.*

And he took the cup, and gave thanks, and gave it to them, saying, *Drink ye all of it:*

For this is my blood of the new testament, which is shed for many for the remission of sins. (Matthew 26: 26-28.)

For I have received of the Lord that which also I delivered unto you, That the Lord Jesus the same night in which he was betrayed took bread:

And when he had given thanks, he brake it, and said, Take, eat: this is my body, which is broken for you: this do in remembrance of me.

After the same manner also he took the cup, when he had supped, saying, This cup is the new testament in my blood: this do ye, as oft as ye drink it, in remembrance of me.

For as often as ye eat this bread, and drink this cup, ye do shew the Lord's death till he come. (1 Corinthians 11: 23-26.)

Unworthily Partaken.

Ye cannot drink the cup of the Lord, and the cup of devils: ye cannot be partakers of the Lord's Table, and of the table of devils. (1 Corinthians 10: 21.)

Wherefore whosoever shall eat this bread, and drink this cup of the Lord, unworthily, shall be guilty of the body and blood of the Lord.

But let a man examine himself, and so let him eat of that bread, and drink of that cup.

For he that eateth and drinketh unworthily, eateth and drinketh damnation to himself, not discerning the Lord's body. (1 Corinthians 11: 27-29.)

COMPASSION.

COM-PAS'SION—sorrow or pity excited by the distress or misfortunes of another or others. Compassion is regarded in the Bible as a good and holy virtue.

REFERENCES.

To him that is afflicted pity should be shewed from his friend; but he forsaketh the fear of the Almighty. (Job 6: 14.)

But as for me, when they were sick, my clothing was sackcloth: I humbled my soul with fasting; and my prayer returned into mine own bosom. (Psalm 35: 13.)

Thus speaketh the Lord of hosts, saying, Execute true judgment, and shew mercy and compassions every man to his brother. (Zechariah 7: 9.)

Rejoice with them that do rejoice, and weep with them that weep. (Romans 12: 15.)

Put on therefore (as the elect of God, holy and beloved) bowels of mercies, kindness, humbleness of mind, meekness, longsuffering. (Colossians 3: 12.)

Finally be ye all of one mind, having compassion one of another, love as

brethren, be pitiful, be courteous. (1 Peter 3: 8.)

Christ's Compassion.

Then Jesus called his disciples unto him, and said, *I have compassion on the multitude, because they continue with me now three days, and have nothing to eat: and I will not send them away fasting, lest they faint in the way.* (Matthew 15: 32.)

So Jesus had compassion on them, and touched their eyes: and immediately their eyes received sight, and they followed him. (Matthew 20: 34.)

For we have not an high Priest which cannot be touched with the feeling of our infirmities: but was in all points tempted like as we are, yet without sin. (Hebrews 4: 15.)

CONCEIT.

CON-CEIT'—improper pride; overweening estimate of one's self; excessive vanity. The Bible utters warnings against this insidious vice.

REFERENCES.

Wo unto them that are wise in their own eyes, and prudent in their own sight! (Isaiah 5: 21.)

Be of the same mind one towards another. Mind not high things, but condescend to men of low estate. Be not wise in your own conceits. (Romans 12: 16.)

CONDEMNATION.

CON'DEM-NA'TION — (1) the declaration that a thing is unfit; (2) passing sentence upon. In the Bible the chief use of the word is in reference to the sentence of sinners and unbelievers.

REFERENCES.
Condemnation for Sin.

Wherefore, as by one man sin entered into the world, and death by sin:

and so death passed upon all men, for that all have sinned. (Hebrews 5: 12.)

For the wages of sin is death; but the gift of God is eternal life through Jesus Christ our Lord. (Hebrews 6: 23.)

He that believeth on him, is not condemned: but he that believeth not, is condemned already, because he hath not believed in the Name of the only begotten Son of God. (John 3: 18.)

Woe unto you, Scribes and Pharisees, hypocrites; for ye devour widows' houses, and for a pretence make long prayer; therefore ye shall receive the greater damnation. (Matthew 23: 14.)

And these shall go away into everlasting punishment: but the righteous into life eternal. (Matthew 25: 46.)

Deliverance from Condemnation.

Verily, verily, I say unto you, He that heareth my word, and believeth on him that sent me, hath everlasting life, and shall not come into condemnation; but is passed from death unto life. (John 5: 24.)

There is therefore now no condemnation to them which are in Christ Jesus, who walk not after the flesh, but after the spirit. (Romans 8: 1.)

CONFESSION.

CON-FES'SION. This word and its derivatives and synonyms is used in many senses in the Scripture; but more often as follows: (1) the act of making known or disclosing, an acknowledgment or an avowal; (2) an admission, the act of yielding, or the act of granting; (3) and chiefly the acknowledgment of misdeeds or sins.

REFERENCES.

Confession of Christ.

Whosoever therefore shall confess me before men, him will I confess also before my Father which is heaven. (Matthew 10: 32.)

Nevertheless, among the chief rulers also, many believed on him; but because of the Pharisees they did not confess him, lest they should be put out of the Synagogue. (John 12: 42.)

That if thou shalt confess with thy mouth the Lord Jesus, and shalt believe in thine heart that God hath raised him from the dead, thou shalt be saved. (Romans 10: 9.)

Whosoever denieth the Son, the same hath not the Father: [but] he that acknowledgeth the Son hath the Father also. (1 John 2: 23.)

Hereby know ye the Spirit of God: Every spirit that confesseth that Jesus Christ is come in the flesh is of God:

And every spirit that confesseth not that Jesus Christ is come in the flesh is not of God: and this is that spirit of antichrist, whereof ye have heard that it should come; and even now already is it in the world. (1 John 4: 2, 3.)

Confession of Sin.

And it shall be, when he shall be guilty in one of these things, that he shall confess that he hath sinned in that thing. (Leviticus 5: 5.)

And Joshua said unto Achan, My son, give, I pray thee, glory to the Lord God of Israel, and make confession unto him; and tell me now what thou hast done, hide it not from me. (Joshua 7: 19.)

If we confess our sins, he is faithful, and just to forgive us our sins, and to cleanse us from all unrighteousness. (1 John 1: 9.)

Confess your faults one to another, and pray one for another, that ye may be healed: the effectual fervent prayer of a righteous man availeth much. (James 5: 16.)

Examples of Confession.

Therefore the people came to Moses, and said, We have sinned, for we have spoken against the Lord, and against thee; pray unto the Lord, that he take away the serpents from us. And Moses prayed for the people. (Numbers 21: 7.)

And Achan answered Joshua, and said, Indeed I have sinned against the Lord God of Israel, and thus and thus have I done. (Joshua 7: 20.)

And Saul said unto Samuel, I have sinned: for I have transgressed the commandment of the Lord, and thy words: because I feared the people, and obeyed their voice. (1 Samuel 15: 24.)

And said, O my God, I am ashamed and blush to lift up my face to thee, my God: for our iniquities are increased over our head, and our trespass is grown up unto the heavens. (Ezra 9: 6.)

CONSCIENCE.

CON'SCIENCE. Conscience is that inward and inborn faculty that enables man to distinguish between right and wrong, judging the moral character of one's actions, and approving or censuring accordingly.

REFERENCES.

Conscience Convicts of Sin.

And he said, I heard thy voice in the garden: and I was afraid, because I was naked; and I hid myself. (Genesis 3: 10.)

And they said one to another, We are verily guilty concerning our brother, in that we saw the anguish of his soul, when he besought us, and we would not hear; therefore is this distress come upon us. (Genesis 42: 21.)

And it came to pass afterward, that David's heart smote him, because he had cut off Saul's skirt. (1 Samuel 24: 5.)

The spirit of man is the candle of the Lord, searching all the inward parts. (Proverbs 20: 27.)

Then Judas, which had betrayed him, when he saw that he was condemned, repented himself, and brought again the thirty pieces of silver to the chief Priests and Elders. (Matthew 27: 3.)

And they which heard it, being convicted by their own conscience, went out one by one, beginning at the eldest, even unto the last: and Jesus was left alone, and the woman standing in the midst. (John 8: 9.)

Which shew the work of the law written in their hearts, their conscience also bearing witness, and their thoughts the mean while accusing or else excusing one another. (Romans 2: 15.)

Conscience Purified.

How much more shall the blood of Christ, who through the eternal Spirit offered himself without spot to God, purge your conscience from dead works, to serve the living God? (Hebrews 9: 14.)

For then would they not have ceased to be offered, because that the worshippers once purged should have had no more conscience of sins? (Hebrews 10: 2.)

Let us draw near with a true heart in full assurance of faith, having our hearts sprinkled from an evil conscience, and our bodies washed with pure water. (Hebrews 2: 22.)

A Good Conscience.

Holding faith, and a good conscience, which some having put away concerning faith, have made shipwreck. (1 Timothy 1: 19.)

Holding the mystery of the faith in a pure conscience. (1 Timothy 3: 9.)

I thank God, whom I serve from my forefathers with pure conscience, that without ceasing I have remembrance of thee in my prayers night and day. (2 Timothy 1: 3.)

Pray for us: for we trust we have a good conscience in all things, willing to live honestly. (Hebrews 13: 18.)

Having a good conscience, that whereas they speak evil of you, as of evildoers, they may be ashamed that falsely accuse your good conversation in Christ. (1 Peter 3: 16.)

Effects of Good Conscience.

And herein do I exercise myself to have always a conscience void of offence toward God, and toward men. (Acts 24: 16.)

For our rejoicing is this, the testimony of our conscience, that in simplicity and godly sincerity, not with fleshly wisdom, but by the grace of God, we have had our conversation in the world, and more abundantly to you-wards. (2 Corinthians 1: 12.)

For this is thankworthy, if a man for conscience toward God endure grief, suffering wrongfully. (2 Peter 2: 19.)

Respect for Another's Conscience.

If any of them that believe not bid you to a feast, and ye be disposed to go, whatsoever is set before you, eat, asking no question for conscience sake.

But if any man say unto you, This is offered in sacrifice unto idols, eat not for his sake that shewed it, and for conscience sake. The earth is the Lord's, and the fulness thereof.

Conscience I say, not thine own, but of the other's: for why is my liberty judged of another man's conscience? (1 Corinthians 10: 27-29.)

CONSOLATION.

CON'SO-LA'TION—comfort and refreshment of spirit in time of distress of mind or body; the alleviation of misery. No other book contains as much consolation for the afflicted, in either mind, body, or estate, as the Bible. To it men and women have gone ever since it has been possible to do so, and have received comfort.

REFERENCES.

The eternal God is thy refuge, and underneath are the everlasting arms: and he shall thrust out the enemy from before thee; and shall say, Destroy them. (Deuteronomy 33: 27.)

For I know that my Redeemer liveth, and that he shall stand at the latter day upon the earth. (Job 19: 25.)

The Lord will strengthen him upon the bed of languishing: thou wilt make all his bed in his sickness. (Psalm 41: 3.)

Why art thou cast down, O my soul? and why art thou disquieted in me? hope thou in God: for I shall yet praise him for the help of his countenance. (Psalm 42: 5.)

Cast thy burden upon the Lord, and he shall sustain thee: he shall never suffer the righteous to be moved. (Psalm 55: 22.)

Now also when I am old and gray-headed, O God, forsake me not; until I have shewed thy strength unto this generation, and thy power to every one that is to come. (Psalm 71: 18.)

Let not your heart be troubled: ye believe in God, believe also in me.

In my Father's house are many mansions; if it were not so, I would have told you: I go to prepare a place for you.

And·if I go and prepare a place for you, I will come again, and receive you unto myself, that where I am, there ye may be also.   (John 14: 1-3.)

For as the sufferings· of Christ abound in us, so our consolation also aboundeth by Christ.   (2 Corinthians 1: 5.)

And he said unto me, My grace is sufficient for thee: for my strength is made perfect in weakness.   Most gladly therefore will I rather glory in my infirmities, that the power of Christ may rest upon me.   (2 Corinthians 12: 9.)

Now our Lord Jesus Christ himself, and God even our Father, which hath loved us, and hath given us everlasting consolation, and good· hope through grace,

Comfort your hearts, and stablish you in every good word and work.   (2 Thessalonians 2: 16, 17.)

CONTENTMENT.

CON-TENT′MENT—satisfaction with one's lot or position; a disposition of mind undisturbed by anxiety or envy.

REFERENCES.

Contentment and Godliness.

Remove far from me vanity and lies; give me neither poverty nor riches; feed me with food convenient for me. (Proverbs 30: 8.)

But godliness with contentment is great gain.   (1 Timothy 6: 6.)

Exhortations to Contentment.

And the soldiers likewise demanded of him, saying, And what shall we do? And he said unto them, *Do violence to no man, neither accuse any falsely, and be content with your wages.*   (Luke 3: 14.)

Let every man abide in the same calling wherein he was called.   (1 Corinthians 7: 20.)

And having food and raiment let us be therewith content.   (1 Timothy 6: 8.)

Let your conversation be without covetousness: and be content with such things as ye have.   For he hath said, I will never leave thee, nor forsake thee. (Hebrews 13: 5.)

CONVERSATION.

CON′VER-SA′TION.   This word is chiefly used in the Bible in its oldest meaning—custom or manner of life and conduct.   In one or two places it is used in its modern form—speech between two or more parties.   Paul uses it in Philippians 3: 20 to indicate citizenship.

REFERENCES.

The wicked have drawn out the sword, and have bent their bow, to cast down the poor and needy, and to slay such as be of upright conversation. (Psalm 37: 14.)

Whoso offereth praise glorifieth me: and to him that ordereth his conversation aright will I shew the salvation of God.   (Psalm 50: 23.)

Let no man despise thy youth; but be thou an example of the believers, in word, in conversation, in charity, in spirit, in faith, in purity.   (1 Timothy 4: 12.)

Who is a wise man and endued with knowledge amongst you? let him shew out of a good conversation his works with meekness of wisdom.   (James 3: 13.)

Only let your conversation be as it becometh the Gospel of Christ, that whether I come and see you, or else be absent, I may hear of your affairs, that ye stand fast in one spirit, with one mind, striving together for the faith of the Gospel. (Philippians 1: 27.)

But as he which hath called you is holy, so be ye holy in all manner of conversation. (1 Peter 1: 15.)

Having your conversation honest among the Gentiles, that whereas they speak against you as evildoers, they may by your good works which they shall behold, glorify God in the day of visitation. (1 Peter 2: 12.)

CONVERSION. (See Repentance.)

CON-VER'SION—literally a turning from one course or state to another. Conversion in its religious sense is the. turning of a sinner from sin to God. It must not be confounded with regeneration, which is the motion of God in the creature, while conversion is the motion of the creature to God, although the turning of the creature is inspired by God. It evidences itself by love of God, delight in his people, attendance upon his ordinances, confidence in his promises, and submission to his authority.

REFERENCES.

Conversion Coming from God.

The law of the Lord is perfect, converting the soul: the testimony of the Lord is sure, making wise the simple. (Psalm 19: 37.)

No man can come to me, except the Father which hath sent me draw him: and I will raise him up at the last day. (John 6: 44.)

Call to Conversion.

Wash you, make you clean: put away the evil of your doings from before mine eyes; cease to do evil;

Learn to do well; seek judgment, relieve the oppressed, judge the fatherless, plead for the widow.

Come now, and let us reason together, saith the Lord: though your sins be as scarlet, they shall be as white as snow; though they be red like crimson, they shall be as wool. (Isaiah 1: 16-18.)

And saying, Repent ye: for the kingdom of heaven is at hand. (Matthew 3: 2.)

From that time Jesus began to preach, and to say, *Repent, for the kingdom of heaven is at hand.* (Matthew 4: 17.)

Then Peter said unto them, Repent, and be baptized every one of you in the Name of Jesus Christ, for the remission of sins, and ye shall receive the gift of the Holy Ghost. (Acts 2: 38.)

And the times of this ignorance God winked at, but now commanded all men every where to repent. (Acts 17: 30.)

Draw nigh to God, and he will draw nigh to you: cleanse your hands ye sinners, and purify your hearts ye double minded. (James 4: 8.)

Prayer for Conversion.

Turn us again, O God of hosts, and cause thy face to shine; and we shall be saved. (Psalm 80: 7.)

Turn us, O God of our salvation, and cause thine anger toward us to cease. (Psalm 85: 4.)

CORINTH.

COR'INTH—a celebrated city of Greece, renowned for its art and beauty as well as for its commerce and wealth. The town that now occupies its site is called Gortho. A Christian church was planted there early after work began among the Gentiles, and the city was the scene of some of Paul's most important labors. Two of his best epistles are directed to the Corinthians.

CORNELIUS.

COR-NE'LI-US. Cornelius was a Roman centurion, or commander of 100 men in the Roman army. His family was one of great distinction and he himself was a man of wealth. He was the first Gentile convert.

Reference.—Acts 10.

COUNSEL.

Coun′sel—advice; critical and instructive opinion. The Bible is full of warnings against evil counsel and commands to obey that which is good.

REFERENCES.

Advantages of Good Counsel.

The way of a fool is right in his own eyes: but he that hearkeneth unto counsel is wise. (Proverbs 12: 15.)

Only by pride cometh contention: but with the well-advised is wisdom. (Proverbs 13: 10.)

Ointment and perfume rejoice the heart: so doth the sweetness of a man's friend by hearty counsel. (Proverbs 27: 9.)

Danger of Rejecting Counsel.

And it came to pass, as he talked with him, that the king said unto him, Art thou made of the king's counsel? forbear; why shouldest thou be smitten? Then the prophet forbare, and said, I know that God hath determined to destroy thee, because thou hast done this, and hast not hearkened unto my counsel. (2 Chronicles 25: 16.)

But ye have set at nought all my counsel, and would none of my reproof: I also will laugh at your calamity: I will mock when your fear cometh. (Proverbs 1: 25, 26.)

But the Pharisees and Lawyers rejected the counsel of God against themselves, being not baptized of him.

And the Lord said, *Whereunto then shall I liken the men of this generation? and to what are they like?* (Luke 7: 30, 31.)

Wicked Counsel Condemned.

He taketh the wise in their own craftiness: and the counsel of the froward is carried headlong. (Job 5: 13.)

Lo, their good is not in their hand: the counsel of the wicked is far from me. (Job 21: 16.)

Blessed is the man that walketh not in the counsel of the ungodly, nor standeth in the way of sinners, nor sitteth in the seat of the scornful. (Psalm 1: 1.)

Destroy thou them, O God; let them fall by their own counsels; cast them out in the multitude of their transgressions; for they have rebelled against thee. (Psalm 5: 10.)

Hide me from the secret counsel of the wicked; from the insurrection of the workers of iniquity. (Psalm 64: 2.)

COURAGE.

Cour′age. Courage is that quality of mind which enables the possessor to encounter danger or difficulties without fear. It is the groundwork of bravery, fortitude, gallantry, intrepidity, all of which are entirely dependent upon it.

REFERENCES.

Exhortations to Courage.

Be strong and of a good courage, fear not, nor be afraid of them: for the Lord thy God, he it is that doth go with thee, he will not fail thee, nor forsake thee. (Deuteronomy 31: 6.)

Only be thou strong and very courageous, that thou mayest observe to do according to all the law which Moses my servant commanded thee: turn not from it to the right hand or to the left, that thou mayest prosper whithersoever thou goest. (Joshua 1: 7.)

Wait on the Lord: be of good courage, and he shall strengthen thine heart: wait, I say, on the Lord. (Psalm 27: 14.)

Courage through Faith.

By faith Abraham when he was called to go out into a place which he should after receive for an inheritance, obeyed, and he went out, not knowing whither he went. (Hebrews 11: 8.)

By faith Abraham when he was tried, offered up Isaac: and he that had received the promises, offered up his only begotten son. (Hebrews 11: 17.)

By faith Moses when he was come to years, refused to be called the son of Pharaoh's daughter,

Choosing rather to suffer affliction with the people of God, than to enjoy the pleasures of sin for a season:

Esteeming the reproach of Christ greater riches than the treasures in Egypt: for he had respect unto the recompense of the reward.

By faith he forsook Egypt, not fearing the wrath of the king: for he endured, as seeing him who is invisible. (Hebrews 11: 24-27.)

COVENANT.

Cov'e-nant. Generally speaking a covenant is a contract or agreement between two, in that each agrees to do something of benefit to the other. In the Bible, however, the word is applied to the promises made by God to man out of His divine graciousness and love. These covenants are known by various names. "The everlasting covenant" was God's promise to confer salvation upon all who come to him through Jesus Christ. The old Levitical covenant, or the old dispensation, was the ancient covenant with the Israelites, which passed away with the new covenant of which Jesus Christ was the seal, otherwise called the new dispensation. There were also divine covenants with individuals, such as those made with Noah, Abraham, and David.

REFERENCES.

God's Covenant with Israel.

And I have also established my covenant with them, to give them the land of Canaan, the land of their pilgrimage, wherein they were strangers. (Exodus 6: 4.)

Now therefore, if ye will obey my voice indeed, and keep my covenant, then ye shall be a peculiar treasure unto me above all people: for all the earth is mine:

And ye shall be unto me a kingdom of priests, and an holy nation. These are the words which thou shalt speak unto the children of Israel. (Exodus 19: 5, 6.)

And the Lord said unto Moses, Write thou these words: for after the tenor of these words I have made a covenant with thee, and with Israel. (Exodus 34: 27.)

The word that came to Jeremiah from the Lord, saying,

Hear ye the words of this covenant, and speak unto the men of Judah, and to the inhabitants of Jerusalem;

And say thou unto them, Thus saith the Lord God of Israel; Cursed be the man that obeyeth not the words of this covenant,

Which I commanded your fathers in the day that I brought them forth out of the land of Egypt, from the iron furnace, saying, Obey my voice, and do them, according to all which I command you: so shall ye be my people, and I will be your God:

That I may perform the oath which I have sworn unto your fathers, to give them a land flowing with milk and honey, as it is this day. Then answered I, and said, So be it, O Lord. (Jeremiah 11: 1-5.)

The New Covenant.

Behold, the days come, saith the Lord, that I will make a new covenant with the house of Israel, and with the house of Judah:

Not according to the covenant that I made with their fathers, in the day that I took them by the hand to bring them out of the land of Egypt; which my covenant they brake, although I was an husband unto them, saith the Lord:

But this shall be the covenant that I will make with the house of Israel; After those days, saith the Lord, I will put my law in their inward parts, and write it in their hearts; and will be their God, and they shall be my people.

And they shall teach no more every man his neighbour, and every man his brother, saying, Know the Lord: for they shall all know me, from the least of them unto the greatest of them, saith the Lord: for I will forgive their iniquity, and I will remember their sin no more. (Jeremiah 31: 31-34.)

And so all Israel shall be saved, as it is written, There shall come out of Sion the Deliverer, and shall turn away ungodliness from Jacob.

For this is my covenant unto them, when I shall take away their sins. (Romans 11: 26, 27.)

Ratified by Christ:

Behold, I will send my messenger, and he shall prepare the way before me: and the Lord, whom ye seek, shall suddenly come to his temple, even the messenger of the covenant, whom ye delight in: behold, he shall come, saith the Lord of hosts. (Malachi 3: 1.)

And this I say, that the Covenant that was confirmed before of God in Christ, the law, which was four hundred and thirty years after, cannot disannul, that it should make the promise of none effect. (Galatians 3: 17.)

But now hath he obtained a more excellent ministry, by how much also he is the Mediator of a better Covenant, which was established upon better promises. (Hebrews 8: 6.)

The Everlasting Covenant.

Incline your ear, and come unto me: hear, and your soul shall live; and I will make an everlasting covenant with you, even the sure mercies of David. (Isaiah 55: 3.)

Nevertheless, I will remember my covenant with thee in the days of thy youth, and I will establish unto thee an everlasting covenant. (Ezekiel 16: 60.)

Moreover I will make a covenant of peace with them; it shall be an everlasting covenant with them: and I will place them, and multiply them, and will set my sanctuary in the midst of them for evermore. (Ezekiel 37: 26.)

Now the God of peace, that brought again from the dead our Lord Jesus, that great shepherd of the sheep, through the blood of the everlasting Covenant,

Make you perfect in every good work to do his will, working in you that which is wellpleasing in his sight, through Jesus Christ, to whom be glory for ever and ever. Amen. (Hebrews 13: 20, 21.)

COVETOUSNESS.

Cov'et-ous-ness—an inordinate desire for the possession of riches or money, or wealth of any sort; also the inordinate desire for the possession of something of supposed value belonging to some other person. The Bible holds up covetousness as a very great sin, and constantly warns mankind against falling victim to it. The tenth-Commandment utters a special warning against it.

REFERENCES.

Covetousness Described.

There is one alone, and there is not a second; yea, he hath neither child nor brother: yet is there no end of all his labour; neither is his eye satisfied with riches: neither saith he, For whom do I labour, and bereave my soul of good? This is also vanity, yea, it is a sore travail. (Ecclesiastes 4: 8.)

He that loveth silver shall not be satisfied with silver; nor he that loveth abundance with increase: this is also vanity.

When goods increase, they are increased that eat them: and what good is there to the owners thereof, saving the beholding of them with their eyes? (Ecclesiastes 5: 10, 11.)

For the love of money is the root of all evil, which while some coveted after, they have erred from the faith, and pierced themselves through with many sorrows. (1 Timothy 6: 10.)

Covetousness Forbidden.

Thou shalt not covet thy neighbour's house, thou shalt not covet thy neighbour's wife, nor his manservant, nor his maidservant, nor his ox, nor his ass, nor any thing that is thy neighbour's. (Exodus 20: 17.)

And he said unto them, *Take heed and beware of covetousness: for a man's life consisteth not in the abundance of the things which he possesseth.* (Luke 12: 15.)

Its Evil Consequences.

And they lay wait for their own blood; they lurk privily for their own lives.

So are the ways of every one that is greedy of gain; which taketh away the life of the owners thereof. (Proverbs 1: 18, 19.)

He that is greedy of gain troubleth his own house; but he that hateth gifts shall live. (Proverbs 15: 27.)

A faithful man shall abound with blessings: but he that maketh haste to be rich shall not be innocent. (Proverbs 28: 20.)

Punishment of Covetousness.

Wo to him that coveteth an evil covetousness to his house, that he may set his nest on high, that he may be delivered from the power of evil! (Habakkuk 2: 9.)

Nor thieves, nor covetous, nor drunkards, nor revilers, nor extortioners, shall inherit the kingdom of God. (1 Corinthians 6: 10.)

CREATION. (See Adam, Eve, God.)

CRE-A'TION—generally, the act of creating or causing to exist; specifically, the bringing into existence of the world and the living and material things in and around it. The story of the Creation is the first thing in the Bible and one of those oftenest read, and yet it is one of the least understood. In telling of the length of time God employed to effect the Creation Moses used a word which has been translated "day" in the singular and "days" in the plural. The word always has been a source of contention, one party holding to the strict reading of the text as it appears, and the other declaring that science disproves by the indisputable testimony of the world itself that the Creation was not brought about in six days of twenty-four hours each.

Both of these views are erroneous; for, when rightly understood, God's works, as seen in the earth, and God's word, as read in the Bible, go hand in hand and prove each other's truth. The trouble has been that each side has been too literal, the one forgetting that it was the method of the writers of Moses's time to write in figurative or allegorical language; and the other blindly seeking to break down Scripture at any cost. Gradually, however, these narrow and obstinate views are being relaxed through the persistent efforts of the best of scholars, scientists, and thinkers; and both sides of the controversy are coming to that point where they can see that scientific truth and religious truth are the children of The Real Truth, God Himself.

Taking the testimony of the Scriptures in the word "day" by giving it a figurative meaning as simply an unfixed division of time instead of the actual twenty-four hours such as we know, and taking the testimony of the earth itself, both are in complete harmony.

Genesis opens with the statement of the beginning of creation in the remotest ages and then passes to the preparation of the earth for the coming of man. This took six periods, which Moses, in the figurative language of his time, called days. This is the Bible testimony. On the part of the earth, the formation of the globe shows the existence of six distinct geological periods or "days" of unknown extent, but at least thousands of years, from the oldest of the rocks down to those formed in the latter part of the sixth period, when man made his appearance. Each one of these periods has characteristics which agree with the statements Moses made with regard to the development of creation. A very wonderful evidence of this is to be found in the period wherein coal was made. The rocks belonging to it show many specimens of the wood and trees from which the coal was formed. This wood shows no rings to tell of sudden or halted growth due to the increase of heat and light in summer and the decrease in winter, and indicates that there was a uniform temperature and very little or very pale light, doubtless due to the vast, continuous fogs that then covered the earth. Coal was made on the fourth day, since it comes in the fourth period of rocks. Moses's account tells of the lifting of great fogs at the latter part of the fourth day and the final letting-in of sunshine.

References.—Genesis 1 and 2.

CROSS.

CROSS. An upright stake with one or more transverse pieces; also a burden or an inflic-

tion. The use of the cross for the execution of criminals dates from very early times, probably originating with the Egyptians many centuries before the time of Christ, by which period it had come into general vogue among all nations. Crucifixion was regarded as the most terrible of all forms of punishment, and the cross itself was the symbol of extreme pain and ignominy. In Christian times it soon became the symbol of martyrdom and redemption. Death after crucifixion was a matter dependent upon the constitution of the sufferer and the nature of the treatment he received. Often life continued for forty-eight hours, while again a spear-thrust or the breaking of the legs of the victim ended his misery through the mercy of the executioners.

REFERENCES.

Christ's Death on the Cross.

And when they were come to the place which is called Calvary, there they crucified him, and the malefactors, one on the right hand, and the other on the left. (Luke 23: 33.)

And being found in fashion as a man, he humbled himself, and became obedient unto death, even the death of the cross. (Philippians 2: 8.)

Looking unto Jesus the author and finisher of our faith; who for the joy that was set before him endured the cross, despising the shame, and is set down at the right hand of the throne of God. (Hebrews 12: 2.)

Power of Christ's Cross.

For Christ sent me not to baptize, but to preach the Gospel; not with wisdom of words, lest the Cross of Christ should be made of none effect.

For the preaching of the Cross is to them that perish foolishness: but unto us which are saved it is the power of God. (1 Corinthians 1: 17, 18.)

Cross to Be Taken Up.

And he that taketh not his cross, and followeth after me, is not worthy of me. (Matthew 10: 38.)

Then said Jesus unto his disciples, *If any man will come after me, let him deny himself, and take up his cross, and follow me.*

For whosoever will save his life, shall lose it: and whosoever will lose his life for my sake, shall find it. (Matthew 16: 24, 25.)

CROWN.

CROWN. An emblem of sovereignty worn on the head by kings and queens. The ancient nations were almost exclusively long-haired, and men and women wore a fillet or band to keep the hair from falling over the eyes. To distinguish rulers from the common people the fillets and bands worn by such individuals were rich in ornament, growth of the custom gradually bringing about the use of heavy metal and jeweled crowns for monarchs and reigning princes. The Bible is full of references to crowns, both literal and figurative.

REFERENCES.

And the soldiers platted a crown of thorns, and put it on his head, and they put on him a purple robe,

And said, Hail king of the Jews: and they smote him with their hands. (John 19: 2, 3.)

Henceforth there is laid up for me a crown of righteousness, which the Lord the righteous judge shall give me at that day: and not to me only, but unto them also that love his appearing. (2 Timothy 4: 8.)

Blessed is the man that endureth temptation: for when he is tried, he shall receive the crown of life, which the Lord hath promised to them that love him. (James 1: 12.)

Fear none of those things which thou

shalt suffer: behold, the devil shall cast some of you into prison, that ye may be tried, and ye shall have tribulation ten days: be thou faithful unto death; and I will give thee a crown of life. (Revelation 2: 10.)

And every man that striveth for the mastery, is temperate in all things: Now they do it to obtain a corruptible crown, but we an incorruptible. (1. Corinthians 9: 25.)

CRUELTY.

CRU'EL-TY—the wilful infliction of injury either physical or otherwise upon others; inhumanity. The Bible teaches that cruelty is a sin and warns against it.

REFERENCES.

The merciful man doeth good to his own soul; but he that is cruel troubleth his own flesh. (Proverbs 11: 17.)

A righteous man regardeth the life of his beast: but the tender mercies of the wicked are cruel. (Proverbs 12: 10.)

As for his father, because he cruelly oppressed, spoiled his brother by violence, and did that which is not good among his people, lo, even he shall die in his iniquity. (Ezekiel 18: 18.)

CURSE. CURSED. CURSING. (See Accursed.)

CURSE. CURS'ED. CURS'ING. To curse is to imprecate or wish evil to a person. It is also a solemn invocation of divine vengeance, and that vengeance itself.

REFERENCES.

The Divine Curse.

And unto Adam he said, Because thou hast hearkened unto the voice of thy wife, and hast eaten of the tree of which I commanded thee, saying, Thou shalt not eat of it: cursed is the ground for thy sake; in sorrow shalt thou eat of it all the days of thy life. (Genesis 3: 17.)

And now art thou cursed from the earth, which hath opened her mouth to receive thy brother's blood from thy hand. (Genesis 4: 11.)

Behold, I set before you this day a blessing and a curse:

A blessing, if ye obey the commandments of the Lord your God which I command you this day;

And a curse, if ye will not obey the commandments of the Lord your God. (Deuteronomy 11: 26-28.)

Human Cursing Forbidden.

And he that curseth his father or his mother, shall surely be put to death. (Exodus 21: 17.)

As he loved cursing, so let it come unto him: as he delighted not in blessing, so let it be far from him. (Psalm 109: 17.)

Out of the same mouth proceedeth blessing and cursing: my brethren, these things ought not so to be. (James 3: 10.)

But I say unto you, Love your enemies, bless them that curse you, do good to them that hate you, and pray for them which despitefully use you, and persecute you. (Matthew 5: 44.)

Bless them which persecute you, bless, and curse not. (Romans 12: 14.)

Additional References.—Deuteronomy 27; Proverbs 11: 26; 27: 14; Matthew 25: 41; Galatians 3: 10; 2 Peter 2: 14.

CYRUS.

Cy′rus—a form of a word the exact meaning and origin of which is unknown, but probably meaning "Sun"; the name of two kings of Persia, one of whom, Cyrus the Great or

Elder, freed the Israelites from the bondage of the Babylonians. This prince lived about 590 B.C., and from the rulership of petty principality raised himself to the throne of the greatest empire of the times. He was very favorable to the Jews, and fulfilled the prophecy of Isaiah as the deliverer of Judah.

References.—Isaiah 44: 28; 45: 1; Daniel 6: 28; 10: 1.

DAGON.

Da′gon—the name of one of the gods of the Philistines, a sort of half-man, half-fish. The principal seat of his worship was Ashdod. His temple was not destroyed until about 150 years before Christ's time.

References.—Judges 16: 23; 1 Samuel 5: 3, 4; 1 Chronicles 10: 10.

DAMASCUS.

Da-mas′cus—a famous city of Syria and probably the oldest town in the world. It existed as early as the days of Abraham and is said to have been founded by that patriarch. No mention is made of it in the Bible from the time of Abraham to that of David, a period of about 800 years, but thereafter mention of it is frequent. It is especially notable by reason of the fact that Paul's conversion took place near it. It is still a thriving place and contains about 150,000 inhabitants. Its history since the time of Christ has been a remarkable one, by reason of the magnificence of the princes that have made it their capital and the battles that have been fought for its possession. It always has been noted for the richness and fineness of its silks, linens, embroideries, and the high quality of the weapons its armories turned out. Its location, climate, and fertility are historical for excellence.

DAMNATION.

Dam-na′tion—a word often used in Scripture, but with various shades of meaning: (1) eternal punishment and total loss of the soul divinely inflicted for some great sin; (2) judgment; (3) punishment, which may be "greater damnation" or, by inference, damnation of a lesser sort.

REFERENCES.

He that believeth and is baptized, shall be saved, but he that believeth not, shall be damned. (Mark 16: 16.)

And shall come forth, they that have done good, unto the resurrection of life, and they that have done evil, unto the resurrection of damnation. (John 5: 29.)

And not rather as we be slanderously reported, and as some affirm that we say, Let us do evil, that good may come? whose damnation is just. (Romans 3: 8.)

Whosoever therefore resisteth the power, resisteth the ordinance of God: and they that resist, shall receive to themselves damnation. (Romans 13: 2.)

That they all might be damned who believe not the truth, but had pleasure in unrighteousness. (2 Thessalonians 2: 12.)

Having damnation, because they have cast off their first faith. (1 Timothy 5: 12.)

And through covetousness shall they with feigned words make merchandise of you, whose judgment now of a long time lingereth not, and their damnation slumbereth not. (2 Peter 2: 3.)

Woe unto you, scribes and Pharisees, hypocrites! for ye devour widows' houses, and for a pretence make long prayer: therefore ye shall receive the greater damnation. (Matthew 23: 14.)

DANIEL.

DAN'IEL—a form of a Hebrew word meaning "God is my judge." Daniel was the name of a remarkable Jewish prophet who lived about 550 B.C., and was the author of one of the books of the Bible. He was born in princely rank in the tribe of Judah, and was one of the noble youths carried away into the Babylonian captivity. From the first he seems to have been a favorite among the Babylonians, doubtless because of his abilities, and was given the name of Belshatzar or Belteshazzar (favorite of Bel). He entered the service of Nebuchadnezzar, and rose to high governmental posts. His interpretations of the monarch's dreams are well known to readers of the Bible. After the fall of Babylon he still continued in high office under the Persian conquerors of Babylon. He is supposed to have died at Susa at the advanced age of ninety years.

REFERENCES.

And the king spake unto Ashpenaz the master of his eunuchs, that he should bring certain of the children of Israel, and of the king's seed, and of the princes;

Children in whom was no blemish, but well favoured, and skilful in all wisdom, and cunning in knowledge, and understanding science, and such as had ability in them to stand in the king's palace, and whom they might teach the learning and the tongue of the Chaldeans.

And the king appointed them a daily provision of the king's meat, and of the wine which he drank: so nourishing them three years, that at the end thereof they might stand before the king.

Now, among these were of the children of Judah, Daniel, Hananiah, Mishael, and Azariah. (Daniel 1: 3-6.)

As for these four children, God gave them knowledge and skill in all learning and wisdom: and Daniel had understanding in all visions and dreams. (Daniel 1: 17.)

Then Daniel answered and said before the king, Let thy gifts be to thyself, and give thy rewards to another; yet I will read the writing unto the king, and make known to him the interpretation. (Daniel 5: 17.)

And this is the writing that was written, MENE, MENE, TEKEL, UPHARSIN.

This is the interpretation of the thing: MENE; God hath numbered thy kingdom, and finished it.

TEKEL; Thou art weighed in the balances, and art found wanting.

PERES; Thy kingdom is divided and given to the Medes and Persians.

Then commanded Belshazzar, and they clothed Daniel with scarlet, and put a chain of gold about his neck, and made a proclamation concerning him, that he should be the third ruler in the kingdom.

In that night was Belshazzar the king of the Chaldeans slain.

And Darius the Median took the kingdom, being about threescore and two years old. (Daniel 5: 25-31.)

It pleased Darius to set over the kingdom an hundred and twenty princes, which should be over the whole kingdom;

And over these three presidents; of whom Daniel was first: that the princes might give accounts unto them, and the king should have no damage.

Then this Daniel was preferred above the presidents and princes, because an excellent spirit was in him; and the king thought to set him over the whole realm. (Daniel 6: 1-3.)

Then these men assembled, and found Daniel praying and making supplication before his God.

Then they came near, and spake before the king concerning the king's decree; Hast thou not signed a decree, that every man that shall ask a petition of any god or man within thirty days, save of thee, O king, shall be cast into the den of lions? The king answered and said, The thing is true, according to the law of the Medes and Persians, which altereth not. (Daniel 6: 11, 12.)

Then the king commanded, and they brought Daniel, and cast him into the den of lions. Now the king spake and said unto Daniel, Thy God whom thou servest continually, he will deliver thee. (Daniel 6: 16.)

Then was the king exceeding glad for him, and commanded that they should take Daniel up out of the den. So Daniel was taken up out of the den, and no manner of hurt was found upon him, because he believed in his God.

And the king commanded, and they brought those men which had accused Daniel, and they cast them into the den of lions, them, their children, and their wives; and the lions had the mastery of them, and brake all their bones in pieces or ever they came at the bottom of the den. (Daniel 6: 23, 24.)

DARKNESS. (See Light.)

DARK'NESS—absence of light. Darkness in the physical sense is mentioned four times in Scripture: as having been existent at the time of the Creation, having been one of the plagues sent upon Egypt before and during the Exodus, and as having been a part of the convulsions of nature attending the Crucifixion. Figuratively, the word is often used to express ignorance or absence of the true religion. It is also used to express sin and misery as opposed to good and happiness.

REFERENCES.

Darkness on Earth.

And the earth was without form, and void; and darkness was upon the face of the deep: and the Spirit of God moved upon the face of the waters.

And God said, Let there be light: and there was light.

And God saw the light, that it was good: and God divided the light from the darkness. (Genesis 1: 2-4.)

And the Lord said unto Moses, Stretch out thine hand toward heaven, that there may be darkness over the land of Egypt, even darkness which may be felt.

And Moses stretched forth his hand toward heaven: and there was a thick darkness in all the land of Egypt three days. (Exodus 10: 21, 22.)

Now from the sixth hour there was darkness over all the land unto the ninth hour. (Matthew 27: 45.)

And the angel of God which went before the camp of Israel, removed, and went behind them; and the pillar of the cloud went from before their face, and stood behind them:

And it came between the camp of the Egyptians and the camp of Israel; and it was a cloud and darkness to them, but it gave light by night to these: so that the one came not near the other all the night. (Exodus 14: 19, 20.)

Darkness Figurative of Punishment.

But the children of the kingdom shall be cast out into outer darkness: there shall be weeping and gnashing of teeth. (Matthew 8: 12.)

Then said the King to the servants, Bind him hand and foot, and take him away, and cast him into outer darkness, there shall be weeping and gnashing of teeth. (Matthew 22: 13.)

For if God spared not the Angels that sinned, but cast them down to hell, and delivered them into chains of darkness, to be reserved unto judgment. (2 Peter 2: 4.)

And the Angels which kept not their first estate, but left their own habitation, he hath reserved in everlasting

chains under darkness, unto the judgment of the great day. (Jude 1: 6.)

Darkness of the Mind and Soul.

Teach us what we shall say unto him; for we cannot order our speech by reason of darkness. (Job 37: 19.)

Who leave the paths of uprightness, to walk in the ways of darkness. (Proverbs 2: 13.)

The wise man's eyes are in his head; but the fool walketh in darkness: and I myself perceived also that one event happeneth to them all. (Ecclesiastes 2: 14.)

The people that walked in darkness have seen a great light: they that dwell in the land of the shadow of death, upon them hath the light shined. (Isaiah 9: 2.)

To open the blind eyes, to bring out the prisoners from the prison, and them that sit in darkness out of the prison house. (Isaiah 42: 7.)

And the light shineth in darkness, and the darkness comprehended it not. (John 1: 5.)

And this is the condemnation, that light is come into the world, and men loved darkness rather than light, because their deeds were evil. (John 3: 19.)

Then spake Jesus again unto them, saying, *I am the light of the world: he that followeth me, shall not walk in darkness, but shall have the light of life.* (John 8: 12.)

Then Jesus said unto them, *Yet a little while is the light with you: walk while ye have the light, lest darkness come upon you: For he that walketh in darkness, knoweth not whither he goeth.* (John 12: 35.)

The night is far spent, the day is at hand: let us therefore cast off the works of darkness, and let us put on the armour of light. (Romans 13: 12.)

For God, who commanded the light to shine out of darkness, hath shined in our hearts, to give the light of the knowledge of the glory of God in the face of Jesus Christ. (1 Corinthians 4: 6.)

Be ye not unequally yoked together with unbelievers: for what fellowship hath righteousness with unrighteousness? and what communion hath light with darkness? (2 Corinthians 6: 14.)

Powers of Darkness.

When I was daily with you in the Temple, ye stretched forth no hands against me: but this is your hour, and the power of darkness. (Luke 22: 53.)

For we wrestle not against flesh and blood, but against principalities, against powers, against the rulers of the darkness of this world, against spiritual wickedness in high places. (Ephesians 6: 12.)

Who hath delivered us from the power of darkness, and hath translated us into the kingdom of his dear Son. (Colossians 1: 13.)

DAVID. (See Absalom, Bathsheba, Saul, Solomon, etc.)

Da'vid—a form of a Hebrew word meaning "beloved." The name of one of the greatest, most human, most romantic, and most interesting figures in the Bible. David was the son of Jesse, a leading man of the tribe of Judah, and was born in Bethlehem about the year 1084 B.C., the youngest of a number of sons. In his early life he tended his father's flocks and was anointed as the successor of Saul as king while he was leading this life. Later he went to Saul's court, was a musician there, and during one of the wars with the Philistines performed a great feat of arms in the slaying of Goliath. After this, and be-

cause of his deeds, Saul grew jealous of the bravery and popularity of the youth, and he was compelled to flee for his life, becoming the leader of a band of discontented Israelites. For a considerable period he was treated as an outlaw, and hunted by his powerful enemy, the king, to whom he showed the greatest magnanimity. At the death of Saul David became king of Judah. More than seven years later, after wars between the supporters of David and those of Ishbosheth, who had reigned over the other tribes of Israel after Saul's death, David came to the kingship of the entire nation.

He reigned over united Israel for thirty-three years, and as a monarch was almost above reproach. The period was a most critical one for the Jews, marking a sort of a transitional stage from the old to a new civilization. David, with his ability as a soldier and statesman, succeeded in consolidating the people and extending the national prestige and influence. The kingdom he left to his son, Solomon, although it had been threatened by serious foreign wars and the rebellions of his elder sons, Absalom and Adonijah, was compact and powerful, and a splendid foundation for the magnificence which later characterized it under the great Solomon.

David's character, in many ways, was a most remarkable one. Few men have succeeded in doing well even one of the dozen different things that he did. He was a shepherd, a soldier, a poet, prophet, priest, king, administrator, a statesman, a heroic leader, a staunch friend, and a most devoted father. Into all of these rôles he threw his immense energy. It can be imagined that a man who could achieve such things must have been one of strong passions. This is true. David had great faults, largely ones that came from strong passions and impetuous traits of disposition. But at the same time he had qualities of soul that were noble. His piety was sublime, and when he sinned his remorse and repentance were of the deepest sort. That he struggled against temptation we know from his writings and from the chronicles others have left. From the Psalms that he wrote, baring his whole soul to his Creator, millions of people have received comfort and uplift, and will continue to receive them until the end of time. David appears to us, in all that we can read or learn of him through study, as one of the most human of all characters in the Bible. His devotion to his people and his years of ministry for their good, his dependence upon God and his piety, and his continual pointing of the way to a higher religious life make him a fitting type of the Christ that was to come from his family a thousand years after his death. This occurred when he was seventy years old. He was buried in Jerusalem, in a tomb which afterwards became the tomb of the Jewish kings. The only word-picture we have descriptive of him shows that in his youth he was good-looking, short of stature, light in complexion, and that he had red hair and blue eyes.

REFERENCES.

David's Life.

And Jesse begat his first-born Eliab, and Abinadab the second, and Shimma the third,

Nethaneel the fourth, Raddai the fifth,

Ozem the sixth, David the seventh. (1 Chronicles 2: 13-15.)

Then Samuel took the horn of oil, and anointed him in the midst of his brethren: and the Spirit of the Lord came upon David from that day forward. So Samuel rose up, and went to Ramah. (1 Samuel 16: 13.)

And David came to Saul, and stood before him: and he loved him greatly; and he became his armourbearer. (1 Samuel 16: 21.)

So David prevailed over the Philistine with a sling and with a stone, and smote the Philistine, and slew him; but there was no sword in the hand of David.

Therefore David ran, and stood upon the Philistine, and took his sword, and drew it out of the sheath thereof, and slew him, and cut off his head therewith. And when the Philistines saw

their champion was dead, they fled. (1 Samuel 17: 50, 51.)

Then Jonathan and David made a covenant, because he loved him as his own soul. (1 Samuel 18: 3.)

And Saul was very wroth, and the saying displeased him; and he said, They have ascribed unto David ten thousands, and to me they have ascribed but thousands: and what can he have more but the kingdom? (1 Samuel 18: 8.)

And Saul sought to smite David even to the wall with the javelin; but he slipped away out of Saul's presence, and he smote the javelin into the wall: and David fled, and escaped that night. (1 Samuel 19: 10.)

David therefore departed thence, and escaped to the cave Adullam: and when his brethren and all his father's house heard it, they went down thither to him.

And every one that was in distress, and every one that was in debt, and every one that was discontented, gathered themselves unto him; and he became a captain over them: and there were with him about four hundred men. (1 Samuel 22: 1, 2.)

And the men of David said unto him, Behold the day of which the Lord said unto thee, Behold, I will deliver thine enemy into thine hand, that thou mayest do to him as it shall seem good unto thee. Then David arose, and cut off the skirt of Saul's robe privily. (1 Samuel 24: 4.)

So David took the spear and the cruse of water from Saul's bolster; and they gat them away, and no man saw it, nor knew it, neither awaked: for they were all asleep; because a deep sleep from the Lord was fallen upon them. (1 Samuel 26: 12.)

And the men of Judah came, and

there they anointed David king over the house of Judah. And they told David, saying, That the men of Jabesh-gilead were they that buried Saul.

And David sent messengers unto the men of Jabesh-gilead, and said unto them, Blessed be ye of the Lord, that ye have shewed this kindness unto your lord, even unto Saul, and have buried him. (2 Samuel 2: 4, 5.)

Now there was long war between the house of Saul and the house of David: but David waxed stronger and stronger, and the house of Saul waxed weaker and weaker. (2 Samuel 3: 1.)

And they brought the head of Ish-bosheth unto David to Hebron, and said to the king, Behold the head of Ish-bosheth the son of Saul thine enemy, which sought thy life; and the Lord hath avenged my lord the king this day of Saul, and of his seed. (2 Samuel 4: 8.)

So all the elders of Israel came to the king to Hebron; and king David made a league with them in Hebron before the Lord: and they anointed David king over Israel.

David was thirty years old when he began to reign, and he reigned forty years.

In Hebron he reigned over Judah seven years and six months: and in Jerusalem he reigned thirty and three years over all Israel and Judah. (2 Samuel 5: 3-5.)

And it came to pass, when the king sat in his house, and the Lord had given him rest round about from all his enemies,

That the king said unto Nathan the prophet, See now, I dwell in an house of cedar, but the ark of God dwelleth within curtains. (2 Samuel 7: 1, 2.)

And it came to pass the same night,

that the word of God came to Nathan, saying,

Go and tell David my servant, Thus saith the Lord, Thou shalt not build me an house to dwell in. (1 Chronicles 17: 3, 4.)

And it shall come to pass, when thy days be expired that thou must go to be with thy fathers, that I will raise up thy seed after thee, which shall be of thy sons; and I will establish his kingdom.

He shall build me an house, and I will establish his throne for ever. (1 Chronicles 17: 11, 12.)

And it came to pass in an eveningtide, that David arose from off his bed, and walked upon the roof of the king's house: and from the roof he saw a woman washing herself; and the woman was very beautiful to look upon.

And David sent and inquired after the woman. And one said, Is not this Bath-sheba the daughter of Eliam, the wife of Uriah the Hittite? (2 Samuel 11: 2, 3.)

Wherefore hast thou despised the commandment of the Lord, to do evil in his sight? thou hast killed Uriah the Hittite with the sword, and hast taken his wife to be thy wife, and hast slain him with the sword of the children of Ammon.

Now therefore the sword shall never depart from thine house; because thou hast despised me, and hast taken the wife of Uriah the Hittite to be thy wife. (2 Samuel 12: 9, 10.)

And David said unto Nathan, I have sinned against the Lord. And Nathan said unto David, The Lord also hath put away thy sin; thou shalt not die.

Howbeit, because by this deed thou hast given great occasion to the enemies of the Lord to blaspheme, the child also that is born unto thee shall surely die. (2 Samuel 12: 13, 14.)

And on this manner did Absalom to all Israel that came to the king for judgment: so Absalom stole the hearts of the men of Israel. (2 Samuel 15: 6.)

But Absalom sent spies throughout all the tribes of Israel, saying, As soon as ye hear the sound of the trumpet, then ye shall say, Absalom reigneth in Hebron. (2 Samuel 15: 10.)

And Absalom sent for Ahithophel the Gilonite, David's counsellor, from his city, even from Giloh, while he offered sacrifices. And the conspiracy was strong; for the people increased continually with Absalom.

And there came a messenger to David, saying, The hearts of the men of Israel are after Absalom.

And David said unto all his servants that were with him at Jerusalem, Arise, and let us flee; for we shall not else escape from Absalom: make speed to depart, lest he overtake us suddenly, and bring evil upon us, and smite the city with the edge of the sword. (2 Samuel 15: 12-14.)

And the king went forth, and all the people after him, and tarried in a place that was far off. (2 Samuel 15: 17.)

And David numbered the people that were with him, and set captains of thousands and captains of hundreds over them.

And David sent forth a third part of the people under the hand of Joab, and a third part under the hand of Abishai the son of Zeruiah, Joab's brother, and a third part under the hand of Ittai the Gittite. And the king said unto the people, I will surely go forth with you myself also.

But the people answered, Thou shalt not go forth: for if we flee away, they will not care for us; neither if half of us die, will they care for us: but now thou art worth ten thousand of us: therefore now it is better that thou succour us out of the city.

And the king said unto them, What seemeth you best I will do. And the king stood by the gate side, and all the people came out by hundreds and by thousands.

And the king commanded Joab and Abishai and Ittai, saying, Deal gently for my sake with the young man, even with Absalom. And all the people heard when the king gave all the captains charge concerning Absalom.

So the people went out into the field against Israel: and the battle was in the wood of Ephraim;

Where the people of Israel were slain before the servants of David, and there was there a great slaughter that day of twenty thousand men. (2 Samuel 18: 1-7.)

And a certain man saw it, and told Joab, and said, Behold, I saw Absalom hanged in an oak. (2 Samuel 18: 10.)

Then said Joab, I may not tarry thus with thee. And he took three darts in his hand, and thrust them through the heart of Absalom, while he was yet alive in the midst of the oak.

And ten young men that bare Joab's armour compassed about and smote Absalom, and slew him. (2 Samuel 18: 14, 15.)

And the king was much moved, and went up to the chamber over the gate, and wept: and as he went, thus he said, O my son Absalom! my son, my son Absalom! would God I had died for thee, O Absalom, my son, my son! (2 Samuel 18: 33.)

And again the anger of the Lord was

kindled against Israel, and he moved David against them to say, Go, number Israel and Judah.

For the king said to Joab the captain of the host, which was with him, Go now through all the tribes of Israel, from Dan even to Beer-sheba, and number ye the people, that I may know the number of the people. (2 Samuel 24: 1, 2.)

Then Adonijah the son of Haggith exalted himself, saying, I will be king: and he prepared him chariots and horsemen, and fifty men to run before him.

And his father had not displeased him at any time in saying, Why hast thou done so? and he also was a very goodly man; and his mother bare him after Absalom. (1 Kings 1: 5, 6.)

Then king David answered and said, Call me Bath-sheba. And she came into the king's presence, and stood before the king.

And the king sware, and said, As the Lord liveth, that hath redeemed my soul out of all distress,

Even as I sware unto thee by the Lord God of Israel, saying, Assuredly Solomon thy son shall reign after me, and he shall sit upon my throne in my stead; even so will I certainly do this day.

Then Bath-sheba bowed with her face to the earth, and did reverence to the king, and said, Let my lord king David live for ever. (1 Kings 1: 28-31.)

And Zadok the priest took a horn of oil out of the tabernacle, and anointed Solomon. And they blew the trumpet; and all the people said, God save king Solomon. (1 Kings 1: 39.)

Now the days of David drew nigh that he should die; and he charged Solomon his son, saying,

I go the way of all the earth: be thou strong therefore, and shew thyself a man;

And keep the charge of the Lord thy God, to walk in his ways, to keep his statutes, and his commandments, and his judgments, and his testimonies, as it is written in the law of Moses, that thou mayest prosper in all that thou doest, and whithersoever thou turnest thyself. (1 Kings 2: 1-3.)

So David slept with his fathers, and was buried in the city of David.

And the days that David reigned over Israel were forty years: seven years reigned he in Hebron, and thirty and three years reigned he in Jerusalem. (1 Kings 2: 10, 11.)

DEACON.

DEA'CON—an English form of a Greek word meaning "ministrant," "helper," or "assistant." In the early days of the Apostolic Church certain officers who were called deacons were appointed to assist the apostles and chiefs, by carrying the bread and wine at communion, receiving contributions, caring for church property, reading, teaching, and catechising. There is no doubt that there was a limit to their work and that certain ministrations were denied to them. They were ordained or set apart, however, by the laying-on of hands. In modern times, the office is pretty much the same as in the early Church. Some of the denominations make the second order of their clergy deacons. The Baptists and allied faiths do not regard the deacon as a separate order of the ministry, but elect laymen to the office.

REFERENCES.

And in those days when the number of the Disciples was multiplied, there arose a murmuring of the Grecians against the Hebrews, because their widows were neglected in the daily ministration.

Then the twelve called the multitude of the Disciples unto them, and said, It is not reason that we should leave the word of God, and serve tables.

Wherefore brethren, look ye out among you seven men of honest report, full of the Holy Ghost, and wisdom, whom we may appoint over this business.

But we will give ourselves continually to prayer, and to the ministry of the word.

And the saying pleased the whole multitude: and they chose Stephen, a man full of faith and of the Holy Ghost, and Philip, and Prochorus, and Nicanor, and Timon, and Permenas, and Nicolas a proselyte of Antioch.

Whom they set before the Apostles: and when they had prayed, they laid their hands on them. (Acts 6: 1-6.)

Likewise must the deacons be grave, not doubletongued, not given to much wine, not greedy of filthy lucre;

Holding the mystery of the faith in a pure conscience.

And let these also first be proved; then let them use the office of a deacon, being found blameless.

Even so must their wives be grave, not slanderers, sober, faithful in all things.

Let the deacons be the husbands of one wife, ruling their children and their own houses well.

For they that have used the office of a deacon well purchase to themselves a good degree, and great boldness in the faith which is in Christ Jesus. (1 Timothy 3: 8-13.)

DEAD SEA. (See Salt Sea.)

DEATH. (See Resurrection.)

DEATH—the cessation of life. The Bible has to do with two kinds of life—natural and spiritual—and therefore with two kinds of death—natural and spiritual. Natural dead are those from whom the breath of life has passed; spiritual dead are those from whom the breath of the spirit has passed—those steeped in wickedness and sin, or void of grace. Christ abolished death in that he arose from the dead and is able to raise mankind from the same state to everlasting life. The Bible is full of references both to the natural and spiritual types of death, and to the natural and spiritual resurrections.

REFERENCES.

General.

There the wicked cease from troubling; and there the weary be at rest. (Job 3: 17.)

So man lieth down, and riseth not: till the heavens be no more, they shall not awake, nor be raised out of their sleep. (Job 14: 12.)

For in death there is no remembrance of thee; in the grave who shall give thee thanks? (Psalm 6: 5.)

Then shall the dust return to the earth as it was: and the spirit shall return unto God who gave it. (Ecclesiastes 12: 7.)

For the grave cannot praise thee, death cannot celebrate thee: they that go down into the pit cannot hope for thy truth. (Isaiah 38: 18.)

Resurrection of the Dead.

And though after my skin worms destroy this body, yet in my flesh shall I see God. (Job 19: 26.)

But God will redeem my soul from the power of the grave: for he shall receive me. Selah. (Psalm 49: 15.)

Thy dead men shall live, together with my dead body shall they arise. Awake and sing, ye that dwell in dust: for thy dew is as the dew of herbs, and the earth shall cast out the dead. (Isaiah 26: 19.)

And many of them that sleep in the dust of the earth shall awake, some to everlasting life, and some to shame and everlasting contempt. (Daniel 12: 2.)

Verily, verily I say unto you, The hour is coming, and now is, when the dead shall hear the voice of the Son of God: and they that hear shall live. (John 5: 25.)

Now if Christ be preached that he rose from the dead, how say some among you that there is no resurrection of the dead?

But if there be no resurrection of the dead, then is Christ not risen. (1 Corinthians 15: 12, 13.)

Persons Raised from the Dead.

By Elijah:

And the Lord heard the voice of Elijah; and the soul of the child came into him again, and he revived. (1 Kings 17: 22.)

By Elisha:

And he went up, and lay upon the child, and put his mouth upon his mouth, and his eyes upon his eyes, and his hands upon his hands: and he stretched himself upon the child; and the flesh of the child waxed warm. (2 Kings 4: 34.)

And it came to pass, as they were burying a man, that behold, they spied a band of men; and they cast the man into the sepulchre of Elisha: and when the man was let down, and touched the bones of Elisha, he revived, and stood up on his feet. (2 Kings 13: 21.)

By Christ:

He said unto them, *Give place, for the maid is not dead, but sleepeth.* And they laughed him to scorn.

But when the people were put forth, he went in, and took her by the hand: and the maid arose. (Matthew 9: 24, 25.)

And he came and touched the bier: and they that bare him stood still. And he said, *Young man, I say unto thee, Arise.*

And he that was dead sat up, and began to speak. And he delivered him to his mother. (Luke 7: 14, 15.)

And when he thus had spoken, he cried with a loud voice, *Lazarus, come forth.*

And he that was dead came forth, bound hand and foot with graveclothes: and his face was bound about with a napkin. Jesus saith unto them, *Loose him, and let him go.* (John 11: 43, 44.)

By Peter:

But Peter put them all forth, and kneeled down, and prayed, and turning him to the body, said, Tabitha, arise. And she opened her eyes, and when she saw Peter, she sat up.

And he gave her his hand, and lift her up: and when he had called the Saints and widows, presented her alive. (Acts 9: 40, 41.)

By Paul:

And there sat in a window a certain young man named Eutychus, being fallen into a deep sleep: and as Paul was long preaching, he sunk down with sleep, and fell down from the third loft, and was taken up dead.

And Paul went down, and fell on him, and embracing him, said, Trouble not yourselves, for his life is in him.

When he therefore was come up again, and had broken bread, and eaten, and talked a long while, even till break of day, so he departed.

And they brought the young man

alive, and were not a little comforted. (Acts 20: 9-12.)

Death Consequence of the Fall.

But of the tree of the knowledge of good and evil, thou shalt not eat of it: for in the day that thou eatest thereof thou shalt surely die. (Genesis 2: 17.)

In the sweat of thy face shalt thou eat bread, till thou return unto the ground; for out of it wast thou taken: for dust thou art, and unto dust shalt thou return. (Genesis 3: 19.)

Wherefore, as by one man sin entered into the world, and death by sin; and so death passed upon all men, for that all have sinned. (Romans 5: 12.)

For the wages of sin is death; but the gift of God is eternal life through Jesus Christ our Lord. (Romans 6: 23.)

For since by man came death, by man came also the resurrection of the dead.

For as in Adam all die, even so in Christ shall all be made alive. (1 Corinthians 15: 21, 22.)

Death Universal.

Man that is born of a woman is of few days, and full of trouble.

He cometh forth like a flower, and is cut down: he fleeth also as a shadow, and continueth not. (Job 14: 1, 2.)

What man is he that liveth, and shall not see death? shall he deliver his soul from the hand of the grave? Selah. (Psalm 89: 48.)

There is no man that hath power over the spirit to retain the spirit: neither hath he power in the day of death: and there is no discharge in that war; neither shall wickedness deliver those that are given to it. (Ecclesiastes 8: 8.)

Death Characterized.

Before I go whence I shall not return, even to the land of darkness, and the shadow of death;

A land of darkness, as darkness itself; and of the shadow of death, without any order, and where the light is as darkness. (Job 10: 21, 22.)

When a few years are come, then I shall go the way whence I shall not return. (Job 16: 22.)

Yea, though I walk through the valley of the shadow of death, I will fear no evil: for thou art with me; thy rod and thy staff they comfort me. (Psalm 23: 4.)

Whatsoever thy hand findeth to do, do it with thy might; for there is no work, nor device, nor knowledge, nor wisdom, in the grave, whither thou goest. (Ecclesiastes 9: 10.)

Death as Punishment.

Whoso sheddeth man's blood, by man shall his blood be shed: for in the image of God made he man. (Genesis 9: 6.)

And set two men, sons of Belial, before him, to bear witness against him, saying, Thou didst blaspheme God and the king. And then carry him out and stone him, that he may die. (1 Kings 21: 10.)

For God commanded, saying, Honour thy father and mother: And he that curseth father or mother, let him die the death. (Matthew 15: 4.)

Death Vanquished by Christ.

Knowing that Christ being raised from the dead dieth no more, death hath no more dominion over him. (Romans 6: 9.)

But is now made manifest by the appearing of our Saviour Jesus Christ, who hath abolished death, and hath brought life and immortality to light through the gospel. (2 Timothy 1: 10.)

Exhortations Concerning Death.

In those days was Hezekiah sick unto death. And the prophet Isaiah the son of Amoz came to him, and said unto him, Thus saith the Lord, Set thine house in order; for thou shalt die, and not live. (2 Kings 20: 1.)

The days of our years are threescore years and ten; and if by reason of strength they be fourscore years, yet is their strength labour and sorrow; for it is soon cut off, and we fly away. (Psalm 90: 10.)

For all flesh is as grass, and all the glory of man as the flower of grass. The grass withereth, and the flower thereof falleth away. (1 Peter 1: 24.)

Persons Exempted from Death.

Enoch:

And Enoch walked with God: and he was not; for God took him. (Genesis 5: 24.)

By faith Enoch was translated, that he should not see death, and was not found, because God had translated him: For before his translation he had this testimony, that he pleased God. (Hebrews 11: 5.)

Elijah:

And it came to pass, as they still went on, and talked, that behold, there appeared a chariot of fire, and horses of fire, and parted them both asunder; and Elijah went up by a whirlwind into heaven. (2 Kings 2: 11.)

Spiritual Death and Deliverance Therefrom.

But Jesus said unto him, *Follow me, and let the dead bury their dead.* (Matthew 8: 22.)

To give light to them that sit in darkness, and in the shadow of death, to guide our feet into the way of peace. (Luke 1: 79.)

Then Jesus said unto them, *Verily, verily, I say unto you, Except ye eat the flesh of the Son of man, and drink his blood, ye have no life in you.* (John 6: 53.)

For if by one man's offence death reigned by one, much more they which receive abundance of grace and of the gift of righteousness, shall reign in life by one, Jesus Christ. (Romans 5: 17.)

Know ye not, that to whom ye yield yourselves servants to obey, his servants ye are to whom ye obey; whether of sin unto death, or of obedience unto righteousness? (Romans 6: 16.)

For to be carnally minded, is death: but to be spiritually minded, is life and peace. (Romans 8: 6.)

And you hath he quickened who were dead in trespasses and sins. (Ephesians 2: 1.)

And you being dead in your sins, and the uncircumcision of your flesh, hath he quickened together with him, having forgiven you all trespasses. (Colossians 2: 13.)

Verily, verily I say unto you, He that heareth my word, and believeth on him that sent me, hath everlasting life, and shall not come into condemnation: but is passed from death unto life. (John 5: 24.)

For in that he died, he died unto sin once: but in that he liveth, he liveth unto God.

Likewise reckon ye also yourselves

to be dead indeed unto sin, but alive unto God, through Jesus Christ our Lord. (Romans 6: 10, 11.)

Wherefore he saith: Awake thou that sleepest, and arise from the dead, and Christ shall give thee light. (Ephesians 5: 14.)

Eternal Death.

And many of them that sleep in the dust of the earth shall awake, some to everlasting life, and some to shame and everlasting contempt. (Daniel 12: 2.)

And fear not them which kill the body, but are not able to kill the soul: but rather fear him which is able to destroy both soul and body in hell. (Matthew 10: 28.)

Then shall he say also unto them on the left hand, Depart from me, ye cursed, into everlasting fire, prepared for the devil and his angels. (Matthew 25: 41.)

Salvation from Eternal Death.

In a moment, in the twinkling of an eye, at the last trump, (for the trumpet shall sound, and the dead shall be raised incorruptible, and we shall be changed.)

For this corruptible must put on incorruption, and this mortal must put on immortality.

So when this corruptible shall have put on incorruption, and this mortal shall have put on immortality, then shall be brought to pass the saying that is written, Death is swallowed up in victory.

O death, where is thy sting? O grave, where is thy victory?

The sting of death is sin; and the strength of sin is the law.

But thanks be to God, which giveth us the victory through our Lord Jesus Christ. (1 Corinthians 15: 52-57.)

DEBORAH.

DEB'O-RAH—a form of a Hebrew word meaning "bee." Deborah was the name of a prophetess and judge of Israel who aided in the overthrow of a Canaanitish attempt to subdue Israel, afterwards writing a song of triumph remarkable for its sublime poetry.

References.—Judges 4 and 5.

DECALOGUE. (See Commandments.)

DEC'A-LOGUE—a form of a Greek name for the Ten Commandments. Used a great deal by modern commentators and writers, as well as ministers and speakers.

DECEIT. (See Lying.)

DE-CEIT'—the act of deceiving or misleading; also any underhand practice or act intended to mislead.

REFERENCES.

The heart is deceitful above all things, and desperately wicked: who can know it? (Jeremiah 17: 9.)

Thou shalt destroy them that speak leasing: the Lord will abhor the bloody and deceitful man. (Psalm 5: 6.)

Thefts, covetousness, wickedness, deceit, lasciviousness, an evil eye, blasphemy, pride, foolishness:

All these evil things come from within, and defile the man. (Mark 7: 22.)

The thoughts of the righteous are right: but the counsels of the wicked are deceit. (Proverbs 12: 5.)

Notable instances of deceit, in additional references: Genesis 3; Genesis 12; Genesis 26; Genesis 27; Judges 4; Joshua 2; 2 Kings 5; Matthew 2; Acts 5.

DELILAH. (See Samson.)

DE-LI'LAH—a form of a Hebrew word meaning "drooping" or "languishing." Delilah was the name of the sweetheart of Samson, who betrayed him to the Philistines. The bribe she received for the act was an enormous one, amounting to about $2,750, a sum vastly greater in Biblical times than now. The name of Delilah has come down through the ages as the synonym for woman's treachery and baseness.

Reference.—Judges 16.

DELUGE. (See Flood.)

DEL'UGE—another term for the Flood, used by many writers and speakers in preference to that term. See Genesis 7 and 8, and full discussion under Flood.

DENIAL.

DE-NI'AL—the act of refusing or disowning. The word is used in the Bible in both ways, but the more important of the references belong to the latter form, and chiefly have to do with denial of Christ.

REFERENCES.

Warnings against Denial.

Be not thou therefore ashamed of the testimony of our Lord, nor of me his prisoner, but be thou partaker of the afflictions of the Gospel according to the power of God. (2 Timothy 1: 8.)

They profess that they know God; but in works they deny him, being abominable, and disobedient, and unto every good work reprobate. (Titus 1: 16.)

But there were false prophets also among the people, even as there shall be false teachers among you, who privily shall bring in damnable heresies, even denying the Lord that brought them, and bring upon themselves swift destruction. (2 Peter 2: 1.)

For there are certain men crept in unawares, who were before of old ordained to this condemnation, ungodly men, turning the grace of our God into lasciviousness, and denying the only Lord God, and our Lord Jesus Christ. (Jude 1: 4.)

Punishment of Denial.

But whosoever shall deny me before men, him will I also deny before my Father which is in heaven. (Matthew 10: 33.)

Whosoever therefore shall be ashamed of me and of my words in this adulterous and sinful generation; of him also shall the Son of man be ashamed, when he cometh in the glory of his Father with the holy angels. (Mark 8: 38.)

If we suffer, we shall also reign with him: if we deny him, he also will deny us. (2 Timothy 2: 12.)

Peter's Denial.

Now Peter sat without in the palace: and a damsel came unto him, saying, Thou also wast with Jesus in Galilee.

But he denied before them all, saying, I know not what thou sayest.

And when he was gone out into the porch, another maid saw him, and said unto them that were there, This fellow was also with Jesus of Nazareth.

And again he denied with an oath, I do not know the man.

And after a while came unto him they that stood by, and said to Peter, Surely thou also art one of them, for thy speech bewrayeth thee.

Then began he to curse and to swear, saying, I know not the man. And immediately the cock crew.

And Peter remembered the words of Jesus, which said unto him, Before the cock crow, thou shalt deny me thrice. And he went out, and wept bitterly. (Matthew 26: 69-75.)

Denial by the Jews.

Then cried they all again, saying, Not this man, but Barabbas. Now

Barabbas was a robber. (John 18: 40.)

But they cried out, Away with him, away with him, crucify him. Pilate saith unto them, Shall I crucify your King? The chief Priests answered, We have no king but Cæsar. (John 19: 15.)

The God of Abraham, and of Isaac, and of Jacob, the God of our fathers, hath glorified his son Jesus, whom ye delivered up, and denied him in the presence of Pilate, when he was determined to let him go. (Acts 3: 13.)

DESPAIR.

DE-SPAIR'—to be hopeless; a state of complete despondency. There are many noble passages in the Bible full of comfort and uplift for those in despair, and Scripture generally teaches the error of abandoning one's self to such moods.

REFERENCES.

And shall say unto them, Hear, O Israel, ye approach this day unto battle against your enemies: let not your hearts faint, fear not, and do not tremble, neither be ye terrified because of them;

For the Lord your God is he that goeth with you, to fight for you against your enemies, to save you. (Deuteronomy 20: 3, 4.)

Be of good courage, and he shall strengthen your heart, all ye that hope in the Lord. (Psalm 31: 24.)

Why art thou cast down, O my soul? and why art thou disquieted within me? hope thou in God: for I shall yet praise him, who is the health of my countenance, and my God. (Psalm 42: 11.)

But they that wait upon the Lord shall renew their strength; they shall mount up with wings as eagles; they shall run, and not be weary; and they walk, and not faint. (Isaiah 40: 31.)

And he spake a parable unto them, to this end, that men ought always to pray, and not to faint. (Luke 18: 1.)

Let not your heart be troubled: ye believe in God, believe also in me. (John 14: 1.)

We are troubled on every side, yet not distressed; we are perplexed, but not in despair;

Persecuted, but not forsaken; cast down, but not destroyed. (2 Corinthians 4: 8, 9.)

And ye have forgotten the exhortation which speaketh unto you as unto children, My son, despise not thou the chastening of the Lord, nor faint when thou art rebuked of him.

For whom the Lord loveth he chasteneth, and scourgeth every son whom he receiveth. (Hebrews 12: 5, 6.)

DEVIL. (See Apollyon, Lucifer, Satan, etc.)

DEV'IL. This word or one of its synonyms is used in many places in Scripture to indicate the power of evil, either figuratively or as the personified spirit of evil itself, just as it is used commonly in modern thought and speech. Some passages refer to it as "demon," although among the old writers a demon was not necessarily an evil thing, but might be a good disembodied spirit. The majority of references, however, have to do with it in its present accepted sense. The Devil is known by many names—Apollyon, Abaddon, Angel of the Bottomless Pit, Evil One, Beelzebub, Lucifer, Satan, the Adversary, etc. Scripture tells us that he rebelled against God and that there was war in heaven and that he and his angels were expelled. We are also told that he is still in rebellion and that the warfare between good and evil—God and the Devil—is constantly going on; but that the Devil finally will be conquered and that he and his angels will be destroyed. The scene of the warfare is now upon earth and the subjects of it the souls of mankind, God constantly striving to win them to Himself, and the Devil seeking to destroy them or bring them into subjection, working in all sorts of ways and under all manner of disguises.

REFERENCES.

History.

And he said unto them, *I beheld Satan as lightning fall from heaven.* (Luke 10: 18.)

And there was war in heaven, Michael and his Angels fought against the dragon, and the dragon fought and his angels,

And prevailed not, neither was their place found any more in heaven.

And the great dragon was cast out, that old serpent, called the devil and Satan, which deceiveth the whole world: he was cast out into the earth, and his angels were cast out with him.

And I heard a loud voice saying in heaven, Now is come salvation, and strength, and the kingdom of our God, and the power of his Christ: for the accuser of our brethren is cast down, which accused them before our God day and night. (Revelation 12: 7-10.)

For if God spared not the angels that sinned, but cast them down to hell, and delivered them into chains of darkness, to be reserved unto judgment. (2 Peter 2: 4.)

Devil's First Work on Earth.

Now the serpent was more subtil than any beast of the field which the Lord God had made. And he said unto the woman, Yea, hath God said, Ye shall not eat of every tree of the garden?

And the woman said unto the serpent, We may eat of the fruit of the trees of the garden:

But of the fruit of the tree which is in the midst of the garden, God hath said, Ye shall not eat of it, neither shall ye touch it, lest ye die.

And the serpent said unto the woman, Ye shall not surely die:

For God doth know that in the day ye eat thereof, then your eyes shall be opened, and ye shall be as gods, knowing good and evil.

And when the woman saw that the tree was good for food, and that it was pleasant to the eyes, and a tree to be desired to make one wise, she took of the fruit thereof, and did eat, and gave also unto her husband with her; and he did eat. (Genesis 3: 1-6.)

And the Lord God said unto the serpent, Because thou hast done this, thou art cursed above all cattle, and above every beast of the field: upon thy belly shalt thou go, and dust shalt thou eat all the days of thy life:

And I will put enmity between thee and the woman, and between thy seed and her seed: it shall bruise thy head, and thou shalt bruise his heel. (Genesis 3: 14, 15.)

Devil Tempts Christ.

Then was Jesus led up of the spirit into the wilderness to be tempted of the devil.

And when he had fasted forty days and forty nights, he was afterward an hungred.

And when the tempter came to him, he said, If thou be the Son of God, command that these stones be made bread.

But he answered and said, *It is written, Man shall not live by bread alone, but by every word that proceedeth out of the mouth of God.*

Then the devil taketh him up into the holy city, and setteth him on a pinnacle of the temple,

And saith unto him, If thou be the Son of God, cast thyself down: for it is written, He shall give his angels charge concerning thee: and in their hands they shall bear thee up, lest at any time thou dash thy foot against a stone.

Jesus said unto him, *It is written again, Thou shalt not tempt the Lord thy God.*

Again, the devil taketh him up into an exceeding high mountain, and sheweth him all the kingdoms of the world, and the glory of them;

And saith unto him, All these things will I give thee, if thou wilt fall down and worship me.

Then saith Jesus unto him, *Get thee hence, Satan: for it is written, Thou shalt worship the Lord thy God, and him only shalt thou serve.*

Then the devil leaveth him, and, behold, angels came and ministered unto him. (Matthew 4: 1-11.)

Powers and Works.

And he shewed me Joshua the high priest standing before the angel of the Lord, and Satan standing at his right hand to resist him. (Zechariah 3: 1.)

When any one heareth the word of the kingdom, and understandeth it not, then cometh the wicked one, and catcheth away that which was sown in his heart: this is he which received seed by the way side. (Matthew 13: 19.)

Ye are of your father the devil, and the lusts of your father ye will do. He was a murderer from the beginning, and abode not in the truth, because there is no truth in him. When he speaketh a lie, he speaketh of his own: for he is a liar, and the father of it. (John 8: 44.)

And no marvel, for Satan himself is transformed into an Angel of light. (2 Corinthians 11: 14.)

Wherefore we would have come unto you, even I Paul, once and again; but Satan hindered us. (1 Thessalonians 2: 18.)

Even him whose coming is after the working of Satan, with all power and signs, and lying wonders. (2 Thessalonians 2: 9.)

Now the Spirit speaketh expressly, that in the latter times some shall depart from the faith, giving heed to seducing spirits, and doctrines of devils. (1 Timothy 4: 1.)

For they are the spirits of devils working miracles, which go forth unto the Kings of the earth, and of the whole world, to gather them to the battle of that great day of God Almighty. (Revelation 16: 14.)

Vanquished by Christ.

He that committeth sin is of the devil; for the devil sinneth from the beginning. For this purpose the Son of God was manifested, that he might destroy the works of the devil. (1 John 3: 8.)

Forasmuch then as the children are partakers of flesh and blood, he also himself likewise took part of the same, that through death he might destroy him that had the power of death, that is, the devil. (Hebrews 2: 14.)

Christians to Resist the Devil.

To whom ye forgive any thing, I forgive also: for if I forgave any thing, to whom I forgave it, for your sakes forgave I it, in the person of Christ,

Lest Satan should get an advantage of us: for we are not ignorant of his devices. (2 Corinthians 2: 10, 11.)

But I fear lest by any means, as the Serpent beguiled Eve through his subtilty, so your minds should be corrupted from the simplicity that is in Christ. (2 Corinthians 11: 3.)

Be ye angry and sin not, let not the sun go down upon your wrath:

Neither give place to the devil. (Ephesians 4: 26, 27.)

Above all, taking the shield of Faith, wherewith ye shall be able to quench all the fiery darts of the wicked. (Ephesians 6: 16.)

Submit yourselves therefore to God: resist the devil, and he will flee from you. (James 4: 7.)

Be sober, be vigilant: because your adversary the devil, as a roaring Lion walketh about, seeking whom he may devour.

Whom resist stedfast in the faith, knowing that the same afflictions are accomplished in your brethren that are in the world. (1 Peter 5: 8, 9.)

And they overcame him by the blood of the Lamb, and by the word of their Testimony, and they loved not their lives unto the death. (Revelation 12: 11.)

DIANA.

DI-AN'A—a celebrated heathen goddess, known to the Greeks, who first worshipped her, as Artemis. One of the most magnificent temples of antiquity was erected in her honor at Ephesus. Her particular symbol was the moon, and her companion deity was Apollo, represented by the sun.

DILIGENCE.

DIL'I-GENCE—constancy, earnestness, application; devoted painstaking and effort to achieve an end. Diligence is one of the many virtues to which the Bible points mankind.

REFERENCES.

Diligence to God.

And said, If thou wilt diligently hearken to the voice of the Lord thy God, and wilt do that which is right in his sight, and wilt give ear to his commandments, and keep all his statutes, I will put none of these diseases upon thee, which I have brought upon the Egyptians: for I am the Lord that healeth thee. (Exodus 15: 26.)

Only take heed to thyself, and keep thy soul diligently, lest thou forget the things which thine eyes have seen, and lest they depart from thy heart all the days of thy life: but teach them thy sons, and thy sons' sons. (Deuteronomy 4: 9.)

Whatsoever is commanded by the God of heaven, let it be diligently done for the house of the God of heaven: for why should there be wrath against the realm of the king and his sons? (Ezra 7: 23.)

Or he that exhorteth, on exhortation: he that giveth, let him do it with simplicity: he that ruleth, with diligence. (Romans 12: 8.)

Diligence in Worldly Affairs.

He becometh poor that dealeth with a slack hand; but the hand of the diligent maketh rich. (Proverbs 10: 4.)

The hand of the diligent shall bear rule: but the slothful shall be under tribute. (Proverbs 12: 24.)

The soul of the sluggard desireth, and hath nothing: but the soul of the diligent shall be made fat. (Proverbs 13: 4.)

DISCIPLE. (See Apostle.)

DIS-CI'PLE—literally, a follower; in a general sense, a scholar or follower of a certain teaching or teacher. The twelve apostles were the original disciples of Christ, but at his death the seventy and all other Christians were given the title. The name is also applied to the followers of John the Baptist and the Pharisees.

References.—Matthew 9: 14; 11: 2; Luke 10; Acts 4: 4; 19: 1.

DISOBEDIENCE.

Dis'o-be'di-ence—refusal or neglect to carry out a command, especially that of a person qualified or empowered to command. The Bible is insistent that those who are disobedient shall be punished, as obedience is one of the first of God's laws. Scripture contains numerous instances of punishment overtaking those who are disobedient.

REFERENCES.

But it shall come to pass, if thou wilt not hearken unto the voice of the Lord thy God, to observe to do all his commandments and his statutes which I command thee this day: that all these curses shall come upon thee, and overtake thee. (Deuteronomy 28: 15.)

For the children of Israel walked forty years in the wilderness, till all the people that were men of war which came out of Egypt were consumed, because they obeyed not the voice of the Lord: unto whom the Lord sware that he would not shew them the land which the Lord sware unto their fathers that he would give us, a land that floweth with milk and honey. (Joshua 5: 6.)

Who gave Jacob for a spoil, and Israel to the robbers? did not the Lord, he against whom we have sinned? for they would not walk in his ways, neither were they obedient unto his law. (Isaiah 42: 24.)

Let no man deceive you with vain words: for because of these things cometh the wrath of God upon the children of disobedience. (Ephesians 5: 6.)

They profess that they know God; but in works they deny him, being abominable, and disobedient, and unto every good work reprobate. (Titus 1: 16.)

For we ourselves also were sometimes foolish, disobedient, deceived, serving divers lusts and pleasures, living in malice and envy, hateful, and hating one another. (Titus 3: 3.)

For if the word spoken by Angels was stedfast, and every transgression and disobedience received a just recompense of reward:

How shall we escape, if we neglect so great salvation, which at the first began to be spoken by the Lord, and was confirmed unto us by them that heard him? (Hebrews 2: 2, 3.)

Additional References and Illustrations.—Genesis 3; Exodus 5; Joshua 7; 1 Samuel 13 and 15; Jonah 1.

DISPENSATION. (See Covenant.)

Dis'pen-sa'tion—the act of giving out, or, that which is given out. In a theological sense dispensations are the systems of rules, promises, and principles laid down at various times by God for his people. There may be said to have been three of these—the Patriarchal, the Jewish, and the Christian, although some writers and commentators recognize only the last two. See Covenant for references.

DIVISION.

Di-vi'sion—the separation of a thing into parts; also discord, disunion. In this latter sense the Bible contains many references calling attention to the necessity for avoiding troubles in churches.

REFERENCES.

Now I beseech you, brethren, mark them which cause divisions and offences, contrary to the doctrine which ye have learned, and avoid them. (Romans 16: 17.)

Now I beseech you, brethren, by the Name of our Lord Jesus Christ, that ye all speak the same thing, and that there be no divisions among you: but that ye be perfectly joined together in the same mind, and in the same judgment. (1 Corinthians 1: 10.)

For ye are yet carnal: for whereas there is among you envying, and strife, and divisions, are ye not carnal, and walk as men? (1 Corinthians 3: 3.)

For first of all when ye come together in the Church, I hear that there be divisions among you, and I partly believe it. (1 Corinthians 11: 18.)

DIVORCE.

DI-VORCE'—literally, any sort of a separation of two things; specifically, the separation of husband and wife. The law of Moses was loosely interpreted by the later Jews and divorces were frequent for absurd causes. Jesus, when appealed to, said, in substance, that divorce without crime on the part of the one put away was opposed to the original divine idea of marriage, which was the making of a bond not to be put asunder by man. Of late years the civilized world has fallen into the same error as the Jews, and the divorce evil has come to be an enormous one. Through the agency of the various denominations an effort is being made to crush the peril, by preventing indiscriminate divorce and re-marriage, and making the only possible ground for divorce the one ground which Christ recognized—unfaithfulness to the marriage vow.

REFERENCES.

Mosaic Divorce.

When a man hath taken a wife, and married her, and it come to pass that she find no favour in his eyes, because he hath found some uncleanness in her: then let him write her a bill of divorcement, and give it in her hand, and send her out of his house.

And when she is departed out of his house, she may go and be another man's wife.

And if the latter husband hate her, and write her a bill of divorcement, and giveth it in her hand, and sendeth her out of his house; or if the latter husband die, which took her to be his wife;

Her former husband, which sent her away, may not take her again to be his wife, after that she is defiled; for that is abomination before the Lord: and thou shalt not cause the land to sin, which the Lord thy God giveth thee for an inheritance. (Deuteronomy 24: 1-4.)

Christ's Law.

It hath been said, Whosoever shall put away his wife, let him give her a writing of divorcement:

But I say unto you, That whosoever shall put away his wife, saving for the cause of fornication, causeth her to commit adultery: and whosoever shall marry her that is divorced committeth adultery. (Matthew 5: 31, 32.)

The Pharisees also came unto him, tempting him, and saying unto him, Is it lawful for a man to put away his wife for every cause?

And he answered and said unto them, *Have ye not read, that he which made them at the beginning made them male and female,*

And said, For this cause shall a man leave father and mother, and shall cleave to his wife: and they twain shall be one flesh?

Wherefore they are no more twain, but one flesh. What therefore God hath joined together, let not man put asunder.

They say unto him, Why did Moses then command to give a writing of divorcement, and to put her away?

He saith unto them, *Moses because of the hardness of your hearts suffered you to put away your wives: but from the beginning it was not so.*

And I say unto you, Whosoever shall put away his wife, except it be for fornication, and shall marry another, committeth adultery: and whoso marrieth her which is put away doth commit adultery. (Matthew 19: 3-9.)

And the Pharisees came to him, and asked him, Is it lawful for a man to put away his wife? tempting him.

And he answered and said unto them, *What did Moses command you?*

And they said, Moses suffered to write a bill of divorcement, and to put her away.

And Jesus answered and said unto them, *For the hardness of your heart he wrote you this precept.*

But from the beginning of the creation God made them male and female.

For this cause shall a man leave his father and mother, and cleave to his wife;

And they twain shall be one flesh: so then they are no more twain, but one flesh.

What therefore God hath joined together, let not man put asunder.

And in the house his disciples asked him again of the same matter.

And he saith unto them, *Whosoever shall put away his wife, and marry another, committeth adultery against her.*

And if a woman shall put away her husband, and be married to another, she committeth adultery. (Mark 10: 2-12.)

DOCTRINE.

Doc′trine—any special code of religion, morals, ethics, or principles taught or delivered; also a system of theology, as Catholic doctrine, Presbyterian doctrine, Baptist doctrine, etc. The doctrine preached by Christ is basic doctrine for all others and the true doctrine.

REFERENCES.

Doctrine of Christ.

And it came to pass, when Jesus had ended these sayings, the people were astonished at his doctrine.

For he taught them as one having authority, and not as the Scribes. (Matthew 7: 28, 29.)

Jesus answered them, *My doctrine is not mine, but his that sent me.*

If any man will do his will, he shall know of the doctrine, whether it be of God, or whether I speak of myself (John 7: 16, 17.)

And they continued stedfastly in the Apostles' doctrine and fellowship, and in breaking of bread, and in prayers. (Acts 2: 42.)

Take heed unto thyself, and unto the doctrine: continue in them: for in doing this, thou shalt both save thyself, and them that hear thee. (1 Timothy 4: 16.)

If any man teach otherwise, and consent not to wholesome words, even the words of our Lord Jesus Christ, and to the doctrine which is according to godliness;

He is proud, knowing nothing, but doting about questions, and strifes of words, whereof cometh envy, strife, railings, evil surmisings. (1 Timothy 6: 3, 4.)

All Scripture is given by inspiration of God, and is profitable for doctrine, for reproof, for correction, for instruction in righteousness,

That the man of God may be perfect, throughly furnished unto all good works. (2 Timothy 3: 16, 17.)

Whosoever transgresseth and abideth not in the doctrine of Christ, hath not God: he that abideth in the doctrine of Christ, he hath both the Father and the Son.

If there come any unto you, and bring not this doctrine, receive him not into your house, neither bid him God speed. (2 John 1: 9, 10.)

False Doctrine.

That we henceforth be no more children, tossed to and fro, and carried about with every wind of doctrine, by the sleight of men, and cunning craftiness, whereby they lie in wait to deceive. (Ephesians 4: 14.)

Now the Spirit speaketh expressly, that in the latter times some shall depart from the faith, giving heed to seducing spirits, and doctrines of devils;

Speaking lies in hypocrisy; having their conscience seared with a hot iron. (1 Timothy 4: 1, 2.)

Preach the word; be instant in season, out of season; reprove, rebuke, exhort with all longsuffering and doctrine.

For the time will come when they will not endure sound doctrine; but after their own lusts shall they heap to themselves teachers, having itching ears;

And they shall turn away their ears from the truth, and shall be turned unto fables. (2 Timothy 4: 2-4.)

DOVE. (See Holy Spirit.)

DOVE—a well-known bird of the pigeon family, many times mentioned in the Bible, from the time Noah used it to find dry land to the later references in the New Testament. Doves were used as sacrifices by the Jews. Figuratively, it was known as the symbol of peace. To Christians it is chiefly known as the symbol of the Holy Ghost, as well as the sign of purity, meekness, and the beauties of righteousness.

References.—Genesis 8: 8; Genesis 15: 9; Psalm 68: 13; Matthew 3: 16; John 1: 32.

DREAM OR DREAMS.

DREAM OR DREAMS. Of all the phenomena that are the results of the workings of the brain and mind that known as dreaming is the most remarkable and mysterious. Science has not yet settled the exact status and causes of the manifestation, but most probably they are caused by the activity of certain functions of the brain and mind while others and the body are asleep, as, for instance, the activity of fancy or imagination during the suspension of judgment or memory or both.

Apparently man has been visited by dreams ever since his creation, since we find references to them in the Bible from the earliest times. The phenomenon was so strange that the ancients often believed they were in communication with God during dreams. It is certain that God has transmitted much of his will and revelation to man in them.

References and Instances.—Genesis 20: 3; 28: 12; 31: 10; 31: 24; 37: 5; 40: 5; Judges 7: 13; 1 Kings 3: 5; Daniel 2 and 4; Matthew 2: 12; 27: 19; Acts 10.

DRINK. DRUNKARDS. (See Temperance.)

DRINK. DRUNK'ARDS. The sin of drunkenness has come down through the ages. There is every indication from both sacred and profane history that the making of strong drink is almost as old as the human race itself, and that, in consequence, drunkards were among the first of the sinners. The Bible utters the most threatening warnings against drunkenness, promising woe and punishment to those who fall into its snare.

REFERENCES.

Drink Forbidden.

He shall separate himself from wine and strong drink, and shall drink no vinegar of wine, or vinegar of strong drink, neither shall he drink any liquor of grapes, nor eat moist grapes, or dried. (Numbers 6: 3.)

It is not for kings, O Lemuel, it is

not for kings to drink wine; nor for princes strong drink:

Lest they drink, and forget the law, and pervert the judgment of any of the afflicted. (Proverbs 31: 4, 5.)

Wine is a mocker, strong drink is raging: and whosoever is deceived thereby is not wise. (Proverbs 20: 1.)

Punishments for Drunkenness.

Wo unto them that rise up early in the morning, that they may follow strong drink; that continue until night, till wine inflame them! (Isaiah 5: 11.)

Wo unto them that are mighty to drink wine, and men of strength to mingle strong drink:

Which justify the wicked for reward, and take away the righteousness of the righteous from him!

Therefore as the fire devoureth the stubble, and the flame consumeth the chaff, so their root shall be as rottenness, and their blossom shall go up as dust: because they have cast away the law of the Lord of hosts, and despised the word of the Holy One of Israel. (Isaiah 5: 22-24.)

Wo to the crown of pride, to the drunkards of Ephraim, whose glorious beauty is a fading flower, which are on the head of the fat valleys of them that are overcome with wine! (Isaiah 28: 11.)

And take heed to yourselves, lest at any time your hearts be overcharged with surfeiting, and drunkenness, and cares of this life, and so that day come upon you unawares. (Luke 21: 34.)

Let us walk honestly, as in the day; not in rioting and drunkenness, not in chambering and wantonness, not in strife and envying. (Romans 13: 13.)

But now I have written unto you, not to keep company, if any man that is called a brother be a fornicator, or covetous, or an idolater, or a railer, or a drunkard, or an extortioner: with such a one, no, not to eat. (1 Corinthians 5: 11.)

Nor thieves, nor covetous, nor drunkards, nor revilers, nor extortioners, shall inherit the kingdom of God. (1 Corinthians 6: 10.)

Envyings, murders, drunkenness, revellings, and such like: of the which I tell you before, as I have also told you in time past, that they which do such things shall not inherit the kingdom of God. (Galatians 5: 21.)

DUST.

Dust—used in the Scripture very often as a symbol for things that are low, humble, impure, contemptuous. It is also used to show the origin of man and the fact that after death man's body must be resolved into its original elements.

REFERENCES.

And the Lord God formed man of the dust of the ground, and breathed into his nostrils the breath of life; and man became a living soul. (Genesis 2: 7.)

In the sweat of thy face shalt thou eat bread, till thou return unto the ground; for out of it wast thou taken: for dust thou art, and unto dust shalt thou return. (Genesis 3: 19.)

And Abraham answered and said, Behold now, I have taken upon me to speak unto the Lord, which am but dust and ashes. (Genesis 18: 27.)

Remember, I beseech thee, that thou hast made me as the clay; and wilt thou bring me into dust again? (Job 10: 9.)

All flesh shall perish together, and man shall turn again unto dust. (Job 34: 15.)

EASTER.

EAS'TER—the Christian festival commemorative of the resurrection of Christ. It is celebrated by almost all faiths and denominations. It had its inception in the feast of the Passover by reason of the fact that Christ was typified by the paschal lamb, to be slain at that time, and after Christ's death it became very easy for the Christian to see the connection between the two events. The name, strangely enough, comes from the name of a Teutonic goddess, Ostera, for whom a solemn feast was observed at about the same season of the year, for which feast the early Roman missionaries substituted the paschal feast.

The word Easter occurs in only one place in the Bible—Acts 12: 4—all the other places where it might be used the word "Passover" taking its place. The cause of this is rather peculiar. "Easter" was the word used in the earlier translations of the Bible, but in the 1611 or Authorized Version the oversight of the translators caused them to miss it, and it never has been altered.

EBENEZER.

EB'EN-E'ZER—a form of a Hebrew word meaning "stone of help." It was the name given to the stone set up by Samuel in commemoration of the help secured from God in giving a victory over the Philistines.

EDEN. (See Adam and Eve.)

E'DEN—the home of Adam and Eve before the Fall. The word is doubtless derived from a very ancient word (edin) meaning "a plain." It now has come to mean "delights," or "pleasantness." The exact location of the Garden of Eden never has been fixed, some authorities placing it in the Euphrates-Tigris valley, while others place it further to the north, in the highlands of Armenia.

EDIFICATION.

ED'I-FI-CA'TION—literally, a building up. When applied to spiritual things the word means advancing, improving, adorning, or comforting the mind and spiritual nature. We receive edification through prayer, hearing the gospel, attending to the Lord's business, reading the Scriptures, and meditation. Much store is set in it by New Testament writers.

REFERENCES.

Let us therefore follow after the things which make for peace, and things wherewith one may edify another. (Romans 14: 19.)

Let every one of us please his neighbour for his good to edification. (Romans 15: 2.)

Now as touching things offered unto idols, we know that we all have knowledge. Knowledge puffeth up, but charity edifieth. (1 Corinthians 8: 1.)

He that speaketh in an unknown tongue, edifieth himself: but he that prophesieth, edifieth the Church.

I would that ye all spake with tongues, but rather that ye prophesied: for greater is he that prophesieth than he that speaketh with tongues, except he interpret, that the Church may receive edifying. (1 Corinthians 14: 4, 5.)

Let no corrupt communication proceed out of your mouth, but that which is good to the use of edifying, that it may minister grace unto the hearers. (Ephesians 4: 29.)

EGYPT.

E'GYPT. This remarkable and mysterious land figures to a large extent in the Bible, as it has in the whole of the world's history. Where its people came from and when are questions the answers to which are lost in the mists of time. It is known, however, that Egypt was a powerful, rich, populous, and civilized nation at the time Abraham began his wanderings. It had huge cities and it was noted for the vast size of its buildings, temples, and monuments. Some of these still exist. To-day, at least five thousand years since they were built, the Pyramids and the Sphinx stand as mute testimonies of the greatness of the ancient people that inhabited the country at that time and was on the decline as a nation even then.

The country is long and shaped somewhat

like a lily. It stretches for many hundred miles along the banks of the Nile. Only the presence of the river makes it inhabitable. Once a year the stream overflows, irrigating the surrounding country and depositing a rich black soil that makes the land a veritable garden. The ruler of Egypt was called pharaoh instead of king. It was the policy of the early pharaohs to keep out of Egypt all foreigners. So long as this policy was followed Egypt was a great nation and extended its conquests in many directions. The influx of Jews, Greeks, and other alien people gradually brought the country to its doom, and it was successively conquered by the Assyrians, Persians, Greeks, and Romans before the time of Christ. Since then it has been the plaything of half-a-dozen nations and conquerors, and nothing is left of its might and power save the memories its ruins can recall.

The Egyptians were, as may be supposed, a nation of idol-worshipers. Their religion was a mixture of nature and beast worship. The priesthood was very learned. Modern scholars have suspected that the Egyptian priests understood and used many of the natural secrets that the wonderful progress of the last century has dragged to light for men of these times. It is believed that some of them had a knowledge of electricity and magnetism as well as hypnotism, employing such knowledge in the conduct of their religious rites. The name of the pharaoh in whose reign the Exodus took place is believed to have been Rameses II. He reigned more than sixty years.

ELEAZAR.

E′LE-A′ZAR—a form of a Hebrew word meaning "God is helper." Eleazar was a very common given name among the Jews. The most important one of the title found in the Bible is the Eleazar who was the son and successor in the high-priesthood of Aaron. He held office in Joshua's time, and seems to have worked in thorough harmony with him.

ELECT AND ELECTION.

E-LECT′ AND E-LEC′TION. These two terms figure to a large extent in Scripture. The former means "chosen" or "selected;" the latter means the act of choosing or selecting.

REFERENCES.

Elect: Christ and God's Chosen.

Behold my servant, whom I uphold; mine elect, in whom my soul delighteth; I have put my Spirit upon him: he shall bring forth judgment to the Gentiles. (Isaiah 42: 1.)

And I will bring forth a seed out of Jacob, and out of Judah an inheritor of my mountains: and mine elect shall inherit it, and my servants shall dwell there. (Isaiah 65: 9.)

Wherefore it is contained in the Scripture, Behold, I lay in Sion a chief corner stone, elect, precious, and he that believeth on him shall not be confounded. (1 Peter 2: 6.)

Elect under the Gospel.

And except those days should be shortened, there should no flesh be saved: but for the elect's sake those days shall be shortened. (Matthew 24: 22.)

And shall not God avenge his own elect, which cry day and night unto him, though he bear long with them? (Luke 18: 7.)

Who shall lay any thing to the charge of God's elect? It is God that justifieth. (Romans 8: 33.)

Even so then at this present time also there is a remnant according to the election of grace.

And if by grace, then is it no more of works: otherwise grace is no more grace. But if it be of works, then is it no more grace, otherwise work is no more work.

What then? Israel hath not obtained that which he seeketh for, but the election hath obtained it, and the rest were blinded. (Romans 11: 5-7.)

Put on therefore, as the elect of God, holy and beloved, bowels of mercies, kindness, humbleness of mind, meekness, longsuffering. (Colossians 3: 12.)

Therefore I endure all things for the elect's sake, that they may also obtain the salvation which is in Christ Jesus, with eternal glory. (2 Timothy 2: 10.)

Election.

For ye see your calling, brethren, how that not many wise men after the flesh, not many mighty, not many noble are called.

But God hath chosen the foolish things of the world, to confound the wise: and God hath chosen the weak things of the world, to confound the things which are mighty:

And base things of the world, and things which are despised, hath God chosen, yea and things which are not, to bring to nought things that are. (1 Corinthians 1: 26-28.)

Knowing, brethren beloved, your election of God. (1 Thessalonians 1: 4.)

Wherefore, the rather, brethren, give diligence to make your calling and election sure: for if ye do these things, ye shall never fall.

For so an entrance shall be ministered unto you abundantly into the everlasting kingdom of our Lord and Saviour Jesus Christ. (2 Peter 1: 10, 11.)

ELI. (See Samuel.)

E′LI—a form of a Hebrew word meaning "summit," "height," or "raised up." Eli was the high-priest and judge of Israel immediately before Samuel. He was a descendant of Aaron, and, though a good and devout man, permitted his sons Hophni and Phinehas to do things that brought down upon them the wrath of God. Samuel warned Eli of the doom that was to overtake his house for this, and later it was realized.

References.—1 Samuel 1; 2; 3; 4.

ELIJAH. (See Elisha.)

E-LI′JAH—a form of a Hebrew word meaning "God-Jehovah." Elijah was the name of one of the most wonderful characters in the Old Testament. Scripture is absolutely silent as to his family and early history, and he is suddenly introduced to the reader without any mention concerning his past. His first utterance is a terrible denunciation of the sins of King Ahab and the prophecy of a three-year drought; and this part of prophet-reformer he consistently carries out to the end of his days, his career being one long struggle against the wickedness of the people. Fleeing from Ahab's wrath, Elijah took refuge near the brook Cherith, there being miraculously cared for by God. Later he went to Zarephath, where he dwelt with a widow, whose dead child he restored to life. Ordered by God to confront Ahab, he obeyed and the result of their meeting was the destruction of the priests of Baal by fire and the end of the drought that had almost ruined Israel. Forced again to flee because of Jezebel, Ahab's wicked wife, Elijah went to the wilderness around Horeb, and there received God's order to anoint Hazael king in Ahab's place and make Elisha his own successor. From this time on he is seen to work almost in conjunction with Elisha. At last, when his work is finished, he is taken off to Heaven in a fiery chariot, his beloved Elisha watching him go.

While the character of Elijah is painted in the Old Testament as unbendingly stern and rigid in its great moral sublimity and wonderful faith, nevertheless there are sidelights upon the man that show him to have been a most lovable character as well. He was hard, and stern, and cold to the sinful, but generous, winning, and loving to the good, and the poor, and the afflicted.

REFERENCES.
Elijah's Life and Works.

And Elijah the Tishbite, who was of the inhabitants of Gilead, said unto Ahab, As the Lord God of Israel liveth, before whom I stand, there shall not be dew nor rain these years, but according to my word. (1 Kings 17: 1.)

So he went and did according unto the word of the Lord: for he went and dwelt by the brook Cherith, that is before Jordan.

And the ravens brought him bread and flesh in the morning, and bread and flesh in the evening; and he drank of the brook. (1 Kings 17: 5, 6.)

And the word of the Lord came unto him, saying,

Arise, get thee to Zarephath, which belongeth to Zidon, and dwell there: behold, I have commanded a widow woman there to sustain thee. (1 Kings 17: 8, 9.)

And he cried unto the Lord, and said, O Lord my God, hast thou also brought evil upon the widow with whom I sojourn, by slaying her son?

And he stretched himself upon the child three times, and cried unto the Lord, and said, O Lord my God, I pray thee, let this child's soul come into him again.

And the Lord heard the voice of Elijah; and the soul of the child came into him again, and he revived. (1 Kings 17: 20-22.)

And Elijah said unto them, Take the prophets of Baal; let not one of them escape. And they took them: and Elijah brought them down to the brook Kishon, and slew them there.

And Elijah said unto Ahab, Get thee up, eat and drink; for there is a sound of abundance of rain. (1 Kings 18: 40, 41.)

So he departed thence, and found Elisha the son of Shaphat, who was plowing with twelve yoke of oxen before him, and he with the twelfth: and Elijah passed by him, and cast his mantle upon him.

And he left the oxen, and ran after Elijah, and said, Let me, I pray thee,

kiss my father and my mother, and then I will follow thee. And he said unto him, Go back again: for what have I done to thee?

And he returned back from him, and took a yoke of oxen, and slew them, and boiled their flesh with the instruments of the oxen, and gave unto the people, and they did eat. Then he arose, and went after Elijah, and ministered unto him. (1 Kings 19: 19-21.)

And it came to pass, when they were gone over, that Elijah said unto Elisha, Ask what I shall do for thee, before I be taken away from thee. And Elisha said, I pray thee, let a double portion of thy spirit be upon me.

And he said, Thou hast asked a hard thing: nevertheless, if thou see me when I am taken from thee, it shall be so unto thee; but if not, it shall not be so.

And it came to pass, as they still went on, and talked, that, behold, there appeared a chariot of fire, and horses of fire, and parted them both asunder; and Elijah went up by a whirlwind into heaven.

And Elisha saw it, and he cried, My father, my father, the chariot of Israel, and the horsemen thereof. And he saw him no more: and he took hold of his own clothes, and rent them in two pieces.

He took up also the mantle of Elijah that fell from him, and went back, and stood by the bank of Jordan. (2 Kings 2: 9-13.)

Elijah at Transfiguration.

And behold, there appeared unto them Moses, and Elias, talking with him.

Then answered Peter, and said unto Jesus, Lord, it is good for us to be here:

If thou wilt, let us make here three tabernacles: one for thee, and one for Moses, and one for Elias. (Matthew 17: 3, 4.)

Forerunner of John the Baptist.

Behold, I will send you Elijah the prophet before the coming of the great and dreadful day of the Lord:

And he shall turn the heart of the fathers to the children, and the heart of the children to their fathers, lest I come and smite the earth with a curse. (Malachi 4: 5, 6.)

For all the Prophets and the Law prophesied until John.

And if ye will receive it, this is Elias which was for to come. (Matthew 11: 13, 14.)

And he shall go before him in the spirit and power of Elias, to turn the hearts of the fathers to the children, and the disobedient to the wisdom of the just, to make ready a people prepared for the Lord. (Luke 1: 17.)

ELISABETH. (See John the Baptist, Zacharias.)

E-LIS'A-BETH—a form of a Hebrew word meaning "God her oath." Elisabeth was the wife of Zacharias, the mother of John the Baptist, and the cousin of Mary the mother of Jesus.

Reference.—Luke 1.

ELISHA. (See Elijah.)

E-LI'SHA—a form of a Hebrew word meaning "God the deliverer." Elisha was the successor of Elijah as Israel's prophet. His whole life, after the translation of Elijah, seems to have been spent in doing good. His character is essentially a different one from that of his predecessor. While we see Elijah's lovableness only occasionally because of the stern things he had to do, we find in everything that Elisha does gentleness and that winning disposition that made him an object of reverence. In this the earnest student can

see God's hand. What Elijah began in tumult and stress, fire and blood, solitude and awe-inspiring visions, Elisha carried to completion in gentleness, healing acts, and loving, peaceful intercourse. Both men worked as God directed and with the means that He gave.

Elisha was prophet for about sixty years. In that time we find him aiding the Israelites to overthrow their enemies and laboring to build up a higher spiritual state, and doing many deeds for the comfort of the poor and the afflicted. He died lamented by all Israel. God, after his death, honored him by permitting the touch of his bones to raise a man from the dead.

REFERENCES.

And the Lord said unto him, Go, return on thy way to the wilderness of Damascus: and when thou comest, anoint Hazael to be king over Syria:

And Jehu the son of Nimshi shalt thou anoint to be king over Israel: and Elisha the son of Shaphat of Abel-meholah shalt thou anoint to be prophet in thy room. (1 Kings 19: 15, 16.)

And he took the mantle of Elijah that fell from him, and smote the waters, and said, Where is the Lord God of Elijah? And when he also had smitten the waters, they parted hither and thither: and Elisha went over.

And when the sons of the prophets which were to view at Jericho saw him, they said, The spirit of Elijah doth rest on Elisha. And they came to meet him, and bowed themselves to the ground before him. (2 Kings 2: 14, 15.)

Now Elisha was fallen sick of his sickness whereof he died. And Joash the king of Israel came down unto him, and wept over his face, and said, O my father, my father! the chariot of Israel, and the horsemen thereof!

And Elisha said unto him, Take bow and arrows. And he took unto him bow and arrows.

And he said to the king of Israel, Put thine hand upon the bow. And he put his hand upon it: and Elisha put his hands upon the king's hands.

And he said, Open the window eastward. And he opened it. Then Elisha said, Shoot. And he shot. And he said, The arrow of the Lord's deliverance, and the arrow of deliverance from Syria: for thou shalt smite the Syrians in Aphek, till thou have consumed them.

And he said, Take the arrows. And he took them. And he said unto the king of Israel, Smite upon the ground. And he smote thrice, and stayed.

And the man of God was wroth with him, and said, Thou shouldest have smitten five or six times; then hadst thou smitten Syria till thou hadst consumed it: whereas now thou shalt smite Syria but thrice.

And Elisha died, and they buried him. And the bands of the Moabites invaded the land at the coming in of the year. (2 Kings 13: 14-20.)

Additional References, Including Miracles. —2 Kings 2: 22; 2: 24; 3: 16; 4: 4; 4: 32; 4: 40; 4: 44; 5: 14; 6: 5; 6: 18; 7: 1; 9: 1; 13: 21.

ENEMIES.

EN'E-MIES—those who are unfriendly or hostile to us; those who wish us evil or do evil to us. The Bible is very explicit as to the way in which we should treat enemies, the New Testament particularly telling us that we should love them and to return good for evil—to do which is the surest test of the Christian character.

REFERENCES.

Treatment of Enemies.

If thou meet thine enemy's ox or his ass going astray, thou shalt surely bring it back to him again.

If thou see the ass of him that hateth thee lying under his burden, and wouldest forbear to help him, thou shalt surely help with him. (Exodus 23: 4, 5.)

And David said to Saul, Wherefore hearest thou men's words, saying, Behold, David seeketh thy hurt?

Behold, this day thine eyes have seen how that the Lord had delivered thee to-day into mine hand in the cave: and some bade me kill thee; but mine eye spared thee; and I said, I will not put forth mine hand against my lord; for he is the Lord's anointed. (1 Samuel 24: 9, 10.)

Rejoice not when thine enemy falleth, and let not thine heart be glad when he stumbleth. (Proverbs 24: 17.)

If thine enemy be hungry, give him bread to eat; and if he be thirsty, give him water to drink:

For thou shalt heap coals of fire upon his head, and the Lord shall reward thee. (Proverbs 25: 21, 22.)

Ye have heard that it hath been said, Thou shalt love thy neighbour, and hate thine enemy.

But I say unto you, Love your enemies, bless them that curse you, do good to them that hate you, and pray for them which despitefully use you, and persecute you. (Matthew 5: 43, 44.)

But love ye your enemies, and do good, and lend, hoping for nothing again: and your reward shall be great, and ye shall be the children of the Highest: for he is kind unto the unthankful, and to the evil. (Luke 6: 35.)

God Delivers from Enemies.

He delivereth me from mine enemies: yea, thou liftest me up above those that rise up against me: thou hast delivered me from the violent man. (Psalm 18: 48.)

For thou hast been a shelter for me, and a strong tower from the enemy. (Psalm 61: 3.)

God's Enemies Punished.

Thy right hand, O Lord, is become glorious in power: thy right hand, O Lord, hath dashed in pieces the enemy. (Exodus 15: 6.)

Let God arise, let his enemies be scattered: let them also that hate him flee before him. (Psalm 68: 1.)

For lo, thine enemies, O Lord, for lo, thine enemies shall perish; all the workers of iniquity shall be scattered. (Psalm 92: 9.)

Therefore saith the Lord, the Lord of hosts, the mighty One of Israel,. Ah, I will ease me of mine adversaries, and avenge me of mine enemies. (Isaiah 1: 24.)

And to you who are troubled, rest with us, when the Lord Jesus shall be revealed from heaven, with his mighty Angels,

In flaming fire, taking vengeance on them that know not God, and that obey not the Gospel of our Lord Jesus Christ. (2 Thessalonians 1: 7, 8.)

Enmity between God and Man.

For to be carnally minded is death; but to be spiritually minded is life and peace.

Because the carnal mind is enmity against God: for it is not subject to the law of God, neither indeed can be. (Romans 8: 6, 7.)

For he is our peace, who hath made both one, and hath broken down the middle wall of partition between us:

Having abolished in his flesh the enmity, even the law of commandments contained in ordinances, for to make in himself of twain one new man, so making peace. (Ephesians 2: 14, 15.)

And (having made peace through the blood of his cross) by him to reconcile all things unto himself, by him, I say, whether they be things in earth, or things in heaven.

And you that were sometimes alienated, and enemies in your mind by wicked works, yet now hath he reconciled. (Colossians 1: 20, 21.)

ENOCH.

E'noch—a form of a Hebrew word meaning "initiated" or "teacher." The Bible mentions a number of persons of this name, as well as a city. The first was the son of Cain, who built a town which he called after himself. The next was the Enoch who "walked with God." He was the son of Jared and the father of Methuselah. We are told that he lived 365 years. He was born about 3,500 B.C. He was such a good man that, according to Moses, he was removed to Heaven without the experience of death.

References.—Genesis 5; Hebrews 11: 5; Jude 1: 14.

ENVY. (See Covetousness.)

En'vy. Envy is that feeling of discontent or uneasiness which makes us covet the good fortunes or possessions of another. The Bible regards envy as a sin, and the whole teaching of the Book, both in the Old and New Testaments, is against it as a stumbling-block to the person who seeks to pursue the religious life.

REFERENCES.

General.

A sound heart is the life of the flesh: but envy the rottenness of the bones. (Proverbs 14: 30.)

Wrath is cruel, and anger is outrageous; but who is able to stand before envy? (Proverbs 27: 4.)

Again, I considered all travail, and every right work, that for this a man is envied of his neighbour. This is also vanity and vexation of spirit. (Ecclesiastes 4: 4.)

Therefore when they were gathered together, Pilate said unto them, Whom will ye that I release unto you? Barabbas, or Jesus, which is called Christ?

For he knew that for envy they had delivered him. (Matthew 27: 17, 18.)

And the Patriarchs, moved with envy, sold Joseph into Egypt: but God was with him. (Acts 7: 9.)

And even as they did not like to retain God in their knowledge, God gave them over to a reprobate mind, to do those things which are not convenient:

Being filled with all unrighteousness, fornication, wickedness, covetousness, maliciousness, full of envy, murder, debate, deceit, malignity, whisperers. (Romans 1: 28, 29.)

For ye are yet carnal: for whereas there is among you envying, and strife, and divisions, are ye not carnal, and walk as men? (1 Corinthians 3: 3.)

For I fear lest when I come, I shall not find you such as I would, and that I shall be found unto you such as ye would not, lest there be debates, envyings, wraths, strifes, backbitings, whisperings, swellings, tumults. (2 Corinthians 12: 20.)

He is proud, knowing nothing, but doting about questions and strifes of words, whereof cometh envy, strife, railings, evil surmisings. (1 Timothy 6: 4.)

Envy Forbidden.

Fret not thyself because of evil doers, neither be thou envious against the workers of iniquity. (Psalm 37: 1.)

Envy thou not the oppressor, and choose none of his ways. (Proverbs 3: 31.)

Let us walk honestly, as in the day; not in rioting and drunkenness, not in chambering and wantonness, not in strife and envying. (Romans 13: 13.)

Wherefore laying aside all malice, and all guile, and hypocrisies, and envies, and evil speakings. (1 Peter 2: 1.)

Consequences of Envy.

For wrath killeth the foolish man, and envy slayeth the silly one. (Job 5: 2.)

Lord, when thy hand is lifted up, they will not see: but they shall see, and be ashamed for their envy at the people; yea, the fire of thine enemies shall devour them. (Isaiah 26: 11.)

For where envying and strife is, there is confusion, and every evil work. (James 3: 16.)

EPHESUS.

EPH'E-SUS—a city of Asia Minor, famous in the time of Christ and for some several centuries later. Ephesus was founded some centuries before the Christian era by the Greeks, and at the time of Christ's birth was one of the largest and finest cities of the East, being noted for its commerce, its art, and its magnificent buildings. Like all Greek cities in their prime, it was most evil and licentious. It possessed one of the wonders of the world in the shape of a great and beautiful temple to the goddess Diana, which was noted for the richness of its priesthood and the number of its worshipers. After the death of Jesus much missionary work was carried on in the place and Paul founded a strong church there. But, like the others of the "seven churches of Asia," it fell into wickedness and was wiped out. To-day nothing is left of Ephesus save heaps of ruins, in which can be found only a trace of its former greatness.

References.—Acts 19 and 20; 1 Corinthians 15: 32; 1 Corinthians 16: 8. See also Paul's Epistle to the Ephesians.

ESAU. (See Isaac, Jacob, Rebekah.)

E'SAU—a form of a Hebrew word meaning "hairy." Esau was the eldest son of Isaac by Rebekah. His warfare with his twin-brother, Jacob, was foretold before their birth. Esau was strong, sturdy, and addicted to the outdoor life of a hunter; Jacob was of a less powerful mold, and given to study. Through craftiness he deprived Esau of his birthright. Esau later lost his father's blessing through being less shrewd than Jacob. After his marriage he became a rich and powerful chieftain in Edom.

References.—Genesis 25; 27; 33; 36.

ESTHER.

Es'ther—a form of a Hebrew word derived from the Persian word sitareh, meaning "star." She was the child of Hebrew parents, born in the vicinity of Babylon during the Exile, and her Hebrew name was Hadassah, Esther being given to her when she became the bride of King Ahasuerus. Her history and what she did for her people will be found in the Bible in the book of Esther, to which the reader is referred.

EUPHRATES.

Eu-phra'tes—the Biblical name for the largest and most important river of Western Asia. It is now called the Phrat. It is a stream about 1,800 miles long and navigable for steamers a large part of the distance. It figures in the Bible a very great deal, having been one of the streams that flowed near Eden. Many notable events occurred on or near its banks.

EVE.   (See Adam, Fall.)

Eve—an Englished form of the feminine style of the Hebrew noun meaning "life." It is the name by which the first woman, Adam's helpmeet, is known. Genesis gives a double account of her creation. After the birth of Seth she disappears from Scripture. Nothing is said concerning when or where she died, or at what age.

REFERENCES.

So God created man in his own image, in the image of God created he him; male and female created he them. (Genesis 1: 27.)

And the Lord God caused a deep sleep to fall upon Adam, and he slept: and he took one of his ribs, and closed up the flesh instead thereof;

And the rib, which the Lord God had taken from man, made he a woman, and brought her unto the man.

And Adam said, This is now bone of my bones, and flesh of my flesh: she shall be called Woman, because she was taken out of Man.   (Genesis 2: 21-23.)

And Adam called his wife's name Eve; because she was the mother of all living. (Genesis 3: 20.)

Now the serpent was more subtil than any beast of the field which the Lord God had made. And he said unto the woman, Yea, hath God said, Ye shall not eat of every tree of the garden?

And the woman said unto the serpent, We may eat of the fruit of the trees of the garden:

But of the fruit of the tree which is in the midst of the garden, God hath said, Ye shall not eat of it, neither shall ye touch it, lest ye die.

And the serpent said unto the woman, Ye shall not surely die:

For God doth know that in the day ye eat thereof, then your eyes shall be opened, and ye shall be as gods, knowing good and evil.

And when the woman saw that the tree was good for food, and that it was pleasant to the eyes, and a tree to be desired to make one wise, she took of the fruit thereof, and did eat, and gave also unto her husband with her; and he did eat. (Genesis 3: 1-6.)

And the Lord God said unto the woman, What is this that thou hast done? And the woman said, The serpent beguiled me, and I did eat. (Genesis 3: 13.)

Unto the woman he said, I will greatly multiply thy sorrow and thy conception; in sorrow thou shalt bring forth children: and thy desire shall be to thy husband, and he shall rule over thee. (Genesis 3: 16.)

EVIL. (See Sin.)

EZEKIEL.

E-ze′ki-el—a form of a Hebrew word meaning "whom God will strengthen." Ezekiel was one of the greater prophets, and lived about the same time as Jeremiah and Daniel. We know that his prophecies were made in captivity; but beyond that fact little is known about him. It is judged from the character of his writings that he was a man of immense energy and vigor, as well as deeply religious and highly spiritual.

Reference.—The book of Ezekiel.

EZRA.

Ez′ra—a form of a Hebrew word meaning "help." The Bible mentions several persons named Ezra. The one of chief importance, however, is the noted priest and scribe who led the second expedition of Israelites back to the fatherland from the Babylonian exile, about the year 458 B.C. This was but a portion of his work. He founded the Great Synagogue at Jerusalem, collected and revised the books of the Old Testament, wrote Chronicles and Ezra himself, and probably Nehemiah and Esther, and set down the basis for the canon of the Old Testament. He died at a very advanced age, said by some to have been 120 years.

FAITH.

FAITH—literally, belief or trust. In the religious sense, faith is the unqualified assent of the mind to the truths of God, either revealed or concealed. The actual word itself occurs but a few times in the Old Testament, but its place is taken by other terms having the same, or almost the same, meaning. In the New Testament its use is very much more frequent and marked, and the presence of faith in the human breast is indicated as an essential to salvation. Paul often refers to it as one of the greatest of human attributes and one of the chief links between God and man.

REFERENCES.

The Nature of Faith.

Now faith is the substance of things hoped for, the evidence of things not seen.

For by it the elders obtained a good report.

Through faith we understand that the worlds were framed by the word of God, so that things which are seen were not made of things which do appear. (Hebrews 11: 1-3.)

Its Power to Justify, Purify, Sanctify.

Therefore we conclude that a man is justified by faith without the deeds of the law. (Romans 3: 28.)

Therefore being justified by faith, we have peace with God through our Lord Jesus Christ:

By whom also we have access by faith into this grace wherein we stand, and rejoice in hope of the glory of God. (Romans 5: 1, 2.)

Knowing that a man is not justified by the works of the law, but by the faith of Jesus Christ, even we have believed in Jesus Christ, that we might be justified by the faith of Christ, and not by the works of the law: for by the works of the law shall no flesh be justified. (Galatians 2: 16.)

And put no difference between us and them, purifying their hearts by faith. (Acts 15: 9.)

To open their eyes, and to turn them from darkness to light, and from the power of Satan unto God, that they may receive forgiveness of sins, and inheritance among them which are sanctified by faith that is in me. (Acts 26: 18.)

Godhead Object of Faith.

And Jesus answering, saith unto them, *Have faith in God.*

For verily I say unto you, that whosoever shall say unto this mountain, Be thou removed, and be thou cast into the sea, and shall not doubt in his heart, but shall believe that those things which he saith shall come to pass: he shall have whatsoever he saith. (Mark 11: 22, 23.)

Let not your heart be troubled: ye believe in God, believe also in me. (John 14: 1.)

But these are written, that ye might believe that Jesus is the Christ the Son of God, and that believing ye might have life through his Name. (John 20: 31.)

Faith Given by the Spirit.

And my speech and my preaching was not with enticing words of man's wisdom, but in demonstration of the Spirit and of power:

That your faith should not stand in the wisdom of men, but in the power of God. (1 Corinthians 2: 4, 5.)

To another faith, by the same spirit: to another the gifts of healing, by the same spirit. (1 Corinthians 12: 9.)

Unity of Faith.

One Lord, one Faith, one Baptism. (Ephesians 4: 5.)

Till we all come in the unity of the faith, and of the knowledge of the Son of God, unto a perfect man, unto the measure of the stature of the fulness of Christ. (Ephesians 4: 13.)

Beloved, when I gave all diligence to write unto you of the common salvation: it was needful for me to write unto you, and exhort you that ye should earnestly contend for the faith which was once delivered unto the Saints. (Jude 1: 3.)

Faith and Salvation.

He that believeth and is baptized shall be saved; but he that believeth not shall be damned. (Mark 16: 16.)

But as many as received him, to them gave he power to become the sons of God, even to them that believe on his Name. (John 1: 12.)

For God so loved the world, that he gave his only begotten Son, that whosoever believeth in him should not perish, but have everlasting life. (John 3: 16.)

He that believeth on the Son hath everlasting life: and he that believeth not the Son shall not see life: but the wrath of God abideth on him. (John 3: 36.)

But that no man is justified by the law in the sight of God, it is evident: for, The just shall live by faith. (Galatians 3: 11.)

For by grace are ye saved, through faith, and that not of yourselves: it is the gift of God. (Ephesians 2: 8.)

And that from a child thou hast known the holy Scriptures, which are able to make thee wise unto salvation through faith which is in Christ Jesus. (2 Timothy 3: 15.)

But without faith it is impossible to please him: for he that cometh to God must believe that he is, and that he is a rewarder of them that diligently seek him. (Hebrews 11: 6.)

Faith Works by Love.

And though I have the gift of prophecy, and understand all mysteries, and all knowledge; and though I have all faith, so that I could remove mountains, and have not charity,* I am nothing. (1 Corinthians 13: 1.)

And now abideth faith, hope, charity,* these three; but the greatest of these is charity.* (1 Corinthians 13: 13.)

For in Jesus Christ neither circumcision availeth any thing, nor uncircumcision, but faith which worketh by love. (Galatians 5: 6.)

Now the end of the commandment is charity, out of a pure heart, and of a good conscience, and of faith unfeigned. (1 Timothy 1: 5.)

Seeing ye have purified your souls in obeying the truth through the Spirit unto unfeigned love of the brethren, see that ye love one another with a pure heart fervently. (1 Peter 1: 22.)

Faith without Works.

Even so faith, if it hath not works, is dead being alone.

Yea, a man may say, Thou hast faith, and I have works: shew me thy faith without thy works, and I will shew thee my faith by my works.

Thou believest that there is one God, thou doest well: the devils also believe, and tremble.

But wilt thou know, O vain man, that faith without works is dead? (James 2: 17-20.)

Brings Peace and Joy.

Therefore being justified by faith, we have peace with God, through our Lord Jesus Christ. (Romans 5: 1.)

Now the God of hope fill you with all joy and peace in believing, that ye may abound in hope through the power of the Holy Ghost. (Romans 15: 13.)

That the trial of your faith, being much more precious than of gold that perisheth, though it be tried with fire, might be found unto praise, and honour, and glory, at the appearing of Jesus Christ:

Whom having not seen, ye love, in whom though now ye see him not, yet believing, ye rejoice with joy unspeakable, and full of glory. (1 Peter 1: 7, 8.)

Blessings from Faith.

And this is the will of him that sent me, that every one which seeth the Son, and believeth on him, may have everlasting life: and I will raise him up at the last day. (John 6: 40.)

Therefore it is of faith, that it might be by grace; to the end the promise might be sure to all the seed; not to that only which is of the law, but to that also which is of the faith of Abraham; who is the father of us all. (Romans 4: 16.)

According to the eternal purpose which he purposed in Christ Jesus our Lord:

In whom we have boldness and access with confidence by the faith of him. (Ephesians 3: 11, 12.)

Neither give heed to fables and endless genealogies, which minister questions, rather than godly edifying which is in faith. (1 Timothy 1: 4.)

Miracles through Faith.

But Jesus turned him about, and when he saw her, he said, *Daughter, be of good comfort, thy faith hath made thee whole.* And the woman was made whole from that hour. (Matthew 9: 22.)

But when Jesus heard it, he answered him, saying, *Fear not, believe only, and she shall be made whole.* (Luke 8: 50.)

And his name through faith in his

* Charity in this sense means love.

name hath made this man strong, whom ye see and know: yea, the faith which is by him hath given him this perfect soundness in the presence of you all. (Acts 3: 16.)

Power of Faith.

And Jesus said unto them, *Because of your unbelief: for verily I say unto you, If ye have faith as a grain of mustard seed, ye shall say unto this mountain, Remove hence to yonder place; and it shall remove; and nothing shall be impossible unto you.* (Matthew 17: 20.)

Jesus said unto him, *If thou canst believe, all things are possible to him that believeth.* (Mark 9: 23.)

For whatsoever is born of God, overcometh the world, and this is the victory that overcometh the world, even our faith. (1 John 5: 4.)

Faith's Trials.

So that we ourselves glory in you in the churches of God for your patience and faith in all your persecutions and tribulations that ye endure. (2 Thessalonians 1: 4.)

By faith Abraham, when he was tried, offered up Isaac: and he that had received the promises offered up his only begotten son. (Hebrews 11: 17.)

Knowing this, that the trying of your faith worketh patience. (James 1: 3.)

That the trial of your faith, being much more precious than of gold that perisheth, though it be tried with fire, might be found unto praise and honour and glory at the appearing of Jesus Christ. (1 Peter 1: 7.)

In Christian's Armor.

Above all, taking the shield of faith, wherewith ye shall be able to quench all the fiery darts of the wicked. (Ephesians 6: 16.)

But let us, who are of the day, be sober, putting on the breastplate of faith and love, and for an helmet, the hope of salvation. (1 Thessalonians 5: 8.)

Constancy in Faith.

Watch ye, stand fast in the faith, quit you like men: be strong. (1 Corinthians 16: 13.)

Examine yourselves, whether ye be in the faith: prove your own selves. Know ye not your own selves, how that Jesus Christ is in you, except ye be reprobates? (2 Corinthians 13: 5.)

Only let your conversation be as it becometh the gospel of Christ: that whether I come and see you, or else be absent, I may hear of your affairs, that ye stand fast in one spirit, with one mind striving together for the faith of the gospel. (Philippians 1: 27.)

As ye have therefore received Christ Jesus the Lord, so walk ye in him:

Rooted and built up in him, and stablished in the faith, as ye have been taught, abounding therein with thanksgiving. (Colossians 2: 6, 7.)

This charge I commit unto thee, son Timothy, according to the prophecies which went before on thee, that thou by them mightest war a good warfare;

Holding faith, and a good conscience; which some having put away concerning faith have made shipwreck. (1 Timothy 1: 18, 19.)

Faithfulness in God's Service.

Who then is a faithful and wise servant, whom his Lord hath made ruler over his household, to give them meat in due season? (Matthew 24: 45.)

But have renounced the hidden things of dishonesty, not walking in craftiness, nor handling the word of God deceitfully, but by manifestation of the truth commending ourselves to every man's conscience in the sight of God. (2 Corinthians 4: 2.)

Beloved, thou doest faithfully whatsoever thou doest to the Brethren, and to strangers:

Which have borne witness of thy charity before the Church: whom if thou bring forward on their journey after a godly sort, thou shalt do well. (3 John 1: 5, 6.)

Faithfulness toward Men.

A tale-bearer revealeth secrets: but he that is of a faithful spirit concealeth the matter. (Proverbs 11: 13.)

A wicked messenger falleth into mischief: but a faithful ambassador is health. (Proverbs 13: 17.)

A faithful witness will not lie: but a false witness will utter lies. (Proverbs 14: 5.)

He that is faithful in that which is least, is faithful also in much: and he that is unjust in the least, is unjust also in much.

If therefore ye have not been faithful in the unrighteous Mammon, who will commit to your trust the true riches?

And if ye have not been faithful in that which is another man's, who shall give you that which is your own? (Luke 16: 10-12.)

Let a man so account of us, as of the ministers of Christ, and stewards of the mysteries of God.

Moreover, it is required in stewards, that a man be found faithful. (1 Corinthians 4: 1, 2.)

And they that have believing masters, let them not despise them, because they are brethren; but rather do them

service, because they are faithful and beloved, partakers of the benefit. These things teach and exhort. (1 Timothy 6: 2.)

FALL. (See Adam, Creation, Eve.)

FALL. The Fall of Man is a theological term which indicates the loss of that state of sinless perfection in which God made his greatest creation, man. God's positive command was transgressed and the disobedience thereby entailed upon succeeding humanity the penalty of sin and suffering and death; salvation only being accorded through the goodness of God and the sacrifice of His Son as the Redeemer of the World.

REFERENCES.

The Command.

And the Lord God commanded the man, saying, Of every tree of the garden thou mayest freely eat:

But of the tree of the knowledge of good and evil, thou shalt not eat of it: for in the day that thou eatest thereof thou shalt surely die. (Genesis 2: 16, 17.)

The Fall and Judgment.

Now the serpent was more subtile than any beast of the field which the Lord God had made. And he said unto the woman, Yea, hath God said, Ye shall not eat of every tree of the garden?

And the woman said unto the serpent, We may eat of the fruit of the trees of the garden:

But of the fruit of the tree which is in the midst of the garden, God hath said, Ye shall not eat of it, neither shall ye touch it, lest ye die.

And the serpent said unto the woman, Ye shall not surely die:

For God doth know that in the day ye eat thereof, then your eyes shall be opened, and ye shall be as gods, knowing good and evil.

And when the woman saw that the tree was good for food, and that it was pleasant to the eyes, and a tree to be desired to make one wise, she took of the fruit thereof, and did eat, and gave also unto her husband with her; and he did eat.

And the eyes of them both were opened, and they knew that they were naked; and they sewed fig leaves together, and made themselves aprons.

And they heard the voice of the Lord God walking in the garden in the cool of the day: and Adam and his wife hid themselves from the presence of the Lord God amongst the trees of the garden.

And the Lord God called unto Adam, and said unto him, Where art thou?

And he said, I heard thy voice in the garden, and I was afraid, because I was naked; and I hid myself.

And he said, Who told thee that thou wast naked? Hast thou eaten of the tree, whereof I commanded thee that thou shouldest not eat?

And the man said, The woman whom thou gavest to be with me, she gave me of the tree, and I did eat.

And the Lord God said unto the woman, What is this that thou hast done? And the woman said, The serpent beguiled me, and I did eat.

And the Lord God said unto the serpent, Because thou hast done this, thou art cursed above all cattle, and above every beast of the field: upon thy belly shalt thou go, and dust shalt thou eat all the days of thy life:

And I will put enmity between thee and the woman, and between thy seed and her seed: it shall bruise thy head, and thou shalt bruise his heel.

Unto the woman he said, I will greatly multiply thy sorrow and thy conception; in sorrow thou shalt bring forth children: and thy desire shall be to thy husband, and he shall rule over thee.

And unto Adam he said, Because thou hast hearkened unto the voice of thy wife, and hast eaten of the tree of which I commanded thee, saying, Thou shalt not eat of it: cursed is the ground for thy sake; in sorrow shalt thou eat of it all the days of thy life;

Thorns also and thistles shall it bring forth to thee; and thou shalt eat the herb of the field:

In the sweat of thy face shalt thou eat bread, till thou return unto the ground; for out of it wast thou taken: for dust thou art, and unto dust shalt thou return. (Genesis 3: 1-19.)

And the Lord God said, Behold, the man is become as one of us, to know good and evil: and now, lest he put forth his hand, and take also of the tree of life, and eat, and live for ever:

Therefore the Lord God sent him forth from the garden of Eden, to till the ground from whence he was taken.

So he drove out the man: and he placed at the east of the garden of Eden Cherubims, and a flaming sword which turned every way, to keep the way of the tree of life. (Genesis 3: 22-24.)

Wherefore, as by one man sin entered into the world, and death by sin; and so death passed upon all men, for that all have sinned. (Romans 5: 12.)

For since by man came death, by man came also the resurrection of the dead.

For as in Adam all die, even so in Christ shall all be made alive. (1 Corinthians 15: 21.)

FATHER. (See Children; for fatherhood of God see God.)

FA'THER. This word is applied in the Scriptures in many senses, the most important of which are: (1) to God as the Father of Christ and of all men; (2) to a male parent; (3) to an ancestor; (4) to a chief or ruler; (5) to the author or source of anything. With relation to its second meaning the Bible is very explicit. It teaches love and veneration for one's parent, as well as obedience and respect. It is equally explicit as to the duty of fathers toward their children, setting forth the needs of love, care, and guidance in the family and religious relations. It also teaches that God is especially watchful for the fatherless. These sentiments, so beautiful and righteous, are an outgrowth of the old Jewish patriarchal system, under which the father of a family was all-powerful.

REFERENCES.

The Duty of Fathers.

For whom the Lord loveth he correcteth; even as a father the son in whom he delighteth. (Proverbs 3: 12.)

He that spareth his rod hateth his son: but he that loveth him chasteneth him betimes. (Proverbs 13: 24.)

Chasten thy son while there is hope, and let not thy soul spare for his crying. (Proverbs 19: 18.)

Foolishness is bound in the heart of a child; but the rod of correction shall drive it far from him. (Proverbs 22: 15.)

Withhold not correction from the child: for if thou beatest him with the rod, he shall not die. (Proverbs 23: 13.)

Correct thy son, and he shall give thee rest; yea, he shall give delight unto thy soul. (Proverbs 29: 17.)

And, ye fathers, provoke not your children to wrath: but bring them up in the nurture and admonition of the Lord. (Ephesians 6: 4.)

Fathers, provoke not your children to anger, lest they be discouraged. (Colossians 3: 21.)

Duty to Fathers.

Honour thy father and thy mother, as the Lord thy God hath commanded thee; that thy days may be prolonged, and that it may go well with thee, in the land which the Lord thy God giveth thee. (Deuteronomy 5: 16.)

Cursed be he that setteth light by his father or his mother: and all the people shall say, Amen. (Deuteronomy 27: 16.)

Ye shall fear every man his mother, and his father, and keep my sabbaths: I am the Lord your God. (Leviticus 19: 3.)

The Fatherless.

Ye shall not afflict any widow, or fatherless child.

If thou afflict them in any wise, and they cry at all unto me, I will surely hear their cry;

And my wrath shall wax hot, and I will kill you with the sword; and your wives shall be widows, and your children fatherless. (Exodus 22: 22-24.)

He doth execute the judgment of the fatherless and widow, and loveth the stranger, in giving him food and raiment. (Deuteronomy 10: 18.)

Cursed be he that perverteth the judgment of the stranger, fatherless, and widow: and all the people shall say, Amen. (Deuteronomy 27: 19.)

Thou hast sent widows away empty, and the arms of the fatherless have been broken.

Therefore snares are round about thee, and sudden fear troubleth thee. (Job 22: 9, 10.)

A father of the fatherless, and a

judge of the widows, is God in his holy habitation. (Psalm 68: 5.)

FAULT.

FAULT—a deviation from the right or a neglect of duty through carelessness or a lack of knowledge rather than through purpose; some error not necessarily a sin.

REFERENCES.

Moreover, if thy brother shall trespass against thee, go and tell him his fault between thee and him alone: if he shall hear thee, thou hast gained thy brother. (Matthew 18: 15.)

Brethren, if a man be overtaken in a fault, ye which are spiritual, restore such a one in the spirit of meekness, considering thyself lest thou also be tempted.

Bear ye one another's burdens, and so fulfill the law of Christ. (Galatians 6: 1, 2.)

Confess your faults one to another, and pray one for another, that ye may be healed. The effectual fervent prayer of a righteous man availeth much. (James 5: 16.)

FEAR.

FEAR—apprehension or dread of impending danger or trouble. All sorts of fears are noted in the Bible, both as to degree and cause. Great stress is laid upon the fear of God as a necessary adjunct to the relations between man and Deity. In the Old Testament this is particularly true; but in the New Testament the degree of fear is reduced and it becomes more of awe and reverence for His greatness and His manifold mercies than of terror.

REFERENCES.
General.

And unto man he said, Behold, the fear of the Lord, that is wisdom; and to depart from evil is understanding. (Job 28: 28.)

The fear of the Lord is the beginning of wisdom: a good understanding have all they that do his commandments: his praise endureth for ever. (Psalm 111: 10.)

The fear of the Lord is the beginning of knowledge: but fools despise wisdom and instruction. (Proverbs 1: 7.)

The fear of the Lord is the beginning of wisdom: and the knowledge of the Holy is understanding. (Proverbs 9: 10.)

Commanded to Fear God.

Thou shalt fear the Lord thy God, and serve him, and shalt swear by his name. (Deuteronomy 6: 13.)

Therefore thou shalt keep the commandments of the Lord thy God, to walk in his ways, and to fear him. (Deuteronomy 8: 6.)

And now, Israel, what doth the Lord thy God require of thee, but to fear the Lord thy God, to walk in all his ways, and to love him, and to serve the Lord thy God with all thy heart and with all thy soul. (Deuteronomy 10: 12.)

Only fear the Lord, and serve him in truth with all your heart: for consider how great things he hath done for you. (1 Samuel 12: 24.)

But the Lord, who brought you up out of the land of Egypt with great power and a stretched out arm, him shall ye fear, and him shall ye worship, and to him shall ye do sacrifice. (2 Kings 17: 36.)

But the Lord your God ye shall fear; and he shall deliver you out of the hand of all your enemies. (2 Kings 17: 39.)

Let all the earth fear the Lord: let all the inhabitants of the world stand in awe of him. (Psalm 33: 8.)

And I say unto you my friends, Be not afraid of them that kill the body, and after that have no more that they can do.

But I will forewarn you whom ye shall fear: Fear him, which after he hath killed hath power to cast into hell: yea, I say unto you, Fear him. (Luke 12: 4, 5.)

Wherefore we receiving a kingdom which cannot be moved, let us have grace, whereby we may serve God acceptably with reverence and godly fear. (Hebrews 12: 28.)

Blessedness of Fearing God.

And Moses said unto the people, Fear not: for God is come to prove you, and that his fear may be before your faces, that ye sin not. (Exodus 20: 20.)

That thou mightest fear the Lord thy God, to keep all his statutes and his commandments, which I command thee, thou, and thy son, and thy son's son, all the days of thy life; and that thy days may be prolonged. (Deuteronomy 6: 2.)

What man is he that feareth the Lord? him shall he teach in the way that he shall choose.

His soul shall dwell at ease; and his seed shall inherit the earth.

The secret of the Lord is with them that fear him; and he will shew them his covenant. (Psalm 25: 12-14.)

Behold, the eye of the Lord is upon them that fear him, upon them that hope in his mercy;

To deliver their soul from death, and to keep them alive in famine. (Psalm 33: 18, 19.)

O fear the Lord, ye his saints: for there is no want to them that fear him. (Psalm 34: 9.)

FELLOWSHIP. (See Communion.)

FEL'LOW-SHIP—the companionship of persons on equal terms; the association together of persons with mutual aims and interests. This is the strict and literal meaning of .the word, and comes nearest to realization, in the religious sense, in the fellowship which exists in a church. With relation to the fellowship of God or Christ with the saints, the saints, out of the benign grace of God and through the sufferings of Christ for them, are permitted the joy of God's and Christ's companionship and association. This is a state better expressed by the word communion.

REFERENCES.

Fellowship of Christ.

God is faithful, by whom ye were called unto the fellowship of his Son Jesus Christ our Lord. (1 Corinthians 1: 9.)

That I may know him, and the power of his resurrection, and the fellowship of his sufferings, being made conformable unto his death. (Philippians 3: 10.)

Fellowship of the Spirit.

If there be therefore any consolation in Christ, if any comfort of love, if any fellowship of the Spirit, if any bowels and mercies,

Fulfil ye my joy, that ye be likeminded, having the same love, being of one accord, of one mind. (Philippians 2: 1, 2.)

Fellowship of the Saints.

And they continued stedfastly in the apostles' doctrine and fellowship, and in breaking of bread, and in prayers. (Acts 2: 42.)

Praying us with much intreaty, that we would receive the gift, and take upon us the fellowship of the ministering to the Saints. (2 Corinthians 8: 4.)

And when James, Cephas, and John,

who seemed to be pillars, perceived the grace that was given unto me, they gave to me and Barnabas the right hands of fellowship, that we should go unto the heathen, and they unto the circumcision. (Galatians 2: 9.)

That which we have seen and heard declare we unto you, that ye also may have fellowship with us: and truly our fellowship is with the Father, and with his Son Jesus Christ. (1 John 1: 3.)

Fellowship with Evil Forbidden.

But I say, that the things which the Gentiles sacrifice, they sacrifice to devils, and not to God: and I would not that ye should have fellowship with devils. (1 Corinthians 10: 20.)

Be ye not unequally yoked together with unbelievers: for what fellowship hath righteousness with unrighteousness? and what communion hath light with darkness? (2 Corinthians 6: 14.)

And have no fellowship with the unfruitful works of darkness, but rather reprove them. (Ephesians 5: 11.)

FILTHINESS. (See Sin.)

FILTH'I-NESS. This word, its source-noun, "filth," and its adjective, "filthy," are used in the Bible in a number of places as figurative of sin. In the original Hebrew and Greek texts the words rendered in English as "filthiness" meant "foul matter" or "anything that soils or defiles."

REFERENCES.

Filthiness of Sin.

How much more abominable and filthy is man, which drinketh iniquity like water? (Job 15: 16.)

They are all gone aside, they are all together become filthy: there is none that doeth good, no, not one. (Psalm 14: 3.)

But we are all as an unclean thing, and all our righteousnesses are as filthy rags; and we all do fade as a leaf; and our iniquities, like the wind, have taken us away. (Isaiah 64: 6.)

In thy filthiness is lewdness: because I have purged thee, and thou wast not purged, thou shalt not be purged from thy filthiness any more till I have caused my fury to rest upon thee. (Ezekiel 24: 13.)

Purification from Filthiness.

When the Lord shall have washed away the filth of the daughters of Zion, and shall have purged the blood of Jerusalem from the midst thereof by the spirit of judgment, and by the spirit of burning. (Isaiah 4: 4.)

And I will scatter thee among the heathen, and disperse thee in the countries, and will consume thy filthiness out of thee. (Ezekiel 22: 15.)

Then will I sprinkle clean water upon you, and ye shall be clean: from all your filthiness, and from all your idols, will I cleanse you. (Ezekiel 36: 25.)

And such were some of you: but ye are washed, but ye are sanctified, but ye are justified in the Name of the Lord Jesus, and by the Spirit of our God. (1 Corinthians 6: 11.)

Having therefore these promises (dearly beloved) let us cleanse ourselves from all filthiness of the flesh and spirit, perfecting holiness in the fear of God. (2 Corinthians 7: 1.)

FIRE.

FIRE. Fire is mentioned in many ways in the Bible, since the Hebrews used it for the various domestic purposes, for warmth, and in their worship of God. Fire was not to be kindled on the Sabbath, and for burnt offerings none could be used except the supernaturally-lighted altar fire. There are a number of instances where fire accompanied divine appearances. The Bible is particularly explicit regarding the use of fire as an instrument of God's judgment and in the place of everlasting torment.

REFERENCES.

God Appears by Fire.

To Moses:

And the Angel of the Lord appeared unto him in a flame of fire out of the midst of a bush; and he looked, and, behold, the bush burned with fire, and the bush was not consumed. (Exodus 3: 2.)

To Israelites:

And the Lord went before them by day in a pillar of a cloud, to lead them the way; and by night in a pillar of fire, to give them light: to go by day and night. (Exodus 13: 21.)

And mount Sinai was altogether on a smoke, because the Lord descended upon it in fire: and the smoke thereof ascended as the smoke of a furnace, and the whole mount quaked greatly. (Exodus 19: 18.)

To Ezekiel:

And I looked, and behold, a whirlwind came out of the north, a great cloud, and a fire infolding itself, and a brightness was about it, and out of the midst thereof as the colour of amber, out of the midst of the fire. (Ezekiel 1: 4.)

To Daniel:

I beheld till the thrones were cast down, and the Ancient of days did sit, whose garment was white as snow, and the hair of his head like the pure wool: his throne was like the fiery flame, and his wheels as burning fire. (Daniel 7: 9.)

Christ to John:

His head and his hairs were white like wool, as white as snow, and his eyes were as a flame of fire,

And his feet like unto fine brass, as if they burned in a furnace: and his voice as the sound of many waters. (Revelation 1: 14, 15.)

Holy Ghost at Pentecost:

And there appeared unto them cloven tongues, like as of fire, and it sat upon each of them.

And they were all filled with the Holy Ghost, and began to speak with other tongues, as the spirit gave them utterance. (Acts 2: 3, 4.)

Fire Emblem of God's Word.

Is not my word like as a fire? saith the Lord; and like a hammer that breaketh the rock in pieces? (Jeremiah 23: 29.)

Fire as Instrument of Judgment.

Then the Lord rained upon Sodom and upon Gomorrah brimstone and fire from the Lord out of heaven. (Genesis 19: 24.)

And Moses stretched forth his rod toward heaven, and the Lord sent thunder and hail, and the fire ran along upon the ground: and the Lord rained hail upon the land of Egypt. (Exodus 9: 23.)

And Nadab and Abihu, the sons of Aaron, took either of them his censer, and put fire therein, and put incense thereon, and offered strange fire before the Lord, which he commanded them not.

And there went out fire from the Lord, and devoured them, and they died before the Lord. (Leviticus 10: 1, 2.)

And when the people complained, it displeased the Lord: and the Lord heard it: and his anger was kindled; and the fire of the Lord burnt among them, and consumed them that were in the uttermost parts of the camp. (Numbers 11: 1.)

And there came out a fire from the Lord, and consumed the two hundred and fifty men that offered incense. (Numbers 16: 35.)

And Elijah answered and said to the captain of fifty, If I be a man of God, then let fire come down from heaven, and consume thee and thy fifty. And there came down fire from heaven, and consumed him and his fifty. (2 Kings 1: 10.)

And to you who are troubled, rest with us, when the Lord Jesus shall be revealed from heaven, with his mighty Angels,

In flaming fire, taking vengeance on them that know not God, and that obey not the Gospel of our Lord Jesus Christ. (2 Thessalonians 1: 7, 8.)

Everlasting Fire.

For a fire is kindled in mine anger, and shall burn unto the lowest hell, and shall consume the earth with her increase, and set on fire the foundations of the mountains. (Deuteronomy 32: 22.)

The sinners in Zion are afraid; fearfulness hath surprised the hypocrites. Who among us shall dwell with the devouring fire? Who among us shall dwell with everlasting burnings? (Isaiah 33: 14.)

And if thy foot offend thee, cut it off: it is better for thee to enter halt into life, than having two feet, to be cast into hell, into the fire that never shall be quenched. (Mark 9: 45.)

FLATTERY.

Flat′ter-y—the act of pleasing another by artful, insincere, and often untruthful, praise. The practice of flattery is a dangerous one, teaching insincerity and leading to lying. The Scriptures utter a number of warnings against it.

REFERENCES.

He that speaketh flattery to his friends, even the eyes of his children shall fail. (Job 17: 5.)

Let me not, I pray you, accept any man's person; neither let me give flattering titles unto man.

For I know not to give flattering titles; in so doing my Maker would soon take me away. (Job 32: 21, 22.)

They speak vanity every one with his neighbour: with flattering lips and with a double heart do they speak.

The Lord shall cut off all flattering lips, and the tongue that speaketh proud things. (Psalm 12: 2, 3.)

For he flattereth himself in his own eyes, until his iniquity be found to be hateful. (Psalm 36: 2.)

Nevertheless they did flatter him with their mouth, and they lied unto him with their tongues. (Psalm 78: 36.)

He that saith unto the wicked, Thou art righteous; him shall the people curse, nations shall abhor him. (Proverbs 24: 24.)

A lying tongue hateth those that are afflicted by it; and a flattering mouth worketh ruin. (Proverbs 26: 28.)

He that rebuketh a man, afterwards shall find more favour than he that flattereth with the tongue. (Proverbs 28: 23.)

A man that flattereth his neighbour spreadeth a net for his feet. (Proverbs 29: 5.)

FLESH.

FLESH. This word appears many times in the Scriptures and with a number of different meanings, the more important of which are (1) the whole of the animal creation, whether man or beast; (2) mankind; (3) the opposite to soul, as modern persons would say, *body and soul*; (4) the actual flesh or tissues of man or beast.

REFERENCES.

Flesh Contrasted with Spirit.

For when we were in the flesh, the motions of sins which were by the law did work in our members, to bring forth fruit unto death. (Romans 7: 5.)

There is therefore now no condemnation to them which are in Christ Jesus, who walk not after the flesh, but after the spirit. (Romans 8: 1.)

Are ye so foolish? having begun in the Spirit, are ye now made perfect by the flesh? (Galatians 3: 3.)

For the flesh lusteth against the Spirit, and the spirit against the flesh: and these are contrary the one to the other: so that ye cannot do the things that ye would. (Galatians 5: 17.)

For he that soweth to his flesh, shall of the flesh reap corruption: but he that soweth to the spirit, shall of the spirit reap life everlasting. (Galatians 6: 8.)

Flesh to Be Subdued.

Having therefore these promises (dearly beloved) let us cleanse ourselves from all filthiness of the flesh and spirit, perfecting holiness in the fear of God. (2 Corinthians 7: 1.)

This I say then, Walk in the spirit, and ye shall not fulfil the lust of the flesh. (Galatians 5: 16.)

In whom also ye are circumcised with the circumcision made without hands, in putting off the body of the sins of the flesh, by the circumcision of Christ. (Colossians 2: 11.)

Forasmuch then as Christ hath suffered for us in the flesh, arm yourselves likewise with the same mind: for he that hath suffered in the flesh, hath ceased from sin:

That he no longer should live the rest of his time in the flesh, to the lusts of men, but to the will of God. (1 Peter 4: 1, 2.)

For all that is in the world, the lust of the flesh, the lust of the eyes, and the pride of life, is not of the Father, but is of the world. (1 John 2: 16.)

God Manifest in Flesh.

And the Word was made flesh, and dwelt among us (and we beheld his glory, the glory as of the only begotten of the Father,) full of grace and truth. (John 1: 14.)

And without controversy, great is the mystery of godliness: God was manifest in the flesh, justified in the Spirit, seen of Angels, preached unto the Gentiles, believed on in the world, received up into glory. (1 Timothy 3: 16.)

For Christ also hath once suffered for sins, the just for the unjust, that he might bring us to God, being put to death in the flesh, but quickened by the Spirit. (1 Peter 3: 18.)

FLOOD.

FLOOD. The Flood is the term commonly given to the great cataclysm described in Genesis 7 and 8, sent by God as a punishment for sin and destroying every living thing on earth except Noah and his family of seven and specimens of the various members of the animal kingdom. There has been a tendency upon the part of some critics and commentators to deny that such a thing as the Flood ever took place upon the ground that science shows no evidence of it in buried remains of the persons, animals, places, and things overwhelmed by it; but such statements are not borne out by facts and reason. In the first place, the Jews are by no means the only race that possess the tradition of a great flood. The Egyptians and Assyrians, both older nations than the Jews, told of such an event. The Hindu races had and still have such a tradition, and so did the ancient Greeks, the Celts, and the Scythians. Strange to say, too, the Chinese possess a legend somewhat similar to the Jewish account, while on this continent the Peruvians, the Aztecs, and some of the North American aborigines, had a flood tradition. What is stranger still, many of the tribes of the South Sea Islands tell similar stories. The investigation of such a tradition thus resolves itself down to an investigation of the extent of the flood rather than to whether or not it happened, which fact seems to be proved by the widespread character of the tradition. If science shows no evidence of a great cataclysm, covering the whole earth, and yet different peoples, separated by vast distances and by oceans, have some knowledge of one, there must have been something of the sort at a time and place from which these different nations could have picked up the tradition. The logical deduction from this is that all of mankind had its origin in one place and from one common stock, and that this place was the scene and the people the victims of a local inundation. This fits in very well with the theory that the cradle of the human race was in Southwestern Asia, that there was a great flood there, and that it happened before the dispersion of the tribes that resulted in the peopling of the world. This is the solution of the problem that has been accepted by the more advanced thinkers among theologians and scientists.

References.—Genesis, chapters 7 and 8.

FOOL.

FOOL. The Bible uses the word "fool" usually to describe a person lacking in moral qualifications rather than intellectual ones; in other words, the Biblical fool is not an idiot or a person of weak mind, but a person who reasons wrong or whose conduct is actuated by other things than right or religion, or a person who through perverseness of will does, and says foolish things.

REFERENCES.

Fools Described.

It is as sport to a fool to do mischief: but a man of understanding hath wisdom. (Proverbs 10: 23.)

A prudent man concealeth knowledge: but the heart of fools proclaimeth foolishness. (Proverbs 12: 23.)

The desire accomplished is sweet to the soul: but it is abomination to fools to depart from evil. (Proverbs 13: 19.)

The wisdom of the prudent is to understand his way: but the folly of fools is deceit.

Fools make a mock at sin: but among the righteous there is favour. (Proverbs 14: 8, 9.)

A wise man feareth, and departeth from evil: but the fool rageth, and is confident. (Proverbs 14: 16.)

Wisdom resteth in the heart of him that hath understanding: but that which is in the midst of fools is made known. (Proverbs 14: 33.)

The tongue of the wise useth knowledge aright: but the mouth of fools poureth out foolishness. (Proverbs 15: 2.)

The lips of the wise disperse knowledge: but the heart of the foolish doeth not so. (Proverbs 15: 7.)

The heart of him that hath understanding seeketh knowledge: but the mouth of fools feedeth on foolishness. (Proverbs 15: 14.)

Understanding is a wellspring of life unto him that hath it: but the instruction of fools is folly. (Proverbs 16: 22.)

Wherefore is there a price in the hand of a fool to get wisdom, seeing he hath no heart to it? (Proverbs 17: 16.)

Wisdom is before him that hath understanding; but the eyes of a fool are in the ends of the earth. (Proverbs 17: 24.)

The fool foldeth his hands together, and eateth his own flesh. (Ecclesiastes 4: 5.)

The words of wise men are heard in quiet more than the cry of him that ruleth among fools. (Ecclesiastes 9: 17.)

Yea also, when he that is a fool walketh by the way, his wisdom faileth him, and he saith to every one that he is a fool. (Ecclesiastes 10: 3.)

Treatment and Punishment.

Speak not in the ears of a fool: for he will despise the wisdom of thy words. (Proverbs 23: 9.)

A whip for the horse, a bridle for the ass, and a rod for the fool's back.

Answer not a fool according to his folly, lest thou also be like unto him.

Answer a fool according to his folly, lest he be wise in his own conceit. (Proverbs 26: 3-5.)

Though thou shouldest bray a fool in a mortar among wheat with a pestle, yet will not his foolishness depart from him. (Proverbs 27: 22.)

For the turning away of the simple shall slay them, and the prosperity of fools shall destroy them. (Proverbs 1: 32.)

The wise in heart will receive commandments: but a prating fool shall fall. (Proverbs 10: 8.)

He that troubleth his own house shall inherit the wind: and the fool shall be servant to the wise of heart. (Proverbs 11: 29.)

He that walketh with wise men shall be wise: but a companion of fools shall be destroyed. (Proverbs 13: 20.)

The words of a wise man's mouth are gracious; but the lips of a fool will swallow up himself. (Ecclesiastes 10: 12.)

FORBEARANCE. (See Longsuffering.)

For-bear'ance—patience with another under trying circumstances. God's people are taught to have forbearance one with another, just as God has forbearance.

REFERENCES.

Forbearance Commended.

I therefore the prisoner of the Lord, beseech you that ye walk worthy of the vocation wherewith ye are called,

With all lowliness and meekness, with longsuffering, forbearing one another in love. (Ephesians 4: 1, 2.)

And ye masters, do the same things unto them, forbearing threatening: knowing that your master also is in heaven, neither is there respect of persons with him. (Ephesians 6: 9.)

Put on therefore (as the elect of God, holy and beloved) bowels of mercies, kindness, humbleness of mind, meekness, longsuffering,

Forbearing one another, and forgiving one another, if any man have a quarrel against any: even as Christ forgave you, so also do ye. (Colossians 3: 12, 13.)

Forbearance of God.

Or despisest thou the riches of his goodness, and forbearance, and longsuffering, not knowing that the goodness of God leadeth thee to repentance? (Romans 2: 4.)

Being justified freely by his grace, through the redemption that is in Jesus Christ:

Whom God hath set forth to be a propitiation, through faith in his blood, to declare his righteousness for the remission of sins that are past, through the forbearance of God. (Romans 3: 24, 25.)

FOREKNOWLEDGE.

FORE-KNOWL'EDGE. Foreknowledge is knowledge of a thing before it happens. In the Scriptural sense foreknowledge is one of the attributes of God, since He knows all things, past, present, and future, and is the Supreme Intelligence.

REFERENCES.

Him, being delivered by the determinate counsel and foreknowledge of God, ye have taken, and by wicked hands have crucified and slain. (Acts 2: 23.)

For whom he did foreknow, he also did predestinate to be conformed to the image of his son, that he might be the firstborn amongst many brethren. (Romans 8: 29.)

God hath not cast away his people which he foreknew. (Romans 11: 2.)

FOREORDINATION. (See Predestination.)

FORGIVENESS.

FOR-GIVE'NESS. The words of the Lord's Prayer embody the gospel of forgiveness— "Forgive us our trespasses as we forgive those who trespass against us." As we forgive so are we forgiven. It is a prerogative of God only to forgive sins, and forgiveness is offered full and free to all those who truly believe. Man is taught to have the forgiving spirit irrespective of repentance of the other party interested.

REFERENCES.

Mutual Forgiveness Commanded.

So shall ye say unto Joseph, Forgive, I pray thee now, the trespass of thy brethren, and their sin; for they did unto thee evil: and now, we pray thee, forgive the trespass of the servants of the God of thy father. And Joseph wept when they spake unto him. (Genesis 50: 17.)

Therefore if thou bring thy gift to the altar, and there rememberest that thy brother hath ought against thee;

Leave there thy gift before the altar, and go thy way; first be reconciled to thy brother, and then come and offer thy gift. (Matthew 5: 23, 24.)

For, if ye forgive men their trespasses, your heavenly Father will also forgive you.

But, if ye forgive not men their trespasses, neither will your Father forgive your trespasses. (Matthew 6: 14, 15.)

Then came Peter to him, and said, Lord, how oft shall my brother sin against me, and I forgive him? till seven times?

Jesus saith unto him, *I say not unto thee, Until seven times: but, Until seventy times seven.* (Matthew 18: 21, 22.)

So likewise shall my heavenly Father do also unto you, if ye from your hearts forgive not every one his brother their trespasses. (Matthew 18: 35.)

And forgive us our sins: for we also forgive every one that is indebted to us. And lead us not into temptation, but deliver us from evil. (Luke 11: 4.)

So that contrariwise, ye ought rather to forgive him, and comfort him, lest perhaps such a one should be swallowed up with overmuch sorrow. (2 Corinthians 2: 7.)

And be ye kind one to another, tender-hearted, forgiving one another, even as God for Christ's sake hath forgiven you. (Ephesians 4: 32.)

Forbearing one another, and forgiving one another, if any man have a quarrel against any: even as Christ forgave you, so also do ye. (Colossians 3: 13.)

Forgiveness Prayed for.

And Moses returned unto the Lord, and said, Oh, this people have sinned a great sin, and have made them gods of gold.

Yet now, if thou wilt forgive their sin: and if not, blot me, I pray thee, out of thy book which thou hast written. (Exodus 32: 31, 32.)

And hearken thou to the supplication of thy servant, and of thy people Israel, when they shall pray toward this place: and hear thou in heaven thy dwelling place: and when thou hearest, forgive. (1 Kings 8: 30.)

Look upon mine affliction and my pain; and forgive all my sins. (Psalm 25: 18.)

I acknowledged my sin unto thee, and mine iniquity have I not hid. I said, I will confess my transgressions unto the Lord; and thou forgavest the iniquity of my sin. Selah. (Psalm 32: 5.)

Have mercy upon me, O God, according to thy loving-kindness: according unto the multitude of thy tender mercies blot out my transgressions.

Wash me thoroughly from mine iniquity, and cleanse me from my sin.

For I acknowledge my transgressions: and my sin is ever before me. (Psalm 51: 1-3.)

Help us, O God of our salvation, for the glory of thy name: and deliver us, and purge away our sins, for thy name's sake. (Psalm 79: 9.)

If thou, Lord, shouldest mark iniquities, O Lord, who shall stand?

But there is forgiveness with thee, that thou mayest be feared. (Psalm 130: 3, 4.)

And forgive us our debts, as we forgive our debtors. (Matthew 6: 12.)

Forgiveness Promised.

If my people, which are called by my name, shall humble themselves, and pray, and seek my face, and turn from their wicked ways; then will I hear from heaven, and will forgive their sin, and will heal their land. (2 Chronicles 7: 14.)

Let the wicked forsake his way, and the unrighteous man his thoughts: and let him return unto the Lord, and he will have mercy upon him; and to our God, for he will abundantly pardon. (Isaiah 55: 7.)

Who is a God like unto thee, that pardoneth iniquity, and passeth by the transgression of the remnant of his heritage? he retaineth not his anger for ever, because he delighteth in mercy. (Micah 7: 18.)

And that repentance and remission of sins should be preached in his Name, among all nations, beginning at Jerusalem. (Luke 24: 47.)

Him hath God exalted with his right hand to be a Prince and a Saviour, for to give repentance to Israel, and forgiveness of sins. (Acts 5: 31.)

To open their eyes, and to turn them from darkness to light, and from the power of Satan unto God, that they may receive forgiveness of sins, and inheritance among them which are sanctified by faith that is in me. (Acts 26: 18.)

In whom we have redemption through his blood, even the forgiveness of sins. (Colossians 1: 14.)

And the prayer of Faith shall save

the sick, and the Lord shall raise him up: and if he have committed sins, they shall be forgiven him. (James 5: 15.)

If we confess our sins, he is faithful and just to forgive us our sins, and to cleanse us from all unrighteousness. (1 John 1: 9.)

FRIENDS.

FRIENDS. Friends and friendship are often mentioned in the Bible, which teaches the beauty and value of good and true friends. The instance of David and Jonathan is one of the most noted examples of this condition of mutual love between persons. The Bible also teaches that certain dangers may arise from evil friends. Men and women are ordered to avoid friendship with the world.

REFERENCES.

Value of Friends.

A man that hath friends must shew himself friendly: and there is a friend that sticketh closer than a brother. (Proverbs 18: 24.)

As in water face answereth to face, so the heart of man to man. (Proverbs 27: 19.)

Can two walk together, except they be agreed? (Amos 3: 3.)

A friend loveth at all times, and a brother is born for adversity. (Proverbs 17: 17.)

Faithful are the wounds of a friend; but the kisses of an enemy are deceitful. (Proverbs 27: 6.)

Thine own friend, and thy father's friend, forsake not; neither go into thy brother's house in the day of thy calamity: for better is a neighbour that is near than a brother far off. (Proverbs 27: 10.)

Two are better than one; because they have a good reward for their labour.

For if they fall, the one will lift up

his fellow: but woe to him that is alone when he falleth; for he hath not another to help him up.

Again, if two lie together, then they have heat: but how can one be warm alone?

And if one prevail against him, two shall withstand him; and a threefold cord is not quickly broken. (Ecclesiastes 4: 9-12.)

Evil Friends.

The soul of the wicked desireth evil: his neighbour findeth no favour in his eyes. (Proverbs 21: 10.)

Make no friendship with an angry man; and with a furious man thou shalt not go;

Lest thou learn his ways, and get a snare to thy soul. (Proverbs 22: 24, 25.)

Confidence in an unfaithful man in time of trouble is like a broken tooth, and a foot out of joint. (Proverbs 25: 19.)

Friendship of David and Jonathan.

And it came to pass, when he had made an end of speaking unto Saul, that the soul of Jonathan was knit with the soul of David, and Jonathan loved him as his own soul.

And Saul took him that day, and would let him go no more home to his father's house.

Then Jonathan and David made a covenant, because he loved him as his own soul. (1 Samuel 18: 1-3.)

Then said Jonathan unto David, Whatsoever thy soul desireth, I will even do it for thee. (1 Samuel 20: 4.)

I am distressed for thee, my brother Jonathan: very pleasant hast thou been unto me: thy love to me was wonderful, passing the love of women. (2 Samuel 1: 26.)

FUTURE. (See Immortality, Life.)

GABRIEL.

GA'BRI-EL—a form of a Hebrew word meaning "the mighty one of God." Gabriel is the name given in the Scriptures to an angel sent by God to communicate certain expressions of His will, notably the birth of Jesus to the Virgin Mary and the birth of John the Baptist to Zacharias. Jewish and Christian writers give Gabriel high rank in the angelic host, both by reason of the importance of his missions and from his own statement that he stood in the presence of God. Scripture, however, is silent as to his rank.

References.—Daniel 8: 16; 9: 21; Luke 1: 19; 1: 26.)

GALATIA.

GA-LA'TIA—a province of the Roman Empire in Asia Minor. The people came of a mixed race. The gospel was introduced into Galatia by Paul, and he wrote to the Galatians the epistle which bears their name.

GALILEE.

GAL'I-LEE—a form of a Hebrew word meaning "a circle." Galilee was the name of one of the three main divisions of Palestine. It lay furthest to the north. It was and is a very pleasant and fruitful country. It is chiefly remarkable, however, because it was the country of Jesus, who was born in one of its chief cities and spent almost the whole of his life there. All of his disciples except the traitor Judas were Galileans. It was in Galilee, too, that He made His first appearance after the Resurrection. The Romans did not look with favor upon the natives of Galilee, for the province was noted for its turbulence and readiness to break into revolt against the Roman rule whenever opportunity offered. Many of its inhabitants were hardy fishermen of the Sea of Galilee.

GAMALIEL.

GA-MA'LI-EL—a form of a Hebrew word meaning "reward of God." There are two men of the name of Gamaliel mentioned in the Bible, but the one of importance is that Gamaliel under whom the apostle Paul studied in his youth and early manhood. He was a man of profound erudition and great scholarship, a Pharisee, a rabbi, and a high member of the Sanhedrin for many years, and probably the president of that body. He was noted as a theologian and authority on the religion of the Hebrews. Through his interference in their behalf the apostles were saved from death (see Acts 5: 34). It has been argued from this that he was a convert to Christianity, but the weight of evidence is very much against such a presumption. The act was due probably to his recognition of the fact that if Christian doctrines were true it would be useless to combat them, and that if false they would leave no lasting impression, while to fight them would only be to repeat religious history which shows that religious opinions only gain strength by opposition.

GATE.

GATE. Gates figure to a large extent in the Bible. Ancient cities, being walled, gates of great strength and size were almost always before the eye of mankind, and therefore came largely into speech, both directly and figuratively. In this last sense we find a number of important references to gates in the Scriptures.

REFERENCES.

Gates of Heaven.

Lift up your heads, O ye gates; and be ye lift up, ye everlasting doors; and the King of glory shall come in. (Psalm 24: 7.)

Open ye the gates, that the righteous nation which keepeth the truth may enter in. (Isaiah 26: 2.)

Gates of Death and Hell.

Have mercy upon me, O Lord: consider my trouble which I suffer of them that hate me, thou that liftest me up from the gates of death. (Psalm 9: 13.)

I said in the cutting off of my days, I shall go to the gates of the grave: I am deprived of the residue of my years. (Isaiah 38: 10.)

And I say also unto thee, That thou art Peter, and upon this rock I will build my church; and the gates of hell shall not prevail against it. (Matthew 16: 18.)

Straight and Wide Gates.

Enter ye in at the strait gate, for wide is the gate, and broad is the way that leadeth to destruction, and many there be which go in thereat:

Because strait is the gate, and narrow is the way which leadeth unto life, and few there be that find it. (Matthew 7: 13, 14.)

Strive to enter in at the strait gate: for many, I say unto you, will seek to enter in, and shall not be able. (Luke 13: 24.)

GENNESARET.

GEN-NES′A-RET. The Sea of Galilee was also known as the Sea of Tiberias and Sea of Gennesaret, from a town of the same name on its shore, the site of which is now lost. It is about 13 miles long and 6 wide. In Christ's time there were nine cities on its shores. Of these only one remains, Tiberias, and it is almost in ruins.

GENTILES.

GEN′TILES—a form of a Latin word which the Jews used to describe certain non-Jewish races. It was applied to all individuals or communities not under the Mosaic law and worshiping Jehovah.

GENTLENESS.

GEN′TLE-NESS—the state of being gentle. The Bible is clear as to the beauty of gentleness as one of the virtues, and all righteous persons are exhorted to cultivate it.

REFERENCES.

But the fruit of the spirit is love, joy, peace, longsuffering, gentleness, goodness, faith. (Galatians 5: 22.)

And the servant of the Lord must not strive: but be gentle unto all men, apt to teach, patient. (2 Timothy 2: 24.)

To speak evil of no man, to be no brawlers, but gentle, shewing all meekness unto all men. (Titus 3: 2.)

GIDEON.

GID′E-ON—a form of a Hebrew word meaning "destroyer." Gideon was the name of the fifth judge of Israel. He lived about 1100 B.C., and was regarded as one of the race's great heroes. His chief work was the defeat of a vast Midianitish army and the overthrow of the galling Midianite power.

References.—Judges 6, 7, and 8.

GIFT.

GIFT — anything voluntarily transferred from one person to another; also some power, talent, or ability given by God to men in general or to an individual.

REFERENCES.

Spiritual Gifts.

The Lord will give strength unto his people; the Lord will bless his people with peace. (Psalm 29: 11.)

Thou hast ascended on high, thou hast led captivity captive: thou hast received gifts for men; yea, for the rebellious also, that the Lord God might dwell among them. (Psalm 68: 18.)

For the Lord God is a sun and shield: the Lord will give grace and glory; no good thing will he withhold from them that walk uprightly. (Psalm 84: 11.)

For the Lord giveth wisdom: out of his mouth cometh knowledge and understanding. (Proverbs 2: 6.)

And I will give them one heart, and I will put a new spirit within you; and I will take the stony heart out of their flesh, and will give them an heart of flesh. (Ezekiel 11: 19.)

Forasmuch then as God gave them

the like gift as he did unto us, who believed on the Lord Jesus Christ: what was I that I could withstand God? (Acts 11: 17.)

Having then gifts, differing according to the grace that is given to us, whether prophecy, let us prophesy according to the proportion of faith. (Romans 12: 6.)

So that ye come behind in no gift; waiting for the coming of our Lord Jesus Christ. (1 Corinthians 1: 7.)

Now there are diversities of gifts, but the same Spirit.

And there are differences of administrations, but the same Lord.

And there are diversities of operations, but it is the same God which worketh all in all.

But the manifestation of the Spirit is given to every man to profit withal.

For to one is given by the Spirit the word of wisdom; to another the word of knowledge by the same Spirit;

To another faith by the same Spirit; to another the gifts of healing by the same Spirit;

To another the working of miracles; to another prophecy; to another discerning of spirits; to another divers kinds of tongues; to another the interpretation of tongues. (1 Corinthians 12: 4-10.)

Follow after charity, and desire spiritual gifts, but rather that ye may prophesy. (1 Corinthians 14: 1.)

Every good gift and every perfect gift is from above, and cometh down from the Father of lights, with whom is no variableness, neither shadow of turning. (James 1: 17.)

Temporal Gifts.

And God said, Let us make man in our image, after our likeness: and let them have dominion over the fish of the sea, and over the fowl of the air, and over the cattle, and over all the earth, and over every creeping thing that creepeth upon the earth. (Genesis 1: 26.)

Therefore God give thee of the dew of heaven, and the fatness of the earth, and plenty of corn and wine. (Genesis 27: 28.)

The young lions do lack, and suffer hunger: but they that seek the Lord shall not want any good thing. (Psalm 34: 10.)

Gift of God and Holy Ghost.

Jesus answered, and said unto her, *If thou knewest the gift of God, and who it is that saith to thee, Give me to drink; thou wouldest have asked of him, and he would have given thee living water.* (John 4: 10.)

Then Peter said unto them, Repent, and be baptized every one of you in the name of Jesus Christ for the remission of sins, and ye shall receive the gift of the Holy Ghost. (Acts 2: 38.)

But Peter said unto him, Thy money perish with thee, because thou hast thought that the gift of God may be purchased with money. (Acts 8: 20.)

Thanks be unto God for his unspeakable gift. (2 Corinthians 9: 15.)

GILBOA. (See Saul.)

GIL-BO'A—meaning "bubbling fountain"—the place where Saul met defeat at the hands of the Philistines and took his own life.

Reference—1 Samuel 31: 1.

GILGAL.

GIL'GAL—meaning "circle" or "wheel." Gilgal was the name of the place where the Israelites first encamped after entering Palestine. It was their headquarters for a part of the time they were engaged in conquering the land. There are several other Gilgals mentioned in Scripture, but none of importance.

Reference.—Joshua 4: 19.

GLUTTONY

GLUT'TON-Y—excess in eating and extravagant indulgence in food. Scripture declares gluttony to be a practice not to be indulged in by the righteous, and condemns it in a number of passages.

REFERENCES.

When thou sittest to eat with a ruler, consider diligently what is before thee:

And put a knife to thy throat, if thou be a man given to appetite. (Proverbs 23: 1, 2.)

Be not among wine-bibbers; among riotous eaters of flesh:

For the drunkard and the glutton shall come to poverty: and drowsiness shall clothe a man with rags. (Proverbs 23: 20, 21.)

Hast thou found honey? eat so much as is sufficient for thee, lest thou be filled therewith, and vomit it. (Proverbs 25: 16.)

For the time past of our life may suffice us to have wrought the will of the Gentiles, when we walked in lasciviousness, lusts, excess of wine, revellings, banquetings, and abominable idolatries. (1 Peter 4: 3.)

But the end of all things is at hand: be ye therefore sober, and watch unto prayer. (1 Peter 4: 7.)

GOD. (See Christ, Gospel, Holy Ghost, Jesus, etc.)

GOD. God is that infinitely great, intelligent, and perfect Being who created the universe and all things in it, and is its supreme ruler and governor. He was neither created nor made, but existed of Himself from all eternity. He is perfect in all ways. He is all mighty in power, all complete in wisdom and knowledge, and all holy in goodness and

grace. His attributes are spirituality, infinity, eternity, immutability, self-sufficiency, perfection, freedom, omnipotence, omniscience, omnipresence, justice, truth, love, mercy, and grace. He is incomprehensible to man in the sense that man cannot come to a full and complete understanding of Him, but He has made sufficient revelations of Himself to man to enable man to know Him. This knowledge of God is innate in man, and it also is acquired. The fullest disclosure of His nature so far made by Him was in the sending of His Son, Jesus the Christ, the god-man, to earth to be a free, living, and acceptable sacrifice and atonement for the sins of the world.

God is God the Father, God the Son, and God the Holy Ghost, three persons and one god, equal in power and co-eternal. This doctrine is not taught in the Old Testament for the reason that God the Son and God the Holy Ghost had not yet been revealed to man, the latter especially not being fully revealed until after the death, resurrection, and ascension of God, the Son. In the New Testament, although not named as the doctrine of the Trinity, the doctrine is clearly and lucidly set forth in the gospels and in the teachings of the personal representatives of Jesus, the apostles.

For God the Jews had two names—Jehovah and Elohim. Elohim was more of an abstract title, signifying pretty much the same as the English word "deity." Jehovah, however, was a more direct and meaningful appellation, signifying the manifest, personal, revealed Elohim.

REFERENCES.

God Described.

As the Lord God Almighty:

And when Abram was ninety years old and nine, the Lord appeared to Abram, and said unto him, I am the Almighty God; walk before me, and be thou perfect. (Genesis 17: 1.)

And I appeared unto Abraham, unto Isaac, and unto Jacob by the name of God Almighty, but by my name JEHOVAH was I not known to them. (Exodus 6: 3.)

I am Alpha and Omega, the beginning and the ending, saith the Lord, which is, and which was, and which is to come, the Almighty. (Revelation 1: 8.)

As the Creator:

In the beginning God created the heaven and the earth. (Genesis 1: 1.)

So God created man in his own image, in the image of God created he him; male and female created he them. (Genesis 1: 27.)

Thou, even thou, art Lord alone; thou hast made heaven, the heaven of heavens, with all their host, the earth, and all things that are therein, the seas, and all that is therein, and thou preservest them all; and the host of heaven worshippeth thee. (Nehemiah 9: 6.)

The heavens declare the glory of God; and the firmament sheweth his handy work. (Psalm 19: 1.)

The heavens are thine, the earth also is thine: as for the world, and the fulness thereof, thou hast founded them. (Psalm 89: 11.)

O Lord of hosts, God of Israel, that dwellest between the cherubims, thou art the God, even thou alone, of all the kingdoms of the earth; thou hast made heaven and earth. (Isaiah 37: 16.)

Drop down, ye heavens, from above, and let the skies pour down righteousness: let the earth open, and let them bring forth salvation, and let righteousness spring up together; I the Lord have created it. (Isaiah 45: 8.)

All things were made by him, and without him was not anything made that was made. (John 1: 3.)

For by him were all things created that are in heaven, and that are in earth, visible and invisible, whether they be thrones, or dominions, or principalities, or powers: all things were created by him, and for him. (Colossians 1: 16.)

As the Father:

At that time Jesus answered, and said, *I thank thee, O Father, Lord of heaven and earth, because thou hast hid these things from the wise and prudent, and hast revealed them unto babes.* (Matthew 11: 25.)

Go ye therefore, and teach all nations, baptizing them in the Name of the Father, and of the Son, and of the holy Ghost. (Matthew 28: 19.)

And he said, *Abba, Father, all things are possible unto thee, take away this cup from me: Nevertheless, not that I will, but what thou wilt.* (Mark 14: 36.)

Then said Jesus, *Father, forgive them, for they know not what they do:* And they parted his raiment, and cast lots. (Luke 23: 34.)

And when Jesus had cried with a loud voice, he said, *Father, into thy hands I commend my spirit:* And having said thus, he gave up the ghost. (Luke 23: 46.)

And the Word was made flesh, and dwelt among us, (and we beheld his glory, the glory as of the only begotten of the Father,) full of grace and truth. (John 1: 14.)

That ye may with one mind and one mouth glorify God, even the Father of our Lord Jesus Christ. (Acts 15: 6.)

But to us there is but one God, the Father, of whom are all things, and we in him, and one Lord Jesus Christ, by whom are all things, and we by him. (1 Corinthians 8: 6.)

Then cometh the end, when he shall have delivered up the kingdom to God even the Father, when he shall have put down all rule, and all authority and power. (1 Corinthians 15: 24.)

Blessed be God, even the Father of our Lord Jesus Christ, the Father of mercies, and the God of all comfort. (2 Corinthians 1: 3.)

And if ye call on the Father, who without respect of persons judgeth according to every man's work, pass the time of your sojourning here in fear. (1 Peter 1: 17.)

God's Attributes.

Eternal:

And Abraham planted a grove in Beer-sheba, and called there on the name of the Lord, the everlasting God. (Genesis 21: 33.)

For I lift up my hand to heaven, and say, I live for ever. (Deuteronomy 32: 40.)

The eternal God is thy refuge, and underneath are the everlasting arms: and he shall thrust out the enemy from before thee; and shall say, Destroy them. (Deuteronomy 33: 27.)

But the Lord shall endure for ever: he hath prepared his throne for judgment. (Psalm 9: 7.)

Before the mountains were brought forth, or ever thou hadst formed the earth and the world, even from everlasting to everlasting, thou art God. (Psalm 90: 2.)

Thy throne is established of old: thou art from everlasting. (Psalm 93: 2.)

But thou, O Lord, shalt endure for ever; and thy remembrance unto all generations. (Psalm 102: 12.)

Thy name, O Lord, endureth for ever; and thy memorial, O Lord, throughout all generations. (Psalm 135: 13.)

The Lord shall reign for ever, even thy God, O Zion, unto all generations. Praise ye the Lord. (Psalm 146: 10.)

For thus saith the high and lofty One that inhabiteth eternity, whose name is Holy; I dwell in the high and holy place, with him also that is of a contrite and humble spirit, to revive the spirit of the humble, and to revive the heart of the contrite ones. (Isaiah 57: 15.)

Doubtless thou art our Father, though Abraham be ignorant of us, and Israel acknowledge us not: thou, O Lord, art our Father, our Redeemer: thy name is from everlasting. (Isaiah 63: 16.)

But the Lord is the true God, he is the living God; and an everlasting King: at his wrath the earth shall tremble, and the nations shall not be able to abide his indignation. (Jeremiah 10: 10.)

Which in his times he shall shew, who is the blessed and only Potentate, the King of kings, and the Lord of lords;

Who only hath immortality, dwelling in the light which no man can approach unto; whom no man hath seen, nor can see: to whom be honour and power everlasting. Amen. (1 Timothy 6: 15, 16.)

But, beloved, be not ignorant of this one thing, that one day is with the Lord as a thousand years, and a thousand years as one day. (2 Peter 3: 8.)

John to the seven churches which are in Asia: Grace be unto you, and peace, from him which is, and which was, and which is to come; and from the seven Spirits which are before his throne. (Revelation 1: 4.)

I am Alpha and Omega, the beginning and the ending, saith the Lord, which is, and which was, and which is to come, the Almighty. (Revelation 1: 8.)

Immutable:

God is not a man, that he should lie; neither the son of man, that he should repent: hath he said, and shall he not do it? or hath he spoken, and shall he not make it good? (Numbers 23: 19.)

And also the Strength of Israel will not lie nor repent: for he is not a man, that he should repent. (1 Samuel 15: 29.)

But he is in one mind, and who can turn him? and what his soul desireth, even that he doeth. (Job 23: 13.)

The counsel of the Lord standeth for ever, the thoughts of his heart to all generations. (Psalm 33: 11.)

For ever, O Lord, thy word is settled in heaven. (Psalm 119: 89.)

For I am the Lord, I change not; therefore ye sons of Jacob are not consumed. (Micah 3: 6.)

Every good gift and every perfect gift is from above, and cometh down from the Father of lights, with whom is no variableness, neither shadow of turning. (James 1: 7.)

Omniscient:

He discovereth deep things out of darkness, and bringeth out to light the shadow of death. (Job 12: 22.)

Hell is naked before him, and destruction hath no covering. (Job 36: 6.)

The Lord looketh from heaven; he beholdeth all the sons of men.

From the place of his habitation he looketh upon all the inhabitants of the earth. (Psalm 33: 13, 14.)

If I say, Surely the darkness shall cover me; even the night shall be light about me.

Yea, the darkness hideth not from thee; but the night shineth as the day: the darkness and the light are both alike to thee. (Psalm 139: 11, 12.)

Great is our Lord, and of great power: his understanding is infinite. (Psalm 147: 5.)

The eyes of the Lord are in every place, beholding the evil and the good. (Proverbs 15: 3.)

Though they dig into hell, thence shall mine hand take them; though they climb to heaven, thence will I bring them down.

And though they hide themselves in the top of Carmel, I will search and take them out thence; and though they be hid from my sight in the bottom of the sea, thence will I command the serpent, and he shall bite them. (Amos 9: 2, 3.)

Known unto God are all his works from the beginning of the world. (Acts 15: 18.)

For if our heart condemn us, God is greater than our heart, and knoweth all things. (1 John 3: 20.)

Omnipresent:

But will God indeed dwell on the earth? behold, the heaven and heaven of heavens cannot contain thee; how much less this house that I have builded? (1 Kings 8: 27.)

But who is able to build him a house, seeing the heaven and heaven of heavens cannot contain him? who am I then, that I should build him a house, save only to burn sacrifice before him? (2 Chronicles 2: 6.)

Whither shall I go from thy Spirit? or whither shall I flee from thy presence?

If I ascend up into heaven, thou art there: if I make my bed in hell, behold, thou art there.

If I take the wings of the morning, and dwell in the uttermost parts of the sea;

Even there shall thy hand lead me, and thy right hand shall hold me. (Psalm 139: 7-10.)

Thus saith the Lord, The heaven is my throne, and the earth is my footstool: where is the house that ye build unto me? and where is the place of my rest? (Isaiah 66: 1.)

Am I a God at hand, saith the Lord, and not a God afar off? (Jeremiah 23: 23.)

That they should seek the Lord, if haply they might feel after him, and find him, though he be not far from every one of us. (Acts 17: 27.)

Omnipotent:

And when Abram was ninety years old and nine, the Lord appeared to Abram, and said unto him, I am the Almighty God; walk before me, and be thou perfect. (Genesis 17: 1.)

And I appeared unto Abraham, unto Isaac, and unto Jacob, by the name of God Almighty; but by my name JEHOVAH was I not known to them. (Exodus 6: 3.)

Behold, happy is the man whom God correcteth: therefore despise not thou the chastening of the Almighty. (Job 5: 17.)

When the Almighty scattered kings in it, it was white as snow in Salmon. (Psalm 68: 14.)

But Jesus beheld them, and said unto them, *With men this is impossible; but with God all things are possible.* (Matthew 19: 26.)

And Jesus looking upon them saith, *With men it is impossible, but not with God: for with God all things are possible.* (Mark 10: 27.)

I am Alpha and Omega, the beginning and the ending, saith the Lord, which is, and which was, and which is

to come, the Almighty. (Revelation 1: 8.)

And I heard as it were the voice of a great multitude, and as the voice of many waters, and as the voice of mighty thunderings, saying, Alleluia: for the Lord God omnipotent reigneth. (Revelation 19: 6.)

Invisible:

And he said, Thou canst not see my face: for there shall no man see me, and live. (Exodus 33: 20.)

No man hath seen God at any time; the only begotten Son, which is in the bosom of the Father, he hath declared him. (John 1: 18.)

And the Father himself, which hath sent me, hath borne witness of me. Ye have neither heard his voice at any time, nor seen his shape. (John 5: 37.)

Now unto the King eternal, immortal, invisible, the only wise God, be honour and glory for ever and ever. Amen. (1 Timothy 1: 17.)

Who only hath immortality, dwelling in the light which no man can approach unto; whom no man hath seen, nor can see: to whom be honour and power everlasting. Amen. (1 Timothy 6: 16.)

Unsearchable:

Canst thou by searching find out God? canst thou find out the Almighty unto perfection? (Job 11: 7.)

Lo, these are parts of his ways; but how little a portion is heard of him? but the thunder of his power who can understand? (Job 26: 14.)

Great is the Lord, and greatly to be praised; and his greatness is unsearchable. (Psalm 145: 3.)

Then I beheld all the work of God, that a man cannot find out the work that is done under the sun: because though a man labour to seek it out, yet he shall not find it; yea, further; though a wise man think to know it, yet shall he not be able to find it. (Ecclesiastes 8: 17.)

O the depth of the riches both of the wisdom and knowledge of God! how unsearchable are his judgments, and his ways past finding out! (Romans 11: 33.)

Unknown:

Behold, God is great, and we know him not, neither can the number of his years be searched out. (Job 36: 26.)

God thundereth marvellously with his voice; great things doeth he, which we cannot comprehend. (Job 37: 5.)

Many, O Lord my God, are thy wonderful works which thou hast done, and thy thoughts which are to us-ward: they cannot be reckoned up in order unto thee: if I would declare and speak of them, they are more than can be numbered. (Psalm 40: 5.)

He hath made every thing beautiful in his time: also he hath set the world in their heart, so that no man can find out the work that God maketh from the beginning to the end. (Ecclesiastes 3: 11.)

Verily thou art a God that hidest thyself, O God of Israel, the Saviour. (Isaiah 45: 15.)

Yet Revealed:

All things are delivered unto me of my Father: and no man knoweth the Son, but the Father; neither knoweth any man the Father, save the Son, and he to whomsoever the Son will reveal him. (Matthew 11: 27.)

Because that which may be known of God is manifest in them, for God hath shewed it unto them.

For the invisible things of him from the Creation of the world are clearly seen, being understood by the things that are made, even his eternal Power and Godhead, so that they are without excuse. (Romans 1: 19, 20.)

But God hath revealed them unto us by his Spirit: for the Spirit searcheth all things, yea, the deep things of God.

For what man knoweth the things of a man, save the spirit of man which is in him? even so the things of God knoweth no man, but the Spirit of God.

Now we have received, not the spirit of the world, but the Spirit which is of God; that we might know the things that are freely given to us of God.

But the natural man receiveth not the things of the Spirit of God: for they are foolishness unto him: neither can he know them, because they are spiritually discerned.

But he that is spiritual judgeth all things, yet he himself is judged of no man.

For who hath known the mind of the Lord, that he may instruct him? But we have the mind of Christ. (1 Corinthians 2: 10-16.)

And we know that the Son of God is come, and hath given us an understanding, that we may know him that is true; and we are in him that is true, even in his Son Jesus Christ. This is the true God, and eternal life. (1 John 5: 20.)

Holy:

For I am the Lord that bringeth you up out of the land of Egypt, to be your God: ye shall therefore be holy, for I am holy. (Leviticus 11: 45.)

Speak unto all the congregation of the children of Israel, and say unto them, Ye shall be holy: for I the Lord your God am holy. (Leviticus 19: 2.)

There is none holy as the Lord: for

there is none besides thee: neither is there any rock like our God. (1 Samuel 2: 2.)

For thou art not a God that hath pleasure in wickedness: neither shall evil dwell with thee. (Psalm 5: 4.)

But thou art holy, O thou that inhabitest the praises of Israel. (Psalm 22: 3.)

Rejoice in the Lord, ye righteous; and give thanks at the remembrance of his holiness. (Psalm 97: 12.)

But the Lord of hosts shall be exalted in judgment, and God that is holy shall be sanctified in righteousness. (Isaiah 5: 16.)

And one cried unto another, and said, Holy, holy, holy, is the Lord of hosts: the whole earth is full of his glory. (Isaiah 6: 3.)

I am the Lord, your Holy One, the Creator of Israel, your King. (Isaiah 43: 15.)

Let no man say when he is tempted, I am tempted of God: for God cannot be tempted with evil, neither tempteth he any man. (James 1: 13.)

But as he which hath called you is holy, so be ye holy in all manner of conversation;

Because it is written, Be ye holy; for I am holy. (1 Peter 1: 15, 16.)

And the four beasts had each of them six wings about him; and they were full of eyes within: and they rest not day and night, saying, Holy, holy, holy, Lord God Almighty, which was, and is, and is to come. (Revelation 4: 8.)

Just:

He is the Rock, his work is perfect: for all his ways are judgment: a God of truth and without iniquity, just and right is he. (Deuteronomy 32: 4.)

Doth God pervert judgment? or doth the Almighty pervert justice? (Job 8: 3.)

For thou hast maintained my right and my cause; thou satest in the throne judging right. (Psalm 9: 4.)

For the righteous Lord loveth righteousness; his countenance doth behold the upright. (Psalm 11: 7.)

He loveth righteousness and judgment: the earth is full of the goodness of the Lord. (Psalm 33: 5.)

Thy righteousness also, O God, is very high, who hast done great things: O God, who is like unto thee! (Psalm 71: 19.)

Justice and judgment are the habitation of thy throne: mercy and truth shall go before thy face. (Psalm 89: 14.)

Clouds and darkness are round about him: righteousness and judgment are the habitation of his throne. (Psalm 97: 2.)

The king's strength also loveth judgment; thou dost establish equity, thou executest judgment and righteousness in Jacob. (Psalm 99: 4.)

Righteous art thou, O Lord, and upright are thy judgments. (Psalm 119: 137.)

The Lord is righteous in all his ways, and holy in all his works. (Psalm 145: 17.)

Yet saith the house of Israel, The way of the Lord is not equal. O house of Israel, are not my ways equal? are not your ways unequal? (Ezekiel 18: 29.)

The just Lord is in the midst thereof; he will not do iniquity: every morning doth he bring his judgment to light, he faileth not; but the unjust knoweth no shame. (Zephaniah 3: 5.)

But we are sure that the judgment of God is according to truth against them which commit such things.

And thinkest thou this, O man, that judgest them which do such things, and doest the same, that thou shalt escape the judgment of God? (Romans 2: 2, 3.)

But if our unrighteousness commend the righteousness of God, what shall we say? Is God unrighteous who taketh vengeance? (I speak as a man,)

God forbid: for then how shall God judge the world? (Romans 3: 5, 6.)

And I heard another out of the altar say, Even so, Lord God Almighty, true and righteous are thy judgments. (Revelation 16: 7.)

Impartial, Faithful, True:

For the Lord your God is God of gods, and Lord of lords, a great God, a mighty, and a terrible, which regardeth not persons, nor taketh reward. (Deuteronomy 10: 17.)

Then Peter opened his mouth, and said, Of a truth I perceive that God is no respecter of persons. (Acts 10: 34.)

For there is no respect of persons with God. (Romans 2: 11.)

But of those who seemed to be somewhat, whatsoever they were, it maketh no matter to me: God accepteth no man's person: for they who seemed to be somewhat in conference added nothing to me. (Galatians 2: 6.)

Knowing that whatsoever good thing any man doeth, the same shall he receive of the Lord, whether he be bond or free. (Ephesians 6: 8.)

But he that doeth wrong shall receive for the wrong which he hath done: and there is no respect of persons. (Colossians 3: 25.)

Know therefore that the Lord thy God, he is God, the faithful God, which keepeth covenant and mercy with them that love him and keep his commandments to a thousand generations. (Deuteronomy 7: 9.)

Who hast kept with thy servant David my father that thou promisedst him: thou spakest also with thy mouth, and hast fulfilled it with thine hand, as it is this day. (I Kings 8: 24.)

Loving, Good, Merciful:

For God so loved the world, that he gave his only begotten Son, that whosoever believeth in him should not perish, but have everlasting life. (John 3: 16.)

Finally, brethren, farewell. Be perfect, be of good comfort, be of one mind, live in peace; and the God of love and peace shall be with you. (2 Corinthians 13: 11.)

The grace of the Lord Jesus Christ, and the love of God, and the communion of the Holy Ghost, be with you all. Amen. (2 Corinthians 13: 14.)

He that loveth not, knoweth not God; for God is love. (1 John 4: 8.)

And we have known and believed the love that God hath to us. God is love; and he that dwelleth in love dwelleth in God, and God in him. (1 John 4: 16.)

O give thanks unto the Lord; for he is good; for his mercy endureth for ever. (1 Chronicles 16: 34.)

O taste and see that the Lord is good: blessed is the man that trusteth in him. (Psalm 34: 8.)

For thou, Lord, art good, and ready to forgive; and plenteous in mercy unto all them that call upon thee. (Psalm 86: 5.)

O give thanks unto the Lord; for he is good: for his mercy endureth for ever. (Psalm 118: 29.)

O give thanks unto the Lord; for he

is good: for his mercy endureth for ever. (Psalm 136: 1.)

They shall abundantly utter the memory of thy great goodness, and shall sing of thy righteousness. (Psalm 145: 7.)

That ye may be the children of your Father which is in heaven: for he maketh his sun to rise on the evil and on the good, and sendeth rain on the just and on the unjust. (Matthew 5: 45.)

And Jesus said unto him, *Why callest thou me good? there is none good but one, that is, God.* (Mark 10: 18.)

Nevertheless for thy great mercies' sake thou didst not utterly consume them, nor forsake them; for thou art a gracious and merciful God. (Nehemiah 9: 31.)

Also unto thee, O Lord, belongeth mercy: for thou renderest to every man according to his work. (Psalm 62: 12.)

The Lord is merciful and gracious, slow to anger, and plenteous in mercy.

He will not always chide: neither will he keep his anger for ever. (Psalm 103: 8, 9.)

It is of the Lord's mercies that we are not consumed, because his compassions fail not. (Lamentations 3: 22.)

To the Lord our God belong mercies and forgiveness, though we have rebelled against him. (Daniel 9: 9.)

Jealous:

Thou shalt not bow down thyself to them, nor serve them: for I the Lord thy God am a jealous God, visiting the iniquity of the fathers upon the children unto the third and fourth generation of them that hate me. (Exodus 20: 5.)

For thou shalt worship no other god: for the Lord, whose name is Jealous, is a jealous God. (Exodus 34: 14.)

For the Lord thy God is a consuming fire, even a jealous God. (Deuteronomy 4: 24.)

They have moved me to jealousy with that which is not God; they have provoked me to anger with their vanities: and I will move them to jealousy with those which are not a people; I will provoke them to anger with a foolish nation. (Deuteronomy 32: 21.)

For they provoked him to anger with their high places, and moved him to jealousy with their graven images. (Psalm 78: 58.)

How long, Lord? wilt thou be angry for ever? shall thy jealousy burn like fire? (Psalm 79: 5.)

God's Characters.

Searcher of Hearts:

And thou, Solomon my son, know thou the God of thy father, and serve him with a perfect heart, and with a willing mind: for the Lord searcheth all hearts, and understandeth all the imaginations of the thoughts: if thou seek him, he will be found of thee; but if thou forsake him, he will cast thee off for ever. (1 Chronicles 28: 9.)

Shall not God search this out? for he knoweth the secrets of the heart. (Psalm 44: 21.)

I the Lord search the heart, I try the reins, even to give every man according to his ways, and according to the fruit of his doings. (Jeremiah 17: 10.)

And they prayed, and said, Thou, Lord, which knowest the hearts of all men, shew whether of these two thou hast chosen. (Acts 1: 24.)

And he that searcheth the hearts knoweth what is the mind of the Spirit, because he maketh intercession for the saints according to the will of God. (Romans 8: 27.)

Disposer of Events:

It is in the power of my hand to do you hurt: but the God of your father spake unto me yesternight, saying, Take thou heed that thou speak not to Jacob either good or bad. (Genesis 31: 29.)

And God sent me before you to preserve you a posterity in the earth, and to save your lives by a great deliverance.

So now it was not you that sent me hither, but God: and he hath made me a father to Pharaoh, and lord of all his house, and a ruler throughout all the land of Egypt. (Genesis 45: 7, 8.)

And Joseph said unto them, Fear not: for am I in the place of God?

But as for you, ye thought evil against me; but God meant it unto good, to bring to pass, as it is this day, to save much people alive. (Genesis 50: 19, 20.)

A man's heart deviseth his way: but the Lord directeth his steps. (Proverbs 16: 9.)

There are many devices in a man's heart; nevertheless the counsel of the Lord, that shall stand. (Proverbs 19: 21.)

Man's goings are of the Lord; how can a man then understand his own way? (Proverbs 20: 24.)

There is no wisdom nor understanding nor counsel against the Lord. (Proverbs 21: 30.)

Then they sought to take him: but no man laid hands on him, because his hour was not yet come. (John 7: 30.)

Supreme Judge:

He is the Lord our God; his judgments are in all the earth. (1 Chronicles 16: 14.)

Shall any teach God knowledge? seeing he judgeth those that are high. (Job 21: 22.)

There the righteous might dispute with him; so should I be delivered forever from my judge. (Job 23: 7.)

The Lord shall judge the people: judge me, O Lord, according to my righteousness, and according to mine integrity that is in me. (Psalm 7: 8.)

And he shall judge the world in righteousness, he shall minister judgment to the people in uprightness. (Psalm 9: 8.)

He shall call to the heavens from above, and to the earth, that he may judge his people. (Psalm 50: 4.)

But God is the judge: he putteth down one, and setteth up another. (Psalm 75: 7.)

Before the Lord: for he cometh, for he cometh to judge the earth: he shall judge the world with righteousness, and the people with his truth. (Psalm 96: 13.)

For I know nothing by myself; yet am I not hereby justified: but he that judgeth me is the Lord.

Therefore judge nothing before the time, until the Lord come, who both will bring to light the hidden things of darkness, and will make manifest the counsels of the hearts: and then shall every man have praise of God. (1 Corinthians 4: 4, 5.)

God's Glory.

Exhibited in Power, Holiness, Majesty, Etc.:

Because I will publish the name of the Lord: ascribe ye greatness unto our God. (Deuteronomy 32: 3.)

Glory and honour are in his presence; strength and gladness are in his place. (1 Chronicles 16: 27.)

But thou, Lord, art most high for evermore. (Psalm 92: 8.)

The Lord reigneth, he is clothed with majesty; the Lord is clothed with strength, wherewith he hath girded himself: the world also is stablished, that it cannot be moved. (Psalm 93: 1.)

The Lord is great in Zion; and he is high above all the people. (Psalm 99: 2.)

Bless the Lord, O my soul. O Lord my God, thou art very great; thou art clothed with honour and majesty. (Psalm 104: 1.)

Cry out and shout, thou inhabitant of Zion: for great is the Holy One of Israel in the midst of thee. (Isaiah 12: 6.)

Behold, the nations are as a drop of a bucket, and are counted as the small dust of the balance: behold, he taketh up the isles as a very little thing. (Isaiah 40: 15.)

But Jesus beheld them, and said unto them, *With men this is impossible; but with God all things are possible.* (Matthew 19: 26.)

And Jesus looking upon them saith, *With men it is impossible, but not with God: for with God all things are possible.* (Mark 10: 27.)

For with God nothing shall be impossible. (Luke 1: 37.)

And he said, *The things which are impossible with men are possible with God.* (Luke 18: 27.)

Exhibited in Christ:

And the Word was made flesh, and dwelt among us, (and we beheld his glory, the glory as of the only begotten of the Father,) full of grace and truth. (John 1: 14.)

For God, who commanded the light to shine out of darkness, hath shined in our hearts, to give the light of the knowledge of the glory of God in the face of Jesus Christ. (2 Corinthians 4: 6.)

Hath in these last days spoken unto us by his Son, whom he hath appointed heir of all things, by whom also he made the worlds;

Who being the brightness of his glory, and the express image of his person, and upholding all things by the word of his power, when he had by himself purged our sins, sat down on the right hand of the Majesty on high. (Hebrews 1: 2, 3.)

Exhibited in His Goodness:

For a multitude of the people, even many of Ephraim, and Manasseh, Issachar and Zebulun, had not cleansed themselves, yet did they eat the passover otherwise than it was written. But Hezekiah prayed for them, saying, The good Lord pardon every one

That prepareth his heart to seek God, the Lord God of his fathers, though he be not cleansed according to the purification of the sanctuary. (2 Chronicles 30: 18, 19.)

Good and upright is the Lord: therefore will he teach sinners in the way. (Psalm 25: 8.)

Oh how great is thy goodness, which thou hast laid up for them that fear thee; which thou hast wrought for them that trust in thee before the sons of men! (Psalm 31: 19.)

He loveth righteousness and judgment: the earth is full of the goodness of the Lord. (Psalm 33: 5.)

Thy congregation hath dwelt therein: thou, O God, hast prepared of thy goodness for the poor. (Psalm 68: 10.)

Thou art good, and doest good; teach me thy statutes. (Psalm 119: 68.)

And he said unto him, *Why callest thou me good? there is none good but one, that is, God: but if thou wilt enter into life, keep the commandments.* (Matthew 19: 17.)

Nevertheless, he left not himself without witness, in that he did good, and gave us rain from heaven, and fruitful seasons, filling our hearts with food and gladness. (Acts 14: 17.)

Or despisest thou the riches of his goodness, and forbearance, and long-suffering, not knowing that the goodness of God leadeth thee to repentance? (Romans 2: 4.)

God's Gifts.

General:

If the Lord delight in us, then he will bring us into this land, and give it us; a land which floweth with milk and honey. (Numbers 14: 8.)

For God giveth to a man that is good in his sight, wisdom, and knowledge, and joy: but to the sinner he giveth travail, to gather and to heap up, that he may give to him that is good before God. (Ecclesiastes 2: 26.)

He that spared not his own Son, but delivered him up for us all, how shall he not with him also freely give us all things? (Romans 8: 32.)

For I would that all men were even as I myself. But every man hath his proper gift of God, one after this manner, and another after that. (1 Corinthians 7: 7.)

Every good gift, and every perfect gift is from above, and cometh down from the Father of lights, with whom is no variableness, neither shadow of turning. (James 1: 17.)

Spiritual:

The Lord will give strength unto his people; the Lord will bless his people with peace. (Psalm 29: 11.)

Thou hast ascended on high, thou hast led captivity captive: thou hast received gifts for men; yea, for the rebellious also, that the Lord God might dwell among them. (Psalm 68: 18.)

I the Lord have called thee in righteousness, and will hold thine hand, and will keep thee, and give thee for a covenant of the people, for a light of the Gentiles. (Isaiah 42: 6.)

And I will give them one heart, and I will put a new spirit within you; and I will take the stony heart out of their flesh, and will give them an heart of flesh. (Ezekiel 11: 19.)

If ye then, being evil, know how to give good gifts unto your children, how much more shall your Father which is in heaven give good things to them that ask him? (Matthew 7: 11.)

Come unto me, all ye that labour and are heavy laden, and I will give you rest. (Matthew 11: 28.)

For God so loved the world, that he gave his only begotten Son: that whosoever believeth in him, should not perish, but have everlasting life. (John 3: 16.)

Jesus answered, and said unto her, *If thou knewest the gift of God, and who it is that saith to thee, Give me to drink; thou wouldest have asked of him, and he would have given thee living water.* (John 4: 10.)

And the glory which thou gavest me I have given them; that they may be one, even as we are one. (John 17: 22.)

But Peter said unto him, Thy money perish with thee, because thou hast thought that the gift of God may be purchased with money. (Acts 8: 20.)

When they heard these things, they held their peace, and glorified God, saying, Then hath God also to the Gentiles granted repentance unto life. (Acts 11: 18.)

And not as it was by one that sinned, so is the gift: for the judgment was by one to condemnation: but the free gift is of many offences unto justification.

For if by one man's offence death reigned by one, much more they which receive abundance of grace and of the gift of righteousness, shall reign in life by one, Jesus Christ. (Romans 5: 16, 17.)

For the wages of sin is death; but the gift of God is eternal life through Jesus Christ our Lord. (Romans 6: 23.)

For by grace are ye saved through faith; and that not of yourselves: it is the gift of God:

Not of works, lest any man should boast. (Ephesians 2: 8, 9.)

But he giveth more grace, wherefore he saith, God resisteth the proud, but giveth grace unto the humble. (James 4: 6.)

Temporal:

And I will give peace in the land, and ye shall lie down, and none shall make you afraid: and I will rid evil beasts out of the land, neither shall the sword go through your land. (Leviticus 26: 6.)

Thus saith God the Lord, he that created the heavens, and stretched them out; he that spread forth the earth, and that which cometh out of it; he that giveth breath unto the people upon it, and spirit to them that walk therein. (Isaiah 42: 5.)

Nevertheless, he left not himself without witness, in that he did good, and gave us rain from heaven, and fruitful seasons, filling our hearts with food and gladness. (Acts 14: 17.)

For every creature of God is good, and nothing to be refused, if it be received with thanksgiving:

For it is sanctified by the word of God, and prayer. (1 Timothy 4: 4, 5.)

Charge them that are rich in this world, that they be not high-minded, nor trust in uncertain riches, but in the living God, who giveth us richly all things to enjoy. (1 Timothy 6: 17.)

God's Names.

And Melchizedek king of Salem brought forth bread and wine: and he was the priest of the most high God. (Genesis 14: 18.)

And God said unto Moses, I AM THAT I AM: And he said, Thus shalt thou say unto the children of Israel, I AM hath sent me unto you. (Exodus 3: 14.)

And I appeared unto Abraham, unto Isaac, and unto Jacob by the name of God Almighty, but by my name JEHOVAH was I not known to them. (Exodus 6: 3.)

For thou shalt worship no other god: for the Lord, whose name is Jealous, is a jealous God. (Exodus 34: 14.)

For who is there of all flesh that hath heard the voice of the living God speaking out of the midst of the fire, as we have, and lived?

Go thou near, and hear all that the Lord our God shall say: and speak thou unto us all that the Lord our God shall speak unto thee; and we will hear it, and do it. (Deuteronomy 5: 26, 27.)

Whom hast thou reproached and blasphemed? and against whom hast thou exalted thy voice, and lifted up thine eyes on high? even against the Holy One of Israel. (2 Kings 19: 22.)

And said, I beseech thee, O Lord God of heaven, the great and terrible God, that keepeth covenant and mercy for them that love him and observe his commandments. (Nehemiah 1: 5.)

Then should I yet have comfort; yea, I would harden myself in sorrow: let him not spare; for I have not concealed the words of the Holy One. (Job 6: 10.)

The mighty God, even the Lord, hath spoken, and called the earth from the rising of the sun unto the going down thereof. (Psalm 50: 1.)

O Lord God of hosts, how long wilt thou be angry against the prayer of thy people? (Psalm 80: 4.)

Sing aloud unto God our strength: make a joyful noise unto the God of Jacob. (Psalm 81: 1.)

Remember now thy Creator in the days of thy youth, while the evil days come not, nor the years draw nigh, when thou shalt say, I have no pleasure in them. (Ecclesiastes 12: 1.)

Therefore saith the Lord, the Lord of hosts, the mighty One of Israel, Ah, I will ease me of mine adversaries, and avenge me of mine enemies. (Isaiah 1: 24.)

Let your light so shine before men, that they may see your good works, and glorify your Father which is in heaven. (Matthew 5: 16.)

And as Esaias said before, Except the Lord of Sabaoth had left us a seed, we had been as Sodoma, and been made like unto Gomorrah. (Romans 9: 29.)

Every good gift, and every perfect gift is from above, and cometh down from the Father of lights, with whom is no variableness, neither shadow of turning. (James 1: 17.)

And he hath on his vesture and on his thigh a name written, KING OF KINGS, AND LORD OF LORDS. (Revelation 19: 16.)

False Gods.

Thou shalt have no other gods before me. (Exodus 20: 3.)

And it shall be, if thou do at all forget the Lord thy God, and walk after other gods, and serve them, and worship them, I testify against you this day that ye shall surely perish. (Deuteronomy 8: 19.)

But the prophet, which shall presume to speak a word in my name, which I have not commanded him to speak, or that shall speak in the name of other gods, even that prophet shall die. (Deuteronomy 18: 20.)

GODLINESS.

GOD'LI-NESS—piety caused by knowledge and love of God, and leading to complete, constant, and cheerful obedience to His commands. It is a virtue many passages in Scripture tell Christians to acquire.

REFERENCES.

I exhort therefore, that, first of all, supplications, prayers, intercessions, and giving of thanks, be made for all men;

For kings, and for all that are in authority; that we may lead a quiet and peaceable life in all godliness and honesty.

For this is good and acceptable in the sight of God our Saviour. (1 Timothy 2: 1-3.)

But refuse profane and old wives' fables, and exercise thyself rather unto godliness.

For bodily exercise profiteth little,

but godliness is profitable unto all things, having promise of the life that now is, and of that which is to come. (1 Timothy 4: 7, 8.)

If any man teach otherwise, and consent not to wholesome words, even the words of our Lord Jesus Christ, and to the doctrine which is according to godliness;

He is proud, knowing nothing, but doting about questions and strifes of words, whereof cometh envy, strife, railings, evil surmisings,

Perverse disputings of men of corrupt minds, and destitute of the truth, supposing that gain is godliness: from such withdraw thyself.

But godliness with contentment is great gain. (1 Timothy 6: 3-6.)

But thou, O man of God, flee these things; and follow after righteousness, godliness, faith, love, patience, meekness. (1 Timothy 6: 11.)

According as his divine power hath given unto us all things that pertain unto life and godliness, through the knowledge of him that hath called us to glory and virtue. (2 Peter 1: 3.)

Seeing then that all these things shall be dissolved, what manner of persons ought ye to be in all holy conversation and godliness. (2 Peter 3: 11.)

GOLGOTHA.

GOL'GO-THA—a form of a Hebrew word meaning "the place of a skull." Golgotha was the name given by the Jews to the hill upon which Christ was crucified. The origin of the word is unsettled, some commentators thinking the hill was a knoll shaped like a skull and others thinking the fact that executions took place there gave it the name. The exact location of it is also unsettled, several sites answering in part the descriptions of Golgotha.

References.—Matthew 27: 33; Mark 15: 22; John 19: 17.

GOLIATH.

GO-LI'ATH—a form of a Hebrew word meaning "exile." Goliath was the name of the Philistine giant whose defeat and death at the hands of the youth David gave such glory to his early career. Goliath is believed to have been more than eleven feet tall.

References.—1 Samuel 17, 21, and 22.

GOMORRAH. (See Sodom.)

GOSHEN.

GO'SHEN—a Hebrew word given as a name to that one of the provinces of Egypt in which the Israelites dwelt. See article on Egypt.

GOSPEL.

GOS'PEL. The word "gospel" comes to us from the Old English word "Godspel," meaning "God story" or "narrative of God." It was early confused with the Anglo-Saxon phrase "god spell," meaning "good story" or "good tidings." So apt was this meaning when the good tidings nature of the gospel, with its message of salvation for all mankind, was considered that the translators of the Authorized Version adopted it, and the compilers of the Revised Version have done the same. This meaning is now generally accepted as the correct one, the central thought of the gospel being that Christ came into the world as its Saviour, certainly the best piece of good tidings and joyful intelligence that could have been brought to mankind.

The word "gospel" naturally became prefixed to each one of the accounts of Christ embodied in the Bible. Of these there are four—Matthew's, Mark's, Luke's, and John's. The distinctive features of these are that Matthew shows Jesus as the promised King of the kingdom of God, Mark depicts Him as the great Prophet, Luke as the special Saviour of sinners, and John as the marvelous Son of God, deity and humanity in one.

REFERENCES.

Its Scope and Power.

And Jesus went about all Galilee, teaching in their synagogues, and preaching the gospel of the kingdom, and healing all manner of sickness and all manner of disease among the people. (Matthew 4: 23.)

And this Gospel of the kingdom shall be preached in all the world, for a witness unto all nations, and then shall the end come. (Matthew 24: 14.)

Now after that John was put in prison, Jesus came into Galilee, preaching the gospel of the kingdom of God,

And saying, The time is fulfilled, and the kingdom of God is at hand: repent ye, and believe the gospel. (Mark 1: 14, 15.)

And the angel said unto them, Fear not: for, behold, I bring you good tidings of great joy, which shall be to all people.

For unto you is born this day in the city of David a Saviour, which is Christ the Lord. (Luke 2: 10, 11.)

Men and brethren, children of the stock of Abraham, and whosoever among you feareth God, to you is the word of this salvation sent. (Acts 13: 26.)

Long time therefore abode they speaking boldly in the Lord, which gave testimony unto the word of his grace, and granted signs and wonders to be done by their hands. (Acts 14: 3.)

Paul, a servant of Jesus Christ, called to be an apostle, separated unto the gospel of God,

(Which he had promised afore by his prophets in the holy scriptures,)

Concerning his Son Jesus Christ our Lord, which was made of the seed of David according to the flesh. (Romans 1: 1-3.)

For God is my witness, whom I serve with my spirit in the gospel of his Son, that without ceasing I make mention of you always in my prayers. (Romans 1: 9.)

For I am not ashamed of the gospel of Christ: for it is the power of God unto salvation to every one that believeth; to the Jew first, and also to the Greek. (Romans 1: 16.)

For the preaching of the cross is to them that perish foolishness; but unto us which are saved it is the power of God. (1 Corinthians 1: 18.)

Now we have received, not the spirit of the world, but the spirit which is of God; that we might know the things that are freely given to us of God.

Which things also we speak, not in the words which man's wisdom teacheth, but which the Holy Ghost teacheth; comparing spiritual things with spiritual. (1 Corinthians 2: 12, 13.)

Moreover, brethren, I declare unto you the gospel which I preached unto you, which also ye have received, and wherein ye stand;

By which also ye are saved, if ye keep in memory what I preached unto you, unless ye have believed in vain. (1 Corinthians 15: 1, 2.)

But if our gospel be hid, it is hid to them that are lost:

In whom the god of this world hath blinded the minds of them which believe not, lest the light of the glorious gospel of Christ, who is the image of God, should shine unto them.

For we preach not ourselves, but Christ Jesus the Lord; and ourselves your servants for Jesus' sake. (2 Corinthians 4: 3-5.)

In whom ye also trusted, after that ye heard the word of truth, the gospel of your salvation: in whom also after that ye believed, ye were sealed with that holy Spirit of promise. (Ephesians 1: 13.)

And your feet shod with the preparation of the gospel of peace. (Ephesians 6: 15.)

Holding forth the word of life; that I may rejoice in the day of Christ, that I have not run in vain, neither laboured in vain. (Philippians 2: 16.)

For the hope which is laid up for you in heaven, whereof ye heard before in the word of the truth of the gospel;

Which is come unto you, as it is in all the world; and bringeth forth fruit, as it doth also in you, since the day ye heard of it, and knew the grace of God in truth. (Colossians 1: 5, 6.)

Let the word of Christ dwell in you richly in all wisdom; teaching and admonishing one another in psalms and hymns and spiritual songs, singing with grace in your hearts to the Lord. (Colossians 3: 16.)

For our gospel came not unto you in word only, but also in power, and in the Holy Ghost, and in much assurance; as ye know what manner of men we were among you for your sake. (1 Thessalonians 1: 5.)

So being affectionately desirous of you, we were willing to have imparted unto you, not the gospel of God only, but also our own souls, because ye were dear unto us. (1 Thessalonians 2: 8.)

For unto us was the gospel preached, as well as unto them: but the word preached did not profit them, not being mixed with faith in them that heard it. (Hebrews 4: 2.)

Unto whom it was revealed, that not unto themselves, but unto us they did minister the things, which are now reported unto you by them that have preached the gospel unto you with the Holy Ghost sent down from heaven; which things the angels desire to look into. (1 Peter 1: 12.)

But the word of the Lord endureth for ever. And this is the word which by the gospel is preached unto you. (1 Peter 1: 25.)

For the time is come that judgment must begin at the house of God: and if it first begin at us, what shall the end be of them that obey not the gospel of God? (1 Peter 4: 17.)

To Whom Preached.

And the scripture, foreseeing that God would justify the heathen through faith, preached before the gospel unto Abraham, saying, In thee shall all nations be blessed. (Galatians 3: 8.)

The blind receive their sight, and the lame walk, the lepers are cleansed, and the deaf hear, the dead are raised up, and the poor have the gospel preached to them. (Matthew 11: 5.)

And the gospel must first be published among all nations. (Mark 13: 10.)

And he said unto them, *Go ye into all the world, and preach the gospel to every creature.* (Mark 16: 15.)

The Spirit of the Lord is upon me, because he hath anointed me to preach the gospel to the poor; he hath sent me to heal the broken-hearted, to preach deliverance to the captives, and recovering of sight to the blind, to set at liberty them that are bruised. (Luke 4: 18.)

For Christ sent me not to baptize, but to preach the gospel: not with wisdom of words, lest the cross of Christ should be made of none effect. (1 Corinthians 1: 17.)

For though I preach the gospel, I have nothing to glory of: for necessity is laid upon me; yea, woe is unto me, if I preach not the gospel! (1 Corinthians 9: 16.)

And I went up by revelation, and communicated unto them that gospel which I preach among the Gentiles, but privately to them which were of reputation, lest by any means I should run, or had run, in vain. (Galatians 2: 2.)

And I saw another angel fly in the midst of heaven, having the everlasting gospel to preach unto them that dwell on the earth, and to every nation, and kindred, and tongue, and people. (Revelation 14: 6.)

Its Admonition to Christians.

For whosoever will save his life shall lose it; but whosoever shall lose his life for my sake and the gospel's, the same shall save it. (Mark 8: 35.)

And I am sure that, when I come unto you, I shall come in the fulness of the blessing of the gospel of Christ. (Romans 15: 29.)

Only let your conversation be as it becometh the gospel of Christ: that whether I come and see you, or else be absent, I may hear of your affairs, that ye stand fast in one spirit, with one mind striving together for the faith of the gospel. (Philippians 1: 27.)

If ye continue in the faith grounded and settled, and be not moved away from the hope of the gospel, which ye have heard, and which was preached to every creature which is under heaven; whereof I Paul am made a minister. (Colossians 1: 23.)

Rejected by Jews.

And when they agreed not among themselves, they departed, after that Paul had spoken one word, Well spake the Holy Ghost by Esaias the prophet unto our fathers,

Saying, Go unto this people, and say, Hearing ye shall hear, and shall not understand; and seeing ye shall see, and not perceive. (Acts 28: 25, 26.)

For this is my covenant unto them, when I shall take away their sins.

As concerning the gospel, they are enemies for your sakes: but as touching the election, they are beloved for the fathers' sakes.

For the gifts and calling of God are without repentance.

For as ye in times past have not believed God, yet have now obtained mercy through their unbelief:

Even so have these also now not believed, that through your mercy they also may obtain mercy.

For God hath concluded them all in unbelief, that he might have mercy upon all. (Romans 11: 27-32.)

From Whom Hid.

But if our Gospel be hid, it is hid to them that are lost:

In whom the God of this world hath blinded the minds of them which believe not, lest the light of the glorious Gospel of Christ, who is the image of God, should shine unto them. (2 Corinthians 4: 3, 4.)

GRACE.

GRACE. Grace will be found in the Scriptures conveying a number of different meanings, including (1) physical beauty; (2) the goodness of God toward man or man toward fellow-man; (3) the forgiving mercy of God as opposed to merit; (4) the gospel generally; (5) certain of God's gifts to man; (6) certain Christian virtues; (7) the future glory or eternal life.

REFERENCES.

Grace of God and Christ.

For the Lord God is a sun and shield: the Lord will give grace and glory; no good thing will he withhold from them that walk uprightly. (Psalm 84: 11.)

And the child grew, and waxed strong in spirit, filled with wisdom, and the grace of God was upon him. (Luke 2: 40.)

And of his fulness have all we received, and grace for grace.

For the Law was given by Moses, but grace and truth came by Jesus Christ. (John 1: 16, 17.)

But none of these things move me, neither count I my life dear unto myself, so that I might finish my course with joy, and the ministry which I have received of the Lord Jesus, to testify the Gospel of the grace of God. (Acts 20: 24.)

Even so then at this present time also there is a remnant according to the election of grace.

And if by grace, then is it no more of works: otherwise grace is no more grace. But if it be of works, then is it no more grace: otherwise work is no more work. (Romans 11: 5, 6.)

But by the grace of God I am what I am: and his grace which was bestowed upon me, was not in vain: But I laboured more abundantly than they all, yet not I, but the grace of God which was with me. (1 Corinthians 15: 10.)

For ye know the grace of our Lord Jesus Christ, that though he was rich, yet for your sakes he became poor, that ye through his poverty might be rich. (2 Corinthians 8: 9.)

Who hath saved us, and called us with an holy calling, not according to our works, but according to his own purpose and grace, which was given us in Christ Jesus before the world began. (2 Timothy 1: 9.)

Likewise, ye younger, submit yourselves unto the elder. Yea, all of you be subject one to another, and be clothed with humility: for God resisteth the proud, and giveth grace to the humble. (1 Peter 5: 5.)

Grace and Salvation.

But we believe that through the grace of the Lord Jesus Christ we shall be saved, even as they. (Acts 15: 11.)

Being justified freely by his grace through the redemption that is in Christ Jesus. (Romans 3: 24.)

Now to him that worketh, is the reward not reckoned of grace, but of debt. (Romans 4: 4.)

But God, who is rich in mercy, for his great love wherewith he loved us,

Even when we were dead in sins, hath quickened us together with Christ, (by grace ye are saved;)

And hath raised us up together, and made us sit together in heavenly places in Christ Jesus:

That in the ages to come he might shew the exceeding riches of his grace in his kindness toward us through Christ Jesus. (Ephesians 2: 4-7.)

Grace's Effects.

For our rejoicing is this, the testimony of our conscience, that in simplicity and godly sincerity, not with fleshly wisdom, but by the grace of God, we have had our conversation in the world, and more abundantly to youward. (2 Corinthians 1: 12.)

And he said unto me, My grace is sufficient for thee: for my strength is made perfect in weakness. Most gladly therefore will I rather glory in my infirmities, that the power of Christ may rest upon me. (2 Corinthians 12: 9.)

For the grace of God that bringeth salvation hath appeared to all men,

Teaching us that, denying ungodliness and worldly lusts, we should live soberly, righteously, and godly, in this present world. (Titus 2: 11, 12.)

As every man hath received the gift, even so minister the same one to another, as good stewards of the manifold grace of God. (1 Peter 4: 10.)

Abusing Grace.

What shall we say then? Shall we continue in sin, that grace may abound? God forbid. How shall we, that are dead to sin, live any longer therein? (Romans 6: 1, 2.)

For sin shall not have dominion over you: for ye are not under the law, but under grace.

What then? shall we sin, because we are not under the law, but under grace? God forbid. (Romans 6: 14, 15.)

For there are certain men crept in unawares, who were before of old ordained to this condemnation, ungodly men, turning the grace of our God into lasciviousness, and denying the only Lord God, and our Lord Jesus Christ. (Jude 1: 4.)

Christ is become of no effect unto you, whosoever of you are justified by the law; ye are fallen from grace. (Galatians 5: 4.)

Exhortations to Grace.

Follow peace with all men, and holiness, without which no man shall see the Lord:

Looking diligently lest any man fail of the grace of God; lest any root of bitterness springing up trouble you, and thereby many be defiled. (Hebrews 12: 14, 15.)

Wherefore we receiving a kingdom which cannot be moved, let us have grace, whereby we may serve God acceptably with reverence and godly fear. (Hebrews 12: 28.)

But the God of all grace, who hath called us unto his eternal glory by Christ Jesus, after that ye have suffered a while, make you perfect, stablish, strengthen, settle you. (2 Peter 3: 10.)

HABAKKUK.

HA-BAK'KUK—a form of a Hebrew word the exact meaning of which is somewhat uncertain. Habakkuk was one of the minor Jewish prophets and flourished about 610 B.C. Little is known of his life. The literary quality of his prophecy is high.

Reference.—The book of Habakkuk.

HAGAR.

HA'GAR—a form of a Hebrew word meaning "stranger." Hagar was one of the slave-women presented to Abraham by the Egyptian pharaoh, and in turn given to Sarah, to be her handmaid. Sarah raised her to the dignity of secondary wife to Abraham and she became the mother of Ishmael. Later, after the birth of Isaac, she and Ishmael gave offense to Sarah and they were both ordered to leave the household. Their wandering and distress are recorded in Scripture. Ishmael became the founder of an extensive tribe.

References.—Genesis 16 and 21.

HAGGAI.

HAG'GAI—a form of a Hebrew word meaning "festive." Haggai was one of the minor prophets. He lived about 535 B.C. Little is known of his personal history.

Reference.—The book of Haggai.

HALLELUJAH.

HAL'LE-LU'JAH—a form of a Hebrew phrase meaning "Praise ye Jah," Jah being one of the forms of the Hebrew word Jehovah, or God.

HAM.

HAM—a form of a Hebrew word meaning "warm," "hot," or "swarthy." Ham was the third son of Noah, and was cursed by his father to the effect that he and his descendants should be slaves and servants to his brothers and their descendants. Ham's sons and their children peopled Egypt, Palestine, Africa, Arabia, and Southwestern Asia generally.

References.—Genesis 9 and 10.

HAMAN.

HA'MAN—the name of the prime minister of King Ahasuerus. He was a foreigner who had been elevated to great rank in the Persian kingdom and conspired against the Jews. The plot, its discovery, Queen Esther's part in the thwarting of it, and the subsequent hanging of Haman on the same gallows he had intended for Mordecai, are graphically told in the book of Esther, to which the reader is referred.

HAND AND HANDS.

HAND AND HANDS. The hand figures to a considerable extent in the Bible. It is often quoted as an indication or symbol of the power of God. The laying-on of hands is shown by the Scripture to have been in use as a means of setting apart men to particular offices or ministries. A ceremonial washing of the hands was an ancient declaration of innocence, especially of blood-guiltiness.

REFERENCES.

God's Hand=Blessing.

Also in Judah the hand of God was to give them one heart to do the commandment of the king and of the princes, by the word of the Lord. (2 Chronicles 30: 12.)

For upon the first day of the first month began he to go up from Babylon, and on the first day of the fifth month came he to Jerusalem, according to the good hand of his God upon him. (Ezra 7: 9.)

Then I told them of the hand of my God which was good upon me; as also the king's words that he had spoken unto me. And they said, Let us rise up and build. So they strengthened their hands for this good work. (Nehemiah 2: 18.)

God's Hand=Chastisement.

For indeed the hand of the Lord was against them, to destroy them from among the host, until they were consumed. (Deuteronomy 2: 15.)

Would ye tarry for them till they were grown? would ye stay for them from having husbands? nay, my daughters; for it grieveth me much for your sakes, that the hand of the Lord is gone out against me. (Ruth 1: 13.)

But he said unto her, Thou speakest as one of the foolish women speaketh. What! shall we receive good at the hand of God, and shall we not receive evil? In all this did not Job sin with his lips. (Job 2: 10.)

Have pity upon me, have pity upon me, O ye my friends; for the hand of God hath touched me. (Job 19: 21.)

Humble yourselves therefore under the mighty hand of God, that he may exalt you in due time. (1 Peter 5: 6.)

Laying=on of Hands.

And thou shalt bring the Levites before the Lord: and the children of Israel shall put their hands upon the Levites:

And Aaron shall offer the Levites before the Lord for an offering of the children of Israel, that they may execute the service of the Lord. (Numbers 8: 10, 11.)

And the Lord said unto Moses, Take thee Joshua the son of Nun, a man in whom is the spirit, and lay thine hand upon him;

And set him before Eleazer the priest, and before all the congregation: and give him a charge in their sight.

And thou shalt put some of thine

honour upon him, that all the congregation of the children of Israel may be obedient. (Numbers 27: 18-20.)

And the saying pleased the whole multitude: and they chose Stephen, a man full of faith and of the Holy Ghost, and Philip, and Prochorus, and Nicanor, and Timon, and Parmenas, and Nicolas a proselyte of Antioch:

Whom they set before the apostles: and when they had prayed, they laid their hands on them. (Acts 6: 5, 6.)

Neglect not the gift that is in thee, which was given thee by prophecy, with the laying on of the hands of the Presbytery. (1 Timothy 4: 14.)

Wherefore I put thee in remembrance that thou stir up the gift of God, which is in thee by the putting on of my hands. (2 Timothy 1: 6.)

Washing of Hands.

And all the elders of that city that are next unto the slain man, shall wash their hands over the heifer that is beheaded in the valley:

And they shall answer and say, Our hands have not shed this blood, neither have our eyes seen it. (Deuteronomy 21: 6.)

I will wash mine hands in innocency: so will I compass thine altar, O Lord. (Psalm 26: 6.)

When Pilate saw that he could prevail nothing, but that rather a tumult was made, he took water, and washed his hands before the multitude, saying, I am innocent of the blood of this just person: see ye to it. (Matthew 27: 24.)

Hands in Prayer.

Hear the voice of my supplications, when I cry unto thee, when I lift up my hands toward thy holy oracle. (Psalm 28: 2.)

Thus will I bless thee while I live: I will lift up my hands in thy name. (Psalm 63: 4.)

Let my prayer be set forth before thee as incense; and the lifting up of my hands as the evening sacrifice. (Psalm 141: 2.)

I stretch forth my hands unto thee: my soul thirsteth after thee, as a thirsty land. Selah. (Psalm 143: 6.)

I will therefore that men pray every where, lifting up holy hands without wrath and doubting. (1 Timothy 2: 8.)

HATRED.

HA'TRED—hate; strong aversion, intense dislike. The emotion of hatred toward one's fellow is one of the passions forbidden in the Bible.

REFERENCES.

If thou see the ass of him that hateth thee lying under his burden, and wouldest forbear to help him, thou shalt surely help with him. (Exodus 23: 5.)

Thou shalt not hate thy brother in thine heart: thou shalt in any wise rebuke thy neighbour, and not suffer sin upon him. (Leviticus 19: 17.)

Hatred stirreth up strifes: but love covereth all sins. (Proverbs 10: 12.)

He that hideth hatred with lying lips, and he that uttereth a slander, is a fool. (Proverbs 10: 18.)

Better is a dinner of herbs where love is, than a stalled ox and hatred therewith. (Proverbs 15: 17.)

Ye have heard that it hath been said, Thou shalt love thy neighbour, and hate thine enemy.

But I say unto you, Love your enemies, bless them that curse you, do good to them that hate you, and pray for them which despitefully use you, and persecute you. (Matthew 5: 43, 44.)

Idolatry, witchcraft, hatred, variance, emulations, wrath, strife, seditions, heresies,

Envyings, murders, drunkenness, revellings, and such like: of the which I tell you before, as I have also told you in time past, that they which do such things shall not inherit the kingdom of God. (Galatians 5: 20, 21.)

For we ourselves also were sometimes foolish, disobedient, deceived, serving divers lusts and pleasures, living in malice and envy, hateful, and hating one another. (Titus 3: 3.)

He that saith he is in the light, and hateth his brother, is in darkness even until now. (1 John 2: 9.)

Whosoever hateth his brother is a murderer: and ye know that no murderer hath eternal life abiding in him. (1 John 3: 15.)

HAUGHTINESS. (See Pride.)

HAUGH′TI-NESS—disdainful and contemptuous pride; arrogance due to excessive pride. Haughtiness is placed by the Bible among the forbidden things. It is unrighteous and lacking in the true Christian spirit.

REFERENCES.

And the afflicted people thou wilt save: but thine eyes are upon the haughty, that thou mayest bring them down. (2 Samuel 22: 28.)

Pride goeth before destruction, and an haughty spirit before a fall. (Proverbs 16: 18.)

The lofty looks of man shall be humbled, and the haughtiness of men shall be bowed down, and the Lord alone shall be exalted in that day. (Isaiah 2: 11.)

And I will punish the world for their evil, and the wicked for their iniquity; and I will cause the arrogancy of the proud to cease, and will lay low the haughtiness of the terrible. (Isaiah 13: 11.)

HEART.

HEART—the organ in the human body which by its motion keeps the blood in circulation—consequently, the seat of life. It is a common thought with mankind that the heart is the seat of all human affections and passions as well as that of life. The ancients, particularly the Jews, also had the idea that the intellect resided in the heart, and, when references to it occur in the Bible, the reader must not lose sight of this fact.

REFERENCES.

Heart of Man.

And God saw that the wickedness of man was great in the earth, and that every imagination of the thoughts of his heart was only evil continually. (Genesis 6: 5.)

And the Lord smelled a sweet savour; and the Lord said in his heart, I will not again curse the ground any more for man's sake; for the imagination of man's heart is evil from his youth: neither will I again smite any more every thing living, as I have done. (Genesis 8: 21.)

Because sentence against an evil work is not executed speedily, therefore the heart of the sons of men is fully set in them to do evil. (Ecclesiastes 8: 11.)

This is an evil among all things that are done under the sun, that there is one event unto all: yea, also the heart of the sons of men is full of evil, and madness is in their heart while they live, and after that they go to the dead. (Ecclesiastes 9: 3.)

The heart is deceitful above all things, and desperately wicked: who can know it? (Jeremiah 17: 9.)

O generation of vipers, how can ye,

being evil, speak good things? for out of the abundance of the heart the mouth speaketh. (Matthew 12: 34.)

But those things which proceed out of the mouth come forth from the heart; and they defile the man.

For out of the heart proceed evil thoughts, murders, adulteries, fornications, thefts, false witness, blasphemies. (Matthew 15: 18, 19.)

A good man out of the good treasure of his heart bringeth forth that which is good; and an evil man out of the evil treasure of his heart bringeth forth that which is evil: for of the abundance of the heart his mouth speaketh. (Luke 6: 45.)

But after thy hardness, and impenitent heart, treasurest up unto thyself wrath, against the day of wrath, and revelation of the righteous judgment of God. (Romans 2: 5.)

Searched and Tried by God.

And thou, Solomon my son, know thou the God of thy father, and serve him with a perfect heart and with a willing mind: for the Lord searcheth all hearts, and understandeth all the imaginations of the thoughts: if thou seek him, he will be found of thee; but if thou forsake him, he will cast thee off for ever. (1 Chronicles 28: 9.)

I know also, my God, that thou triest the heart, and hast pleasure in uprightness. As for me, in the uprightness of mine heart I have willingly offered all these things: and now have I seen with joy thy people, which are present here, to offer willingly unto thee. (1 Chronicles 29: 17.)

Shall not God search this out? for he knoweth the secrets of the heart. (Psalm 44: 21.)

Search me, O God, and know my heart: try me, and know my thoughts. (Psalm 129: 23.)

Every way of a man is right in his own eyes: but the Lord pondereth the hearts. (Proverbs 21: 2.)

If thou sayest, Behold, we knew it not; doth not he that pondereth the heart consider it? and he that keepeth thy soul, doth not he know it? and shall not he render to every man according to his works? (Proverbs 24: 12.)

Made Better by God.

For God who commanded the light to shine out of darkness, hath shined in our hearts, to give the light of the knowledge of the glory of God in the face of Jesus Christ. (2 Corinthians 4: 6.)

Wait on the Lord: be of good courage, and he shall strengthen thine heart: wait, I say, on the Lord. (Psalm 27: 14.)

The preparations of the heart in man, and the answer of the tongue, is from the Lord. (Proverbs 16: 1.)

To the end he may stablish your hearts unblameable in holiness before God even our Father, at the coming of our Lord Jesus Christ with all his Saints. (1 Thessalonians 3: 13.)

Promise of a New Heart.

And I will give them an heart to know me, that I am the Lord: and they shall be my people, and I will be their God: for they shall return unto me with their whole heart. (Jeremiah 24: 7.)

And I will give them one heart and one way, that they may fear me for ever, for the good of them, and of their children after them. (Jeremiah 32: 39.)

A new heart also will I give you, and a new spirit will I put within you: and

I will take away the stony heart out of your flesh, and I will give you an heart of flesh. (Ezekiel 36: 26.)

HEAVEN.

HEAV'EN—a word used in the Bible to indicate a number of different things and conditions, the more important of which are (1) the sky, or firmament above the earth; (2) the dwelling-place of God, the angels, and the blessed; (3) the abode of the blessed after death; (4) the assembly of God and the blessed collectively; (5) any place or condition of supreme happiness or comfort. The Bible paints in no uncertain colors the delights of Heaven, but the pen of man is quite incapable of telling all that Heaven must be, so we can have no distinct conception of it.

REFERENCES.

The Firmament as Heaven.

In the beginning God created the heaven and the earth. (Genesis 1: 1.)

And God called the firmament Heaven. And the evening and the morning were the second day. (Genesis 1: 8.)

O Lord our Lord, how excellent is thy name in all the earth! who hast set thy glory above the heavens. (Psalm 8: 1.)

It is he that sitteth upon the circle of the earth, and the inhabitants thereof are as grasshoppers; that stretcheth out the heavens as a curtain, and spreadeth them out as a tent to dwell in. (Isaiah 40: 22.)

God's Dwelling-Place.

And hearken thou to the supplication of thy servant, and of thy people Israel, when they shall pray toward this place: and hear thou in heaven thy dwelling-place: and when thou hearest, forgive. (1 Kings 8: 30.)

He that sitteth in the heavens shall laugh: the Lord shall have them in derision. (Psalm 2: 4.)

But our God is in the heavens; he hath done whatsoever he hath pleased. (Psalm 115: 3.)

Unto thee lift I up mine eyes, O thou that dwellest in the heavens. (Psalm 123: 1.)

Thus saith the Lord, The heaven is my throne, and the earth is my footstool: where is the house that ye build unto me? and where is the place of my rest? (Isaiah 66: 1.)

After this manner therefore pray ye: Our Father which art in heaven, Hallowed be thy name.

Thy kingdom come. Thy will be done in earth, as it is in heaven. (Matthew 6: 9, 10.)

Heaven is my throne, and earth is my footstool: What house will ye build me, saith the Lord? Or what is the place of my rest? (Acts 7: 49.)

Now of the things which we have spoken, this is the sum: we have such an high Priest, who is set on the right hand of the throne of the Majesty in the heavens. (Hebrews 8: 1.)

Happiness in Heaven.

Thou wilt shew me the path of life: in thy presence is fulness of joy; at thy right hand there are pleasures for evermore. (Psalm 16: 11.)

They shall not hunger nor thirst, neither shall the heat nor sun smite them: for he that hath mercy on them shall lead them, even by the springs of water shall he guide them. (Isaiah 49: 10.)

Rejoice, and be exceeding glad: for great is your reward in heaven: for so persecuted they the prophets which were before you. (Matthew 5: 12.)

Then shall the righteous shine forth

as the sun in the kingdom of their Father. Who hath ears to hear, let him hear. (Matthew 13: 43.)

In my Father's house are many mansions: if it were not so, I would have told you. I go to prepare a place for you. (John 14: 2.)

But as it is written, Eye hath not seen, nor ear heard, neither have entered into the heart of man, the things which God hath prepared for them that love him. (1 Corinthians 2: 9.)

To an inheritance incorruptible, and undefiled, and that fadeth not away, reserved in heaven for you. (1 Peter 1: 4.)

They shall hunger no more, neither thirst any more, neither shall the Sun light on them, nor any heat.

For the Lamb, which is in the midst of the throne, shall feed them, and shall lead them unto living fountains of waters: and God shall wipe away all tears from their eyes. (Revelation 7: 16, 17.)

And I heard a voice from heaven, saying unto me, Write, Blessed are the dead which die in the Lord, from henceforth, yea, saith the Spirit, that they may rest from their labours, and their works do follow them. (Revelation 14: 13.)

And God shall wipe away all tears from their eyes: and there shall be no more death, neither sorrow, nor crying, neither shall there be any more pain: for the former things are passed away. (Revelation 21: 4.)

Those Who Enter Heaven.

Blessed are the poor in spirit: for theirs is the kingdom of heaven. (Matthew 5: 3.)

Not every one that saith unto me, Lord, Lord, shall enter into the kingdom of heaven; but he that doeth the will of my Father which is in heaven. (Matthew 7: 21.)

Then shall the King say unto them on his right hand, Come, ye blessed of my Father, inherit the kingdom prepared for you from the foundation of the world. (Matthew 25: 34.)

And if children, then heirs, heirs of God, and joint-heirs with Christ: if so be that we suffer with him, that we may be also glorified together. (Romans 8: 17.)

But ye are come unto mount Sion, and unto the city of the living God the heavenly Jerusalem, and to an innumerable company of Angels:

To the general assembly, and Church of the firstborn which are written in heaven, and to God the Judge of all, and to the spirits of just men made perfect. (Hebrews 12: 22, 23.)

After this I beheld, and lo, a great multitude which no man could number, of all nations, and kindreds, and people, and tongues, stood before the throne, and before the Lamb, clothed with white robes, and palms in their hands. (Revelation 7: 9.)

And I said unto him, Sir, thou knowest. And he said to me, These are they which came out of great tribulation, and have washed their robes, and made them white in the blood of the Lamb. (Revelation 7: 14.)

Those Who Enter Not.

Many will say to me in that day, Lord, Lord, have we not prophesied in thy name? and in thy name have cast out devils? and in thy name done many wonderful works?

And then will I profess unto them, I never knew you: depart from me, ye that work iniquity. (Matthew 7: 22, 23.)

Then shall he say also unto them on the left hand, Depart from me, ye cursed, into everlasting fire, prepared for the devil and his angels:

For I was an hungered, and ye gave me no meat: I was thirsty, and ye gave me no drink:

I was a stranger, and ye took me not in: naked, and ye clothed me not: sick, and in prison, and ye visited me not. (Matthew 25: 41-43.)

Then shall ye begin to say, We have eaten and drunk in thy presence, and thou hast taught in our streets.

But he shall say, I tell you, I know you not whence ye are; depart from me, all ye workers of iniquity. (Luke 13: 26, 27.)

But the fearful, and unbelieving, and the abominable, and murderers, and whoremongers, and sorcerers, and idolaters, and all liars, shall have their part in the lake which burneth with fire and brimstone: which is the second death. (Revelation 21: 8.)

Heaven a Secure Abode.

But lay up for yourselves treasures in heaven, where neither moth nor rust doth corrupt, and where thieves do not break through nor steal. (Matthew 16: 20.)

But now they desire a better country, that is, a heavenly: wherefore God is not ashamed to be called their God: for he hath prepared for them a city. (Hebrews 11: 16.)

HEBREW. (See Israel, Israelites.)

HE'BREW. The appellation of Hebrew is really the name given to the Israelites by other nations and not the people's own distinctive name for themselves. The origin of the term is not known definitely, some ascribing it to a word meaning "ancestor" and others to a word meaning "to pass over." It is now generally applied to all members of the race as sons of Abraham. It is also specially applied to the language of the Jews.

HELL. (See Devil, Satan, etc.)

HELL. "Hell" came to the English language from the Anglo-Saxon. In old English it was used to designate the world of the dead generally, or the place of departed spirits, with all the sad and painful associations of the dark beyond. Modern English, however, has given it a more specific meaning—the place to which impenitent and damned spirits go finally; the abode of Satan, and the condition of punishment reserved for outcast sinners and wrongdoers.

In the Bible the word Hell is often used in this sense. The other words meaning about the same thing are Hades, which comes from the Greek; Sheol, which was the Hebrew term, and Gehenna.

REFERENCES.

Hell as the Grave.

He seeing this before, spake of the resurrection of Christ, that his soul was not left in hell, neither his flesh did see corruption. (Acts 2: 31.)

O death, where is thy sting? O grave, where is thy victory? (1 Corinthians 15: 55.)

And the sea gave up the dead which were in it: and death and hell delivered up the dead which were in them: and they were judged every man according to their works.

And death and hell were cast into the lake of fire: this is the second death. (Revelation 20: 13, 14.)

Hell Place of Torment.

And thou, Capernaum, which art exalted unto heaven, shalt be brought down to hell: for if the mighty works, which have been done in thee, had been done in Sodom, it would have remained until this day. (Matthew 11: 23.)

And shall cast them into a furnace of fire: there shall be wailing and gnashing of teeth. (Matthew 13: 42.)

And in hell he lifted up his eyes, being in torments, and seeth Abraham afar off, and Lazarus in his bosom. (Luke 16: 23.)

For if God spared not the Angels that sinned, but cast them down to hell, and delivered them into chains of darkness, to be reserved unto judgment. (2 Peter 2: 4.)

The same shall drink of the wine of the wrath of God, which is poured out without mixture into the cup of his indignation, and he shall be tormented with fire and brimstone, in the presence of the holy Angels, and in the presence of the Lamb:

And the smoke of their torment ascendeth up for ever and ever. And they have no rest day nor night, who worship the beast and his image, and whosoever receiveth the mark of his name. (Revelation 14: 10, 11.)

And the devil that deceived them, was cast into the lake of fire and brimstone, where the beast and the false prophet are, and shall be tormented day and night, for ever and ever. (Revelation 20: 10.)

And whosoever was not found written in the book of life, was cast into the lake of fire. (Revelation 20: 15.)

Those Sent to Hell.

The wicked shall be turned into hell, and all the nations that forget God. (Psalm 9: 17.)

But I say unto you, That whosoever is angry with his brother without a cause shall be in danger of the judgment: and whosoever shall say to his brother, Raca, shall be in danger of the council: but whosoever shall say, Thou

fool, shall be in danger of hell fire. (Matthew 5: 22.)

Woe unto you, scribes and Pharisees, hypocrites! for ye compass sea and land to make one proselyte, and when he is made, ye make him twofold more the child of hell than yourselves. (Matthew 23: 15.)

And when he had opened the fourth seal, I heard the voice of the fourth beast say, Come and see.

And I looked, and behold a pale horse: and his name that sat on him was Death, and Hell followed with him. And power was given unto them over the fourth part of the earth, to kill with sword, and with hunger, and with death, and with the beasts of the earth. (Revelation 6: 7, 8.)

HERESY.

HER'E-SY—an opinion held in opposition to the established or authorized doctrine of a church or sect or denomination, especially when it is of a nature likely to cause a division or separation; a lack of orthodox or sound belief. Scripture teaches the serious and dangerous nature of heresy, showing that it tends to subvert the religion of the Lord Jesus Christ, and warns against it.

REFERENCES.

For first of all, when ye come together in the church, I hear that there be divisions among you; and I partly believe it.

For there must be also heresies among you, that they which are approved may be made manifest among you. (1 Corinthians 11: 18, 19.)

Now the works of the flesh are manifest, which are these, adultery, fornication, uncleanness, lasciviousness,

Idolatry, witchcraft, hatred, variance, emulations, wrath, strife, seditions, heresies. (Galatians 5: 19, 20.)

But there were false prophets also among the people, even as there shall be false teachers among you, who privily shall bring in damnable heresies, even denying the Lord that bought them, and bring upon themselves swift destruction. (2 Peter 2: 1.)

Now I beseech you, brethren, mark them which cause divisions and offences contrary to the doctrine which ye have learned; and avoid them. (Romans 16: 17.)

Now I beseech you, brethren, by the Name of our Lord Jesus Christ, that ye all speak the same thing, and that there be no divisions among you: but that ye be perfectly joined together in the same mind, and in the same judgment. (1 Corinthians 1: 10.)

For God is not the author of confusion, but of peace, as in all churches of the saints. (1 Corinthians 14: 33.)

HEROD.

HER'OD. The large number of Herods mentioned in the gospels often causes some confusion to the reader. The name Herod was the family name of a line of bad but powerful rulers of Judea under the authority of Rome. They enjoyed the title of king, although they were responsible to the Roman Cæsar for all their acts. With one or two exceptions, the Herodian family was thoroughly bad. At the same time they were thoroughly capable. The head and founder of the family, Herod the Great, was a monster of iniquity, his whole reign being one series of murders and bloodshed. His only good work was the rebuilding of the temple at Jerusalem. Even this, however, was not destined to stand, despite the fact that the Master walked and talked within its walls. It was destroyed in the sack of Jerusalem by the troops of the Roman Emperor Titus. This Herod was the one who tried to bring about the death of the infant Jesus by killing the children in Bethlehem. His son, Herod Antipas, was on the throne when Jesus went up to Jerusalem for the last time, and sent Jesus to Pilate for trial. Herodias, the woman who brought about the death of John the Baptist, was his wife.

References.—Matthew 2 (for Herod the Great); Matthew 14 (for Herod Antipas).

HEZEKIAH.

HEZ'E-KI'AH—a form of a Hebrew word meaning "strength of Jehovah." Hezekiah was the twelfth king of Judah and one of the best of Judah's kingly line, although he was the son of the idolater Ahaz. He was born about 726 B.C., ascended the throne when about twenty-five years old, and reigned twenty-nine years. One of the first acts of his reign was to do away with the idol-worship that had grown up under his father and restore the true faith. He then turned his attention to win back the cities captured by the Philistines. His success in these military operations led him to refuse tribute to Assyria, which nation had already destroyed the kingdom of Israel and led away the ten tribes captive. This act brought to his doors an Assyrian army, and Hezekiah was forced to make terms by despoiling the Temple of gold to give to the Assyrians, who promptly broke faith, and were just as promptly punished by God, who in a night destroyed 180,000 of them by plague. Hezekiah fell ill, and, after earnest prayer, was told by the prophet Isaiah that God would spare his life for fifteen years. The remainder of his reign appears to have been peaceable and prosperous.

References.—2 Kings 16; 18; 19; 20.

HOLINESS.

HO'LI-NESS—moral purity; freedom from sin; purity; high state of religious feeling. The Bible mentions two sorts of holiness—that of God, which is perfect, and that of man, which is man's attempt to follow in the way of God. It is a grace that the Scripture enjoins man, in a number of places, to acquire.

REFERENCES.

For I am the Lord your God: ye shall therefore sanctify yourselves, and ye shall be holy; for I am holy: neither shall ye defile yourselves with any manner of creeping thing that creepeth upon the earth. (Leviticus 11: 44.)

Sanctify yourselves therefore and be ye holy: for I am the Lord your God.

And ye shall keep my statutes, and do them: I am the Lord which sanctify you. (Leviticus 20: 7.)

That ye may remember, and do all my commandments, and be holy unto your God. (Numbers 15: 40.)

In holiness and righteousness before him, all the days of our life. (Luke 1: 75.)

I beseech you therefore, brethren, by the mercies of God, that ye present your bodies a living sacrifice, holy, acceptable unto God, which is your reasonable service. (Romans 12: 1.)

Having therefore these promises, dearly beloved, let us cleanse ourselves from all filthiness of the flesh and spirit, perfecting holiness in the fear of God. (2 Corinthians 7: 1.)

According as he hath chosen us in him, before the foundation of the world, that we should be holy, and without blame before him in love. (Ephesians 1: 4.)

And that ye put on that new man, which after God is created in righteousness, and true holiness. (Ephesians 4: 24.)

Put on therefore, as the elect of God, holy and beloved, bowels of mercies, kindness, humbleness of mind, meekness, longsuffering. (Colossians 3: 12.)

Follow peace with all men, and holiness, without which no man shall see the Lord. (Hebrews 12: 14.)

But as he which hath called you is holy, so be ye holy in all manner of conversation;

Because it is written, Be ye holy, for I am holy. (1 Peter 1: 15, 16.)

Seeing then that all these things shall be dissolved, What manner of persons ought ye to be in all holy conversation, and godliness? (2 Peter 3: 11.)

He that is unjust, let him be unjust still: and he which is filthy, let him be filthy still: and he that is righteous, let him be righteous still: and he that is holy, let him be holy still. (Revelation 22: 11.)

HOLY GHOST. (See Christ, God, Jesus, Trinity.)

HOʼLY GHOST—the third person of the Trinity of God the Father, God the Son and God the Holy Ghost, also called the Holy Spirit. The orthodox doctrine of Christianity teaches that the Holy Ghost is a part of the Godhead, co-equal and co-eternal; in other words, that as God the Son is God by reason of eternal affiliation, so God the Holy Ghost is God by reason of procession, the doctrine holding that God the Holy Ghost proceeds from the Father and the Son. This is set forth in the three great creeds—generally in the Apostles', and specifically in the Nicene and Athanasian. The divinity and office of the Holy Ghost are clearly taught in the New Testament, but in the Old Testament we find references only by prophecy and inference, although the Spirit of God is often mentioned. Complete revelation of the Holy Ghost did not come until after the death and ascension of Jesus Christ, therefore that which is now thoroughly understood by Christianity was but imperfectly grasped by the people of patriarchal times. With the present light enjoyed by Christianity it is clear that many things from the time of Samuel were direct operations of the Holy Ghost. We also find manifestations of the Holy Ghost in events immediately prior to the birth of Jesus, and during His life and work with His disciples, and we also find the Master making references to the Spirit, as well as giving the promise to send the Comforter after His passing. This was fulfilled after His ascension, at which time the dispensation of the Holy Ghost to man may be said to have begun. All this was foreshadowed by the Master, chiefly, perhaps, in the command to baptize in the name of the Father, Son, and Holy Ghost.

REFERENCES.

Attributes.

Eternal:

How much more shall the blood of Christ, who through the eternal Spirit offered himself without spot to God, purge your conscience from dead works, to serve the living God? (Hebrews 9: 14.)

Omnipresent:

Whither shall I go from thy Spirit? or whither shall I flee from thy presence?

If I ascend up into heaven, thou art there: if I make my bed in hell, behold thou art there.

If I take the wings of the morning, and dwell in the uttermost parts of the sea;

Even there shall thy hand lead me, and thy right hand shall hold me.

If I say, Surely the darkness shall cover me; even the night shall be light about me.

Yea, the darkness hideth not from thee; but the night shineth as the day: the darkness and the light are both alike to thee. (Psalm 139: 7-12.)

Omniscient:

But God hath revealed them unto us by his Spirit: for the Spirit searcheth all things, yea, the deep things of God. (1 Corinthians 2: 10.)

Omnipotent:

The Spirit of God hath made me, and the breath of the Almighty hath given me life. (Job 33: 4.)

And the Angel answered and said unto her, The holy Ghost shall come upon thee, and the power of the Highest shall overshadow thee. Therefore also that holy thing which shall be born of thee, shall be called the son of God. (Luke 1: 35.)

Through mighty signs and wonders, by the power of the Spirit of God, so that from Jerusalem, and round about unto Illyricum, I have fully preached the Gospel of Christ. (Romans 15: 19.)

Proceeds from Father and Son:

But the Comforter, which is the Holy Ghost, whom the Father will send in my name, he shall teach you all things, and bring all things to your remembrance, whatsoever I have said unto you. (John 14: 26.)

But when the Comforter is come, whom I will send unto you from the Father, even the Spirit of truth, which proceedeth from the Father, he shall testify of me. (John 15: 26.)

And when he had said this, he breathed on them, and saith unto them, *Receive ye the Holy Ghost.* (John 20: 22.)

For it is not ye that speak, but the Spirit of your Father which speaketh in you. (Matthew 10: 20.)

Howbeit when he, the Spirit of truth, is come, he will guide you into all truth: for he shall not speak of himself; but whatsoever he shall hear, that shall he speak: and he will shew you things to come.

He shall glorify me: for he shall receive of mine, and shall shew it unto you.

All things that the Father hath are mine: therefore said I, that he shall take of mine, and shall shew it unto you. (John 16: 13-15.)

If ye be reproached for the Name of Christ, happy are ye, for the spirit of glory, and of God resteth upon you: on their part he is evil spoken of, but on your part he is glorified. (1 Peter 4: 14.)

Offices, Etc.

Author of New Birth:

Jesus answered, *Verily, verily, I say unto thee, Except a man be born of water and of the Spirit, he cannot enter into the kingdom of God.*

That which is born of the flesh is flesh; and that which is born of the Spirit is spirit. (John 3: 5, 6.)

Appointing and Directing Ministers:

As they ministered to the Lord, and fasted, the Holy Ghost said, Separate me Barnabas and Saul, for the work whereunto I have called them. (Acts 13: 2.)

So they, being sent forth by the Holy Ghost, departed unto Seleucia, and from thence they sailed to Cyprus. (Acts 13: 4.)

Take heed therefore unto yourselves, and to all the flock, over the which the Holy Ghost hath made you overseers, to feed the Church of God, which he hath purchased with his own blood. (Acts 20: 28.)

Now when they had gone throughout Phrygia, and the region of Galatia, and were forbidden of the Holy Ghost to preach the word in Asia,

After they were come to Mysia, they assayed to go into Bithynia: but the Spirit suffered them not. (Acts 16: 6, 7.)

Can Be Vexed, Resisted, Tempted:

But they rebelled, and vexed his Holy Spirit: therefore he was turned to be their enemy, and he fought against them. (Isaiah 63: 10.)

Ye stiffnecked and uncircumcised in heart, and ears, ye do always resist the Holy Ghost: as your fathers did, so do ye. (Acts 7: 51.)

Then Peter said unto her, How is it that ye have agreed together, to tempt the Spirit of the Lord? behold, the feet of them which have buried thy husband are at the door, and shall carry thee out. (Acts 5: 9.)

Comforter, Sanctifier, Helper:

The Spirit of the Lord God is upon me; because the Lord hath anointed me to preach good tidings unto the meek; he hath sent me to bind up the brokenhearted, to proclaim liberty to the captives, and the opening of the prison to them that are bound;

To proclaim the acceptable year of the Lord, and the day of vengeance of our God; to comfort all that mourn. (Isaiah 61: 1, 2.)

And I will pray the Father, and he shall give you another Comforter, that he may abide with you for ever;

Even the Spirit of truth; whom the world cannot receive, because it seeth him not, neither knoweth him: but ye know him; for he dwelleth with you, and shall be in you. (John 14: 16, 17.)

But when the Comforter is come, whom I will send unto you from the Father, even the Spirit of truth, which proceedeth from the Father, he shall testify of me. (John 15: 26.)

And the heathen shall know that I the Lord do sanctify Israel, when my sanctuary shall be in the midst of them for evermore. (Ezekiel 37: 28.)

That I should be the minister of Jesus Christ to the Gentiles, ministering the gospel of God, that the offering up of the Gentiles might be acceptable, being sanctified by the Holy Ghost. (Romans 15: 16.)

Then had the churches rest throughout all Judæa and Galilee and Samaria, and were edified; and walking in the fear of the Lord, and in the comfort of the Holy Ghost, were multiplied. (Acts 9: 31.)

Likewise the spirit also helpeth our infirmities: for we know not what we should pray for as we ought: but the spirit itself maketh intercession for us with groanings which cannot be uttered. (Romans 8: 26.)

And hope maketh not ashamed, because the love of God is shed abroad in our hearts, by the Holy Ghost, which is given unto us. (Romans 3: 5.)

For the kingdom of God is not meat and drink; but righteousness, and peace, and joy in the Holy Ghost. (Romans 14: 17.)

For we through the spirit wait for the hope of righteousness by faith. (Galatians 5: 5.)

But the fruit of the spirit is love, joy, peace, longsuffering, gentleness, goodness, faith. (Galatians 5: 22.)

Dwells with Saints:

Even the Spirit of truth; whom the world cannot receive, because it seeth him not, neither knoweth him: but ye know him; for he dwelleth with you, and shall be in you. (John 14: 17.)

What? know ye not that your body is the temple of the Holy Ghost which is in you, which ye have of God, and ye are not your own? (1 Corinthians 6: 19.)

Has Own Power and Will:

Now the God of hope fill you with all joy and peace in believing, that ye may abound in hope through the power of the Holy Ghost. (Romans 15: 13.)

But all these worketh that one and the selfsame spirit, dividing to every man severally as he will. (1 Corinthians 12: 11.)

Inspiring Scripture:

Men and brethren, this scripture must needs have been fulfilled, which the Holy Ghost by the mouth of David spake before concerning Judas, which was guide to them that took Jesus. (Acts 1: 16.)

Of which salvation the Prophets have inquired, and searched diligently, who prophesied of the grace that should come unto you,

Searching what, or what manner of time the Spirit of Christ which was in them did signify, when it testified beforehand the sufferings of Christ, and the glory that should follow.

Unto whom it was revealed, that not unto themselves, but unto us, they did minister the things which are now reported unto you by them that have preached the Gospel unto you, with the Holy Ghost sent down from heaven, which things the Angels desire to look into. (1 Peter 1: 10-12.)

For the prophecy came not in old time by the will of man: but holy men of God spake as they were moved by the Holy Ghost. (2 Peter 1: 21.)

Source of Wisdom and Power:

And the Spirit of the Lord shall rest upon him, the spirit of wisdom and understanding, the spirit of counsel and might, the spirit of knowledge and of the fear of the Lord. (Isaiah 11: 2.)

But the Comforter, which is the Holy Ghost, whom the Father will send in my name, he shall teach you all things, and bring all things to your remembrance, whatsoever I have said unto you. (John 14: 26.)

For to one is given by the spirit the

word of wisdom, to another the word of knowledge, by the same spirit. (1 Corinthians 12: 8.)

But if I cast out devils by the Spirit of God, then the kingdom of God is come unto you. (Matthew 12: 28.)

Through mighty signs and wonders, by the power of the Spirit of God, so that from Jerusalem, and round about unto Illyricum, I have fully preached the Gospel of Christ. (Romans 15: 19.)

Strives with and Convinces Sinners:

And the Lord said, My Spirit shall not always strive with man, for that he also is flesh: yet his days shall be an hundred and twenty years. (Genesis 6: 3.)

And when he is come, he will reprove the world of sin, and of righteousness, and of judgment:

Of sin, because they believe not on me;

Of righteousness, because I go to my Father, and ye see me no more;

Of judgment, because the prince of this world is judged. (John 16: 8-11.)

The Witness:

Whereof the Holy Ghost also is a witness to us: for after that he had said before,

This is the covenant that I will make with them after those days, saith the Lord, I will put my laws into their hearts, and in their minds will I write them;

And their sins and iniquities will I remember no more. (Hebrews 10: 15-17.)

If we receive the witness of men, the witness of God is greater: for this is the witness of God which he hath testified of his Son. (1 John 5: 9.)

Gift of the Holy Ghost.

By the Father:

Thou gavest also thy good Spirit to instruct them, and withheldest not thy manna from their mouth, and gavest them water for their thirst. (Nehemiah 9: 20.)

By the Son:

And when he had said this, he breathed on them, and saith unto them, *Receive ye the Holy Ghost.* (John 20: 22.)

After the Ascension:

(But this spake he of the Spirit, which they that believe on him should receive: for the Holy Ghost was not yet given; because that Jesus was not yet glorified.) (John 7: 39.)

In Answer to Prayer:

If ye then, being evil, know how to give good gifts unto your children: how much more shall your heavenly Father give the Holy Spirit to them that ask him? (Luke 11: 13.)

After Repentance and Baptism:

Then Peter said unto them, Repent, and be baptized every one of you in the name of Jesus Christ for the remission of sins, and ye shall receive the gift of the Holy Ghost. (Acts 2: 38.)

While Peter yet spake these words, the Holy Ghost fell on all them which heard the word.

And they of the circumcision which believed were astonished, as many as came with Peter, because that on the Gentiles also was poured out the gift of the Holy Ghost. (Acts 10: 44, 45.)

Holy Ghost's Qualities:

Until the Spirit be poured upon us from on high, and the wilderness be a fruitful field, and the fruitful field be counted for a forest. (Isaiah 32: 15.)

As for me, this is my covenant with them, saith the Lord; My Spirit that is upon thee, and my words which I have put in thy mouth, shall not depart out of thy mouth, nor out of the mouth of thy seed, nor out of the mouth of thy seed's seed, saith the Lord, from henceforth and for ever. (Isaiah 59: 21.)

Neither will I hide my face any more from them: for I have poured out my Spirit upon the house of Israel, saith the Lord God. (Ezekiel 39: 29.)

Now he which stablisheth us with you in Christ, and hath anointed us, is God,

Who hath also sealed us, and given the earnest of the Spirit in our hearts. (2 Corinthians 1: 21, 22.)

That the blessing of Abraham might come on the Gentiles, through Jesus Christ: that we might receive the promise of the Spirit through faith. (Galatians 3: 14.)

And he that keepeth his commandments dwelleth in him, and he in him: and hereby we know that he abideth in us, by the spirit which he hath given us. (1 John 3: 24.)

Symbols and Emblems of Holy Ghost.

Dove:

And Jesus, when he was baptized, went up straightway out of the water: and lo, the heavens were opened unto him, and he saw the Spirit of God descending like a dove, and lighting upon him. (Matthew 3: 16.)

Fire:

I indeed baptize you with water unto repentance: but he that cometh after me is mightier than I, whose shoes I am not worthy to bear: he shall bap-

tize you with the Holy Ghost, and with fire. (Matthew 3: 11.)

Oil:

But the anointing which ye have received of him, abideth in you: and ye need not that any man teach you: But, as the same anointing teacheth you of all things, and is truth, and is no lie: and even as it hath taught you, ye shall abide in him. (1 John 2: 27.)

Rain and Dew:

And I will make them and the places round about my hill a blessing; and I will cause the shower to come down in his season; there shall be showers of blessing. (Ezekiel 34: 26.)

Seal:

Who hath also sealed us, and given the earnest of the Spirit in our hearts. (2 Corinthians 1: 22.)

Tongues:

And there appeared unto them cloven tongues like as of fire, and it sat upon each of them.

And they were all filled with the Holy Ghost, and began to speak with other tongues, as the Spirit gave them utterance. (Acts 2: 3, 4.)

Voice:

Also I heard the voice of the Lord, saying, Whom shall I send, and who will go for us? Then said I, Here am I; send me. (Isaiah 6: 8.)

Water:

Jesus answered, *Verily, verily, I say unto thee, Except a man be born of water and of the Spirit, he cannot enter into the kingdom of God.* (John 3: 5.)

Sin against Holy Ghost:

Wherefore I say unto you, All manner of sin and blasphemy shall be for-

given unto men: but the blasphemy against the Holy Ghost shall not be forgiven unto men.

And whosoever speaketh a word against the Son of man, it shall be forgiven him: but whosoever speaketh against the Holy Ghost, it shall not be forgiven him, neither in this world, neither in the world to come. (Matthew 12: 31, 32.)

Verily I say unto you, All sins shall be forgiven unto the sons of men, and blasphemies wherewith soever they shall blaspheme:

But he that shall blaspheme against the Holy Ghost hath never forgiveness, but is in danger of eternal damnation. (Mark 3: 28, 29.)

And whosoever speaketh a word against the Son of man, it shall be forgiven him: but whosoever speaketh against the Holy Ghost it shall not be forgiven. (Luke 12: 10.)

If any man see his brother sin a sin which is not unto death, he shall ask, and he shall give him life for them that sin not unto death. There is a sin unto death: I do not say that he shall pray for it. (1 John 5: 16.)

For it is impossible for those who were once enlightened, and have tasted of the heavenly gift, and were made partakers of the Holy Ghost,

And have tasted the good word of God, and the powers of the world to come,

If they shall fall away, to renew them again unto repentance; seeing they crucify to themselves the Son of God afresh, and put him to an open shame. (Hebrews 6: 4-6.)

For if we sin wilfully after that we have received the knowledge of the truth, there remaineth no more sacrifice for sins. (Hebrews 10: 26.)

HONESTY.

HON'ES-TY—the state of being honest; integrity, sincerity, truthfulness, straightforwardness of speech or conduct. No man can be a Christian or follow the Master's teaching unless he is honest. The Bible contains many exhortations to honesty.

REFERENCES.

Better is a little with righteousness, than great revenues without right. (Proverbs 16: 8.)

Seest thou a man diligent in his business? he shall stand before kings; he shall not stand before mean men. (Proverbs 22: 29.)

Withhold not good from them to whom it is due, when it is in the power of thine hand to do it.

Say not unto thy neighbour, Go, and come again, and to-morrow I will give; when thou hast it by thee. (Proverbs 3: 27, 28.)

The wicked borroweth and payeth not again: but the righteous sheweth mercy, and giveth. (Psalm 37: 21.)

Recompense to no man evil for evil. Provide things honest in the sight of all men. (Romans 12: 17.)

Let us walk honestly as in the day, not in rioting and drunkenness, not in chambering and wantonness, not in strife and envying. (Romans 13: 13.)

Providing for honest things, not only in the sight of the Lord, but in the sight of men. (2 Corinthians 8: 21.)

Now I pray to God that ye do no evil, not that we should appear approved, but that ye should do that which is honest, though we be as reprobates. (2 Corinthians 13: 7.)

Finally, brethren, whatsoever things are true, whatsoever things are honest, whatsoever things are just, whatsoever things are pure, whatsoever things are lovely, whatsoever things are of good report: if there be any virtue, and if there be any praise, think on these things. (Philippians 4: 8.)

That ye may walk honestly toward them that are without, and that ye may have lack of nothing. (1 Thessalonians 4: 12.)

I exhort therefore, that first of all, supplications, prayers, intercessions, and giving of thanks be made for all men:

For Kings, and for all that are in authority, that we may lead a quiet and peaceable life in all godliness and honesty. (1 Timothy 2: 1, 2.)

Pray for us: for we trust we have a good conscience in all things, willing to live honestly. (Hebrews 13: 18.)

HONOR. (Spelled "honour" throughout the Bible.)

Hon′or—used chiefly in the Bible to mean respect, esteem, reverence, deference. The Scriptures teach that honor should be paid to God, that parents should be honored, that the ruler or rulers of a country should receive honor, that all persons in authority should receive the honor due their rank and position.

REFERENCES.

Honor Due to God.

Give unto the Lord the glory due unto his name; worship the Lord in the beauty of holiness. (Psalm 29: 2.)

Let my mouth be filled with thy praise and with thy honour all the day. (Psalm 71: 8.)

I will speak of the glorious honour of thy majesty, and of thy wondrous works. (Psalm 145: 5.)

A son honoureth his father, and a servant his master: if then I be a father, where is mine honour? and if I be a master, where is my fear? saith the Lord of hosts unto you, O priests, that despise my name. And ye say,

Wherein have we despised thy name? (Malachi 1: 6.)

Now unto the king eternal, immortal, invisible, the only wise God, be honour and glory for ever and ever. Amen. (1 Timothy 1: 17.)

Thou art worthy, O Lord, to receive glory, and honour, and power: for thou hast created all things, and for thy pleasure they are, and were created. (Revelation 4: 11.)

And every creature which is in heaven, and on the earth, and under the earth, and such as are in the sea, and all that are in them, heard I, saying, Blessing, honour, glory, and power be unto him that sitteth upon the Throne, and unto the Lamb for ever and ever. (Revelation 5: 13.)

Honor Granted by God.

And I have also given thee that which thou hast not asked, both riches, and honour: so that there shall not be any among the kings like unto thee all thy days. (1 Kings 3: 13.)

The Jews had light, and gladness, and joy, and honour. (Esther 8: 16.)

Length of days is in her right hand; and in her left hand riches and honour. (Proverbs 3: 16.)

Exalt her, and she shall promote thee: she shall bring thee to honour, when thou dost embrace her. (Proverbs 4: 8.)

Riches and honour are with me; yea, durable riches and righteousness. (Proverbs 8: 18.)

By humility and the fear of the Lord are riches, and honour, and life. (Proverbs 22: 4.)

A man's pride shall bring him low: but honour shall uphold the humble in spirit. (Proverbs 29: 23.)

O thou king, the most high God gave

Nebuchadnezzar thy father a kingdom, and majesty, and glory, and honour. (Daniel 5: 18.)

If any man serve me, let him follow me; and where I am, there shall also my servant be: if any man serve me, him will my Father honour. (John 12: 26.)

Honor Due to Parents.

Honour thy father and thy mother; that thy days may be long upon the land which the Lord thy God giveth thee. (Exodus 20: 12.)

For God commanded, saying, Honour thy father and mother: and, He that curseth father or mother, let him die the death.

But ye say, Whosoever shall say to his father or his mother, It is a gift, by whatsoever thou mightest be profited by me;

And honour not his father or his mother, he shall be free. Thus have ye made the commandment of God of none effect by your tradition. (Matthew 15: 4-6.)

Honor to the Aged.

Thou shalt rise up before the hoary head, and honour the face of the old man, and fear thy God: I am the Lord. (Leviticus 19: 32.)

Honor to Rulers, Etc.

Honour all men. Love the brotherhood. Fear God. Honour the King. (1 Peter 2: 17.)

HOPE.

HOPE. Hope is one of the most uplifting emotions of which man is capable. It is the desire for some good, with the expectation of obtaining it; pleasing expectancy; the cherishing of an aim with the thought of attaining it. With it there is always a certain amount of joy or pleasure. It is one of man's most natural passions, given him by God for the purpose of making him better, since it enables him to bear better his burdens and infuses strength when he is weak or worn.

REFERENCES.

Good Hope.

Therefore my heart is glad, and my glory rejoiceth: my flesh also shall rest in hope. (Psalm 16: 9.)

Be of good courage, and he shall strengthen your heart, all ye that hope in the Lord. (Psalm 31: 24.)

And have hope towards God, which they themselves also allow, that there shall be a resurrection of the dead, both of the just and unjust. (Acts 24: 15.)

Now the God of hope fill you with all joy and peace in believing, that ye may abound in hope, through the power of the Holy Ghost. (Ronians 15: 13.)

Now our Lord Jesus Christ himself, and God, even our Father, which hath loved us, and hath given us everlasting consolation and good hope through grace. (2 Thessalonians 2: 16.)

Hopes of Wicked Perish.

So are the paths of all that forget God; and the hypocrite's hope shall perish. (Job 8: 13.)

But the eyes of the wicked shall fail, and they shall not escape, and their hope shall be as the giving up of the ghost. (Job 11: 20.)

That at that time ye were without Christ, being aliens from the commonwealth of Israel, and strangers from the covenants of promise, having no hope, and without God in the world. (Ephesians 2: 12.)

Hope's Comfort.

And thou shalt be secure, because there is hope; yea, thou shalt dig about thee, and thou shalt take thy rest in safety. (Job 11: 18.)

Happy is he that hath the God of Jacob for his help, whose hope is in the Lord his God. (Psalm 146: 5.)

Blessed is the man that trusteth in the Lord, and whose hope the Lord is. (Jeremiah 17: 7.)

Rejoicing in hope, patient in tribulation, continuing instant in prayer. (Romans 12: 12.)

For whatsoever things were written aforetime, were written for our learning, that we through patience and comfort of the Scriptures might have hope. (Romans 15: 4.)

And now abideth faith, hope, charity, these three, but the greatest of these is charity. (1 Corinthians 13: 13.)

There is one body, and one spirit, even as ye are called in one hope of your calling. (Ephesians 4: 4.)

For the hope which is laid up for you in heaven, whereof ye heard before in the word of the truth of the Gospel. (Colossians 1: 5.)

But Christ as a Son over his own house, whose house are we, if we hold fast the confidence, and the rejoicing of the hope firm unto the end. (Hebrews 3: 6.)

Hope's Encouragement.

Why art thou cast down, O my soul? and why art thou disquieted in me? hope thou in God: for I shall yet praise him for the help of his countenance. (Psalm 42: 5.)

Let Israel hope in the Lord: for with the Lord there is mercy, and with him is plenteous redemption. (Psalm 130: 7.)

It is good that a man should both hope and quietly wait for the salvation of the Lord. (Lamentations 3: 26.)

Turn you to the strong hold, ye prisoners of hope: even to-day do I declare that I will render double unto thee. (Zechariah 9: 12.)

If ye continue in the faith grounded and settled, and be not moved away from the hope of the Gospel, which ye have heard, and which was preached to every creature which is under heaven, whereof I Paul am made a Minister. (Colossians 1: 23.)

Looking for that blessed hope, and the glorious appearing of the great God, and our Saviour Jesus Christ. (Titus 2: 13.)

And we desire, that every one of you do shew the same diligence, to the full assurance of hope unto the end. (Hebrews 6: 11.)

Wherefore gird up the loins of your mind, be sober, and hope to the end, for the grace that is to be brought unto you at the revelation of Jesus Christ. (1 Peter 1: 13.)

Hope's Effects.

And hope maketh not ashamed; because the love of God is shed abroad in our hearts by the Holy Ghost which is given unto us. (Romans 5: 5.)

For we are saved by hope: but hope that is seen is not hope: for what a man seeth, why doth he yet hope for?

But if we hope for that we see not, then do we with patience wait for it. (Romans 8: 24, 25.)

Hope God's Gift.

For we through the Spirit wait for the hope of righteousness by faith. (Galatians 5: 5.)

Now our Lord Jesus Christ himself, and God even our Father, which hath loved us, and hath given us everlasting consolation, and good hope through grace. (2 Thessalonians 2: 16.)

In hope of eternal life, which God that cannot lie, promised before the world began. (Titus 1: 2.)

Blessed be the God and Father of our Lord Jesus Christ, which according to his abundant mercy hath begotten us again unto a lively hope, by the resurrection of Jesus Christ from the dead. (1 Peter 1: 3.)

HOREB. (See Sinai.)

HOSANNA.

Ho-san'na—a very ancient Hebrew exclamation meaning "Save now!" or "Succor now!" It was used as an exclamation of praise to the Lord or for the calling down of blessings. The shouts of "Hosanna" raised at the Master's public entry into Jerusalem may be taken to mean: "Lord, preserve this Son of David and give him many favors and blessings!"

References.—Matthew 21: 9; Mark 11: 9, 10; John 12: 13.

HOSEA.

Ho-se'a—a form of a Hebrew word meaning "deliverer." Hosea was one of the most remarkable of the minor prophets. He lived about 785 B.C. Little is known with exactness of his birth and parentage and the name of the tribe to which he belonged. That his life must have been filled with tragedy may be gathered from his book and the terrible and bloody history of the time in which he wrote.

Reference.—The book of Hosea.

HOSHEA.

Ho-she'a—a form of a Hebrew word meaning "God is help." Hoshea was the last king of Israel. He conspired against his predecessor, Pekah, and slew him, later usurping the throne. His reign was bloody and wicked. Shalmaneser, the Assyrian king, attacked him about the year 720 B.C., defeated the Israelite army, and sent the ten tribes

composing the kingdom into captivity beyond the Euphrates river.

References.—2 Kings 15 and 17.

HOSPITALITY.

Hos-pi-tal'i-ty—the act or practice of being hospitable; the reception or entertainment of persons—either friends or strangers—without reward. Hospitality was a very common virtue in Biblical times, and indeed it continues to be in most Eastern countries. The Bible teaches it as a Christian trait.

REFERENCES.

Be not forgetful to entertain strangers: for thereby some have entertained angels unawares. (Hebrews 13: 2.)

Use hospitality one to another without grudging.

As every man hath received the gift, even so minister the same one to another, as good stewards of the manifold grace of God. (1 Peter 4: 9, 10.)

Beloved, thou doest faithfully whatsoever thou doest to the brethren, and to strangers;

Which have borne witness of thy charity before the church: whom if thou bring forward on their journey after a godly sort, thou shalt do well:

Because that for his name's sake they went forth, taking nothing of the Gentiles,

We therefore ought to receive such, that we might be fellow helpers to the truth. (3 John 1: 5-8.)

If there come any unto you, and bring not this doctrine, receive him not into your house, neither bid him God speed:

For he that biddeth him God speed is partaker of his evil deeds. (2 John 1: 10, 11.)

I wrote unto the church: but Diotrephes, who loveth to have the preëminence among them, receiveth us not.

Wherefore, if I come, I will remember his deeds which he doeth, prating against us with malicious words: and not content therewith, neither doth he himself receive the brethren, and forbiddeth them that would, and casteth them out of the church. (3 John 1: 9, 10.)

For whosoever shall give you a cup of water to drink in my name, because ye belong to Christ, verily I say unto you, he shall not lose his reward. (Mark 9: 41.)

HUMILITY.

Hu-mil'i-ty—the state of being humble; freedom from pride and arrogance; a modest estimate of one's worth, or a sense of unworthiness through imperfection or sinfulness; lowliness; meekness. Humility, as a characteristic of the Christian, is one of the effects of the divine grace upon the human mind and soul. It is by no means to be regarded as meanness or baseness, but it is a medium between foolish and ignominious self-effacement and pride and vainglory. When we are humble we do not attribute to ourselves any goodness or virtue that we do not have, we do not overrate ourselves, we do not take immoderate delight in ourselves, we realize our imperfections, and we ascribe all our goodness and good works to God. The Bible teaches that humility is pleasing to God, and we have, as a pattern of humility, the Master Himself.

REFERENCES.

Humility Becoming.

And Abraham answered and said, Behold now, I have taken upon me to speak unto the Lord, which am but dust and ashes. (Genesis 18: 27.)

Lord, my heart is not haughty, nor mine eyes lofty: neither do I exercise myself in great matters, or in things too high for me. (Psalm 131: 1.)

Surely I am more brutish than any man, and have not the understanding of a man.

I neither learned wisdom, nor have the knowledge of the holy. (Proverbs 30: 2, 3.)

Humility Commanded.

At the same time came the disciples unto Jesus, saying, Who is the greatest in the kingdom of heaven?

And Jesus called a little child unto him, and set him in the midst of them,

And said, *Verily I say unto you, Except ye be converted, and become as little children, ye shall not enter into the kingdom of heaven.*

Whosoever therefore shall humble himself as this little child, the same is greatest in the kingdom of heaven. (Matthew 18: 1-4.)

But Jesus called them unto him, and said, *Ye know that the princes of the Gentiles exercise dominion over them, and they that are great exercise authority upon them.*

But it shall not be so among you: but whosoever will be great among you, let him be your minister;

And whosoever will be chief among you, let him be your servant. (Matthew 20: 25-27.)

But he that is greatest among you shall be your servant.

And whosoever shall exalt himself shall be abased; and he that shall humble himself shall be exalted. (Matthew 23: 11, 12.)

And he put forth a parable to those which were bidden, when he marked how they chose out the chief rooms; saying unto them,

When thou art bidden of any man to a wedding, sit not down in the highest room; lest a more honourable man than thou be bidden of him;

And he that bade thee and him come and say to thee, Give this man place;

and thou begin with shame to take the lowest room.

But when thou art bidden, go and sit thou in the lowest room; that when he that bade thee cometh, he may say unto thee, Friend, go up higher: then shalt thou have worship in the presence of them that sit at meat with thee.

For whosoever exalteth himself shall be abased; and he that humbleth himself shall be exalted. (Luke 14: 7-11.)

For I say, through the grace given unto me, to every man that is among you, not to think of himself more highly than he ought to think; but to think soberly, according as God hath dealt to every man the measure of faith. (Romans 12: 3.)

And if any man think that he knoweth any thing, he knoweth nothing yet as he ought to know. (1 Corinthians 8: 2.)

Let nothing be done through strife or vainglory; but in lowliness of mind let each esteem other better than themselves. (Philippians 2: 3.)

My brethren, be not many masters, knowing that we shall receive the greater condemnation. (James 3: 1.)

Humble yourselves in the sight of the Lord, and he shall lift you up. (James 4: 10.)

Humble yourselves therefore under the mighty hand of God, that he may exalt you in due time. (1 Peter 5: 6.)

Humility Rewarded.

Seest thou how Ahab humbleth himself before me? because he humbleth himself before me, I will not bring the evil in his days: but in his son's days will I bring the evil upon his house. (1 Kings 21: 29.)

Because thine heart was tender, and thou didst humble thyself before God,

when thou heardest his words against this place, and against the inhabitants thereof, and humbledst thyself before me, and didst rend thy clothes, and weep before me; I have even heard thee also, saith the Lord. (2 Chronicles 34: 27.)

Though the Lord be high, yet hath he respect unto the lowly: but the proud he knoweth afar off. (Psalm 138: 6.)

When pride cometh, then cometh shame: but with the lowly is wisdom. (Proverbs 11: 2.)

The fear of the Lord is the instruction of wisdom; and before honour is humility. (Proverbs 15: 33.)

Better it is to be of an humble spirit with the lowly, than to divide the spoil with the proud. (Proverbs 16: 19.)

Before destruction the heart of man is haughty; and before honour is humility. (Proverbs 18: 12.)

By humility and the fear of the Lord are riches, and honour, and life. (Proverbs 22: 4.)

But he giveth more grace. Wherefore he saith, God resisteth the proud, but giveth grace unto the humble. (James 4: 6.)

Likewise, ye younger, submit yourselves unto the elder. Yea, all of you be subject one to another, and be clothed with humility: for God resisteth the proud, and giveth grace to the humble. (1 Peter 5: 5.)

And he spake this parable unto certain which trusted in themselves that they were righteous, and despised others:

Two men went up into the temple to pray; the one a Pharisee, and the other a publican.

The Pharisee stood and prayed thus with himself, God, I thank thee, that I am not as other men are, extortioners, unjust, adulterers, or even as this publican.

I fast twice in the week, I give tithes of all that I possess.

And the publican, standing afar off, would not lift up so much as his eyes unto heaven, but smote upon his breast, saying, God be merciful to me a sinner.

I tell you, this man went down to his house justified rather than the other: for every one that exalteth himself shall be abased; and he that humbleth himself shall be exalted. (Luke 18: 9-14.)

HYPOCRITE AND HYPOCRISY.

HYP'O-CRITE AND HY-POC'RI-SY. A hypocrite is one who seems or professes to be what he is not, especially in the matter of religion. Hypocrisy is the act or practice of being a hypocrite. It is a deadly sin, since it is a profession of religion where none is felt or where none exists. It has been used from time immemorial by men and women for the basest kinds of purposes, and almost always with some personal and selfish aim. The Scriptures are full of warnings against hypocrisy and show that the hypocrite has little hope of reaching the kingdom of Heaven.

REFERENCES.

Hypocrisy Condemned.

Upright men shall be astonied at this, and the innocent shall stir up himself against the hypocrite. (Job 17: 8.)

For there is no faithfulness in their mouth; their inward part is very wickedness; their throat is an open sepulchre; they flatter with their tongue. (Psalm 5: 9.)

Wherefore the Lord said, Forasmuch as this people draw near me with their mouth, and with their lips do honour me, but have removed their heart far from me, and their fear toward me is taught by the precept of men:

Therefore, behold, I will proceed to do a marvellous work among this people, even a marvellous work and a wonder: for the wisdom of their wise men shall perish, and the understanding of their prudent men shall be hid. (Isaiah 29: 13, 14.)

The vile person shall be no more called liberal, nor the churl said to be bountiful.

For the vile person will speak villany, and his heart will work iniquity, to practise hypocrisy, and to utter error against the Lord, to make empty the soul of the hungry; and he will cause the drink of the thirsty to fail. (Isaiah 32: 5, 6.)

And they come unto thee as the people cometh, and they sit before thee as my people, and they hear thy words, but they will not do them: for with their mouth they shew much love, but their heart goeth after their covetousness. (Ezekiel 33: 31.)

No man can serve two masters: for either he will hate the one, and love the other; or else he will hold to the one, and despise the other. Ye cannot serve God and mammon. (Matthew 6: 24.)

Ye hypocrites, well did Esaias prophesy of you, saying,

This people draweth nigh unto me with their mouth, and honoureth me with their lips; but their heart is far from me.

But in vain they do worship me, teaching for doctrines the commandments of men. (Matthew 15: 7-9.)

But woe unto you, scribes and Pharisees, hypocrites! for ye shut up the kingdom of heaven against men: for ye neither go in yourselves, neither suffer ye them that are entering to go in.

Woe unto you, scribes and Pharisees, hypocrites! for ye devour widows' houses, and for a pretence make long prayer: therefore ye shall receive the greater damnation. (Matthew 23: 13, 14.)

Woe unto you, scribes and Pharisees, hypocrites! for ye pay tithe of mint and anise and cummin, and have omitted the weightier matters of the law, judgment, mercy and faith: these ought ye to have done, and not to leave the other undone.

Ye blind guides, which strain at a gnat, and swallow a camel.

Woe unto you, scribes and Pharisees, hypocrites! for ye make clean the outside of the cup and of the platter, but within they are full of extortion and excess.

Thou blind Pharisee, cleanse first that which is within the cup and platter, that the outside of them may be clean also.

Woe unto you, scribes and Pharisees, hypocrites! for ye are like unto whited sepulchres, which indeed appear beautiful outward, but are within full of dead men's bones, and of all uncleanness.

Even so ye also outwardly appear righteous unto men, but within ye are full of hypocrisy and iniquity.

Woe unto you, scribes and Pharisees, hypocrites! because ye build the tombs of the prophets, and garnish the sepulchres of the righteous,

And say, If we had been in the days of our fathers, we would not have been partakers with them in the blood of the prophets.

Wherefore ye be witnesses unto yourselves, that ye are the children of them which killed the prophets. (Matthew 23: 23-31.)

An instructor of the foolish, a teacher of babes, which hast the form of knowledge and of the truth in the law.

Thou therefore which teachest another, teachest thou not thyself? thou that preachest a man should not steal, dost thou steal?

Thou that sayest a man should not commit adultery, dost thou commit adultery? thou that abhorrest idols, dost thou commit sacrilege?

Thou that makest thy boast of the law, through breaking the law dishonourest thou God? (Romans 2: 20-23.)

They profess that they know God; but in works they deny him, being abominable, and disobedient, and unto every good work reprobate. (Titus 1: 16.)

Hypocrisy's Punishment.

So are the paths of all that forget God; and the hypocrite's hope shall perish:

Whose hope shall be cut off, and whose trust shall be a spider's web. (Job 8: 13, 14.)

Knowest thou not this of old, since man was placed upon earth,

That the triumphing of the wicked is short, and the joy of the hypocrite but for a moment?

Though his excellency mount up to the heavens, and his head reach unto the clouds;

Yet he shall perish for ever like his own dung: they which have seen him shall say, Where is he?

He shall fly away as a dream, and shall not be found: yea, he shall be chased away as a vision of the night.

The eye also which saw him shall see him no more; neither shall his place any more behold him.

His children shall seek to please the poor, and his hands shall restore their goods.

His bones are full of the sin of his

youth, which shall lie down with him in the dust. (Job 20: 4-11.)

For what is the hope of the hypocrite, though he hath gained, when God taketh away his soul? (Job 27: 8.)

But the hypocrites in heart heap up wrath: they cry not when he bindeth them.

They die in youth, and their life is among the unclean. (Job 36: 13, 14.)

But unto the wicked God saith, What hast thou to do to declare my statutes, or that thou shouldest take my covenant in thy mouth?

Seeing thou hatest instruction, and castest my words behind thee. (Psalm 50: 16, 17.)

IDLE. (See Diligence.)

I'DLE—unemployed; not turned to appropriate or good use; thoughtless, unprofitable; slothful or sluggish. The Bible shows idleness to be all of the preceding things and cautions mankind against falling into such a state.

REFERENCES.

Idleness Reproved.

Go to the ant, thou sluggard; consider her ways, and be wise:

Which having no guide, overseer, or ruler,

Provideth her meat in the summer, and gathereth her food in the harvest.

How long wilt thou sleep, O sluggard? when wilt thou arise out of thy sleep?

Yet a little sleep, a little slumber, a little folding of the hands to sleep:

So shall thy poverty come as one that travelleth, and thy want as an armed man. (Proverbs 6: 6-11.)

He also that is slothful in his work is brother to him that is a great waster. (Proverbs 18: 9.)

I went by the field of the slothful, and by the vineyard of the man void of understanding;

And lo, it was all grown over with thorns, and nettles had covered the face thereof, and the stone wall thereof was broken down. (Proverbs 24: 30, 31.)

Not slothful in business: fervent in spirit, serving the Lord. (Romans 12: 11.)

And that ye study to be quiet, and to do your own business, and to work with your own hands, (as we commanded you). (1 Thessalonians 4: 11.)

For even when we were with you, this we commanded you, that if any would not work, neither should he eat.

For we hear that there are some which walk among you disorderly, working not at all, but are busybodies. (2 Thessalonians 3: 10, 11.)

That ye be not slothful, but followers of them who through faith and patience inherit the promises. (Hebrews 6: 12.)

Idleness a Poverty Producer.

He becometh poor that dealeth with a slack hand; but the hand of the diligent maketh rich.

He that gathereth in summer is a wise son: but he that sleepeth in harvest is a son that causeth shame. (Proverbs 10: 4, 5.)

The hand of the diligent shall bear rule: but the slothful shall be under tribute. (Proverbs 12: 24.)

The soul of the sluggard desireth, and hath nothing: but the soul of the diligent shall be made fat. (Proverbs 13: 4.)

Slothfulness casteth into a deep sleep; and an idle soul shall suffer hunger. (Proverbs 19: 15.)

The sluggard will not plough by reason of the cold; therefore shall he beg in harvest, and have nothing. (Proverbs 20: 4.)

Love not sleep, lest thou come to poverty; open thine eyes, and thou shalt be satisfied with bread. (Proverbs 20: 13.)

By much slothfulness the building decayeth; and through idleness of the hands the house droppeth through. (Ecclesiastes 10: 18.)

Idleness a Source of Evil-Speaking.

And withal they learn to be idle, wandering about from house to house; and not only idle, but tattlers also, and busybodies, speaking things which they ought not. (1 Timothy 4: 13.)

Idleness a Cause of Ignorance.

The sluggard is wiser in his own conceit than seven men that can render a reason. (Proverbs 26: 16.)

All ye beasts of the field, come to devour, yea, all ye beasts in the forest.

His watchmen are blind: they are all ignorant, they are all dumb dogs, they cannot bark; sleeping, lying down, loving to slumber. (Isaiah 56: 9, 10.)

Then shall we know, if we follow on to know the Lord: his going forth is prepared as the morning; and he shall come unto us as the rain, as the latter and former rain unto the earth. (Hosea 6: 3.)

IGNORANCE.

IG'NO-RANCE—the condition of being without knowledge, either in general or as to a particular object or for a particular reason. The word "ignorance" is often used by modern people to denote illiteracy, or lack of education. This, however, is only one of the word's meanings, and where it is encountered in the Bible, should be given to it only after much thought and examination of the references. Ignorance often can be willful and obstinate.

REFERENCES.

For I bear them record, that they have a zeal of God, but not according to knowledge.

For they being ignorant of God's righteousness, and going about to establish their own righteousness, have not submitted themselves unto the righteousness of God. (Romans 10: 2, 3.)

For this they willingly are ignorant of, that by the word of God the heavens were of old, and the earth standing out of the water, and in the water,

Whereby the world that then was, being overflowed with water, perished. (2 Peter 3: 5, 6.)

Moreover, brethren, I would not that ye should be ignorant, how that all our fathers were under the cloud, and all passed through the sea. (1 Corinthians 10: 1.)

Now concerning spiritual gifts, brethren, I would not have you ignorant. (1 Corinthians 12: 1.)

But I would not have you to be ignorant, brethren, concerning them which are asleep, that ye sorrow not, even as others which have no hope. (1 Thessalonians 4: 13.)

But (beloved) be not ignorant of this one thing, that one day is with the Lord as a thousand years, and a thousand years as one day. (2 Peter 3: 8.)

IMMORTALITY. (See Death.)

IM'MOR-TAL'I-TY—the quality or state of being immortal or exempted from death or annihilation; unending existence. Christians pretty generally believe in the doctrine of immortality, although some hold that only those who accept Christ will be fortunate enough to win immortality. As a matter of fact, immortality is one of the doctrines of modern natural religion, it being held that the body is distinct from the soul, and at death when the body passes away the soul is not affected by the change. Many of the ancients held the same view of the deathlessness of the soul. It was taught by the Old Testament writers, but not so clearly as those of the New Testament, as Jesus set it forth in language not to be misunderstood.

REFERENCES.

Immortality of God.

Now unto the King eternal, immortal, invisible, the only wise God, be honour and glory for ever and ever. Amen. (1 Timothy 1: 17.)

Who only hath immortality, dwelling in the light which no man can approach unto, whom no man hath seen, nor can see: to whom be honour and power everlasting. Amen. (1 Timothy 6: 16.)

Immortality of Man.

But after thy hardness, and impenitent heart, treasurest up unto thyself wrath, against the day of wrath, and revelation of the righteous judgment of God:

Who will render to every man according to his deeds:

To them, who by patient continuance in well doing seek for glory, and honour, and immortality, eternal life. (Romans 2: 5-7.)

For this corruptible must put on incorruption, and this mortal must put on immortality.

So when this corruptible shall have put on incorruption, and this mortal shall have put on immortality, then shall be brought to pass the saying that is written, Death is swallowed up in victory. (1 Corinthians 15: 53, 54.)

INCARNATION.

IN'CAR-NA'TION—the act of clothing with flesh; the state of being in a human form.

"Incarnation" is the word applied to the union of the second person of the Godhead with a human form; in other words, the coming to earth as a man of God the Son.

REFERENCES.

But while he thought on these things, behold, the Angel of the Lord appeared unto him in a dream, saying, Joseph thou son of David, fear not to take unto thee Mary thy wife; for that which is conceived in her, is of the Holy Ghost.

And she shall bring forth a son, and thou shalt call his Name Jesus: for he shall save his people from their sins. (Matthew 1: 20, 21.)

But when the fulness of the time was come, God sent forth his Son made of a woman, made under the law,

To redeem them that were under the law, that we might receive the adoption of sons. (Galatians 4: 4, 5.)

For I came down from heaven, not to do mine own will, but the will of him that sent me. (John 6: 38.)

INDUSTRY. (See Diligence, Idle.)

IN'DUS-TRY—diligence in any employment or pursuit, either mental or physical. The Bible is full of references to industry and the need for it. Industry is made almost a part of religion, on the basis that what God has given to us we should use to the best of our abilities.

REFERENCES.

General.

Much food is in the tillage of the poor: but there is that is destroyed for want of judgment. (Proverbs 13: 23.)

Not slothful in business; fervent in spirit; serving the Lord. (Romans 12: 11.)

Let him that stole steal no more: but rather let him labour, working with his hands the thing which is good, that he may have to give to him that needeth. (Ephesians 4: 28.)

And that ye study to be quiet, and to do your own business, and to work with your own hands, as we commanded you;

That ye may walk honestly toward them that are without, and that ye may have lack of nothing. (1 Thessalonians 4: 11, 12.)

For even when we were with you, this we commanded you, that if any would not work, neither should he eat.

For we hear that there are some which walk among you disorderly, working not at all, but are busybodies.

Now them that are such we command and exhort by our Lord Jesus Christ, that with quietness they work, and eat their own bread. (2 Thessalonians 3: 10-12.)

The husbandman that laboureth must be first partaker of the fruits. (2 Timothy 2: 6.)

The Blessings and Rewards of Industry.

And the man Jeroboam was a mighty man of valour: and Solomon seeing the young man that he was industrious, he made him ruler over all the charge of the house of Joseph. (1 Kings 11: 28.)

Wealth gotten by vanity shall be diminished: but he that gathereth by labour shall increase. (Proverbs 13: 11.)

In all labour there is profit: but the talk of the lips tendeth only to penury. (Proverbs 14: 23.)

He that laboureth, laboureth for himself; for his mouth craveth it of him. (Proverbs 16: 26.)

Love not sleep, lest thou come to poverty: open thine eyes, and thou shalt be satisfied with bread. (Proverbs 20: 13.)

The thoughts of the diligent tend only to plenteousness; but of every one that is hasty only to want. (Proverbs 21: 5.)

Be thou diligent to know the state of thy flocks, and look well to thy herds:

For riches are not for ever: and doth the crown endure to every generation?

The hay appeareth, and the tender grass sheweth itself, and herbs of the mountains are gathered.

The lambs are for thy clothing, and the goats are the price of the field.

And thou shalt have goats' milk enough for thy food, for the food of thy household, and for the maintenance for thy maidens. (Proverbs 27: 23-27.)

Behold that which I have seen: it is good and comely for one to eat and to drink, and to enjoy the good of all his labour that he taketh under the sun all the days of his life, which God giveth him: for it is his portion. (Ecclesiastes 5: 18.)

INJUSTICE.

IN-JUS'TICE—lack of justice and equity; violation of the right of another or others; wrong; unfairness. Scripture warns us against doing injustice, showing us that we always should be careful of the rights of others and that we should deal fairly in everything we do.

REFERENCES.

Warnings against Injustice.

Thou shalt neither vex a stranger, nor oppress him: for ye were strangers in the land of Egypt. (Exodus 22: 21.)

Thou shalt not wrest the judgment of thy poor in his cause. (Exodus 23: 6.)

Ye shall do no unrighteousness in judgment; thou shalt not respect the person of the poor, nor honour the person of the mighty: but in righteousness shalt thou judge thy neighbour. (Leviticus 19: 15.)

Thou shalt not wrest judgment; thou shalt not respect persons, neither take a gift: for a gift doth blind the eyes of the wise, and pervert the words of the righteous.

That which is altogether just shalt thou follow, that thou mayest live, and inherit the land which the Lord thy God giveth thee. (Deuteronomy 16: 19, 20.)

Thou shalt not pervert the judgment of the stranger, nor of the fatherless, nor take a widow's raiment to pledge. (Deuteronomy 24: 17.)

If I did despise the cause of my manservant or of my maid-servant, when they contended with me;

What then shall I do when God riseth up? and when he visiteth, what shall I answer him? (Job 31: 13, 14.)

Thus saith the Lord; Execute ye judgment and righteousness, and deliver the spoiled out of the hand of the oppressor: and do no wrong, do no violence to the stranger, the fatherless, nor the widow, neither shed innocent blood in this place. (Jeremiah 22: 3.)

He that is faithful in that which is least is faithful also in much: and he that is unjust in the least is unjust also in much. (Luke 16: 10.)

Results of Injustice.

When a wicked man dieth, his expectation shall perish: and the hope of unjust men perisheth. (Proverbs 11: 7.)

He that by usury and unjust gain increaseth his substance, he shall gather it for him that will pity the poor. (Proverbs 28: 8.)

That no man go beyond and defraud his brother in any matter, because that the Lord is the avenger of all such; as we also have forewarned you, and testified. (1 Thessalonians 4: 6.)

The Lord knoweth how to deliver the godly out of temptations, and to reserve the unjust unto the day of judgment to be punished. (2 Peter 2: 9.)

INSPIRATION.

In'spi-ra'tion—the supernatural divine influence on the prophets, apostles, etc., by which they were qualified to communicate religious truth, either by word of mouth or by writings; also the power at any time, even now, for man to receive religious truth. The word is also used to denote that truth itself.

REFERENCES.

Inspiration of Scripture.

All Scripture is given by inspiration of God, and is profitable for doctrine, for reproof, for correction, for instruction in righteousness,

That the man of God may be perfect, throughly furnished unto all good works. (2 Timothy 3: 16, 17.)

As he spake by the mouth of his holy Prophets, which have been since the world began. (Luke 1: 70.)

Knowing this first, that no prophecy of the Scripture is of any private Interpretation:

For the prophecy came not in old time by the will of man: but holy men of God spake as they were moved by the Holy Ghost. (2 Peter 1: 20, 21.)

God who at sundry times, and in divers manners, spake in time past unto the Fathers by the Prophets. (Hebrew 1: 1.)

INTEGRITY.

In-teg'ri-ty—the state of being morally sound or whole; freedom from corrupting influence or motive; honesty; uprightness; rectitude. The Bible regards integrity in the same light as it does honesty—as a necessity for the living of the Christian life.

REFERENCES.

Behold, here I am: witness against me before the Lord, and before his anointed; whose ox have I taken? or whose ass have I taken? or whom have I defrauded? whom have I oppressed? or of whose hand have I received any bribe to blind mine eyes therewith? and I will restore it you. (1 Samuel 12: 3.)

Moreover, they reckoned not with the men, into whose hand they delivered the money to be bestowed on workmen: for they dealt faithfully. (2 Kings 12: 15.)

Howbeit, there was no reckoning made with them of the money that was delivered into their hand, because they dealt faithfully. (2 Kings 22: 7.)

And the Lord said unto Satan, Hast thou considered my servant Job, that there is none like him in the earth, a perfect and an upright man, one that feareth God, and escheweth evil? and still he holdeth fast his integrity, although thou movedst me against him, to destroy him without cause. (Job 2: 3.)

The Lord shall judge the people: judge me, O Lord, according to my righteousness, and according to mine integrity that is in me. (Psalm 7: 8.)

Judge me, O Lord; for I have walked in mine integrity: I have trusted also in the Lord; therefore I shall not slide. (Psalm 26: 1.)

And as for me, thou upholdest me in mine integrity, and settest me before thy face for ever. (Psalm 41: 12.)

The integrity of the upright shall guide them: but the perverseness of transgressors shall destroy them. (Proverbs 11: 3.)

Better is the poor that walketh in his integrity, than he that is perverse in his lips, and is a fool. (Proverbs 19: 1.)

The just man walketh in his integrity: his children are blessed after him. (Proverbs 20: 7.)

INTERCESSION.

IN'TER-CES'SION—the act of mediating between two persons for the purpose of effecting a reconciliation or for making a prayer or petition to one for the other. Sometimes the intercessor is against the second party, although rarely. One of the great offices of Christ Jesus is that of intercession, when in His Capacity of Mediator he intercedes with God the Father for mankind, serving to illustrate the power and majesty of the Father and the grace and wisdom of the Son. The Bible also teaches us that the Holy Ghost makes intercession for us. Mankind also can intercede when they go to God the Father with their prayers for their fellows.

REFERENCES.

Intercession of Christ.

Then said Jesus, *Father, forgive them; for they know not what they do.* And they parted his raiment, and cast lots. (Luke 23: 34.)

Who is he that condemneth? It is Christ that died, yea rather that is risen again, who is even at the right hand of God, who also maketh intercession for us. (Romans 8: 34.)

Wherefore he is able also to save them to the uttermost, that come unto God by him, seeing he ever liveth to make intercession for them. (Hebrews 7: 25.)

My little children, these things write I unto you, that ye sin not. And if any man sin, we have an Advocate with the

Father, Jesus Christ the righteous. (1 John 2: 1.)

Christ's Intercession.

Therefore will I divide him a portion with the great, and he shall divide the spoil with the strong; because he hath poured out his soul unto death: and he was numbered with the transgressors; and he bare the sin of many, and made intercession for the transgressors. (Isaiah 53: 12.)

Holy Ghost's Intercession.

Likewise the Spirit also helpeth our infirmities: for we know not what we should pray for as we ought: but the Spirit itself maketh intercession for us with groanings which cannot be uttered. (Romans 8: 26.)

Intercession for All Men.

I exhort therefore, that, first of all, supplications, prayers, intercessions, and giving of thanks, be made for all men;

For kings, and for all that are in authority; that we may lead a quiet and peaceable life in all godliness and honesty.

For this is good and acceptable in the sight of God our Saviour;

Who will have all men to be saved, and to come unto the knowledge of the truth. (1 Timothy 2: 1-4.)

Praying always with all prayer and supplication in the Spirit, and watching thereunto with all perseverance and supplication for all saints. (Ephesians 6: 18.)

Requests for Intercession.

Now I beseech you, brethren, for the Lord Jesus Christ's sake, and for the love of the Spirit, that ye strive together with me in your prayers to God for me. (Romans 15: 30.)

You also helping together by prayer for us, that for the gift bestowed upon us by the means of many persons, thanks may be given by many on our behalf. (2 Corinthians 1: 11.)

Withal, praying also for us, that God would open unto us a door of utterance, to speak the mystery of Christ, for which I am also in bonds. (Colossians 4: 3.)

Brethren, pray for us. (1 Thessalonians 5: 25.)

Finally, brethren, pray for us, that the word of the Lord may have free course, and be glorified, even as it is with you. (2 Thessalonians 3: 1.)

Pray for us: for we trust we have a good conscience, in all things willing to live honestly.

But I beseech you the rather to do this, that I may be restored to you the sooner. (Hebrews 13: 18, 19.)

ISAAC. (See Abraham, Esau, Jacob, Israelites, Sarah.)

I'saac—a form of a Hebrew word meaning "mocking laughter." Isaac was the only son of Abraham and Sarah and was born about the year 1896 B.C., while his parents were in their old age. Abraham had been promised a child by God, and for a long time Ishmael, the son of Hagar, was supposed to be the fulfillment of the divine word, but later God showed Abraham that such was not the case. In the early part of his life Isaac almost became a human sacrifice to God through his father's great faith. At forty he wedded his beautiful cousin Rebekah. He seems to have entertained great fear that she would be carried off from him. At sixty Esau and Jacob were born, the latter being his mother's favorite. Because of his failed eyesight Jacob managed to secure the old man's blessing after he had succeeded in depriving Esau of his birthright. He died very wealthy at a very advanced age.

Isaac's character has been the subject of much argument as well as criticism. His memory has sometimes been reviled for his denial of his wife and for permitting Jacob to enjoy the proceeds of his deceptions in which his brother Esau was the loser. These objections, however, do not seem to weigh with the consistent and patient fortitude with which Isaac bore his many griefs and troubles. He was a dutiful son, a loving husband, and the father of a household where he could not always make order reign, because of the warring elements within it. Unquestionably, Isaac was a man who suffered and bore his sufferings heroically. There is no doubt but that he won respect and esteem from the men of his times, while in the Hebrew mind he is inseparably linked with Abraham and Jacob, his father and his son.

REFERENCES.

And God said unto Abraham, As for Sarai thy wife, thou shalt not call her name Sarai, but Sarah shall her name be.

And I will bless her, and give thee a son also of her: yea, I will bless her, and she shall be a mother of nations; kings of people shall be of her.

Then Abraham fell upon his face, and laughed, and said in his heart, Shall a child be born unto him that is an hundred years old? and shall Sarah, that is ninety years old, bear? (Genesis 17: 15-17.)

And Abraham called the name of his son that was born unto him, whom Sarah bare to him, Isaac. (Genesis 21: 3.)

And it came to pass after these things, that God did tempt Abraham, and said unto him, Abraham: and he said, Behold, here I am.

And he said, Take now thy son, thine only son Isaac, whom thou lovest, and get thee into the land of Moriah; and offer him there for a burnt-offering upon one of the mountains which I will tell thee of. (Genesis 22: 1, 2.)

And they came to the place which God had told him of; and Abraham built an altar there, and laid the wood in order, and bound Isaac his son, and laid him on the altar upon the wood.

And Abraham stretched forth his hand, and took the knife to slay his son.

And the angel of the Lord called unto him out of heaven, and said, Abraham, Abraham: and he said, Here am I.

And he said, Lay not thine hand upon the lad, neither do thou any thing unto him: for now I know that thou fearest God, seeing thou hast not withheld thy son, thine only son from me.

And Abraham lifted up his eyes, and looked, and behold behind him a ram caught in a thicket by his horns: and Abraham went and took the ram, and offered him up for a burnt-offering in the stead of his son. (Genesis 22: 9-13.)

And Isaac brought her into his mother Sarah's tent, and took Rebekah, and she became his wife; and he loved her: and Isaac was comforted after his mother's death. (Genesis 24: 67.)

And Jacob went near unto Isaac his father; and he felt him, and said, The voice is Jacob's voice, but the hands are the hands of Esau.

And he discerned him not, because his hands were hairy, as his brother Esau's hands: so he blessed him.

And he said, Art thou my very son Esau? And he said, I am.

And he said, Bring it near to me, and I will eat of my son's venison, that my soul may bless thee. And he brought it near to him, and he did eat: and he brought him wine, and he drank.

And his father Isaac said unto him, Come near now, and kiss me, my son.

And he came near, and kissed him: and he smelled the smell of his raiment, and blessed him, and said, See, the smell of my son is as the smell of a field which the Lord hath blessed:

Therefore God give thee of the dew of heaven, and the fatness of the earth, and plenty of corn and wine:

Let people serve thee, and nations bow down to thee: be lord over thy brethren, and let thy mother's sons bow down to thee: cursed be every one that curseth thee, and blessed be he that blesseth thee.

And it came to pass, as soon as Isaac had made an end of blessing Jacob, and Jacob was yet scarce gone out from the presence of Isaac his father, that Esau his brother came in from his hunting. (Genesis 27: 22-30.)

And the days of Isaac were an hundred and fourscore years.

And Isaac gave up the ghost and died, and was gathered unto his people, being old and full of days; and his sons Esau and Jacob buried him. (Genesis 35: 28, 29.)

ISAIAH.

I-SA'IAH (pronounced Izayah or Izay-yah) —a form of a Hebrew word meaning "Jah is helper." The name is often written Esaias. Isaiah was one of the greatest of all the prophets, and certainly the greatest of those who wrote their prophecies in the form of a book. Of his personal history we know very little. He appears to have been born about the year 765 B.C. He is said to have been of the Hebrew royal family. The period of his life was in times that were exceedingly troubled, the Hebrews suffering from the combined ill effects of bad kings and the dangers arising from the cruel and warlike Assyrians, who were then at the height of their power as a nation of conquerors. His prophecies were threefold in character—to condemn the sins of his people, to call them to repentance, and to foretell the coming of the Messiah. In this latter respect he was the chief of the prophets, for to him God revealed much of

the advent, character, ministry, teaching, sufferings, and death of Jesus, as well as the extension and glory of His kingdom. His thought and language are always lofty and dignified, stamping his work with the highest mark of literary excellence. There is a tradition that Isaiah suffered martyrdom in the reign of King Manasseh by being sawn in half, but there is no definite proof to show that such was the case.

Reference.—The entire book of Isaiah.

ISCARIOT. (See Judas Iscariot.)

ISHMAEL.

ISH'MA-EL (pronounced Ishmale)—a form of a Hebrew word meaning "God hears." Ishmael was the son of Abraham and Hagar, and was born about fourteen years before Isaac. Not long thereafter he and his mother were cast off from the family by reason of the anger of Sarah, Abraham's wife, and wandered through the wilderness into what is now Arabia. Ishmael's descendants became a part of the Arabian race and remain so to this day. The pure Arabs are descendants of Joktan, son of Eber, great-great-grandson of Shem.

References.—Genesis, chapters 16, 17, 21, and 25.

ISRAEL. (See Israelites, Jacob, Jews, Judah.)

IS'RA-EL—a form of a Hebrew word meaning "a prince with God" or "soldier of God." Israel was the name given to Jacob by God after wrestling with the angel. (See Genesis 32: 22-30.) It also became the racial name of the Hebrews (see Israelites and Jews), as well as the name of the combined nation and the name of one of the two kingdoms founded after the split of the united twelve tribes. (See Israelites for history of the kingdom of Israel; see Jews for history of the Israelites as a race.)

ISRAELITES.

IS'RA-EL-ITES—the name given to the descendants of Abraham, Isaac, and Jacob, as well as to one of the two kingdoms set up after the nation was divided. This division was caused by the rivalry that always had existed between the tribes of Judah and Ephraim from the time of the conquest of Canaan. The twelve tribes composing the nation always were more or less unsettled by this rivalry. The influence of Samuel and Saul, who were of the tribe of Benjamin, acted as a balance of power for a considerable time, but at Saul's death the trouble between Judah and Ephraim broke out afresh. David's brilliant and masterful rule, together with the peaceful and yet splendid reign of his son Solomon, brought the two wings of the nation together in reunion, but after the death of Solomon the national bond again became sundered. In the year 975 B.C. Solomon's son, Rehoboam, found himself confronting a revolt headed by Jeroboam, an Ephraimite. He was too weak to put it down, with the result that Jeroboam was able to take away from him all the nation save the tribe of Judah, the Levites, and a part of Benjamin. Rehoboam clung to his part which became the kingdom of Judah, and Jeroboam set up for himself a kingdom which came to be called the kingdom of Israel. (See Judah for history of kingdom of Judah.)

Jeroboam's kingdom, possessing the majority of the Hebrew race and the greater part of the land, rose rapidly in power and for fifty years or more maintained a considerable degree of power and influence, although the people gave themselves over to idolatries of all sorts. The act, however, was a fatal one, and foreshadowed the downfall of the race, for as soon as the period of prosperity had passed the doom of the kingdom was apparent. Wars and troubles of many kinds set in, while on the East the growing might of Assyria and its warlike and cruel people showed how the fortunes of Israel were to end. In 250 years no less than nineteen kings occupied the throne and finally, in 721 B.C., the Assyrians, under their conqueror king, Shalmaneser, invaded Israel, took Samaria, destroyed the kingdom, and carried the ten tribes away into captivity beyond the river Euphrates. Here the old tribal formation soon became lost, and the people, already far departed from the worship of Jehovah, fell under the influence of the idolatrous Assyrian religion. At the end of the Captivity some of the Jews went back to Palestine, and made an effort to begin a na-

tional life anew, but with no success, for there never again was a united Hebrew nation.

JACOB. (See Abraham, Isaac, Joseph, Rebekah, Leah, Rachel, etc.)

JA′COB—a form of a Hebrew word meaning "heel-catcher" or "supplanter." Jacob was the younger of twin sons born about 1836 B.C. to Isaac by his wife Rebekah, the other being Esau. He was his mother's favorite. Through stratagem he bought his elder brother's birthright and secured his father's blessing in material things. Later, when he left home to seek a wife, Isaac confirmed this blessing, adding to it that of the spiritual promises made by God to Abraham and Isaac. Jacob fell in love with Rachel, the daughter of Laban, who shrewdly made Jacob serve fourteen years for the woman of his choice and marry her sister Leah as well. Late in life he migrated to Egypt because of famine in his own land, and died there. The change of his name from Jacob to Israel occurred before the journey to Egypt. Jacob had decided to leave Laban, with whom he had been for a number of years after he had married, and who had become jealous of his son-in-law's prosperity. To return to his own land he had to go through that of his brother Esau, of whom he was afraid and sought to appease by presents. The night before meeting Esau he wrestled with an unknown antagonist, who proved to be an angel. The angel overcame him and then gave him his new name of Israel. The character of Jacob has been a subject of great discussion. It leaves a much less favorable impression than that of any other of the patriarchs, because of the deceit practiced upon his father and the defrauding of Esau of his birthright. Many commentators are inclined to cast the entire blame for both of these acts upon the maternal favoritism of Rebekah. Taking another view, it may be said that Jacob's earlier life, with its unquestionable sin, was but preparatory to the splendid and exalted faith and goodness of his latter days. His service for Rachel shows him to have been a man capable of immense and unswerving devotion and loyalty, while his treatment of his children indicates that he was a good father. All of his later life gives proof of his deep piety and faith and trust in God.

REFERENCES.

Jacob's Youth.

And the boys grew: and Esau was a cunning hunter, a man of the field; and Jacob was a plain man, dwelling in tents.

And Isaac loved Esau, because he did eat of his venison: but Rebekah loved Jacob. (Genesis 25: 27, 28.)

Obtains Birthright.

And Esau said to Jacob, Feed me, I pray thee, with that same red pottage; for I am faint: therefore was his name called Edom.

And Jacob said, Sell me this day thy birthright.

And Esau said, Behold, I am at the point to die: and what profit shall this birthright do to me?

And Jacob said, Swear to me this day; and he sware unto him: and he sold his birthright unto Jacob. (Genesis 25: 30-33.)

Obtains Blessing.

And he came unto his father, and said, My father: and he said, Here am I; who art thou, my son?

And Jacob said unto his father, I am Esau thy firstborn; I have done according as thou badest me: arise, I pray thee, sit and eat of my venison, that thy soul may bless me.

And Isaac said unto his son, How is it that thou hast found it so quickly, my son? And he said, Because the Lord thy God brought it to me.

And Isaac said unto Jacob, Come near, I pray thee, that I may feel thee, my son, whether thou be my very son Esau or not.

And Jacob went near unto Isaac his father; and he felt him, and said, The voice is Jacob's voice, but the hands are the hands of Esau.

And he discerned him not, because his hands were hairy, as his brother Esau's hands: so he blessed him. (Genesis 27: 18-23.)

The Dream and Promise.

And he dreamed, and behold a ladder set up on the earth, and the top of it reached to heaven: and behold the angels of God ascending and descending on it.

And, behold, the Lord stood above it, and said, I am the Lord God of Abraham thy father, and the God of Isaac: the land whereon thou liest, to thee will I give it, and to thy seed;

And thy seed shall be as the dust of the earth: and thou shalt spread abroad to the west, and to the east, and to the north, and to the south: and in thee and in thy seed shall all the families of the earth be blessed.

And, behold, I am with thee, and will keep thee in all places whither thou goest, and will bring thee again into this land; for I will not leave thee, until I have done that which I have spoken to thee of. (Genesis 28: 12-15.)

And Jacob was left alone; and there wrestled a man with him until the breaking of the day.

And when he saw that he prevailed not against him, he touched the hollow of his thigh; and the hollow of Jacob's thigh was out of joint, as he wrestled with him.

And he said, Let me go, for the day breaketh. And he said, I will not let thee go, except thou bless me.

And he said unto him, What is thy name? And he said, Jacob.

And he said, Thy name shall be called no more Jacob, but Israel: for as a prince hast thou power with God and with men, and hast prevailed. (Genesis 32: 24-28.)

Jacob's Children.

The sons of Leah; Reuben, Jacob's firstborn, and Simeon, and Levi, and Judah, and Issachar, and Zebulun:

The sons of Rachel; Joseph, and Benjamin:

And the sons of Bilhah, Rachel's handmaid; Dan, and Naphtali:

And the sons of Zilpah, Leah's handmaid; Gad, and Asher. These are the sons of Jacob, which were born to him in Padanaram. (Genesis 35: 23-26.)

Blesses His Sons and Dies.

And Jacob called unto his sons, and said, Gather yourselves together, that I may tell you that which shall befall you in the last days.

Gather yourselves together, and hear, ye sons of Jacob; and hearken unto Israel your father. (Genesis 49: 1, 2.)

All these are the twelve tribes of Israel: and this is it that their father spake unto them, and blessed them; every one according to his blessing he blessed them. (Genesis 49: 28.)

And when Jacob had made an end of commanding his sons, he gathered up his feet into the bed, and yielded up the ghost, and was gathered unto his people. (Genesis 49: 23.)

JAH. (See Jehovah.)

JAH—a form of a Hebrew word meaning "Lord." Jah is a short form of the word "Jehovah." It is chiefly used in making up Hebrew proper names.

JAMES.

JAMES—a name derived from the name "Jacob" through changes made in passing from one language to another. There are three persons named James mentioned in the Bible. They appear only in the New Testament and are:

1. *James, the son of Zebedee*—a Galilean fisherman and one of the first four of the disciples. He was a brother of the evangelist John and was almost always singled out by Jesus when there was some special duty to be done. He appears to have been a man of high resolution and determined character. He was the first of the disciples to die a martyr's death, and indeed the only one the manner of whose death is exactly known. (See Matthew 4: 21; Acts 12: 2.)

2. *James, the son of Alphæus*—also called James the Less. Little is known regarding him. (See Matthew 10: 3.)

3. *James, "the brother of the Lord."* There is much confusion over this James, due to the difference in opinion which exists over the question as to whether or not the Lord had any brothers. Certain passages in Matthew and Mark indicate that He had (Matthew 13: 55; Mark 6: 3), but certain critics think that the somewhat lax nature of stating relationship which was in vogue in the time of Jesus is responsible for the opinion, and that in reality the brothers and sisters mentioned were first cousins of the Lord. This theory makes the name of the mother of James the same as the mother of Jesus, which also was not an uncommon thing in the case of sisters in the days of the Master. There is also an opinion to the effect that this James was the son of Joseph by a marriage prior to that with Mary, the belief being held by some that Joseph was a widower at the time he wedded the mother of our Lord. This would give strong basis for James being called "the brother of the Lord." But on the whole, the matter is very much unsettled.

The Epistle of James comes in for its share of uncertainty also in respect to the identity of its author, its authorship being credited, by various thinkers, either to one of the three men of the name mentioned above, or to an unknown James.

JAPHETH.

JA'PHETH—a form of a Hebrew word meaning "widespread." Japheth was one of the sons of Noah. He is understood to have been the progenitor of the races which settled Europe and Western Asia.

References.—Genesis 9: 27; Genesis 10: 1; 1 Chronicles 1: 4.

JEALOUS AND JEALOUSY.

JEAL'OUS-Y—a word used in the Bible to express several types of a certain emotion: (1) uneasiness from the fear that some one may rob us of the affections or regard of a loved one; (2) God's sensitiveness for the regard of His people that they do not turn astray to other gods; (3) God's sensitiveness for the faith of his people. The Bible teaches that there are two sorts of jealousy—one righteous, such as God's and man's when it is aroused by proper motives of concern for the loved ones; and the other unrighteous, the latter based upon the selfish desire of the one entertaining it.

REFERENCES.

God's Jealousy.

Thou shalt not bow down thyself to them, nor serve them: For I the Lord thy God am a jealous God, visiting the iniquity of the fathers upon the children unto the third and fourth generation of them that hate me. (Exodus 20: 5.)

The Lord will not spare him, but then the anger of the Lord and his jealousy shall smoke against that man, and all the curses that are written in this book shall lie upon him, and the Lord shall blot out his name from under heaven. (Deuteronomy 29: 20.)

For they provoked him to anger with their high places, and moved him to jealousy with their graven images. (Psalm 78: 58.)

Neither their silver nor their gold shall be able to deliver them in the day of the Lord's wrath; but the whole land shall be devoured by the fire of his jealousy: for he shall make even a speedy riddance of all them that dwell in the land. (Zephaniah 1: 18.)

Do we provoke the Lord to jealousy?

are we stronger than he? (1 Corinthians 10: 22.)

Human Jealousy.

For jealousy is the rage of a man: therefore he will not spare in the day of vengeance.

He will not regard any ransom; neither will he rest content, though thou givest many gifts. (Proverbs 6: 34, 35.)

Set me as a seal upon thine heart, as a seal upon thine arm: for love is strong as death; jealousy is cruel as the grave: the coals thereof are coals of fire, which hath a most vehement flame. (Song of Solomon 8: 6.)

And I will judge thee, as women that break wedlock and shed blood are judged; and I will give thee blood in fury and jealousy. (Ezekiel 16: 38.)

JEHOSHAPHAT.

JE-HOSH'A-PHAT—a form of a Hebrew word meaning "Jehovah judged." Jehoshaphat was the fourth king of the kingdom of Judah and is reckoned to have been one of the best of the Hebrew monarchs. He reigned twenty-five years. He did away with much of the idolatry that infested the people and by his good and wise government contributed much to the advancement of the little kingdom and the fact that it long outlived the kingdom of Israel. He enjoyed much of the good counsel of Elisha. His greatest fault seems to have been a somewhat fiery temper.

References.—1 Kings 15: 24; 1 Kings 22: 50; 2 Chronicles 17 and 21.

JEHOVAH. (See God.)

JE-HO'VAH—a form of a Hebrew word meaning "the existing one," or, as more freely translated, "The Lord." The exact pronunciation of the word in the Hebrew has been lost, the Jews having always avoided uttering it, using some other word meaning the same thing or some derivative. This was a custom brought about originally by reverence for

God, to whom the name of Jehovah was given. Leviticus 24: 16 was the apparent basis for the custom, which seems to have degenerated into a superstition.

JEHU.

JE'HU—a form of a Hebrew word meaning "Jah is he." Jehu was the eleventh king of Israel and was noted for the energetic and determined manner in which he set about stamping out idolatry in his kingdom. Anointed king by the order of Elisha, Jehu began rebellion against the monarch then on the throne, Joram. He put Joram to death, had his wicked mother, Jezebel, killed, and exterminated what was left of the line of Ahab in fulfillment of an old prophecy. But Jehu, despite his energy, fell short of doing away with all of Israel's idolatry, and therefore fell under divine displeasure.

References.—2 Kings 9 and 10.

JEPHTHAH.

JEPH'THAH—a form of a Hebrew word meaning "he will open." Jephthah was the ninth judge of Israel. Before reaching this dignity he was the leader of a band of free-lance soldiers. As such he was summoned by the tribes to overthrow the yoke of the Ammonites. Before departing upon the campaign he made a vow to God to give Him as an offering, if he should be victorious, whatever should come forth first from his house on his return. He defeated the Ammonites, and the first to come from his house was his own daughter. It formerly was supposed that the girl was given as a burnt-offering, but latter-day commentaries are inclined to doubt this, inclining to the belief that she became vowed to virginity.

Reference.—Judges 11.

JEREMIAH.

JER'E-MI'AH—a form of a Hebrew word meaning "Jah will rise" or "Jah throws." Jeremiah was the name of one of the foremost of the Hebrew prophets. He was born about 650 B.C. and was the son of a priest. His work was done in the days when the kingdom of Judah was falling and during the time of the early Babylonian captivity. He told the people what would happen to them for their wickednesses and was thrown into prison for it, being actually a prisoner when Jerusalem was taken. The Babylonian conquerors permitted him to go back to his native land and continue his work. It was fruitless, and he is said to have died in exile in Egypt. His literary style is exceedingly high. His two contributions to the Bible are the book of Jeremiah and Lamentations.

References.—The book of Jeremiah and Lamentations.

JERICHO.

JER'I-CHO—a form of a Hebrew word probably meaning "a fragrant place." Jericho was the name of a noted place in the Jordan valley at the point where the river enters the Dead Sea. It was the first city taken by the Israelites after crossing the Jordan. The miraculous manner of its fall is related in Joshua 6: 20. At that time it was large and populous, and the center of a spot of great abundance and fertility. A squalid little village now occupies a part of the old site of the place, and it seems to have lived up to the curse pronounced upon it by the Israelites.

JERUSALEM. (See David, Jesus, Jews, Judah, Solomon, Titus.)

JE-RU'SA-LEM—a form of a Hebrew word meaning "founded peaceful," or "the foundation of peace." Jerusalem is the name of the most famous city of the world—the City of David, the Holy City, the city just outside of which Jesus the Christ died, the city for which such a vast amount of human blood has been shed since by Christian and Crusader, and Infidel and Moslem. It is located about thirty-five miles east of Joppa and the Mediterranean Sea, on a high tableland, which, in reality, is the crest of a range of splendid hills. The place itself is built upon a cluster of hills, which include Mount Zion, the Mount of Olives, Mount Moriah, and one or two others.

Just when it was founded is not known, but it must have been at a very ancient time, for the place was known in the days of Abraham as the city of Salem. Years afterward, the Israelites, making their conquering way through the land of Canaan, under Joshua, took a part of it. This was about 1,444 years before the birth of Christ. Little is heard about it thereafter until David's time, when he made himself the master of it, and thenceforth one of its titles was "the city of David." Under the sway of David and Solomon it rose rapidly in beauty, splendor, and power, and even after the division of the race of the Jews into two kingdoms it continued to be the great Jewish city. When the decline of Hebrew power set in, the magnificent place attracted the eye of the Babylonians and Assyrians, although it fell first to the Egyptians. After this event (B.C. 970) it went through various fortunes, and in B.C. 588 it was captured after a three years' siege by the forces of Nebuchadnezzar, the king of Babylon, who almost destroyed it. After the fall of the Babylonian empire, at the hands of the conquering Persians, Jerusalem began to see better days. The Persian kings permitted such of the exiled Jews as desired to return to their holy city, the Temple was rebuilt, and it seemed that the place was well on its way to recover its glory. Even under Alexander the Great it was permitted to go unmolested, although that conqueror originally intended to destroy it for its loyalty to the Persians, whom he had defeated.

Following Alexander there ensued another period of varying fortunes. In about B.C. 167 Antiochus Epiphanes captured the city, plundered it, razed its walls, and set up the worship of Jupiter in the Temple. The Maccabean revolt changed the ownership of the city to the Jews once more and they enjoyed it for almost a century. Then the Roman general, Pompey, took the city, no less than 12,000 Jews falling in a massacre that resulted from the capture. Pompey left the Temple treasure untouched, but a few years later another Roman general, Crassus, removed them. Shortly after, the Herodian family appeared upon the scene, as kings under the authority of Rome, and once again Jerusalem began to take on an air of splendor. Under Herod the Great, the Temple was rebuilt even more magnificent in style than it had been in Solomon's day, and when Jesus was a youth the city was at the very height of its grandeur.

It might almost seem that God permitted Jerusalem to grow magnificent beyond its for-

mer beauty so that its shame and sorrow might be the greater. After the rejection of Jesus by His own people and His crucifixion the vials of the divine wrath were preparing. In A.D. 70, about thirty-eight years after the tragedy of Golgotha, the Roman general, Titus, laid siege to the city. It held out for forty-two months—until the inhabitants and defenders actually were forced to eat their own children for food. Then it fell, and Titus, in his wrath, almost wiped it off the face of the earth. With this practical destruction of the city and the attendant horrors of the siege were fulfilled two great prophecies. The first (Deuteronomy 38: 57 et seq.) came from the lips of Moses more than 1,500 years before, and the second Christ's own prophecy that the place should be destroyed (Matthew 24 and Luke 19: 41-44). How wonderfully this all was carried out we see when we learn that even the old foundations of the Temple, that had stood for more than eleven hundred years, were overturned, stone for stone, by the treasure-hunting Romans. No one ever will know how many persons perished in the siege and the assault and the butchery which followed. It was the end of Jerusalem as the holy city of the Jews.

The city's modern history is very eventful. For fifty years after the capture of the place by Titus it was hardly more than a heap of ruins. Then the Romans partially rebuilt it, and the Jews made an effort to restore the Temple. But God's hand was against such a restoration. We are credibly informed that mysterious fires broke out at nights and destroyed such work as had been done and that fires even manifested themselves in the foundations and drove the workmen away. An earthquake also seems to have added its "Thou shalt not" to the rebuilding of the edifice Christ said should be destroyed. The history of the city is almost a blank from the time of Titus to that of Emperor Constantine. This prince, his interest awakened by his exceedingly pious mother, the Empress Helena, gave the place much attention, and in A.D. 335 a magnificent church was built on the supposed site of the Holy Sepulchre. During the following three hundred years the city gradually reassumed some of its old glory and beauty. In A.D. 614 the Persians captured it, and in 636 the Arabians obtained possession.

From this date onward to the year 1000 Jerusalem enjoyed a period of quiet and peace. Then the wars known as the Crusades broke out. On one side were the Christians from Europe fighting for the recovery of the Holy Sepulchre, while on the other were the Moslems, or followers of Mohammed. In 1099, after a siege of forty days, the Christians, under Godfrey of Bouillon, took the city by storm and a dreadful massacre followed. A kingdom was set up, with Godfrey as king. This monarchy lasted eighty-eight years. Then the Moslems got possession again, and since then they have managed to retain it, save for one or two short periods which are of little historical importance.

The present population of the city is about 60,000, about half of which are Jews. It is only a ghost of the splendid city which it was in its glory. Yet thousands of Christians visit it yearly to make pious pilgrimages to the place wherein the Master once trod.

JESUS. (See Christ, God, Holy Ghost, Trinity, etc.)

JE′SUS—the ordinary designation of the incarnate Son of God and Saviour of mankind, being the English form of the Greek version of the Hebrew name Joshua or Jeshua. This name originally was Jehoshua, meaning "Saviour" or "Help of Jehovah," but was abbreviated to the forms given above. Jesus was the Lord's proper name, just as David, or Paul, or John, or Mark were the proper names of the men who bore them. Christ is an official title, just as are the titles "the Baptist," "the Apostle," or "the King." To distinguish Him from other persons who bore the same name, it not being an uncommon one among the Hebrews, He is often called Jesus of Nazareth. The present article will deal with His human life, teachings, and work. They are the subjects of the New Testament, and form the historical and doctrinal foundations of Christianity. The gospels of Matthew, Mark, Luke, and John do not tell all of His life in detail, but seek to give a general picture. Each writer viewed it from a different point, and one often saw things others did not. John, for instance, devotes a great

amount of his gospel to the last three months of His life. So far as is known the order in which they were written is (1) Mark's—about 66 A.D.; (2) Matthew's—about 70-80 A.D.; (3) Luke's—about 80 A.D.; (4) John's—about 85-96 A.D.

We cannot be absolutely sure of the date of either Jesus' birth or death, because of certain confusion which exists regarding the years. The most modern research and thought gives the probable year of His birth as B.C. 4 and that of His death A.D. 30 or 31. The same doubt exists as to the duration of His ministry, opinion being divided as to whether it was one, two, or three years. After all, these things are entirely immaterial and unimportant, since it is what He taught and how He taught that are the things to be considered, rather than the mere questions of months, or days, or years.

Of His family we have almost complete record. Joseph and Mary were of the best blood of the race of Israel. Yet Joseph was not only a poor man but a hard-working one. They were of Nazareth in Galilee, where the religious air was much purer than in Judea and Jerusalem, where Pharisaism was the ruling doctrine. His coming had been prophesied from away back in the past, but the Jews, beaten, cowed, and dispersed by their powerful enemies, looked not for a Prince of Peace. What they expected was a great and wonderful soldier and conqueror, who would set his heel upon the necks of their foes instead of winning the world by love and self-sacrifice. This was the attitude of a majority of the Jews up to the very hour of Jesus' death, thus fulfilling the Scripture that He should be despised and rejected by His own people.

Jesus was born in Bethlehem, a Judean town, for the reason that Joseph and Mary had gone there to meet the tax-gatherer to be enrolled, Joseph being taxed in that town because he was of the line of David, and therefore accredited to Bethlehem, although his place of residence was Nazareth. The announcement of God's angel to Mary and Joseph of His coming birth took place in Nazareth. No sooner was the babe born that trouble began. Three wise men from the East appeared before Herod the King, asking where they could find the new-born King of the Jews that they might do homage to him. This and the stories of the shepherds about the celestial music which had greeted the Saviour's birth—stories that doubtless had reached Herod's ears—caused the wicked king to wish to slay the babe, in whom he could only see a pretender to the throne. To escape Herod, Joseph was divinely ordered to take Jesus into Egypt until Herod died.

Of the first thirty years of the Master's life we do not know much save the little that Luke tells us of His boyhood. After He was twelve years old we know nothing with authority except what is inferred in those beautiful words of strength and promise in Luke 2: 51 and 52: "And he went down with them, and came to Nazareth, and was subject unto them: but his mother kept all these sayings in her heart. And Jesus increased in wisdom and stature, and in favour with God and man." These few words mean without doubt that in His home relations He was a dutiful, obedient son and a kind and loving brother, and that outside of His home life He was a good neighbor and friend; that in business relations He was faithful; that as a worker at His trade He was skilled, capable, and industrious; that with respect to the state and the political government under which He lived He was a well-informed, intelligent, and law-abiding citizen, and that He was a close student of the religious history and doctrine of the time. His habits of Sabbath observance while a boy and during His early manhood were doubtless similar to those of the good Sunday-school scholar and Christian of the present time.

There is also little doubt but that He followed Joseph's trade of carpenter and supported His mother after Joseph's death, which seems to have occurred during His later youth. All the years concerning which the gospels are silent were years of preparation for the ministry which was to end in the Great Sacrifice upon Calvary. Whether He knew what His mission was to be we know not. It may have been that He knew; it may have been that it was revealed to Him on the coming of John the Baptist. Either way, His obedience to the will of His Father is a beautiful thing to contemplate.

With His baptism began the work for which He was sent. First He was tempted. Put to the proof He proved steadfast. Then He called His first disciples and set about that marvelous work of which it is said: "He went about doing good." His first miracle was performed at Cana in Galilee, where, at a wedding feast, He turned water into wine. Following this was a season of healing and preaching, but His first great utterance of which we have a complete account was the Sermon on the Mount. Wonderful as it was, still greater things were to come in the parables. Next came the choice of the twelve and their sending forth to preach the word. This led up to the feeding of the thousands and the breaking of the news to the disciples that He was to suffer death, with which was coupled the announcement of the founding of His Church. Six days later came the Transfiguration, and then the disciples, if indeed they needed proof, knew that the Man they followed was truly the Son of God. But much more was to come before He was to be sacrificed. Twice more was He to foretell his passion, many more parables was He to utter, many more sick were to feel His healing touch, and much more good was he to do.

At last came the time. He and His disciples went up to Jerusalem to the Passover knowing what was to happen. He entered the holy city in triumph; only seven days later He departed from it carrying His cross to the place where He was to die. During that time He was not idle. There was much to be done and little time in which to do it. But it was done, and at last the departing Master sat in a little upper room eating a farewell meal with His followers. There he instituted the beautiful ordinance by which Christians partake symbolically of His body and blood in memory of Him and to their spiritual sustenance, and promised to send them the Comforter. Events now trod upon each other's heels. The betrayal, Peter's denial, the trials before the Sanhedrin and Pilate, the condemnation, and finally the agony on Calvary succeeded each other. Dead—but living in the sense that His sacrifice of Himself for man was never to perish and to benefit the human race for all time—they laid Him in the sepulchre, from which on the third day He arose. Ten times thereafter He appeared to His people and forty days after His resurrection He ascended into Heaven, leaving the work He had begun and the Church He had founded to be carried on by the devoted band of men He had left behind.

Considering Jesus simply in His character as a man and a teacher we cannot but be astounded at the marvelous character of His work. In the course of a ministry which certainly could not have extended over a longer period than thirty months, we find that he overturned a system of ethics that had endured for nearly two thousand years, revised and purified the world's old and diseased code of morals, gave the death-blow to paganisms, and set up His own ethics, morals, and religion to the extent that they will stand for all time without change. And these three things —ethics, morals, and religion—are of such a character that they are not only good for one race of men but for all races, and not only intended for yesterday but for to-morrow as well as for to-day. By the old systems men could live or they could die. By the systems that Jesus laid down men can do both equally well, for beyond the grave they have the hope of everlasting life and the promise of salvation by remission of sin through His blood.

Strange as it may seem, every tangible evidence of Him has passed from the world. Nothing of Him has endured save His redemption of us, His promises to us, His commands to us, and the Church He gave us. We do not know what His face looked like; we do not know the actual spot of His birthplace; His home in Nazareth is gone; we are not sure just where Calvary is; we do not know whether the sepulchre in which He was laid still exists. All these things are hidden from us—doubtless by divine intention. God would have us know alone that His Son loved and died for us.

REFERENCES.

Birth and Infancy.

Annunciation to Mary:

And the Angel said unto her, Fear not, Mary, for thou hast found favour with God.

And behold, thou shalt conceive in thy womb, and bring forth a son, and shalt call his name Jesus.

He shall be great, and shall be called the son of the Highest, and the Lord God shall give unto him the throne of his father David.

And he shall reign over the house of Jacob for ever, and of his kingdom there shall be no end. (Luke 1: 30-33.)

Annunciation to Joseph:

And Joseph also went up from Galilee, out of the city of Nazareth, into Judæa, unto the city of David, which is called Bethlehem, (because he was of the house and lineage of David,)

To be taxed with Mary his espoused wife, being great with child.

And so it was, that while they were there, the days were accomplished that she should be delivered.

And she brought forth her firstborn son, and wrapped him in swaddling clothes, and laid him in a manger, because there was no room for them in the Inn. (Luke 2: 4-7.)

Annunciation to the Shepherds:

And the Angel said unto them, Fear not: For behold, I bring you good tidings of great joy, which shall be to all people.

For unto you is born this day, in the city of David, a Saviour, which is Christ the Lord.

And this shall be a sign unto you; ye shall find the babe wrapped in swaddling clothes lying in a manger.

And suddenly there was with the Angel a multitude of the heavenly host praising God, and saying,

Glory to God in the highest, and on earth peace, good will toward men.

And it came to pass, as the Angels were gone away from them into heaven, the shepherds said one to another, Let us now go even unto Bethlehem, and see this thing which is come to pass, which the Lord hath made known unto us.

And they came with haste, and found Mary and Joseph, and the babe lying in a manger. (Luke 2: 10-16.)

Annunciation to the Wise Men:

Now when Jesus was born in Bethlehem of Judæa, in the days of Herod the king, behold, there came Wise men from the East to Jerusalem,

Saying, Where is he that is born King of the Jews? for we have seen his Star in the East, and are come to worship him. (Matthew 2: 1, 2.)

And when they were departed, behold, the Angel of the Lord appeareth to Joseph in a dream, saying, Arise and take the young child, and his mother, and flee into Egypt, and be thou there until I bring thee word: for Herod will seek the young child, to destroy him.

When he arose, he took the young child and his mother by night, and departed into Egypt:

And was there until the death of Herod, that it might be fulfilled which was spoken of the Lord by the Prophet, saying, Out of Egypt have I called my son. (Matthew 2: 13-15.)

Boyhood.

Now his parents went to Jerusalem every year, at the feast of the Passover.

And when he was twelve years old, they went up to Jerusalem, after the custom of the feast. (Luke 2: 41, 42.)

And it came to pass, that after three days they found him in the Temple, sitting in the midst of the Doctors, both hearing them, and asking them ques-

And all that heard him were astonished at his understanding, and answers.

And when they saw him, they were amazed: and his mother said unto him, Son, why hast thou thus dealt with us? Behold, thy father and I have sought thee sorrowing.

And he said unto them, *How is it that ye sought me? Wist ye not that I must be about my Father's business?*

And they understood not the saying which he spake unto them.

And he went down with them, and came to Nazareth, and was subject unto them: but his mother kept all these sayings in her heart.

And Jesus increased in wisdom and stature, and in favour with God and man. (Luke 2: 46-52.)

Baptism and Ministry.

But John forbade him, saying, I have need to be baptized of thee, and comest thou to me?

And Jesus answering said unto him, *Suffer it to be so now: for thus it becometh us to fulfil all righteousness.* Then he suffered him.

And Jesus, when he was baptized, went up straightway out of the water: and, lo, the heavens were opened unto him, and he saw the Spirit of God descending like a dove, and lighting upon him:

And lo a voice from heaven, saying, This is my beloved Son, in whom I am well pleased. (Matthew 3: 14-17.)

And he came to Nazareth, where he had been brought up: and, as his custom was, he went into the synagogue on the sabbath day, and stood up for to read.

And there was delivered unto him the book of the prophet Esaias. And when he had opened the book, he found the place where it was written,

The Spirit of the Lord is upon me, because he hath anointed me to preach the gospel to the poor; he hath sent me to heal the broken-hearted, to preach deliverance to the captives, and recovering of sight to the blind, to set at liberty them that are bruised,

To preach the acceptable year of the Lord.

And he closed the book, and he gave it again to the minister, and sat down. And the eyes of all them that were in the synagogue were fastened on him.

And he began to say unto them, *This day is this scripture fulfilled in your ears.* (Luke 4: 16-21.)

First Disciples Chosen.

And so was also James, and John, the sons of Zebedee, which were partners with Simon. And Jesus said unto Simon, *Fear not; from henceforth thou shalt catch men.*

And when they had brought their ships to land, they forsook all, and followed him. (Luke 5: 10, 11.)

Opposition Begins.

As they went out, behold, they brought to him a dumb man possessed with a devil.

And when the devil was cast out, the dumb spake: and the multitudes marvelled, saying, It was never so seen in Israel.

But the Pharisees said, He casteth out devils through the prince of the devils. (Matthew 9: 32-34.)

Preaching and Healing.

And Jesus went about all the cities and villages, teaching in their synagogues, and preaching the gospel of the kingdom, and healing every sickness and every disease among the people.

But when he saw the multitudes, he was moved with compassion on them, because they fainted, and were scattered abroad, as sheep having no shepherd.

Then saith he unto his disciples, *The harvest truly is plenteous, but the labourers are few;*

Pray ye therefore the Lord of the harvest, that he will send forth labourers into his harvest. (Matthew 10: 35-38.)

Disciples Sent Forth.

And when he had called unto him his twelve disciples, he gave them power against unclean spirits, to cast them out, and to heal all manner of sickness and all manner of disease. (Matthew 11: 1.)

Church Established.

And Simon Peter answered and said, Thou art the Christ, the Son of the living God.

And Jesus answered and said unto him, *Blessed art thou, Simon Bar-jona: for flesh and blood hath not revealed it unto thee, but my Father which is in heaven.*

And I say also unto thee, That thou art Peter, and upon this rock I will build my church; and the gates of hell shall not prevail against it. (Matthew 16: 16-18.)

Death and Suffering Foretold.

Then charged he his disciples that they should tell no man that he was Jesus the Christ.

From that time forth began Jesus to shew unto his disciples, how that he must go unto Jerusalem, and suffer many things of the elders and chief priests and scribes, and be killed, and be raised again the third day. (Matthew 16: 20, 21.)

The Transfiguration.

And after six days Jesus taketh Peter, James, and John his brother, and bringeth them up into an high mountain apart,

And was transfigured before them: and his face did shine as the sun, and his raiment was white as the light. (Matthew 17: 1, 2.)

And as they came down from the mountain, Jesus charged them, saying, *Tell the vision to no man, until the Son of man be risen again from the dead.* (Matthew 17: 9.)

Last Journey to Jerusalem and Triumphal Entry.

And Jesus going up to Jerusalem took the twelve disciples apart in the way, and said unto them,

Behold, we go up to Jerusalem; and the Son of man shall be betrayed unto the chief priests and unto the scribes, and they shall condemn him to death,

And shall deliver him to the Gentiles to mock, and to scourge, and to crucify him: and the third day he shall rise again. (Matthew 20: 17-19.)

On the next day much people that were come to the feast, when they heard that Jesus was coming to Jerusalem,

Took branches of palm trees, and went forth to meet him, and cried, Hosanna: Blessed is the King of Israel that cometh in the name of the Lord. (John 12: 12, 13.)

Indicates Judas as Traitor.

And as they did eat, he said, *Verily I say unto you, that one of you shall betray me.*

And they were exceeding sorrowful, and began every one of them to say unto him, Lord, is it I?

And he answered and said, *He that dippeth his hand with me in the dish, the same shall betray me.*

The Son of man goeth as it is written of him: but woe unto that man by whom the Son of man is betrayed! it had been good for that man if he had not been born.

Then Judas, which betrayed him, answered and said, Master, is it I? He said unto him, *Thou hast said.* (Matthew 26: 21-25.)

Institutes Lord's Supper.

And as they were eating, Jesus took bread, and blessed it, and brake it, and gave it to the disciples, and said, *Take, eat; this is my body.*

And he took the cup, and gave thanks, and gave it to them, saying, *Drink ye all of it;*

For this is my blood of the new testament, which is shed for many for the remission of sins. (Matthew 26: 26-28.)

The Agony in the Garden.

Then cometh Jesus with them unto a place called Gethsemane, and saith unto the disciples, *Sit ye here, while I go and pray yonder.*

And he took with him Peter and the two sons of Zebedee, and began to be sorrowful and very heavy.

Then saith he unto them, *My soul is exceeding sorrowful, even unto death: tarry ye here, and watch with me.*

And he went a little farther, and fell on his face, and prayed, saying, *O my Father, if it be possible, let this cup pass from me: nevertheless not as I will, but as thou wilt.*

And he cometh unto the disciples, and findeth them asleep, and saith unto Peter, *What, could ye not watch with me one hour?*

Watch and pray, that ye enter not into temptation: the spirit indeed is willing, but the flesh is weak.

He went away again the second time, and prayed, saying, *O my Father, if this cup may not pass away from me, except I drink it, thy will be done.*

And he came and found them asleep again: for their eyes were heavy.

And he left them, and went away again, and prayed the third time, saying the same words. (Matthew 26: 36-44.)

The Betrayal.

And while he yet spake, lo, Judas, one of the twelve, came, and with him a great multitude with swords and staves, from the chief priests and elders of the people.

Now he that betrayed him gave them a sign, saying, Whomsoever I shall kiss, that same is he: hold him fast.

And forthwith he came to Jesus, and said, Hail, master; and kissed him. (Matthew 26: 47-49.)

Trial and Condemnation.

Now the chief priests, and elders, and all the council, sought false witness against Jesus, to put him to death;

But found none: yea, though many false witnesses came, yet found they none. At the last came two false witnesses,

And said, This fellow said, I am able to destroy the temple of God, and to build it in three days.

And the high priest arose, and said unto him, Answerest thou nothing? what is it which these witness against thee?

But Jesus held his peace. And the high priest answered and said unto him, I adjure thee by the living God, that thou tell us whether thou be the Christ, the Son of God.

Jesus saith unto him, Thou hast said: nevertheless I say unto you, Hereafter shall ye see the Son of man sitting on the right hand of power, and coming in the clouds of heaven. (Matthew 26: 59-64.)

And when they had bound him, they led him away, and delivered him to Pontius Pilate the governor. (Matthew 27: 2.)

Pilate saith unto them, What shall I do then with Jesus which is called Christ? They all say unto him, Let him be crucified.

And the governor said, Why, what evil hath he done? But they cried out the more, saying, Let him be crucified.

When Pilate saw that he could prevail nothing, but that rather a tumult was made, he took water, and washed his hands before the multitude, saying, I am innocent of the blood of this just person: see ye to it.

Then answered all the people, and said, His blood be on us, and on our children. (Matthew 27: 22-25.)

The Crucifixion.

And they crucified him, and parted his garments, casting lots: that it might be fulfilled which was spoken by the prophet, They parted my garments among them, and upon my vesture did they cast lots. (Matthew 27: 35.)

Now when the centurion, and they that were with him, watching Jesus, saw the earthquake, and those things that were done, they feared greatly, saying, Truly this was the Son of God. (Matthew 27: 54.)

The Burial.

When the even was come, there came a rich man of Arimathæa, named Joseph, who also himself was Jesus' disciple:

He went to Pilate, and begged the body of Jesus. Then Pilate commanded the body to be delivered.

And when Joseph had taken the body, he wrapped it in a clean linen cloth,

And laid it in his own new tomb, which he had hewn out in the rock: and he rolled a great stone to the door of the sepulchre, and departed. (Matthew 27: 57-60.)

The Resurrection.

And when the sabbath was past, Mary Magdalene, and Mary the mother of James, and Salome, had bought sweet spices, that they might come and anoint him.

And very early in the morning the first day of the week, they came unto the sepulchre at the rising of the sun.

And they said among themselves, Who shall roll us away the stone from the door of the sepulchre?

And when they looked, they saw that the stone was rolled away: for it was very great.

And entering into the sepulchre, they saw a young man sitting on the right side, clothed in a long white garment; and they were affrighted.

And he saith unto them, Be not affrighted: Ye seek Jesus of Nazareth, which was crucified: he is risen; he is not here: behold the place where they laid him. (Luke 16: 1-6.)

Appearances After Resurrection and Before Ascension.

1. *To Mary Magdalene:*

Now when Jesus was risen early the first day of the week, he appeared first to Mary Magdalene, out of whom he had cast seven devils. (Mark 16: 9.)

(See also John 20: 11-18.)

2. *To Other Women:*

And as they went to tell his disciples, behold Jesus met them, saying, *All hail.* And they came and held him by the feet, and worshipped him.

Then said Jesus unto them, *Be not afraid: go tell my brethren that they go into Galilee, and there shall they see me.* (Matthew 28: 9, 10.)

3. *To Two Disciples Near Emmaus:*

After that he appeared in another form unto two of them, as they walked, and went into the country. (Mark 16: 12.)

(See also Luke 24: 13-28.)

4. *To Simon:*

Saying, The Lord is risen indeed, and hath appeared to Simon. (Luke 24: 34.)

5. *To Ten Apostles:*

And as they thus spake, Jesus himself stood in the midst of them, and saith unto them, *Peace be unto you.* (Luke 24: 36.)

(See also John 20: 19-23.)

6. *To Eleven Apostles:*

Afterward he appeared unto the eleven as they sat at meat, and upbraided them with their unbelief and hardness of heart, because they believed not them which had seen him after he was risen.

And he said unto them, *Go ye into all the world, and preach the gospel to every creature.*

He that believeth and is baptized shall be saved; but he that believeth not shall be damned.

And these signs shall follow them that believe; In my name shall they cast out devils; they shall speak with new tongues;

They shall take up serpents; and if they drink any deadly thing, it shall not hurt them; they shall lay hands on the sick, and they shall recover. (Mark 16: 14-18.)

(See also John 20: 26-29.)

7. *To Disciples at Sea of Tiberias:*

After these things Jesus shewed himself again to the disciples at the sea of Tiberias; and on this wise shewed he himself. (John 21: 1.)

(See remainder of chapter.)

8. *To Disciples on a Mount in Galilee:*

Then the eleven disciples went away into Galilee, into a mountain where Jesus had appointed them.

And when they saw him, they worshipped him: but some doubted.

And Jesus came and spake unto them, saying, *All power is given unto me in heaven and in earth.*

Go ye therefore, and teach all nations, baptizing them in the name of the Father, and of the Son, and of the Holy Ghost:

Teaching them to observe all things whatsoever I have commanded you: and, lo, I am with you alway, even unto the end of the world. (Matthew 28: 16-20.)

9. *To 500 at Once:*

After that, he was seen of above five hundred brethren at once; of whom the greater part remain unto this present, but some are fallen asleep. (1 Corinthians 15: 6.)

10. *To James:*

After that, he was seen of James; then of all the apostles. (1 Corinthians 15: 7.)

The Ascension.

And he led them out as far as to Bethany, and he lifted up his hands, and blessed them.

And it came to pass, while he blessed them, he was parted from them, and carried up into heaven. (Luke 24: 50, 51.)

Appearances After Ascension.

1. *To Stephen:*

But he, being full of the Holy Ghost, looked up stedfastly into heaven, and saw the glory of God, and Jesus standing on the right hand of God,

And said, Behold, I see the heavens opened, and the Son of man standing on the right hand of God. (Acts 7: 55, 56.)

2. *To Paul:*

And last of all he was seen of me also, as of one born out of due time. (1 Corinthians 15: 8.)

3. *To John:*

And I turned to see the voice that spake with me. And being turned, I saw seven golden candlesticks;

And in the midst of the seven candlesticks one like unto the Son of man, clothed with a garment down to the foot, and girt about the paps with a golden girdle. (Revelation 1: 12, 13.)

Jesus' Teaching.

Preaches repentance at Galilee, Matthew 4: 17; at Nazareth, Luke 4: 16-19.

Preaches the gospel of the kingdom, Matthew 4: 23; Mark 1: 14.

Testimony concerning John the Baptist, Matthew 11: 7; Luke 7: 24; 20: 4.

Preaches respecting the Father and the Son to the Jews, John 5; 8: 18, 42; 10: 15; 12: 23; on the bread of life, John 6: 26; on the seed of Abraham, John 8: 21; on the traditions of the elders, Matthew 15: 1; Mark 7: 1.

Answers Pharisees, Matthew 12: 38; 16: 1; Mark 8: 11; Luke 11: 16; 12: 54; John 2: 18.

Lesson to disciples on humility, John 13: 14-16.

Teaches Scribes and Pharisees, Matthew 23; Mark 12; Luke 11: 37; 20: 45.

Prophesies destruction of Jerusalem, etc., Matthew 24; Mark 13; Luke 13: 34; 17: 20; 19: 41; 21.

Invites weary to rest, Matthew 11: 23.

Talks on suffering for the Gospel, Matthew 10: 37; Luke 14: 26.

Talks on marriage, Matthew 19; Mark 10.

    riches, Matthew 19: 16; Mark 10: 17; Luke 12: 13; 18: 18.

    tribute, Matthew 22: 15; Mark 12: 13; Luke 20: 20.

    resurrection, Matthew 22: 23; Mark 12: 18.

    two great commandments, Matthew 22: 35; Mark 12: 28.

    widow's mite, Mark 12: 41; Luke 21: 1.

    watchfulness, Matthew 24: 42; Mark 13: 33; Luke 12: 35; 21: 34.

    last judgment, Matthew 25: 31.

    faith, Matthew 8.

    those who follow him, Luke 9: 23-57.

    fasting, Matthew 9: 14; Mark 2: 18; Luke 5: 33.

    blasphemy, Matthew 12: 31; Mark 3: 28; Luke 11: 15.

    His brethren, Matthew 12: 46; Mark 3: 31; Luke 8: 19.

Sermon on the Mount—Matthew 5, 6, and 7.

Contains—The Beatitudes (those who are blessed), 5: 5-11; salt of the earth, 5: 13; light of the world, 5: 14; righteousness of the Scribes and Pharisees, 5: 20; anger, 5: 22;

"thou fool," 5: 22; reconciliation, 5: 24; adultery, 5: 27; the hand and the eye, 5: 29, 30; divorce, 5: 32, 33; oaths, 5: 33; eye for an eye, 5: 38; love to neighbor and enemy, 5: 43; perfection, 5: 48; almsgiving, 6: 1; prayer, 6: 5-7; Lord's Prayer, 6: 9-13; fasting, 6: 16; treasure on earth and in heaven, 6: 19-21; evil eye, 6: 23; two masters, 6: 24; God and Mammon, 6: 24; taking thought, 6: 25-33; seeking kingdom of God, 6: 33; judging not, 7: 1-3; ask, seek, find, 7: 7-11; straight gate, 7: 13; false prophets, 7: 15; grapes, thorns, figs, thistles, 7: 16-20; good and bad trees, 7: 17; hearers and doers, 7: 23, 24; house on sand and house on rock, 7: 24-27.

Jesus' Parables.

Of wise and foolish builders, Matthew 7: 24-27.

    children of the bridechamber, Matthew 9: 15; Luke 5: 34, 35.

    new cloth and old garment, Matthew 9: 13; Luke 5: 36.

    new wine and new bottles, Matthew 9: 17.

    unclean spirit, Matthew 12: 43.

    sower, Matthew 13: 3-9, 18-23; Luke 8: 5-15.

    the tares, Matthew 13: 24-43.

    mustard seed, Matthew 13: 31, 32; Luke 13: 19.

    leaven, Matthew 13: 33.

    hidden treasure, Matthew 13: 44.

    pearl of great price, Matthew 13: 45, 46.

    net cast into the sea, Matthew 13: 47-50.

    meats defiling not, Matthew 15: 10-15.

    unmerciful servant, Matthew 18: 23-35.

    hired laborers, Matthew 20: 1-16.

    the two sons, Matthew 21: 28-32.

    the wicked husbandmen, Matthew 21: 33-45.

    marriage of the king's son, Matthew 22: 2-14.

    the fig tree, Matthew 24: 32-34.

    man of the house watching, Matthew 24: 43.

    faithful and evil servants, Matthew 24: 45-51.

    the ten virgins, Matthew 25: 1-13.

    the talents, Matthew 25: 14-30.

    kingdom divided against itself, Mark 3: 24.

Jesus' Parables (continued).

Of house divided against itself, Mark 3: 25.

    strong man armed, Mark 3: 27; Luke 11: 21.

    seed growing secretly, Mark 4: 26-29.

    the lighted candle, Mark 4: 21; Luke 11: 33-36.

    man taking a far journey, Mark 13: 34-37.

    blind leading the blind, Luke 6: 39.

    the beam and the mote, Luke 6: 41, 42.

    the tree and its fruit, Luke 6: 43-45.

    creditor and debtors, Luke 7: 41-47.

    the good Samaritan, Luke 10: 30-37.

    the friend at midnight, Luke 11: 5-9.

    the rich fool, Luke 12: 16-21.

    the cloud and the wind, Luke 12: 54-57.

    the barren fig tree, Luke 13: 6-9.

    chief seats at the feast, Luke 14: 7-11.

    builder of a tower, Luke 14: 28-30, 33.

    the king going to war, Luke 14: 31-33.

    the savor of salt, Luke 14: 34, 35.

    the lost sheep, Luke 15: 3-7.

    the lost piece of silver, Luke 15: 8-10.

    the prodigal son, Luke 15: 11-32.

    the unjust steward, Luke 16: 1-8.

    the rich man and Lazarus, Luke 16: 19-31.

    unprofitable servant, Luke 17: 7.

    importunate widow, Luke 18: 1-8.

    the Pharisee and the Publican, Luke 18: 9-14.

    the pounds, Luke 19: 12-27.

    the Bread of Life, John 6: 47.

    the Good Shepherd, John 10: 1-6.

    the Vine and the branches, John 15: 1-5.

Jesus' Miracles.

    Water turned into wine, John 2: 6-10.

    Nobleman's son healed, John 4: 46-53.

    Centurion's servant healed, Matthew 8: 5-13.

    Draughts of fishes, Luke 5: 4-6; John 21: 6.

    Devils cast out, Matthew 8: 28-32; 9: 32, 33; 15: 22-28; 17: 14-18; Mark 1: 23-27.

    Peter's mother-in-law healed, Matthew 8: 14, 15.

    Lepers cleansed, Matthew 8: 3; Luke 17: 14.

    Paralytic healed, Mark 2: 3-12.

    Withered hand restored, Matthew 12: 10-13.

    Impotent man healed, John 5: 5-9.

    Dead raised to life, Matthew 9: 18, 19; 9: 23-25; Luke 7: 12-15; John 11: 11-44.

    Issue of blood stopped, Matthew 9: 20-22.

    Blind restored to sight, Matthew 9: 27-30; Mark 8: 22-25; John 9: 1-7.

    The deaf and dumb cured, Mark 7: 32-35.

    The multitude fed, Matthew 14: 15-21; 15: 32-38.

    Walking on the sea, Matthew 14: 25-27.

    The tribute money, Matthew 17: 27.

    The tempest stilled, Matthew 8: 23-26; Mark 4: 37; Luke 8: 23.

    Sudden arrival of ship, John 6: 21.

    Woman healed of infirmity, Luke 13: 11-13.

    Dropsy cured, Luke 14: 2-4.

    Fig tree blighted, Matthew 21: 19.

    Malchus healed, Luke 22: 50, 51.

Miracles performed before the messengers of John, John 7: 21, 22.

Different diseases healed, Matthew 4: 23, 24; 14: 14; 15: 30; Mark 1: 34; Luke 6: 17, 19.

Character of Jesus.

Holy:

And the angel answered and said unto her, The Holy Ghost shall come upon thee, and the power of the Highest shall overshadow thee: therefore also that holy thing which shall be born of thee shall be called the Son of God. (Luke 1: 35.)

For of a truth against thy holy child Jesus, whom thou hast anointed, both Herod, and Pontius Pilate, with the Gentiles, and the people of Israel, were gathered together. (Acts 4: 27.)

And to the angel of the church in Philadelphia write; These things saith he that is holy, he that is true, he that hath the key of David, he that openeth, and no man shutteth; and shutteth, and no man openeth. (Revelation 3: 7.)

Righteous:

He shall see of the travail of his soul, and shall be satisfied: by his knowledge shall my righteous servant justify many; for he shall bear their iniquities. (Isaiah 53: 11.)

Thou hast loved righteousness, and hated iniquity; therefore God, even thy God, hath anointed thee with the oil of gladness above thy fellows. (Hebrews 1: 9.)

Good:

And, behold, one came and said unto him, Good Master, what good thing shall I do, that I may have eternal life? (Matthew 19: 16.)

Faithful:

And righteousness shall be the girdle of his loins, and faithfulness the girdle of his reins. (Isaiah 11: 5.)

Faithful is he that calleth you, who also will do it. (1 Thessalonians 5: 24.)

True:

And the Word was made flesh, and dwelt among us, (and we beheld his glory, the glory as of the only begotten of the Father,) full of grace and truth. (John 1: 14.)

He that speaketh of himself seeketh his own glory: but he that seeketh his glory that sent him, the same is true, and no unrighteousness is in him. (John 7: 18.)

And we know that the Son of God is come, and hath given us an understanding, that we may know him that is true, and we are in him that is true, even in his Son Jesus Christ. This is the true God, and eternal life. (1 John 5: 20.)

Just:

Rejoice greatly, O daughter of Zion; shout, O daughter of Jerusalem: behold, thy King cometh unto thee: he is just, and having salvation; lowly, and riding upon an ass, and upon a colt the foal of an ass. (Zechariah 9: 9.)

I can of mine own self do nothing: as I hear, I judge: and my judgment is just; because I seek not mine own will, but the will of the Father which hath sent me. (John 5: 30.)

And he said, The God of our fathers hath chosen thee, that thou shouldest know his will, and see that Just One, and shouldest hear the voice of his mouth. (Acts 22: 14.)

Guileless:

And he made his grave with the wicked, and with the rich in his death; because he had done no violence, neither was any deceit in his mouth. (Isaiah 53: 9.)

Who did no sin, neither was guile found in his mouth. (1 Peter 2: 22.)

Sinless:

For he hath made him to be sin for us, who knew no sin; that we might be made the righteousness of God in him. (2 Corinthians 5: 21.)

Spotless:

But with the precious blood of Christ, as of a lamb without blemish and without spot. (1 Peter 1: 19.)

Innocent:

Saying, I have sinned in that I have betrayed the innocent blood. And they said, What is that to us? see thou to that. (Matthew 27: 4.)

Undefiled:

For such an high priest became us, who is holy, harmless, undefiled, separate from sinners, and made higher than the heavens. (Hebrews 7: 26.)

Obedient to the Father:

Jesus saith unto them, *My meat is to do the will of him that sent me, and to finish his work.* (John 14: 34.)

If ye keep my commandments, ye shall abide in my love; even as I have kept my Father's commandments, and abide in his love. (John 15: 10.)

Subject to Earthly Parents:

And he went down with them, and came to Nazareth, and was subject unto them: but his mother kept all these sayings in her heart. (Luke 2: 51.)

Zealous:

And he said unto them, *How is it that ye sought me? wist ye not that I must be about my Father's business?* (Luke 2: 49.)

Meek and Lowly:

He was oppressed, and he was afflicted, yet he opened not his mouth: he is brought as a lamb to the slaughter, and as a sheep before her shearers is dumb, so he openeth not his mouth. (Isaiah 53: 7.)

Take my yoke upon you, and learn of me: for I am meek and lowly in heart: and ye shall find rest unto your souls. (Matthew 11: 29.)

Resigned:

Saying, *Father, if thou be willing, remove this cup from me: nevertheless not my will, but thine, be done.* (Luke 22: 42.)

Longsuffering:

Howbeit for this cause I obtained mercy, that in me first Jesus Christ might shew forth all longsuffering, for a pattern to them which should hereafter believe on him to life everlasting. (1 Timothy 1: 16.)

Compassionate:

He shall feed his flock like a shepherd: he shall gather the lambs with his arm, and carry them in his bosom, and shall gently lead those that are with young. (Isaiah 40: 11.)

Then Jesus called his disciples unto him, and said, *I have compassion on the multitude, because they continue with me now three days, and have nothing to eat: and I will not send them away fasting, lest they faint in the way.* (Matthew 15: 32.)

And when the Lord saw her, he had compassion on her, and said unto her, *Weep not.* (Luke 7: 13.)

And when he was come near, he beheld the city, and wept over it. (Luke 19: 41.)

Benevolent:

And Jesus went about all Galilee, teaching in their synagogues, and preaching the gospel of the kingdom, and healing all manner of sickness and all manner of disease among the people. (Matthew 4: 23.)

How God anointed Jesus of Nazareth with the Holy Ghost and with power: who went about doing good, and healing all that were oppressed of the devil; for God was with them. (Acts 10: 38.)

Loving:

Now before the feast of the passover, when Jesus knew that his hour was come that he should depart out of this world unto the Father, having loved his own which were in the world, he loved them unto the end. (John 13: 1.)

Greater love hath no man than this, that a man lay down his life for his friends. (John 15: 13.)

Humble:

For whether is greater, he that sitteth at meat, or he that serveth? is not he that sitteth at meat? but I am among you as he that serveth. (Luke 22: 27.)

And being found in fashion as a man, He humbled himself, and became obedient unto death, even the death of the cross. (Philippians 2: 8.)

Self-denying:

And Jesus saith unto him, *The foxes have holes, and the birds of the air have nests; but the Son of man hath not where to lay his head.* (Matthew 8: 20.)

For ye know the grace of our Lord Jesus Christ, that, though he was rich, yet for your sakes he became poor, that ye through his poverty might be rich. (2 Corinthians 8: 9.)

Forgiving:

Then said Jesus, *Father, forgive them; for they know not what they do.* And they parted his raiment, and cast lots. (Luke 23: 34.)

JEWS. (See Israel, Israelites, Judah, etc.)

JEWS. The word "Jew" is a corruption of the word "Judah" and seems to have been applied first to the people of the tribe of Judah, and thence to the Israelite race in general. It is first found in the Bible in 2 Kings 16: 6. The history of the Jews, as a people, is of very great interest. It may be said to have begun with the emigation of Abraham from Ur about the year 2000 B.C. He went into Palestine, leading a nomadic life, which was followed by his descendants for several generations, a very numerous tribe being finally built up. About the year 1700 B.C. the race removed itself to Egypt, and promptly fell under the yoke of the Egyptians, although at first their condition was extremely good by reason of the power exercised by Joseph. The Pharaoh finally turned the Jews into a race of slaves, forcing them to various sorts of labor, chief of which was work on the vast buildings he was erecting. But a deliverer was raised up for them in the person of Moses. About the year 1400 B.C. they succeeded in escaping from the land of their oppression. By this time they numbered several millions of people and were divided into twelve tribes. Led by Moses, they marched forth into the wilderness to the east of Egypt, receiving at Sinai the law of the Ten Commandments and a statement of the general policy that was to be pursued by them as a nation. A sacrificial system was set up and a priesthood developed, the whole forming a theocratic government of the strongest kind. For a period of forty years the race kept to the wilderness, developing itself for the career of conquest it was to enter upon in Palestine. This large and fine country was in possession of many warlike tribes, and the business of turning them out occupied a long period of years. Moses having died before this period, the leadership was in the hands of Joshua, a soldier of great capabilities. The conquest, however, was not completed by arms entirely, for the original inhabitants managed to retain a number of cities. The tribes settled down to a rather loose confederacy under tribal chiefs, gradually absorbing the alien races, and trusting for general government to leaders who were called judges. Samuel, the last judge, gave the Jews their first king in Saul, and from that time to the dispersion the government was a monarchy. Under David and Solomon the nation reached its greatest strength and power. At the latter's death tribal jealousy brought about troubles which ended in the formation of a second monarchy, the race being known as the kingdom of Israel and the kingdom of Judah. National unity having been lost, the Jews fell an easy prey to the neighboring powerful and warlike peoples. First the Egyptian and then the Assyrian and Babylonian kings subdued the Jews, the latter carrying the conquered Israelites into captivity. The overthrow of the Babylonian empire by the Persians gave the Jews a chance to become a nation again, but there was no strong leader to profit by the opportunity.

One conqueror after another brought the race under subjection, and finally the Roman domination destroyed the last hope that a new Jewish nation might arise. Other great national influences rose, and gradually the Jews became dispersed over the face of the earth— a people without a land, without a home, and driven here and there by persecution, yet always believing that the promised Messiah would come and deliver them from bondage. Jesus as a Messiah they could not understand because He was a deliverer by peace and gentleness, whereas they had been taught to look for a soldier of the Joshua or David type. Therefore they rejected Him. The dispersion of the race continued throughout the years of the Roman domination and afterwards. Now there is not a nation upon earth that does not have its Jews.

No national race is so old as the Jewish people, yet none is so widely separated. Through it all, however, they have maintained their customs and traditions, and, to a certain extent, their religion, for the feasts, fasts, and rites celebrated in an orthodox Jewish synagogue to-day are pretty much the same as they were twenty-five centuries ago, while they still await the coming of the Messiah.

The Israelites, as a race, have exercised a great amount of influence upon the history of the world. Not a little of this has been due to the persecutions they have endured—and probably no other race has suffered so much from other races. In all lands and in all ages they have been at the mercy of some stronger people. This can be noticed even in the present, although most countries now permit the Jew full and free citizenship and common rights with other subjects or citizens. They have given some great men to the world in all departments of civilization—science, the arts, literature, and especially to commerce, business, and finance. In Europe Jewish financiers are in almost complete control through the great family of the Rothschilds, while in this country a vast amount of power, political, social, and commercial, is wielded by men of the race of Abraham, Isaac, and Jacob. But that they ever will become a reunited nation, with a land and home for themselves, is beyond the hopes of the most sanguine and optimistic of the race.

JEZEBEL.

JEZ'E-BEL—a form of a Hebrew word meaning "chaste." Jezebel was the daughter of a king of Tyre and wife of the wicked Israelite king, Ahab. She succeeded easily in leading him to set up the licentious worship of the Tyrian gods, and the pair brought down upon Israel the wrath of God. After Ahab's death Jezebel assumed the regency for her son Joram and later gave him the benefit of her wicked counsel. After Joram's death at the hands of Jehu she taunted the latter and he put her to death. Her name has become a byword for all that is bad and vicious in woman.

References.—1 Kings 16, 18, 19, 21; 2 Kings 9: 30.

JOAB.

Jo'AB—a form of a Hebrew word meaning "Jehovah the father." Joab was a nephew of David and commander of David's army. He slew Abner in consequence of a blood-feud and later was appointed to the chief command of the Jewish forces for bravery displayed at the storming of Mount Zion. He was devoted to David and showed his loyalty at the most critical times. David proved ungrateful, and while he lay upon his deathbed Joab cast his lot with Adonijah. On the collapse of Adonijah's rebellion Solomon had Joab killed, despite the fact that he had taken refuge at the temple altar. He was a splendid soldier, but most unscrupulous, save where the interests of the people and the king were at stake.

References.—2 Samuel 3, 8, 14, 18, 19, 20, 24; 1 Kings 1 and 2.

JOB.

JOB—a form of a Hebrew word meaning "returning." Job is the hero of one of the most remarkable books of the Bible. He is pictured as having been a most devout and good man, sorely afflicted by Satan with the permission of God as a test of his faith. Job complains and takes issue with God. There is lengthy argument between Job and his friends, the subject of which is how the afflictions of the righteous and the prosperity of the wicked can be consistent with God's justice. Job several times challenges God to settle the question. Another friend, Elihu, takes a part in the discussion, showing Job the error of his way, and God Himself speaks to Job out of a whirlwind. Job sees the enormity of his wrongdoings in complaining against the Almighty and repents sincerely and fully, whereupon God restores him to health and riches.

There has been much debate among Bible scholars and students as to the character of this book, chiefly as to whether Job was an historical personage and what was the period in which he lived, and what was the period in which the work was written. These things are not definitely settled and are of small moment beside the splendid truths that the book itself conveys. There is no question concerning the high literary character of the book, which would be a monument to the literary ability of any age. As a work teaching true and great lessons and pointing a sublime religious moral, Job takes its place among the very foremost of Scripture.

JOHN.

JOHN—a corruption of the Hebrew name Jehohanan, meaning "favored by Jehovah." The Bible mentions a number of persons named John, chief of whom are John the Baptist, who, so far as we know, wrote nothing that remains to this day; John the disciple, who wrote the gospel and epistles bearing his name and the book of Revelation; and Mark, who wrote the Gospel by Mark, and whose surname was John.

1. John the Baptist, "the forerunner of Jesus Christ," was the son of Zacharias and Elisabeth, who was a cousin of Mary, the mother of Jesus. He was six months older than his Master. His parents were informed by the angel Gabriel of his forthcoming birth. He was trained in the most pious and devout manner for the remarkable and holy office he was destined to fill. In the fullness of time he came forth from the desert to take up his ministry, garbed like the ancient prophets in skins and exhibiting all their austerity of life and manner. He called upon the Jews to repent, thus preparing the way for the work of the Lord. He soon gathered around him a number of disciples and went about baptizing all who came to him. There is no question but that John could have given Jesus much trouble in the beginning of His ministry had he chosen to assume the higher office, but he was faithful to his divine trust, and always showed in his talks that he was but the messenger of another higher and more holy than he. This is clearly set forth when he met Jesus, asking baptism at the Master's hands in preference to giving it. The remainder of John's ministry is somewhat obscure. It is likely, however, that he continued in his work subordinate to Jesus. The manner of his death is well known. He took Herod the king to task for marrying his brother Philip's wife, Herodias, and the latter, in revenge, claimed his head as a reward for her daughter's shame in dancing before the king and his drunken and debauched court. John was forthwith executed by order of Herod.

2. John the disciple, often called "the beloved disciple" because of the special favor shown to him by Jesus, was a Galilean fisherman of a well-to-do family. With James and Peter he seems to have been chosen for many particular and delicate tasks. For a long time he seems to have misunderstood the nature of the Lord's mission, expecting like other Jews that the Master would set up some sort of political government or military kingdom. The Master loved John for his mild and affectionate disposition, although we know that at times he could show great zeal and impetuosity, as, for example, when he wanted to call down fire from heaven. After the Ascension he continued to live in Jerusalem, and about A.D. 65 he went to Ephesus. From there he was exiled to Patmos, but seems to have returned to Ephesus before his death. All of his writings show a very high degree of spirituality and imagination, in strict keeping with the character of the man as we know it from the testimony of others.

JONAH.

JO'NAH—a form of a Hebrew word meaning "dove." Jonah was one of the minor prophets. He lived about 840 B.C.
Reference.—The book of Jonah.

JONATHAN.

JON'A-THAN—a form of a Hebrew word meaning "God-given." Jonathan was the eldest son of Saul and heir to the throne. The nobility of his character is shown clearly by the readiness with which he surrendered this heirship to David, whom he believed to have been chosen by God for the kingly dignity. A friendship of the most devoted type existed between him and David, enduring through the terrible days when Saul was seeking David's life. After Jonathan's death, David sang his eulogy in terms that are unmatched for exquisite dignity and pathos, and he declared that his affection was "wonderful, passing the love of women."

References.—1 Samuel 13, 18, 31; 2 Samuel 1.

JORDAN.

JOR'DAN—a form of a Hebrew word meaning "the descender." Jordan is the name of Palestine's chief river, which the Scriptures have made one of the most famous streams in the world, an importance which is chiefly historic, for the river itself is neither beautiful nor commercially of much value. It rises on the slopes of Mount Hermon and flows about 200 miles, emptying into the Dead Sea. In its waters Jesus was baptized, while centuries before it marked the end of the wanderings of the Israelites, who crossed it to begin the conquest of Canaan. It is mentioned 180 times in the Old Testament and 15 times in the New Testament.

JOSEPH.

JO'SEPH—a form of a Hebrew word meaning "he will increase." The Bible contains records of ten persons named Joseph, only three of whom, however, are of importance: (1) Joseph, the son of Jacob; (2) Joseph, the husband of Mary, the mother of Jesus; (3) Joseph of Arimathea.

1. Joseph was the first child Rachel bore to Jacob. He came into the world about B.C. 1726, near Damascus. Up to the age of seventeen we have little or nothing of his history. At that time he excited the envy and jealousy of his brothers by reason of his father's love, and they secretly sold him as a slave to a band of Ishmaelites, who took him to Egypt. The brothers deluded Jacob into believing the boy dead. The Ishmaelites, on reaching Egypt, sold Joseph to Potiphar, a high official of the government, and he rose to power and influence in Potiphar's household. Incurring the deep displeasure of Potiphar's wife, Joseph was cast into prison, but through the interpretation of dreams for the governor of the prison and for the pharaoh himself, he was released and raised to the position of viceroy. Not long after this Joseph's brethren came to Egypt, and during the course of their stay he made himself known to them. The pharaoh, through favor to Joseph, told him to invite his family to settle in the land, which was done, thus laying the foundation for the future bondage of the Israelites. He lived many years, taking care of his aged father and showering favors upon his brothers.

The character of Joseph is, next to that of Jesus, the most lovable and beautiful in the Bible. In all the record of him there is nothing to justify a word of reproach or criticism. He had great faith, he was steadfast in resistance to temptation, and he constantly returned good for evil. Unquestionably he is nearer the type of Jesus than any other Bible character.

2. Joseph, the husband of Mary, was the son of Heli (or Jacob), and a descendant of David. Tradition says that he was well advanced in years when Jesus was born, but there is no means of verifying this. After the birth of Jesus and the return from Egypt, Joseph gradually disappears, the last mention of him being with reference to the trip to Jerusalem, upon which Jesus was found disputing with the doctors. He is supposed to have died a considerable time prior to the crucifixion.

3. Joseph of Arimathea was a wealthy Hebrew, secretly one of the followers of Jesus. After the crucifixion he begged the body of the Master from the government and buried it in his new private tomb.

REFERENCES.

Joseph, the Son of Jacob.

And she called his name Joseph; and said, The Lord shall add to me another son. (Genesis 30: 24.)

Now Israel loved Joseph more than all his children, because he was the son of his old age: and he made him a coat of many colours.

And when his brethren saw that their father loved him more than all his brethren, they hated him, and could not speak peaceably unto him. (Genesis 37: 3, 4.)

Then there passed by Midianites,

merchantmen; and they drew and lifted up Joseph out of the pit, and sold Joseph to the Ishmaelites for twenty pieces of silver: and they brought Joseph into Egypt. (Genesis 37: 28.)

And Joseph was brought down to Egypt: and Potiphar, an officer of Pharaoh, captain of the guard, an Egyptian, bought him of the hands of the Ishmaelites, which had brought him down thither. (Genesis 39: 1.)

And it came to pass, when his master heard the words of his wife, which she spake unto him, saying, After this manner did thy servant to me; that his wrath was kindled.

And Joseph's master took him, and put him into the prison, a place where the king's prisoners were bound: and he was there in the prison.

But the Lord was with Joseph, and shewed him mercy, and gave him favour in the sight of the keeper of the prison. (Genesis 39: 19-21.)

And Pharaoh said unto his servants, Can we find such a one as this is, a man in whom the spirit of God is?

And Pharaoh said unto Joseph, Forasmuch as God hath shewed thee all this, there is none so discreet and wise as thou art:

Thou shalt be over my house, and according unto thy word shall all my people be ruled: only in the throne will I be greater than thou. (Genesis 41: 38-40.)

And the sons of Israel came to buy corn among those that came: for the famine was in the land of Canaan.

And Joseph was the governor over the land, and he it was that sold to all the people of the land: and Joseph's brethren came, and bowed down themselves before him with their faces to the earth.

And Joseph saw his brethren, and he knew them, but made himself strange unto them, and spake roughly unto them; and he said unto them, Whence come ye? And they said, From the land of Canaan to buy food.

And Joseph knew his brethren, but they knew not him. (Genesis 42: 5-8.)

Then Joseph could not refrain himself before all them that stood by him; and he cried, Cause every man to go out from me. And there stood no man with him, while Joseph made himself known unto his brethren. (Genesis 45: 1.)

And Pharaoh said unto Joseph, Say unto thy brethren, This do ye; lade your beasts, and go, get you unto the land of Canaan;

And take your father and your households, and come unto me: and I will give you the good of the land of Egypt, and ye shall eat the fat of the land. (Genesis 45: 17, 18.)

And Joseph dwelt in Egypt, he, and his father's house: and Joseph lived a hundred and ten years.

And Joseph saw Ephraim's children of the third generation: the children also of Machir the son of Manasseh were brought up upon Joseph's knees.

And Joseph said unto his brethren, I die; and God will surely visit you, and bring you out of this land unto the land which he sware to Abraham, to Isaac, and to Jacob. (Genesis 50: 22-24.)

Joseph, the Husband of Mary.

And Jacob begat Joseph the husband of Mary, of whom was born Jesus, who is called Christ. (Matthew 1: 16.)

Then Joseph, her husband, being a just man, and not willing to make her a publick example, was minded to put her away privily.

But while he thought on these things,

behold, the angel of the Lord appeared unto him in a dream, saying, Joseph, thou son of David, fear not to take unto thee Mary thy wife: for that which is conceived in her is of the Holy Ghost. (Matthew 1: 19, 20.)

Then Joseph being raised from sleep did as the angel of the Lord had bidden him, and took unto him his wife. (Matthew 1: 24.)

And when they were departed, behold, the angel of the Lord appeareth to Joseph in a dream, saying, Arise, and take the young child and his mother, and flee into Egypt, and be thou there until I bring thee word: for Herod will seek the young child to destroy him.

When he arose, he took the young child and his mother by night, and departed into Egypt. (Matthew 2: 13, 14.)

But when Herod was dead, behold, an angel of the Lord appeareth in a dream to Joseph in Egypt,

Saying, Arise, and take the young child and his mother, and go into the land of Israel: for they are dead which sought the young child's life.

And he arose, and took the young child and his mother, and came into the land of Israel. (Matthew 2: 19-21.)

Joseph of Arimathea.

When the even was come, there came a rich man of Arimathæa, named Joseph, who also himself was Jesus' disciple:

He went to Pilate, and begged the body of Jesus. Then Pilate commanded the body to be delivered.

And when Joseph had taken the body, he wrapped it in a clean linen cloth,

And laid it in his own new tomb, which he had hewn out in the rock: and he rolled a great stone to the door

of the sepulchre, and departed. (Matthew 27: 57-60.)

JOSHUA.

JOSH'U-A—a form of the Hebrew word "Jehoshua" and one of the earlier forms of the name "Jesus." Joshua was the son of Nun and the successor of Moses as the leader of the Israelites. He was a soldier of uncommon ability as well as a man eminently fitted for the leadership of a people like the Jews. He was one of the twelve spies sent out to examine the land of Canaan and, with Caleb, reserved to enter the land. He led a life almost entirely free from blemish, and is regarded as having been of the type of Christ. He died at a very advanced age.

References.—Exodus 17, 24, 32, 33; Numbers 13, 27, 34; Deuteronomy 1, 3, 34; Joshua 1, 3, 4, 5, 6, 7, 8, 10, 12, 14, 22, 23, 24.

JOY.

Joy—that passion or emotion excited by the acquisition or the expectation of good; pleasure caused by good fortune, or the like; gladness, delight.

REFERENCES.
General.

Then he said unto them, Go your way, eat the fat, and drink the sweet, and send portions unto them for whom nothing is prepared: for this day is holy unto our Lord: neither be ye sorry; for the joy of the Lord is your strength. (Nehemiah 8: 10.)

Thou wilt shew me the path of life: in thy presence is fulness of joy; at thy right hand there are pleasures for evermore. (Psalm 16: 11.)

In thy name shall they rejoice all the day: and in thy righteousness shall they be exalted. (Psalm 89: 16.)

Let Israel rejoice in him that made him: let the children of Zion be joyful in their King. (Psalm 149: 2.)

It shall blossom abundantly, and rejoice, even with joy and singing: the glory of Lebanon shall be given unto it, the excellency of Carmel and Sharon, they shall see the glory of the Lord, and the excellency of our God. (Isaiah 35: 2.)

Whereas thou hast been forsaken and hated, so that no man went through thee, I will make thee an eternal excellency, a joy of many generations. (Isaiah 60: 15.)

I will greatly rejoice in the Lord, my soul shall be joyful in my God; for he hath clothed me with the garments of salvation, he hath covered me with the robe of righteousness, as a bridegroom decketh himself with ornaments, and as a bride adorneth herself with her jewels. (Isaiah 61: 10.)

Notwithstanding in this rejoice not, that the spirits are subject unto you; but rather rejoice, because your names are written in heaven. (Luke 10: 20.)

These things have I spoken unto you, that my joy might remain in you, and that your joy might be full. (John 15: 11.)

For the kingdom of God is not meat and drink; but righteousness, and peace, and joy in the Holy Ghost. (Romans 14: 17.)

And ye became followers of us, and of the Lord, having received the word in much affliction, with joy of the Holy Ghost. (1 Thessalonians 1: 6.)

Joy of Wicked Is Folly.

That the triumphing of the wicked is short, and the joy of the hypocrite but for a moment. (Job 20: 5.)

Folly is joy to him that is destitute of wisdom: but a man of understanding walketh uprightly. (Proverbs 15: 21.)

And whatsoever mine eyes desired I kept not from them, I withheld not my heart from any joy; for my heart rejoiced in all my labour: and this was my portion of all my labour. (Ecclesiastes 2: 10.)

And gladness is taken away, and joy out of the plentiful field; and in the vineyards there shall be no singing, neither shall there be shouting: the treaders shall tread out no wine in their presses; I have made their vintage shouting to cease. (Isaiah 16: 10.)

Be afflicted, and mourn, and weep: let your laughter be turned to mourning, and your joy to heaviness. (James 4: 9.)

Joy Follows Grief.

For his anger endureth but a moment; in his favour is life: weeping may endure for a night, but joy cometh in the morning. (Psalm 30: 5.)

They that sow in tears shall reap in joy.

He that goeth forth and weepeth, bearing precious seed, shall doubtless come again with rejoicing, bringing his sheaves with him. (Psalm 125: 5, 6.)

And the ransomed of the Lord shall return, and come to Zion with songs and everlasting joy upon their heads: they shall obtain joy and gladness, and sorrow and sighing shall flee away. (Isaiah 35: 10.)

To appoint unto them that mourn in Zion, to give unto them beauty for ashes, the oil of joy for mourning, the garment of praise for the spirit of heaviness; that they might be called Trees of righteousness, The planting of the Lord, that he might be glorified. (Isaiah 61: 3.)

Rejoice ye with Jerusalem, and be glad with her, all ye that love her: rejoice for joy with her, all ye that mourn for her. (Isaiah 66: 10.)

Then shall the virgin rejoice in the dance, both young men and old together, for I will turn their mourning into joy, and will comfort them, and make them rejoice from their sorrow. (Jeremiah 31: 13.)

Verily, verily, I say unto you, That ye shall weep and lament, but the world shall rejoice: and ye shall be sorrowful, but your sorrow shall be turned into joy. (John 16: 20.)

As sorrowful, yet alway rejoicing; as poor, yet making many rich; as having nothing, and yet possessing all things. (2 Corinthians 6: 10.)

My brethren, count it all joy when ye fall into divers temptations. (James 1: 2.)

Joy Over Repenting Sinner.

I say unto you, that likewise joy shall be in heaven over one sinner that repenteth, more than over ninety and nine just persons, which need no repentance. (Luke 15: 7.)

Likewise, I say unto you, there is joy in the presence of the angels of God over one sinner that repenteth. (Luke 15: 10.)

Joy in Hymns.

Speaking to yourselves in psalms and hymns and spiritual songs, singing and making melody in your heart to the Lord. (Ephesians 5: 19.)

Let the word of Christ dwell in you richly in all wisdom; teaching and admonishing one another in psalms and hymns and spiritual songs, singing with grace in your hearts to the Lord. (Colossians 3: 16.)

Is any among you afflicted? let him pray. Is any merry? let him sing psalms. (James 5: 13.)

JUDAH. (See David, Israel, Israelites, Jews, etc.)

JU'DAH—a form of a Hebrew word meaning "celebrated." Judah was the name of the fourth son of Jacob and Leah. It also became the name of one of the twelve Hebrew tribes as well as one of the two kingdoms of the Israelites. Judah, Jacob's son, is better known to Bible readers than any of the other sons of the patriarch except Joseph. He acted a very manly part in the dealings of the brethren with Joseph in Egypt, and took a high place in the affairs of the nation. From his line descended David and Jesus.

The kingdom of Judah had its inception with the revolt of the ten tribes, but it was really a continuation of the kingdom of Saul and David. It lasted 487 years, and 133 years longer than its larger neighbor, Israel. It was more compact and wealthier than Israel and should have lasted even longer, but decay was caused by the contest between church and state, the priesthood gradually depriving the king of power. Twice the royal line was almost destroyed in the factional wars. Jerusalem was several times plundered by conquerors before the kingdom eventually fell into the hands of the Babylonians.

JUDAS OR JUDE.

JU'DAS OR JUDE. Judas is the Greek form of the Hebrew name Judah, and is borne by a number of persons named in the New Testament—Judas Lebbeus or Thaddeus, one of the apostles; Judas, surnamed Barsabas; Judas or Jude, named as one of the brothers of the Lord; and Judas Iscariot, who betrayed the Lord. We know little about any of them save Iscariot. He was a native of Kerioth, a village of Judah. He seems to have been a man of much ability and strong passions and emotions. Just what were the motives that led him to the betrayal mankind has never been able to solve definitely. We know that he was the treasurer of the little company of disciples and that he had been guilty of stealing from the funds. We also know that he loved money for the sake of its increase. For these reasons it has long been thought that he delivered Jesus to the Jews for the double sake of hiding his theft and for the reward he might gain. On the other hand the price of betrayal was small—about equal to $19 in modern money—and Judas' repentance and suicidal remorse are not in consonance with the character of a man who would do such a deed for the sake of money. We are told that Jesus knew who was to betray Him and we are also told that He ordered Judas to do the thing that he was to do quickly. Many critics have thought that Judas held to the belief that Jesus should manifest His power in some great and miraculous way and become the sort of Messiah all Israel expected, that he was angry at the meekness and peaceful character of the Master and that the whole betrayal was a sudden, mad, and impetuous act, bitterly regretted when the traitor saw the full fruits of it. This view is supported in a great measure by the subsequent acts of Judas as well as his words. And on the whole, we must not forget that the tragedy was destined by divine will to take place, and that in God's infinite wisdom some one had to be the instrument for the carrying out of the plan for the salvation of the world.

References.—Matthew 26: 14, 47; Mark 14: 10, 43; Luke 22: 3, 47; John 13: 26; 18: 2.

JUDGE AND JUDGES.

Judges are frequently mentioned in the Bible. In the first place, men who were given such a title governed Israel for a period of more than 400 years before the days of the kings. The system was introduced by Moses. They were, for the most part, men of strong and upright character and were given wide magisterial and military powers. Secondly, the Scriptures call attention to the fact that judges must exercise the duties of their office in becoming manner, that they must not be unjust, etc.

REFERENCES.

Judges' Functions.

And let them judge the people at all seasons: and it shall be, that every great matter they shall bring unto thee, but every small matter they shall judge: so shall it be easier for thyself, and they shall bear the burden with thee. (Exodus 18: 22.)

Ye shall do no unrighteousness in judgment; thou shalt not respect the person of the poor, nor honour the person of the mighty: but in righteousness shalt thou judge thy neighbour. (Leviticus 19: 15.)

And I charged your judges at that time, saying, Hear the causes between your brethren, and judge righteously between every man and his brother, and the stranger that is with him. (Deuteronomy 1: 16.)

And said to the judges, Take heed what ye do: for ye judge not for man, but for the Lord, who is with you in the judgment.

Wherefore now let the fear of the Lord be upon you; take heed and do it: for there is no iniquity with the Lord our God, nor respect of persons, nor taking of gifts. (2 Chronicles 19: 6, 7.)

Unjust Judges.

And his sons walked not in his ways, but turned aside after lucre, and took bribes, and perverted judgment. (1 Samuel 16: 3.)

Thy princes are rebellious, and companions of thieves: every one loveth gifts, and followeth after rewards: they judge not the fatherless, neither doth the cause of the widow come unto them. (Isaiah 1: 23.)

He that justifieth the wicked, and he that condemneth the just, even they both are abomination to the Lord. (Proverbs 17: 15.)

He that saith unto the wicked, Thou art righteous; him shall the people curse, nations shall abhor him. (Proverbs 24: 24.)

Woe unto them that decree unrighteous decrees, and that write grievousness which they have prescribed;

To turn aside the needy from judgment, and to take away the right from the poor of my people, that widows may be their prey, and that they may rob the fatherless! (Isaiah 10: 1, 2.)

Cautions Respecting Judging.

Judge not, that ye be not judged.

For with what judgment ye judge, ye shall be judged: and with what measure ye mete, it shall be measured to you again. (Matthew 7: 1, 2.)

Judge not, and ye shall not be judged: condemn not, and ye shall not be condemned: forgive, and ye shall be forgiven. (Luke 6: 37.)

Judge not according to the appearance, but judge righteous judgment. (John 7: 24.)

Therefore thou art inexcusable, O man, whosoever thou art that judgest: for wherein thou judgest another, thou condemnest thyself; for thou that judgest doest the same things.

But we are sure that the judgment of God is according to truth against them which commit such things.

And thinkest thou this, O man, that judgest them which do such things, and doest the same, that thou shalt escape the judgment of God? (Romans 2: 1-3.)

Speak not evil one of another, brethren. He that speaketh evil of his brother, and judgeth his brother, speaketh evil of the law, and judgeth the law: but if thou judge the law, thou art not a doer of the law, but a judge.

There is one lawgiver, who is able to save and to destroy: who art thou that judgest another? (James 4: 11, 12.)

JUDGMENT, THE LAST. (See Millennium, Resurrection, etc.)

JUDG'MENT. The Last Judgment or The Day of Judgment or The Great Day or The Last Day is the time when, according to the teaching of the Bible, Christ will judge the world. The character of the occasion as well as the nature of Christ's judgment are fully set out in Scripture, although not so fully understood by mankind, different denominations and different minds drawing many different conclusions from the references.

REFERENCES.

The Last Judgment Foretold.

Then shall the trees of the wood sing out at the presence of the Lord, because he cometh to judge the earth. (1 Chronicles 16: 33.)

But the Lord shall endure for ever: he hath prepared his throne for judgment.

And he shall judge the world in righteousness, he shall minister judgment to the people in uprightness. (Psalm 9: 7, 8.)

Before the Lord; for he cometh, for he cometh to judge the earth: he shall judge the world with righteousness, and the people with his truth. (Psalm 96: 13.)

I said in mine heart, God shall judge the righteous and the wicked: for there is a time there for every purpose and for every work. (Ecclesiastes 3: 17.)

For God shall bring every work into judgment, with every secret thing, whether it be good, or whether it be evil. (Ecclesiastes 12: 14.)

Because he hath appointed a day, in the which he will judge the world in righteousness by that man whom he hath ordained; whereof he hath given assurance unto all men, in that he hath raised him from the dead. (Acts 17: 31.)

In the day when God shall judge the secrets of men by Jesus Christ according to my gospel. (Romans 2: 16.)

For we must all appear before the

judgment seat of Christ; that every one may receive the things done in his body, according to that he hath done, whether it be good or bad. (2 Corinthians 5: 10.)

And as it is appointed unto men once to die, but after this the judgment:

So Christ was once offered to bear the sins of many; and unto them that look for him shall he appear the second time without sin unto salvation. (Hebrews 9: 27, 28.)

But the heavens and the earth, which are now, by the same word are kept in store, reserved unto fire against the day of judgment and perdition of ungodly men. (2 Peter 3: 7.)

The Last Judgment Described.

Our God shall come, and shall not keep silence: a fire shall devour before him, and it shall be very tempestuous round about him.

He shall call to the heavens from above, and to the earth, that he may judge his people.

Gather my saints together unto me; those that have made a covenant with me by sacrifice.

And the heavens shall declare his righteousness: for God is judge himself. Selah. (Psalm 50: 3-6.)

I beheld till the thrones were cast down, and the Ancient of days did sit, whose garment was white as snow, and the hair of his head like the pure wool: his throne was like the fiery flame, and his wheels as burning fire.

A fiery stream issued and came forth from before him: thousand thousands ministered unto him, and ten thousand times ten thousand stood before him: the judgment was set, and the books were opened. (Daniel 7: 9, 10.)

When the Son of man shall come in his glory, and all the holy angels with him, then shall he sit upon the throne of his glory:

And before him shall be gathered all nations; and he shall separate them one from another, as a shepherd divideth his sheep from the goats:

And he shall set the sheep on his right hand, but the goats on the left. (Matthew 25: 31-33.)

In flaming fire taking vengeance on them that know not God, and that obey not the gospel of our Lord Jesus Christ. (2 Thessalonians 1: 8.)

And I beheld when he had opened the sixth seal, and, lo, there was a great earthquake; and the sun became black as sackcloth of hair, and the moon became as blood;

And the stars of heaven fell unto the earth, even as a fig tree casteth her untimely figs, when she is shaken of a mighty wind.

And the heaven departed as a scroll when it is rolled together; and every mountain and island were moved out of their places.

And the kings of the earth, and the great men, and the rich men, and the chief captains, and the mighty men, and every bondman, and every free man, hid themselves in the dens and in the rocks of the mountains;

And said to the mountains and rocks, Fall on us, and hide us from the face of him that sitteth on the throne, and from the wrath of the Lamb:

For the great day of his wrath is come; and who shall be able to stand? (Revelation 6: 12-17.)

And I saw a great white throne, and him that sat on it, from whose face the earth and the heaven fled away; and there was found no place for them.

And I saw the dead, small and great,

stand before God; and the books were opened: and another book was opened, which is the book of life: and the dead were judged out of those things which were written in the books, according to their works.

And the sea gave up the dead which were in it; and death and hell delivered up the dead which were in them: and they were judged every man according to their works.

And death and hell were cast into the lake of fire. This is the second death.

And whosoever was not found written in the book of life was cast into the lake of fire. (Revelation 20: 11-15.)

Hope of Christians in Last Judgment.

Who shall lay any thing to the charge of God's elect? It is God that justifieth. (Romans 8: 33.)

Therefore judge nothing before the time, until the Lord come, who both will bring to light the hidden things of darkness, and will make manifest the counsels of the hearts: and then shall every man have praise of God. (1 Corinthians 4: 5.)

For I am now ready to be offered, and the time of my departure is at hand.

I have fought a good fight, I have finished my course, I have kept the faith:

Henceforth there is laid up for me a crown of righteousness, which the Lord, the righteous judge, shall give me at that day: and not to me only, but unto all them also that love his appearing. (2 Timothy 4: 6-8.)

And now, little children, abide in him; that when he shall appear, we may have confidence, and not be ashamed before him at his coming. (1 John 2: 28.)

Herein is our love made perfect, that we may have boldness in the day of judgment: because as he is, so are we in this world. (1 John 4: 17.)

JUSTICE.

Jus'tice—the rendering to every one of his or her due right, reward, or punishment; conformity to the principles of righteousness and rectitude; conformity to truth and reality in thoughts or opinions and conduct. The Bible contains many injunctions looking toward the establishment of justice in the thoughts, actions, and motives of mankind. Justice indeed is one of the foundation principles of the Ten Commandments, the Golden Rule, while in the doctrines of Christianity it holds a commanding position.

God's justice is that perfection whereby He is infinitely righteous and just in all His principles and acts and wise, good, and perfect in His treatment of man. His justice is of two sorts: remunerative, by which He gives rewards for goodness, and punitive, by which He deals out punishment for evil.

REFERENCES.

God's Justice.

He is the Rock, his work is perfect: for all his ways are judgment: a God of truth and without iniquity, just and right is he. (Deuteronomy 32: 4.)

Shall mortal man be more just than God? shall a man be more pure than his Maker? (Job 4: 17.)

Doth God pervert judgment? or doth the Almighty pervert justice? (Job 8: 3.)

Yea, surely God will not do wickedly, neither will the Almighty pervert judgment. (Job 34: 12.)

The just Lord is in the midst thereof; he will not do iniquity: every morning doth he bring his judgment to light, he faileth not; but the unjust knoweth no shame. (Zephaniah 3: 5.)

If we confess our sins, he is faithful and just to forgive us our sins, and to cleanse us from all unrighteousness. (1 John 1: 9.)

And they sing the song of Moses the servant of God, and the song of the Lamb, saying, Great and marvellous are thy works, Lord God Almighty; just and true are thy ways, thou King of saints. (Revelation 15: 3.)

Man Commanded to Do Justice.

Ye shall do no unrighteousness in judgment, in meteyard, in weight, or in measure.

Just balances, just weights, a just ephah, and a just hin shall ye have: I am the Lord your God, which brought you out of the land of Egypt. (Leviticus 19: 35, 36.)

Judges and officers shalt thou make thee in all thy gates, which the Lord thy God giveth thee, throughout thy tribes: and they shall judge the people with just judgment. (Deuteronomy 16: 18.)

Defend the poor and fatherless: do justice to the afflicted and needy. (Psalm 82: 3.)

The curse of the Lord is in the house of the wicked: but he blesseth the habitation of the just. (Proverbs 3: 33.)

Thus saith the Lord; Execute ye judgment and righteousness, and deliver the spoiled out of the hand of the oppressor: and do no wrong, do no violence to the stranger, the fatherless, nor the widow, neither shed innocent blood in this place. (Jeremiah 22: 3.)

He hath shewed thee, O man, what is good; and what doth the Lord require of thee, but to do justly, and to love mercy, and to walk humbly with thy God? (Micah 6: 8.)

Therefore all things whatsoever ye would that men should do to you, do ye even so to them: for this is the law and the prophets. (Matthew 7: 12.)

Finally, brethren, whatsoever things are true, whatsoever things are honest, whatsoever things are just, whatsoever things are pure, whatsoever things are lovely, whatsoever things are of good report; if there be any virtue, and if there be any praise, think on these things. (Philippians 4: 8.)

Render therefore to all their dues: tribute to whom tribute is due; custom to whom custom; fear to whom fear; honour to whom honour.

Owe no man anything, but to love one another: for he that loveth another hath fulfilled the law. (Romans 13: 7, 8.)

Masters, give unto your servants that which is just and equal; knowing that ye also have a Master in heaven. (Colossians 4: 1.)

JUSTIFICATION.

JUS'TI-FI-CA'TION—the act of justifying or the state of being justified. This word is used in the Bible to indicate the judicial act of God by which the sinner is declared innocent or without sin or the effects of sin. This is not the result of the justified one's works but by the righteousness of Christ, and the faith of the justified one in Him. By the deeds of the law—that is, obedience to the law—there shall be no justification in God's sight. The faith that brings about the working of Christ's justifying righteousness is a full and living one. These facts are the bases for the doctrine of justification. Different denominations take more or less different views of the matter, but none leaves the essential groundwork.

REFERENCES.

Behold, his soul which is lifted up, is not upright in him: but the just shall live by his faith. (Habakkuk 2: 4.)

And by him all that believe are justified from all things, from which ye could not be justified by the law of Moses. (Acts 13: 39.)

For therein is the righteousness of God revealed from faith to faith: as it is written, The just shall live by faith. (Romans 1: 17.)

Therefore by the deeds of the law there shall no flesh be justified in his sight: for by the law is the knowledge of sin.

But now the righteousness of God without the law is manifested, being witnessed by the law and the prophets;

Even the righteousness of God which is by faith of Jesus Christ unto all and upon all them that believe: for there is no difference:

For all have sinned, and come short of the glory of God;

Being justified freely by his grace through the redemption that is in Christ Jesus:

Whom God hath set forth to be a propitiation through faith in his blood, to declare his righteousness for the remission of sins that are past, through the forbearance of God;

To declare, I say, at this time his righteousness: that he might be just, and the justifier of him which believeth in Jesus.

Where is boasting then? It is excluded. By what law? of works? Nay: but by the law of faith.

Therefore we conclude that a man is justified by faith without the deeds of the law. (Romans 3: 20-28.)

Therefore being justified by faith, we have peace with God through our Lord Jesus Christ:

By whom also we have access by faith into this grace wherein we stand, and rejoice in hope of the glory of God. (Romans 5: 1, 2.)

But that no man is justified by the law in the sight of God, it is evident: for, The just shall live by faith.

And the law is not of faith: but, The man that doeth them shall live in them. (Galatians 3: 11, 12.)

KEDAR.

KE'DAR—a form of a Hebrew word meaning "black." Kedar was the second son of Ishmael and became the founder of a famous tribe of Arabians. It is through descent from the tribe of Kedar that Mohammed, the celebrated prophet and leader of the Moslems, traced his descent from Abraham.

KINDNESS.

KIND'NESS—the state or quality of being kind; beneficence; benevolence; goodness of heart or disposition. The Bible enjoins us to kindness. This means not only to our fellow-man, but to animals as well. Kindness is regarded as one of the jewels of the Christian crown.

REFERENCES.

The desire of a man is his kindness: and a poor man is better than a liar. (Proverbs 19: 22.)

She openeth her mouth with wisdom; and in her tongue is the law of kindness. (Proverbs 31: 26.)

Be kindly affectioned one to another with brotherly love; in honour preferring one another. (Romans 12: 10.)

Charity suffereth long, and is kind; charity envieth not; charity vaunteth not itself, is not puffed up. (1 Corinthians 13: 4.)

By pureness, by knowledge, by longsuffering, by kindness, by the Holy Ghost, by love unfeigned. (2 Corinthians 6: 6.)

And be ye kind one to another, tender-hearted, forgiving one another, even as God for Christ's sake hath forgiven you. (Ephesians 4: 32.)

Put on therefore, as the elect of God, holy and beloved, bowels of mercies, kindness, humbleness of mind, meekness, longsuffering. (Colossians 3: 12.)

And to godliness brotherly kindness; and to brotherly kindness charity. (2 Peter 1: 7.)

KING.

KING—a chief ruler or sovereign; a person who rules a nation, usually one of a family that has given other sovereigns to the throne. In the Old Testament we find numerous examples of kings who ruled over a single city instead of a country. This form of government had its origin in the lands of which we read in the Bible. With relation to the Hebrews it was the original idea of Moses never to have a king in Israel save God, who would be represented in the government by priests. This form of government is called a theocracy. Later he foresaw that a visible king would be needed and arranged for it (Deuteronomy 17: 14). The custom of anointing with oil the head of the monarch seems to have had its origin in Egypt, from whence Moses doubtless borrowed it, giving it a much higher and spiritual meaning. From this custom springs the phrase that a king is one of "the Lord's anointed."

REFERENCES.

Kings Chosen by God.

When thou art come unto the land which the Lord thy God giveth thee, and shalt possess it, and shalt dwell therein, and shalt say, I will set a king over me, like as all the nations that are about me. (Deuteronomy 17: 14.)

And when Samuel saw Saul, the Lord said unto him, Behold the man whom I spake to thee of! this same shall reign over my people. (1 Samuel 9: 17.)

And the Lord said unto Samuel, How long wilt thou mourn for Saul, seeing I have rejected him from reigning over Israel? fill thine horn with oil, and go, I will send thee to Jesse the Bethlehem-

ite: for I have provided me a king among his sons. (1 Samuel 16: 1.)

But I will take the kingdom out of his son's hand, and will give it unto thee, even ten tribes. (1 Kings 11: 35.)

And the Lord said unto him, Go, return on thy way to the wilderness of Damascus: and when thou comest, anoint Hazael to be king over Syria. (1 Kings 19: 15.)

Howbeit the Lord God of Israel chose me before all the house of my father to be king over Israel for ever: for he hath chosen Judah to be the ruler; and of the house of Judah, the house of my father; and among the sons of my father he liked me to make me king over all Israel. (1 Chronicles 28: 4.)

And he changeth the times and the seasons: he removeth kings, and setteth up kings; he giveth wisdom unto the wise, and knowledge to them that know understanding. (Daniel 2: 21.)

Duties and Admonitions.

Be wise now therefore, O ye kings: be instructed, ye judges of the earth. (Psalm 2: 10.)

It is the glory of God to conceal a thing: but the honour of kings is to search out a matter,

The heaven for height, and the earth for depth, and the heart of kings is unsearchable. (Proverbs 25: 2, 3.)

It is not for kings, O Lemuel, it is not for kings to drink wine; nor for princes strong drink:

Lest they drink, and forget the law, and pervert the judgment of any of the afflicted. (Proverbs 31: 4, 5.)

Honor Due to Kings.

My son, fear thou the Lord and the king: and meddle not with them that are given to change. (Proverbs 24: 21.)

Put not forth thyself in the presence of the king, and stand not in the place of great men. (Proverbs 25: 6.)

I counsel thee to keep the king's commandment, and that in regard of the oath of God. (Ecclesiastes 8: 2.)

Curse not the king, no not in thy thought; and curse not the rich in thy bedchamber: for a bird of the air shall carry the voice, and that which hath wings shall tell the matter. (Ecclesiastes 10: 20.)

KINGDOM OF GOD, CHRIST, HEAVEN.

King'dom. The kingdom of God is God's universal dominion over all things, and in it He preserves, protects, gives laws, and regulates all things, dispensing favors or judgments as pleases Him.

The kingdom of Christ is His Church as well as that blessed state in which He will rule with His Father.

The kingdom of Heaven is that state of glory wherein God and Christ rule and shall rule, and to which the blessed will be called to their reward as citizens.

REFERENCES.

The Kingdom of God.

Thine, O Lord, is the greatness, and the power, and the glory, and the victory, and the majesty: for all that is in the heaven and in the earth is thine; thine is the kingdom, O Lord, and thou art exalted as head above all. (1 Chronicles 29: 11.)

For the kingdom is the Lord's: and he is the governor among the nations. (Psalm 22: 28.)

Thy throne, O God, is for ever and ever: the sceptre of thy kingdom is a right sceptre. (Psalm 45: 6.)

They shall speak of the glory of thy kingdom, and talk of thy power;

To make known to the sons of men his mighty acts, and the glorious majesty of his kingdom.

Thy kingdom is an everlasting kingdom, and thy dominion endureth throughout all generations. (Psalm 145: 11-13.)

Then the moon shall be confounded, and the sun ashamed, when the Lord of hosts shall reign in mount Zion, and in Jerusalem, and before his ancients gloriously. (Isaiah 24: 23.)

And in the days of these kings shall the God of heaven set up a kingdom, which shall never be destroyed: and the kingdom shall not be left to other people, but it shall break in pieces and consume all these kingdoms, and it shall stand for ever. (Daniel 2: 44.)

For the kingdom of God is not meat and drink; but righteousness, and peace, and joy in the Holy Ghost. (Romans 14: 17.)

Kingdom of Christ.

For unto us a child is born, unto us a son is given: and the government shall be upon his shoulder: and his name shall be called Wonderful, Counsellor, The Mighty God, The Everlasting Father, The Prince of Peace.

Of the increase of his government and peace there shall be no end, upon the throne of David, and upon his kingdom to order it, and to establish it with judgment and with justice from henceforth even for ever. The zeal of the Lord of hosts will perform this. (Isaiah 9: 6, 7.)

Behold, a King shall reign in righteousness, and princes shall rule in judgment. (Isaiah 32: 1.)

Verily I say unto you, There be some standing here, which shall not taste of death, till they see the Son of man coming in his kingdom. (Matthew 16: 28.)

Jesus answered, *My kingdom is not of this world: if my kingdom were of this world, then would my servants fight, that I should not be delivered to the Jews: but now is my kingdom not from hence.* (John 18: 36.)

For so an entrance shall be ministered unto you abundantly into the everlasting kingdom of our Lord and Saviour Jesus Christ. (2 Peter 1: 11.)

Kingdom of Heaven.

In those days came John the Baptist, preaching in the wilderness of Judæa,

And saying, Repent ye: for the kingdom of heaven is at hand. (Matthew 3: 1, 2.)

And I say unto you, That many shall come from the east and west, and shall sit down with Abraham, and Isaac, and Jacob, in the kingdom of heaven. (Matthew 8: 11.)

Verily I say unto you, Among them that are born of women there hath not risen a greater than John the Baptist: notwithstanding he that is least in the kingdom of heaven is greater than he. (Matthew 11: 11.)

He answered and said unto them, *Because it is given unto you to know the mysteries of the kingdom of heaven, but to them it is not given.* (Matthew 13: 11.)

Who Shall Enter the Kingdom of Heaven.

Blessed are the poor in spirit: for theirs is the kingdom of heaven. (Matthew 5: 3.)

Not every one that saith unto me, Lord, Lord, shall enter into the kingdom of heaven; but he that doeth the will of my Father which is in heaven. (Matthew 7: 21.)

And Jesus said unto him, No man,

having put his hand to the plow, and looking back, is fit for the kingdom of God. (Luke 9: 62.)

Jesus answered and said unto him, *Verily, verily, I say unto thee, Except a man be born again, he cannot see the kingdom of God.* (John 3: 3.)

Confirming the souls of the disciples, and exhorting them to continue in the faith, and that we must through much tribulation enter into the kingdom of God. (Acts 14: 22.)

For the kingdom of God is not meat and drink; but righteousness, and peace, and joy in the Holy Ghost. (Romans 14: 17.)

Now this I say, brethren, that flesh and blood cannot inherit the kingdom of God; neither doth corruption inherit incorruption. (1 Corinthians 15: 50.)

Which is a manifest token of the righteous judgment of God, that ye may be counted worthy of the kingdom of God, for which ye also suffer:

Seeing it is a righteous thing with God to recompense tribulation to them that trouble you. (2 Thessalonians 1: 5, 6.)

KISS.

Kiss. The kiss has been known as the token of love and affection from time immemorial. The ancients used it to symbolize various things—affection, salutation, respect, veneration, submission, homage, and even worship and the end of enmity. Many references to it and its various uses are to be found in the Bible.

REFERENCES.

Kiss a Holy Salute.

Salute one another with an holy kiss. The churches of Christ salute you. (Romans 16: 16.)

All the brethren greet you. Greet ye

one another with an holy kiss. (1 Corinthians 16: 20.)

Greet one another with an holy kiss. (2 Corinthians 13: 12.)

Kiss a Mark of Affection.

And he came near, and kissed him: and he smelled the smell of his raiment, and blessed him, and said, See, the smell of my son is as the smell of a field which the Lord hath blessed. (Genesis 27: 27.)

And Jacob kissed Rachel, and lifted up his voice, and wept. (Genesis 29: 11.)

Moreover, he kissed all his brethren, and wept upon them: and after that his brethren talked with him. (Genesis 45: 15.)

Then Samuel took a vial of oil, and poured it upon his head, and kissed him, and said, Is it not because the Lord hath anointed thee to be captain over his inheritance? (1 Samuel 10: 1.)

And as soon as the lad was gone, David arose out of a place toward the south, and fell on his face to the ground, and bowed himself three times: and they kissed one another, and wept one with another, until David exceeded. (1 Samuel 20: 41.)

And stood at his feet behind him weeping, and began to wash his feet with tears, and did wipe them with the hairs of her head, and kissed his feet, and anointed them with the ointment. (Luke 7: 38.)

And he arose, and came to his father. But when he was yet a great way off, his father saw him, and had compassion, and ran, and fell on his neck, and kissed him. (Luke 15: 20.)

And they all wept sore, and fell on Paul's neck, and kissed him. (Acts 20: 37.)

Treacherous Kiss.

And Joab said to Amasa, Art thou in health, my brother? And Joab took Amasa by the beard with the right hand to kiss him.

But Amasa took no heed to the sword that was in Joab's hand: so he smote him therewith in the fifth rib, and shed out his bowels to the ground, and struck him not again; and he died. So Joab and Abishai his brother pursued after Sheba the son of Bichri. (2 Samuel 20: 9, 10.)

Now he that betrayed him gave them a sign, saying, Whomsoever I shall kiss, that same is he: hold him fast.

And forthwith he came to Jesus, and said, Hail, master; and kissed him. (Matthew 26: 48, 49.)

KNOWLEDGE.

KNOWL'EDGE—the act or state of knowing; clear understanding of fact, truth, or duty; enlightenment; learning; scholarship. The word "knowledge" is used in the Bible to denote the foregoing definitions and is also used in a religious sense to indicate the perfect wisdom of God and the lesser religious wisdom of man and his more or less complete understanding of God and divine truths.

REFERENCES.

Knowledge Given by God.

And I have filled him with the spirit of God, in wisdom, and in understanding, and in knowledge, and in all manner of workmanship. (Exodus 31: 3.)

And God said to Solomon, Because this was in thine heart, and thou hast not asked riches, wealth, or honour, nor the life of thine enemies, neither yet hast asked long life; but hast asked wisdom and knowledge for thyself, that thou mayest judge my people, over whom I have made thee king:

Wisdom and knowledge is granted

unto thee; and I will give thee riches, and wealth, and honour, such as none of the kings have had that have been before thee, neither shall there any after thee have the like. (2 Chronicles 1: 11, 12.)

Teach me good judgment and knowledge: for I have believed thy commandments. (Psalm 119: 66.)

For the Lord giveth wisdom: out of his mouth cometh knowledge and understanding. (Proverbs 2: 6.)

For God giveth to a man that is good in his sight, wisdom, and knowledge, and joy: but to the sinner he giveth travail, to gather and to heap up, that he may give to him that is good before God. This also is vanity and vexation of spirit. (Ecclesiastes 2: 26.)

Whom shall he teach knowledge? and whom shall he make to understand doctrine? them that are weaned from the milk, and drawn from the breasts.

For precept must be upon precept, precept upon precept; line upon line, line upon line; here a little, and there a little. (Isaiah 28: 9, 10.)

And he changeth the times and the seasons: he removeth kings, and setteth up kings; he giveth wisdom unto the wise, and knowledge to them that know understanding. (Daniel 2: 21.)

At that time Jesus answered and said, *I thank thee, O Father, Lord of heaven and earth, because thou hast hid these things from the wise and prudent, and hast revealed them unto babes.* (Matthew 11: 25.)

He answered and said unto them, *Because it is given unto you to know the mysteries of the kingdom of heaven, but to them it is not given.* (Matthew 13: 11.)

Now we have received, not the spirit of the world, but the spirit which is of God; that we might know the things that are freely given to us of God.

Which things also we speak, not in the words which man's wisdom teacheth, but which the Holy Ghost teacheth; comparing spiritual things with spiritual. (1 Corinthians 2: 12, 13.)

For to one is given by the Spirit the word of wisdom; to another the word of knowledge by the same Spirit. (1 Corinthians 12: 8.)

Benefits of Knowledge.

The fear of the Lord is the beginning of knowledge: but fools despise wisdom and instruction. (Proverbs 1: 7.)

Get wisdom, get understanding: forget it not; neither decline from the words of my mouth.

Forsake her not, and she shall preserve thee: love her, and she shall keep thee.

Wisdom is the principal thing; therefore get wisdom: and with all thy getting get understanding. (Proverbs 4: 5-7.)

Give instruction to a wise man, and he will be yet wiser: teach a just man, and he will increase in learning.

The fear of the Lord is the beginning of wisdom: and the knowledge of the Holy is understanding. (Proverbs 9: 9, 10.)

Wise men lay up knowledge: but the mouth of the foolish is near destruction. (Proverbs 10: 14.)

Whoso loveth instruction loveth knowledge: but he that hateth reproof is brutish. (Proverbs 12: 1.)

Every prudent man dealeth with knowledge: but a fool layeth open his folly. (Proverbs 13: 16.)

For wisdom is a defence, and money is a defence: but the excellency of knowledge is, that wisdom giveth life to them that have it. (Ecclesiastes 7: 12.)

Till we all come in the unity of the faith, and of the knowledge of the Son of God, unto a perfect man, unto the measure of the stature of the fulness of Christ. (Ephesians 4: 13.)

Who is a wise man and endued with knowledge among you? let him shew out of a good conversation his works with meekness of wisdom. (James 3: 13.)

For if after they have escaped the pollutions of the world through the knowledge of the Lord and Saviour Jesus Christ, they are again entangled therein, and overcome, the latter end is worse with them than the beginning. (2 Peter 2: 20.)

Lack of Knowledge.

How long, ye simple ones, will ye love simplicity? and the scorners delight in their scorning, and fools hate knowledge? (Proverbs 1: 22.)

Also, that the soul be without knowledge, it is not good; and he that hasteth with his feet sinneth. (Proverbs 19: 2.)

For my people is foolish, they have not known me; they are sottish children, and they have none understanding; they are wise to do evil, but to do good they have no knowledge. (Jeremiah 4: 22.)

My people are destroyed for lack of knowledge: because thou hast rejected knowledge, I will also reject thee, that thou shalt be no priest to me: seeing thou hast forgotten the law of thy God, I will also forget thy children. (Hosea 4: 6.)

And even as they did not like to retain God in their knowledge, God gave them over to a reprobate mind, to do those things which are not convenient. (Romans 1: 28.)

Awake to righteousness, and sin not; for some have not the knowledge of God: I speak this to your shame. (Romans 15: 34.)

Knowledge Prayed for and Sought.

For this cause we also, since the day we heard it, do not cease to pray for you, and to desire that ye might be filled with the knowledge of his will in all wisdom and spiritual understanding;

That ye might walk worthy of the Lord unto all pleasing, being fruitful in every good work, and increasing in the knowledge of God. (Colossians 1: 9, 10.)

But grow in grace, and in the knowledge of our Lord and Saviour Jesus Christ. To him be glory both now and for ever. Amen. (2 Peter 3: 18.)

Knowledge's Responsibility.

Professing themselves to be wise, they became fools. (Romans 1: 22.)

Behold, thou art called a Jew, and restest in the law, and makest thy boast of God,

And knowest his will, and approvest the things that are more excellent, being instructed out of the law;

And art confident that thou thyself art a guide of the blind, a light of them which are in darkness,

An instructor of the foolish, a teacher of babes, which hast the form of knowledge and of the truth in the law. (Romans 2: 17-20.)

Therefore to him that knoweth to do good, and doeth it not, to him it is sin. (James 4: 17.)

Imperfection of Man's Knowledge.

For there is a man whose labour is in wisdom, and in knowledge, and in equity; yet to a man that hath not laboured therein shall he leave it for his portion. This also is vanity and a great evil. (Ecclesiastes 2: 21.)

That frustrateth the tokens of the liars, and maketh diviners mad; that turneth wise men backward, and maketh their knowledge foolish. (Isaiah 44: 25.)

For it is written, I will destroy the wisdom of the wise, and will bring to nothing the understanding of the prudent.

Where is the wise? where is the scribe? where is the disputer of this world? hath not God made foolish the wisdom of this world?

For after that in the wisdom of God the world by wisdom knew not God, it pleased God by the foolishness of preaching to save them that believe. (1 Corinthians 1: 19-21.)

Let no man deceive himself. If any man among you seemeth to be wise in this world, let him become a fool, that he may be wise.

For the wisdom of this world is foolishness with God. For it is written, He taketh the wise in their own craftiness.

And again, The Lord knoweth the thoughts of the wise, that they are vain. (1 Corinthians 3: 18-20.)

LABAN.

LA'BAN—a form of a Hebrew word meaning "white." Laban was the brother of Rebekah and the father of the two wives of Jacob, Rachel and Leah. By a shrewd trick he forced Jacob to serve him fourteen years for the privilege of marrying the two women.
References.—Genesis 24, 29, 30, 31.

LABOR. (Spelled "labour" throughout the Bible.)

LA'BOR—physical toil or bodily exertion; work; hard muscular effort directed toward some useful end. After the sin of Adam and Eve labor was set forth by God as the primeval curse, man being condemned to earn his bread by the sweat of his brow, a phrase which aptly illustrates the character of labor. But labor is by no means an everlasting curse, nor is it degrading nor without its blessing, as the Scriptures definitely show it to be pleasing to God.

REFERENCES.

Labor Ordained for Man.

In the sweat of thy face shalt thou eat bread, till thou return unto the ground; for out of it wast thou taken: for dust thou art, and unto dust shalt thou return. (Genesis 3: 19.)

Man goeth forth unto his work and to his labour until the evening. (Psalm 104: 23.)

Labor Blessed by God.

The labour of the righteous tendeth to life: the fruit of the wicked to sin. (Proverbs 10: 16.)

Wealth gotten by vanity shall be diminished: but he that gathereth by labour shall increase. (Proverbs 13: 11.)

There is nothing better for a man than that he should eat and drink, and that he should make his soul enjoy good in his labour. This also I saw, that it was from the hand of God. (Ecclesiastes 2: 24.)

The sleep of a labouring man is sweet, whether he eat little or much: but the abundance of the rich will not suffer him to sleep. (Ecclesiastes 5: 12.)

Every man also to whom God hath given riches and wealth, and hath given him power to eat thereof, and to take his portion, and to rejoice in his labour; this is the gift of God. (Ecclesiastes 5: 19.)

Sabbath Labor Forbidden.

Remember the sabbath day, to keep it holy.

Six days shalt thou labour, and do all thy work:

But the seventh day is the sabbath of the Lord thy God: in it thou shalt not do any work, thou, nor thy son, nor thy daughter, thy manservant, nor thy maidservant, nor thy cattle, nor thy stranger that is within thy gates:

For in six days the Lord made heaven and earth, the sea, and all that in them is, and rested the seventh day: wherefore the Lord blessed the sabbath day, and hallowed it. (Exodus 20: 8-11.)

Lawful to Labor for Good on Sabbath.

And the ruler of the synagogue answered with indignation, because that Jesus had healed on the sabbath day, and said unto the people, There are six days in which men ought to work: in them therefore come and be healed, and not on the sabbath day.

The Lord then answered him, and said, *Thou hypocrite, doth not each one of you on the sabbath loose his ox or his ass from the stall, and lead him away to watering?* (Luke 13: 14, 15.)

And Jesus answering spake unto the lawyers and Pharisees, saying, *Is it lawful to heal on the sabbath day?*

And they held their peace. And he took him, and healed him, and let him go;

And answered them, saying, *Which of you shall have an ass or an ox fallen into a pit, and will not straightway pull him out on the sabbath day?*

And they could not answer him again to these things. (Luke 14: 3-6.)

The Laborer's Hire.

And in the same house remain, eat-ing and drinking such things as they give: for the labourer is worthy of his hire. Go not from house to house. (Luke 10: 7.)

For the scripture saith, Thou shalt not muzzle the ox that treadeth out the corn. And, The labourer is worthy of his reward. (1 Timothy 5: 18.)

LAW.

LAW—a rule of conduct enforced by a higher authority than the persons to whom it is given. In the Bible we find God's law. The Old Testament is often called the Law. It originally was laid down to the Hebrews through Moses; and while it had special application to them and special requirements they were bound to observe, the fundamentals of it were universal. In later Jewish times rigid observance of the law brought into existence the hard, cold sect of the Pharisees, who gave greater attention to splitting hairs over the commands of God than they did to giving Him honor and worship, thus developing a degree of hypocrisy without an equal. The statement that Christ abolished the law must not be taken literally. What He did was to indicate that by the law no man could be justified; that rigid and hypocritical adherence to it was worth nothing to a man without the love of God in his heart; that He came to shed His blood to secure forgiveness of transgressions and to pave with His body and blood the way for the coming of the Holy Ghost, who should give guidance to all who were His true disciples. Thus does it come about that for Christians certain features of the old Mosaic ceremonial law, with special references to rites and sacrifices, are abolished. God's fundamental Law, the Ten Commandments, were not abolished and continue to be the basis, along with the two new commandments that Jesus gave, of right Christian living.

REFERENCES.

Law Given to Adam and Noah.

And the Lord God commanded the man, saying, Of every tree of the garden thou mayest freely eat:

But of the tree of the knowledge of

good and evil, thou shalt not eat of it: for in the day that thou eatest thereof thou shalt surely die. (Genesis 3: 16, 17.)

And surely your blood of your lives will I require: at the hand of every beast will I require it, and at the hand of man; at the hand of every man's brother will I require the life of man.

Whoso sheddeth man's blood, by man shall his blood be shed: for in the image of God made he man. (Genesis 9: 5, 6.)

Law Proclaimed Through Moses.

And Moses went up unto God, and the Lord called unto him out of the mountain, saying, Thus shalt thou say to the house of Jacob, and tell the children of Israel;

Ye have seen what I did unto the Egyptians, and how I bare you on eagles' wings, and brought you unto myself.

Now therefore, if ye will obey my voice indeed, and keep my covenant, then ye shall be a peculiar treasure unto me above all people: for all the earth is mine:

And ye shall be unto me a kingdom of priests, and a holy nation. These are the words which thou shalt speak unto the children of Israel. (Exodus 19: 3-6.)

And Moses called all Israel, and said unto them, Hear, O Israel, the statutes and judgments which I speak in your ears this day, that ye may learn them, and keep and do them. (Deuteronomy 5: 1.)

Entire Obedience Demanded.

Cursed be he that confirmeth not all the words of this law to do them: and all the people shall say, Amen. (Deuteronomy 27: 26.)

For as many as are of the works of the law are under the curse: for it is written, Cursed is every one that continueth not in all things which are written in the book of the law to do them. (Galatians 3: 10.)

For whosoever shall keep the whole law, and yet offend in one point, he is guilty of all. (James 2: 10.)

The Law Good.

The law of the Lord is perfect, converting the soul: the testimony of the Lord is sure, making wise the simple.

The statutes of the Lord are right, rejoicing the heart: the commandment of the Lord is pure, enlightening the eyes. (Psalm 19: 7, 8.)

Wherefore the law is holy, and the commandment holy, and just, and good. (Romans 7: 12.)

All Men Guilty Under the Law.

Now we know that what things soever the law saith, it saith to them who are under the law: that every mouth may be stopped, and all the world may become guilty before God.

Therefore by the deeds of the law there shall no flesh be justified in his sight: for by the law is the knowledge of sin. (Romans 3: 19, 20.)

Fulfilled in Christ.

Think not that I am come to destroy the law, or the prophets: I am not come to destroy, but to fulfil.

For verily I say unto you, Till heaven and earth pass, one jot or one tittle shall in no wise pass from the law, till all be fulfilled.

Whosoever therefore shall break one of these least commandments, and shall teach men so, he shall be called the least in the kingdom of heaven: but whoso-

ever shall do and teach them, the same shall be called great in the kingdom of heaven. (Matthew 5: 17-19.)

Therefore as by the offence of one judgment came upon all men to condemnation; even so by the righteousness of one the free gift came upon all men unto justification of life.

For as by one man's disobedience many were made sinners, so by the obedience of one shall many be made righteous.

Moreover the law entered, that the offence might abound. But where sin abounded, grace did much more abound:

That as sin hath reigned unto death, even so might grace reign through righteousness unto eternal life by Jesus Christ our Lord. (Romans 5: 18-21.)

Abolished in Christ.

Forasmuch as we have heard, that certain which went out from us have troubled you with words, subverting your souls, saying, Ye must be circumcised, and keep the law: to whom we gave no such commandment. (Acts 15: 24.)

Knowing that a man is not justified by the works of the law, but by the faith of Jesus Christ, even we have believed in Jesus Christ, that we might be justified by the faith of Christ, and not by the works of the law: for by the works of the law shall no flesh be justified. (Galatians 2: 16.)

And this I say, that the covenant, that was confirmed before of God in Christ, the law, which was four hundred and thirty years after, cannot disannul, that it should make the promise of none effect.

For if the inheritance be of the law,

it is no more of promise: but God gave it to Abraham by promise.

Wherefore then serveth the law? It was added because of transgressions, till the seed should come to whom the promise was made; and it was ordained by angels in the hand of a mediator.

Now a mediator is not a mediator of one, but God is one.

Is the law then against the promises of God? God forbid: for if there had been a law given which could have given life, verily righteousness should have been by the law.

But the scripture hath concluded all under sin, that the promise by faith of Jesus Christ might be given to them that believe.

But before faith came, we were kept under the law, shut up unto the faith which should afterwards be revealed.

Wherefore the law was our schoolmaster to bring us unto Christ, that we might be justified by faith.

But after that faith is come, we are no longer under a schoolmaster. (Galatians 3: 17-25.)

But now in Christ Jesus ye who sometimes were far off are made nigh by the blood of Christ.

For he is our peace, who hath made both one, and hath broken down the middle wall of partition between us;

Having abolished in his flesh the enmity, even the law of commandments contained in ordinances; for to make in himself of twain one new man, so making peace;

And that he might reconcile both unto God in one body by the cross, having slain the enmity thereby. (Ephesians 2: 13-16.)

Blotting out the handwriting of ordinances that was against us, which was contrary to us, and took it out of the way, nailing it to his cross. (Colossians 2: 14.)

For the law made nothing perfect, but the bringing in of a better hope did; by the which we draw nigh unto God.

And inasmuch as not without an oath he was made priest:

(For those priests were made without an oath; but this with an oath by him that said unto him, The Lord sware and will not repent, Thou art a priest for ever after the order of Melchisedec:)

By so much was Jesus made a surety of a better testament. (Hebrews 7: 19-22.)

Christians Redeemed.

For the law was given by Moses, but grace and truth came by Jesus Christ. (John 1: 17.)

And by him all that believe are justified from all things, from which ye could not be justified by the law of Moses. (Acts 13: 39.)

For Christ is the end of the law for righteousness to every one that believeth.

For Moses describeth the righteousness which is of the law, That the man which doeth those things shall live by them.

But the righteousness which is of faith speaketh on this wise, Say not in thine heart, Who shall ascend into heaven? (that is, to bring Christ down from above:)

Or, who shall descend into the deep? (that is, to bring up Christ again from the dead.)

But what saith it? The word is nigh thee, even in thy mouth, and in thy heart: that is, the word of faith, which we preach;

That if thou shalt confess with thy mouth the Lord Jesus, and shalt believe in thine heart that God hath raised him from the dead, thou shalt be saved. (Romans 10: 4-9.)

O foolish Galatians, who hath bewitched you, that ye should not obey the truth, before whose eyes Jesus Christ hath been evidently set forth, crucified among you?

This only would I learn of you, Received ye the Spirit by the works of the law, or by the hearing of faith?

Are ye so foolish? having begun in the Spirit, are ye now made perfect by the flesh?

Have ye suffered so many things in vain? if it be yet in vain.

He therefore that ministereth to you the Spirit, and worketh miracles among you, doeth he it by the works of the law, or by the hearing of faith?

Even as Abraham believed God, and it was accounted to him for righteousness.

Know ye therefore that they which are of faith, the same are the children of Abraham.

And the scripture, foreseeing that God would justify the heathen through faith, preached before the gospel unto Abraham, saying, In thee shall all nations be blessed.

So then they which be of faith are blessed with faithful Abraham.

For as many as are of the works of the law are under the curse: for it is written, Cursed is every one that continueth not in all things which are written in the book of the law to do them.

But that no man is justified by the law in the sight of God, it is evident: for, The just shall live by faith.

And the law is not of faith: but, The man that doeth them shall live in them.

Christ hath redeemed us from the

curse of the law, being made a curse for us: for it is written, Cursed is every one that hangeth on a tree:

That the blessing of Abraham might come on the Gentiles through Jesus Christ; that we might receive the promise of the Spirit through faith. (Galatians 3: 1-14.)

LAZARUS.

LAZ'A-RUS—a Greek form of the Hebrew name "Eleazar," meaning "God is his helper." The name of Lazarus is mentioned in two connections in the Scriptures—as the name of the brother of Martha and Mary, whom Jesus raised from the dead, and again as the chief character of one of the Master's most noted parables, the rich man and the beggar, Lazarus.

References.—John 11 and 12; Luke 16 (parable).

LEAH. (See Jacob, Laban, Rachel.)

LE'AH—a form of a Hebrew word meaning "wearied." Leah was one of the wives of Jacob. She had little share in his affections, however. Her life seems to have been a sad one.

References.—Genesis 29, 30, 31, 33, 49.

LEBANON.

LEB'A-NON—a form of a Hebrew word meaning "white from snow." Lebanon is the name of two ranges of mountains of Palestine, noted for their remarkable beauty and the magnificent cedars that grew upon them.

LEPROSY.

LEP'RO-SY—the name of a peculiar disease of the skin. Leprosy seems to have had its origin as a disease in Asia Minor or the surrounding country many ages ago. Persons afflicted with it were regarded as unclean and were forced to keep themselves away from healthy persons. To be a leper was to be an outcast and eventually to suffer a lonely and terrible death. In almost all times there has been a tendency to confuse with leprosy a very much more horrible and deadly disease that should be known as elephantiasis. The

true leprosy is rarely contagious except by long association with a diseased person and has none of the sickening features of elephantiasis. Most modern so-called leper colonies are composed of persons suffering with the latter disease.

LEVI.

LE'VI—a form of a Hebrew word meaning "joining" or "adhering." Levi was the third son of Jacob and Leah. His descendants, the Levites, became the Hebrew priesthood.

LIBERALITY.

LIB'ER-AL'I-TY—the act, quality, or state of being liberal; generosity; also candor and charity. The Bible contains many injunctions to the faithful to cultivate the grace of liberality, not only in giving to God and the poor but in our relations to our fellow-men.

REFERENCES.

If there be among you a poor man of one of thy brethren within any of thy gates in thy land which the Lord thy God giveth thee, thou shalt not harden thine heart, nor shut thine hand from thy poor brother:

But thou shalt open thine hand wide unto him, and shalt surely lend him sufficient for his need, in that which he wanteth.

Beware that there be not a thought in thy wicked heart, saying, The seventh year, the year of release, is at hand; and thine eye be evil against thy poor brother, and thou givest him nought; and he cry unto the Lord against thee, and it be sin unto thee.

Thou shalt surely give him, and thine heart shall not be grieved when thou givest unto him: because that for this thing the Lord thy God shall bless thee in all thy works, and in all that thou puttest thine hand unto.

For the poor shall never cease out of the land: therefore I command thee, saying, Thou shalt open thine hand wide unto thy brother, to thy poor, and to thy needy, in thy land.

And if thy brother, a Hebrew man, or a Hebrew woman, be sold unto thee, and serve thee six years; then in the seventh year thou shalt let him go free from thee.

And when thou sendest him out free from thee, thou shalt not let him go away empty:

Thou shalt furnish him liberally out of thy flock, and out of thy floor, and out of thy winepress: of that wherewith the Lord thy God hath blessed thee thou shalt give unto him.

And thou shalt remember that thou wast a bondman in the land of Egypt, and the Lord thy God redeemed thee: therefore I command thee this thing to-day. (Deuteronomy 15: 7-15.)

The liberal soul shall be made fat: and he that watereth shall be watered also himself. (Proverbs 11: 25.)

But the liberal deviseth liberal things; and by liberal things shall he stand. (Isaiah 32: 8.)

LIBERTY.

LIB'ER-TY—the state of being free; exemption from the will of another person claiming ownership of services or person. Liberty is one of the most valuable heritages of modern man. In the past, few men enjoyed it; under present conditions there are few who do not enjoy it. It is one of the results of advancing civilization. Where there is no liberty there can be no progress. This is especially true of religious affairs. It has only been since the right of man to worship God according to the dictates of his conscience has been recognized that evangelical religion has made definite and distinct headway. The old policy of combining the Church and the State gave men narrow views and resulted in persecutions and troubles. Nowadays this yoke is almost entirely thrown off.

REFERENCES.

Liberty Bestowed by the Gospel.

Because the creature itself also shall be delivered from the bondage of corruption into the glorious liberty of the children of God. (Romans 8: 21.)

Now the Lord is that Spirit: and where the Spirit of the Lord is, there is liberty. (2 Corinthians 3: 17.)

Stand fast therefore in the liberty wherewith Christ hath made us free, and be not entangled again with the yoke of bondage. (Galatians 5: 1.)

But whoso looketh into the perfect law of liberty, and continueth therein, he being not a forgetful hearer, but a doer of the work, this man shall be blessed in his deed. (James 1: 25.)

The Spirit of the Lord God is upon me, because the Lord hath anointed me to preach good tidings unto the meek; he hath sent me to bind up the broken-hearted, to proclaim liberty to the captives, and the opening of the prison to them that are bound. (Isaiah 61: 1.)

Liberty Not to Be Abused.

But take heed lest by any means this liberty of yours become a stumbling-block to them that are weak. (1 Corinthians 8: 9.)

For, brethren, ye have been called unto liberty; only use not liberty for an occasion to the flesh, but by love serve one another. (Galatians 5: 13.)

For so is the will of God, that with well doing ye may put to silence the ignorance of foolish men:

As free, and not using your liberty for a cloke of maliciousness, but as the servants of God. (1 Peter 2: 15, 16.)

For this is thankworthy, if a man for conscience toward God endure grief, suffering wrongfully.

For what glory is it, if, when ye be

buffeted for your faults, ye shall take it patiently? but if, when ye do well, and suffer for it, ye take it patiently, this is acceptable with God. (1 Peter 2: 19, 20.)

LIFE. (See Death, Immortality, Resurrection.)

LIFE—that state which begins with birth or germination and ends in death or complete decay; also the period during which such a state continues or exists; the union of soul and body; the opposite of death. In the natural order of things life must have an end. This ending is called death. In the providence of God both life and death are mysteries. The secret of the beginning of life is hidden from us as well as the secret of the things after death. We simply know that life and death happen. We also know that God gave each one of us an immortal soul to live in the mortal body. Having done so He makes the promise of eternal life (or happiness) for it after the death of the mortal body if we win it by our conduct during life, or eternal death (punishment) if we merit it. Taking these facts as a basis, the future life may be considered as follows: Often we wake from dreams to either a sense of happiness or trouble, as the nature of the dream may have been. A similar condition may exist the moment after death.

REFERENCES.

Life the Gift of God.

And the Lord God formed man of the dust of the ground, and breathed into his nostrils the breath of life; and man became a living soul. (Genesis 2: 7.)

Who knoweth not in all these that the hand of the Lord hath wrought this?

In whose hand is the soul of every living thing, and the breath of all mankind. (Job 12: 9, 10.)

Thy righteousness is like the great mountains; thy judgments are a great deep: O Lord, thou preservest man and beast. (Psalm 36: 6.)

For in him we live, and move, and have our being; as certain also of your own poets have said, For we are also his offspring. (Acts 17: 28.)

Long Life Promised.

Honour thy father and thy mother: that thy days may be long upon the land which the Lord thy God giveth thee. (Exodus 20: 12.)

Ye shall walk in all the ways which the Lord your God hath commanded you, that ye may live, and that it may be well with you, and that ye may prolong your days in the land which ye shall possess. (Deuteronomy 5: 33.)

My son, forget not my law; but let thine heart keep my commandments:

For length of days, and long life, and peace shall they add to thee. (Proverbs 3: 1, 2.)

Life's Vanity and Uncertainty.

Is there not an appointed time to man upon earth? are not his days also like the days of a hireling? (Job 7: 1.)

Now my days are swifter than a post: they flee away, they see no good.

They are passed away as the swift ships: as the eagle that hasteth to the prey. (Job 9: 25, 26.)

Man that is born of a woman is of few days, and full of trouble.

He cometh forth like a flower, and is cut down: he fleeth also as a shadow, and continueth not. (Job 14: 1, 2.)

Behold, thou hast made my days as a handbreadth; and mine age is as nothing before thee: verily every man at his best state is altogether vanity. Selah.

Surely every man walketh in a vain shew: surely they are disquieted in vain: he heapeth up riches, and knoweth not who shall gather them. (Psalm 39: 5, 6.)

Remember how short my time is: wherefore hast thou made all men in vain?

What man is he that liveth, and shall not see death? shall he deliver his soul from the hand of the grave? Selah. (Psalm 89: 47, 48.)

For a thousand years in thy sight are but as yesterday when it is past, and as a watch in the night.

Thou carriest them away as with a flood; they are as a sleep; in the morning they are like grass which groweth up.

In the morning it flourisheth, and groweth up; in the evening it is cut down, and withereth. (Psalm 90: 4-6.)

For who knoweth what is good for man in this life, all the days of his vain life which he spendeth as a shadow? for who can tell a man what shall be after him under the sun? (Ecclesiastes 6: 12.)

Mine age is departed, and is removed from me as a shepherd's tent: I have cut off like a weaver my life: he will cut me off with pining sickness: from day even to night wilt thou make an end of me. (Isaiah 38: 12.)

Go to now, ye that say, To day or to morrow we will go into such a city, and continue there a year, and buy and sell, and get gain:

Whereas ye know not what shall be on the morrow. For what is your life? It is even a vapour, that appeareth for a little time, and then vanisheth away.

For that ye ought to say, If the Lord will, we shall live, and do this, or that. (James 4: 13-15.)

For all flesh is as grass, and all the glory of man as the flower of grass. The grass withereth, and the flower thereof falleth away. (1 Peter 1: 24.)

The Right Mode of Living.

In holiness and righteousness before him, all the days of our life. (Luke 1: 75.)

If it be possible, as much as lieth in you, live peaceably with all men. (Romans 12: 18.)

For none of us liveth to himself, and no man dieth to himself.

For whether we live, we live unto the Lord; and whether we die, we die unto the Lord: whether we live therefore, or die, we are the Lord's. (Romans 14: 7, 8.)

For to me to live is Christ, and to die is gain.

But if I live in the flesh, this is the fruit of my labour: yet what I shall choose I wot not. (Philippians 1: 21, 22.)

Spiritual Life.

Therefore we are buried with him by baptism into death: that like as Christ was raised up from the dead by the glory of the Father, even so we also should walk in newness of life. (Romans 6: 4.)

I am crucified with Christ: nevertheless I live; yet not I, but Christ liveth in me: and the life which I now live in the flesh I live by the faith of the Son of God, who loved me, and gave himself for me. (Galatians 2: 20.)

And you hath he quickened, who were dead in trespasses and sins. (Ephesians 2: 1.)

For ye are dead, and your life is hid with Christ in God. (Colossians 3: 3.)

Eternal Life.

As the dew of Hermon, and as the dew that descended upon the mountains of Zion: for there the Lord commanded the blessing, even life for evermore. (Psalm 133: 3.)

Labour not for the meat which perisheth, but for that meat which endureth unto everlasting life, which the Son of man shall give unto you: for him hath God the Father sealed. (John 6: 27.)

Whoso eateth my flesh, and drinketh my blood, hath eternal life; and I will raise him up at the last day. (John 6: 54.)

And I give unto them eternal life; and they shall never perish, neither shall any man pluck them out of my hand. (John 10: 28.)

As thou hast given him power over all flesh, that he should give eternal life to as many as thou hast given him.

And this is life eternal, that they might know thee the only true God, and Jesus Christ whom thou hast sent. (John 17: 2, 3.)

Who will render to every man according to his deeds:

To them who by patient continuance in well doing seek for glory and honour and immortality, eternal life. (Romans 2: 6, 7.)

For the wages of sin is death; but the gift of God is eternal life through Jesus Christ our Lord. (Romans 6: 23.)

For the life was manifested, and we have seen it, and bear witness, and shew unto you that eternal life, which was with the Father, and was manifested unto us. (1 John 1: 2.)

And this is the promise that he hath promised us, even eternal life. (1 John 2: 25.)

Keep yourselves in the love of God, looking for the mercy of our Lord Jesus Christ unto eternal life. (Jude 1: 21.)

He that hath an ear, let him hear what the Spirit saith unto the churches; To him that overcometh will I give to eat of the tree of life, which is in the midst of the paradise of God. (Revelation 2: 7.)

And he said unto me, It is done. I am Alpha and Omega, the beginning and the end. I will give unto him that is athirst of the fountain of the water of life freely. (Revelation 21: 6.)

And as Moses lifted up the serpent in the wilderness, even so must the Son of man be lifted up:

That whosoever believeth in him should not perish, but have eternal life.

For God so loved the world, that he gave his only begotten Son, that whosoever believeth in him should not perish, but have everlasting life. (John 3: 14-16.)

Verily, verily, I say unto you, He that heareth my word, and believeth on him that sent me, hath everlasting life, and shall not come into condemnation; but is passed from death unto life.

Verily, verily, I say unto you, The hour is coming, and now is, when the dead shall hear the voice of the Son of God: and they that hear shall live.

For as the Father hath life in himself; so hath he given to the Son to have life in himself. (John 3: 24-26.)

LIGHT. (See Darkness.)

LIGHT—the opposite of dark. Light is that force, agent, or action in nature which by its operation upon the organs of sight renders objects visible. The word is also used in a figurative sense to denote illumination of the mind. Both uses of the word are to be found in the Bible. Jesus Christ is called the Light of the world because of His power of illuminating the mind of man and of acting as a guiding beacon to His followers.

REFERENCES.

Light Comes from God.

And God said, Let there be light: and there was light.

And God saw the light, that it was good: and God divided the light from the darkness.

And God called the light Day, and the darkness he called Night. And the evening and the morning were the first day. (Genesis 1: 3-5.)

Thus saith the Lord, which giveth the sun for a light by day, and the ordinances of the moon and of the stars for a light by night, which divideth the sea when the waves thereof roar; The Lord of hosts is his name. (Jeremiah 31: 35.)

Light a Type of God's Favor.

And Moses stretched forth his hand toward heaven; and there was a thick darkness in all the land of Egypt three days:

They saw not one another, neither rose any from his place for three days: but all the children of Israel had light in their dwellings. (Exodus 10: 22, 23.)

There be many that say, Who will shew us any good? Lord, lift thou up the light of thy countenance upon us. (Psalm 4: 6.)

The Lord is my light and my salvation; whom shall I fear? the Lord is the strength of my life; of whom shall I be afraid? (Psalm 27: 1.)

Light is sown for the righteous, and gladness for the upright in heart. (Psalm 97: 11.)

The people that walked in darkness have seen a great light: they that dwell in the land of the shadow of death, upon them hath the light shined. (Isaiah 9: 2.)

The sun shall be no more thy light by day; neither for brightness shall the moon give light unto thee: but the Lord shall be unto thee an everlasting light, and thy God thy glory. (Isaiah 60: 19.)

God's Word Produces Light.

The statutes of the Lord are right, rejoicing the heart: the commandment of the Lord is pure, enlightening the eyes. (Psalm 19: 8.)

Thy word is a lamp unto my feet, and a light unto my path. (Psalm 119: 105.)

The entrance of thy words giveth light; it giveth understanding unto the simple. (Psalm 119: 130.)

For the commandment is a lamp; and the law is light; and reproofs of instruction are the way of life. (Proverbs 6: 23.)

Christ the Light of the World.

A light to lighten the Gentiles, and the glory of thy people Israel. (Luke 2: 32.)

In him was life; and the life was the light of men.

And the light shineth in darkness; and the darkness comprehended it not. (John 1: 4, 5.)

And this is the condemnation, that light is come into the world, and men loved darkness rather than light, because their deeds were evil.

For every one that doeth evil hateth the light, neither cometh to the light, lest his deeds should be reproved. (John 3: 19, 20.)

Then spake Jesus again unto them, saying, *I am the light of the world: he that followeth me shall not walk in darkness, but shall have the light of life.* (John 8: 12.)

Then Jesus said unto them, *Yet a little while is the light with you. Walk while ye have the light, lest darkness come upon you: for he that walketh in darkness knoweth not whither he goeth.*

While ye have light, believe in the light, that ye may be the children of light. These things spake Jesus, and departed, and did hide himself from them. (John 12: 35, 36.)

And the city had no need of the sun, neither of the moon, to shine in it: for the glory of God did lighten it, and the Lamb is the light thereof.

And the nations of them which are saved shall walk in the light of it: and the kings of the earth do bring their glory and honour into it. (Revelation 21: 23, 24.)

LORD'S DAY. (See Sabbath, Sunday.)

LORD'S PRAYER. (See Prayer.)

LORD'S SUPPER. (See Communion, Fellowship.)

LOT.

Lot—a form of a Hebrew word meaning "a covering." Lot was the name of the nephew of Abraham who accompanied that patriarch from the land of the Chaldees. Eventually they separated and Lot seems to have taken up his residence in or near the wicked cities of Sodom and Gomorrah, from whence he and his family fled just prior to their destruction. We are told that his wife was turned into a pillar of salt because she looked back at them during the flight. Lot's descendants were the Moabites and Ammonites.

References.—Genesis 13, 14, 19, etc.

LOVE. (See Marriage, etc.)

Love—that emotion expressive of the good will or affection or kindness which human beings entertain one for another; also the expression of the emotion in words or acts calculated to gratify or benefit another; also the union of these two ideas in a higher and nobler sense. This development of the emotion is particularly evidenced in the attitude of God toward man, and shown in the giving by God through Jesus Christ all those things necessary for the salvation of man. Love to Christ by man is the natural offspring of Christ's love to man. The great measure and test of love is self-sacrifice, the surrender of self and the ambitions of self, the abandonment of self in devotion to another, or to others, the latter a type of love approaching the perfect type of the love of Christ. The province of love is to uplift and exalt. In mankind it is always more or less imperfect, in consequence of which we find distorted and degenerated specimens of love, in affections for things that are vile, or sinful, or degrading, such as love of money, love of pleasure, love of self, etc.

REFERENCES.

Love Is of God and from God.

He that loveth not knoweth not God; for God is love.

In this was manifested the love of God toward us, because that God sent his only begotten Son into the world, that we might live through him. (1 John 4: 8, 9.)

Love to God Commanded.

And thou shalt love the Lord thy God with all thine heart, and with all thy soul, and with all thy might. (Deuteronomy 6: 5.)

Therefore thou shalt love the Lord thy God, and keep his charge, and his statutes, and his judgments, and his commandments, alway. (Deuteronomy 11: 1.)

But take diligent heed to do the commandment and the law, which Moses the servant of the Lord charged you, to love the Lord your God, and to walk in all his ways, and to keep his commandments, and to cleave unto him, and to serve him with all your heart and with all your soul. (Joshua 22: 5.)

He that loveth father or mother more than me is not worthy of me: and he that loveth son or daughter more than me is not worthy of me. (Matthew 10: 37.)

Master, which is the great commandment in the law?

Jesus said unto him, *Thou shalt love the Lord thy God with all thy heart, and with all thy soul, and with all thy mind.*

This is the first and great commandment. (Matthew 22: 36-38.)

And one of the scribes came, and having heard them reasoning together, and perceiving that he had answered them well, asked him, Which is the first commandment of all? (Mark 12: 28.)

And thou shalt love the Lord thy God with all thy heart, and with all thy soul, and with all thy mind, and with all thy strength: this is the first commandment. (Mark 12: 30.)

And to love him with all the heart, and with all the understanding, and with all the soul, and with all the strength, and to love his neighbour as himself, is more than all whole burnt offerings and sacrifices. (Mark 12: 33.)

That thou mayest love the Lord thy God, and that thou mayest obey his voice, and that thou mayest cleave unto him: for he is thy life, and the length of thy days: that thou mayest dwell in the land which the Lord sware unto thy fathers, to Abraham, to Isaac, and to Jacob, to give them. (Deuteronomy 30: 20.)

Because he hath set his love upon me, therefore will I deliver him: I will set him on high, because he hath known my name. (Psalm 91: 14.)

The Lord preserveth all them that love him: but all the wicked will he destroy. (Psalm 145: 20.)

I love them that love me; and those that seek me early shall find me. (Proverbs 8: 17.)

But as it is written, Eye hath not seen, nor ear heard, neither have entered into the heart of man, the things which God hath prepared for them that love him. (1 Corinthians 2: 9.)

But if any man love God, the same is known of him. (1 Corinthians 8: 3.)

Herein is our love made perfect, that we may have boldness in the day of judgment: because as he is, so are we in this world.

There is no fear in love; but perfect love casteth out fear: because fear hath torment. He that feareth is not made perfect in love. (1 John 4: 17, 18.)

Brotherly Love.

A new commandment I give unto you, That ye love one another; as I have loved you, that ye also love one another.

By this shall all men know that ye are my disciples, if ye have love one to another. (John 13: 34, 35.)

This is my commandment, *That ye love one another, as I have loved you.* (John 15: 12.)

Let love be without dissimulation. Abhor that which is evil; cleave to that which is good.

Be kindly affectioned one to another with brotherly love; in honour preferring one another. (Romans 12: 9, 10.)

But as touching brotherly love ye need not that I write unto you: for ye yourselves are taught of God to love one another. (1 Thessalonians 4: 9.)

Let brotherly love continue. (Hebrews 13: 1.)

Seeing ye have purified your souls in

obeying the truth through the Spirit unto unfeigned love of the brethren, see that ye love one another with a pure heart fervently. (1 Peter 1: 22.)

And above all things have fervent charity among yourselves: for charity shall cover the multitude of sins. (1 Peter 4: 8.)

In this the children of God are manifest, and the children of the devil: whosoever doeth not righteousness is not of God, neither he that loveth not his brother.

For this is the message that ye heard from the beginning, that we should love one another. (1 John 3: 10, 11.)

We know that we have passed from death unto life, because we love the brethren. He that loveth not his brother abideth in death. (1 John 3: 14.)

Beloved, let us love one another: for love is of God; and every one that loveth is born of God, and knoweth God. (1 John 4: 7.)

Beloved, if God so loved us, we ought also to love one another. (1 John 4: 11.)

If a man say, I love God, and hateth his brother, he is a liar: for he that loveth not his brother whom he hath seen, how can he love God whom he hath not seen?

And this commandment have we from him, That he who loveth God love his brother also. (1 John 4: 20, 21.)

Though I speak with the tongues of men and of angels, and have not charity, I am become as sounding brass, or a tinkling cymbal.

And though I have the gift of prophecy, and understand all mysteries, and all knowledge; and though I have all faith, so that I could remove mountains, and have not charity, I am nothing.

And though I bestow all my goods to feed the poor, and though I give my body to be burned, and have not charity, it profiteth me nothing.

Charity suffereth long, and is kind; charity envieth not; charity vaunteth not itself, is not puffed up,

Doth not behave itself unseemly, seeketh not her own, is not easily provoked, thinketh no evil;

Rejoiceth not in iniquity, but rejoiceth in the truth;

Beareth all things, believeth all things, hopeth all things, endureth all things.

Charity never faileth: but whether there be prophecies, they shall fail; whether there be tongues, they shall cease; whether there be knowledge, it shall vanish away. (1 Corinthians 13: 1-8.)

*And now abideth faith, hope, charity, these three; but the greatest of these is charity. (1 Corinthians 13: 13.)

And this is love, that we walk after his commandments. This is the commandment, That, as ye have heard from the beginning, ye should walk in it. (2 John 1: 6.)

Law of Love to Man.

Therefore all things whatsoever ye would that men should do to you, do ye even so to them: for this is the law and the prophets. (Matthew 7: 12.)

Honour thy father and thy mother: and, Thou shalt love thy neighbour as thyself. (Matthew 19: 19.)

And the second is like unto it, Thou shalt love thy neighbour as thyself. (Matthew 22: 39.)

And the second is like, namely this,

---

* Every time CHARITY occurs in the above it should without doubt be rendered LOVE.

Thou shalt love thy neighbour as thyself. There is none other commandment greater than these. (Mark 12: 31.)

Owe no man anything, but to love one another: for he that loveth another hath fulfilled the law.

For this, Thou shalt not commit adultery, Thou shalt not kill, Thou shalt not steal, Thou shalt not bear false witness, Thou shalt not covet; and if there be any other commandment, it is briefly comprehended in this saying, namely, Thou shalt love thy neighbour as thyself.

Love worketh no ill to his neighbour: therefore love is the fulfilling of the law. (Romans 13: 8-10.)

The Measure of the Fullness of Love.

And Jesus answering said unto him, *Simon, I have somewhat to say unto thee.* And he saith, Master, say on.

There was a certain creditor which had two debtors: the one owed five hundred pence, and the other fifty.

And when they had nothing to pay, he frankly forgave them both. Tell me therefore, which of them will love him most?

Simon answered and said, I suppose that he, to whom he forgave most. And he said unto him, *Thou hast rightly judged.* (Luke 7: 40-43.)

For all the law is fulfilled in one word, even in this; Thou shalt love thy neighbour as thyself. (Galatians 5: 14.)

If ye fulfil the royal law according to the Scripture, Thou shalt love thy neighbour as thyself, ye do well. (James 2: 8.)

LUKE.

LUKE—the Englished form of the Greek proper name Loukas (Latin, Lucas or Lu-

canus), meaning "born at daylight." Luke, chiefly known to modern Christians as the writer of the gospel bearing his name, and the book of the Acts, appears to have been a Syro-Greek of the city of Antioch and early converted to Christianity. There is a tradition that he was one of the 70 and one of the two that saw Jesus at Emmaus, but of this latter statement there is no confirmation. He was an educated man and a physician. He also was an able helper to Paul and accompanied the great apostle to the Gentiles to Jerusalem and to Rome. It is said that he suffered martyrdom, but when, where, and how we have no means of knowing.

LYING.

LY'ING—the act of telling a lie; also the state of being a lie or a falsehood. Lying is one of the sins against which the Bible strongly inveighs. The doom of liars is also carefully pointed out. Nevertheless it is one of the most common of offences, and has been in all ages. Prevarication is a form of lying, since the motive to mislead by statement is as present in it as in the full-fledged lie.

REFERENCES.

These six things doth the Lord hate; yea, seven are an abomination unto him:

A proud look, a lying tongue, and hands that shed innocent blood,

A heart that deviseth wicked imaginations, feet that be swift in running to mischief,

A false witness that speaketh lies, and he that soweth discord among brethren. (Proverbs 6: 16-19.)

Lying lips are abomination to the Lord: but they that deal truly are his delight. (Proverbs 12: 22.)

Ye shall not steal, neither deal falsely, neither lie one to another. (Leviticus 19: 11.)

Lie not one to another, seeing that ye have put off the old man with his deeds. (Colossians 3: 9.)

Ye are of your father the devil, and the lusts of your father ye will do. He was a murderer from the beginning, and abode not in the truth, because there is no truth in him. When he speaketh a lie, he speaketh of his own: for he is a liar, and the father of it. (John 8: 44.)

But the fearful, and unbelieving, and the abominable, and murderers, and whoremongers, and sorcerers, and idolaters, and all liars, shall have their part in the lake which burneth with fire and brimstone: which is the second death. (Revelation 21: 8.)

And there shall in no wise enter into it any thing that defileth, neither whatsoever worketh abomination, or maketh a lie: but they which are written in the Lamb's book of life. (Revelation 21: 27.)

For without are dogs, and sorcerers, and whoremongers, and murderers, and idolaters, and whosoever loveth and maketh a lie. (Revelation 22: 15.)

MACEDONIA. (See Paul.)

MAC-E-DO′NI-A (so named from its mythical founder, Macedon)—a large country to the north of Greece, extending to the Balkan mountains. It originally was the home of a hardy and warlike race, who gave to the world two great conquerors, Philip of Macedon and his son, Alexander the Great. It was the first country of Europe to receive the gospel, Paul and his companions preaching there on the inspired invitation of its people: "Come over into Macedonia, and help us." (Acts 16: 9.)

MACHPELAH.

MACH-PE′LAH—a form of a Hebrew word meaning "twofold" or "double." Machpelah was the name of a plot of ground containing a large cave which Abraham bought for use as a family sepulchre. In it were buried Abraham, Isaac, Rebekah, and Leah. Under the great mosque at Hebron there is a cave which is said to be the cave of Machpelah.

MAGDALA. (See Mary.)

MAG-DA′LA—a form of a Hebrew word meaning "tower." Magdala was a village on the Sea of Galilee, the home of Mary Magdalene, that is, Mary of Magdala.

MAGDALENE. (See Mary.)

MAGI.

MA′GI—the name of one of the six tribes of the Mede nation. They were of the priestly caste, occupying the same position among the Medes as did the Levites among the Hebrews. They were men of the most learned type and were credited with having penetrated many of the secrets of nature which the Egyptian and Chaldean priesthood had acquired, secrets that gave them enormous influence over the people, who believed that they were capable of performing acts of magic and miracles. Many of them were free from idolatrous superstition and welcomed such knowledge of the true God as the Hebrew could carry to them. Indeed, it seems that their religion, in its original form, was a sort of worship of Jehovah, although they had not the knowledge of Him that the Hebrews had, nor did they call Him by that name.

The "wise men from the East" who came to find the infant Jesus and worship Him were men of the tribe of the Magi. We are told that they were guided by a star, which after it had led them to Bethlehem had performed its functions and disappeared, God sending them back another way to their own country through the guidance of a dream. The gifts they brought were entirely typical of the rank of Jesus—gold to show His kingly dignity, frankincense to show their adoration of Him as the Son of God, and myrrh to indicate the bitterness of His Passion. Tradition gives their names as Gaspar, Melchoir, and Balthasar, but, of course, there is absolutely no confirmation of this. To this day the Greek Church celebrates in almost regal splendor a festival commemorating the visit.

MAJESTY.

MAJ'ES-TY—the dignity and authority of sovereign power. The majesty of God and Christ passes that of the kings and rulers of the earth to a limitless degree.

REFERENCES.

Thine, O Lord, is the greatness, and the power, and the glory, and the victory, and the majesty: for all that is in the heaven and in the earth is thine; thine is the kingdom, O Lord, and thou art exalted as head above all. (1 Chronicles 29: 11.)

Fair weather cometh out of the north: with God is terrible majesty. (Job 37: 22.)

The Lord reigneth, he is clothed with majesty; the Lord is clothed with strength, wherewith he hath girded himself: the world also is stablished, that it cannot be moved. (Psalm 93: 1.)

Honour and majesty are before him: strength and beauty are in his sanctuary. (Psalm 96: 6.)

They shall lift up their voice, they shall sing for the majesty of the Lord, they shall cry aloud from the sea. (Isaiah 24: 14.)

For we have not followed cunningly devised fables, when we made known unto you the power and coming of our Lord Jesus Christ, but were eyewitnesses of his majesty. (2 Peter 1: 16.)

MALACHI.

MAL'A-CHI—a form of a Hebrew word meaning "my angel." Malachi was the last of the minor prophets. His book is therefore the last of the canon of the Old Testament. He lived about the year 400 B.C. His prophecy is along the same lines as his contemporary, Nehemiah.

Reference.—The book of Malachi.

MALICE.

MAL'ICE—violent hatred, leading to the doing of evil things against the object of it. Malice is akin to malevolence and malignity. The Bible warns us against the harboring of malice in our hearts, and the passion is generally regarded as one of the worst of sins against our fellow-man.

REFERENCES.

Whoso mocketh the poor reproacheth his Maker: and he that is glad at calamities shall not be unpunished. (Proverbs 17: 5.)

Rejoice not when thine enemy falleth, and let not thine heart be glad when he stumbleth:

Lest the Lord see it, and it displease him, and he turn away his wrath from him. (Proverbs 24: 17, 18.)

Therefore let us keep the feast, not with old leaven, neither with the leaven of malice and wickedness; but with the unleavened bread of sincerity and truth. (1 Corinthians 5: 8.)

Brethren, be not children in understanding: howbeit in malice be ye children, but in understanding be men. (1 Corinthians 14: 20.)

Let all bitterness, and wrath, and anger, and clamour, and evil speaking be put away from you, with all malice. (Ephesians 4: 31.)

But now ye also put off all these; anger, wrath, malice, blasphemy, filthy communication out of your mouth. (Colossians 3: 8.)

For we ourselves also were sometimes foolish, disobedient, deceived, serving divers lusts and pleasures, living in malice and envy, hateful, and hating one another. (Titus 3: 3.)

Grudge not one against another, brethren, lest ye be condemned: behold, the judge standeth before the door. (James 5: 9.)

Wherefore laying aside all malice, and all guile, and hypocrisies, and envies, and all evil speakings,

As newborn babes, desire the sincere milk of the word, that ye may grow thereby. (1 Peter 2: 1, 2.)

MAMMON. (See Riches.)

MAM'MON—a word from the Chaldee meaning "riches" or "wealth." The Master, in using the term, personified it and placed it in opposition to God as a sort of idolatry. His meaning in an oft quoted but not well understood scripture appears to have been to "make friends of the mammon of unrighteousness," by spending wealth in a manner to benefit and bless poor saints, so that they may intercede with God for blessings upon you here and obtain for you His gracious pardon and be gratefully waiting on the golden shore to welcome and receive you into the "everlasting habitation."

REFERENCES.

No man can serve two masters: for either he will hate the one, and love the other; or else he will hold to the one, and despise the other. Ye cannot serve God and mammon. (Matthew 16: 24.)

And I say unto you, Make to yourselves friends of the mammon of unrighteousness; that, when ye fail, they may receive you into everlasting habitations.

He that is faithful in that which is least is faithful also in much: and he that is unjust in the least is unjust also in much.

If therefore ye have not been faithful in the unrighteous mammon, who will commit to your trust the true riches?

And if ye have not been faithful in that which is another man's, who shall give you that which is your own?

No servant can serve two masters:

for either he will hate the one, and love the other; or else he will hold to the one, and despise the other. Ye cannot serve God and mammon. (Luke 16: 9-13.)

MAN.

MAN—the English generic name for the human race; also the name for the male type of the human race as opposed to the female type.

The human mind has puzzled much over the origin of mankind and the meaning of the verses in Genesis telling of the creation of the human race. For years thinkers on this subject were divided into two distinct classes—those who insisted upon a literal rendering of the Mosaic text to the effect that man was made by God from earth, into which the breath of life was breathed, and those who insisted that the passages were written in allegory and that what Moses intended to show was simply the divine hand in the development of man from the animal kingdom, a theory proved, so far as the human mind is capable of proving a theory, by the achievements and advancement of science. The warfare between these two schools of thought was bitter, those standing for the literal reading of Genesis accusing the others of atheism, infidelity, etc., and the scientists declaring their antagonists to be narrow-minded and possessed of mental visions obscured by too great devotion to their religious faith. In later years, however, a new school of thought has arisen, having among its members men whose religious goodstanding and scientific attainments could not be impugned. This school contends that there is nothing in science to nullify the Mosaic statement that man was made from earth and the breath of life breathed into him, and that likewise there is nothing in religious dogma to nullify the position that man is an evolution of the animal. They declare, on the other hand, that the evolution of man from animal is one of the surest proofs of the loving-kindness of God for His created things, that it is a part of the divine plan for the improvement of creation and the gradual drawing nearer to God of the things to which He gave life, a plan which is taught in all Scripture, and a part of which was the coming to earth of the Son of God and the shedding of the Son's blood for the redemption of the human race. All these things, this school declares, are part and parcel of God's loving and helpful regard for His creation, manifested since the beginning of things and to be manifested until the end of time. They trace it in the gradual development of all forms of life and human attainments, pointing out that man, through the God-given benefits of civilization and religious liberty, is immeasurably higher as a human being, and closer to his God as a creature made in the likeness of that God, than he was in the time of Moses, or David, or in the days when Jesus lived, or in the Middle Ages, or in the times when religious liberty was barely rearing its head under Luther and the Reformation. This improvement (or evolution), they contend, will continue to go on until the time when God in His wisdom will see fit to come again to earth in the shape of the glorified Christ, as promised to us in the Scripture by Jesus the Christ Himself.

While this school of thought takes the position that Moses' statement that man was made from dust and that the breath of life was breathed into him is allegorical, and in strict keeping with the methods of communicating such things in Moses' time, they do not take any stock in the statements of the other side that man originated in half a dozen places at once, which for a long time was a favorite argument against the truth of the Mosaic position. They declare that all evidences assemble to show that man did originate in one place, as Moses said. To prove this they offer the fact that widely-separated races have similar traditions—such as the Creation, the garden of Eden or its counterpart, the Flood or destruction of a large part of the race by a deluge, and one or two other universal traditions; the universal practice of early mankind to sacrifice to supernatural beings they called gods; the widespread diffusion of serpent worship and nature worship among aboriginal peoples; the similarity of certain customs, such as skull-squeezing for infants, tattooing and marking the flesh among peoples separated by vast distances of land and water; the indications in language that back in the past there was a common tongue

spoken by all men; and chief of all the physiological fact that all mankind has the same number of bones, muscles, organs, nerves, and functions, regardless of color, native land, or degree of culture or civilization. As has been said, this school numbers among its members men whose religious orthodoxy and scientific eminence cannot be questioned—men of all shades of faith, Baptist, Methodist, Presbyterian, Episcopalian, Roman Catholic, and Jew; doctors, historians, philologists, and naturalists—and for the most part they bitterly resent the attitudes of the other sides of the controversy.

REFERENCES.

Man's Creation and Fall.

And God said, Let us make man in our image, after our likeness: and let them have dominion over the fish of the sea, and over the fowl of the air, and over the cattle, and over all the earth, and over every creeping thing that creepeth upon the earth.

So God created man in his own image, in the image of God created he him; male and female created he them. (Genesis 1: 26, 27.)

And the Lord God formed man of the dust of the ground, and breathed into his nostrils the breath of life; and man became a living soul. (Genesis 2: 7.)

And the Lord God called unto Adam, and said unto him, Where art thou?

And he said, I heard thy voice in the garden: and I was afraid, because I was naked; and I hid myself.

And he said, Who told thee that thou wast naked? Hast thou eaten of the tree whereof I commanded thee, that thou shouldest not eat?

And the man said, The woman whom thou gavest to be with me, she gave me of the tree, and I did eat. (Genesis 3: 9-12.)

And the Lord God said, Behold, the

man is become as one of us, to know good and evil: and now, lest he put forth his hand, and take also of the tree of life, and eat, and live for ever:

Therefore the Lord God sent him forth from the garden of Eden, to till the ground from whence he was taken.

So he drove out the man: and he placed at the east of the garden of Eden cherubim, and a flaming sword which turned every way, to keep the way of the tree of life. (Genesis 3: 22-24.)

Man's Dignity.

And God blessed them, and God said unto them, Be fruitful, and multiply, and replenish the earth, and subdue it: and have dominion over the fish of the sea, and over the fowl of the air, and over every living thing that moveth upon the earth.

And God said, Behold, I have given you every herb bearing seed, which is upon the face of all the earth, and every tree, in the which is the fruit of a tree yielding seed; to you it shall be for meat.

And to every beast of the earth, and to every fowl of the air, and to every thing that creepeth upon the earth, wherein there is life, I have given every green herb for meat: and it was so. (Genesis 1: 28-30.)

Man's Depravity and Sin Universal.

And God saw that the wickedness of man was great in the earth, and that every imagination of the thoughts of his heart was only evil continually. (Genesis 6: 5.)

The earth also was corrupt before God; and the earth was filled with violence.

And God looked upon the earth, and, behold, it was corrupt; for all flesh had corrupted his way upon the earth. (Genesis 6: 11, 12.)

They have corrupted themselves, their spot is not the spot of his children: they are a perverse and crooked generation. (Deuteronomy 32: 5.)

Behold, he putteth no trust in his saints; yea, the heavens are not clean in his sight.

How much more abominable and filthy is man, which drinketh iniquity like water? (Job 15: 15, 16.)

The fool hath said in his heart, There is no God. They are corrupt, they have done abominable works, there is none that doeth good.

The Lord looked down from heaven upon the children of men, to see if there were any that did understand, and seek God.

They are all gone aside, they are all together become filthy: there is none that doeth good, no, not one. (Psalm 14: 1-3.)

The fool hath said in his heart, There is no God. Corrupt are they, and have done abominable iniquity: there is none that doeth good.

God looked down from heaven upon the children of men, to see if they were any that did understand, that did seek God.

Every one of them is gone back: they are altogether become filthy; there is none that doeth good, no, not one. (Psalm 53: 1-3.)

For all this they sinned still, and believed not for his wondrous works. (Psalm 78: 32.)

Most men will proclaim every one his own goodness: but a faithful man who can find? (Proverbs 20: 6.)

Who can say, I have made my heart clean, I am pure from my sin? Proverbs 20: 9.)

Behold, this have I found, saith the Preacher, counting one by one, to find out the account;

Which yet my soul seeketh, but I find not: one man among a thousand have I found; but a woman among all those have I not found.

Lo, this only have I found, that God hath made man upright; but they have sought out many inventions. (Ecclesiastes 7: 27-29.)

Because sentence against an evil work is not executed speedily, therefore the heart of the sons of men is fully set in them to do evil. (Ecclesiastes 8: 11.)

Wherefore will ye plead with me? ye all have transgressed against me, saith the Lord. (Jeremiah 2: 29.)

Yet thou sayest, Because I am innocent, surely his anger shall turn from me. Behold, I will plead with thee, because thou sayest, I have not sinned. (Jeremiah 2: 35.)

And ye have done worse than your fathers; for, behold, ye walk every one after the imagination of his evil heart, that they may not hearken unto me. (Jeremiah 16: 12.)

But those things which proceed out of the mouth come forth from the heart; and they defile the man.

For out of the heart proceed evil thoughts, murders, adulteries, fornications, thefts, false witness, blasphemies:

These are the things which defile a man: but to eat with unwashen hands defileth not a man. (Matthew 15: 18-20.)

And he said, That which cometh out of the man, that defileth the man.

For from within, out of the heart of men, proceed evil thoughts, adulteries, fornications, murders,

Thefts, covetousness, wickedness, *deceit, lasciviousness, an evil eye, blasphemy, pride, foolishness:*

All these evil things come from within, and defile the man. (Mark 7: 20-23.)

Do not think that I will accuse you to the Father: there is one that accuseth you, even Moses, in whom ye trust. (John 5: 45.)

Man's Imperfection and Weakness.

O our God, wilt thou not judge them? for we have no might against this great company that cometh against us; neither know we what to do: but our eyes are upon thee. (2 Chronicles 20: 12.)

Which of you by taking thought can add one cubit unto his stature? (Matthew 6: 27.)

So then it is not of him that willeth, nor of him that runneth, but of God that sheweth mercy. (Romans 9: 16.)

So then neither is he that planteth any thing, neither he that watereth; but God that giveth the increase. (1 Corinthians 3: 7.)

Not that we are sufficient of ourselves to think any thing as of ourselves; but our sufficiency is of God. (2 Corinthians 3: 5.)

Man Made to Suffer.

Although affliction cometh not forth of the dust, neither doth trouble spring out of the ground:

Yet man is born unto trouble, as the sparks fly upward. (Job 5: 6, 7.)

Man that is born of a woman is of few days, and full of trouble.

He cometh forth like a flower, and is cut down: he fleeth also as a shadow, and continueth not. (Job 14: 1, 2.)

Lord, make me to know mine end, and the measure of my days, what it is; that I may know how frail I am. (Psalm 39: 4.)

Confirming the souls of the disciples, and exhorting them to continue in the faith, and that we must through much tribulation enter into the kingdom of God. (Acts 14: 22.)

For we know that the whole creation groaneth and travaileth in pain together until now.

And not only they, but ourselves also, which have the firstfruits of the Spirit, even we ourselves groan within ourselves, waiting for the adoption, to wit, the redemption of our body. (Romans 8: 22, 23.)

Ignorance of Man.

For inquire, I pray thee, of the former age, and prepare thyself to the search of thy fathers:

(For we are but of yesterday, and know nothing, because our days upon earth are a shadow:)

Shall not they teach thee, and tell thee, and utter words out of their heart? (Job 8: 8-10.)

For vain man would be wise, though man be born like a wild ass's colt. (Job 11: 12.)

But where shall wisdom be found? and where is the place of understanding?

Man knoweth not the price thereof; neither is it found in the land of the living. (Job 28: 12, 13.)

There is a way that seemeth right unto a man; but the end thereof are the ways of death. (Proverbs 16: 25.)

Boast not thyself of to-morrow; for thou knowest not what a day may bring forth. (Proverbs 27: 1.)

Then I beheld all the work of God, that a man cannot find out the work that is done under the sun: because though a man labour to seek it out, yet he shall not find it; yea further; though a wise man think to know it yet shall he not be able to find it. (Ecclesiastes 8: 17.)

We grope for the wall like the blind, and we grope as if we had no eyes: we stumble at noonday as in the night; we are in desolate places as dead men. (Isaiah 59: 10.)

Where is the wise? where is the scribe? where is the disputer of this world? hath not God made foolish the wisdom of this world?

For after that in the wisdom of God the world by wisdom knew not God, it pleased God by the foolishness of preaching to save them that believe. (1 Corinthians 1: 20, 21.)

And if any man think that he knoweth any thing, he knoweth nothing yet as he ought to know. (1 Corinthians 8: 2.)

Whereas ye know not what shall be on the morrow. For what is your life? It is even a vapour, that appeareth for a little time, and then vanisheth away. (James 4: 14.)

Mortality of Man.

Yet ye shall be brought to the grave, and shall remain in the tomb.

The clods of the valley shall be sweet unto him, and every man shall draw after him, as there are innumerable before him. (Job 21: 32, 33.)

All they that be fat upon earth shall eat and worship: all they that go down to the dust shall bow before him: and none can keep alive his own soul. (Psalm 22: 29.)

What man is he that liveth, and shall not see death? shall he deliver his soul from the hand of the grave? Selah. (Psalm 79: 48.)

One generation passeth away, and another generation cometh: but the earth abideth for ever. (Ecclesiastes 1: 4.)

I considered all the living which walk under the sun, with the second child that shall stand up in his stead. (Ecclesiastes 4: 15.)

Yea, though he live a thousand years twice told, yet hath he seen no good: do not all go to one place? (Ecclesiastes 6: 6.)

There is no man that hath power over the spirit to retain the spirit; neither hath he power in the day of death: and there is no discharge in that war; neither shall wickedness deliver those that are given to it. (Ecclesiastes 8: 8.)

Your fathers, where are they? and the prophets, do they live for ever? (Zechariah 1: 5.)

And they truly were many priests, because they were not suffered to continue by reason of death. (Hebrews 7: 23.)

Vanity of Man's Life.

Like sheep they are laid in the grave; death shall feed on them; and the upright shall have dominion over them in the morning; and their beauty shall consume in the grave from their dwelling. (Psalm 49: 14.)

Vanity of vanities, saith the Preacher, vanity of vanities; all is vanity.

What profit hath a man of all his labour which he taketh under the sun?

One generation passeth away, and another generation cometh: but the earth abideth for ever. (Ecclesiastes 1: 2-4.)

Man's Duty.

Let us hear the conclusion of the whole matter: Fear God, and keep his commandments: for this is the whole duty of man. (Ecclesiastes 12: 13.)

He hath shewed thee, O man, what is good; and what doth the Lord require of thee, but to do justly, and to love mercy, and to walk humbly with thy God? (Micah 6: 8.)

And this is his commandment, That we should believe on the name of his Son Jesus Christ, and love one another, as he gave us commandment. (1 John 3: 23.)

Man's Redemption.

But God commendeth his love toward us, in that, while we were yet sinners, Christ died for us.

Much more then, being now justified by his blood, we shall be saved from wrath through him.

For if, when we were enemies, we were reconciled to God by the death of his Son, much more, being reconciled, we shall be saved by his life.

And not only so, but we also joy in God through our Lord Jesus Christ, by whom we have now received the atonement.

Wherefore, as by one man sin entered into the world, and death by sin; and so death passed upon all men, for that all have sinned:

(For until the law sin was in the world: but sin is not imputed when there is no law.

Nevertheless death reigned from Adam to Moses, even over them that had not sinned after the similitude of Adam's transgression, who is the figure of him that was to come.

But not as the offence, so also is the free gift. For if through the offence of one many be dead, much more the grace of God, and the gift by grace, which is by one man, Jesus Christ, hath abounded unto many.

And not as it was by one that sinned,

so is the gift: for the judgment was by one to condemnation, but the free gift is of many offences unto justification.

For if by one man's offence death reigned by one; much more they which receive abundance of grace and of the gift of righteousness shall reign in life by one, Jesus Christ.)

Therefore as by the offence of one judgment came upon all men to condemnation; even so by the righteousness of one the free gift came upon all men unto justification of life.

For as by one man's disobedience many were made sinners, so by the obedience of one shall many be made righteous. (Romans 5: 8-19.)

And as we have borne the image of the earthy, we shall also bear the image of the heavenly. (1 Corinthians 15: 49.)

For our conversation is in heaven; from whence also we look for the Saviour, the Lord Jesus Christ:

Who shall change our vile body, that it may be fashioned like unto his glorious body, according to the working whereby he is able even to subdue all things unto himself. (Philippians 3: 20, 21.)

Giving thanks unto the Father, which hath made us meet to be partakers of the inheritance of the saints in light:

Who hath delivered us from the power of darkness, and hath translated us into the kingdom of his dear Son:

In whom we have redemption through his blood, even the forgiveness of sins. (Colossians 1: 12-14.)

But one in a certain place testified, saying, What is man, that thou art mindful of him? or the son of man, that thou visitest him?

Thou madest him a little lower than the angels; thou crownedst him with glory and honour, and didst set him over the works of thy hands:

Thou hast put all things in subjection under his feet. For in that he put all in subjection under him, he left nothing that is not put under him. But now we see not yet all things put under him.

But we see Jesus, who was made a little lower than the angels for the suffering of death, crowned with glory and honour; that he by the grace of God should taste death for every man.

For it became him, for whom are all things, and by whom are all things, in bringing many sons unto glory, to make the captain of their salvation perfect through sufferings.

For both he that sanctifieth and they who are sanctified are all of one: for which cause he is not ashamed to call them brethren,

Saying, I will declare thy name unto my brethren, in the midst of the church will I sing praise unto thee.

And again, I will put my trust in him. And again, Behold I and the children which God hath given me.

Forasmuch then as the children are partakers of flesh and blood, he also himself likewise took part of the same; that through death he might destroy him that had the power of death, that is, the devil;

And deliver them who through fear of death were all their lifetime subject to bondage.

For verily he took not on him the nature of angels; but he took on him the seed of Abraham.

Wherefore in all things it behoved him to be made like unto his brethren, that he might be a merciful and faithful high priest in things pertaining to

God, to make reconciliation for the sins of the people. (Hebrews 2: 6-17.)

MANNA.

MAN'NA—a form of a Hebrew word or word-phrase meaning "what is it?" Manna was the name given to the food miraculously supplied by God to the Israelites during their forty years of wandering in the desert. When they beheld it they uttered the word-phrase which eventually became its name. It was like no other thing in the way of food they had seen, nor was its strange falling from Heaven with the dew likely to lead them to any natural explanation of its presence. Botanists, naturalists, and scientists have made many researches and efforts to identify known natural substances with the Scriptural manna, but have failed to find anything that answers the descriptions among the articles of which they have knowledge.

REFERENCES.

Then said the Lord unto Moses, Behold, I will rain bread from heaven for you; and the people shall go out and gather a certain rate every day, that I may prove them, whether they will walk in my law, or no. (Exodus 16: 4.)

And when the dew that lay was gone up, behold, upon the face of the wilderness there lay a small round thing, as small as the hoar frost on the ground.

And when the children of Israel saw it, they said one to another, It is manna: for they wist not what it was. And Moses said unto them, This is the bread which the Lord hath given you to eat. (Exodus 16: 14, 15.)

And Moses said, Let no man leave of it till the morning.

Notwithstanding they hearkened not unto Moses; but some of them left of it until the morning, and it bred worms, and stank: and Moses was wroth with them.

And they gathered it every morning, every man according to his eating: and when the sun waxed hot, it melted. (Exodus 16: 19-21.)

And the house of Israel called the name thereof Manna: and it was like coriander seed, white; and the taste of it was like wafers made with honey. (Exodus 16: 31.)

And the children of Israel did eat manna forty years, until they came to a land inhabited: they did eat manna, until they came unto the borders of the land of Canaan. (Exodus 16: 35.)

But now our soul is dried away: there is nothing at all, besides this manna, before our eyes.

And the manna was as coriander seed, and the colour thereof as the colour of bdellium.

And the people went about, and gathered it, and ground it in mills, or beat it in a mortar, and baked it in pans, and made cakes of it: and the taste of it was as the taste of fresh oil.

And when the dew fell upon the camp in the night, the manna fell upon it. (Numbers 11: 6-9.)

And the manna ceased on the morrow after they had eaten of the old corn of the land: neither had the children of Israel manna any more; but they did eat of the fruit of the land of Canaan that year. (Joshua 5: 12.)

And he humbled thee, and suffered thee to hunger, and fed thee with manna, which thou knewest not, neither did thy fathers know; that he might make thee know that man doth not live by bread only, but by every word that proceedeth out of the mouth of the Lord doth man live. (Deuteronomy 8: 3.)

Who fed thee in the wilderness with manna, which thy fathers knew not, that he might humble thee, and that he might prove thee, to do thee good at thy latter end. (Deuteronomy 8: 16.)

Thou gavest also thy good Spirit to instruct them, and withheldest not thy manna from their mouth, and gavest them water for their thirst. (Nehemiah 9: 20.)

Though he had commanded the clouds from above, and opened the doors of heaven,

And had rained down manna upon them to eat, and had given them of the corn of heaven.

Man did eat angels' food: he sent them meat to the full. (Psalm 78: 23-25.)

Our fathers did eat manna in the desert; as it is written, He gave them bread from heaven to eat. (John 6: 31.)

MARK.

MARK—an Englished form of the Latin proper name Marcus, meaning "a hammer" or "sprung from Mars." Mark is the name by which we know one of the evangelists or gospel writers, whose surname was John. In the Acts he is simply called John or Mark. He is supposed to have been an early convert from Judaism and to have lived in Jerusalem, where his mother, whose name was Mary, had a house where the apostles were accustomed to assemble. There is some evidence also that he was a relative—possibly a cousin—of Barnabas. He seems to have accompanied Paul on his first missionary journey and then to have left the great apostle because of some disagreement. Later they were reconciled, and Mark accompanied Paul to Rome and shared the apostle's first and second captivity there. There is also some evidence to the effect that Mark was a companion and interpreter to Peter for a time. Thus it appears that Mark was a good servant of the early Church. His gospel is believed to have been written through or by reason of his association with Peter. It is a narrative of the Saviour's actions, rather than of His discourses.

MARRIAGE.

MAR'RIAGE—the legal union for life of a man and a woman; matrimony; wedlock. Of the divine institution of marriage there can be no question. Eve was made as a helpmeet for Adam, the first man, and the whole description of the mating of the pair in Eden is of a type calculated to convey an exalted idea of the relation. Further on, from the lips of the Master Himself we have the divine approval of marriage and sundry statements that show the attitude of divinity toward it. Unquestionably, God's intention in creating the marriage bond was that there should be one wife to one husband and *vice versa;* in other words, that marriages should be monogamous and not polygamous; that nothing should sever the relationship except death or the adultery of one or the other of the parties. These points are covered by the facts that only one wife was made for Adam and the statements of Jesus, who said that man might not put away his wife save for the one cause as well as "What therefore God hath joined together let not man put asunder." The divine attitude is perfectly clear and perfectly intelligible to mankind, absolutely nothing being left to inference, guesswork, or construction.

From the earliest times, however, the institution of marriage has been distorted by mankind to suit his convenience. "Putting away" or divorce has been practiced at the will of both man and woman, while polygamy is found among all peoples and in all times. In latter days open polygamy has been generally regarded as unlawful, although for many years it was practiced by the Mormons, and is still practiced, although in secret. The great modern evil connected with the bond of marriage is divorce. In recent years there has been a headlong tendency among almost all classes toward divorce, the courts recognizing very many causes for legal separation over and above the one cause mentioned by Jesus. So widespread has the evil become that it has grown into a menace to society, threatening to overturn moral standards that are vital to the existence of the human race. Within the last few years the clergy of the various denominations have more or less gotten together to break up the custom of marrying divorced persons, knowing that since remarriage is usually the thing sought after in divorce cases to refuse to perform the marriage ceremony in such cases would be striking at the root of the evil.

REFERENCES.

Marriage Instituted by God.

And the Lord God said, It is not good that the man should be alone: I will make him a help meet for him.

And out of the ground the Lord God formed every beast of the field, and every fowl of the air; and brought them unto Adam to see what he would call them: and whatsoever Adam called every living creature, that was the name thereof:

And Adam gave names to all cattle, and to the fowl of the air, and to every beast of the field: but for Adam there was not found a help meet for him.

And the Lord God caused a deep sleep to fall upon Adam, and he slept; and he took one of his ribs, and closed up the flesh instead thereof.

And the rib, which the Lord God had taken from man, made he a woman, and brought her unto the man.

And Adam said, This is now bone of my bones, and flesh of my flesh: she shall be called Woman, because she was taken out of man.

Therefore shall a man leave his father and his mother, and shall cleave unto his wife: and they shall be one flesh. (Genesis 2: 18-24.)

Marriage Approved and Discussed by Christ.

The Pharisees also came unto him, tempting him, and saying unto him, Is it lawful for a man to put away his wife for every cause?

And he answered and said unto them, *Have ye not read that he which*

made them at the beginning made them male and female,

And said, For this cause shall a man leave father and mother, and shall cleave to his wife: and they twain shall be one flesh?

Wherefore they are no more twain, but one flesh. What therefore God hath joined together, let not man put asunder.

They say unto him, Why did Moses then command to give a writing of divorcement, and to put her away?

He saith unto them, *Moses because of the hardness of your hearts suffered you to put away your wives: but from the beginning it was not so.*

And I say unto you, Whosoever shall put away his wife, except it be for fornication, and shall marry another, committeth adultery: and whoso marrieth her which is put away doth commit adultery. (Matthew 19: 3-9.)

And the Pharisees came to him, and asked him, Is it lawful for a man to put away his wife? tempting him.

And he answered and said unto them, *What did Moses command you?*

And they said, Moses suffered to write a bill of divorcement, and to put her away.

And Jesus answered and said unto them, *For the hardness of your heart he wrote you this precept.*

But from the beginning of the creation God made them male and female.

For this cause shall a man leave his father and mother, and cleave to his wife;

And they twain shall be one flesh: so then they are no more twain, but one flesh.

What therefore God hath joined together, let not man put asunder.

And in the house his disciples asked him again of the same matter.

And he saith unto them, *Whosoever shall put away his wife, and marry another, committeth adultery against her.*

And if a woman shall put away her husband, and be married to another, she committeth adultery.   Mark 10: 2-12.)

The same day came to him the Sadducees, which say that there is no resurrection, and asked him,

Saying, Master, Moses said, If a man die, having no children, his brother shall marry his wife, and raise up seed unto his brother.

Now there were with us seven brethren: and the first, when he had married a wife, deceased, and, having no issue, left his wife unto his brother:

Likewise the second also, and the third, unto the seventh.

And last of all the woman died also.

Therefore in the resurrection whose wife shall she be of the seven? for they all had her.

Jesus answered and said unto them, *Ye do err, not knowing the scriptures, nor the power of God.*

For in the resurrection they neither marry, nor are given in marriage, but are as the angels of God in heaven. (Matthew 22: 23-30.)

Obligations of Marriage.

For the woman which hath an husband, is bound by the law to her husband, so long as he liveth: but if the husband be dead, she is loosed from the law of the husband.

So then if, while her husband liveth, she be married to another man, she shall be called an adulteress: but if her husband be dead, she is free from that law, so that she is no adulteress, though she be married to another man. (Romans 7: 2, 3.)

And unto the married I command, yet not I, but the Lord, Let not the wife depart from her husband:

But and if she depart, let her remain unmarried, or be reconciled to her husband: and let not the husband put away his wife.

But to the rest speak I, not the Lord, If any brother hath a wife that believeth not, and she be pleased to dwell with him, let him not put her away.

And the woman which hath an husband that believeth not, and if he be pleased to dwell with her, let her not leave him.

For the unbelieving husband is sanctified by the wife, and the unbelieving wife is sanctified by the husband; else were your children unclean, but now are they holy.

But if the unbelieving depart, let him depart. A brother or a sister is not under bondage in such cases: but God hath called us to peace.

For what knowest thou, O wife, whether thou shalt save thy husband? or how knowest thou, O man, whether thou shalt save thy wife? (1 Corinthians 7: 10-16.)

Wives, submit yourselves unto your own husbands, as unto the Lord.

For the husband is the head of the wife, even as Christ is the head of the Church: and he is the saviour of the body.

Therefore as the Church is subject unto Christ, so let the wives be to their own husbands in every thing.

Husbands, love your wives, even as Christ also loved the Church, and gave himself for it:

That he might sanctify and cleanse

it with the washing of water, by the word,

That he might present it to himself a glorious Church, not having spot or wrinkle, or any such thing: but that it should be holy and without blemish.

So ought men to love their wives, as their own bodies: he that loveth his wife, loveth himself.

For no man ever yet hated his own flesh: but nourisheth and cherisheth it, even as the Lord the Church:

For we are members of his body, of his flesh, and of his bones.

For this cause shall a man leave his father and mother, and shall be joined unto his wife, and they two shall be one flesh.

This is a great mystery: but I speak concerning Christ and the Church.

Nevertheless, let every one of you in particular, so love his wife even as himself, and the wife see that she reverence her husband. (Ephesians 5: 22-33.)

Marriage Honorable.

Marriage is honourable in all, and the bed undefiled: but whoremongers and adulterers God will judge. (Hebrews 13: 4.)

MARTHA.

MAR'THA—a form of a Hebrew word of somewhat obscure sense—probably meaning "a lady." Martha is the name of quite a well-known character of the New Testament, the sister of Lazarus and Mary of Bethany. She appears as the bustling, energetic housewife, who, when visited by the Master, gave her whole attention to his entertainment as a guest worthy of the best her house afforded, forgetting all of His spiritual greatness and the good His teaching could do her. This was in notable opposition to the acts of her sister, Mary, who eagerly listened to every word the Master uttered. Later, at the raising of Laza-

rus, she failed to grasp the spiritual and mystic significance of Jesus' words, and suffered rebuke which brought from her full confession of faith in Him. The character is one of the most interesting in Scripture.

References.—Luke 10: 38; John 11: 5, 21.

MARY.

MA'RY—the English form of a Hebrew proper name meaning "rebellion." The name Mary is found applied to six different women mentioned in the New Testament, as follows: (1) Mary, the mother of Jesus; (2) Mary Magdalene; (3) Mary, the sister of Lazarus and Martha; (4) Mary, the sister of the Lord's mother and wife to Cleophas or Alphæus; (5) Mary, the mother of John, surnamed Mark; (6) Mary, a Christian woman of Rome, mentioned by Paul.

1. Mary, the mother of Jesus, was of the line of David, blood that was accounted the best in all Israel. Of her early life we know little, the first event of her history of which we have any knowledge being what is known to sacred writers as the Annunciation—that is, the notification to her by the angel Gabriel that she was to become the mother of the Christ or Messiah, an honor that every woman of Israel craved by reason of the favor God would thus show her. She communicated the news immediately to Elisabeth, also highly favored of God through becoming the mother of John the Baptist. Mary's song of rejoicing (Luke 1: 46-55) has come down to us in the Scripture as one of the most beautiful hymns of adoration ever uttered by the human tongue. After the birth of the Lord, Mary is seen in Scripture only in glimpses. They are: Offerings in the temple according to the law of Moses (Luke 1: 22, *sq.*); her return with her husband to Nazareth (Luke 2: 39); their habit of annually visiting Jerusalem at the Feast of the Passover (verse 41); the appearance of the Magi, which seems to have occurred at one of these periodic visits (Matt. 2: 1-12); the flight of the holy family into Egypt, and their return, after the death of Herod, to Nazareth (verses 13-23); the scene which occurred on another of those periodic visits, when, after having proceeded two days' journey on her way homeward, she discovered that her son was not in the company, and,

on returning to Jerusalem, found him sitting in the temple with the doctors of the law, "both hearing them and asking them questions" (Luke 2: 42-52); her appearance and conduct at the marriage feast in Cana of Galilee (John 2: 1, sq.); her attempt in the synagogue at Capernaum to induce Jesus to desist from teaching (Matt. 2: 46, sq.); her accompanying of her son when he went up to Jerusalem immediately before his crucifixion; her following him to Calvary; her being consigned by him while hanging on the cross to the care of his beloved apostle John, who from that time took her to reside in his house (John 9: 25, sq.); and her associating with the disciples at Jerusalem after his ascension (Acts 1: 14). We have no exact knowledge as to when and where she died. There are traditions that she lived in Ephesus in the household of John, "the beloved disciple," and that she died there about A.D. 63. Her character, as the Bible gives it to us, was that of the most tender, patient, faithful, devout, loving, and humble of women, immeasurably thankful for the blessedness bestowed upon her.

2. Mary Magdalene has been very much wronged by commentators and the world in general as having been supposed to have been a woman of depraved character. Even in modern times the word "Magdalene" is synonymous with fallen womanhood. Mary Magdalene unquestionably got her second name from Magdala, the Galilean town from which she came, and not from any taint of evil. On the other hand, we find that she must have been of good family since she was the companion of persons attached to Herod's court, while her physical wretchedness is shown in the fact that she had been possessed of "seven devils" and that after they had gone out of her she, with other devout women, ministered to Jesus. In the Master's last hours and at His Resurrection she was an important witness, and she was, in fact, the first to whom the risen Saviour showed Himself. Thus were her sublime faith and devotion rewarded. We know nothing of her later life or her death.

3. Mary, the sister of Lazarus and Martha, was a woman of a very high spiritual type, a fact which is shown in a study of her actions in the presence of the Lord and a comparison of them with those of her sister Martha (see article on Martha). She showed her love and veneration and her understanding of the mystical nature of Jesus' life and mission and approaching death by anointing His feet with costly ointment. Her station seems to have been always at the feet of the Master. We know nothing of her after life or her death.

4. Mary, the wife of Cleophas or Alphæus, seems to have been the sister of the Lord's mother. The fact that two sisters bore the same given name is not strange, since such things often occurred in the time of Jesus. The circumstance, however, has given rise to many misunderstandings and puzzles in the minds of modern readers unfamiliar with the customs of the time. This Mary was one of the holy women who were witnesses of the Master's last hours and His Resurrection.

5. Mary, the mother of John, surnamed Mark, appears to have been a good and devout woman, who was a sister to Barnabas. We know little of her save that the apostles were accustomed to assemble at her home.

6. The Mary of whom Paul speaks in Romans 16: 6 was a Roman woman, doubtless a convert. We know little of her, save that she treated the apostle with kindness—which seems to be the reason why he mentioned her name.

MASTER.

MAS′TER. This word is used in a number of different senses in the Bible, chief among which are (1) owner; (2) lord; (3) chief; (4) instructor; (5) head of a household.

REFERENCES.

Duties of Masters.

But the seventh day is the sabbath of the Lord thy God: in it thou shalt not do any work, thou, nor thy son, nor thy daughter, thy manservant, nor thy maidservant, nor thy cattle, nor thy stranger that is within thy gates. (Exodus 20: 10.)

Thou shalt not defraud thy neighbour, neither rob him: the wages of him that is hired shall not abide with thee all night until the morning. (Leviticus 19: 13.)

Thou shalt not oppress a hired servant that is poor and needy, whether he be of thy brethren, or of thy strangers that are in thy land within thy gates:

At his day thou shalt give him his hire, neither shall the sun go down upon it; for he is poor, and setteth his heart upon it: lest he cry against thee unto the Lord, and it be sin unto thee. (Deuteronomy 24: 14, 15.)

If I did despise the cause of my manservant or of my maidservant, when they contended with me;

What then shall I do when God riseth up? and when he visiteth, what shall I answer him? (Job 31: 13, 14.)

Woe unto him that buildeth his house by unrighteousness, and his chambers by wrong; that useth his neighbour's service without wages, and giveth him not for his work. (Jeremiah 22: 13.)

And, ye masters, do the same things unto them, forbearing threatening: knowing that your Master also is in heaven; neither is there respect of persons with him. (Ephesians 6: 9.)

Masters, give unto your servants that which is just and equal; knowing that ye also have a Master in heaven. (Colossians 4: 1.)

Behold, the hire of the labourers who have reaped down your fields, which is of you kept back by fraud, crieth: and the cries of them which have reaped are entered into the ears of the Lord of Sabaoth. (James 5: 4.)

MATTHEW.

MAT'THEW—a form of a Hebrew word meaning "the gift of Jehovah." Matthew, also called Levi, is said to have been a son of Alphæus. If such is the truth then he was a relative of Jesus. He held a government position of a humble sort—a kind of deputy collector of customs. The fact that he seems to have known Jesus before he was called to be a disciple is good evidence that he was related to Jesus. Of his life after the crucifixion we have no safe knowledge. We are told by tradition that he preached especially to the Jews. The gospel bearing his name is the longest and in some respects the most complete of all the gospels.

MATTHIAS.

MAT-THI'AS—equivalent to Matthew. Matthias was one of the 70, and was chosen by lot to supply the vacancy caused by the treason and death of Judas. It is significant that this choosing by lot was done in the time intervening between Ascension and Pentecost, a period when the followers of Christ were without the leadership of the Master and without the guidance of the Holy Ghost. The choice was a legitimate procedure of human wisdom, and while on a lower level than the selection of the original Twelve and Paul was nevertheless effective and proper. He unquestionably suffered martyrdom, although the scene of his death is not known.

MEDDLERS AND MEDDLING. (See Busy-bodies.)

MEDES.

MEDES—the name of a people inhabiting a country called Media. Media lay to the eastward of Assyria and Babylonia. The people were a hardy race, full of martial spirit and vigor. They were noted for the inflexibility of their laws. They existed for a time as an independent monarchy and then were absorbed into the Persian state. Their priesthood was very learned.

MEDIATOR. (See Advocate, Christ, Jesus.)

ME'DI-A'TOR—a person who intervenes between two other persons for the purpose of effecting a reconciliation or settling a dispute or quarrel; a peacemaker. One of the offices of Jesus the Christ is to be a mediator between the offended God the Father and His earthly children. In this connection we find a number of passages in Scripture.

REFERENCES.

Jesus saith unto him, *I am the way, the truth, and the life: no man cometh unto the Father, but by me.* (John 14: 6.)

And in that day ye shall ask me nothing. Verily, verily, I say unto you, Whatsoever ye shall ask the Father in my name, he will give it you. (John 16: 23.)

At that day ye shall ask in my name: and I say not unto you, that I will pray the Father for you:

For the Father himself loveth you, because ye have loved me, and have believed that I came out from God. (John 16: 26, 27.)

And now I am no more in the world, but these are in the world, and I come to thee. Holy Father, keep through thine own name those whom thou hast given me, that they may be one, as we are. (John 17: 11.)

Neither pray I for these alone, but for them also which shall believe on me through their word. (John 17: 24.)

Who is he that condemneth? It is Christ that died, yea rather, that is risen again, who is even at the right hand of God, who also maketh intercession for us. (Romans 8: 34.)

In whom we have boldness and access with confidence by the faith of him. (Ephesians 3: 12.)

And whatsoever ye do in word or deed, do all in the name of the Lord Jesus, giving thanks to God and the Father by him. (Colossians 3: 17.)

Wherefore he is able also to save them to the uttermost that come unto God by him, seeing he ever liveth to make intercession for them. (Hebrews 7: 25.)

And for this cause he is the mediator of the new testament, that by means of death, for the redemption of the transgressions that were under the first testament, they which are called might receive the promise of eternal inheritance. (Hebrews 9: 15.)

For Christ is not entered into the holy places made with hands, which are the figures of the true; but into heaven itself, now to appear in the presence of God for us. (Hebrews 9: 24.)

And to Jesus the mediator of the new covenant, and to the blood of sprinkling, that speaketh better things than that of Abel. (Hebrews 12: 24.)

My little children, these things write I unto you, that ye sin not. And if any man sin, we have an advocate with the Father, Jesus Christ the righteous. (1 John 2: 1.)

MEDITATION.

MED'I-TA'TION—the act of giving a subject close and profound consideration and study; used especially with reference to thought upon religious affairs or subjects connected with the welfare of the soul. The Bible suggests the wisdom and benefits of meditation. Wisdom and spirituality come from it, as well as the peace which a philosophical outlook upon life, its joys and griefs, realized hopes and disappointments, struggles and triumphs, can bring.

REFERENCES.

And these words which I command thee this day, shall be in thine heart. (Deuteronomy 6: 6.)

Therefore shall ye lay up these my words in your heart and in your soul, and bind them for a sign upon your hand, that they may be as frontlets between your eyes. (Deuteronomy 11: 18.)

And he said unto them, Set your hearts unto all the words which I testify among you this day, which ye shall command your children to observe to do, all the words of this law. (Deuteronomy 32: 46.)

This book of the law shall not depart out of thy mouth; but thou shalt meditate therein day and night, that thou mayest observe to do according to all that is written therein: for then thou shalt make thy way prosperous, and then thou shalt have good success. (Joshua 1: 8.)

But his delight is in the law of the Lord: and in his law doth he meditate day and night.

And he shall be like a tree planted by the rivers of water, that bringeth forth his fruit in his season; his leaf also shall not wither; and whatsoever he doeth shall prosper. (Psalm 1: 2, 3.)

I will meditate in thy precepts, and have respect unto thy ways. (Psalm 119: 15.)

Princes also did sit and speak against me: but thy servant did meditate in thy statutes. (Psalm 119: 23.)

O how love I thy law! it is my meditation all the day. (Psalm 119: 97.)

Mine eyes prevent the night watches, that I might meditate in thy word. (Psalm 119: 48.)

Meditate upon these things; give thyself wholly to them; that thy profiting may appear to all.

Take heed unto thyself, and unto the doctrine; continue in them: for in doing this thou shalt both save thyself, and them that hear thee. (1 Timothy 4: 15, 16.)

MEEKNESS. (Humility.)

MEEK'NESS—mildness of temper; a state of being not easily provoked or irritated; patience under injury; humbleness; submissiveness. Meekness is a grace the Bible assures us we should earnestly endeavor to acquire. It is not a common attribute of man, and

therefore we are taught to cultivate it, taking as our example the character of our Lord, whose meekness was one of his most distinguishing traits. Special rewards are promised those who succeed in obtaining this grace.

REFERENCES.

Christ an Example of Meekness.

Take my yoke upon you, and learn of me: for I am meek and lowly in heart: and ye shall find rest unto your souls. (Matthew 11: 29.)

Now I Paul myself beseech you by the meekness and gentleness of Christ, who in presence am base among you, but being absent am bold toward you. (2 Corinthians 10: 1.)

Exhortations to Meekness.

Seek ye the Lord, all ye meek of the earth, which have wrought his judgment; seek righteousness, seek meekness: it may be ye shall be hid in the day of the Lord's anger. (Zephaniah 2: 3.)

Meekness, temperance: against such there is no law. (Galatians 5: 23.)

Brethren, if a man be overtaken in a fault, ye which are spiritual, restore such a one in the spirit of meekness, considering thyself lest thou also be tempted. (Galatians 6: 1.)

I therefore, the prisoner of the Lord, beseech you that ye walk worthy of the vocation wherewith ye are called,

With all lowliness and meekness, with longsuffering, forbearing one another in love. (Ephesians 4: 1, 2.)

Put on therefore, as the elect of God, holy and beloved, bowels of mercies, kindness, humbleness of mind, meekness, longsuffering. (Colossians 3: 12.)

But thou, O man of God, flee these things; and follow after righteousness, godliness, faith, love, patience, meekness. (1 Timothy 6: 11.)

And the servant of the Lord must not strive: but be gentle unto all men, apt to teach, patient,

In meekness instructing those that oppose themselves, if God peradventure will give them repentance to the acknowledging of the truth.

And that they may recover themselves out of the snare of the devil, who are taken captive by him at his will. (2 Timothy 2: 24-26.)

To speak evil of no man, to be no brawlers, but gentle, shewing all meekness unto all men. (Titus 3: 2.)

Wherefore lay apart all filthiness, and superfluity of naughtiness, and receive with meekness the engrafted word, which is able to save your souls. (James 1: 21.)

Who is a wise man and endued with knowledge amongst you? let him shew out of a good conversation his works with meekness of wisdom. (James 3: 13.)

But let it be the hidden man of the heart, in that which is not corruptible, even the ornament of a meek and quiet spirit, which is in the sight of God of great price. (1 Peter 3: 4.)

But sanctify the Lord God in your hearts, and be ready always to give an answer to every man that asketh you a reason of the hope that is in you, with meekness and fear. (1 Peter 3: 15.)

Meekness Blessed by God.

The meek shall eat and be satisfied: they shall praise the Lord that seek him: your heart shall live for ever. (Psalm 22: 26.)

The meek will he guide in judgment: and the meek will he teach his way. (Psalm 25: 9.)

But the meek shall inherit the earth; and shall delight themselves in the abundance of peace. (Psalm 37: 11.)

The humble shall see this, and be glad: and your heart shall live that seek God. (Psalm 69: 32.)

Thou didst cause judgment to be heard from heaven; the earth feared and was still,

When God arose to judgment, to save all the meek of the earth. Selah. (Psalm 76: 8, 9.)

The Lord lifteth up the meek: he casteth the wicked down to the ground. (Psalm 47: 6.)

But with righteousness shall he judge the poor, and reprove with equity for the meek of the earth: and he shall smite the earth with the rod of his mouth, and with the breath of his lips shall he slay the wicked. (Isaiah 11: 4.)

The meek also shall increase their joy in the Lord, and the poor among men shall rejoice in the Holy One of Israel. (Isaiah 29: 19.)

The Spirit of the Lord God is upon me, because the Lord hath anointed me to preach good tidings unto the meek; he hath sent me to bind up the brokenhearted, to proclaim liberty to the captives, and the opening of the prison to them that are bound. (Isaiah 61: 1 and Luke 4: 18.)

Blessed are the meek: for they shall inherit the earth. (Matthew 5: 5.)

MELCHIZEDEK.

MEL-CHIZ'E-DEK—a form of a Hebrew word meaning "king of righteousness." Melchizedek was the name of a priest-king of Jerusalem who lived in the time of Abraham. He was a worshiper of Jehovah, although where he received the faith we have no means of knowing, since the whole region round about Jerusalem, and in fact the whole of

Palestine at this period, was given over to idolatry. Abraham recognized Melchizedek's kingly and priestly dignity by paying tithes to him, while of Melchizedek himself it is written that he gave Abraham his blessing and refreshments of bread and wine for himself and his hungry followers. Writers and commentators for many generations have recognized in this ancient priest and king a type of the Christ, and still others have seen in the bread and wine sacrificial and sacramental meaning. A few have seen fit to think Melchizedek was an earthly appearance of Christ. We can be content, however, with believing Melchizedek to have been the forerunning type of the Master. The orthodox Jews, who refused to receive Jesus as the Christ, were inclined to cavil at his priesthood because He did not fulfill the strict letter of the Levirate law, so far as they could see. Paul, whose vision on this subject was not obscured by Pharisaism or Sadduceeism, pointed out very clearly that the "order of Melchizedek" was of a higher type of priesthood than the Levirate, and that Abraham, the patriarchal ancestor to whom they loved to point, had recognized the superiority by paying tribute of tithes and homage to the Jerusalem priest-king, and that this fact in itself should make the Jews understand that there was a higher priesthood than the Aaronic and Levirate. Paul's effort to make the Jews see in Christ a priest "of the order of Melchizedek" was almost fruitless.

REFERENCES.

Melchizedek Blesses Abraham.

And Melchizedek king of Salem brought forth bread and wine: and he was the priest of the most high God.

And he blessed him, and said, Blessed be Abram of the most high God, possessor of heaven and earth:

And blessed be the most high God, which hath delivered thine enemies into thy hand. And he gave him tithes of all. (Genesis 14: 18-20.)

The Two Orders Compared.

The Lord hath sworn, and will not repent, Thou art a priest for ever after the order of Melchizedek. (Psalm 110: 4.)

And no man taketh this honour unto himself, but he that is called of God, as was Aaron.

So also, Christ glorified not himself, to be made an High Priest: but he that said unto him, Thou art my Son, to day have I begotten thee.

As he saith also in another place, Thou art a Priest for ever after the order of Melchisedec.

Who in the days of his flesh, when he had offered up prayers and supplications, with strong crying and tears, unto him that was able to save him from death, and was heard, in that he feared.

Though he were a Son, yet learned he obedience by the things which he suffered:

And being made perfect, he became the author of eternal salvation unto all them that obey him,

Called of God an high Priest after the order of Melchisedec:

Of whom we have many things to say, and hard to be uttered, seeing ye are dull of hearing. (Hebrews 5: 4-11.)

For when God made promise to Abraham, because he could swear by no greater, he sware by himself,

Saying, Surely, blessing I will bless thee, and multiplying I will multiply thee.

And so after he had patiently endured, he obtained the promise.

For men verily swear by the greater, and an oath for confirmation is to them an end of all strife.

Wherein God willing more abundantly to shew unto the heirs of promise the immutability of his counsel, confirmed it by an oath:

That by two immutable things, in

which it was impossible for God to lie, we might have a strong consolation, who have fled for refuge to lay hold upon the hope set before us.

Which hope we have as an anchor of the soul both sure and stedfast, and which entereth into that within the veil,

Whither the forerunner is for us entered; even Jesus, made an high Priest for ever after the order of Melchisedec. (Hebrews 6: 13-20.)

For this Melchisedec, king of Salem, priest of the most high God, who met Abraham returning from the slaughter of the kings, and blessed him;

To whom also Abraham gave a tenth part of all; first being by interpretation King of righteousness, and after that also King of Salem, which is, King of peace;

Without father, without mother, without descent, having neither beginning of days, nor end of life; but made like unto the Son of God; abideth a priest continually. (Hebrews 7: 1-3.)

MELITA.

MEL'I-TA—the ancient name of the modern island of Malta, upon the coast of which Paul was shipwrecked while on his way to Rome. A bay on the north side of the island is pointed out as the scene of the shipwreck and is called by the name of the apostle. The island was colonized by the Phœnicians as early as the year 1000 B.C.

MENE.

ME'NE—the first word of the phrase supernaturally written on the wall at the feast of Belshazzar and translated by Daniel. The phrase was "Mene, mene, tekel, upharsin." Literally translated the words mean, "He is numbered, he is numbered, they are divided." The words are pure Chaldee, and as such they easily could have been read by the Babylonian king and his scribes or learned men. It is therefore to be supposed that they were writ-

ten in some other character than Chaldee, since Daniel was the only man who could translate them. This is the view taken by most commentators, and they add that the character was probably the very ancient Hebrew of the time of Moses, a text with which Daniel unquestionably was familiar.

Reference.—Daniel 5: 25-28.

MERCY. (See Compassion, Pity, etc.)

MER'CY—affectionate pity to those who are needy, distressed, or suffering, either in mind or body or estate; kindness or compassion to those who are in need of them; a high type of benevolence. Mercy is one of the striking attributes of God. The Scriptures point out the elevating quality of this grace when possessed by man, and advise mankind to cultivate it. Special rewards are promised to those who are truly merciful. Mercy to a fallen foe has been regarded in all ages as one of the surest indications of nobility of character, approaching the godlike in the character of its exaltation.

REFERENCES.

Mercy of God.

But he, being full of compassion, forgave their iniquity, and destroyed them not: yea, many a time turned he his anger away, and did not stir up all his wrath. (Psalm 78: 38.)

The Lord is merciful and gracious, slow to anger, and plenteous in mercy. (Psalm 103: 8.)

And therefore will the Lord wait, that he may be gracious unto you, and therefore will he be exalted, that he may have mercy upon you: for the Lord is a God of judgment: blessed are all they that wait for him. (Isaiah 30: 18.)

Let the wicked forsake his way, and the unrighteous man his thoughts: and let him return unto the Lord, and he will have mercy upon him; and to our God, for he will abundantly pardon. (Isaiah 54: 7.)

But though he cause grief, yet will he have compassion according to the multitude of his mercies.

For he doth not afflict willingly, nor grieve the children of men. (Lamentations 3: 32, 33.)

Supplication for Mercy.

Be merciful, O Lord, unto thy people Israel, whom thou hast redeemed, and lay not innocent blood unto thy people of Israel's charge. And the blood shall be forgiven them. (Deuteronomy 21: 8.)

And hearken thou to the supplication of thy servant, and of thy people Israel, when they shall pray toward this place: and hear thou in heaven thy dwelling-place: and when thou hearest, forgive. (1 Kings 8: 30.)

Now therefore, our God, the great, the mighty, and the terrible God, who keepest covenant and mercy, let not all the trouble seem little before thee, that hath come upon us, on our kings, on our princes, and on our priests, and on our prophets, and on our fathers, and on all thy people, since the time of the kings of Assyria unto this day. (Nehemiah 9: 32.)

Have mercy upon me, O God, according to thy loving-kindness: according unto the multitude of thy tender mercies blot out my transgressions. (Psalm 51: 1.)

O Lord, according to all thy righteousness, I beseech thee, let thine anger and thy fury be turned away from thy city Jerusalem, thy holy mountain: because for our sins, and for the iniquities of our fathers, Jerusalem and thy people are become a reproach to all that are about us. (Daniel 9: 16.)

O Lord, I have heard thy speech and was afraid: O Lord, revive thy work in the midst of the years, in the midst of the years make known; in wrath remember mercy. (Habakkuk 3: 2.)

Mercy Commanded.

Let not mercy and truth forsake thee: bind them about thy neck; write them upon the table of thine heart:

So shalt thou find favour and good understanding in the sight of God and man. (Proverbs 3: 3, 4.)

Thus speaketh the Lord of hosts, saying, Execute true judgment, and shew mercy and compassions every man to his brother:

And oppress not the widow, nor the fatherless, the stranger, nor the poor; and let none of you imagine evil against his brother in your heart. (Zechariah 7: 9, 10.)

Be ye therefore merciful, as your Father also is merciful. (Luke 6: 36.)

Dearly beloved, avenge not yourselves, but rather give place unto wrath: for it is written, Vengeance is mine, I will repay, saith the Lord.

Therefore if thine enemy hunger, feed him: if he thirst, give him drink. For in so doing thou shalt heap coals of fire on his head.

Be not overcome of evil, but overcome evil with good. (Romans 12: 19-21.)

If there be therefore any consolation in Christ, if any comfort of love, if any fellowship of the Spirit, if any bowels and mercies. (Philippians 2: 1.)

For he shall have judgment without mercy, that hath shewed no mercy, and mercy rejoiceth against judgment. (James 2: 13.)

The Merciful Are Blessed.

The merciful man doeth good to his own soul; but he that is cruel troubleth his own flesh. (Proverbs 11: 17.)

Blessed are the merciful: for they shall obtain mercy. (Matthew 5: 7.)

MESHACH. (See Abednego, Shadrach.)

ME'SHACH—a form of a Chaldee word meaning "ram." Meshach was the Babylonian name given to one of the three Hebrew princes cast into the fiery furnace by Nebuchadnezzar and miraculously saved from harm.

Reference.—Daniel 1 and 3.

MESOPOTAMIA.

MES'O-PO-TA'MI-A—a form of a Greek word meaning "the country between the two rivers." Mesopotamia is one of the most celebrated lands of the whole earth. It is that stretch of country between the rivers Tigris and Euphrates in Southwestern Asia. It is about 700 miles long. In the Bible it is largely known by the name Aram-Naharaim, Mesopotamia being the name given to it after the conquest of it by Alexander the Great. It included Assyria and a large part of Babylonia. It unquestionably was the Ur of the Chaldees, known to Abraham.

MESSIAH. (See Christ.)

MES-SI'AH—a form of a Hebrew word meaning "the anointed one." The early Jews seem to have applied the term somewhat indiscriminately at first to the kingly as well as to the priestly dignity, since both were anointed as a symbol of their office. Later it came to be regarded as the name of the earthly manifestation of God the Jews expected. They insisted that the Messiah would be an earthly prince of great military strength and believed he would set them free from the yoke of other nations and either destroy the enemies of Israel or render them tributary. The coming of the Messiah as a prince of peace and gentleness they were utterly unable to comprehend and promptly rejected Him. Modern Christianity understands the Messiah as the Redeemer of man, Christ Jesus, but the Jewish theology still refuses to recognize this, their attitude being exactly the same to-day as it was when the Jewish populace of Jerusalem selected Jesus for crucifixion in preference to the robber Barabbas.

Christianity can see the old prophecies fulfilled; the Jew of the orthodox faith cannot. To the Christian eye everything promised by God has been brought about by His stupendous and adorable power; to the Jew the coming of the Messiah is still a thing of the future.

References.—See references under Christ.

METHUSELAH.

ME-THU'SE-LAH—a form of a Hebrew word meaning "man of the dart." Methuselah was the son of Enoch and remarkable as being the oldest of those antediluvian patriarchs whose great ages are recorded in Genesis 5. The figures indicate that he was 969 years old when he died.

Reference.—Genesis 5.

MICAH.

MI'CAH—a form of a Hebrew word meaning "who is like Jehovah." Micah was one of the twelve minor prophets and a contemporary with Isaiah. He lived about 725 B.C. The book bearing his name is not an individual discourse, but a sort of compilation of them in substance. Micah is specially interesting because of the fact that he foretold the name of the birthplace of the Saviour (Micah 5: 2).

Reference.—The book of Micah.

MICHAEL.

MI'CHA-EL—a form of a Hebrew word meaning "who is like God." A number of different persons bearing the name Michael appear in Scripture, but the most important of them is the angel Michael. His name is mentioned three times, the passages showing that he was deputized by God to keep special watch over the Hebrew nation, that he disputed with Satan over the body of Moses, and that he and his host warred successfully against Satan and his host when the wicked angels rebelled.

References.—Daniel 10: 13-21; Jude 1: 9; Revelation 12: 7-9.

MIDIANITES.

MID'I-AN-ITES—the name of a people supposed to have been descended from Abraham's son, Midian. They appear to have peopled northern Arabia. They gave the Israelites a great deal of trouble until overthrown by Gideon.

MILLENNIUM.

Mil-len'ni-um—a word formed from two Latin words (*mille* a thousand and *annus* a year) and meaning "a thousand years." The word especially means the thousand years, mentioned in the 20th chapter of Revelation, during which holiness is to be triumphant throughout the world and the saints living and reigning with Christ. The idea of a reign of goodness at the close of earthly things is by no means a new one. The Jews had it long before the time of Jesus, supposing that the Messiah would come to earth and reign during that time in Jerusalem, the ancient royal city of the Hebraic race. They conceived this period would be a sort of a golden age in which Judaism would be triumphant over the whole earth. Accompanying this were various other ideas of a more or less personal nature, varying with the degree of refinement and culture of the person entertaining them. With some the millennial period was conjectured to be a time of the highest sensual delights, while others of a more esthetic and spiritual nature had higher and purer conceptions. Some of these ideas, if not all, appear to have been taken up in the time of Christ, and in special relation to Him by what is known as the Judaizing Christians. The apostles themselves seem to have had somewhat similar views until after the Ascension and Pentecost, when through the Holy Ghost they were given to know something of the higher truths, and schooled to wait His second coming in His own good time, which they conceived to be at the time of the final judgment of the world.

In our own times the question of the Millennium has attracted a great deal of attention and given rise to a great deal of debate. The question was and is not whether there will be any such thing as the Millennium, but whether the Lord would come before the thousand years began and reign during them, or whether He would come at their close. Those who favored the first view were called "pre-millennialites" and those who favored the latter proposition were called "postmillennialites." Whatever the merits of either side of this debate (which is by no means closed) there are many persons entirely unconnected with it who believe the world to be very close to the opening of the millennial period. It would be futile to go into the arguments on this score, but it may be fitting to call attention to that Scripture which declares, from the lips of the Master Himself, that no man knows the day or the hour when the Son of God will come. But to show the tendency of the religious times toward better things the author feels at liberty to quote from his own work upon the subject ("The Church-member's Guide," pp. 211-213):

"The present time seems to be the golden age of religious progress. At no period in the past has there been such a vast array of consecrated men and women working for the cause of the Master. Never has there been such freedom of thought and worship as there is at this time. Never has the true missionary spirit been shown as now. Instead of one or two faiths fighting and persecuting each other there are scores earnestly working for the spread of the kingdom. There is rivalry, of course, but there is no persecution and no meting out of death to the man who does not believe as you do, or does not attend the church you attend.

"What does this indicate? If we examine history, especially history from the time of Christ, we find that great religious changes make their appearance at intervals of about 800 years. From the days of the Master to the time of Charlemagne was a period of 800 years. In it rose the Christian faith and the power of the popes was developed. In the next 800 years the power of the popes was abused and finally fell, for by the year 1600 the grip of Rome on religion had been loosed. The next period of 800 years will bring us to the year 2400. That something better than that which now exists must come is the only logical deduction, since something better has come at the end of each period in the past.

"What is it to be? No man knows; no man can tell. If we look back over the past 400 years we see vast changes on every side and in everything. If a man in the year 1507 had said that in the year 1907 men would talk by means of a wire charged with electricity over many hundreds of miles or would send messages by it, or travel in a railway train at the rate of sixty miles an hour, or cross the Atlantic Ocean in six days, he would have been put into a madhouse or a jail. And yet these things have come to pass. What, then, will the year 2407 bring?

"God alone knows, and man can but speculate and make guesses. If the human, finite mind could pierce the veil of the future man would be worse instead of better. God, in His wisdom, so has arranged things that man cannot tell for a certainty to-day what is going to happen to-morrow and He is immeasurably good to us in keeping from our knowledge what the year 2407 is to bring forth. But of this we can be sure: The world is growing better, not worse. The Church is achieving vast works for the extension of the faith and the tragedy that took place on Golgotha 1900 years ago is bearing its fruit of salvation for those who will accept it.

"So let us live, then, that whatever may come to the world in the next few centuries men may be better and nearer to God in that time. Let us always sing:

'Thy kingdom come, O God! Thy rule, O
    Christ, begin!
Break with Thine iron rod the tyrannies of
    sin.

.   .   .   .

We pray Thee, Lord, arise, and come in
    Thy great might;
Revive our longing eyes, which languish for
    Thy sight.' "

REFERENCES.

The Universal Triumph of Christianity.

All the ends of the world shall remember and turn unto the Lord: and all the kindreds of the nations shall worship before thee. (Psalm 22: 27.)

A seed shall serve him; it shall be accounted to the Lord for a generation.

They shall come, and shall declare his righteousness unto a people that shall be born, that he hath done this. (Psalm 22: 30, 31.)

And it shall come to pass in the last days, that the mountain of the Lord's house shall be established in the top of the mountains, and shall be exalted above the hills; and all nations shall flow unto it.

And many people shall go and say, Come ye, and let us go up to the mountain of the Lord, to the house of the God of Jacob; and he will teach us of his ways, and we will walk in his paths: for out of Zion shall go forth the law, and the word of the Lord from Jerusalem. (Isaiah 2: 2, 3.)

The lofty looks of man shall be humbled, and the haughtiness of men shall be bowed down; and the Lord alone shall be exalted in that day.

For the day of the Lord of hosts shall be upon every one that is proud and lofty, and upon every one that is lifted up; and he shall be brought low:

And upon all the cedars of Lebanon, that are high and lifted up, and upon all the oaks of Bashan,

And upon all the high mountains, and upon all the hills that are lifted up,

And upon every high tower, and upon every fenced wall,

And upon all the ships of Tarshish, and upon all pleasant pictures.

And the loftiness of man shall be bowed down, and the haughtiness of men shall be made low; and the Lord alone shall be exalted in that day. (Isaiah 2: 9-17.)

Universal Peace.

Come, behold the works of the Lord, what desolations he hath made in the earth.

He maketh wars to cease unto the end of the earth; he breaketh the bow, and cutteth the spear in sunder; he burneth the chariot in the fire. (Psalm 46: 8, 9.)

And he shall judge among the nations, and shall rebuke many people: and they shall beat their swords into ploughshares, and their spears into pruninghooks: nation shall not lift up sword against nation, neither shall ye learn war any more.

O house of Jacob, come ye, and let us walk in the light of the Lord. (Isaiah 2: 4, 5.)

For every battle of the warrior is with confused noise, and garments rolled in blood; but this shall be with burning and fuel of fire. (Isaiah 9: 5.)

The wolf also shall dwell with the lamb, and the leopard shall lie down with the kid; and the calf and the young lion and the fatling together; and a little child shall lead them.

And the cow and the bear shall feed; their young ones shall lie down together: and the lion shall eat straw like the ox.

And the sucking child shall play on the hole of the asp, and the weaned child shall put his hand on the cockatrice' den.

They shall not hurt nor destroy in all my holy mountain: for the earth shall be full of the knowledge of the Lord, as the waters cover the sea. (Isaiah 11: 6-9.)

The Binding and Loosing of Satan.

And I saw an angel come down from heaven, having the key of the bottomless pit and a great chain in his hand.

And he laid hold on the dragon, that old serpent, which is the Devil, and Satan, and bound him a thousand years,

And cast him into the bottomless pit, and shut him up, and set a seal upon him, that he should deceive the nations no more, till the thousand years should be fulfilled: and after that he must be loosed a little season.

And I saw thrones, and they sat upon them, and judgment was given unto them: and I saw the souls of them that were beheaded for the witness of Jesus, and for the word of God, and which had not worshipped the beast, neither his image, neither had received his mark upon their foreheads, or in their hands; and they lived and reigned with Christ a thousand years.

But the rest of the dead lived not again until the thousand years were finished. This is the first resurrection.

Blessed and holy is he that hath part in the first resurrection: on such the second death hath no power, but they shall be priests of God and of Christ, and shall reign with him a thousand years.

And when the thousand years are expired, Satan shall be loosed out of his prison,

And shall go out to deceive the nations which are in the four quarters of the earth, Gog and Magog, to gather them together to battle: the number of whom is as the sand of the sea.

And they went up on the breadth of the earth, and compassed the camp of the saints about, and the beloved city: and fire came down from God out of heaven, and devoured them.

And the devil that deceived them was cast into the lake of fire and brimstone, where the beast and the false prophet are, and shall be tormented day and night for ever and ever. (Revelation 20: 1-10.)

Christ's Second Coming.

Time Not Revealed:

But of that day and hour knoweth no man, no, not the angels of heaven, but my Father only. (Matthew 24: 36.)

Coming Will Be Sudden:

But of the times and the seasons, brethren, ye have no need that I write unto you.

For yourselves know perfectly that the day of the Lord so cometh as a thief in the night.

For when they shall say, Peace and safety; then sudden destruction cometh upon them, as travail upon a woman with child; and they shall not escape.

But ye, brethren, are not in darkness, that that day should overtake you as a thief. (1 Thessalonians 5: 1-4.)

Behold, I come as a thief. Blessed is he that watcheth, and keepeth his garments, lest he walk naked, and they see his shame. (Revelation 16: 15.)

But as the days of Noe were, so shall also the coming of the Son of man be.

For as in the days that were before the flood they were eating and drinking, marrying and giving in marriage, until the day that Noe entered into the ark,

And knew not until the flood came, and took them all away; so shall also the coming of the Son of man be. (Matthew 24: 37-39.)

And as it was in the days of Noe, so shall it be also in the days of the Son of man.

They did eat, they drank, they married wives, they were given in marriage, unitl the day that Noe entered into the ark, and the flood came, and destroyed them all.

Likewise also as it was in the days of Lot; they did eat, they drank, they bought, they sold, they planted, they builded;

But the same day that Lot went out of Sodom it rained fire and brimstone from heaven, and destroyed them all.

Even thus shall it be in the day when the Son of man is revealed. (Luke 17: 26-30.)

For as the lightning cometh out of the east, and shineth even unto the west; so shall also the coming of the Son of man be. (Matthew 24: 27.)

Certainty of His Coming:

Then Peter, turning about, seeth the disciple whom Jesus loved following; which also leaned on his breast at supper, and said, Lord, which is he that betrayeth thee?

Peter seeing him saith to Jesus, Lord, and what shall this man do?

Jesus saith unto him, *If I will that he tarry till I come, what is that to thee? follow thou me.* (John 21: 20-22.)

Coming to Be Glorious:

Whosoever therefore shall be ashamed of me and of my words, in this adulterous and sinful generation, of him also shall the Son of man be ashamed, when he cometh in the glory of his Father with the holy angels. (Mark 8: 38.)

And then shall they see the Son of man coming in the clouds with great power and glory. (Mark 13: 26.)

Holding forth the word of life; that it may rejoice in the day of Christ, that I have not run in vain, neither laboured in vain. (Philippians 2: 16.)

For our conversation is in heaven; from whence also we look for the Saviour, the Lord Jesus Christ. (Philippians 3: 20.)

For what is our hope, or joy, or crown of rejoicing? Are not even ye in the presence of our Lord Jesus Christ at his coming?

For ye are our glory and joy. (1 Thessalonians 2: 19, 20.)

Looking for that blessed hope, and the glorious appearing of the great God and our Saviour Jesus Christ. (Titus 2: 13.)

Signs of His Coming:

And there shall be signs in the sun, and in the moon, and in the stars; and upon the earth distress of nations, with perplexity; the sea and the waves roaring;

Men's hearts failing them for fear, and for looking after those things which are coming on the earth: for the powers of heaven shall be shaken.

And then shall they see the Son of man coming in a cloud with power and great glory.

And when these things begin to come to pass, then look up, and lift up your heads; for your redemption draweth nigh.

And he spake to them a parable; *Behold the fig tree, and all the trees;*

When they now shoot forth, ye see and know of your own selves that summer is now nigh at hand.

So likewise ye, when ye see these things come to pass, know ye that the kingdom of God is nigh at hand.

Verily I say unto you, This generation shall not pass away, till all be fulfilled. (Luke 21: 25-32.)

MINISTER AND MINISTRY. (See Call.)

MIN'IS-TER—one who serves; in a special sense, one who performs sacerdotal duties, or is duly authorized to act as the pastor of a church, to preach and to administer the ordinances and sacraments.

MIN'IS-TRY—the whole body of ministers or clergy; the ecclesiastical calling; the state of being a minister; the act of ministering.

The ministry is the highest of all human callings. To be a minister means to serve God in the highest manner possible to man. In the first place there must be a special spir-itual fitness in the man, and this unquestionably is the result of direct divine intervention. It has been generally given the designation of "call," by which is meant that the special spiritual fitness is God's mandate to the person possessing it to enter upon the work of guiding souls to God, to expounding and preaching the word of God and the gospel of salvation, and to carrying out the various ordinances and sacraments laid down by God. Ministers are required to be pure and holy in life, to be full of faith and righteousness, and to possess the graces and virtues which raise them up above the common type of man and bring them closer to God, from whom they receive their commission to act. Beyond these spiritual qualifications there are certain others, including knowledge of God's word and a certain amount of special education, although some denominations are willing to forego this latter qualification, and finally the consent and authorization of the sect or denomination to which they belong, such consent and authorization being given usually after a period of probationary work in a minor capacity. These are wise and proper safeguards, to which no doubt God gives full consent, for the purpose of maintaining the purity and excellence of the whole body of God's authorized servants upon earth.

With regard to the relations of the people of the Church toward the ministry we are told to honor, obey, and support them, to give heed to their exhortations, to follow the spiritual advice they give us, and to consider their dignity and office. On their part, they are told to be worthy ministers, to live uprightly and to remember that they are the chosen servants of the Master, for the upbuilding and continuance of His earthly kingdom.

REFERENCES.

General.

But we will give ourselves continually to prayer, and to the ministry of the word. (Acts 6: 4.)

But none of these things move me, neither count I my life dear unto myself, so that I might finish my course with joy, and the ministry which I have received of the Lord Jesus, to testify the Gospel of the grace of God. (Acts 20: 24.)

Having then gifts, differing according to the grace that is given to us, whether prophecy, let us prophesy according to the proportion of faith.

Or ministry, let us wait on our ministering: or he that teacheth, on teaching:

Or he that exhorteth, on exhortation: he that giveth, let him do it with simplicity: he that ruleth, with diligence: he that sheweth mercy, with cheerfulness. (Romans 12: 6-8.)

I beseech you, brethren, (ye know the house of Stephanas, that it is the firstfruits of Achaia, and that they have addicted themselves to the ministry of the Saints,)

That ye submit yourselves unto such, and to every one that helpeth with us and laboureth. (1 Corinthians 11: 15, 16.)

Wherefore holy brethren, partakers of the heavenly calling, consider the Apostle and high Priest of our profession Christ Jesus,

Who was faithful to him that appointed him, as also Moses was faithful in all his house.

For this man was counted worthy of more glory than Moses, inasmuch as he who hath builded the house hath more honour than the house.

For every house is builded by some man, but he that built all things is God.

And Moses verily was faithful in all his house as a servant, for a testimony of those things which were to be spoken after. (Hebrews 3: 1-5.)

Be not thou therefore ashamed of the testimony of our Lord, nor of me his prisoner, but be thou partaker of the afflictions of the Gospel according to the power of God,

Who hath saved us, and called us with an holy calling, not according to our works, but according to his own purpose and grace, which was given us in Christ Jesus, before the world began,

But is now made manifest by the appearing of our Saviour Jesus Christ, who hath abolished death, and hath brought life and immortality to light, through the Gospel:

Whereunto I am appointed a Preacher, and an Apostle, and a teacher of the Gentiles. (2 Thessalonians 1: 8-11.)

But ye are a chosen generation, a royal Priesthood, an holy nation, a peculiar people, that ye should shew forth the praises of him who hath called you out of darkness into his marvellous light. (1 Peter 2: 9.)

Divine Appointment.

Now therefore go, and I will be with thy mouth, and teach thee what thou shalt say.

And he said, O my Lord, send, I pray thee, by the hand of him whom thou wilt send. (Exodus 4: 12, 13.)

The Lord gave the word: great was the company of those that published it. (Psalm 68: 11.)

Paul, a servant of Jesus Christ, called to be an apostle, separated unto the gospel of God. (Romans 1: 1.)

Now he which stablisheth us with you in Christ, and hath anointed us, is God. (2 Corinthians 1: 24.)

For we are unto God a sweet savour of Christ, in them that are saved, and in them that perish:

To the one we are the savour of death unto death; and to the other the savour of life unto life. And who is sufficient for these things?

For we are not as many, which corrupt the word of God: but as of sincerity, but as of God, in the sight of God speak we in Christ. (2 Corinthians 2: 15-17.)

Do we begin again to commend ourselves? or need we, as some others, epistles of commendation to you, or letters of commendation from you? (2 Corinthians 3: 1.)

Now then we are ambassadors for Christ, as though God did beseech you by us: we pray you in Christ's stead, be ye reconciled to God. (2 Corinthians 5: 20.)

Paul, an apostle, (not of men, neither by man, but by Jesus Christ, and God the Father, who raised him from the dead.) (Galatians 1: 1.)

From henceforth let no man trouble me: for I bear in my body the marks of the Lord Jesus. (Galatians 6: 17.)

The eyes of your understanding being enlightened; that ye may know what is the hope of his calling, and what the riches of the glory of his inheritance in the saints. (Ephesians 1: 18.)

I therefore, the prisoner of the Lord, beseech you that ye walk worthy of the vocation wherewith ye are called. (Ephesians 4: 1.)

I press toward the mark for the prize of the high calling of God in Christ Jesus. (Philippians 3: 14.)

Wherefore also we pray always for you, that our God would count you worthy of this calling, and fulfill all the good pleasure of his goodness, and the work of faith with power;

That the name of our Lord Jesus Christ may be glorified in you, and ye in him, according to the grace of our God, and the Lord Jesus Christ. (2 Thessalonians 1: 11, 12.)

Neglect not the gift that is in thee, which was given thee by prophecy, with the laying on of the hands of the presbytery. (1 Timothy 4: 14.)

Who hath saved us, and called us with an holy calling, not according to our works, but according to his own purpose and grace, which was given us in Christ Jesus, before the world began. (2 Timothy 1: 9.)

See that ye refuse not him that speaketh. For if they escaped not who refused him that spake on earth, much more shall not we escape, if we turn away from him that speaketh from heaven. (Hebrews 12: 25.)

But ye are a chosen generation, a royal priesthood, an holy nation, a peculiar people; that ye should shew forth the praises of him who hath called you out of darkness into his marvellous light. (1 Peter 2: 9.)

But the anointing which ye have received of him abideth in you, and ye need not that any man teach you: but as the same anointing teacheth you of all things, and is truth, and is no lie, and even as it hath taught you, ye shall abide in him. (1 John 2: 27.)

We are of God: he that knoweth God heareth us; he that is not of God heareth not us. Hereby know we the spirit of truth, and the spirit of error. (1 John 4: 6.)

Field and Power.

He answered and said unto them, *He that soweth the good seed is the Son of man;*

The field is the world; the good seed are the children of the kingdom; but the tares are the children of the wicked one;

The enemy that sowed them is the devil; the harvest is the end of the world; and the reapers are the angels.

As therefore the tares are gathered and burned in the fire; so shall it be in the end of this world. (Matthew 13: 37-40.)

Go ye therefore, and teach all nations, baptizing them in the name of the Father, and of the Son, and of the Holy Ghost:

Teaching them to observe all things whatsoever I have commanded you: and, lo, I am with you alway, even unto the end of the world. Amen. (Matthew 28: 19, 20.)

Say not ye, There are yet four months, and then cometh harvest? behold, I say unto you, Lift up your eyes, and look on the fields; for they are white already to harvest. (John 4: 35.)

Duties of Ministers.

To Preach True Doctrine:

But we preach Christ crucified, unto the Jews a stumblingblock, and unto the Greeks foolishness:

But unto them which are called, both Jews and Greeks, Christ, the power of God, and the wisdom of God. (1 Corinthians 1: 23, 24.)

And I, brethren, when I came to you, came not with excellency of speech, or of wisdom, declaring unto you the testimony of God.

For I determined not to know any thing among you, save Jesus Christ, and him crucified.

And I was with you in weakness, and in fear, and in much trembling.

And my speech and my preaching was not with enticing words of man's wisdom, but in demonstration of the Spirit and of power:

That your faith should not stand in the wisdom of men, but in the power of God. (1 Corinthians 2: 1-5.)

For we are labourers together with God, ye are God's husbandry, ye are God's building.

According to the grace of God which is given unto me, as a wise masterbuilder I have laid the foundation, and another buildeth thereon. But let every man take heed how he buildeth thereupon.

For other foundation can no man lay, than that is laid, which is Jesus Christ.

Now if any man build upon this foundation, gold, silver, precious stones, wood, hay, stubble:

Every man's work shall be made manifest. For the day shall declare it, because it shall be revealed by fire, and the fire shall try every man's work of what sort it is. (1 Corinthians 3: 9 13.)

For we preach not ourselves, but Christ Jesus the Lord, and ourselves your servants for Jesus' sake.

For God who commanded the light to shine out of darkness, hath shined in our hearts, to give the light of the knowledge of the glory of God in the face of Jesus Christ.

But we have this treasure in earthen vessels, that the excellency of the power may be of God, and not of us. (2 Corinthians 4: 5-7.)

Knowing therefore the terror of the Lord, we persuade men; but we are made manifest unto God, and I trust also, are made manifest in your consciences.

For we commend not ourselves again unto you, but give you occasion to glory on our behalf, that you may have somewhat to answer them which glory in appearance, and not in heart.

For whether we be beside ourselves,

it is to God: or whether we be sober, it is for your cause. (2 Corinthians 5: 11-13.)

To Shun Error:

For I know this, that after my departing shall grievous wolves enter in among you, not sparing the flock.

Also of your own selves shall men arise, speaking perverse things, to draw away disciples after them.

Therefore watch, and remember, that by the space of three years I ceased not to warn every one night and day with tears. (Acts 20: 29-31.)

From which some having swerved have turned aside into vain jangling;

Desiring to be teachers of the law; understanding neither what they say, nor whereof they affirm. (1 Timothy 1: 6, 7.)

If any man teach otherwise, and consent not to wholesome words, even the words of our Lord Jesus Christ, and to the doctrine which is according to godliness;

He is proud, knowing nothing, but doting about questions and strifes of words, whereof cometh envy, strife, railings, evil surmisings,

Perverse disputings of men of corrupt minds, and destitute of the truth, supposing that gain is godliness: from such withdraw thyself. (1 Timothy 6: 3-5.)

But shun profane and vain babblings: for they will increase unto more ungodliness.

And their word will eat as doth a canker: of whom is Hymeneus and Philetus;

Who concerning the truth have erred, saying that the resurrection is past already; and overthrow the faith of some. (2 Timothy 2: 16-18.)

To Avoid Useless Discussions:

Neither give heed to fables and endless genealogies, which minister questions, rather than godly edifying which is in faith: so do. (1 Timothy 1: 4.)

If thou put the brethren in remembrance of these things, thou shalt be a good minister of Jesus Christ, nourished up in the words of faith and of good doctrine, whereunto thou hast attained.

But refuse profane and old wives' fables, and exercise thyself rather unto godliness. (1 Timothy 4: 6, 7.)

O Timothy, keep that which is committed to thy trust, avoiding profane and vain babblings, and oppositions of science falsely so called. (1 Timothy 6: 20.)

Of these things put them in remembrance, charging them before the Lord, that they strive not about words to no profit, but to the subverting of the hearers.

Study to shew thyself approved unto God, a workman that needeth not to be ashamed, rightly dividing the word of truth. (2 Timothy 2: 14, 15.)

But foolish and unlearned questions avoid, knowing that they do gender strifes. (2 Timothy 2: 23.)

But avoid foolish questions, and genealogies, and contentions, and strivings about the law; for they are unprofitable and vain. (Titus 3: 9.)

To Reprove, Kindly yet with Force:

Brethren, I beseech you, be as I am; for I am as ye are: ye have not injured me at all.

Ye know how through infirmity of the flesh I preached the gospel unto you at the first.

And my temptation which was in my flesh ye despised not, nor rejected; but received me as an angel of God, even as Christ Jesus.

Where is then the blessedness ye spake of? for I bear you record, that, if it had been possible, ye would have plucked out your own eyes, and have given them to me.

Am I therefore become your enemy, because I tell you the truth? (Galatians 4: 12-16.)

Now some are puffed up, as though I would not come to you.

But I will come to you shortly, if the Lord will, and will know, not the speech of them which are puffed up, but the power.

What will ye? shall I come unto you with a rod, or in love, and in the spirit of meekness? (1 Corinthians 4: 18-21.)

Now in this that I declare unto you I praise you not, that ye come together not for the better, but for the worse.

For first of all, when ye come together in the church, I hear that there be divisions among you; and I partly believe it. (1 Corinthians 11: 17, 18.)

This is the third time I am coming to you. In the mouth of two or three witnesses shall every word be established.

I told you before, and foretell you, as if I were present, the second time; and being absent now I write to them which heretofore have sinned, and to all other, that, if I come again, I will not spare. (2 Corinthians 13: 1, 2.)

Therefore I write these things being absent, lest being present I should use sharpness, according to the power which the Lord hath given me to edification, and not to destruction. (2 Corinthians 13: 10.)

For do I now persuade men, or God? or do I seek to please men? for if I yet pleased men, I should not be the servant of Christ. (Galatians 1: 10.)

To Set a Good Example:

In all things shewing thyself a pattern of good works: in doctrine shewing uncorruptness, gravity, sincerity,

Sound speech, that cannot be condemned; that he that is of the contrary part may be ashamed, having no evil thing to say of you. (Titus 2: 7, 8.)

To Maintain Decency and Order:

How is it then, brethren? when ye come together, every one of you hath a psalm, hath a doctrine, hath a tongue, hath a revelation, hath an interpretation. Let all things be done unto edifying.

If any man speak in an unknown tongue, let it be by two, or at the most by three, and that by course; and let one interpret.

But if there be no interpreter, let him keep silence in the church; and let him speak to himself, and to God. (1 Corinthians 14: 26-28.)

Let your women keep silence in the churches: for it is not permitted unto them to speak; but they are commanded to be under obedience, as also saith the law.

And if they will learn any thing, let them ask their husbands at home: for it is a shame for women to speak in the church. (1 Corinthians 14: 34, 35.)

Let all things be done decently and in order. (1 Corinthians 14: 40.)

Ministerial Graces and Qualifications.

Knowledge and Discretion:

And he spake a parable unto them; *Can the blind lead the blind? shall they not both fall into the ditch?* (Luke 6: 39.)

But what I do, that I will do, that I may cut off occasion from them which desire occasion; that wherein they glory, they may be found even as we.

For such are false apostles, deceitful workers, transforming themselves into the apostles of Christ. (2 Corinthians 11: 12, 13.)

And I went up by revelation, and communicated unto them that gospel which I preach among the Gentiles, but privately to them which were of reputation, lest by any means I should run, or had run, in vain. (Galatians 2: 2.)

Truthfulness:

But as God is true, our word toward you was not yea and nay. (2 Corinthians 1: 18.)

Therefore, seeing we have this ministry, as we have received mercy, we faint not;

But have renounced the hidden things of dishonesty, not walking in craftiness, nor handling the word of God deceitfully; but, by manifestation of the truth, commending ourselves to every man's conscience in the sight of God. (2 Corinthians 4: 1, 2.)

For we can do nothing against the truth, but for the truth. (2 Corinthians 13: 8.)

For yourselves, brethren, know our entrance in unto you, that it was not in vain:

But even after that we had suffered before, and were shamefully entreated, as ye know, at Philippi, we were bold in our God to speak unto you the gospel of God with much contention. (1 Thessalonians 2: 1, 2.)

For neither at any time used we flattering words, as ye know, nor a cloak of covetousness; God is witness. (1 Thessalonians 2: 5.)

Gentleness:

I write not these things to shame you, but as my beloved sons I warn you.

For though ye have ten thousand instructors in Christ, yet have ye not many fathers: for in Christ Jesus I have forgotten you through the gospel.

Wherefore I beseech you, be ye followers of me. (1 Corinthians 4: 14-16.)

For out of much affliction and anguish of heart I wrote unto you with many tears; not that ye should be grieved, but that ye might know the love which I have more abundantly unto you.

But if any have caused grief, he hath not grieved me, but in part: that I may not overcharge you all.

Sufficient to such a man is this punishment, which was inflicted of many.

So that contrariwise ye ought rather to forgive him, and comfort him, lest perhaps such a one should be swallowed up with overmuch sorrow.

Wherefore I beseech you that ye would confirm your love toward him.

For to this end also did I write, that I might know the proof of you, whether ye be obedient in all things.

To whom ye forgive any thing, I forgive also: for if I forgave any thing, to whom I forgave it, for your sakes forgave I it in the person of Christ. (2 Corinthians 2: 4-10.)

But we were gentle among you, even as a nurse cherisheth her children:

So being affectionately desirous of you, we were willing to have imparted unto you, not the gospel of God only, but also our own souls, because ye were dear unto us. (1 Thessalonians 2: 7, 8.)

Forbearance:

For if he that cometh preacheth another Jesus, whom we have not preached, or if ye receive another spirit, which ye have not received, or another gospel, which ye have not accepted, ye might well bear with him. (2 Corinthians 11: 4.)

Some indeed preach Christ even of envy and strife; and some also of good will:

The one preach Christ of contention, not sincerely, supposing to add affliction to my bonds:

But the other of love, knowing that I am set for the defence of the gospel.

What then? notwithstanding, every way, whether in pretence, or in truth, Christ is preached; and I therein do rejoice, yea, and will rejoice. (Philippians 1: 15-18.)

Meekness and Humility:

For whether is greater, he that sitteth at meat, or he that serveth? is not he that sitteth at meat? but I am among you as he that serveth. (Luke 22: 27.)

If I then, your Lord and Master, have washed your feet; ye also ought to wash one another's feet. (John 13: 14.)

I have planted, Apollos watered; but God gave the increase.

So then neither is he that planteth any thing, neither he that watereth; but God that giveth the increase. (1 Corinthians 3: 6, 7.)

We are fools for Christ's sake, but ye are wise in Christ; we are weak, but ye are strong; ye are honourable, but we are despised. (1 Corinthians 4: 10.)

But we have this treasure in earthen vessels, that the excellency of the power may be of God, and not of us. (2 Corinthians 4: 7.)

Now I Paul myself beseech you by the meekness and gentleness of Christ, who in presence am base among you, but being absent am bold toward you:

But I beseech you, that I may not be bold when I am present with that confidence, wherewith I think to be bold against some, which think of us as if we walked according to the flesh. (2 Corinthians 10: 1, 2.)

And the servant of the Lord must not strive; but be gentle unto all men, apt to teach, patient;

In meekness instructing those that oppose themselves; if God peradventure will give them repentance to the acknowledging of the truth. (2 Timothy 2: 24, 25.)

To speak evil of no man, to be no brawlers, but gentle, shewing all meekness unto all men. (Titus 3: 2.)

Firmness:

But neither Titus, who was with me, being a Greek, was compelled to be circumcised:

And that because of false brethren unawares brought in, who came in privily to spy out our liberty which we have in Christ Jesus, that they might bring us into bondage:

To whom we gave place by subjection, no, not for an hour; that the truth of the gospel might continue with you. (Galatians 2: 3-5.)

Blamelessness:

Giving no offence in any thing, that the ministry be not blamed. (2 Corinthians 6: 3.)

By pureness, by knowledge, by longsuffering, by kindness, by the Holy Ghost, by love unfeigned,

By the word of truth, by the power

of God, by the armour of righteousness on the right hand and on the left. (2 Corinthians 6: 6, 7.)

Ye are witnesses, and God also, how holily and justly and unblameably we behaved ourselves among you that believe. (1 Thessalonians 2: 10.)

But thou, O man of God, flee these things; and follow after righteousness, godliness, faith, love, patience, meekness. (1 Timothy 6: 11.)

Flee also youthful lusts: but follow righteousness, faith, charity, peace, with them that call on the Lord out of a pure heart. (2 Timothy 2: 22.)

Zeal and Devotion:

For God is my witness, whom I serve with my spirit in the gospel of his Son, that without ceasing I make mention of you always in my prayers;

Making request, if by any means now at length I might have a prosperous journey by the will of God to come unto you.

For I long to see you, that I may impart unto you some spiritual gift, to the end ye may be established;

That is, that I may be comforted together with you by the mutual faith both of you and me. (Romans 1: 9-12.)

For none of us liveth to himself, and no man dieth to himself. (Romans 14: 7.)

For we commend not ourselves again unto you, but give you occasion to glory on our behalf, that ye may have somewhat to answer them which glory in appearance, and not in heart.

For whether we be beside ourselves, it is to God: or whether we be sober, it is for your cause. (2 Corinthians 5: 12, 13.)

The Reward of the Ministry.

Say not ye, There are yet four months, and then cometh harvest? behold, I say unto you, Lift up your eyes, and look on the fields; for they are white already to harvest.

And he that reapeth receiveth wages, and gathereth fruit unto life eternal: that both he that soweth and he that reapeth may rejoice together.

And herein is that saying true, One soweth, and another reapeth.

I sent you to reap that whereon ye bestowed no labour: other men laboured, and ye are entered into their labours. (John 4: 35-38.)

For I know that this shall turn to my salvation through your prayer, and the supply of the spirit of Jesus Christ,

According to my earnest expectation, and my hope, that in nothing I shall be ashamed, but that with all boldness, as always, so now also Christ shall be magnified in my body, whether it be by life or by death.

For to me to live is Christ, and to die is gain. (Philippians 1: 19-21.)

For I am now ready to be offered, and the time of my departure is at hand.

I have fought a good fight, I have finished my course, I have kept the faith.

Henceforth there is laid up for me a crown of righteousness, which the Lord the righteous judge shall give me at that day: and not to me only, but unto them also that love his appearing. (2 Timothy 4: 6-8.)

MIRACLE. (See Appendix for table of miracles.)

MIR′A-CLE—a wonder, or a wonderful thing; specifically, an event or effect contrary to the established laws or constitution of nature.

In understanding miracles we must first

understand that God, in His wisdom, established a certain set of laws and rules for the working of His creation, for the maintenance of the universe, for the life and death of mankind, and for the germination, growth, and decay of the vegetable kingdom, etc. These rules are what we know as and call the laws of nature. Any interference with the working of these uniform rules or laws of nature on the part of man brings about confusion or disorder, and if man were able to interfere with that part of these laws which regulates the motions of the earth or the stars annihilation would ensue. But, if for some reason of His own, for the good of mankind or in His infinite wisdom, which sees so much farther than man sees, it is necessary to deviate from His fixed laws and rules, then unquestionably the will of God brings about such deviations, which to us are known under the name of miracles.

We find, in various parts of the Bible, instances where God saw that it was necessary to permit these deviations from His laws as part of His plans for the welfare of man and the betterment of the human race. A number of them occur in Old Testament times, chiefly through the medium of Aaron, Moses, Elijah, and Elisha. By far the larger number took place in New Testament times, through the medium of Jesus and some of the more favored of the apostles. The cause for these miracles is instantly apparent—they were to convince humanity of the divine character and mission of Jesus, to aid in laying the foundations of the Christian Church, and to maintain that Church until it was sufficiently strong to maintain itself. Thus the Bible shows that when miracles are necessary for the carrying out of God's purposes the laws of nature are suspended either in whole or in part, or for a longer or a shorter period, as best suits their Maker. In Old Testament times miracles were necessary to preserve or aid God's chosen people, the Jews, from the royal line of which the human element in the Messiah was to spring. In New Testament times miracles were necessary to prove to a doubting world Jesus' Messiahship. The need for miracles being passed God ceases to deviate from His laws, which He knows to be sufficient to answer all the purposes of average times. We find this proved by the fact that in the 400 years between the times of Malachi and Jesus there is no record of a miracle, while after the Apostolic Church was thoroughly established and capable of taking care of itself, the working of miracles gradually ceased, and there is no satisfactory record of any since that time.

MIRIAM. (See Aaron, Moses.)

MIR'I-AM—a form of a Hebrew word meaning "bitterness." Miriam was the elder sister of Aaron and Moses. She is supposed to have watched the infant Moses when he was exposed upon the Nile for the Egyptian princess to pick up. She was held in high esteem by the Israelites as the sister of their leader and priest. After the escape from Egypt and the passage of the Red Sea she celebrated the events in a wonderful song of triumph, which is one of the most spirited and inspiring things in the Bible. The arrival of Moses' wife Zipporah seems to have caused Miriam much jealousy, and she excited Aaron to sedition. God afflicted her with leprosy, only recovering through the intervention of Moses. She died in the fortieth year of the Israelites' wanderings.

References.—See references to Aaron and Moses; also Exodus 15: 21.

MISCHIEF.

MIS'CHIEF—harm or damage; especially disarrangement of order caused by some human agency or some human being. The Bible issues warning to man to avoid mischief.

REFERENCES.

Behold, he travaileth with iniquity, and hath conceived mischief, and brought forth falsehood.

He made a pit, and digged it, and is fallen into the ditch which he made.

His mischief shall return upon his own head, and his violent dealing shall come down upon his own pate. (Psalm 7: 14-16.)

Deliver me, O Lord, from the evil man: preserve me from the violent man;

Which imagine mischiefs in their heart; continually are they gathered together for war. (Psalm 140: 1, 2.)

Whoso diggeth a pit shall fall therein: and he that rolleth a stone, it will return upon him. (Proverbs 26: 27)

Wo to thee that spoilest, and thou wast not spoiled; and dealest treacherously, and they dealt not treacherously with thee! when thou shalt cease to spoil, thou shalt be spoiled; and when thou shalt make an end to deal treacherously, they shall deal treacherously with thee. (Isaiah 33: 1.)

And said, O full of all subtilty and all mischief, thou child of the devil, thou enemy of all righteousness, wilt thou not cease to pervert the right ways of the Lord? (Acts 13: 10.)

MITE.

MITE—the smallest coin known to the Hebrew at the time of Christ. Its value was about one-eighth of a cent. It was made famous by the words of Christ in reference to it when the widow gave two into the treasury.

REFERENCES.

And there came a certain poor widow, and she threw in two mites, which make a farthing.

And he called unto him his disciples, and saith unto them, *Verily I say unto you, That this poor widow hath cast more in, than all they which have cast into the treasury:*

For all they did cast in of their abundance; but she of her want did cast in all that she had, even all her living. (Mark 12: 42-44.)

MOABITES.

MO'AB-ITES—the name of a tribe descended from Moab, the son of Lot by his eldest daughter, and therefore related to the Israelites. Despite this relationship there appear to have been almost continual wars between the two nations when the Israelites reached and settled down in Canaan. Traces of their cities have become lost, thus fulfilling the prophecies of Jeremiah. Reference as to origin, Genesis 19: 36, 37.

MOLECH.

MO'LECH—a form of a Hebrew phrase meaning "the ruler." Molech (also called Moloch) was the chief deity of the Ammonites. His worship spread to the Phœnicians and the Israelites. It was a most terrible idolatry, one of the features of it being the sacrifice of infants, who were placed in the arms of the statue of the god and slowly burned to death, the arms of the idol being hollow, whereby they could be, and were at the time of making sacrifices, filled with fire. Investigators have thought that these sacrifices had their origin in the memory of the terrible calamity which happened to Sodom and Gomorrah, as a result of which the Ammonites came into existence, they being descendants of Lot. It is supposed the Ammonites sought in the sacrifices to appease the god of fire, thus preventing a recurrence of what they conceived to be his destroying anger.

MONEY. (See Avarice, Covetousness, Mammon, etc.)

MON'EY—whatever commodity or thing the people of any country have agreed or are required to accept as the medium of payment for labor or goods. In very ancient times money consisted of cattle or animals or grains or any products of the soil or man's labor. Later precious stones or metals were used, but it was not for a long time that the head or token of the ruler began to be stamped upon pieces of metal to give it a national character. In some places cattle and products still continue to be used as money. Some savage races use shells, beads, the teeth of animals or large fishes. In a number of passages the Bible teaches us the worth of money and its value as a thing with which to do good and to bring happiness; but it is equally clear on the score of inordinate love of money, declaring it to be a sin for which man shall be held strictly accountable.

REFERENCES.

But Jesus perceived their wickedness, and said, *Why tempt ye me, ye hypocrites?*

Shew me the tribute money. And they brought unto him a penny.

And he saith unto them, *Whose is this image and superscription?*

They say unto him, Caesar's. Then saith he unto them, *Render therefore unto Caesar the things which are Caesar's; and unto God the things that are God's.* (Matthew 22: 18-21.)

And Jesus sat over against the treasury, and beheld how the people cast money into the treasury: and many that were rich cast in much.

And there came a certain poor widow, and she threw in two mites, which make a farthing.

And he called unto him his disciples, and saith unto them, *Verily I say unto you, That this poor widow hath cast more in, than all they which have cast into the treasury:*

For all they did cast in of their abundance; but she of her want did cast in all that she had, even all her living. (Mark 12: 41-44.)

And Judas Iscariot, one of the twelve, went unto the chief priests, to betray him unto them.

And when they heard it, they were glad, and promised to give him money. And he sought how he might conveniently betray him. (Mark 14: 10, 11.)

For the love of money is the root of all evil: which while some coveted after, they have erred from the faith, and pierced themselves through with many sorrows. (1 Timothy 6: 10.)

MORDECAI. (See Esther, Haman.)

Mor'de-cai—a Hebrew form of a Persian word meaning "little man." Mordecai was the uncle and guardian of Esther. He was an officer of the Persian King's court and learned of Haman's plot against the Hebrew race, and communicated it to Esther, with the result that Haman lost his life for his plotting. For the deliverance from this plot to massacre the whole nation the Jews instituted the Feast of Purim, which they celebrate to this day.

Reference.—The book of Esther.

MORTALITY. (See Death, Immortality, Life, etc.)

Mor-tal'i-ty—the state of being subject to death. All things that have life are in a state of mortality—that is, they are subject to death.

REFERENCES.

And though after my skin worms destroy this body, yet in my flesh shall I see God. (Job 19: 26.)

But if the Spirit of him that raised up Jesus from the dead dwell in you, he that raised up Christ from the dead shall also quicken your mortal bodies by his Spirit that dwelleth in you. (Romans 8: 11.)

For this corruptible must put on incorruption, and this mortal must put on immortality.

So when this corruptible shall have put on incorruption, and this mortal shall have put on immortality, then shall be brought to pass the saying that is written, Death is swallowed up in victory.

O death, where is thy sting? O grave, where is thy victory?

The sting of death is sin; and the strength of sin is the law.

But thanks be to God, which giveth us the victory through our Lord Jesus Christ. (1 Corinthians 15: 53-57.)

For we which live are alway delivered unto death for Jesus' sake, that the life also of Jesus might be made manifest in our mortal flesh.

So then death worketh in us, but life in you. (2 Corinthians 4: 11, 12.)

For we that are in this tabernacle do groan, being burdened: not for that we would be unclothed, but clothed upon, that mortality might be swallowed up of life. (2 Corinthians 5: 4.)

MOSES. (See Aaron, Exodus, Jews, Miriam, etc.)

Mo'ses—a form of a Hebrew word meaning "drawn out of the water." We can see very readily why the name of Moses was given to the infant who was destined by God to become the great leader and lawgiver of the Hebrew race. He was the son of Amram and Jochebed, members of the tribe of Levi. The pharaoh then on the throne was an enemy of the Jews and had decreed that all male Jew children were to be put to death. Moses' parents, doubtless divinely guided, made an ark or small boat and sent the infant adrift upon the Nile, watched by his sister, Miriam. This seems to have been done so that the babe would fall into the hands of the pharaoh's daughter when she came with her women to bathe. This fell out as planned, and the Egyptian princess, who was childless, adopted the infant. Moses grew up in the Pharaonic court and was given the very best education possible in those times—which means that he was educated for the Egyptian priesthood, a priesthood full of the highest learning and familiar with many secrets of nature kept from the common people and used as the source of what was popularly believed to be magic and miracles. But Moses, when he grew up, threw in his lot with his own people, although offered royal honors and high posts in the priesthood. Fleeing from Egypt, because he had killed an Egyptian who was taskmaster over the Israelites, he went to the land of Midian and became a shepherd under Jethro, his future father-in-law. During his life as a shepherd he received his divine commission to become the deliverer of his people, which commission was confirmed to him by a series of miracles. Returning to Egypt he led his fellow-Israelites out to the forty years of wandering in the desert. During this time

he was the mouthpiece of God in the communication of the law and the covenants. For the sins of impatience and presumption at the waters of Meribah (Numbers 20: 10-12) he was not permitted by God to cross the Jordan into the Promised Land. He died at the age of 120 on the top of Mount Pisgah, from whence he viewed Canaan. Even the Jews did not know where he was buried.

The character of Moses is one of the most sublime in all history, whether sacred or profane. For love of his God and faith in Him and in His people he gave up the greatest of honors in Egypt, the throne of which was apparently within his reach. His work as Israel's leader and lawgiver during the years of wandering must have been exceedingly difficult and wearing, and yet at the end he asked for nothing and took nothing. All the rewards went to others, so far as he could give them, and even though he earned the right of being called the father of his people, that honor was already given to another, Abraham. But God in His goodness has taken care that Moses shall never be forgotten, and he lives in the memory of man through the sheer force of his greatness, by far the greatest of all the great characters of the Old Testament. In him there is none of the shiftiness that Abraham, Isaac, and Jacob could show on occasions, and we find in him none of the dark sins that here and there disfigured the life of David. He is the only mortal to whom Jesus compared Himself. The only blot he possessed was a certain impatience, a fault which brought about the fatal incident at Meribah. The only other character in Scripture that compares with him is the gigantic one of Paul, the great apostle to the Gentiles.

REFERENCES.

Birth and Early History.

And the woman conceived and bare a son: and when she saw him that he was a goodly child, she hid him three months.

And when she could not longer hide him, she took for him an ark of bulrushes, and daubed it with slime and with pitch, and put the child therein;

and she laid it in the flags by the river's brink.

And his sister stood afar off, to wit what would be done to him.

And the daughter of Pharaoh came down to wash herself at the river; and her maidens walked along by the river's side: and when she saw the ark among the flags, she sent her maid to fetch it.

And when she had opened it, she saw the child: and, behold, the babe wept. And she had compassion on him, and said, This is one of the Hebrews' children.

Then said his sister to Pharaoh's daughter, Shall I go and call to thee a nurse of the Hebrew women, that she may nurse the child for thee?

And Pharaoh's daughter said to her, Go. And the maid went and called the child's mother.

And Pharaoh's daughter said unto her, Take this child away, and nurse it for me, and I will give thee thy wages. And the woman took the child, and nursed it.

And the child grew, and she brought him unto Pharaoh's daughter, and he became her son. And she called his name Moses: and she said, Because I drew him out of the water. (Exodus 2: 2-10.)

His Call to Leadership.

And it came to pass, in process of time, that the king of Egypt died: and the children of Israel sighed by reason of the bondage, and they cried, and their cry came up unto God by reason of the bondage. (Exodus 2: 23.)

Now Moses kept the flock of Jethro his father in law, the priest of Midian: and he led the flock to the back side of the desert, and came to the mountain of God, even to Horeb.

And the Angel of the Lord appeared unto him in a flame of fire out of the midst of a bush: and he looked, and, behold, the bush burned with fire, and the bush was not consumed.

And Moses said, I will now turn aside, and see this great sight, why the bush is not burnt.

And when the Lord saw that he turned aside to see, God called unto him out of the midst of the bush, and said, Moses, Moses. And he said, Here am I. (Exodus 3: 1-4.)

Come now therefore, and I will send thee unto Pharaoh, that thou mayest bring forth my people the children of Israel out of Egypt.

And Moses said unto God, Who am I, that I should go unto Pharaoh, and that I should bring forth the children of Israel out of Egypt?

And he said, Certainly I will be with thee; and this shall be a token unto thee, that I have sent thee: When thou hast brought forth the people out of Egypt, ye shall serve God upon this mountain. (Exodus 3: 10-12.)

The Exodus.

Now the sojourning of the children of Israel who dwelt in Egypt was four hundred and thirty years.

And it came to pass at the end of the four hundred and thirty years, even the selfsame day it came to pass, that all the hosts of the Lord went out from the land of Egypt. (Exodus 12: 40, 41.)

And the Egyptians pursued, and went in after them to the midst of the sea, even all Pharaoh's horses, his chariots, and his horsemen.

And it came to pass, that in the morning watch the Lord looked unto the host of the Egyptians through the pillar of fire and of the cloud, and troubled the host of the Egyptians.

And took off their chariot wheels, that they drave them heavily: so that the Egyptians said, Let us flee from the face of Israel; for the Lord fighteth for them against the Egyptians.

And the Lord said unto Moses, Stretch out thine hand over the sea, that the waters may come again upon the Egyptians, upon their chariots, and upon their horsemen.

And Moses stretched forth his hand over the sea, and the sea returned to his strength when the morning appeared; and the Egyptians fled against it; and the Lord overthrew the Egyptians in the midst of the sea.

And the waters returned, and covered the chariots, and the horsemen, and all the host of Pharaoh that came into the sea after them; there remained not so much as one of them.

But the children of Israel walked upon dry land in the midst of the sea; and the waters were a wall unto them on their right hand, and on their left.

Thus the Lord saved Israel that day out of the hand of the Egyptians; and Israel saw the Egyptians dead upon the sea shore.

And Israel saw that great work which the Lord did upon the Egyptians: and the people feared the Lord, and believed the Lord, and his servant Moses. (Exodus 14: 23-31.)

Receives the Law.

And the Lord said unto Moses, Come up to me into the mount, and be there: and I will give thee tables of stone, and a law, and commandments which I have written; that thou mayest teach them.

And Moses rose up, and his minister

Joshua; and Moses went up into the mount of God.

And he said unto the elders, Tarry ye here for us, until we come again unto you: and, behold, Aaron and Hur are with you: if any man have any matters to do, let him come unto them.

And Moses went up into the mount, and a cloud covered the mount.

And the glory of the Lord abode upon mount Sinai, and the cloud covered it six days; and the seventh day he called unto Moses out of the midst of the cloud.

And the sight of the glory of the Lord was like devouring fire on the top of the mount in the eyes of the children of Israel.

And Moses went into the midst of the cloud, and gat him up into the mount: and Moses was in the mount forty days and forty nights. (Exodus 24: 12-18.)

And Moses turned, and went down from the mount, and the two tables of the testimony were in his hand: the tables were written on both their sides; on the one side and on the other were they written.

And the tables were the work of God, and the writing was the writing of God, graven upon the tables. (Exodus 32: 15, 16.)

And it came to pass, as soon as he came nigh unto the camp, that he saw the calf, and the dancing: and Moses' anger waxed hot, and he cast the tables out of his hands, and brake them beneath the mount. (Exodus 32: 19.)

And the Lord said unto Moses, Hew thee two tables of stone like unto the first: and I will write upon these tables the words that were in the first tables, which thou brakest. (Exodus 34: 1.)

And he was there with the Lord forty days and forty nights; he did neither eat bread, nor drink water. And he wrote upon the tables the words of the covenant, the ten commandments.

And it came to pass, when Moses came down from mount Sinai with the two tables of testimony in Moses' hand, when he came down from the mount, that Moses wist not that the skin of his face shone while he talked with him. (Exodus 34: 28, 29.)

Moses' Sin.

And the Lord spake unto Moses, saying,

Take the rod, and gather thou the assembly together, thou and Aaron thy brother, and speak ye unto the rock before their eyes; and it shall give forth his water, and thou shalt bring forth to them water out of the rock: so thou shalt give the congregation and their beasts drink.

And Moses took the rod from before the Lord, as he commanded him.

And Moses and Aaron gathered the congregation together before the rock, and he said unto them, Hear now, ye rebels; must we fetch you water out of this rock?

And Moses lifted up his hand, and with his rod he smote the rock twice: and the water came out abundantly, and the congregation drank, and their beasts also.

And the Lord spake unto Moses and Aaron, Because ye believed me not, to sanctify me in the eyes of the children of Israel, therefore ye shall not bring this congregation into the land which I have given them. (Numbers 20: 7-12.)

Told of His Coming Death.

And the Lord said unto Moses, Get thee up into this mount Abarim, and see the land which I have given unto the children of Israel.

And when thou hast seen it, thou also shalt be gathered unto thy people, as Aaron thy brother was gathered.

For ye rebelled against my commandment in the desert of Zin, in the strife of the congregation, to sanctify me at the water before their eyes: that is the water of Meribah in Kadesh in the wilderness of Zin.

And Moses spake unto the Lord, saying,

Let the Lord, the God of the spirits of all flesh, set a man over the congregation,

Which may go out before them, and which may go in before them, and which may lead them out, and which may bring them in; that the congregation of the Lord be not as sheep which have no shepherd.

And the Lord said unto Moses, Take thee Joshua the son of Nun, a man in whom is the spirit, and lay thine hand upon him. (Numbers 27: 12-18.)

Prophesies Israel's Fate and of Christ.

Furthermore the Lord was angry with me for your sakes, and sware that I should not go over Jordan, and that I should not go in unto that good land, which the Lord thy God giveth thee for an inheritance:

But I must die in this land, I must not go over Jordan: but ye shall go over, and possess that good land.

Take heed unto yourselves, lest ye forget the covenant of the Lord your God, which he made with you, and make you a graven image, or the likeness of any thing, which the Lord thy God hath forbidden thee.

For the Lord thy God is a consuming fire, even a jealous God.

When thou shalt beget children, and children's children, and ye shall have remained long in the land, and shall corrupt yourselves, and make a graven image, or the likeness of any thing, and shall do evil in the sight of the Lord thy God, to provoke him to anger;

I call heaven and earth to witness against you this day, that ye shall soon utterly perish from off the land whereunto ye go over Jordan to possess it; ye shall not prolong your days upon it, but shall utterly be destroyed.

And the Lord shall scatter you among the nations, and ye shall be left few in number among the heathen, whither the Lord shall lead you. (Deuteronomy 4: 21-27.)

And the Lord said unto me, They have well spoken that which they have spoken.

I will raise them up a Prophet from among their brethren, like unto thee, and will put my words in his mouth; and he shall speak unto them all that I shall command him.

And it shall come to pass, that whosoever will not hearken unto my words which he shall speak in my name, I will require it of him. (Deuteronomy 18: 17-19.)

Moses' Death.

And Moses went up from the plains of Moab unto the mountain of Nebo, to the top of Pisgah, that is over against Jericho: and the Lord shewed him all the land of Gilead, unto Dan,

And all Naphtali, and the land of Ephraim, and Manasseh, and all the land of Judah, unto the utmost sea,

And the south, and the plain of the valley of Jericho, the city of palm trees, unto Zoar.

And the Lord said unto him, This is the land which I sware unto Abraham, unto Isaac, and unto Jacob, saying, I will give it unto thy seed: I have caused thee to see it with thine eyes, but thou shalt not go over thither.

So Moses the servant of the Lord died there in the land of Moab, according to the word of the Lord.

And he buried him in a valley in the land of Moab, over against Bethpeor: but no man knoweth of his sepulchre unto this day. (Deuteronomy 34: 1-6.)

Seen at the Transfiguration.

And there appeared unto them Elias with Moses: and they were talking with Jesus. (Mark 9: 4.)

MOTHER. (See Father, Etc.)

MOTH'ER—the female parent. Mother is a word strangely alike in a large number of languages, showing evidences of a common origin and a single primitive form. The Israelites gave great respect and veneration to mothers, a respect which has been imitated by most Christian races and due to womankind as one of the honors and rewards of motherhood.

REFERENCES.

Honour thy father and thy mother: that thy days may be long upon the land which the Lord thy God giveth thee. (Exodus 20: 12.)

My son, hear the instruction of thy father, and forsake not the law of thy mother. (Proverbs 1: 8.)

He that wasteth his father, and chaseth away his mother, is a son that causeth shame, and bringeth reproach. (Proverbs 19: 26.)

Hearken unto thy father that begat thee, and despise not thy mother when she is old. (Proverbs 23: 22.)

MOUTH.

MOUTH—the opening in the head of all types of the animal kingdom through which food is taken and from which the sounds of the voice issue. We find plenteous references to the mouth in Scripture both in a figurative and a literal sense.

REFERENCES.

Mouth of God.

And he humbled thee, and suffered thee to hunger, and fed thee with manna, which thou knewest not, neither did thy fathers know; that he might make thee know that man doth not live by bread only, but by every word that proceedeth out of the mouth of the Lord, doth man live. (Deuteronomy 8: 3.)

But he answered and said, *It is written, Man shall not live by bread alone, but by every word that proceedeth out of the mouth of God.* (Matthew 4: 4.)

Mouth of Babes.

Out of the mouth of babes and sucklings hast thou ordained strength because of thine enemies, that thou mightest still the enemy and the avenger. (Psalm 8: 2.)

And said unto him, Hearest thou what these say? And Jesus saith unto them, *Yea; have ye never read, Out of the mouth of babes and sucklings thou hast perfected praise?* (Matthew 21: 16.)

Mouth of the Wicked.

But the king shall rejoice in God; every one that sweareth by him shall glory: but the mouth of them that speak lies shall be stopped. (Psalm 63: 11.)

The righteous shall see it, and rejoice: and all iniquity shall stop her mouth. (Psalm 107: 42.)

For the mouth of the wicked and the mouth of the deceitful are opened against me; they have spoken against me with a lying tongue. (Psalm 109: 2.)

Put away from thee a froward mouth, and perverse lips put far from thee. (Proverbs 4: 24.)

A naughty person, a wicked man, walketh with a froward mouth. (Proverbs 6: 12.)

An ungodly witness scorneth judgment: and the mouth of the wicked devoureth iniquity. (Proverbs 19: 28.)

Now we know that what things soever the law saith, it saith to them who are under the law: that every mouth may be stopped, and all the world may become guilty before God. (Romans 3: 19.)

Mouth of the Righteous.

The mouth of the righteous speaketh wisdom, and his tongue talketh of judgment. (Psalm 37: 30.)

The mouth of the just bringeth forth wisdom: but the froward tongue shall be cut out. (Proverbs 10: 31.)

The words of a wise man's mouth are gracious; but the lips of a fool will swallow up himself. (Ecclesiastes 10: 12.)

Mouth of the Fool.

In the mouth of the foolish is a rod of pride: but the lips of the wise shall preserve them. (Proverbs 14: 3.)

The tongue of the wise useth knowledge aright: but the mouth of fools poureth out foolishness. (Proverbs 15: 3.)

A fool's mouth is his destruction, and his lips are the snare of his soul. (Proverbs 18: 7.)

The legs of the lame are not equal: so is a parable in the mouth of fools. (Proverbs 26: 7.)

MURDER.

Mur'der—the malicious killing of a human being. In all times and in all ages the offense of murder has been an outrage upon God as the destruction of a thing made in His likeness as well as an offense to man in the taking off of a member of society. Killings done in accident or in the defense of life are not to be regarded as murders, although many of the ancient races did not so distinguish, and permitted blood-revenge for them the same as for actual murder. The command of God regarding the shedding of human blood is very explicit. No matter what the conditions the killing of a human being, except in accident or through actual defense of life, is murder. In recent years there has sprung up a theory that under certain circumstances killings are not to be classed as murder, but instead are given some euphonious name, such as "justifiable homicide" or the like. The theory, however, is without the light of clear logic and reason and by no means in consonance with the teaching of God's word.

REFERENCES.

The murderer rising with the light killeth the poor and needy, and in the night is as a thief. (Job 24: 14.)

He sitteth in the lurking places of the villages: in the secret places doth he murder the innocent: his eyes are privily set against the poor. (Psalm 10: 8.)

And surely your blood of your lives will I require: at the hand of every beast will I require it, and at the hand of man; at the hand of every man's brother will I require the life of man.

Whoso sheddeth man's blood, by man shall his blood be shed: for in the image of God made he man. (Genesis 9: 5, 6.)

He that smiteth a man, so that he die, shall be surely put to death. (Exodus 21: 12.)

But if a man come presumptuously upon his neighbour, to slay him with guile; thou shalt take him from mine altar, that he may die. (Exodus 21: 14.)

Thou shalt not kill. (Deuteronomy 5: 17.)

Cursed be he that smiteth his neighbour secretly: and all the people shall say, Amen.

Cursed be he that taketh reward to slay an innocent person: and all the people shall say, Amen. (Deuteronomy 27: 24-25.)

Whosoever hateth his brother is a murderer: and ye know that no murderer hath eternal life abiding in him. (1 John 3: 15.)

MUSIC.

Mu'sic—the science and art of tones and pleasing sounds arranged in melody or harmony and melody combined. According to the Bible the first record of music is reference to Jubal, a descendant of Cain. Jubal is said to have invented certain musical instruments, and the art in a rude form probably existed prior to his time. His inventions were not the harp and the organ as we know them, but what was known to the ancients as the lyre and the Pandean pipes, the modern evolutions of which are the first-named instruments—that is, harp and organ. Music was used socially from a very early date. The same is probably true with relation to it as an accompaniment to religious services. David, we know, was a musician, and music was used in the religious services and worship of God by his people almost from the earliest times. The names given to the instruments of David's time are not, however, the names by which the Jews knew them, but those which, in the minds of the Bible translators, best fitted the Jewish words. Religion has inspired some of the grandest of musical compositions, notably the majestic oratorios of Handel, all of which are on sacred subjects.

REFERENCES.

And his brother's name was Jubal: he was the father of all such as handle the harp and organ. (Genesis 4: 21.)

Praise the Lord with harp: sing unto him with the psaltery and an instrument of ten strings.

Sing unto him a new song; play skilfully with a loud noise. (Psalm 33: 2, 3.)

Sing aloud unto God our strength: make a joyful noise unto the God of Jacob.

Take a psalm, and bring hither the timbrel, the pleasant harp with the psaltery.

Blow up the trumpet in the new moon, in the time appointed, on our solemn feast day. (Psalm 81: 1-3.)

Make a joyful noise unto the Lord, all the earth: make a loud noise, and rejoice, and sing praise.

Sing unto the Lord with the harp; with the harp, and the voice of a psalm.

With trumpets and sound of cornet make a joyful noise before the Lord, the King. (Psalm 98: 4-6.)

Sing unto him, sing psalms unto him; talk ye of all his wondrous works. (Psalm 105: 2.)

Speaking to yourselves in psalms and hymns and spiritual songs, singing and making melody in your heart to the Lord. (Ephesians 5: 19.)

Let the word of Christ dwell in you richly in all wisdom; teaching and admonishing one another in psalms and hymns and spiritual songs, singing with grace in your hearts to the Lord. (Colossians 3: 16.)

MYSTERY.

Mys'ter-y—specifically, something that is beyond ordinary or human comprehension; something that has not been or cannot be explained. The word was used in the religious sense to tell of things that had been hidden, but were then revealed. It is still (and better) used to describe things which we are unable, by reason of our limited knowledge and understanding, to comprehend or explain. There are mysteries concerning life and death and God which God is not yet willing we should understand, and which may not be revealed to us until the last day.

REFERENCES.

Mystery of the Kingdom of God.

Made Known by Christ:

And he said unto them, *Unto you it is given to know the mystery of the kingdom of God: but unto them that are without, all these things are done in parables:*

That seeing they may see, and not perceive; and hearing they may hear, and not understand; lest at any time they should be converted, and their sins should be forgiven them. (Mark 4: 11.)

Having made known unto us the mystery of his will, according to his good pleasure which he hath purposed in himself:

That in the dispensation of the fulness of times he might gather together in one all things in Christ, both which are in heaven, and which are on earth; even in him. (Ephesians 1: 9, 10.)

How that by revelation he made known unto me the mystery; (as I wrote afore in few words,

Whereby, when ye read, ye may understand my knowledge in the mystery of Christ)

Which in other ages was not made known unto the sons of men, as it is now revealed unto his holy apostles and prophets by the Spirit;

That the Gentiles should be fellowheirs, and of the same body, and partakers of his promise in Christ by the gospel. (Ephesians 3: 3-6.)

And without controversy great is the mystery of godliness: God was manifest in the flesh, justified in the Spirit, seen of angels, preached unto the Gentiles, believed on in the world, received up into glory. (1 Timothy 3: 16.)

Made Known to and by Apostles:

Let a man so account of us, as of the ministers of Christ, and stewards of the mysteries of God. (1 Corinthians 4: 1.)

And though I have the gift of prophecy, and understand all mysteries, and all knowledge; and though I have all faith, so that I could remove mountains, and have not charity, I am nothing. (1 Corinthians 13: 2.)

And for me, that utterance may be given unto me, that I may open my mouth boldly, to make known the mystery of the gospel,

For which I am an ambassador in bonds: that therein I may speak boldly, as I ought to speak. (Ephesians 6: 19, 20.)

That their hearts might be comforted, being knit together in love, and unto all riches of the full assurance of understanding, to the acknowledgement of the mystery of God, and of the Father, and of Christ;

In whom are hid all the treasures of wisdom and knowledge. (Colossians 2: 2, 3.)

Mystery of Raising the Dead.

Behold, I shew you a mystery; We shall not all sleep, but we shall all be changed,

In a moment, in the twinkling of an eye, at the last trump: for the trumpet shall sound, and the dead shall be raised incorruptible, and we shall be changed. (1 Corinthians 15: 51, 52.)

Mystery of Iniquity.

For the mystery of iniquity doth already work: only he who now letteth will let, until he be taken out of the way. (2 Thessalonians 2: 7.)

And upon her forehead was a name written, MYSTERY, BABYLON THE GREAT, THE MOTHER OF HARLOTS AND ABOMINATIONS OF THE EARTH.

And I saw the woman drunken with the blood of the saints, and with the blood of the martyrs of Jesus: and when I saw her, I wondered with great admiration.

And the angel said unto me, Wherefore didst thou marvel? I will tell thee the mystery of the woman, and of the beast that carrieth her, which hath the seven heads and ten horns.

The beast that thou sawest was, and is not; and shall ascend out of the bottomless pit, and go into perdition: and they that dwell on the earth shall wonder, whose names were not written in the book of life from the foundation of the world, when they behold the beast that was, and is not, and yet is. (Revelation 17: 5-8.)

NAAMAN.

Na'a-man—a form of a Hebrew word meaning "pleasantness." Naaman was the commander of the armies of Damascus and a leper. Hearing of the things done by the prophet Elisha he journeyed to meet him. Elisha declined to see him, but told him to go and bathe seven times in the Jordan. Naaman was inclined to be angry at what he considered foolishness, but obeyed and was cured. The cure resulted in his conversion to the religion of the true God.

Reference.—2 Kings 5.

NABAL. (See Abigail.)

Na'bal—a form of a Hebrew word meaning "stupid" or "foolish." Nabal was a wealthy farmer and stock-raiser living in Judah, but a man of harsh and forbidding nature. David sent to him to requisition provisions for his men, who had been protecting

Nabal's property. Nabal refused angrily and with insolence, whereupon David set out to punish him. Nabal's wife, Abigail, met David, and by tact and good sense averted his anger. When she told her husband of the danger he had been in, he had what seems to have been a stroke of apoplexy and died. David was so impressed with Abigail that he made her his wife. The incident occurred about B.C. 1061.

Reference.—1 Samuel 25.

NABOTH.

NA'BOTH—a form of a Hebrew word meaning "fruit." Naboth was the proprietor of a rich vineyard near Jezreel, which adjoined the palace of King Ahab, who coveted the ground. His wicked wife, Jezebel, plotted to get it for him, and falsely accused Naboth of blasphemy, and had him stoned to death, his estates thus becoming confiscate to the crown. For the act Elijah pronounced a terrible curse upon Ahab and his house, all of which was fulfilled.

References.—1 Kings 21; 2 Kings 9.

NAHUM.

NA'HUM—a form of a Hebrew word meaning "consolation." Nahum was one of the minor prophets. He lived about 735 B.C. His literary style is most elegant.

Reference.—The book of Nahum.

NAME.

NAME—the word or title by which a person, place, or thing is known. In the Bible we find great stress laid upon names. Almost always they give us some insight into the character of the person bearing them or a clue to his or her origin. In several instances we find a change of name in order to more fittingly describe the person or to show an altered condition. The Bible also instructs us to venerate the name of God and Christ. The value of a good name—that is, a good character—is also pointed out.

REFERENCES.

The Name of God.

And I appeared unto Abraham, unto Isaac, and unto Jacob, by the name of God Almighty; but by my name JEHOVAH was I not known to them. (Exodus 6: 3.)

That men may know that thou, whose name alone is JEHOVAH, art the Most High over all the earth. (Psalm 83: 18.)

Honor Due to Name of God.

Thou shalt not take the name of the Lord thy God in vain: for the Lord will not hold him guiltless that taketh his name in vain. (Exodus 20: 7.)

If thou wilt not observe to do all the words of this law that are written in this book, that thou mayest fear this glorious and fearful name, THE LORD THY GOD. (Exodus 28: 58.)

O magnify the Lord with me and let us exalt his name together. (Psalm 34: 3.) .

His name shall endure for ever: his name shall be continued as long as the sun: and men shall be blessed in him: all nations shall call him blessed. (Psalm 72: 17.)

He sent redemption unto his people: he hath commanded his covenant for ever: holy and reverend is his name. (Psalm 111: 9.)

For all people will walk every one in the name of his god, and we will walk in the name of the Lord our God for ever and ever. (Micah 4: 5.)

Let as many servants as are under the yoke count their own masters worthy of all honour, that the name of God and his doctrine be not blasphemed. (1 Timothy 6: 1.)

Prayer in Name of Christ.

And whatsoever ye shall ask in my name, that will I do, that the Father may be glorified in the Son.

If ye shall ask any thing in my name, I will do it. (John 14: 13, 14.)

And in that day ye shall ask me nothing. Verily, verily, I say unto you, Whatsoever ye shall ask the Father in my name, he will give it you.

Hitherto have ye asked nothing in my name: ask, and ye shall receive, that your joy may be full. (John 16: 23, 24.)

Giving thanks always for all things unto God, and the Father, in the Name of our Lord Jesus Christ. (Ephesians 5: 20.)

And whatsoever ye do in word or deed, do all in the Name of the Lord Jesus, giving thanks to God and the Father, by him. (Colossians 3: 17.)

By him therefore let us offer the sacrifice of praise to God continually, that is, the fruit of our lips, giving thanks to his Name. (Hebrews 13: 15.)

Miracles in Christ's Name.

Then Peter said, Silver and gold have I none, but such as I have, give I thee: In the Name of Jesus Christ of Nazareth, rise up and walk. (Acts 3: 6.)

Be it known unto you all, and to all the people of Israel, that by the Name of Jesus Christ of Nazareth, whom ye crucified, whom God raised from the dead, even by him, doth this man stand here before you, whole. (Acts 4: 10.)

Then certain of the vagabond Jews, exorcists, took upon them to call over them which had evil spirits the Name of the Lord Jesus, saying, We adjure you by Jesus whom Paul preacheth.

And there were seven sons of one Sceva, a Jew, and chief of the Priests, which did so.

And the evil spirit answered, and said, Jesus I know, and Paul I know, but who are ye?

And the man in whom the evil spirit was, leapt on them, and overcame them, and prevailed against them, so that they fled out of that house naked and wounded. (Acts 19: 13-16.)

Value of Good Name.

A good name is rather to be chosen than great riches, and loving favour rather than silver and gold. (Proverbs 22: 1.)

A good name is better than precious ointment; and the day of death than the day of one's birth. (Ecclesiastes 7: 1.)

Names Changed.

Neither shall thy name any more be called Abram, but thy name shall be Abraham; for a father of many nations have I made thee. (Genesis 17: 5.)

And God said unto Abraham, As for Sarai thy wife, thou shalt not call her name Sarai, but Sarah shall her name be. (Genesis 17: 15.)

And he said, Thy name shall be called no more Jacob, but Israel: for as a prince hast thou power with God and with men, and hast prevailed. (Genesis 32: 28.)

And David comforted Bathsheba his wife, and went in unto her, and lay with her: and she bare a son, and he called his name Solomon: and the Lord loved him.

And he sent by the hand of Nathan the prophet; and he called his name Jedidiah, because of the Lord. (2 Samuel 12: 24, 25.)

Unto whom the prince of the eunuchs gave names: for he gave unto Daniel the name of Belteshazzar; and to Hananiah, of Shadrach; and to Mishael, of Meshach; and to Azariah, of Abednego. (Daniel 1: 7.)

And Simon he surnamed Peter;

And James the son of Zebedee, and John the brother of James; and he surnamed them Boanerges, which is, The sons of thunder. (Mark 3: 16, 17.)

Then Saul, (who also is called Paul,) filled with the Holy Ghost, set his eyes on him. (Acts 13: 9.)

NAOMI. (See Ruth.)

NA-O'MI—a form of a Hebrew word meaning "my pleasantness and delight." Wife of Elimelech and mother-in-law of Ruth.

NAPHTALI.

NAPH'TA-LI—a form of a Hebrew word meaning "my wrestling." Naphtali was the sixth son of Jacob. The Hebrew tribe of Naphtali was descended from him. The men of Naphtali were noted for the readiness with which they responded to the national call to arms.

NATHAN.

NA'THAN—a form of a Hebrew word meaning "gift" or "given." Nathan was a Hebrew prophet who lived in the times of David and Solomon. His first appearance of importance is with regard to the unauthorized approval he gave to David's plan for the building of the Temple, an approval which finally he had to retract. Later we find him reproving David for his sin in the case of Bath-sheba and Uriah. He probably brought up Solomon under his care. He died some time in Solomon's reign.

References.—2 Samuel 7: 12; 1 Kings 1; 1 Chronicles 29; 2 Chronicles 9.

NATHANAEL.

NA-THAN'A-EL—a form of a Hebrew word meaning "given of God." Nathanael was one of the Twelve. He was from Cana of Galilee, and the man who spoke the famous words, "Can any good thing come out of Nazareth?" when spoken to by Philip regarding Jesus. But he accepted the Saviour and appears to have suffered martyrdom for him.

References.—John 1: 45; John 21: 2.

NAZARETH. (See Jesus.)

NAZ'A-RETH—a form of a Hebrew word meaning (probably) "the branch." Nazareth was the name of a small Galilean town noted because of the fact that Jesus spent the greater part of his life there and received its name as a part of His own. The place is not mentioned in the Old Testament. It seems to have been held in contempt by the Jerusalem Jews. This was for several reasons. Galilee was regarded as low, provincial, uncultured, and of little repute by the Jews in and around the royal city. Nazareth itself had gotten a bad name by reason of the somewhat turbulent nature of its people, who were nothing loath to show their contempt for the Jerusalem Jews, who groaned under the weight of the Roman rule, while the Galileans rejoiced in a certain amount of independence due to their remoteness. The town is still in existence and is rather prettier in a simple way than other towns of Palestine. The inhabitants are farmers or stock-raisers, or small artisans or tradesmen.

NEBUCHADNEZZAR. (See Babylon, Daniel.)

NEB-U-CHAD-NEZ'ZAR—a Hebrew form of a Chaldee proper name or name-phrase, probably meaning "Nebo, prince of the gods." Nebuchadnezzar was the son of Nabopolassar, under whom the Babylonian empire was brought into concrete shape. He was born about 630 B.C., ascended the throne on the death of his father in 610 B.C., and reigned about forty years. He figures very prominently in the Bible. While still only the crown prince he invaded Judah and subdued it, carrying Jehoiakim, the king, away captive, along with many others. His elevation to the throne followed immediately. He restored Jehoiakim to his kingdom under promise of tribute, but in order to put down Judah's rebellions made several campaigns toward Jerusalem, in the last of which he plundered the Temple, and left it to be almost destroyed by his chief general. Among the Hebrew captives of his first visit was Daniel, and to him Nebuchadnezzar showed special favor, rising to be the king's first minister. He elevated his realm to very great splendor and beautified Babylon—already magnificent—

with many wonderful buildings, temples, and palaces. For his queen, Amytis, he built a huge series of hanging gardens, which have been classed among the wonders of the world. They were made to imitate the splendid and flowery groves of her native country, Media. Exalted beyond measure by his power and pride, Nebuchadnezzar was punished by God, who sent to him a most awful disease. It lasted for seven years, and while possessed by it he ran around on all fours like a dog, living on bones and offal and grasses, and sleeping naked in the open—indeed, reverting to a state of complete animalism. The disease is not unknown to modern physicians. It is a very rare form of mania.

References.—Daniel 2, 3, 4, etc.

NEHEMIAH.

NE-HE-MI'AH—a form of a Hebrew word meaning "comforted of Jehovah." Nehemiah was a noted Jewish prophet and patriot. He lived about 470-400 B.C. He seems to have been of the royal house of Judah and one of the members of the Captivity. He had a position as cupbearer to the Persian monarch, Artaxerxes Longimanus, and succeeded in getting his master to send him back to Palestine to rebuild Jerusalem. He did a part of this work, but the most important thing he did was to reërect the city wall and set on foot many reforms among the people that still lived in the ancient Hebrew capital. He was twice governor of Jerusalem, and also wrote the book that bears his name. He died at a very advanced age.

Reference.—Book of Nehemiah.

NEIGHBORS. (See Fellowship.)

NEIGH'BORS—persons who are members of the same community and live close to each other. This is the strict and literal meaning of the word, but Jesus gave it a much wider and broader definition when he included the whole world as neighbors, and illustrated it by the parable of the good Samaritan. Thus it is that Christianity has as one of its fundamentals the brotherhood of man, and as one of its most sublime tenets the loving of thy neighbor as thyself.

REFERENCES.

Thou shalt not bear false witness against thy neighbour.

Thou shalt not covet thy neighbour's house, thou shalt not covet thy neighbour's wife, nor his manservant, nor his maidservant, nor his ox, nor his ass, nor any thing that is thy neighbour's. (Exodus 20: 16, 17.)

Thou shalt not avenge, nor bear any grudge against the children of thy people, but thou shalt love thy neighbour as thyself: I am the Lord. (Leviticus 19: 18.)

Cursed be he that removeth his neighbour's landmark: and all the people shall say, Amen. (Deuteronomy 27: 17.)

Say not unto thy neighbour, Go, and come again, and to-morrow I will give; when thou hast it by thee. (Proverbs 3: 28.)

Be not a witness against thy neighbour without cause; and deceive not with thy lips.

Say not, I will do so to him as he hath done to me: I will render to the man according to his work. (Proverbs 24: 28, 29.)

Go not forth hastily to strive, lest thou know not what to do in the end thereof, when thy neighbour hath put thee to shame. (Proverbs 25: 8.)

Withdraw thy foot from thy neighbour's house; lest he be weary of thee, and so hate thee.

A man that beareth false witness against his neighbour is a maul, and a sword, and a sharp arrow. (Proverbs 25: 17, 18.)

And the second is like, namely this, Thou shalt love thy neighbour as thyself. There is none other commandment greater than these.

And the scribe said unto him, Well,

Master, thou hast said the truth: for there is one God· and there is none other but he:

And to love him with all the heart, and with all the understanding, and with all the soul, and with all the strength, and to love his neighbour as himself, is more than all whole burnt offerings and sacrifices.

And when Jesus saw that he answered discreetly, he said unto him. *Thou art not far from the kingdom of God.* And no man after that durst ask him any question. (Mark 12: 31-34.)

For this, Thou shalt not commit adultery, Thou shalt not kill, Thou shalt not steal, Thou shalt not bear false witness, Thou shalt not covet; and if there be any other commandment, it is briefly comprehended in this saying, namely, Thou shalt love thy neighbour as thyself.

Love worketh no ill to his neighbour: therefore love is the fulfilling of the law. (Romans 13: 9, 10.)

For all the law is fulfilled in one word, even in this; Thou shalt love thy neighbour as thyself.

But if ye bite and devour one another, take heed that ye be not consumed one of another. (Galatians 5: 14.)

If ye fulfil the royal law, according to the Scripture, Thou shalt love thy neighbour as thyself, ye do well. (James 2: 8.)

NICODEMUS.

Nic'o-de'mus—a word of somewhat uncertain origin, but probably from a Greek word meaning "conqueror of the people." Nicodemus was a wealthy Jew, a Pharisee and a member of the Sanhedrin. He was impressed by Jesus' teachings, but being afraid to seek Him openly, paid a visit by night, receiving instructions from the Master. He aided Joseph of Arimathea to bury the crucified Lord. Tradition says that later he openly avowed himself a follower of Christ, but there is no evidence to support this.

References.—John 3, 7, and 19.

NIGHT. (See Day.)

Night—the opposite of day; used often in the Scripture in a figurative sense to express darkness of the spiritual understanding.

REFERENCES.

And God called the light Day, and the darkness he called Night: and the evening and the morning were the first day. (Genesis 1: 5.)

Day unto day uttereth speech, and night unto night sheweth knowledge. (Psalm 19: 2.)

I must work the works of him that sent me, while it is day: the night cometh, when no man can work. (John 9: 4.)

The night is far spent, the day is at hand: let us therefore cast off the works of darkness, and let us put on the armour of light. (Romans 13: 12.)

Ye are all the children of light, and the children of the day: we are not of the night nor of darkness.

Therefore let us not sleep, as do others; but let us watch and be sober.

For they that sleep, sleep in the night; and they that be drunken are drunken in the night. (1 Thessalonians 5: 5.)

And the gates of it shall not be shut at all by day: for there shall be no night there. (Revelation 21: 25.)

Thy sun shall no more go down; neither shall thy moon withdraw itself: for the Lord shall be thine everlasting light, and the days of thy mourning shall be ended. (Isaiah 60: 20.)

NINEVEH. (See Assyria, Babylon.)

Nin'e-veh — a Chaldee - Hebrew word meaning "the dwelling of Ninus." Nineveh was one of the greatest cities of the ancient world; to-day naught remains of it but some scattered heaps or mounds, not even the ruins of buildings being left to show traces of that which was once the queen city of the world. It was a city of vastnesses of all sorts, vast buildings, vast wealth, vast power, vast sins, vast licentiousness, and vast evil, and, as was prophecied, it has been wiped utterly from the face of the earth.

Researches show that Nineveh must have been founded at least 2,500 years before Christ and probably earlier. It originally was a colony established by the Babylonians (probably under that Asshur, who became the founder of the Assyrian kingdom). As the Assyrian monarchy grew, so did Nineveh, which the kings made their capital. Finally it became greater than its mother city, and at one time waged such successful war against it that Babylon and the Babylonian empire for a time became a subject state. But like Babylon, it fell a victim to the Persian conqueror and then to the Greeks and Romans.

Of its wickednesses we have plenty of evidence throughout the Bible. Its men were bold, cruel, warlike, and grasping; its women licentious and evil. In Jonah we learn a little of the badness of the place.

At its zenith of wealth and power the place was of enormous extent, equal in size to any of the great capitals of the modern world. One old historian tells us that its walls were no less than 72 miles in circumference or perimeter. The same writer says they were 100 feet high and wide enough for three war chariots to drive abreast, and that there were 1,500 towers around them. Under Sargon, Shalmaneser, and Tiglath-Pileser, its most famous kings, its treasure-houses and palaces were full of the plunder of the then known world.

NOAH. (See Flood.)

No'ah—a form of a Hebrew word meaning "rest" or "quiet." Noah's place in the Bible is familiar to every reader or student of the Book. Of his early history we have little or no knowledge save that he was the son of the second Lamech and the tenth in line from Adam. Genesis tells us of the wrath of God against mankind for wicked-

ness and God's intention to save Noah and his family and certain specimens of animal life in order to populate the world after venting His wrath by destroying man by a vast flood. Noah, following the divine command, built an ark and went into it with his family and the animals, thus passing unscathed through the flood which raged. Noah's first act, after reaching dry land again, was to offer thankful sacrifices to God. His sons, Shem, Ham, and Japhet, became the fathers of the new human race.

REFERENCES.

And Lamech lived a hundred eighty and two years, and begat a son:

And he called his name Noah, saying, This same shall comfort us concerning our work and toil of our hands, because of the ground which the Lord hath cursed. (Genesis 5: 28, 29.)

And the Lord said, I will destroy man whom I have created from the face of the earth; both man and beast, and the creeping thing, and the fowls of the air; for it repenteth me that I have made them.

But Noah found grace in the eyes of the Lord.

These are the generations of Noah: Noah was a just man and perfect in his generations, and Noah walked with God.

And Noah begat three sons, Shem, Ham, and Japheth.

The earth also was corrupt before God; and the earth was filled with violence.

And God looked upon the earth, and behold, it was corrupt; for all flesh had corrupted his way upon the earth.

And God said unto Noah, The end of all flesh is come before me; for the earth is filled with violence through them; and behold, I will destroy them with the earth.

Make thee an ark of gopher wood;

rooms shalt thou make in the ark, and shalt pitch it within and without with pitch. (Genesis 6: 7-14.)

And the Lord said unto Noah, Come thou and all thy house into the ark; for thee have I seen righteous before me in this generation.

Of every clean beast thou shalt take to thee by sevens, the male and his female: and of beasts that are not clean by two, the male and his female.

Of fowls also of the air by sevens, the male and the female; to keep seed alive upon the face of all the earth. (Genesis 7: 1-3.)

And Noah was six hundred years old when the flood of waters was upon the earth.

And Noah went in, and his sons, and his wife, and his sons' wives with him, into the ark, because of the waters of the flood. (Genesis 7: 6, 7.)

And in the second month, on the seven and twentieth day of the month, was the earth dried.

And God spake unto Noah, saying,

Go forth of the ark, thou, and thy wife, and thy sons, and thy sons' wives with thee.

Bring forth with thee every living thing that is with thee, of all flesh, both of fowl, and of cattle, and of every creeping thing that creepeth upon the earth; that they may breed abundantly in the earth, and be fruitful, and multiply upon the earth.

And Noah went forth, and his sons, and his wife, and his sons' wives with him:

Every beast, every creeping thing, and every fowl, and whatsoever creepeth upon the earth, after their kinds, went forth out of the ark.

And Noah builded an altar unto the Lord; and took of every clean beast, and of every clean fowl, and offered burnt offerings on the altar. (Genesis 8: 14-20.)

And Noah lived after the flood three hundred and fifty years.

And all the days of Noah were nine hundred and fifty years: and he died. (Genesis 9: 28, 29.)

OATH.

OATH—strictly speaking an appeal to God to witness the truth of a statement. Thus there are two parts to an oath—the human declaration and the divine attestation asked for by the person declaring. The sacred nature of the act must be apparent, and therefore persons taking false oaths commit one of the most deadly of sins. It is usual to take oath upon the Bible, but the Jew, who does not recognize the inspired nature of all the Scriptures, takes oath only upon the first five books, otherwise known as the Pentateuch, which are the books of the Law to him. The condemnation passed upon the oath by the Master during the course of the Sermon on the Mount has been regarded as forbidding the taking of an oath upon all occasions. A single glance at this position should show the fallacy of it, and indicate that what the Saviour had reference to was the indiscriminate swearing that went on in His times between man and man. That the Saviour meant to forbid the judicial oath, or oath in a court of law, is unthinkable, for He Himself did not hesitate to make oath before the high priest. The apostles quite well understood the Master's meaning, for they recognized the oath and its nature and used it. (See 2 Corinthians 11: 31 and Galatians 1: 20.)

REFERENCES.

Christ's Teaching Concerning Oaths.

Pharisaic Casuistry Denounced:

Woe unto you, scribes and Pharisees, hypocrites! for ye compass sea and land to make one proselyte; and when he is made, ye make him twofold more the child of hell than yourselves.

Woe unto you, ye blind guides, which

say, Whosoever shall swear by the temple, it is nothing; but whosoever shall swear by the gold of the temple, he is a debtor!

Ye fools and blind: for whether is greater the gold, or the temple that sanctifieth the gold?

And, Whosoever shall swear by the altar, it is nothing; but whosoever sweareth by the gift that is upon it, he is guilty.

Ye fools and blind; for whether is greater, the gift, or the altar that sanctifieth the gift?

Whoso therefore shall swear by the altar, sweareth by it, and by all things thereon.

And whoso shall swear by the temple, sweareth by it, and by him that dwelleth therein.

And he that shall swear by heaven, sweareth by the throne of God, and by him that sitteth thereon. (Matthew 23: 15-22.)

Swearing Forbidden:

Again, ye have heard that it hath been said by them of old time, Thou shalt not forswear thyself, but shalt perform unto the Lord thine oaths:

But I say unto you, Swear not at all; neither by heaven; for it is God's throne:

Nor by the earth; for it is his footstool: neither by Jerusalem; for it is the city of the great King.

Neither shalt thou swear by thy head, because thou canst not make one hair white or black.

But let your communication be, Yea, yea; Nay, nay: for whatsoever is more than these cometh of evil. (Matthew 5: 33-37.)

But above all things, my brethren, swear not, neither by heaven, neither by the earth, neither by any other oath: but let your yea be yea; and your nay, nay; lest ye fall into condemnation. (James 5: 12.)

Judicial Oaths: Apostolic Oaths.

But Jesus held his peace. And the high priest answered and said unto him, I adjure thee by the living God, that thou tell us whether thou be the Christ, the Son of God.

Jesus saith unto him, *Thou hast said: nevertheless I say unto you, Hereafter shall ye see the Son of man sitting on the right hand of power, and coming in the clouds of heaven.* (Matthew 26: 63, 64.)

The God and Father of our Lord Jesus Christ, which is blessed for evermore, knoweth that I lie not. (2 Corinthians 11: 31.)

Now the things which I write unto you, behold, before God, I lie not. (Galatians 1: 20.)

I protest by your rejoicing which I have in Christ Jesus our Lord, I die daily. (1 Corinthians 15: 31.)

Moreover I call God for a record upon my soul, that to spare you I came not as yet unto Corinth. (2 Corinthians 1: 23.)

OBADIAH.

O-BA-DI′AH—a form of a Hebrew word meaning "servant of Jehovah." Obadiah was the name of several persons mentioned in Scripture, the most important of whom is the prophet Obadiah. He is supposed to have lived and written about the year 600 B.C. We know nothing of his life and have but a fragment of his work as a prophet.

Reference.—The book of Obadiah.

OBEDIENCE.

O-BE′DI-ENCE—the act of conforming to the command of a superior out of due regard for his authority. Obedience is one of the fundamentals necessary to the Christian life. Faith in itself is simply a form of obedience, while the more active forms of it are in keeping the commands of God. For our example we have the obedience to God the Father of Jesus Christ, God the Son. We can easily see in His life passages where the human side of Him asserted itself, and where, tempted as we are, the human man in Him was put to the test. And yet, with what wonderful self-effacement He came forth from the trial obedient even unto death. A sublime illustration of this obedience is to be found in His prayer in the garden of Gethsemane to have the cup of sorrow and death pass from him, if it were God's will. We see in this the strivings of the man nature against the awful agonies He knew he was to undergo on the cross.

REFERENCES.

Obedience of Christ.

And he taketh with him Peter and James and John, and began to be sore amazed, and to be very heavy;

And saith unto them, *My soul is exceeding sorrowful unto death: tarry ye here, and watch.*

And he went forward a little, and fell on the ground, and prayed that, if it were possible, the hour might pass from him.

And he said, *Abba, Father, all things are possible unto thee; take away this cup from me: nevertheless not what I will, but what thou wilt.*

And he cometh, and findeth them sleeping, and saith unto Peter, *Simon, sleepest thou? couldest not thou watch one hour?*

Watch ye and pray, lest ye enter into temptation. The spirit truly is ready, but the flesh is weak.

And again he went away, and prayed, and spake the same words.

And when he returned, he found them asleep again, (for their eyes were heavy,) neither wist they what to answer him.

And he cometh the third time, and saith unto them, *Sleep on now, and take your rest: it is enough, the hour is come; behold, the Son of man is betrayed into the hands of sinners.*

Rise up, let us go; lo, he that betrayeth me is at hand. (Mark 14: 33-42.)

For as by one man's disobedience many were made sinners: so by the obedience of one shall many be made righteous. (Romans 5: 19.)

And being found in fashion as a man, he humbled himself, and became obedient unto death, even the death of the Cross. (Philippians 2: 8.)

Who in the days of his flesh, when he had offered up prayers and supplications with strong crying and tears unto him that was able to save him from death, and was heard in that he feared;

Though he were a Son, yet learned he obedience by the things which he suffered. (Hebrews 5: 7, 8.)

Obedience to God Enjoined.

Now therefore, if ye will obey my voice indeed, and keep my covenant, then ye shall be a peculiar treasure unto me above all people: for all the earth is mine. (Exodus 19: 5.)

Beware of him, and obey his voice, provoke him not; for he will not pardon your transgressions: for my name is in him.

But if thou shalt indeed obey his voice, and do all that I speak; then I will be an enemy unto thine enemies, and an adversary unto thine adversaries. (Exodus 23: 21, 22.)

Therefore thou shalt love the Lord thy God, and keep his charge, and his statutes, and his judgments, and his commandments, always. (Deuteronomy 11: 1.)

Behold, I set before you this day a blessing and a curse:

A blessing, if ye obey the commandments of the Lord your God which I command you this day;

And a curse, if ye will not obey the commandments of the Lord your God, but turn aside out of the way which I command you this day, to go after other gods which ye have not known. (Deuteronomy 11: 26-28.)

If ye be willing and obedient, ye shall eat the good of the land:

But if ye refuse and rebel, ye shall be devoured with the sword: for the mouth of the Lord hath spoken it. (Isaiah 1: 19, 20.)

But this thing commanded I them, saying, Obey my voice, and I will be your God, and ye shall be my people: and walk ye in all the ways that I have commanded you, that it may be well unto you. (Jeremiah 7: 23.)

Therefore now amend your ways and your doings, and obey the voice of the Lord your God; and the Lord will repent him of the evil that he hath pronounced against you. (Jeremiah 26: 13.)

Then Peter and the other Apostles answered, and said, We ought to obey God rather than men. (Acts 5: 29.)

But whoso looketh into the perfect law of liberty, and continueth therein, he being not a forgetful hearer, but a doer of the work, this man shall be blessed in his deed. (James 1: 25.)

Blessings of Obedience.

And it shall come to pass, if thou shalt hearken diligently unto the voice of the Lord thy God, to observe and to do all his commandments which I command thee this day: that the Lord thy God will set thee on high above all nations of the earth:

And all these blessings shall come on thee, and overtake thee, if thou shalt hearken unto the voice of the Lord thy God.

Blessed shalt thou be in the city, and blessed shalt thou be in the field.

Blessed shall be the fruit of thy body, and the fruit of thy ground, and the fruit of thy cattle, the increase of thy kine, and the flocks of thy sheep.

Blessed shall be thy basket and thy store.

Blessed shalt thou be when thou comest in, and blessed shalt thou be when thou goest out. (Deuteronomy 28: 1-6.)

Not every one that saith unto me, Lord, Lord, shall enter into the kingdom of heaven; but he that doeth the will of my Father which is in heaven.

Many will say to me in that day, Lord, Lord, have we not prophesied in thy name? and in thy name have cast out devils? and in thy name done many wonderful works?

And then will I profess unto them, I never knew you: depart from me, ye that work iniquity.

Therefore whosoever heareth these sayings of mine, and doeth them, I will liken him unto a wise man, which built his house upon a rock:

And the rain descended, and the floods came, and the winds blew, and beat upon that house; and it fell not: for it was founded upon a rock.

And every one that heareth these sayings of mine, and doeth them not, shall be likened unto a foolish man, which built his house upon the sand:

And the rain descended, and the floods came, and the winds blew, and beat upon that house, and it fell: and great was the fall of it. (Matthew 7: 21-27.)

By faith Abraham, when he was called to go out into a place which he should after receive for an inheritance, obeyed; and he went out, not knowing whither he went. (Hebrews 11: 8.)

Seeing ye have purified your souls in obeying the truth to the Spirit, unto unfeigned love of the brethren: see that ye love one another with a pure heart fervently. (1 Peter 1: 22.)

Blessed are they that do his commandments, that they may have right to the tree of life, and may enter in through the gates into the city. (Revelation 22: 14.)

Obedience Preferred Before Sacrifice.

And Samuel said, Hath the Lord as great delight in burnt-offerings and sacrifices, as in obeying the voice of the Lord? Behold, to obey is better than sacrifice, and to hearken than the fat of rams. (1 Samuel 15: 22.)

Obedience to the Faith.

For if I have boasted any thing to him of you, I am not ashamed; but as we spake all things to you in truth, even so our boasting which I made before Titus, is found a truth.

And his inward affection is more abundant toward you, whilst he remembereth the obedience of you all, how with fear and trembling you received him. (2 Corinthians 7: 14, 15.)

Elect, according to the foreknowledge of God the Father, through sanctification of the Spirit unto obedience, and sprinkling of the blood of Jesus Christ: Grace unto you and peace be multiplied. (1 Peter 1: 2.)

Domestic and Governmental Obedience.

Children, obey your parents in the Lord: for this is right. (Ephesians 6: 1.)

Children, obey your parents in all things, for this is well pleasing unto the Lord. (Colossians 3: 20.)

To be discreet, chaste, keepers at home, good, obedient to their own husbands, that the word of God be not blasphemed. (Titus 2: 5.)

Servants, be obedient to them that are your masters according to the flesh, with fear and trembling, in singleness of your heart, as unto Christ:

Not with eyeservice as menpleasers, but as the servants of Christ, doing the will of God from the heart. (Ephesians 6: 5, 6.)

Obey them that have the rule over you, and submit yourselves: for they watch for your souls, as they that must give account, that they may do it with joy, and not with grief: for that is unprofitable for you. (Hebrews 13: 17.)

OFFENSE. (See Sin.)

OF-FENSE'—the act of offending, either by sin or crime, affront or injury. Offense by all of the four means given above is indicated in various passages of Scripture. The word is spelled "offence" in Scripture.

REFERENCES.
Giving of Offense Deprecated.

Give none offence, neither to the Jews, nor to the Gentiles, nor to the Church of God. (1 Corinthians 10: 32.)

Giving no offence in any thing, that the ministry be not blamed. (2 Corinthians 6: 3.)

That ye may approve things that are excellent, that ye may be sincere and without offence till the day of Christ. (Philippians 1: 10.)

Woe Because of Offenses (Sin).

Woe unto the world because of offences! for it must needs be that offences come; but woe to that man by whom the offence cometh!

Remedies for Offenses.

If the spirit of the ruler rise up against thee, leave not thy place; for yielding pacifieth great offences. (Ecclesiastes 10: 4.)

And if thy right eye offend thee, pluck it out, and cast it from thee: for it is profitable for thee that one of thy members should perish, and not that thy whole body should be cast into hell.

And if thy right hand offend thee, cut it off, and cast it from thee: for it is profitable for thee that one of thy members should perish, and not that thy whole body should be cast into hell. (Matthew 5: 29, 30.)

Wherefore if thy hand or thy foot offend thee, cut them off, and cast them from thee: it is better for thee to enter into life halt or maimed, rather than having two hands or two feet to be cast into everlasting fire.

And if thine eye offend thee, pluck it out, and cast it from thee: it is better for thee to enter into life with one eye, rather than having two eyes to be cast into hell fire. (Matthew 18: 8, 9.)

And whosoever shall offend one of these little ones that believe in me, it is better for him that a millstone were hanged about his neck, and he were cast into the sea. (Mark 9: 42.)

Now I beseech you, brethren, mark them which cause divisions and offences contrary to the doctrine which ye have learned; and avoid them.

For they that are such serve not our Lord Jesus Christ, but their own belly; and by good words and fair speeches deceive the hearts of the simple. (Romans 16: 17, 18.)

Christ Delivered for Our Offenses.

But for us also, to whom it shall be imputed, if we believe on him that raised up Jesus our Lord from the dead;

Who was delivered for our offences, and was raised again for our justification. (Romans 4: 24, 25.)

OLIVET OR OLIVES, MOUNT OF.

OL'I-VET—another name for the Mount of Olives, a range of hills near Jerusalem, so named because of the large number of olive trees which grew upon its slopes.

OMNIPOTENCE. (See Christ, God.)

OMNIPRESENCE. (See Christ, God.)

OMNISCIENCE. (See Christ, God.)

OPPRESSION. (See Bondage.)

OP-PRES'SION — the act of oppressing; working hardship or injustice upon another because of superior strength or power; tyranny; unnecessary severity or cruelty. Oppression is one of the sins into which mankind falls simply because he is mankind and is inclined to show forth his power over such persons as are weaker than he. The Bible utters warnings throughout its length over the needless exercise of tyranny and severity. When inclined to oppress those who are weaker than we, or who are at our mercy, we should remember the merciful nature of God, who never indulges in oppression, although His power is so immeasurably greater than ours.

REFERENCES.

Thou shalt neither vex a stranger, nor oppress him: for ye were strangers in the land of Egypt.

Ye shall not afflict any widow, or fatherless child.

If thou afflict them in any wise, and

they cry at all unto me, I will surely hear their cry;

And my wrath shall wax hot, and I will kill you with the sword; and your wives shall be widows, and your children fatherless. (Exodus 22: 21-24.)

And if thou sell aught unto thy neighbour, or buyest aught of thy neighbour's hand, ye shall not oppress one another. (Leviticus 25: 14.)

He shall dwell with thee, even among you in that place which he shall choose in one of thy gates where it liketh him best: thou shalt not oppress him. (Deuteronomy 23: 16.)

Thou shalt not oppress an hired servant that is poor and needy, whether he be of thy brethren, or of thy strangers that are in thy land within thy gates. (Deuteronomy 24: 14.)

For the oppression of the poor, for the sighing of the needy, now will I arise, saith the Lord; I will set him in safety from him that puffeth at him. (Psalm 12: 5.)

Trust not in oppression, and become not vain in robbery: if riches increase, set not your heart upon them. (Psalm 62: 10.)

So I returned, and considered all the oppressions that are done under the sun: and behold the tears of such as were oppressed, and they had no comforter; and on the side of their oppressors there was power; but they had no comforter. (Ecclesiastes 4: 1.)

If thou seest the oppression of the poor, and violent perverting of judgment and justice in a province, marvel not at the matter: for he that is higher than the highest regardeth; and there be higher than they. (Ecclesiastes 5: 8.)

Learn to do well; seek judgment, relieve the oppressed, judge the father-less, plead for the widow. (Isaiah 1: 17.)

Wo unto them that decree unrighteous decrees, and that write grievousness which they have prescribed;

To turn aside the needy from judgment, and to take away the right from the poor of my people, that widows may be their prey, and that they may rob the fatherless!

And what will ye do in the day of visitation, and in the desolation which shall come from far? to whom will ye flee for help? and where will ye leave your glory?

Without me they shall bow down under the prisoners, and they shall fall under the slain. For all this his anger is not turned away, but his hand is stretched out still. (Isaiah 10: 1-4.)

Is not this the fast that I have chosen? to loose the bands of wickedness, to undo the heavy burdens, and to let the oppressed go free, and that ye break every yoke? (Isaiah 58: 6.)

In thee have they set light by father and mother: in the midst of thee have they dealt by oppression with the stranger: in thee have they vexed the fatherless and the widow. (Ezekiel 22: 7.)

Wo to them that devise iniquity, and work evil upon their beds! when the morning is light, they practise it, because it is in the power of their hand.

And they covet fields, and take them by violence; and houses, and take them away: so they oppress a man and his house, even a man and his heritage.

Therefore thus saith the Lord; Behold, against this family do I devise an evil, from which ye shall not remove your necks; neither shall ye go haughtily: for this time is evil. (Micah 2: 1-3.)

And I will come near to you to judgment: and I will be a swift witness against the sorcerers, and against the adulterers, and against false swearers, and against those that oppress the hireling in his wages, the widow, and the fatherless, and that turn aside the stranger from his right, and fear not me, saith the Lord of hosts. (Malachi 3: 5.)

Behold, the hire of the labourers which have reaped down your fields, which is of you kept back by fraud, crieth: and the cries of them which have reaped are entered into the ears of the Lord of Sabaoth. (James 5: 4.)

ORACLE.

Or'a-cle—strictly speaking, the answer of a god or something reputed to be a god to a question propounded by a worshiper. Scripturally, the word has a wider meaning. The old prophets were called oracles because they were the mouthpieces of God, and the Scriptures are called oracles because they were inspired by God. The sanctuary of the Temple was also called the oracle, as the holy of holies.

REFERENCES.

The Scriptures as Oracles.

This is he that was in the Church in the wilderness with the Angel which spake to him in the mount Sina, and with our fathers: who received the lively oracles, to give unto us. (Acts 7: 38.)

What advantage then hath the Jew? or what profit is there of circumcision?

Much every way: chiefly, because that unto them were committed the Oracles of God. (Romans 3: 1, 2.)

For when for the time ye ought to be teachers, ye have need that one teach you again which be the first principles of the oracles of God; and are become such as have need of milk, and not of strong meat. (Hebrews 5: 12.)

If any man speak, let him speak as the oracles of God: if any man minister, let him do it as of the ability which God giveth, that God in all things may be glorified through Jesus Christ, to whom be praise and dominion for ever and ever. Amen. (1 Peter 4: 11.)

ORDER.

Or'der—regular arrangement; established rule or custom to prevent confusion; also the decorum of public assemblages or civil life. In various passages the Scriptures point out the necessity for order, especially in the worship of God and in the churches.

REFERENCES.

Let all things be done decently, and in order. (1 Corinthians 14: 40.)

For this cause left I thee in Crete, that thou shouldest set in order the things that are wanting, and ordain Elders in every city, as I had appointed thee. (Titus 1: 5.)

ORDINANCES.

Or'di-nanc-es — ecclesiastical rites and ceremonies. The ordinances are certain institutions of divine order and authority relating to the worship of God. They may be named as (1) Baptism; (2) The Lord's Supper; (3) public ministry or preaching or reading the word; (4) hearing the gospel; (5) prayer; (6) singing of psalms and hymns; (7) fasting; (8) solemn thanksgivings. Some denominations do not recognize all of the above as essential ordinances, holding that only the Lord's Supper and Baptism are ordinances in the complete sense of the word. Still other denominations hold that one or two institutions other than the first two are ordinances. Scriptural authority for the above-named will be found below.

REFERENCES.

Baptism.

Go ye therefore, and teach all nations, baptizing them in the name of the

Father, and of the Son, and of the Holy Ghost. (Matthew 28: 19.)

The Lord's Supper.

And he took the cup, and gave thanks and said, *Take this, and divide it among yourselves:*

For I say unto you, I will not drink of the fruit of the vine, until the kingdom of God shall come.

And he took bread, and gave thanks, and brake it, and gave unto them, saying, *This is my body which is given for you: this do in remembrance of me.*

Likewise also the cup after supper, saying, *This cup is the new testament in my blood, which is shed for you.* (Luke 22: 17-20.)

Public Ministry.

And he said unto them, *Go ye into all the world, and preach the gospel to every creature.* (Mark 16: 15.)

Hearing the Gospel.

If any man have ears to hear, let him hear. (Mark 4: 23.)

Public Prayer.

After this manner therefore pray ye: Our Father which art in heaven, Hallowed be thy name.

Thy kingdom come. Thy will be done in earth, as it is in heaven.

Give us this day our daily bread.

And forgive us our debts, as we forgive our debtors.

And lead us not into temptation, but deliver us from evil: For thine is the kingdom, and the power, and the glory, for ever. Amen. (Matthew 6: 9-13.)

Singing of Psalms.

Let the word of Christ dwell in you richly in all wisdom; teaching and admonishing one another in psalms and hymns and spiritual songs, singing with grace in your hearts to the Lord. (Colossians 3: 16.)

Fasting.

Blessed are they which do hunger and thirst after righteousness: for they shall be filled. (Matthew 5: 6.)

And Jesus said unto them, *Can the children of the bridechamber mourn, as long as the bridegroom is with them? but the days will come, when the bridegroom shall be taken from them, and then shall they fast.* (Matthew 9: 15.)

Solemn Thanksgiving.

In every thing give thanks: for this is the will of God in Christ Jesus concerning you. (1 Thessalonians 5: 18.)

ORDINATION.

OR'DI-NA'TION—the act or state of being ordained or ordered, constituted, or set apart, as for the ministry or the diaconate. Ordination is the setting forth to the world the right of the ordained person to officiate as a minister of the gospel and to practice and celebrate those ordinances that God, in His wisdom, saw fit to establish for the maintenance of His Church. It is a time of intense solemnity, for after the ceremony has been performed the ordained one has become a special servant and minister of God, in a different and more responsible relation to the Master than the ordinary human being.

REFERENCES.

Mode and Use of Ordination.

And the saying pleased the whole multitude: and they chose Stephen, a man full of faith and of the Holy Ghost, and Philip, and Prochorus, and Nicanor, and Timon, and Permenas, and Nicolas a proselyte of Antioch.

Whom they set before the Apostles:

and when they had prayed, they laid their hands on them. (Acts 6: 5, 6.)

And when they had ordained them Elders in every Church, and had prayed with fasting, they commended them to the Lord, on whom they believed. (Acts 14: 23.)

Whereunto I am ordained a preacher, and an Apostle (I speak the truth in Christ, and lie not), a teacher of the Gentiles in faith and verity. (1 Timothy 2: 7.)

Neglect not the gift that is in thee, which was given thee by prophecy, with the laying on of the hands of the presbytery. (1 Timothy 4: 14.)

And the things that thou hast heard of me among many witnesses, the same commit thou to faithful men, who shall be able to teach others also. (2 Timothy 2: 2.)

For this cause left I thee in Crete, that thou shouldest set in order the things that are wanting, and ordain elders in every city, as I had appointed thee. (Titus 1: 5.)

OSTENTATION. (See Boasting, Pride.)

Os'ten-ta'tion — ambitious, proud, and unnecessary display; pretentious parade of one's wealth in dress, manner, speech, or mode of living. The vice of ostentation forms the subject of a number of passages of Scripture. It is against the principle and theory of Christianity, as well as being a useless and foolish vanity.

REFERENCES.

Whoso boasteth himself of a false gift is like clouds and wind without rain. (Proverbs 25: 14.)

Boast not thyself of to-morrow; for thou knowest not what a day may bring forth.

Let another man praise thee, and not thine own mouth; a stranger, and not thine own lips. (Proverbs 27: 1, 2.)

Take heed that ye do not your alms before men, to be seen of them: otherwise ye have no reward of your Father which is in heaven.

Therefore when thou doest thine alms, do not sound a trumpet before thee, as the hypocrites do in the synagogues and in the streets, that they may have glory of men. Verily I say unto you, They have their reward.

But when thou doest alms, let not thy left hand know what thy right hand doeth:

That thine alms may be in secret: and thy Father which seeth in secret himself shall reward thee openly. (Matthew 6: 1-4.)

PARABLE. (See Appendix.)

Par'a-ble—a short, fictitious, and comparative narrative of something which might occur in real life, from which a moral is pointed or a lesson taught. The parable as a means of teaching was used by the Hebrew teachers from the earliest times, and arrived at its highest development in the parables of Jesus. It was a form specially adapted to a low class of minds. The most ignorant people could absorb and digest a parable where they could not begin to comprehend a thing taught in direct language. This was doubtless due to the story or narrative form of it, impressing a series of facts upon the mind, each fact containing some germ of the truth the teacher sought to impart.

Jesus made His parables things of actual life, and they form the most characteristic and beautiful passages of his teachings. They number, as we get them, about thirty, but unquestionably in the course of His ministry he spoke many more. They are susceptible of arrangement into four groups, which, if followed in proper rotation, give a splendid idea of the Master's teaching and the things He taught. These groups are set out below, only single references being used, the choice being given to the best of the forms:

First Group: Christ's Kingdom.

1. Wicked Husbandmen (Matt. 21: 33-44). The fate of those who abuse their privileges and refuse to enter the kingdom.

2. The Rich Fool (Luke 12: 16-21). The vanity of all worldly things without the kingdom.

3. The Marriage of the King's Son (Matt. 22: 1-14). Danger of rejecting the invitations of the kingdom.

4. The Barren Fig-tree (Luke 13: 6-9). Danger of delay.

5. The Great Supper (Luke 14: 15-24). Outward privileges useless without a personal use of the means of salvation.

6. The Pearl of Great Price (Matt. 13: 45, 46). The kingdom to be sought for alone.

7. The Hid Treasure (Matt. 13: 44). Sacrifice for the kingdom when found.

8. The Rich Man and Lazarus (Luke 16: 19-31). The kingdom in the estimate of God and of man.

Second Group: The Kingdom and the Human Heart.

9. The Sower (Matt. 13: 3-8). Preparation of the heart.

10. The Seed Growing Secretly (Mark 4: 26-29). The kingdom grows in the heart silently and constantly.

11. The Tares and the Wheat (Matt. 13: 24-30). Difficulties in the way of the kingdom.

12. The Mustard-seed (Matt. 13: 31, 32). Outward growth of the kingdom.

13. The Leaven in the Meal (Matt. 13: 33). Inward growth.

Third Group: The Kingdom Manifested.

14. The Two Debtors (Luke 7: 41-43). The kingdom appears in obedience springing from love.

15. The Good Samaritan (Luke 10: 30-37). Aid in love, which knows no limits and spares no pains.

16. The Two Sons (Matt. 21: 28). In the obedience of deeds not words.

17. The Unmerciful Servant (Matt. 18: 23-35). In mercy and forgiveness without limit.

18. The Unjust Steward (Luke 16: 1-9). In wise and energetic improvement of temporal advantages.

19. The Friend at Midnight (Luke 11: 5-8). In constant prayer.

20. The Unjust Judge (Luke 18: 1-8). Persevering prayer.

21. The Pharisee and Publican (Luke 18: 9-14). In humility and contrition.

22. The Laborers in the Vineyard (Matt. 20: 1-16). Unselfish rejoicing in the salvation of others.

23. The Lost Sheep (Matt. 17).

24. The Lost Piece of Money (Luke 15: 8-10).

25. The Prodigal Son (Luke 15: 11-32). In acknowledging the wisdom and beauty of receiving sinners, and in a missionary spirit.

26. The Unprofitable Servant (Luke 17: 7-10.) Confessing all that we can do is nothing.

27. The Ten Virgins (Matt. 25: 1-13). Preparation for the coming of the Lord.

28. The Talents (Matt. 25: 14-30). Active preparation for the coming of the Lord.

Fourth Group: The Kingdom Consummated.

29. The Pounds (Luke 19: 11-27). The final reckoning.

30. The Draw-net (Matt. 13: 47-50). The final separation.

(See Jesus for complete references to parables, in the various gospels.)

Old Testament Parables.

1. The Ewe Lamb—Nathan to David (2 Samuel 12: 1-4).

2. The Two Brethren—by the widow of Tekoah (2 Samuel 14: 1-11).

3. The Escaped Captive—by one of the sons of the prophets to Ahab (1 Kings 20: 35-40).

4. The Vineyard and the Grapes—Isaiah to Judah and Jerusalem (Isaiah 5: 1-7).

5. The Eagle and the Vine—Ezekiel to Israel (Ezekiel 17: 3-10).

6. The Lion's Whelps—Ezekiel to Israel (Ezekiel 19: 2-9).

7. The Boiling Pot — Ezekiel to Israel (Ezekiel 24: 3-5).

FABULOUS PARABLES.

1. The Trees Choosing a King—Jotham to the Shechemites (Judges 9: 7-15).
2. Micaiah's Dream (1 Kings 22: 19-23).
3. The Thistle and the Cedar (Jehoash to Amaziah (2 Kings 14: 9).
(See Appendix for tables of parables.)

PARACLETE. (See Comforter, Holy Ghost.)

PAR'A-CLETE—the English form of a Greek word meaning "one who pleads another's cause before a judge." It is one of the names applied to the Holy Ghost.

PARADISE. (See Eden, Heaven.)

PAR'A-DISE—generally, some place or state of bliss, or region or state wherein great happiness and felicity is to be enjoyed. The Bible utilizes the word to indicate (1) the Garden of Eden; (2) the abode of justified and sanctified souls, or Heaven; and (3) a state of happiness.

PARDON. (See Forgiveness, Sin, etc.)

PAR'DON—forgiveness; remission of punishment for an act of sin or injury. The Bible teaches us to pardon and forgive our enemies just as God is willing and ready to pardon and forgive our offenses against Him. Pardon for sin is one of the results of faith and repentance.

REFERENCES.

And why dost thou not pardon my transgression, and take away mine iniquity? for now shall I sleep in the dust; and thou shalt seek me in the morning, but I shall not be. (Job 7: 21.)

Remember not the sins of my youth, nor my transgressions: according to thy mercy remember thou me for thy goodness' sake, O Lord. (Psalm 25: 7.)

For thy name's sake, O Lord, pardon mine iniquity; for it is great. (Psalm 25: 11.)

Look upon mine affliction and my pain; and forgive all my sins. (Psalm 25: 18.)

Deliver me from all my transgressions: make me not the reproach of the foolish. (Psalm 39: 8.)

Have mercy upon me, O God, according to thy lovingkindness: according unto the multitude of thy tender mercies blot out my transgressions. (Psalm 51: 1.)

Make me to hear joy and gladness; that the bones which thou hast broken may rejoice.

Hide thy face from my sins, and blot out all mine iniquities. (Psalm 51: 8, 9.)

Deliver me from bloodguiltiness, O God, thou God of my salvation: and my tongue shall sing aloud of thy righteousness. (Psalm 51: 14.)

PARENTS. (See Children.)

PAR'ENTS—a name properly given to a father or mother, but also extended to their fathers and mothers upward in a direct line. As our divine Parent is good to us, His word counsels us to be good to our earthly parents. We are ordered to honor them in one of the commands of the Decalogue, and otherwise in the Bible told to set forth our love and obedience.

REFERENCES.

Duty to Parents.

Honour thy father and thy mother: that thy days may be long upon the land which the Lord thy God giveth thee. (Exodus 20: 12.)

Ye shall fear every man his mother and his father, and keep my sabbaths: I am the Lord your God. (Leviticus 19: 3.)

For God commanded, saying, Honour thy father and mother: and, He that curseth father or mother, let him die the death.

But ye say, Whosoever shall say to his father or his mother, It is a gift, by whatsoever thou mightest be profited by me;

And honour not his father or his mother, he shall be free. Thus have ye made the commandment of God of none effect by your tradition. (Matthew 15: 4-6.)

Honour thy father and thy mother: and, Thou shalt love thy neighbour as thyself. (Matthew 19: 19.)

Honour thy father and mother; which is the first commandment with promise;

That it may be well with thee, and thou mayest live long on the earth. (Ephesians 6: 2, 3.)

Duty of Parents.

He that spareth his rod hateth his son: but he that loveth him chasteneth him betimes. (Proverbs 13: 24.)

Chasten thy son while there is hope, and let not thy soul spare for his crying. (Proverbs 19: 18.)

Train up a child in the way he should go: and when he is old, he will not depart from it. (Proverbs 22: 6.)

Foolishness is bound in the heart of a child; but the rod of correction shall drive it far from him. (Proverbs 22: 15.)

Withhold not correction from the child: for if thou beatest him with the rod, he shall not die.

Thou shalt beat him with the rod, and shalt deliver his soul from hell. (Proverbs 23: 13, 14.)

If a son shall ask bread of any of you that is a father, will ye give him a stone? or if he ask a fish, will he for a fish give him a serpent?

Or if he shall ask an egg, will he offer him a scorpion?

If ye then, being evil, know how to give good gifts unto your children: how much more shall your heavenly Father give the Holy Spirit to them that ask him? (Luke 11: 11-13.)

And, ye fathers, provoke not your children to wrath: but bring them up in the nurture and admonition of the Lord. (Ephesians 6: 4.)

Fathers, provoke not your children to anger, lest they be discouraged. (Colossians 3: 21.)

But if any provide not for his own, and specially for those of his own house, he hath denied the faith, and is worse than an infidel. (1 Timothy 5: 8.)

PARTIALITY. (See Judgment.)

PAR'TI-AL'I-TY—the act of showing undue favor to one person or one thing over another person or thing; unjust bias of mind. The Bible regards partiality as an unfairness of which man should not be guilty and condemns it.

REFERENCES.

Ye shall do no unrighteousness in judgment; thou shalt not respect the person of the poor, nor honour the person of the mighty: but in righteousness shalt thou judge thy neighbour. (Leviticus 19: 15.)

Ye shall not respect persons in judgment; but ye shall hear the small as well as the great; ye shall not be afraid of the face of man; for the judgment is God's: and the cause that is too hard for you, bring it unto me, and I will hear it. (Deuteronomy 1: 17.)

Therefore have I also made you contemptible and base before all the people, according as ye have not kept my ways, but have been partial in the law. (Malachi 2: 9.)

I charge thee before God, and the Lord Jesus Christ, and the elect Angels, that thou observe these things without preferring one before another, doing nothing by partiality. (1 Timothy 5: 21.)

Are ye not then partial in yourselves, and are become judges of evil thoughts? (James 2: 4.)

But the wisdom that is from above, is first pure, then peaceable, gentle, and easy to be intreated, full of mercy, and good fruits, without partiality, and without hypocrisy. (James 3: 17.)

PASSOVER.

PASS'O-VER—the most important feast in the Jewish religious calendar. It was instituted to commemorate the saving of the Hebrew firstborn in Egypt at the time when God, smiting with death the firstborn of the Egyptians, passed over the houses of the Jews, which were marked with the blood of a lamb. The Jews have continued to observe the feast to the present day, sacrificing a lamb for the occasion. Beyond this historical significance, which is confined to the Hebrews, the Passover has a typical meaning. To the Christian it sets forth the great fact and consequences of the sacrifice of Jesus Christ in the shedding of His blood for the sins of the world (1 Corinthians 5: 7). Thus Jesus became the Paschal Lamb. The Jews, in roasting the Lamb of sacrifice, invariably used two transverse sticks thrust through the body in the shape of a cross. Even this, we see, is typical of the cross upon which Christ died.

REFERENCES.

Passover Instituted.

And this day shall be unto you for a memorial; and ye shall keep it a feast to the Lord throughout your generations: ye shall keep it a feast by an ordinance for ever. (Exodus 12: 14.)

And ye shall observe the feast of unleavened bread; for in this selfsame day have I brought your armies out of the land of Egypt: therefore shall ye observe this day in your generations by an ordinance for ever. (Exodus 12: 17.)

And ye shall observe this thing for an ordinance to thee and to thy sons for ever.

And it shall come to pass, when ye be come to the land which the Lord will give you, according as he hath promised, that ye shall keep this service.

And it shall come to pass, when your children shall say unto you, What mean ye by this service?

That ye shall say, It is the sacrifice of the Lord's passover, who passed over the houses of the children of Israel in Egypt, when he smote the Egyptians, and delivered our houses. And the people bowed the head and worshipped. (Exodus 12: 24-27.)

It is a night to be much observed unto the Lord for bringing them out from the land of Egypt: this is that night of the Lord to be observed of all the children of Israel in their generations. (Exodus 12: 42.)

Christ's Last Passover.

Now the first day of the feast of unleavened bread the disciples came to Jesus, saying unto him, Where wilt thou that we prepare for thee to eat the passover?

And he said, Go into the city to such a man, and say unto him, The Master saith, My time is at hand; I will keep the passover at thy house with my disciples.

And the disciples did as Jesus had appointed them; and they made ready the passover.

Now when the even was come, he sat down with the twelve. (Matthew 26: 17-20.)

Significance to Christians.

Purge out therefore the old leaven, that ye may be a new lump, as ye are unleavened. For even Christ our passover is sacrificed for us:

Therefore let us keep the feast, not with old leaven, neither. with the leaven of malice and wickedness; but with the unleavened bread of sincerity and truth. (1 Corinthians 5: 7, 8.)

PATIENCE.

PA'TIENCE—the state or quality of being patient; bearing suffering, trouble, disappointment, waiting, or trials with fortitude; uncomplaining endurance of evils or wrongs. There must be discrimination between patience and resignation. Patience implies the self-possession of the spirit and indicates a certain quietness and repose. Resignation is submission. One of the many virtues taught in Scripture is patience. It is a noble quality and one of the jewels of the Christian crown. Unless we have patience we are exceedingly liable to sin unwittingly because of the thousand and one petty annoyances of life, which harass the temper and leave us open to temptation.

REFERENCES.

Patience Under Affliction.

Surely it is meet to be said unto God, I have borne chastisement, I will not offend any more:

That which I see not teach thou me: If I have done iniquity, I will do no more. (Job 34: 31, 32.)

My son, despise not the chastening of the Lord; neither be weary of his correction. (Proverbs 3: 11.)

It is good for a man that he bear the yoke in his youth.

He sitteth alone and keepeth silence, because he hath borne it upon him.

He putteth his mouth in the dust; if so be there may be hope. (Lamentations 3: 27-29.)

And ye have forgotten the exhortation which speaketh unto you as unto children, My son, despise not thou the chastening of the Lord, nor faint when thou art rebuked of him. (Hebrews 12: 5.)

Exhortations to Patience.

Better is the end of a thing than the beginning thereof: and the patient in spirit is better than the proud in spirit. (Ecclesiastes 7: 8.)

In your patience possess ye your souls. (Luke 21: 19.)

Strengthened with all might, according to his glorious power, unto all patience and longsuffering with joyfulness. (Colossians 1: 11.)

Now we exhort you, brethren, warn them that are unruly, comfort the feebleminded, support the weak, be patient toward all men. (1 Thessalonians 5: 14.)

And so, after he had patiently endured, he obtained the promise. (Hebrews 6: 15.)

For ye have need of patience, that, after ye have done the will of God, ye might receive the promise. (Hebrews 10: 36.)

Knowing this, that the trying of your faith worketh patience.

But let patience have her perfect work, that ye may be perfect and entire, wanting nothing. (James 1: 3, 4.)

Be patient therefore, brethren, unto the coming of the Lord. Behold, the husbandman waiteth for the precious fruit of the earth, and hath long patience for it, until he receive the early and latter rain.

Be ye also patient; stablish your hearts: for the coming of the Lord draweth nigh. (James 5: 7, 8.)

Behold, we count them happy which

endure. Ye have heard of the patience of Job, and have seen the end of the Lord; that the Lord is very pitiful, and of tender mercy. (James 5: 11.)

PAUL.

PAUL—the Greek form of the name of the great apostle to the Gentiles, the original form of whose name, according to the Hebrew, was Saul, meaning "asked for."

The life and works of Paul, if we did but know the whole of them, would doubtless form one of the greatest of religious romances. Paul was born in the city of Tarsus, in Cilicia, about the year A.D. 5. His father, a Jew, seems to have rendered some service to the Roman government for which he was given the right of free Roman citizenship, which, under the Roman law, descended to his son. The family unquestionably was well-to-do, a fact deduced from the splendid education given to the future apostle. Tarsus in those days was a great seat of learning, and here Saul (as he was called in the Hebrew) went to school. At the same time he learned a trade, as did every Hebrew boy. This trade was the making of tent-cloth and tents. Later we find him using this trade as a means of self-support. Having arrived at the proper age, he was sent to Jerusalem; there to study for the Jewish ministry under the famous scholar and teacher, Gamaliel, who was a strict Pharisee. Paul's remarkable ability and mental powers doubtless attracted the admiration of Gamaliel, who is said to have specially favored his young pupil. We can imagine him a young man about the time of Christ's death, filled full of zeal for the Hebrew faith and of contempt and derision for the new faith of Christ. Having been educated among the strictest of the Pharisees, we easily can see a reason for the persecutions he heaped upon Jesus' followers. At this time he was just as devoted to the Pharisees as he afterwards became to the cause of the Master; and the Scriptures tell us how he pursued and persecuted the Christians and took part, although a passive one, in the martyrdom of the sainted Stephen.

But God had a use for this persecutor. He was to be the chosen vessel of His ministra-

tions to the Gentiles, and He was to convert him in a special and distinct way. This came about while Paul was on his way to Damascus, there to carry out certain plans for the further persecution of the Christians. He was struck to the ground by a sudden vision from Heaven and heard the voice of the Master calling to him. He realized instantly what had happened and bowed to the Divine Will, as he said: "Lord, what wilt thou have me to do?" His baptism and consecration to the cause followed. After this he seems to have spent three years in Arabia, doubtless in preparation for the gigantic work he was to do for the Master during the remainder of his life. On his return we find that he was received at first with suspicion until the apostles had assured their following that he was no longer the persecutor but an apostle like themselves.

His first work was done in Damascus, where he had once been the center of anti-Christian tyranny. The orthodox Jews naturally hated him, and we can imagine that more than once he must have barely escaped with his life from them. From Damascus he went to Jerusalem, and from there to Antioch, and from there back to Jerusalem again. At this period he was assigned to a general missionary journey—his first—and he set out through Asia Minor, using for the first time the name of Paul. On the second missionary journey the faith was taken across the continental boundary into Europe. After the third missionary journey the Jews, who still hated him with consuming force, succeeded in getting him flung into jail on the charge of desecrating the temple of their faith. His enemies almost killed him, but he was rescued by the Roman soldiery, and for a time kept in chains. By reason of his Roman citizenship and the right of appeal to Cæsar it carried with it, he was sent to Rome, a voyage which proved full of miracle.

After this, accounts are at fault. We know that he must have spent several years in Rome (and yet he seems not to have been in prison all that time), and that for a period of two years at least he was active in missionary work in the Eternal City. It is probable that he was released shortly after his arrival, and then devoted his time to work for the cause, and that later on he was thrown into prison by the Roman authorities, only to go from his cell to the place of martyrdom. It seems unquestionable that he was beheaded, probably on one of the hills outside of Rome. It is said that he went from Rome, during the interim between imprisonments, to Asia Minor and to Spain, but our authorities for this are meager.

The character of Paul is one of the most remarkable in all history, either sacred or profane. It is the sum of human zeal, self-sacrifice, and devotion, so far as its physical and personal side go. Besides, during it he was active in another sense, employing his wonderful literary ability in the composition of those magnificent epistles and communications to the churches he had established and to his fellow-laborers. The Pauline writings are especially vigorous in instruction, in good sense, and in doctrine. Their writer was a man of indomitable energy, of tireless activity, and almost superhuman patience. He feared nothing save the displeasure of his Master, and he had perfect faith in the wisdom, righteousness, and love of that Master. He wanted to do nothing but to spend and be spent in that Master's cause, knowing full well that for fighting the good fight, running the straight course, and keeping the faith God would reward him. For his ministry, which extended over a period of at least thirty years, he was splendidly fitted by education, temperament, and character. Physically, his trials must have been enormous, for tradition shows that he was small, weak, and not always in good health. Indeed, in personal appearance there seems to have been little in the great apostle to command admiration, while he realized some shortcoming unknown to us which he called "a thorn in the flesh." The spirit and courage of the man must have been simply tremendous, and he leaves behind a glory that is imperishable. No other human figure in the New Testament compares with him, and he is a fit companion for the mighty majesty of Moses and Elijah in the Old Testament. His writings are read to-day in more than one hundred and fifty different languages, while all over the world there are churches that bear his name.

REFERENCES.

Paul as a Persecutor.

And cast him out of the city, and stoned him: and the witnesses laid down their clothes at a young man's feet, whose name was Saul. (Acts 7: 58.)

And Saul was consenting unto his death. And at that time there was a great persecution against the Church which was at Jerusalem, and they were all scattered abroad throughout the regions of Judæa, and Samaria, except the Apostles.

And devout men carried Stephen to his burial, and made great lamentation over him.

As for Saul, he made havoc of the Church, entering into every house, and haling men and women committed them to prison. (Acts 8: 1-3.)

And Saul, yet breathing out threatenings and slaughter against the disciples of the Lord, went unto the high Priest,

And desired of him letters to Damascus, to the Synagogues, that if he found any of this way, whether they were men or women, he might bring them bound unto Jerusalem. (Acts 9: 1, 2.)

And I persecuted this way unto the death, binding and delivering into prisons both men and women.

As also the high Priest doth bear me witness, and all the estate of the elders: from whom also I received letters unto the brethren, and went to Damascus, to bring them which were there, bound unto Jerusalem, for to be punished. (Acts 22: 4, 5.)

I verily thought with myself, that I ought to do many things contrary to the name of Jesus of Nazareth:

Which thing I also did in Jerusalem,

and many of the Saints did I shut up in prison, having received authority from the chief Priests, and when they were put to death, I gave my voice against them.

And I punished them oft in every Synagogue, and compelled them to blaspheme, and being exceedingly mad against them, I persecuted them even unto strange cities. (Acts 26: 9-11.)

For I am the least of the Apostles, that am not meet to be called an Apostle, because I persecuted the Church of God. (1 Corinthians 15: 9.)

For ye have heard of my conversation in time past in the Jews' religion, how that beyond measure I persecuted the Church of God, and wasted it:

And profited in the Jews' religion above many my equals in mine own nation, being more exceedingly zealous of the traditions of my fathers. (Galatians 1: 13, 14.)

Concerning zeal, persecuting the Church; touching the righteousness which is in the law, blameless. (Philippians 3: 6.)

Who was before a blasphemer, and a persecutor, and injurious. But I obtained mercy, because I did it ignorantly, in unbelief. (1 Timothy 1: 13.)

Paul's Conversion.

And as he journeyed, he came near Damascus: and suddenly there shined round about him a light from heaven:

And he fell to the earth, and heard a voice saying unto him, *Saul, Saul, why persecutest thou me?*

And he said, Who art thou, Lord? And the Lord said, *I am Jesus whom thou persecutest: it is hard for thee to kick against the pricks.*

And he trembling and astonished said, Lord, what wilt thou have me to do? And the Lord said unto him, *Arise, and go into the city, and it shall be told thee what thou must do.*

And the men which journeyed with him stood speechless, hearing a voice, but seeing no man.

And Saul arose from the earth; and when his eyes were opened, he saw no man: but they led him by the hand, and brought him into Damascus.

And he was three days without sight, and neither did eat nor drink.

And there was a certain disciple at Damascus, named Ananias; and to him said the Lord in a vision, *Ananias.* And he said, Behold, I am here, Lord.

And the Lord said unto him, *Arise, and go into the street which is called Straight, and enquire in the house of Judas for one called Saul, of Tarsus: for, behold, he prayeth,*

And hath seen in a vision a man named Ananias coming in, and putting his hand on him, that he might receive his sight.

Then Ananias answered, Lord, I have heard by many of this man, how much evil he hath done to thy saints at Jerusalem:

And here he hath authority from the chief priests to bind all that call on thy name.

But the Lord said unto him, *Go thy way: for he is a chosen vessel unto me, to bear my name before the Gentiles, and kings, and the children of Israel:*

For I will shew him how great things he must suffer for my name's sake.

And Ananias went his way, and entered into the house; and putting his hands on him said, Brother Saul, the Lord, even Jesus, that appeared unto thee in the way as thou camest, hath sent me, that thou mightest receive thy sight, and be filled with the Holy Ghost.

And immediately there fell from his eyes as it had been scales: and he received sight forthwith, and arose, and was baptized.

And when he had received meat, he was strengthened. Then was Saul certain days with the disciples which were at Damascus.

And straightway he preached Christ in the synagogues, that he is the Son of God. (Acts 9: 3-20.)

His Ministry.

Now there were in the church that was at Antioch certain prophets and teachers; as Barnabas, and Simeon that was called Niger, and Lucius of Cyrene, and Manaen, which had been brought up with Herod the tetrarch, and Saul.

As they ministered to the Lord, and fasted, the Holy Ghost said, Separate me Barnabas and Saul for the work whereunto I have called them.

And when they had fasted and prayed, and laid their hands on them, they sent them away. (Acts 13: 1-3.)

But when they departed from Perga, they came to Antioch in Pisidia, and went into the synagogue on the sabbath day, and sat down. (Acts 13: 14.)

And it came to pass in Iconium, that they went both together into the synagogue of the Jews, and so spake, that a great multitude both of the Jews and also of the Greeks believed. (Acts 14: 1.)

And when they had preached the gospel to that city, and had taught many, they returned again to Lystra, and to Iconium, and Antioch,

Confirming the souls of the disciples, and exhorting them to continue in the faith, and that we must through much tribulation enter into the kingdom of God.

And when they had ordained them elders in every church, and had prayed with fasting, they commended them to the Lord, on whom they believed.

And after they had passed throughout Pisidia, they came to Pamphylia.

And when they had preached the word in Perga, they went down into Attalia:

And thence sailed to Antioch, from whence they had been recommended to the grace of God for the work which they fulfilled. (Acts 14: 21-26.)

Paul also and Barnabas continued in Antioch, teaching and preaching the word of the Lord, with many others also.

And some days after Paul said unto Barnabas, Let us go again and visit our brethren in every city where we have preached the word of the Lord, and see how they do.

And Barnabas determined to take with them John, whose surname was Mark.

But Paul thought not good to take him with them, who departed from them from Pamphylia, and went not with them to the work.

And the contention was so sharp between them, that they departed asunder one from the other: and so Barnabas took Mark, and sailed unto Cyprus;

And Paul chose Silas, and departed, being recommended by the brethren unto the grace of God.

And he went through Syria and Cilicia, confirming the churches. (Acts 15: 35-41.)

After they were come to Mysia, they assayed to go into Bithynia: but the Spirit suffered them not.

And they passing by Mysia came down to Troas.

And a vision appeared to Paul in the night; There stood a man of Macedonia, and prayed him, saying, Come over into Macedonia, and help us.

And after he had seen the vision, immediately we endeavoured to go into Macedonia, assuredly gathering that the Lord had called us for to preach the gospel unto them.

Therefore loosing from Troas, we came with a straight course to Samothracia, and the next day to Neapolis;

And from thence to Philippi, which is the chief city of that part of Macedonia, and a colony: and we were in that city abiding certain days. (Acts 16: 7-12.)

Miraculous Release from Prison.

And at midnight Paul and Silas prayed, and sang praises unto God: and the prisoners heard them.

And suddenly there was a great earthquake, so that the foundations of the prison were shaken: and immediately all the doors were opened, and every one's bands were loosed.

And the keeper of the prison awaking out of his sleep, and seeing the prison doors open, he drew out his sword, and would have killed himself, supposing that the prisoners had been fled.

But Paul cried with a loud voice, saying, Do thyself no harm: for we are all here.

Then he called for a light, and sprang in, and came trembling, and fell down before Paul and Silas,

And brought them out, and said, Sirs, what must I do to be saved?

And they said, Believe on the Lord Jesus Christ, and thou shalt be saved, and thy house.

And they spake unto him the word of the Lord, and to all that were in his house.

And he took them the same hour of the night, and washed their stripes; and was baptized, he and all his, straightway. (Acts 16: 25-33.)

And then immediately the brethren sent away Paul to go as it were to the sea: but Silas and Timotheus abode there still.

And they that conducted Paul brought him unto Athens: and receiving a commandment unto Silas and Timotheus for to come to him with all speed, they departed.

Now while Paul waited for them at Athens, his spirit was stirred in him, when he saw the city wholly given to idolatry. (Acts 17: 14-16.)

After these things Paul departed from Athens, and came to Corinth. (Acts 18: 1.)

Gives the Holy Ghost.

And it came to pass, that, while Apollos was at Corinth, Paul having passed through the upper coasts came to Ephesus: and finding certain disciples,

He said unto them, Have ye received the Holy Ghost since ye believed? And they said unto him, We have not so much as heard whether there be any Holy Ghost.

And he said unto them, Unto what then were ye baptized? And they said, Unto John's baptism.

Then said Paul, John verily baptized with the baptism of repentance, saying unto the people, that they should believe on him which should come after him, that is, on Christ Jesus.

When they heard this, they were baptized in the name of the Lord Jesus.

And when Paul had laid his hands

upon them, the Holy Ghost came on them; and they spake with tongues, and prophesied.

And all the men were about twelve.

And he went into the synagogue, and spake boldly for the space of three months, disputing and persuading the things concerning the kingdom of God.

But when divers were hardened, and believed not, but spake evil of that way before the multitude, he departed from them, and separated the disciples, disputing daily in the school of one Tyrannus.

And this continued by the space of two years; so that all they which dwelt in Asia heard the word of the Lord Jesus, both Jews and Greeks.

And God wrought special miracles by the hands of Paul:

So that from his body were brought unto the sick handkerchiefs or aprons, and the diseases departed from them, and the evil spirits went out of them. (Acts 19: 1-12.)

Imprisonment Prophesied.

And the next day we that were of Paul's company departed, and came unto Cæsarea: and we entered into the house of Philip the evangelist, which was one of the seven; and abode with him.

And the same man had four daughters, virgins, which did prophesy.

And as we tarried there many days, there came down from Judæa a certain prophet, named Agabus.

And when he was come unto us, he took Paul's girdle, and bound his own hands and feet, and said, Thus saith the Holy Ghost, So shall the Jews at Jerusalem bind the man that owneth this girdle, and shall deliver him into the hands of the Gentiles.

And when we heard these things, both we, and they of that place, besought him not to go up to Jerusalem.

Then Paul answered, What mean ye to weep and to break mine heart? for I am ready not to be bound only, but also to die at Jerusalem for the name of the Lord Jesus.

And when he would not be persuaded, we ceased, saying, The will of the Lord be done. (Acts 21: 8-14.)

And when the seven days were almost ended, the Jews which were of Asia, when they saw him in the temple, stirred up all the people, and laid hands on him,

Crying out, Men of Israel, help: This is the man, that teacheth all men every where against the people, and the law, and this place: and further brought Greeks also into the temple, and hath polluted this holy place. (Acts 21: 27, 28.)

And as they bound him with thongs, Paul said unto the centurion that stood by, Is it lawful for you to scourge a man that is a Roman, and uncondemned?

When the centurion heard that, he went and told the chief captain, saying, Take heed what thou doest: for this man is a Roman.

Then the chief captain came, and said unto him, Tell me, art thou a Roman? He said, Yea.

And the chief captain answered, With a great sum obtained I this freedom. And Paul said, But I was free born.

Then straightway they departed from him which should have examined him: and the chief captain also was afraid, after he knew that he was a Roman, and because he had bound him. (Acts 22: 25-29.)

And the night following the Lord stood by him, and said, Be of good cheer, Paul: for as thou hast testified of me in Jerusalem, so must thou bear witness also at Rome. (Acts 23: 11.)

Then the soldiers, as it was commanded them, took Paul, and brought him by night to Antipatris.

On the morrow they left the horsemen to go with him, and returned to the castle:

Who, when they came to Cæsarea, and delivered the epistle to the governor, presented Paul also before him. (Acts 23: 31-33.)

Appeals to Cæsar.

And he commanded a centurion to keep Paul, and to let him have liberty, and that he should forbid none of his acquaintance to minister or come unto him.

And after certain days, when Felix came with his wife Drusilla, which was a Jewess, he sent for Paul, and heard him concerning the faith in Christ.

And as he reasoned of righteousness, temperance, and judgment to come, Felix trembled, and answered, Go thy way for this time; when I have a convenient season, I will call for thee.

He hoped also that money should have been given him of Paul, that he might loose him: wherefore he sent for him the oftener, and communed with him.

But after two years Porcius Festus came into Felix' room: and Felix, willing to shew the Jews a pleasure, left Paul bound. (Acts 24: 23-27.)

Then Festus, when he had conferred with the council, answered, Hast thou appealed unto Cæsar? unto Cæsar shalt thou go. (Acts 25: 12.)

Before Agrippa.

Then Agrippa said unto Paul, Thou art permitted to speak for thyself. Then Paul stretched forth the hand, and answered for himself. (Acts 26: 1.)

And as he thus spake for himself, Festus said with a loud voice, Paul, thou art beside thyself; much learning doth make thee mad.

But he said, I am not mad, most noble Festus; but speak forth the words of truth and soberness.

For the king knoweth of these things, before whom also I speak freely: for I am persuaded that none of these things are hidden from him; for this thing was not done in a corner.

King Agrippa, believest thou the prophets? I know that thou believest.

Then Agrippa said unto Paul, Almost thou persuadest me to be a Christian.

And Paul said, I would to God, that not only thou, but also all that hear me this day, were both almost, and altogether such as I am, except these bonds. (Acts 26: 24-29.)

Sets Out for Rome.

And when it was determined that we should sail into Italy, they delivered Paul and certain other prisoners unto one named Julius, a centurion of Augustus' band. (Acts 27: 1.)

And when neither sun nor stars in many days appeared, and no small tempest lay on us, all hope that we should be saved was then taken away. (Acts 27: 20.)

Tempest and Wreck.

And now I exhort you to be of good cheer: for there shall be no loss of any man's life among you, but of the ship.

For there stood by me this night the angel of God, whose I am, and whom I serve,

Saying, Fear not, Paul; thou must be brought before Cæsar: and, lo, God hath given thee all them that sail with thee.

Wherefore, sirs, be of good cheer: for I believe God, that it shall be even as it was told me. (Acts 27: 22-25.)

And falling into a place where two seas met, they ran the ship aground; and the forepart stuck fast, and remained unmoveable, but the hinder part was broken with the violence of the waves. (Acts 27: 41.)

Miracle of the Viper.

And when they were escaped, then they knew that the island was called Melita.

And the barbarous people shewed us no little kindness: for they kindled a fire, and received us every one, because of the present rain, and because of the cold.

And when Paul had gathered a bundle of sticks, and laid them on the fire, there came a viper out of the heat, and fastened on his hand.

And when the barbarians saw the venomous beast hang on his hand, they said among themselves, No doubt this man is a murderer, whom, though he hath escaped the sea, yet vengeance suffereth not to live.

And he shook off the beast into the fire, and felt no harm.

Howbeit they looked when he should have swollen, or fallen down dead suddenly: but after they had looked a great while, and saw no harm come to him, they changed their minds, and said that he was a god. (Acts 28: 1-6.)

Dwells in Rome.

And when we came to Rome, the Centurion delivered the prisoners to the Captain of the guard: but Paul was suffered to dwell by himself, with a soldier that kept him. (Acts 28: 16.)

And Paul dwelt two whole years in his own hired house, and received all that came in unto him,

Preaching the kingdom of God, and teaching those things which concern the Lord Jesus Christ, with all confidence, no man forbidding him. (Acts 28: 30, 31.)

Foretells His Death.

But watch thou in all things, endure afflictions, do the work of an evangelist, make full proof of thy ministry.

For I am now ready to be offered, and the time of my departure is at hand.

I have fought a good fight, I have finished my course, I have kept the faith:

Henceforth there is laid up for me a crown of righteousness, which the Lord, the righteous judge, shall give me at that day: and not to me only, but unto all them also that love his appearing. (2 Timothy 4: 5-8.)

Paul's Writings.

(a) *Chronologically.*

1 and 2 Thessalonians, written A.D. 52, 53, from Corinth.

Galatians, written A.D. 56-57, from Ephesus.

1 Corinthians, written A.D. 57, from Ephesus.

2 Corinthians, written A.D. 57, from Macedonia.

Romans, written A.D. 58, from Corinth.

Colossians, Ephesians, Philippians, and Philemon, written A.D. 61-63, from Rome.

Hebrews, written A.D. 64 (?), from Italy.

1 Timothy and Titus, written A.D. 65 or 57 (?), from Macedonia.

2 Timothy, written A.D. 67 or 64 (?), from Rome.

The time of the composition of the Pastoral Epistles depends upon the question of the second Roman captivity. The Second Epistle to Timothy was at all events the last, whether written in the first or second captivity.

(b) *Topically.*

Romans and Galatians: doctrines of sin and grace.

1 and 2 Corinthians: moral and practical questions.

Colossians and Philippians: person of Christ.

Ephesians: the Church of Christ.

1 and 2 Thessalonians: the second advent.

1 and 2 Timothy and Titus: church government and pastoral care.

Philemon: slavery.

Hebrews: the eternal priesthood and sacrifice of Christ.

PEACE.

PEACE—a state of quiet or tranquillity; freedom from disturbance or agitation; calm; repose.

REFERENCES.

Peace to Be Sought of God.

And seek the peace of the city whither I have caused you to be carried away captives, and pray unto the Lord for it: for in the peace thereof shall ye have peace. (Jeremiah 29: 7.)

I exhort therefore, that, first of all, supplications, prayers, intercessions, and giving of thanks, be made for all men;

For kings, and for all that are in authority; that we may lead a quiet and peaceable life in all godliness and honesty. (1 Timothy 2: 1, 2.)

Bestowed by God.

And I will give peace in the land, and ye shall lie down, and none shall make you afraid: and I will rid evil beasts

out of the land, neither shall the sword go through your land. (Leviticus 26: 6.)

Their blood shall therefore return upon the head of Joab, and upon the head of his seed for ever: but upon David, and upon his seed, and upon his house, and upon his throne, shall there be peace for ever from the Lord. (1 Kings 2: 33.)

When a man's ways please the Lord, he maketh even his enemies to be at peace with him. (Proverbs 16: 7.)

I form the light, and create darkness: I make peace, and create evil: I the Lord do all these things. (Isaiah 45: 7.)

Then said I, Ah Lord God! behold, the prophets say unto them, Ye shall not see the sword, neither shall ye have famine; but I will give you assured peace in this place. (Jeremiah 14: 13.)

Peace Should Be Maintained.

Depart from evil, and do good; seek peace, and pursue it. (Psalm 34: 14.)

Blessed are the peacemakers: for they shall be called the children of God. (Matthew 5: 9.)

If it be possible, as much as lieth in you, live peaceably with all men. (Romans 12: 18.)

Let us therefore follow after the things which make for peace, and things wherewith one may edify another. (Romans 14: 19.)

But if the unbelieving depart, let him depart. A brother or a sister is not under bondage in such cases: but God hath called us to peace. (1 Corinthians 7: 15.)

Endeavouring to keep the unity of the Spirit in the bond of peace. (Ephesians 4: 3.)

And to esteem them very highly in love for their work's sake. And be at peace among yourselves. (1 Thessalonians 5: 13.)

Flee also youthful lusts: but follow righteousness, faith, charity, peace, with them that call on the Lord out of a pure heart. (2 Timothy 2: 22.)

And the fruit of righteousness is sown in peace of them that make peace. (James 3: 18.)

Let him eschew evil, and do good; let him seek peace, and ensue it. (1 Peter 3: 11.)

Spiritual Peace God's Gift.

Peace I leave with you, my peace I give unto you: not as the world giveth, give I unto you. Let not your heart be troubled, neither let it be afraid. (John 14: 27.)

The word which God sent unto the children of Israel, preaching peace by Jesus Christ: (he is Lord of all). (Acts 10: 36.)

To all that be in Rome, beloved of God, called to be saints: Grace to you and peace from God our Father, and the Lord Jesus Christ. (Romans 1: 7.)

Therefore being justified by faith, we have peace with God through our Lord Jesus Christ. (Romans 5: 1.)

For to be carnally minded is death; but to be spiritually minded is life and peace. (Romans 8: 6.)

For the kingdom of God is not meat and drink; but righteousness, and peace, and joy in the Holy Ghost. (Romans 14: 17.)

And the peace of God, which passeth all understanding, shall keep your hearts and minds through Christ Jesus. (Philippians 4: 7.)

And let the peace of God rule in your hearts, to the which also ye are called in one body; and be ye thankful. (Colossians 3: 15.)

And the very God of peace sanctify you wholly; and I pray God your whole spirit and soul and body be preserved blameless unto the coming of our Lord Jesus Christ. (1 Thessalonians 5: 23.)

Now the Lord of peace himself give you peace always by all means. The Lord be with you all. (2 Thessalonians 3: 16.)

John to the seven churches which are in Asia: Grace be unto you, and peace, from him which is, and which was, and which is to come; and from the seven Spirits which are before his throne. (Revelation 1: 4.)

Peace Denied to the Wicked.

And as Jehu entered in at the gate, she said, Had Zimri peace, who slew his master? (2 Kings 9: 31.)

There is no peace, saith the Lord, unto the wicked. (Isaiah 48: 22.)

The way of peace they know not: and there is no judgment in their goings: they have made them crooked paths; whosoever goeth therein shall not know peace. (Isaiah 59: 8.)

The spoilers are come upon all high places through the wilderness: for the sword of the Lord shall devour from the one end of the land even to the other end of the land: no flesh shall have peace. (Jeremiah 12: 12.)

Destruction cometh; and they shall seek peace, and there shall be none. (Ezekiel 7: 25.)

Peace Promised.

The Lord will give strength unto his people; the Lord will bless his people with peace. (Psalm 29: 11.)

I will hear what God the Lord will speak: for he will speak peace unto his people, and to his saints: but let them not turn again to folly. (Psalm 85: 8.)

Peace I leave with you, my peace I give unto you: not as the world giveth, give I unto you. Let not your heart be troubled, neither let it be afraid. (John 14: 27.)

And as many as walk according to this rule, peace be on them, and mercy, and upon the Israel of God. (Galatians 6: 16.)

Peace be to the brethren, and love with faith, from God the Father and the Lord Jesus Christ. (Ephesians 6: 23.)

Peace in Earth and Heaven.

And suddenly there was with the angel a multitude of the heavenly host praising God, and saying,

Glory to God in the highest, and on earth peace, good will toward men. (Luke 2: 13, 14.)

And when he was come nigh, even now at the descent of the mount of Olives, the whole multitude of the disciples began to rejoice and praise God with a loud voice for all the mighty works that they had seen;

Saying, Blessed be the King that cometh in the name of the Lord: peace in heaven, and glory in the highest. (Luke 19: 37, 38.)

PENTATEUCH.

PEN'TA-TEUCH—the Greek name for the first five books of the Bible. The name means "five-fold book." The Jews called the books "the hatorah" or law. It is the only part of the Bible they recognize as specially inspired.

PENTECOST. (See Holy Ghost.)

PEN'TE-COST—the Greek name for the Jewish Feast of Weeks, which was celebrated on the fiftieth day from the Passover. Pentecost means, broadly, "fiftieth day." To the Christian, however, the day of Pentecost has a far stronger and more beautiful significance. It is the day on which the Church of Christ really had its birth through the coming of the Holy Ghost.

REFERENCES.

And when the day of Pentecost was fully come, they were all with one accord in one place.

And suddenly there came a sound from heaven as of a rushing mighty wind, and it filled all the house where they were sitting.

And there appeared unto them cloven tongues like as of fire, and it sat upon each of them.

And they were all filled with the Holy Ghost, and began to speak with other tongues, as the Spirit gave them utterance.

And there were dwelling at Jerusalem Jews, devout men, out of every nation under heaven.

Now when this was noised abroad, the multitude came together, and were confounded, because that every man heard them speak in his own language.

And they were all amazed and marvelled, saying one to another, Behold, are not all these which speak Galilæans?

And how hear we every man in our own tongue, wherein we were born?

Parthians, and Medes, and Elamites, and the dwellers in Mesopotamia, and in Judæa, and Cappadocia, in Pontus, and Asia,

Phrygia, and Pamphylia, in Egypt, and in the parts of Libya about Cyrene, and strangers of Rome, Jews and proselytes,

Cretes and Arabians, we do hear them speak in our tongues the wonderful works of God.

And they were all amazed, and were

in doubt, saying one to another, What meaneth this?

Others mocking said, These men are full of new wine.

Put Peter, standing up with the eleven, lifted up his voice, and said unto them, Ye men of Judæa, and all ye that dwell at Jerusalem, be this known unto you, and hearken to my words:

For these are not drunken, as ye suppose, seeing it is but the third hour of the day.

But this is that which was spoken by the prophet Joel;

And it shall come to pass in the last days, saith God, I will pour out of my Spirit upon all flesh: and your sons and your daughters shall prophesy, and your young men shall see visions, and your old men shall dream dreams:

And on my servants and on my handmaidens I will pour out in those days of my Spirit; and they shall prophesy:

And I will shew wonders in heaven above, and signs in the earth beneath; blood, and fire, and vapour of smoke:

The sun shall be turned into darkness, and the moon into blood, before that great and notable day of the Lord come:

And it shall come to pass, that whosoever shall call on the name of the Lord shall be saved. (Acts 2: 1-21.)

PERFECTION.

Per-fec'tion—the quality or state of being perfect or complete, so that nothing is wanting; the highest attainable state of excellence. Perfection in any sense of the word is not possible with mankind. God alone is perfect in Himself, and the justified are made perfect through His grace, in the future state. We are taught by Scripture, however, to strive to walk in that perfection manifested by Jesus.

REFERENCES.
Perfection Not in Man.

How much less shall I answer him, and choose out my words to reason with him?

Whom, though I were righteous, yet would I not answer, but I would make supplication to my judge. (Job 9: 14, 15.)

If I justify myself, mine own mouth shall condemn me: if I say, I am perfect, it shall also prove me perverse.

Though I were perfect, yet would I not know my soul: I would despise my life. (Job 9: 20, 21.)

If I say, I will forget my complaint, I will leave off my heaviness, and comfort myself;

I am afraid of all my sorrows, I know that thou wilt not hold me innocent.

If I be wicked, why then labour I in vain?

If I wash myself with snow water, and make my hands never so clean;

Yet shalt thou plunge me in the ditch, and mine own clothes shall abhor me. (Job 9: 27-30.)

And enter not into judgment with thy servant: for in thy sight shall no man living be justified. (Psalm 143: 2.)

For there is not a just man upon earth, that doeth good, and sinneth not. (Ecclesiastes 7: 20.)

Not as though I had already attained, either were already perfect: but I follow after, if that I may apprehend that for which also I am apprehended of Christ Jesus.

Brethren, I count not myself to have apprehended: but this one thing I do, forgetting those things which are behind, and reaching forth unto those things which are before,

I press toward the mark for the prize

of the high calling of God in Christ Jesus. (Philippians 3: 12-14.)

If we say that we have no sin, we deceive ourselves, and the truth is not in us. (1 John 1: 8.)

If we say that we have not sinned, we make him a liar, and his word is not in us. (1 John 1: 10.)

Perfection to Be Striven For.

Ye shall observe to do therefore as the Lord your God hath commanded you: ye shall not turn aside to the right hand or to the left. (Deuteronomy 5: 32.)

Thou shalt be perfect with the Lord thy God. (Deuteronomy 18: 13.)

Be ye therefore very courageous to keep and to do all that is written in the book of the law of Moses, that ye turn not aside therefrom to the right hand or to the left. (Joshua 23: 6.)

Let your heart therefore be perfect with the Lord our God, to walk in his statutes, and to keep his commandments, as at this day. (1 Kings 8: 61.)

I will behave myself wisely in a perfect way. O when wilt thou come unto me? I will walk within my house with a perfect heart. (Psalm 101: 2.)

But put ye on the Lord Jesus Christ, and make not provision for the flesh, to fulfil the lusts thereof, (Romans 13:14.)

Having therefore these promises, dearly beloved, let us cleanse ourselves from all filthiness of the flesh and spirit, perfecting holiness in the fear of God. (2 Corinthians 7: 1.)

For we are glad, when we are weak, and ye are strong: and this also we wish, even your perfection. (2 Corinthians 13: 9.)

Finally, brethren, farewell. Be perfect, be of good comfort, be of one mind, live in peace; and the God of love and peace shall be with you. (2 Corinthians 13: 11.)

Till we all come in the unity of the faith, and of the knowledge of the Son of God, unto a perfect man, unto the measure of the stature of the fulness of Christ:

That we henceforth be no more children, tossed to and fro, and carried about with every wind of doctrine, by the sleight of men, and cunning craftiness, whereby they lie in wait to deceive. (Ephesians 4: 13, 14.)

That ye may approve things that are excellent; that ye may be sincere and without offence till the day of Christ. (Philippians 1: 10.)

That ye may be blameless and harmless, the sons of God, without rebuke, in the midst of a crooked and perverse nation, among whom ye shine as lights in the world. (Philippians 2: 15.)

And you, that were sometime alienated and enemies in your mind by wicked works, yet now hath he reconciled

In the body of his flesh through death, to present you holy and unblameable and unreproveable in his sight. (Colossians 1: 21, 22.)

PERJURY.

Per'ju-ry—the act of swearing falsely or breaking an oath. Perjury is not only a very great crime in the eyes of man, but it is condemned by God.

REFERENCES.

Thou shalt not bear false witness against thy neighbour. (Exodus 20: 16.)

And ye shall not swear by my name falsely, neither shalt thou profane the name of thy God: I am the Lord. (Leviticus 19: 12.)

Then said he unto me, This is the

curse that goeth forth over the face of the whole earth: for every one that stealeth shall be cut off as on this side, according to it; and every one that sweareth shall be cut off as on that side, according to it.

I will bring it forth, saith the Lord of hosts, and it shall enter into the house of the thief, and into the house of him that sweareth falsely by my name: and it shall remain in the midst of his house, and shall consume it with the timber thereof and the stones thereof. (Zechariah 5: 3, 4.)

And let none of you imagine evil in your hearts against his neighbour; and love no false oath. (Zechariah 8: 17.)

PERSECUTION.

PER'SE-CU'TION—the act of pursuing with hostile intentions, and to seek after and to improve all occasions for doing other persons or a person an injury. In a Scriptural sense persecution was the active and malignant opposition which the Christians of all ages, save the present, have met with from the enemies of Christ or from pagans. In the early days of the Church persecution was of a particularly terrible sort, men, women, and children being exposed to the brutalities of the populace or thrown to the animals in the Roman arenas. There were ten of these periods, extending off and on from A.D. 64, in the times of Nero, to A.D. 303, in the reign of Diocletian. But, whether the persecution was in the remote past, or in the Middle Ages, or in later times, the Church has always been strong in meeting trials or death, and has grown and prospered under the lash of tyranny.

REFERENCES.

Persecution Foretold and Expected.

Wherefore, behold, I send unto you prophets, and wise men, and scribes: and some of them ye shall kill and crucify; and some of them shall ye scourge in your synagogues, and persecute them from city to city. (Matthew 23: 34.)

Now the brother shall betray the brother to death, and the father the son; and children shall rise up against their parents, and shall cause them to be put to death. (Mark 13: 12.)

Go your ways: behold, I send you forth as lambs among wolves. (Luke 10: 3.)

Therefore also said the wisdom of God, I will send them prophets and apostles, and some of them they shall slay and persecute. (Luke 11: 49.)

I am come to send fire on the earth; and what will I, if it be already kindled?

But I have a baptism to be baptized with; and how am I straitened till it be accomplished!

Suppose ye that I am come to give peace on earth? I tell you, Nay; but rather division:

For from henceforth there shall be five in one house divided, three against two, and two against three.

The father shall be divided against the son, and the son against the father; the mother against the daughter, and the daughter against the mother; the mother in law against her daughter in law, and the daughter in law against her mother in law. (Luke 12: 49-53.)

But before all these, they shall lay their hands on you, and persecute you, delivering you up to the synagogues, and into prisons, being brought before kings and rulers for my name's sake.

And it shall turn to you for a testimony. (Luke 21: 12, 13.)

And ye shall be betrayed both by parents, and brethren, and kinsfolk, and friends; and some of you shall they cause to be put to death. (Luke 21: 16.)

Remember the word that I said unto you, The servant is not greater than his lord. If they have persecuted me, they will also persecute you; if they have kept my saying, they will keep yours also.

But all these things will they do unto you for my name's sake, because they know not him that sent me. (John 15: 20, 21.)

They shall put you out of the synagogues: yea, the time cometh, that whosoever killeth you will think that he doeth God service.

And these things will they do unto you, because they have not known the Father, nor me. (John 16: 2, 3.)

For I will shew him how great things he must suffer for my name's sake. (Acts 9: 16.)

Confirming the souls of the disciples, and exhorting them to continue in the faith, and that we must through much tribulation enter into the kingdom of God. (Acts 14: 22.)

And now, behold, I go bound in the spirit unto Jerusalem, not knowing the things that shall befall me there:

Save that the Holy Ghost witnesseth in every city, saying that bonds and afflictions abide me. (Acts 20: 22, 23.)

For I think that God hath set forth us the apostles last, as it were appointed to death: for we are made a spectacle unto the world, and to angels, and to men. (1 Corinthians 4: 9.)

That no man should be moved by these afflictions: for yourselves know that we are appointed thereunto.

For verily, when we were with you, we told you before that we should suffer tribulation; even as it came to pass, and ye know. (1 Thessalonians 3: 3, 4.)

Yea, and all that will live godly in Christ Jesus shall suffer persecution. (2 Timothy 3: 12.)

Ye have not yet resisted unto blood, striving against sin. (Hebrews 12: 4.)

Endurance of Persecution.

We are troubled on every side, yet not distressed; we are perplexed, but not in despair;

Persecuted, but not forsaken; cast down, but not destroyed. (2 Corinthians 4: 8, 9.)

And in nothing terrified by your adversaries: which is to them an evident token of perdition, but to you of salvation, and that of God. (Philippians 1: 28.)

For the which cause I also suffer these things: nevertheless I am not ashamed; for I know whom I have believed, and am persuaded that he is able to keep that which I have committed unto him against that day. (2 Timothy 1: 12.)

Beloved, think it not strange concerning the fiery trial which is to try you, as though some strange thing happened unto you:

But rejoice, inasmuch as ye are partakers of Christ's sufferings; that, when his glory shall be revealed, ye may be glad also with exceeding joy. (1 Peter 4: 12, 13.)

Yet if any man suffer as a Christian, let him not be ashamed; but let him glorify God on this behalf. (1 Peter 4: 16.)

Persecution Blessed.

Blessed are they which are persecuted for righteousness' sake: for theirs is the kingdom of heaven.

Blessed are ye, when men shall revile you, and persecute you, and shall say all manner of evil against you falsely, for my sake.

Rejoice, and be exceeding glad: for

great is your reward in heaven: for so persecuted they the prophets which were before you. (Matthew 5: 10-12.)

Whosoever therefore shall confess me before men, him will I confess also before my Father which is in heaven.

But whosoever shall deny me before men, him will I also deny before my Father which is in heaven. (Matthew 10: 32, 33.)

For whosoever will save his life shall lose it: but whosoever shall lose his life for my sake and the gospel's, the same shall save it. (Mark 8: 35.)

And Jesus answered and said, Verily I say unto you, There is no man that hath left house, or brethren, or sisters, or father, or mother, or wife, or children, or lands, for my sake, and the gospel's,

But he shall receive a hundredfold now in this time, houses, and brethren, and sisters, and mothers, and children, and lands, with persecutions; and in the world to come eternal life. (Mark 10: 29, 30.)

And ye shall be hated of all men for my name's sake: but he that shall endure unto the end, the same shall be saved. (Mark 13: 13.)

PERSEVERANCE. (See Steadfastness.)

PER'SE-VER'ANCE—the act or state of persisting in anything undertaken; continued pursuit or prosecution of any business or plan or effort. The Bible, in many passages, enjoins us to perseverance, particularly with reference to the things that are good and holy.

REFERENCES.

But he that shall endure unto the end, the same shall be saved. (Matthew 24: 13.)

And Jesus said unto him, No man, having put his hand to the plow, and looking back, is fit for the kingdom of God. (Luke 9: 62.)

Now when the Congregation was broken up, many of the Jews and religious Proselytes followed Paul and Barnabas, who speaking to them, persuaded them to continue in the grace of God. (Acts 13: 43.)

Therefore my beloved brethren, be ye stedfast, unmoveable, always abounding in the work of the Lord, forasmuch as you know that your labour is not in vain in the Lord. (1 Corinthians 15: 58.)

Watch ye, stand fast in the faith, quit you like men: be strong. (1 Corinthians 16: 13.)

Praying always with all prayer and supplication in the Spirit, and watching thereunto with all perseverance and supplication for all saints. (Ephesians 6: 18.)

If ye continue in the faith grounded and settled, and be not moved away from the hope of the gospel, which ye have heard, and which was preached to every creature which is under heaven; whereof I Paul am made a minister. (Colossians 1: 23.)

But ye, brethren, be not weary in well doing. (2 Thessalonians 3: 13.)

That thou keep this commandment without spot, unrebukeable, until the appearing of our Lord Jesus Christ. (1 Timothy 6: 14.)

But Christ as a son over his own house; whose house are we, if we hold fast the confidence and the rejoicing of the hope firm unto the end. (Hebrews 3: 6.)

But exhort one another daily, while it is called To day; lest any of you be hardened through the deceitfulness of sin.

For we are made partakers of Christ,

if we hold the beginning of our confidence stedfast unto the end. (Hebrews 3: 13, 14.)

Let us hold fast the profession of our faith without wavering (for he is faithful that promised). (Hebrews 10: 23.)

Now the just shall live by faith: but if any man draw back, my soul shall have no pleasure in him.

But we are not of them who draw back unto perdition: but of them that believe, to the saving of the soul. (Hebrews 10: 38, 39.)

Ye therefore, beloved, seeing ye know these things before, beware lest ye also being led away with the error of the wicked, fall from your own stedfastness. (2 Peter 3: 17.)

Fear none of those things which thou shalt suffer: behold, the devil shall cast some of you into prison, that ye may be tried, and ye shall have tribulation ten days: be thou faithful unto death, and I will give thee a crown of life. (Revelation 2: 10.)

But that which ye have already, hold fast till I come.

And he that overcometh, and keepeth my works unto the end, to him will I give power over the nations. (Revelation 2: 25, 26.)

PETER.

PE′TER—the English form of a Greek word meaning "a rock" or "a stone," given to Simon the son of Jonas, one of the earliest of the disciples, as well as one of the greatest.

Peter was a native of Bethsaida, a Galilee fishing-town, and with his brother Andrew pursued the occupation of a fisherman. He probably was a disciple of John the Baptist before the ministry of Jesus began. Andrew met Jesus before Peter and then presented his brother to the Master, on which occasion Jesus gave him the name of Cephas, which in Greek is Petros, from which we get the English Peter. From the first we find Peter

taking a sort of leadership among the apostles, acting as spokesman for them in their intercourse with Jesus, and generally showing those qualities of ardent attachment and zeal, which were so strong a part of his nature. The incidents of the gospels throw much light upon Peter's character—the attempt to walk upon the sea to his Master, his unhesitating avowals of faith in Jesus' Messiahship, his rash but affectionate rebuke of the Lord for speaking of suffering and death as a part of His divine mission, his horror at the thought that his beloved Master desired to wash his feet, and the denial he made of Jesus after his vaunting avowal that he never would deny Him, and his subsequent bitter sorrow and repentance. Peter, we see in this series of incidents, was only a mortal man and a Jew who had a different idea as to what the Messiah should be. After the crucifixion, we find an entirely different Peter. Knowledge and wisdom had come to him through Jesus' death and resurrection, and his whole course of thought and action changed. He was just as zealous and active as ever, but his rashness and impetuosity had gone. We know that he spent the remainder of his life in active and useful ministry. On one occasion Paul felt it necessary to rebuke him, and strange to say not because of rash or impetuous acts, but for apparent weakness and timidity—a truly strange thing when we consider the man's former character. He suffered martyrdom, probably at Rome and with his head downward, about the same time as Paul.

REFERENCES.

Call and Sending Forth.

And Jesus, walking by the sea of Galilee, saw two brethren, Simon called Peter, and Andrew his brother, casting a net into the sea: for they were fishers.

And he saith unto them, *Follow me, and I will make you fishers of men.* (Matthew 4: 18, 19.)

Now when he had left speaking, he said unto Simon, *Launch out into the deep, and let down your nets for a draught.*

And Simon answering said unto

him, Master, we have toiled all the night, and have taken nothing: nevertheless at thy word I will let down the net.

And when they had this done, they inclosed a great multitude of fishes: and their net brake.

And they beckoned unto their partners, which were in the other ship, that they should come and help them. And they came, and filled both the ships, so that they began to sink.

When Simon Peter saw it, he fell down at Jesus' knees, saying, Depart from me; for I am a sinful man, O Lord. (Luke 5: 4-8.)

Tries to Walk on Water.

And Peter answered him and said, Lord, if it be thou, bid me come unto thee on the water.

And he said, *Come.* And when Peter was come down out of the ship, he walked on the water, to go to Jesus.

But when he saw the wind boisterous, he was afraid; and beginning to sink, he cried, saying, Lord, save me.

And immediately Jesus stretched forth his hand, and caught him, and said unto him, *O thou of little faith, wherefore didst thou doubt?* (Matthew 14: 28-31.)

Confesses Jesus' Messiahship.

And Simon Peter answered and said, Thou art the Christ, the Son of the living God.

And Jesus answered and said unto him, *Blessed art thou, Simon Bar-jona: for flesh and blood hath not revealed it unto thee, but my Father which is in heaven.*

And I say also unto thee, That thou art Peter, and upon this rock I will build my church; and the gates of hell shall not prevail against it.

And I will give unto thee the keys of the kingdom of heaven: and whatsoever thou shalt bind on earth shall be bound in heaven: and whatsoever thou shalt loose on earth shall be loosed in heaven. (Matthew 16: 16-19.)

Witnesses the Transfiguration.

And after six days Jesus taketh Peter, James, and John his brother, and bringeth them up into an high mountain apart,

And was transfigured before them: and his face did shine as the sun, and his raiment was white as the light.

And, behold, there appeared unto them Moses and Elias talking with him.

Then answered Peter, and said unto Jesus, Lord, it is good for us to be here: if thou wilt, let us make here three tabernacles; one for thee, and one for Moses, and one for Elias. (Matthew 17: 1-4.)

Denies Christ.

And the Lord said, *Simon, Simon, behold, Satan hath desired to have you, that he may sift you as wheat:*

But I have prayed for thee, that thy faith fail not: and when thou art converted, strengthen thy brethren.

And he said unto him, Lord, I am ready to go with thee, both into prison, and to death.

And he said, *I tell thee, Peter, the cock shall not crow this day, before that thou shalt thrice deny that thou knowest me.* (Luke 22: 31-34.)

Then took they him, and led him, and brought him into the high priest's house. And Peter followed afar off.

And when they had kindled a fire in

the midst of the hall, and were set down together, Peter sat down among them.

But a certain maid beheld him as he sat by the fire, and earnestly looked upon him, and said, This man was also with him.

And he denied him, saying, Woman, I know him not.

And after a little while another saw him, and said, Thou art also of them. And Peter said, Man, I am not.

And about the space of one hour after another confidently affirmed, saying, Of a truth this fellow also was with him: for he is a Galilæan.

And Peter said, Man, I know not what thou sayest. And immediately, while he yet spake, the cock crew.

And the Lord turned, and looked upon Peter. And Peter remembered the word of the Lord, how he had said unto him, Before the cock crow, thou shalt deny me thrice.

And Peter went out, and wept bitterly. (Luke 22: 51-62.)

Jesus Foretells Peter's Martyrdom.

He saith unto him the third time, *Simon, son of Jonas, lovest thou me?* Peter was grieved because he said unto him the third time, Lovest thou me? And he said unto him, Lord, thou knowest all things; thou knowest that I love thee. Jesus saith unto him, *Feed my sheep.*

Verily, verily, I say unto thee, When thou wast young, thou girdedst thyself, and walkedst whither thou wouldest: but when thou shalt be old, thou shalt stretch forth thy hands, and another shall gird thee, and carry thee whither thou wouldest not.

This spake he, signifying by what death he should glorify God. And when he had spoken this, he saith unto him, *Follow me.* (John 21: 17-19.)

Teaches Boldly.

And they called them, and commanded them not to speak at all nor teach in the name of Jesus.

But Peter and John answered and said unto them, Whether it be right in the sight of God to hearken unto you more than unto God, judge ye.

For we cannot but speak the things which we have seen and heard.

So when they had further threatened them, they let them go, finding nothing how they might punish them, because of the people: for all men glorified God for that which was done. (Acts 4: 18-21.)

Delivered from Prison.

Peter therefore was kept in prison: but prayer was made without ceasing of the church unto God for him.

And when Herod would have brought him forth, the same night Peter was sleeping between two soldiers, bound with two chains: and the keepers before the door kept the prison.

And, behold, the angel of the Lord came upon him, and a light shined in the prison: and he smote Peter on the side, and raised him up, saying, Arise up quickly. And his chains fell off from his hands.

And the angel said unto him, Gird thyself, and bind on thy sandals. And so he did. And he saith unto him, Cast thy garment about thee, and follow me.

And he went out, and followed him; and wist not that it was true which was done by the angel; but thought he saw a vision. (Acts 12: 5-9.)

Foretells His Death.

Yea, I think it meet, as long as I am in this tabernacle, to stir you up by putting you in remembrance;

Knowing that shortly I must put off this my tabernacle, even as our Lord Jesus Christ hath shewed me.

Moreover I will endeavour that ye may be able after my decease to have these things always in remembrance.

For we have not followed cunningly devised fables, when we made known unto you the power and coming of our Lord Jesus Christ, but were eyewitnesses of his majesty. (2 Peter 1: 13-16.)

PHARAOH.

PHA'RAOH (usually pronounced as though spelled "faro")—meaning "the sun." The name was applied to the monarchs of Egypt as their official title. Quite a number of them figure in the pages of the Old Testament. Roughly, they were the pharaoh Abraham knew, the one who befriended Joseph, the one who "knew not Joseph," the one of the oppression, the one of the Exodus, probably a son of the pharaoh of the oppression, and several others, one of whom gave his daughter to Solomon as a wife.

PHARISEE.

PHAR'I-SEE — meaning "the separated." The Pharisees were one of the three sects into which Judaism was divided at the period of Christ. Those of them that were not hypocrites were fanatics. The sect doubtless had its origin in the changed conditions manifested among the Israelites after the return from the second captivity, when the purity of the old Hebrewism gave place to the impure Judaism. The Pharisees insisted upon keeping all the formal laws of Moses to the very last letter, especially those with reference to clean and unclean things. The first record we have of them as a distinct and recognized sect is about the year 150 B.C. They rapidly grew to power and eminence, craftily making themselves the popular party by declaring that God had given to all men alike the kingdom, the

priesthood, and holiness. By the time of Christ they entirely dominated Hebrew politics and society. Christ's protests against their greed, rascality, and hypocrisy naturally made them His enemies, and they pursued Him vindictively until they brought about His condemnation and death.

PHILIP.

PHIL'IP—a form of a Greek word meaning "a lover of horses." The reader meets in the New Testament four persons bearing the name of Philip—one Philip the apostle, and the other Philip the evangelist, one of the original seven deacons. The other two Philips were unimportant sons of Herod the Great.

PHILIPPI.

PHI-LIP'PI—a city of Macedonia, named in honor of Philip of Macedon. Later it seems to have been a Roman colony. Not far from it was fought a great battle, one of the most decisive ones in history. The result of it turned the Roman republic into a monarchy. Paul several times visited the church formed in the place, and wrote one of his epistles to its members.

PHILISTINES.

PHI-LIS'TINES—the name of a people who inhabited the country of Philistia. The name means "emigrant" or "wandering." The Philistines held a small strip of territory on the coast, and are supposed originally to have come from Egypt as colonists. They were a strong, warlike, and powerful people, and gave the Israelites a vast amount of trouble.

PILATE, PONTIUS.

PI'LATE. Pontius Pilate was the sixth Roman procurator or governor of Judea, having been appointed to the office by the emperor Tiberius to succeed Valerius Gratus. He held office ten years, and during them Jesus the Christ was brought before him by the Jews for trial. Pilate was a man who could deal out evenhanded justice when policy or his own personal ends did not interfere.

We can see that he favored the release of Jesus because he found Him innocent of wrong. Although Jesus had been tried and condemned by His own countrymen, they had not the power of executing Him, a power which rested entirely with Pilate, who could have ordered the Master's release and the Jews would not have been able to gainsay him. But as soon as he realized that personal danger might attend such action or that the Jews might complain to Rome, he weakly submitted to their wishes. Not long after the crucifixion Pilate got into political trouble and was ordered home to Rome to appear before the emperor. In the meantime, however, the emperor died and Pilate escaped punishment. He eventually committed suicide while in exile.

References.—Matthew 27; Mark 15; Luke 23; John 18 and 19.

PITY. (See Compassion, Kindness, Mercy.)

Pɪᴛ'ʏ—compassion or mercy for the suffering or distress of others. Pity is one of the divine virtues. With God it is in a state of perfection, while in mankind the amount possessed varies according to the quality of the spiritual nature.

REFERENCES.

Have pity upon me, have pity upon me, O ye my friends; for the hand of God hath touched me. (Job 19: 21.)

Reproach hath broken my heart; and I am full of heaviness: and I looked for some to take pity, but there was none; and for comforters, but I found none. (Proverbs 69: 20.)

He that hath pity upon the poor, lendeth unto the Lord; and that which he hath given will he pay him again. (Proverbs 19: 17.)

Shouldest not thou also have had compassion on thy fellowservant, even as I had pity on thee? (Matthew 18: 33.)

PLEASURES. (See Happiness, Joy, Sin.)

Pʟᴇᴀs'ᴜʀᴇ—the gratification of the senses or the mind; agreeable sensations or emotions; amusement. Pleasures are of two sorts—those that are harmful to the Christian and religious life, and those that make us enjoy that life better by making us realize the extent of God's plans for us by giving us good things. Worldly pleasures are placed by the Bible in the class of hurtful pleasures, and we are warned to avoid them.

REFERENCES.
Vanity of Worldly Pleasures.

I said in mine heart, Go to now, I will prove thee with mirth; therefore enjoy pleasure: and behold, this also is vanity.

I said of laughter, It is mad: and of mirth, What doeth it?

I sought in mine heart to give myself unto wine, yet acquainting mine heart with wisdom; and to lay hold on folly, till I might see what was that good for the sons of men, which they should do under the heaven all the days of their life.

I made me great works; I builded me houses; I planted me vineyards;

I made me gardens and orchards, and I planted trees in them of all kind of fruits:

I made me pools of water, to water therewith the wood that bringeth forth trees:

I got me servants and maidens, and had servants born in my house; also I had great possessions of great and small cattle above all that were in Jerusalem before me;

I gathered me also silver and gold, and the peculiar treasure of kings, and of the provinces; I gat me men-singers and women-singers, and the delights of the sons of men, as musical instruments, and that of all sorts.

So I was great, and increased more than all that were before me in Jerusalem: also my wisdom remained with me.

And whatsoever mine eyes desired I kept not from them, I withheld not my heart from any joy; for my heart rejoiced in all my labour: and this was my portion of all my labour.

Then I looked on all the works that my hands had wrought, and on the labour that I had laboured to do: and behold, all was vanity and vexation of spirit, and there was no profit under the sun. (Ecclesiastes 2: 1-11.)

Effects of Worldly Pleasure.

And that which fell among thorns are they, which, when they have heard, go forth, and are choked with cares and riches and pleasures of this life, and bring no fruit to perfection. (Luke 8: 14.)

Go to now, ye rich men, weep and howl for your miseries that shall come upon you.

Your riches are corrupted, and your garments are motheaten.

Your gold and silver is cankered; and the rust of them shall be a witness against you, and shall eat your flesh as it were fire. Ye have heaped treasure together for the last days.

Behold, the hire of the labourers who have reaped down your fields, which is of you kept back by fraud, crieth: and the cries of them which have reaped are entered into the ears of the Lord of sabaoth.

Ye have lived in pleasure on the earth, and been wanton; ye have nourished your hearts, as in a day of slaughter. (James 5: 1-5.)

But these, as natural brute beasts made to be taken and destroyed, speak evil of the things that they understand not, and shall utterly perish in their own corruption,

And shall receive the reward of unrighteousness, as they that count it pleasure to riot in the day time: Spots they are and blemishes, sporting themselves with their own deceivings, while they feast with you:

Having eyes full of adultery and that cannot cease from sin, beguiling unstable souls: an heart they have exercised with covetous practices: cursed children. (2 Peter 2: 12-14.)

Commands and Warnings against Worldly Pleasure.

Traitors, heady, highminded, lovers of pleasures more than lovers of God,

Having a form of godliness, but denying the power thereof: from such turn away.

For of this sort are they which creep into houses, and lead captive silly women laden with sins, led away with divers lusts,

Ever learning, and never able to come to the knowledge of the truth. (2 Timothy 3: 4-7.)

For we ourselves also were sometimes foolish, disobedient, deceived, serving divers lusts and pleasures, living in malice and envy, hateful, and hating one another. (Titus 3: 3.)

Forasmuch then as Christ hath suffered for us in the flesh, arm yourselves likewise with the same mind: for he that hath suffered in the flesh hath ceased from sin;

That he no longer should live the rest of his time in the flesh to the lusts of men, but to the will of God.

For the time past of our life may suffice us to have wrought the will of the Gentiles, when we walked in lasciviousness, lusts, excess of wine, revelings, banquetings, and abominable idolatries:

Wherein they think it strange that ye run not with them to the same excess of riot, speaking evil of you:

Who shall give account to him that is ready to judge the quick and the dead.

For for this cause was the gospel preached also to them that are dead, that they might be judged according to men in the flesh, but live according to God in the spirit. (1 Peter 4: 1-6.)

PLENTY.

PLEN'TY — a full or adequate supply; enough and to spare; abundance. The Bible shows us very conclusively that plenty, like all other things, comes from God, and that we are not sufficiently thankful to Him for it. When we are poor and have little we are inclined to go to Him with prayers and petitions that He gives us, but when He has given and with openhanded generosity, we rarely seek Him to return our praise and thanks. It is a human failing, but we should strive to overcome it.

REFERENCES.

And the Lord shall make thee plenteous in goods, in the fruit of thy body, and in the fruit of thy cattle, and in the fruit of thy ground, in the land which the Lord sware unto thy fathers to give thee. (Deuteronomy 28: 11.)

Thou crownest the year with thy goodness; and thy paths drop fatness.

They drop upon the pastures of the wilderness: and the little hills rejoice on every side.

The pastures are clothed with flocks; the valleys also are covered over with corn; they shout for joy, they also sing. (Psalm 65: 11-13.)

Thou, O God, didst send a plentiful rain, whereby thou didst confirm thine inheritance, when it was weary. (Psalm 68: 9.)

Rid me, and deliver me from the hand of strange children, whose mouth speaketh vanity, and their right hand is a right hand of falsehood:

That our sons may be as plants grown up in their youth; that our daughters may be as cornerstones, polished after the similitude of a palace:

That our garners may be full, affording all manner of store; that our sheep may bring forth thousands and ten thousands in our streets:

That our oxen may be strong to labour; that there be no breaking in, nor going out; that there be no complaining in our streets.

Happy is that people, that is in such a case: yea, happy is that people, whose God is the Lord. (Psalm 144: 11-15.)

And ye shall eat in plenty, and be satisfied, and praise the name of the Lord your God, that hath dealt wondrously with you: and my people shall never be ashamed. (Joel 2: 26.)

POOR. (See Riches.)

POOR. We find the word "poor" used in the Bible to indicate a number of different conditions, namely: (1) Destitute of property or the good things of life; needy or indigent; (2) destitute of such qualities as are desirable or might be expected; (3) worthy of pity or sympathy; (4) free from self-assertion or not proud or arrogant, otherwise the meek.

The Bible bids us be good to the poor in that it advises almsgiving and kindness to those who have less of worldly goods than we. It also counsels us to be generous, kind, and considerate toward those things or persons that are poor in the sense of qualities, giving from our own store of qualities to help them, or, in the case of inanimate things, to remember that they are creations of God. To the "poor in spirit" or the meek are promised great rewards.

REFERENCES.
The Poor Always to Be Found.

For the poor shall never cease out of the land: therefore I command thee, saying, Thou shalt open thine hand wide unto thy brother, to thy poor, and to thy needy, in thy land. (Deuteronomy 15: 11.)

For ye have the poor always with you; but me ye have not always. (Matthew 26: 11.)

For ye have the poor with you always, and whensoever ye will ye may do them good: but me ye have not always. (Mark 14: 7.)

The Condition of the Poor.

They turn the needy out of the way: the poor of the earth hide themselves together. (Job 24: 4.)

There is that maketh himself rich, yet hath nothing: there is that maketh himself poor, yet hath great riches.

The ransom of a man's life are his riches: but the poor heareth not rebuke. (Proverbs 13: 7, 8.)

The poor useth entreaties; but the rich answereth roughly. (Job 18: 23.)

Wealth maketh many friends; but the poor is separated from his neighbour. (Job 19: 4.)

Now there was found in it a poor wise man, and he by his wisdom delivered the city; yet no man remembered that same poor man.

Then said I, Wisdom is better than strength: nevertheless the poor man's wisdom is despised, and his words are not heard. (Ecclesiastes 9: 15, 16.)

Hearken, my beloved brethren, Hath not God chosen the poor of this world rich in faith, and heirs of the kingdom which he hath promised to them that love him? (James 2: 5.)

Causes for Poverty.

How long wilt thou sleep, O sluggard? when wilt thou arise out of thy sleep?

Yet a little sleep, a little slumber, a little folding of the hands to sleep:

So shall thy poverty come as one that travelleth, and thy want as an armed man. (Proverbs 6: 9-11.)

He becometh poor that dealeth with a slack hand; but the hand of the diligent maketh rich. (Proverbs 10: 4.)

For the drunkard and the glutton shall come to poverty: and drowsiness shall clothe a man with rags. (Proverbs 23: 21.)

He that tilleth his land shall have plenty of bread: but he that followeth after vain persons shall have poverty enough. (Proverbs 28: 19.)

He that hasteth to be rich hath an evil eye, and considereth not that poverty shall come upon him. (Proverbs 28: 22.)

Oppression of Poor Condemned.

If thou lend money to any of my people that is poor by thee, thou shalt not be to him as an usurer, neither shalt thou lay upon him usury. (Exodus 22: 25.)

If there be among you a poor man of one of thy brethren within any of thy gates in thy land which the Lord thy God giveth thee, thou shalt not harden thy heart, nor shut thine hand from thy poor brother. (Deuteronomy 15: 7.)

Defend the poor and fatherless: do justice to the afflicted and needy.

Deliver the poor and needy: rid them out of the hand of the wicked. (Psalm 82: 3, 4.)

He that oppresseth the poor reproacheth his Maker: but he that honoureth him hath mercy on the poor. (Proverbs 14: 31.)

Whoso mocketh the poor reproacheth his Maker: and he that is glad at calamities shall not be unpunished. (Proverbs 17: 5.)

He that oppresseth the poor to increase his riches, and he that giveth to the rich, shall surely come to want. (Proverbs 22: 16.)

Rob not the poor, because he is poor: neither oppress the afflicted in the gate:

For the Lord will plead their cause, and spoil the soul of those that spoiled them. (Proverbs 22: 22, 23.)

The Lord will enter into judgment with the ancients of his people, and the princes thereof; for ye have eaten up the vineyard; the spoil of the poor is in your houses.

What mean ye that ye beat my people to pieces, and grind the faces of the poor? saith the Lord God of hosts. (Isaiah 3: 14, 15.)

Thus saith the Lord; For three transgressions of Israel, and for four, I will not turn away the punishment thereof: because they sold the righteous for silver, and the poor for a pair of shoes;

That pant after the dust of the earth on the head of the poor, and turn aside the way of the meek. (Amos 2: 6, 7.)

Forasmuch, therefore, as your treading is upon the poor, and ye take from him burdens of wheat: ye have built houses of hewn stone, but ye shall not dwell in them; ye have planted pleasant vineyards, but ye shall not drink wine of them. (Amos 5: 11.)

And oppress not the widow, nor the fatherless, the stranger, nor the poor; and let none of you imagine evil against his brother in your heart. (Zechariah 7: 10.)

For if there come unto your assembly a man with a gold ring, in goodly apparel, and there come in also a poor man in vile raiment;

And ye have respect to him that weareth the gay clothing, and say unto him, Sit thou here in a good place; and say to the poor, Stand thou there, or sit here under my footstool:

Are ye not then partial in yourselves, and are become judges of evil thoughts? (James 2: 2-4.)

Poor to Be Kindly Treated.

And six years thou shalt sow thy land, and shalt gather in the fruits thereof:

But the seventh year thou shalt let it rest and lie still; that the poor of thy people may eat: and what they leave the beasts of the field shall eat. In like manner thou shalt deal with thy vineyard, and with thy oliveyard. (Exodus 23: 10, 11.)

And thou shalt not glean thy vineyard, neither shalt thou gather every grape of thy vineyard; thou shalt leave them for the poor and stranger: I am the Lord your God. (Leviticus 19: 10.)

If thy brother be waxen poor, and hath sold away some of his possession, and if any of his kin come to redeem it, then shall he redeem that which his brother sold. (Leviticus 25: 25.)

If there be among you a poor man of one of thy brethren within any of thy gates in thy land which the Lord thy God giveth thee, thou shalt not harden thine heart, nor shut thine hand from thy poor brother:

But thou shalt open thine hand wide unto him, and shalt surely lend him sufficient for his need, in that which he wanteth. (Deuteronomy 15: 7, 8.)

Blessed is he that considereth the poor: the Lord will deliver him in time of trouble.

The Lord will preserve him, and keep him alive; and he shall be blessed upon the earth: and thou wilt not deliver him unto the will of his enemies.

The Lord will strengthen him upon the bed of languishing: thou wilt make all his bed in his sickness. (Psalm 41: 1-3.)

He that despiseth his neighbour sinneth: but he that hath mercy on the poor, happy is he. (Proverbs 14: 21.)

Only they would that we should remember the poor, the same which I also was forward to do. (Galatians 2: 10.)

God Considers the Poor.

But he saveth the poor from the sword, from their mouth, and from the hand of the mighty.

So the poor hath hope, and iniquity stoppeth her mouth. (Job 5: 15, 16.)

For the needy shall not always be forgotten: the expectation of the poor shall not perish for ever. (Psalm 9: 18.)

Thy congregation hath dwelt therein: thou, O God, hast prepared of thy goodness for the poor. (Psalm 68: 10.)

For the Lord heareth the poor, and despiseth not his prisoners. (Psalm 69: 33.)

He shall judge thy people with righteousness, and thy poor with judgment. (Psalm 72: 2.)

He will regard the prayer of the destitute, and not despise their prayer. (Psalm 102: 17.)

He raiseth up the poor out of the dust, and lifteth the needy out of the dunghill;

That he may set him with princes, even with the princes of his people. (Psalm 113: 7, 8.)

I will abundantly bless her provision: I will satisfy her poor with bread. (Psalm 132: 15.)

And he said unto his disciples, *Therefore I say unto you, Take no thought for your life, what ye shall eat; neither for the body, what ye shall put on.*

The life is more than meat, and the body is more than raiment.

Consider the ravens: for they neither sow nor reap; which neither have storehouse nor barn; and God feedeth them: how much more are ye better than the fowls?

And which of you with taking thought can add to his stature one cubit?

If ye then be not able to do that thing which is least, why take ye thought for the rest?

Consider the lilies how they grow: they toil not, they spin not; and yet I say unto you, that Solomon in all his glory was not arrayed like one of these.

If then God so clothe the grass, which is to day in the field, and to morrow is cast into the oven; how much more will he clothe you, O ye of little faith?

And seek not ye what ye shall eat, or what ye shall drink, neither be ye of doubtful mind.

For all these things do the nations of the world seek after: and your Father knoweth that ye have need of these things.

But rather seek ye the kingdom of God; and all these things shall be added unto you.

Fear not, little flock; for it is your Father's good pleasure to give you the kingdom. (Luke 12: 22-32.)

The Church's Care for the Poor.

And in those days when the number of the Disciples was multiplied, there arose a murmuring of the Grecians against the Hebrews, because their widows were neglected in the daily ministration.

Then the twelve called the multitude of the Disciples unto them, and said, It is not reason that we should leave the word of God, and serve tables.

Wherefore, brethren, look ye out among you seven men of honest report, full of the Holy Ghost, and wisdom, whom we may appoint over this business. (Acts 6: 1-3.)

Therefore I thought it necessary to exhort the brethren, that they would go before unto you, and make up beforehand your bounty, whereof ye had notice before, that the same might be ready, as a matter of bounty, and not as of covetousness.

But this I say, He which soweth sparingly shall reap also sparingly; and he which soweth bountifully shall reap also bountifully.

Every man according as he purposeth in his heart, so let him give; not grudgingly, or of necessity: for God loveth a cheerful giver.

And God is able to make all grace abound toward you; that ye, always having all sufficiency in all things, may abound to every good work:

(As it is written, He hath dispersed abroad; he hath given to the poor: his righteousness remaineth for ever.

Now he that ministereth seed to the sower both minister bread for your food, and multiply your seed sown, and increase the fruits of your righteousness;)

Being enriched in every thing to all bountifulness, which causeth through us thanksgiving to God. (2 Corinthians 9: 5-11.)

Only they would that we should remember the poor; the same which I also was forward to do. (Galatians 2: 10.)

Christ Blesses the Poor in Spirit.

For all those things hath mine hand made, and all those things have been, saith the Lord: but to this man will I look, even to him that is poor and of a contrite spirit, and trembleth at my word. (Isaiah 66: 2.)

Blessed are the poor in spirit: for theirs is the kingdom of heaven. (Matthew 5: 3.)

And he lifted up his eyes on his disciples, and said, *Blessed be ye poor: for yours is the kingdom of God.* (Luke 6: 20.)

POTIPHAR. (See Joseph.)

Pot′i-phar—a Hebrew form of an Egyptian name, probably meaning "belonging to the sun." Potiphar was the name of the Egyptian official to whom Joseph was sold by the tradesmen who bought him from his brethren. Potiphar's treatment of Joseph after the latter had been cast into prison at the instance of Potiphar's wife indicates that he found reason to believe the young Hebrew innocent of the charges made against him.

Reference.—Genesis 39.

POTTAGE. (See Esau, Jacob.)

Pot′tage—a dish made by boiling lentils, rice, parsley, or flour with bits of meat, the whole forming a sort of thick, meaty soup. The preparation is almost as old as mankind, and still forms a very favorite article of diet in the East.

PRAISE.

Praise—honor rendered for worth; approval; laudation; especially in the Scriptural sense, joyful tribute or homage rendered to the Divine Being. The Bible is full of exhortations and directions to God's people to render to Him proper praise and honor, with gladness and thanksgiving for His manifold mercies and goodnesses to us and to all men. Praise is a part of the Christian life.

REFERENCES.

Praise to God.

The Lord is my strength and song, and he is become my salvation: he is my God, and I will prepare him a habitation; my father's God, and I will exalt him. (Exodus 15: 2.)

Hear, O ye kings; give ear, O ye princes; I, even I, will sing unto the Lord; I will sing praise to the Lord God of Israel. (Judges 5: 3.)

Therefore I will give thanks unto thee, O Lord, among the heathen, and I will sing praises unto thy name. (2 Samuel 22: 50.)

Sing unto him, sing psalms unto him, talk ye of all his wondrous works. (1 Chronicles 16: 9.)

Declare his glory among the heathen; his marvelous works among all nations. (1 Chronicles 16: 24.)

Blessed be the Lord God of Israel for ever and ever. And all the people said, Amen, and praised the Lord. (1 Chronicles 16: 36.)

Now, therefore, our God, we thank thee, and praise thy glorious name. (1 Chronicles 29: 13.)

I will praise the Lord according to his righteousness: and will sing praise to the name of the Lord most high. (Psalm 5: 17.)

I will praise thee, O Lord, with my whole heart; I will shew forth all thy marvellous works. (Psalm 9: 1.)

Sing praises to the Lord, which dwelleth in Zion: declare among the people his doings. (Psalm 9: 11.)

Be thou exalted, Lord, in thine own strength: so will we sing and praise thy power. (Psalm 21: 13.)

Ye that fear the Lord, praise him; all ye the seed of Jacob, glorify him; and fear him, all ye the seed of Israel. (Psalm 22: 23.)

O magnify the Lord with me, and let us exalt his name together. (Psalm 34: 3.)

And in that day shall ye say, Praise the Lord, call upon his name, declare his doings among the people, make mention. that his name is exalted. (Isaiah 12: 4.)

The Lord hath brought forth our righteousness: come, and let us declare in Zion the work of the Lord our God. (Jeremiah 51: 10.)

Now I Nebuchadnezzar praise and extol and honour the King of heaven, all whose works are truth, and his ways judgment: and those that walk in pride he is able to abase. (Daniel 4: 37.)

And ye shall eat in plenty, and be satisfied, and praise the name of the Lord your God, that hath dealt wondrously with you: and my people shall never be ashamed. (Joel 2: 26.)

And Mary said, My soul doth magnify the Lord,

And my spirit hath rejoiced in God my Saviour. (Luke 1: 46, 47.)

Praise in Public Worship.

That I may shew forth all thy praise in the gates of the daughter of Zion: I will rejoice in thy salvation. (Psalm 9: 14.)

My foot standeth in an even place; in the congregations will I bless the Lord. (Psalm 26: 12.)

I will give thee thanks in the great congregation: I will praise thee among much people. (Psalm 35: 18.)

Bless ye God in the congregations, even the Lord, from the fountain of Israel. (Psalm 68: 26.)

And the heavens shall praise thy wonders, O Lord: thy faithfulness also in the congregation of the saints. (Psalm 89: 5.)

Enter into his gates with thanksgiving, and into his courts with praise: be thankful unto him, and bless his name. (Psalm 100: 4.)

Let them exalt him also in the congregation of the people, and praise him in the assembly of the elders. (Psalm 107: 32.)

PRAYER.

PRAYER—the act of addressing thanksgiving, adoration, supplication, or intercession to God.

Prayer is one of the first and sweetest duties of the Christian toward God. By it he approaches the personal ear of his Maker, pouring out his thanks for life, preservation, and salvation, glorifying God, asking aid, assistance, grace, or strength, or making intercession for some other person. It is one of the surest means of attaining a higher type of spirituality, as well as one of the strongest of staffs upon which to lean when we are weak or troubled. Earnest, continued prayer invariably brings peace when we are at war with ourselves, for God never fails to listen to the call of those who come to Him in distress of mind and ask Him to give of His infinite strength to support them. But in asking God for things we must never forget that His knowledge and wisdom are infinitely greater than ours, and that we must not expect Him to grant our wishes if in His sight they are not expedient or will be harmful to us. His own Son, in the garden of Gethsemane, addressed Him from the human side of his nature and asked Him to let the cup of Calvary pass from Him, if it should be His will. But Jesus was willing to let everything rest in the hands of his Father, obeying Him in all things. No prayer should pass the lips of man without the thought, either spoken or in the heart: "Thy will, O Lord, not mine, be done."

Much has been said in argument regarding the proper posture for prayer. Unquestionably kneeling is the one in which we show the greatest reverence and love for our Maker, but after all it is the frame of mind which we are in, and not the actual posture, that shows our heart's feelings. Kneeling, sitting, standing, bowing the head, or prostrate, we should pray with faith, repentance, sincerity, fervency, and in the name of Christ.

REFERENCES.

Objects and Occasions of Prayer.

And say ye, Save us, O God of our salvation, and gather us together, and deliver us from the heathen, that we may give thanks to thy holy name, and glory in thy praise. (1 Chronicles 16: 35.)

He shall pray unto God, and he will be favourable unto him: and he shall see his face with joy: for he will render unto man his righteousness. (Job 33: 26.)

Pray for the peace of Jerusalem: they shall prosper that love thee. (Psalm 132: 6.)

But I say unto you, Love your enemies, bless them that curse you, do good to them that hate you, and pray for them which despitefully use you, and persecute you. (Matthew 5: 44.)

Pray ye therefore the Lord of the harvest, that he will send forth labourers into his harvest. (Matthew 9: 38.)

Watch and pray, that ye enter not into temptation: the spirit indeed is willing, but the flesh is weak. (Matthew 26: 41.)

And the publican, standing afar off, would not lift up so much as his eyes unto heaven, but smote upon his breast, saying, God be merciful to me a sinner. (Luke 18: 13.)

And he cried, saying, Jesus, thou son of David, have mercy on me. (Luke 18: 38.)

Now I beseech you, brethren, for the Lord Jesus Christ's sake, and for the love of the Spirit, that ye strive together with me in your prayers to God for me. (Romans 15: 30.)

Is any among you afflicted? let him pray. Is any merry? let him sing Psalms. (James 5: 13.)

But the end of all things is at hand: be ye therefore sober and watch unto prayer. (1 Peter 4: 7.)

Prayer Commanded.

Seek ye the Lord while he may be found, call ye upon him while he is near. (Isaiah 55: 6.)

Ask, and it shall be given you; seek, and ye shall find; knock, and it shall be opened unto you:

For every one that asketh receiveth; and he that seeketh findeth; and to him that knocketh it shall be opened. (Matthew 7: 7, 8.)

Watch and pray, that ye enter not into temptation: the spirit indeed is willing, but the flesh is weak. (Matthew 26: 41.)

And he spake a parable unto them to this end, that men ought always to pray, and not to faint. (Luke 18: 1.)

Watch ye therefore, and pray always, that ye may be accounted worthy to escape all these things that shall come to pass, and to stand before the Son of man. (Luke 21: 36.)

Praying always with all prayer and supplication in the Spirit, and watching thereunto with all perseverance and supplication for all saints. (Ephesians 6: 18.)

Be careful for nothing: but in every thing by prayer and supplication with thanksgiving let your request be made known unto God. (Philippians 4: 6.)

Continue in prayer, and watch in the same with thanksgiving. (Colossians 4: 2.)

Pray without ceasing. (1 Thessalonians 5: 17.)

Brethren, pray for us. (1 Thessalonians 5: 25.)

I exhort therefore, that, first of all, supplications, prayers, intercessions, and giving of thanks, be made for all men;

For kings, and for all that are in authority; that we may lead a quiet and peaceable life in all godliness and honesty.

For this is good and acceptable in the sight of God our Saviour;

Who will have all men to be saved, and to come unto the knowledge of the truth. (1 Timothy 2: 1-4.)

I will therefore that men pray every where, lifting up holy hands, without wrath and doubting. (1 Timothy 2: 8.)

Encouragement to Prayer.

He shall pray unto God, and he will be favourable unto him: and he shall see his face with joy: for he will render unto man his righteousness. (Job 33: 26.)

The Lord hath heard my supplication; the Lord will receive my prayer. (Psalm 6: 9.)

For this shall every one that is godly pray unto thee in a time when thou mayest be found: surely in the floods of great waters they shall not come nigh unto him. (Psalm 32: 6.)

But verily God hath heard me; he hath attended to the voice of my prayer.

Blessed be God, which hath not turned away my prayer, nor his mercy from me. (Psalm 66: 19, 20.)

And it shall come to pass, that before they call, I will answer; and while they are yet speaking, I will hear. (Isaiah 65: 24.)

And I will bring the third part through the fire, and will refine them as silver is refined, and will try them as gold is tried: they shall call on my name, and I will hear them; I will say, It is my people; and they shall say, The Lord is my God. (Zechariah 13: 9.)

Again I say unto you, That if two of you shall agree on earth as touching any thing that they shall ask, it shall be done for them of my Father which is in heaven. (Matthew 18: 19.)

And all things, whatsoever ye shall ask in prayer, believing, ye shall receive. (Matthew 21: 22.)

Therefore I say unto you, What things soever ye desire, when ye pray, believe that ye receive them, and ye shall have them. (Mark 11: 24.)

And I say unto you, Ask, and it shall be given you; seek, and ye shall find; knock, and it shall be opened unto you. (Luke 11: 9.)

For whosoever shall call upon the Name of the Lord, shall be saved. (Romans 10: 13.)

If any of you lack wisdom, let him ask of God, that giveth to all men liberally, and upbraideth not: and it shall be given him.

But let him ask in faith, nothing wavering: for he that wavereth is like a wave of the sea, driven with the wind, and tossed. (James 1: 5, 6.)

Prayers Heard and Answered.

Lord, thou hast heard the desire of the humble: thou wilt prepare their heart, thou wilt cause thine ear to hear. (Psalm 10: 17.)

O thou that hearest prayer, unto thee shall all flesh come. (Psalm 65: 2.)

Moses and Aaron among his priests, and Samuel among them that call upon his name; they called upon the Lord, and he answered them. (Psalm 99: 6.)

Then shalt thou call, and the Lord shall answer; thou shalt cry, and he shall say, Here I am. If thou take away from the midst of thee the yoke, the putting forth of the finger, and speaking vanity. (Isaiah 58: 9.)

Proper Offering of Prayer.

The Lord is nigh unto all them that call upon him, to all that call upon him in truth. (Psalm 145: 18.)

Be not rash with thy mouth, and let not thine heart be hasty to utter any thing before God: for God is in heaven, and thou upon earth: therefore let thy words be few. (Ecclesiastes 5: 2.)

And when thou prayest, thou shalt not be as the hypocrites are: for they love to pray standing in the synagogues and in the corners of the streets, that they may be seen of men. Verily I say unto you, They have their reward.

But thou, when thou prayest, enter into thy closet, and when thou hast shut thy door, pray to thy Father which is in secret; and thy Father which seeth in secret shall reward thee openly.

But when ye pray, use not vain repetitions, as the heathen do: for they think that they shall be heard for their much speaking.

Be not ye therefore like unto them: for your Father knoweth what things ye have need of, before ye ask him. (Matthew 6: 5-8.)

And he went a little farther, and fell on his face, and prayed, saying, *O my Father, if it be possible, let this cup pass from me: nevertheless not as I will, but as thou wilt.* (Matthew 26: 39.)

And when ye stand praying, forgive, if ye have ought against any: that your Father also which is in heaven may forgive you your trespasses.

But if ye do not forgive, neither will your Father which is in heaven forgive your trespasses. (Mark 11: 25, 26.)

Now we know that God heareth not sinners: but if any man be a worshipper of God, and doeth his will, him he heareth. (John 9: 31.)

If ye abide in me, and my words abide in you, ye shall ask what ye will, and it shall be done unto you. (John 15: 7.)

Rejoicing in hope; patient in tribulation; continuing instant in prayer. (Romans 12: 12.)

Continue in prayer, and watch in the same with thanksgiving. (Colossians 4: 2.)

Now she that is a widow indeed, and desolate, trusteth in God, and continueth in supplications and prayers night and day. (1 Timothy 5: 5.)

But without faith it is impossible to please him: for he that cometh to God, must believe that he is, and that he is a rewarder of them that diligently seek him. (Hebrews 11: 6.)

Draw nigh to God, and he will draw nigh to you: cleanse your hands ye sinners, and purify your hearts ye double minded. (James 4: 8.)

Pray through and in the Name of Christ.

At that day ye shall ask in my name: and I say not unto you, that I will pray the Father for you. (John 16: 26.)

For through him we both have an access by one Spirit unto the Father. (Ephesians 2: 18.)

Having therefore, brethren, boldness to enter into the Holiest by the blood of Jesus. (Hebrews 10: 19.)

Posture for Prayer.

And they fell upon their faces, and said, O God, the God of the spirits of all flesh, shall one man sin, and wilt thou be wroth with all the congregation? (Numbers 16: 22.)

And Solomon stood before the altar of the Lord in the presence of all the congregation of Israel, and spread forth his hands toward heaven:

And he said, Lord God of Israel, there is no God like thee, in heaven above, or on earth beneath, who keepest covenant and mercy with thy servants that walk before thee with all their heart. (1 Kings 8: 22, 23.)

And David lifted up his eyes, and saw the angel of the Lord stand between the earth and the heaven, having a drawn sword in his hand, stretched out over Jerusalem. Then David and the elders of Israel, who were clothed in sackcloth, fell upon their faces. (1 Chronicles 21: 16.)

Hear the voice of my supplications, when I cry unto thee, when I lift up my hands toward thy holy oracle. (Psalm 28: 2.)

O come, let us worship and bow down: let us kneel before the Lord our maker. (Psalm 95: 6.)

Arise, cry out in the night: in the beginning of the watches pour out thy heart like water before the face of the Lord: lift up thine hands toward him for the life of thy young children, that faint for hunger in the top of every street. (Lamentations 2: 19.)

And he was withdrawn from them about a stone's cast, and kneeled down, and prayed. (Luke 22: 41.)

Wicked and Hypocritical Prayer Condemned.

Set thou a wicked man over him: and let Satan stand at his right hand.

When he shall be judged, let him be condemned: and let his prayer become sin. (Psalm 109: 6, 7.)

Hé that turneth away his ear from hearing the law, even his prayer shall be abomination. (Proverbs 28: 9.)

And when thou prayest, thou shalt not be as the hypocrites are: for they love to pray standing in the synagogues and in the corners of the streets, that they may be seen of men. Verily I say unto you, They have their reward. (Matthew 6: 5.)

The Lord's Prayer.

Matthew's Form:

After this manner therefore pray ye: Our Father which art in heaven, Hallowed be thy name.

Thy kingdom come. Thy will be done in earth, as it is in heaven.

Give us this day our daily bread.

And forgive us our debts, as we forgive our debtors.

And lead us not into temptation, but deliver us from evil: For thine is the kingdom, and the power, and the glory, for ever. Amen. · (Matthew 6: 9-13.)

Luke's Form:

And it came to pass, that, as he was praying in a certain place, when he ceased, one of his disciples said unto him, Lord, teach us to pray, as John also taught his disciples.

And he said unto them, *When ye pray, say, Our Father which art in heaven, Hallowed be thy name. Thy kingdom come. Thy will be done, as in heaven, so in earth.*

Give us day by day our daily bread.

And forgive us our sins; for we also forgive every one that is indebted to us. And lead us not into temptation; but deliver us from evil. (Luke 11: 1-4.)

PREACHING. (See Minister.)

PREACH'ING—public discoursing upon religious subjects, usually from a Scriptural text. Preaching is one of the most common forms for the circulation of the Gospel and religious truths, or the deliverance of homilies upon the Christian life. The prophets all were preachers, and Jesus Himself did a vast amount of His ministerial work in this manner, as also did the apostles. Since the complete establishment of the Church, the preacher has come to be recognized as a member of a sacred profession, and in modern years he has been specially trained and educated for it.

REFERENCES.

Gospel of Christ to Be Preached.

From that time Jesus began to preach, and to say, *Repent: for the kingdom of heaven is at hand.* (Matthew 4: 17.)

Go ye therefore, and teach all nations, baptizing them in the name of the Father, and of the Son, and of the Holy Ghost. (Matthew 28: 19.)

Now after that John was put in prison, Jesus came into Galilee, preaching the gospel of the kingdom of God. (Mark 1: 14.)

And he said unto them, *Go ye into all the world, and preach the gospel to every creature.* (Mark 16: 15.)

And there was delivered unto him the book of the prophet Esaias. And when he had opened the book, he found the place where it was written,

The Spirit of the Lord is upon me, because he hath anointed me to preach the gospel to the poor; he hath sent me to heal the brokenhearted, to preach deliverance to the captives, and recovering of sight to the blind, to set at liberty them that are bruised,

To preach the acceptable year of the Lord. (Luke 4: 17-19.)

Jesus said unto him, *Let the dead bury their dead: but go thou and preach the kingdom of God.* (Luke 9: 60.)

And that repentance and remission

of sins should be preached in his name among all nations, beginning at Jerusalem. (Luke 24: 47.)

But Philip was found at Azotus: and passing through he preached in all the cities, till he came to Cæsarea. (Acts 10: 40.)

But what saith it? The word is nigh thee, even in thy mouth, and in thy heart, that is the word of faith which we preach,

That if thou shalt confess with thy mouth the Lord Jesus, and shalt believe in thine heart that God hath raised him from the dead, thou shalt be saved. (Romans 10: 8, 9.)

For Christ sent me not to baptize, but to preach the Gospel: not with wisdom of words, lest the Cross of Christ should be made of none effect.

For the preaching of the Cross is to them that perish foolishness: but unto us which are saved it is the power of God. (1 Corinthians 1: 17, 18.)

PREDESTINATION.

PRE-DES'TI-NA'TION—the name given by theologians to the divine purpose regarding mankind, nations, and individuals. The exact meaning of certain passages of Scripture regarding God's attitude toward man and salvation have proved to be very fruitful sources of controversy for many generations. The older Calvinists, or followers of John Calvin, believed that certain members of the human race had been foreordained and predestinated by God to salvation and everlasting life and others foredoomed to everlasting punishment and that Christ's atonement was limited to these predestinated ones. On the other hand, the followers of Arminius, who lived in the generation following Calvin, maintained that Christ's atonement was for all mankind and that whosoever would might profit by it through faith and confession, thus taking the position that those whom God predestinated were all those who accept Him and His Son,

and that those foredoomed are those who do not. This article makes no pretence of discussing the merits of either side of the argument.

REFERENCES.

For whom he did foreknow, he also did predestinate to be conformed to the image of his Son, that he might be the firstborn among many brethren.

Moreover whom he did predestinate, them he also called: and whom he called, them he also justified: and whom he justified, them he also glorified. (Romans 8: 29, 30.)

Therefore hath he mercy on whom he will have mercy, and whom he will he hardeneth.

Thou wilt say then unto me, Why doth he yet find fault? For who hath resisted his will?

Nay but, O man, who art thou that repliest against God? Shall the thing formed say to him that formed it, Why hast thou made me thus?

Hath not the potter power over the clay, of the same lump to make one vessel unto honour, and another unto dishonour?

What if God, willing to shew his wrath, and to make his power known, endured with much longsuffering the vessels of wrath fitted to destruction:

And that he might make known the riches of his glory on the vessels of mercy, which he had afore prepared unto glory,

Even us, whom he hath called, not of the Jews only, but also of the Gentiles?

As he saith also in Osee, I will call them my people, which were not my people; and her beloved, which was not beloved.

And it shall come to pass, that in the place where it was said unto them, Ye are not my people; there shall they be called the children of the living God. (Romans 9: 18-26.)

But what saith it? The word is nigh thee, even in thy mouth, and in thy heart: that is, the word of faith, which we preach;

That if thou shalt confess with thy mouth the Lord Jesus, and shalt believe in thine heart that God hath raised him from the dead, thou shalt be saved.

For with the heart man believeth unto righteousness; and with the mouth confession is made unto salvation.

For the scripture saith, Whosoever believeth on him shall not be ashamed.

For there is no difference between the Jew and the Greek: for the same Lord over all is rich unto all that call upon him.

For whosoever shall call upon the name of the Lord shall be saved.

How then shall they call on him in whom they have not believed? and how shall they believe in him of whom they have not heard? and how shall they hear without a preacher?

And how shall they preach, except they be sent? as it is written, How beautiful are the feet of them that preach the gospel of peace, and bring glad tidings of good things!

But they have not all obeyed the gospel. For Esaias saith, Lord, who hath believed our report? (Romans 10: 8-16.)

Paul, an apostle of Jesus Christ by the will of God, to the saints which are at Ephesus, and to the faithful in Christ Jesus:

Grace be to you, and peace, from God our Father, and from the Lord Jesus Christ.

Blessed be the God and Father of our Lord Jesus Christ, who hath blessed us with all spiritual blessings in heavenly places in Christ:

According as he hath chosen us in him before the foundation of the world, that we should be holy and without blame before him in love:

Having predestinated us unto the adoption of children by Jesus Christ to himself, according to the good pleasure of his will,

To the praise of the glory of his grace, wherein he hath made us accepted in the beloved.

In whom we have redemption through his blood, the forgiveness of sins, according to the riches of his grace;

Wherein he hath abounded toward us in all wisdom and prudence;

Having made known unto us the mystery of his will, according to his good pleasure which he hath purposed in himself:

That in the dispensation of the fulness of times he might gather together in one all things in Christ, both which are in heaven, and which are on earth; even in him:

In whom also we have obtained an inheritance, being predestinated according to the purpose of him who worketh all things after the counsel of his own will:

That we should be to the praise of his glory, who first trusted in Christ.

In whom ye also trusted, after that ye heard the word of truth, the gospel of your salvation: in whom also after that ye believed, ye were sealed with that Holy Spirit of promise,

Which is the earnest of our inheritance until the redemption of the purchased possession, unto the praise of his glory. (Ephesians 1: 1-14.)

PRIDE. (See Conceit, Ostentation, Vanity.)

PRIDE—the state or quality of being proud or having inordinate self-esteem; conceit of one's talents, ability, wealth, station, etc.; disdainful behavior; contempt for those beneath us in station.

Pride is regarded in Scripture as a vice, and we are told to shun it as an evil thing, and as a vanity which leads only to destruction.

One sort of pride is a good thing. In this sense pride means an appreciation of one's position as a Christian and a member of the human family and an abhorrence of doing anything that is unworthy of such high stations; proper self-respect and self-esteem; otherwise a decent and respectable elevation of character.

REFERENCES.
General.

Talk no more so exceeding proudly; let not arrogancy come out of your mouth: for the Lord is a God of knowledge, and by him actions are weighed. (1 Samuel 2: 3.)

These six things doth the Lord hate; yea, seven are an abomination unto him:

A proud look, a lying tongue, and hands that shed innocent blood. (Proverbs 6: 16, 17.)

The fear of the Lord is to hate evil: pride, and arrogancy, and the evil way, and the froward mouth, do I hate. (Proverbs 8: 13.)

Every one that is proud in heart is an abomination to the Lord: though hand join in hand, he shall not be unpunished. (Proverbs 16: 5.)

A high look and a proud heart, and the ploughing of the wicked, is sin. (Proverbs 21: 4.)

But when his heart was lifted up, and his mind hardened in pride, he was deposed from his kingly throne, and they took his glory from him. (Daniel 5: 20.)

For I say, through the grace given unto me, to every man that is among you, not to think of himself more highly than he ought to think; but to think soberly, according as God hath dealt to every man the measure of faith. (Romans 12: 3.)

Be of the same mind one toward another. Mind not high things, but condescend to men of low estate. Be not wise in your own conceits. (Romans 12: 16.)

Origin of Pride.

And Hezekiah hearkened unto them, and shewed them all the house of his precious things, the silver, and the gold, and the spices, and the precious ointment, and all the house of his armour, and all that was found in his treasures: there was nothing in his house, nor in all his dominion, that Hezekiah shewed them not. (2 Kings 20: 13.)

In that day shalt thou not be ashamed for all thy doings, wherein thou hast transgressed against me: for then I will take away out of the midst of thee them that rejoice in thy pride, and thou shalt no more be haughty because of my holy mountain. (Zephaniah 3: 11.)

The Pharisee stood and prayed thus with himself, God, I thank thee, that I am not as other men are, extortioners, unjust, adulterers, or even as this publican.

I fast twice in the week, I give tithes of all that I possess. (Luke 18: 11, 12.)

Now as touching things offered unto idols, we know that we all have knowledge. Knowledge puffeth up: but Charity edifieth.

And if any man think that he knoweth any thing, he knoweth nothing yet as he ought to know. (1 Corinthians 8: 1, 2.)

Not a novice, lest being lifted up with pride, he fall into the condemnation of the devil. (1 Timothy 3: 6.)

Evil Results of Pride.

The wicked in his pride doth persecute the poor: let them be taken in the devices that they have imagined. (Psalm 10: 2.)

Only by pride cometh contention: but with the well-advised is wisdom. (Proverbs 13: 10.)

Proud and haughty scorner is his name, who dealeth in proud wrath. (Proverbs 21: 24.)

He that is of a proud heart stirreth up strife: but he that putteth his trust in the Lord shall be made fat. (Proverbs 28: 25.)

Thy terribleness hath deceived thee, and the pride of thine heart, O thou that dwellest in the clefts of the rock, that holdest the height of the hill: though thou shouldest make thy nest as high as the eagle, I will bring thee down from thence, saith the Lord. (Jeremiah 49: 16.)

Shame and Destruction Follows Pride.

When pride cometh, then cometh shame: but with the lowly is wisdom. (Proverbs 11: 2.)

Pride goeth before destruction, and an haughty spirit before a fall.

Better it is to be of an humble spirit with the lowly, than to divide the spoil with the proud. (Proverbs 16: 18, 19.)

Before destruction the heart of man is haughty, and before honour is humility. (Proverbs 18: 12.)

The crown of pride, the drunkards of Ephraim, shall be trodden under feet. (Isaiah 28: 3.)

PRIESTHOOD. (See Aaron, Call, Ministry, etc.)

PRIEST'HOOD—any order of priests or ministers. The scope of the present article is to deal with the Hebrew priesthood, the Christian ministry having been discussed in its proper place elsewhere. In the early days of the Hebrew nation there was no definite order of priests, the head of the family occupying the position with reference to his own household, the eldest son succeeding his father. Under the Mosaic system the tribe of Levi was substituted for the patriarchal rule in religious affairs, and the Hebrews were promised that if they kept the law they would be made a kingdom of priests, a holy nation, and a peculiar people—that is, a people set apart. The candidate for orders was required to prove his descent from Aaron and to be without bodily blemish. Tithes were set apart for the support of the priesthood, and besides there were many valuable perquisites or fees. In later times the entire body became corrupted by making the office of priest a post for the amassing of much wealth, and this largely contributed to the downfall of the nation.

PRINCE.

PRINCE—the son of a king or ruler of royal birth; also a person high in authority as a noble; also used as a generic name for a ruler or sovereign. We find the term used in various parts of the Bible. Christ is called the Prince of Peace and the Devil is given a title of prince to show his sovereignty over evil things.

REFERENCES.

Christ Prince of Peace and Life.

For unto us a child is born, unto us a son is given: and the government shall be upon his shoulder: and his name shall be called Wonderful, Counsellor, The Mighty God, The Everlasting Father, The Prince of Peace. (Isaiah 9: 6.)

And killed the Prince of life, whom God hath raised from the dead, whereof we are witnesses. (Acts 3: 15.)

Devil Prince of This World and Powers of the Air.

Now is the judgment of this world: now shall the prince of this world be cast out. (John 12: 31.)

Hereafter I will not talk much with you: for the prince of this world cometh, and hath nothing in me. (John 14: 30.)

Wherein in time past ye walked according to the course of this world, according to the prince of the power of the air, the spirit that now worketh in the children of disobedience. (Ephesians 2: 2.)

Christ's Miracles Ascribed to Prince of Devils.

But the Pharisees said, He casteth out devils through the prince of the devils. (Matthew 9: 34.)

But when the Pharisees heard it, they said, This fellow doth not cast out devils, but by Beelzebub the prince of the devils. (Matthew 12: 24.)

And the scribes which came down from Jerusalem said, He hath Beelzebub, and by the prince of the devils casteth he out devils.

And he called them unto him, and said unto them in parables, *How can Satan cast out Satan?* (Mark 3: 22, 23.)

PROFANITY. (See Blasphemy, Oath, etc.)

PROFESSION. (See Confession.)

Pro-fes'sion—public avowal or declaration; open acknowledgment; also a solemn vow or promise.

Profession of faith, or open acknowledgment of belief in Christ, is a primal requirement of Christianity. We are told to come out squarely before the world confessing our faith in God the Father, Jesus Christ the Son, and the Holy Ghost. This is a declaration of allegiance and definite act of enlistment under the banner of Christ, who died for our salvation. To this profession we are told to hold fast, since through it we and our principles are known to the world.

REFERENCES.

Fight the good fight of faith, lay hold on eternal life, whereunto thou art also called, and hast professed a good profession before many witnesses. (1 Timothy 6: 12.)

Seeing then that we have a great high Priest, that is passed into the heavens, Jesus the Son of God, let us hold fast our profession. (Hebrews 4: 14.)

Let us hold fast the profession of our faith without wavering; (for he is faithful that promised;)

And let us consider one another to provoke unto love and to good works. (Hebrews 10: 23, 24.)

PROMISE. (See Covenant.)

Prom'ise—a declaration made by one person to another to do, or to refrain from doing, a thing, a declaration which gives the person receiving it the right to expect the performance of the thing or its non-performance, according to the nature of the declaration.

The Bible is full from cover to cover of the promises of God to man. The greatest of these is the promise of salvation through faith. We find it foretold away back in the Old Testament in the time of Moses, and running on down thence to the final chapters of Revelation. And this is but one of the many promises of God. All are contingent upon something or other, wherein God shows His goodness and wisdom. If we love Him and keep His commandments He has promised us certain rewards; if we display the virtues He loves in us He promises us other rewards; if we believe in His Son we have the promise of eternal life. God's promises are not like those of men: He never breaks them. If we fail to win the fulfillment of the promise, we must search our own hearts and lives to find the reason.

REFERENCES.

Promises of God.

To Mankind from the Fall:

And I will put enmity between thee and the woman, and between thy seed and her seed; it shall bruise thy head, and thou shalt bruise his heel. (Genesis 3: 15.)

To Noah:

And the Lord smelled a sweet savour; and the Lord said in his heart, I will not again curse the ground any more for man's sake; for the imagination of man's heart is evil from his youth: neither will I again smite any more every thing living, as I have done.

While the earth remaineth, seed-time and harvest, and cold and heat, and summer and winter, and day and night, shall not cease. (Genesis 8: 21, 22.)

And I, behold, I establish my covenant with you, and with your seed after you;

And with every living creature that is with you, of the fowl, of the cattle, and of every beast of the earth with you, from all that go out of the ark, to every beast of the earth.

And I will establish my covenant with you; neither shall all flesh be cut off any more by the waters of a flood; neither shall there any more be a flood to destroy the earth. (Genesis 9: 9-11.)

To Abraham:

For all the land which thou seest, to thee will I give it, and to thy seed for ever.

And I will make thy seed as the dust of the earth: so that if a man can number the dust of the earth, then shall thy seed also be numbered. (Genesis 13: 15, 16.)

And I will make thee exceedingly fruitful, and I will make nations of thee; and kings shall come out of thee.

And I will establish my covenant between me and thee, and thy seed after thee, in their generations, for an everlasting covenant; to be a God unto thee, and to thy seed after thee. (Genesis 17: 6, 7.)

And said, By myself have I sworn, saith the Lord, for because thou hast done this thing, and hast not withheld thy son, thine only son:

That in blessing I will bless thee, and in multiplying I will multiply thy seed as the stars of the heaven, and as the sand which is upon the seashore; and thy seed shall possess the gate of his enemies;

And in thy seed shall all the nations of the earth be blessed; because thou hast obeyed my voice. (Genesis 22: 16-18.)

To David:

And as since the time that I commanded judges to be over my people Israel, and have caused thee to rest from all thine enemies. Also the Lord telleth thee that he will make thee an house.

And when thy days be fulfilled, and thou shalt sleep with thy fathers, I will set up thy seed after thee, which shall proceed out of thy bowels, and I will establish his kingdom.

He shall build an house for my name, and I will stablish the throne of his kingdom for ever.

I will be his father, and he shall be my son. If he commit iniquity, I will chasten him with the rod of men, and with the stripes of the children of men. (2 Samuel 7: 11-14.)

Promises of Christ.

But seek ye first the kingdom of God, and his righteousness; and all these things shall be added unto you. (Matthew 6: 33.)

Ask, and it shall be given you; seek, and ye shall find; knock, and it shall be opened unto you. (Matthew 7: 7.)

He that receiveth you receiveth me, and he that receiveth me receiveth him that sent me.

He that receiveth a prophet in the name of a prophet shall receive a prophet's reward; and he that receiveth a righteous man in the name of a righteous man shall receive a righteous man's reward.

And whosoever shall give to drink unto one of these little ones a cup of cold water only in the name of a disciple, verily I say unto you, he shall in no wise lose his reward. (Matthew 10: 39-42.)

Come unto me, all ye that labour and are heavy laden, and I will give you rest. (Matthew 11: 28.)

For whosoever shall do the will of my Father which is in heaven, the same is my brother, and sister, and mother. (Matthew 12: 50.)

And I say also unto thee, That thou art Peter, and upon this rock I will build my church; and the gates of hell shall not prevail against it.

And I will give unto thee the keys of the kingdom of heaven: and whatsoever thou shalt bind on earth shall be bound in heaven: and whatsoever thou shalt loose on earth shall be loosed in heaven. (Matthew 16: 18, 19.)

Then said Jesus unto his disciples, *If any man will come after me, let him deny himself, and take up his cross, and follow me.*

For whosoever will save his life shall lose it: and whosoever will lose his life for my sake shall find it. (Matthew 16: 24, 25.)

And Jesus said unto them, *Because of your unbelief: for verily I say unto you, If ye have faith as a grain of mustard seed, ye shall say unto this mountain, Remove hence to yonder place; and it shall remove; and nothing shall be impossible unto you.* (Matthew 17: 20.)

And Jesus said unto them, *Verily I say unto you, That ye which have followed me, in the regeneration when the Son of man shall sit in the throne of his glory, ye also shall sit upon twelve thrones, judging the twelve tribes of Israel.*

And every one that hath forsaken houses, or brethren, or sisters, or father, or mother, or wife, or children, or lands, for my name's sake, shall receive an hundredfold, and shall inherit everlasting life.

But many that are first shall be last; and the last shall be first. (Matthew 19: 28-30.)

Teaching them to observe all things whatsoever I have commanded you: and, lo, I am with you alway, even unto the end of the world. Amen. (Matthew 28: 20.)

Fear not, little flock; for it is your Father's good pleasure to give you the kingdom. (Luke 12: 32.)

Verily, verily, I say unto you, He that believeth on me, the works that I do shall he do also; and greater works than these shall he do; because I go unto my Father.

And whatsoever ye shall ask in my name, that will I do, that the Father may be glorified in the Son.

If ye shall ask any thing in my name, I will do it. (John 14: 12-14.)

Promise of the Gospel.

I have made a covenant with my chosen, I have sworn unto David my servant,

Thy seed will I establish for ever, and build up thy throne to all generations. Selah. (Psalm 89: 3, 4.)

Paul, a servant of Jesus Christ, called to be an Apostle, separated unto the Gospel of God,

(Which he had promised afore by his Prophets in the holy Scriptures,)

Concerning his Son Jesus Christ our Lord, which was made of the seed of David according to the flesh,

And declared to be the Son of God, with power, according to the Spirit of holiness, by the resurrection from the dead. (Romans 1: 1-4.)

That the Gentiles should be fellow-heirs, and of the same body, and partakers of his promise in Christ, by the Gospel. (Ephesians 3: 6.)

Paul an Apostle of Jesus Christ by the will of God, according to the promise of life, which is in Christ Jesus. (2 Timothy 1: 1.)

For when God made promise to Abraham, because he could swear by no greater, he sware by himself,

Saying, Surely blessing I will bless thee, and multiplying I will multiply thee.

And so, after he had patiently endured, he obtained the promise.

For men verily swear by the greater: and an oath for confirmation is to them an end of all strife.

Wherein God, willing more abundantly to shew unto the heirs of promise the immutability of his counsel, confirmed it by an oath:

That by two immutable things, in which it was impossible for God to lie, we might have a strong consolation, who have fled for refuge to lay hold upon the hope set before us:

Which hope we have as an anchor of the soul, both sure and stedfast, and which entereth into that within the veil;

Whither the forerunner is for us entered, even Jesus, made an high priest for ever after the order of Melchisedec. (Hebrews 6: 13-20.)

God's Promises Unbreakable and Precious.

God is not a man, that he should lie; neither the son of man, that he should repent: hath he said, and shall he not do it? or hath he spoken, and shall he not make it good? (Numbers 23: 19.)

Know therefore that the Lord thy God, he is God, the faithful God, which keepeth covenant and mercy with them that love him and keep his commandments to a thousand generations. (Deuteronomy 7: 9.)

And behold, this day I am going the way of all the earth; and ye know in all your hearts and in all your souls, that not one thing hath failed of all the good things which the Lord your God spake concerning you; all are come to pass unto you, and not one thing hath failed thereof.

Therefore it shall come to pass, that as all good things are come upon you, which the Lord your God promised you; so shall the Lord bring upon you all evil things, until he have destroyed you from off this good land which the Lord your God hath given you. (Joshua 23: 14, 15.)

Blessed be the Lord, that hath given rest unto his people Israel, according to all that he promised: there hath not failed one word of all his good promise, which he promised by the hand of Moses his servant. (1 Kings 8: 56.)

For all the promises of God in him

are Yea, and in him Amen, unto the glory of God by us. (2 Corinthians 1: 20.)

Is the law then against the promises of God? God forbid: for if there had been a law given which could have given life, verily righteousness should have been by the law.

But the Scripture hath concluded all under sin, that the promise by faith of Jesus Christ might be given to them that believe. (Galatians 3: 21, 22.)

Whereby are given unto us exceeding great and precious promises, that by these you might be partakers of the divine nature, having escaped the corruption that is in the world through lust. (2 Peter 1: 4.)

God Remembers His Promises.

For he remembered his holy promise, and Abraham his servant. (Psalm 105: 42.)

He hath holpen his servant Israel, in remembrance of his mercy,

As he spake to our fathers, to Abraham, and to his seed for ever. (Luke 1: 54, 55.)

Come now, and let us reason together, saith the Lord: though your sins be as scarlet, they shall be as white as snow; though they be red like crimson, they shall be as wool.

If ye be willing and obedient, ye shall eat the good of the land:

But if ye refuse and rebel, ye shall be devoured with the sword: for the mouth of the Lord hath spoken it. (Isaiah 1: 18-20.)

Or let him take hold of my strength, that he may make peace with me, and he shall make peace with me. (Isaiah 27: 5.)

I, even I, am he that blotteth out thy transgressions for mine own sake, and will not remember thy sins. (Isaiah 43: 25.)

I have blotted out, as a thick cloud, thy transgressions, and as a cloud, thy sins: return unto me; for I have redeemed thee. (Isaiah 44: 22.)

Promises to the Repentant and Returning.

Ho, every one that thirsteth, come ye to the waters, and he that hath no money; come ye, buy, and eat; yea, come, buy wine and milk without money and without price.

Wherefore do ye spend money for that which is not bread? and your labour for that which satisfieth not? hearken diligently unto me, and eat ye that which is good, and let your soul delight itself in fatness.

Incline your ear, and come unto me: hear, and your soul shall live; and I will make an everlasting covenant with you, even the sure mercies of David.

Behold, I have given him for a witness to the people, a leader and commander to the people. (Isaiah 55: 1-4.)

And they shall teach no more every man his neighbour, and every man his brother, saying, Know the Lord: for they shall all know me, from the least of them unto the greatest of them, saith the Lord: for I will forgive their iniquity, and I will remember their sin no more. (Jeremiah 31: 34.)

And I will cleanse them from all their iniquity, whereby they have sinned against me; and I will pardon all their iniquities, whereby they have sinned, and whereby they have transgressed against me. (Jeremiah 33: 8.)

None of his sins that he hath committed shall be mentioned unto him: he hath done that which is lawful and right; he shall surely live. (Ezekiel 33: 16.)

And will be a Father unto you, and ye shall be my sons and daughters, saith the Lord Almighty. (2 Corinthians 6: 18.)

Having therefore these promises, dearly beloved, let us cleanse ourselves from all filthiness of the flesh and spirit, perfecting holiness in the fear of God. (2 Corinthians 7: 1.)

God Promises to Uphold and Perfect.

For the arms of the wicked shall be broken: but the Lord upholdeth the righteous. (Psalm 37: 17.)

My flesh and my heart faileth: but God is the strength of my heart, and my portion for ever. (Psalm 73: 26.)

For the Lord God is a sun and shield: the Lord will give grace and glory; no good thing will he withhold from them that walk uprightly. (Psalm 84: 11.)

He giveth power to the faint; and to them that have no might he increaseth strength. (Isaiah 40: 29.)

Fear thou not; for I am with thee: be not dismayed; for I am thy God: I will strengthen thee; yea, I will help thee; yea, I will uphold thee with the right hand of my righteousness. (Isaiah 41: 10.)

And even to your old age I am he: and even to hoar hairs will I carry you: I have made, and I will bear; even I will carry, and will deliver you. (Isaiah 46: 4.)

For thus saith the Lord of hosts: After the glory hath he sent me unto the nations which spoiled you: for he that toucheth you, toucheth the apple of his eye.

For behold, I will shake my hand upon them, and they shall be a spoil to their servants: and ye shall know that the Lord of hosts hath sent me. (Zechariah 2: 8, 9.)

And I will strengthen them in the Lord; and they shall walk up and down in his name, saith the Lord. (Zechariah 10: 12.)

But the Comforter, which is the Holy Ghost, whom the Father will send in my name, he shall teach you all things, and bring all things to your remembrance, whatsoever I have said unto you. (John 14: 26.)

And the God of peace shall bruise Satan under your feet shortly. The grace of our Lord Jesus Christ be with you. Amen. (Romans 16: 20.)

There hath no temptation taken you, but such as is common to man: but God is faithful, who will not suffer you to be tempted above that you are able: but will with the temptation also make a way to escape, that ye may be able to bear it. (1 Corinthians 10: 13.)

But thanks be to God, which giveth us the victory, through our Lord Jesus Christ. (1 Corinthians 15: 57.)

And he said unto me, My grace is sufficient for thee: for my strength is made perfect in weakness. Most gladly therefore will I rather glory in my infirmities, that the power of Christ may rest upon me. (1 Corinthians 12: 9.)

Blessed be the God and Father of our Lord Jesus Christ, who hath blessed us with all spiritual blessings in heavenly places in Christ. (Ephesians 1: 3.)

Promises to the Poor and Fatherless, Etc.

He doth execute the judgment of the fatherless and widow, and loveth the stranger, in giving him food and raiment. (Deuteronomy 10: 18.)

And he shall judge the world in righteousness, he shall minister judgment to the people in uprightness.

The Lord also will be a refuge for the oppressed, a refuge in times of trouble. (Psalm 9: 8, 9.)

Thou hast seen it; for thou beholdest mischief and spite, to requite it with thy hand: the poor committeth himself unto thee; thou art the helper of the fatherless. (Psalm 10: 14.)

A father of the fatherless, and a judge of the widows, is God in his holy habitation.

God setteth the solitary in families: he bringeth out those which are bound with chains: but the rebellious dwell in a dry land. (Psalm 68: 5, 6.)

For the Lord heareth the poor, and despiseth not his prisoners. (Psalm 69: 33.)

For he shall deliver the needy when he crieth; the poor also, and him that hath no helper.

He shall spare the poor and needy, and shall save the souls of the needy.

He shall redeem their soul from deceit and violence: and precious shall their blood be in his sight. (Psalm 72: 12-14.)

He will regard the prayer of the destitute, and not despise their prayer. (Psalm 102: 17.)

For he shall stand at the right hand of the poor, to save him from those that condemn his soul. (Psalm 109: 31.)

He raiseth up the poor out of the dust, and lifteth the needy out of the dunghill;

That he may set him with princes, even with the princes of his people.

He maketh the barren woman to keep house, and to be a joyful mother of children. Praise ye the Lord. (Psalm 113: 7-9.)

Leave thy fatherless children, I will preserve them alive; and let thy widows trust in me. (Jeremiah 49: 11.)

Promises of Temporal Blessings.

And ye shall serve the Lord your God, and he shall bless thy bread, and thy water; and I will take sickness away from the midst of thee. (Exodus 23: 25.)

And I will give peace in the land, and ye shall lie down, and none shall make you afraid: and I will rid evil beasts out of the land, neither shall the sword go through your land. (Leviticus 26: 60.)

O fear the Lord, ye his saints; for there is no want to them that fear him.

The young lions do lack, and suffer hunger: but they that seek the Lord shall not want any good thing. (Psalm 34: 9, 10.)

Trust in the Lord, and do good; so shalt thou dwell in the land, and verily thou shalt be fed. (Psalm 37: 3.)

Honour the Lord with thy substance, and with the firstfruits of all thine increase:

So shall thy barns be filled with plenty, and thy presses shall burst out with new wine. (Proverbs 3: 9, 10.)

Therefore I say unto you, Take no thought for your life, what ye shall eat, or what ye shall drink; nor yet for your body, what ye shall put on. Is not the life more than meat, and the body than raiment?

Behold the fowls of the air: for they sow not, neither do they reap, nor gather into barns; yet your heavenly Father feedeth them. Are ye not much better than they? (Matthew 6: 25, 26.)

But my God shall supply all your need according to his riches in glory by Christ Jesus. (Philippians 4: 19.)

For bodily exercise profiteth little: but godliness is profitable unto all things, having promise of the life that now is, and of that which is to come. (1 Timothy 4: 8.)

PROPHECY. (See Prophets; see also Prophecies regarding Christ in Appendix.)

PROPH'E-CY—literally, a foretelling; specifically, a foretelling of such things or events as can be known only to God.

One of the ways in which God communicated His will to man, and no doubt still does so in a way in which we cannot now understand, was by means of prophecy through the mouths of specially selected men and women, whom we call prophets. In the same manner God made revelations of Himself and His plans for mankind. A notable instance of this is to be seen in the prophecies relating to Jesus Christ, the Saviour, whose miraculous birth, ministry, mission, death, and resurrection were subjects foretold by prophets centuries before the coming of the Man of Sorrows Himself. In the Appendix to this volume will be found set out this particular series of revelations and their fulfillment, to which the reader is referred. Prophetic revelations may be said to begin in the Bible with Moses. They continue on down to the time of John at the end of the Apostolic Age, and some of the most remarkable of them are to be found in John's marvelous book of Revelation. A vast amount of these prophecies have been fulfilled. Others, notably those of John, which relate to the things of the final days, remain yet to be fulfilled. Divine inspiration is, of course, the basis of all prophecy. We find it communicated to mortals in a number of different ways, chief of which were visions and dreams. In turn, the communication by the prophet to the people and the world varied, doubtless because of differences in spiritual temperament and mental or literary ability. In Isaiah we find the prophetic sense—if such we can call the divine revelation—most highly developed. Isaiah's prophecies were clear, concise, and extraordinarily descriptive. Daniel's prophecies were of a highly imaginative type, and clothed in splendid allegory and figures. The reader is referred to Daniel 7 and 8 for a remarkable instance of this—the prophecy of the four kingdoms.

REFERENCES.

(For prophecies relating to Christ and their fulfillment see Appendix.)

God the Author of Prophecy.

Thus saith the Lord the King of Israel, and his Redeemer the Lord of hosts; I am the first, and I am the last; and besides me there is no God.

And who, as I, shall call, and shall declare it, and set it in order for me, since I appointed the ancient people? and the things that are coming, and shall come, let them shew unto them.

Fear ye not, neither be afraid: have not I told thee from that time, and have declared it? ye are even my witnesses. Is there a God besides me? yea, there is no God; I know not any. (Isaiah 44: 6-8.)

Tell ye, and bring them near; yea, let them take counsel together: who hath declared this from ancient time? who hath told it from that time? have not I the Lord? and there is no God else besides me; a just God and a Saviour; there is none besides me. (Isaiah 45: 21.)

As he spake by the mouth of his holy prophets, which have been since the world began. (Luke 1: 70.)

We have also a more sure word of prophecy; whereunto ye do well that ye take heed, as unto a light that shineth in a dark place, until the day dawn, and the day star arise in your hearts:

Knowing this first, that no prophecy of the scripture is of any private interpretation.

For the prophecy came not in old time by the will of man: but holy men of God spake as they were moved by the Holy Ghost. (2 Peter 1: 19-21.)

The Revelation of Jesus Christ,

which God gave unto him, to shew unto his servants things which must shortly come to pass; and he sent and signified it by his angel unto his servant John:

Who bare record of the word of God, and of the testimony of Jesus Christ, and of all things that he saw.

Blessed is he that readeth, and they that hear the words of this prophecy, and keep those things which are written therein: for the time is at hand. (Revelation 1: 1-3.)

Prophecy the Gift of Christ and the Holy Ghost.

For to one is given by the Spirit the word of wisdom; to another the word of knowledge by the same Spirit;

To another faith by the same Spirit; to another the gifts of healing by the same Spirit;

To another the working of miracles; to another prophecy; to another discerning of spirits; to another divers kinds of tongues; to another the interpretation of tongues:

But all these worketh that one and the self-same Spirit, dividing to every man severally as he will.

For as the body is one, and hath many members, and all the members of that one body, being many, are one body: so also is Christ. (1 Corinthians 12: 8-12.)

And he gave some, apostles; and some, prophets; and some, evangelists; and some, pastors and teachers. (Ephesians 4: 11.)

And I will give power unto my two witnesses, and they shall prophesy a thousand two hundred and threescore days, clothed in sackcloth. (Revelation 11: 3.)

Prophecy to Be Received with Faith.

And they rose early in the morning, and went forth into the wilderness of Tekoa: and as they went forth, Jehoshaphat stood and said, Hear me, O Judah, and ye inhabitants of Jerusalem; Believe in the Lord your God, so shall ye be established; believe his prophets, so shall ye prosper. (2 Chronicles 20: 20.)

Then he said unto them, *O fools, and slow of heart to believe all that the prophets have spoken.* (Luke 24: 25.)

Despise not prophesyings. (1 Thessalonians 5: 20.)

PROPHETS. (See Prophecy; see also Tabulated List of Prophets and Prophecies in Appendix.)

PROPH'ETS—the human beings to whom God made revelations regarding His will for communication to mankind. They were very many, especially in the days prior to the coming of Christ, and we have no means of learning exactly their number. The Old Testament (excluding Moses from the list) contains the writings of sixteen of the foremost of them, divided into two groups, four major and twelve minor prophets. We find in the patriarchal days some glimmerings of the prophetic office, but the first of the prophets can be said to have been Moses. The last appears to have been Malachi. They lived in the most extreme simplicity, even to poverty and want. They can be regarded as types or forerunners of the Christ Himself. In the New Testament John the Baptist is the first prophet we meet. Jesus was a prophet in two senses, because of His two natures, the human and divine, and is the Prophet of His Church in all ages. The last prophet of the New Testament is John, the author of Revelation.

It readily can be imagined that wicked men imitated the office of the prophet for the achievement of personal aims. We find several of them in the Old Testament, while the New Testament utters warnings against their appearance.

References.—See Appendix for list of prophets, with references, and the specific nature of their prophecies.

PROPITIATION.

Pro-pi'ti-a'tion—theologically, an atonement or atoning sacrifice. One of the names given to Jesus Christ.

REFERENCES.

Being justified freely by his grace through the redemption that is in Christ Jesus:

Whom God hath set forth to be a propitiation through faith in his blood, to declare his righteousness for the remission of sins that are past, through the forbearance of God. (Romans 3: 24, 25.)

And he is the propitiation for our sins: and not for ours only, but also for the sins of the whole world. (1 John 2: 2.)

Herein is love, not that we loved God, but that he loved us, and sent his Son to be the propitiation for our sins. (1 John 4: 10.)

PROSPERITY.

Pros-per'i-ty—the quality or state of being prosperous, or having plenty of anything or things good or desirable; successful progress in any business or enterprise.

REFERENCES.

Prosperity of the Righteous.

They shall be abundantly satisfied with the fatness of thy house; and thou shalt make them drink of the river of thy pleasures. (Psalm 36: 8.)

But the meek shall inherit the earth; and shall delight themselves in the abundance of peace. (Psalm 37: 11.)

The Lord knoweth the days of the upright: and their inheritance shall be for ever.

They shall not be ashamed in the evil time: and in the days of famine they shall be satisfied. (Psalm 37: 18, 19.)

All the horns of the wicked also will I cut off; but the horns of the righteous shall be exalted. (Psalm 75: 10.)

For the Lord God is a sun and shield: the Lord will give grace and glory; no good thing will he withhold from them that walk uprightly. (Psalm 84: 11.)

The righteous shall flourish like the palm tree; he shall grow like a cedar in Lebanon. (Psalm 92: 12.)

Prosperity of the Wicked.

I have seen the foolish taking root: but suddenly I cursed his habitation. (Job 5: 3.)

The earth is given into the hand of the wicked: he covereth the faces of the judges thereof; if not, where, and who is he? (Job 9: 24.)

The tabernacles of robbers prosper, and they that provoke God are secure; into whose hand God bringeth abundantly. (Job 12: 6.)

They spend their days in wealth, and in a moment go down to the grave. (Job 21: 13.)

Yet he filled their houses with good things: but the counsel of the wicked is far from me. (Job 22: 18.)

He draweth also the mighty with his power: he riseth up, and no man is sure of life.

Though it be given him to be in safety, whereon he resteth; yet his eyes are upon their ways.

They are exalted for a little while, but are gone and brought low: they are taken out of the way as all other, and cut off as the tops of the ears of corn. (Job 24: 22-24.)

They are not in trouble as other men; neither are they plagued like other men.

Therefore pride compasseth them about as a chain; violence covereth them as a garment.

Their eyes stand out with fatness: they have more than heart could wish. (Psalm 73: 5-7.)

Behold, these are the ungodly, who prosper in the world; they increase in riches. (Psalm 73: 12.)

Though a sinner do evil a hundred times, and his days be prolonged, yet surely I know that it shall be well with them that fear God, which fear before him:

But it shall not be well with the wicked, neither shall he prolong his days, which are as a shadow; because he feareth not before God. (Ecclesiastes 8: 12, 13.)

As a cage is full of birds, so are their houses full of deceit: therefore they are become great and waxen rich. (Jeremiah 5: 27.)

Dangers of Prosperity.

And it shall be, when the Lord thy God shall have brought thee into the land which he sware unto thy fathers, to Abraham, to Isaac, and to Jacob, to give thee great and goodly cities, which thou buildedst not,

And houses full of all good things, which thou filledst not, and wells digged, which thou diggedst not, vineyards and olive trees, which thou plantedst not; when thou shalt have eaten and be full;

Then beware lest thou forget the Lord, which brought thee forth out of the land of Egypt, from the house of bondage. (Deuteronomy 6: 10-12.)

For the turning away of the simple shall slay them, and the prosperity of fools shall destroy them. (Proverbs 1: 32.)

Remove far from me vanity and lies; give me neither proverty nor riches; feed me with food convenient for me:

Lest I be full, and deny thee, and say, Who is the Lord? or lest I be poor, and steal, and take the name of my God in vain. (Proverbs 30: 8, 9.)

But woe unto you that are rich! for ye have received your consolation.

Woe unto you that are full! for ye shall hunger. Woe unto you that laugh now! for ye shall mourn and weep. (Luke 6: 24, 25.)

And he spake a parable unto them, saying, *The ground of a certain rich man brought forth plentifully:*

And he thought within himself, saying, What shall I do, because I have no room where to bestow my fruits?

And he said, This will I do: I will pull down my barns, and build greater; and there will I bestow all my fruits and my goods.

And I will say to my soul, Soul, thou hast much goods laid up for many years; take thine ease, eat, drink, and be merry.

But God said unto him, Thou fool, this night thy soul shall be required of thee: then whose shall those things be, which thou hast provided?

So is he that layeth up treasure for himself, and is not rich toward God. (Luke 12: 16-21.)

There was a certain rich man, which was clothed in purple and fine linen, and fared sumptuously every day:

And there was a certain beggar named Lazarus, which was laid at his gate, full of sores,

And desiring to be fed with the crumbs which fell from the rich man's

table: moreover the dogs came and licked his sores.

And it came to pass, that the beggar died, and was carried by the angels into Abraham's bosom: the rich man also died, and was buried;

And in hell he lift up his eyes, being in torments, and seeth Abraham afar off, and Lazarus in his bosom.

And he cried and said, Father Abraham, have mercy on me, and send Lazarus, that he may dip the tip of his finger in water, and cool my tongue; for I am tormented in this flame.

But Abraham said, Son, remember that thou in thy lifetime receivedst thy good things, and likewise Lazarus evil things: but now he is comforted, and thou art tormented. (Luke 16: 19-25.)

Go to now, ye rich men, weep and howl for your miseries that shall come upon you.

Your riches are corrupted, and your garments are motheaten.

Your gold and silver is cankered; and the rust of them shall be a witness against you, and shall eat your flesh as it were fire. Ye have heaped treasure together for the last days. (James 5: 1-3.)

PROVIDENCE.

Prov'i-dence—the manifestation of the watchfulness and care God exercises over His creatures; the providence of God or God's providence.

REFERENCES.

While the earth remaineth, seedtime and harvest, and cold and heat, and summer and winter, and day and night shall not cease. (Genesis 8: 22.)

Thy righteousness is like the great mountains; thy judgments are a great deep: O Lord, thou preservest man and beast.

How excellent is thy lovingkindness, O God! therefore the children of men put their trust under the shadow of thy wings. (Psalm 36: 6, 7.)

That thou givest them they gather: thou openest thine hand, they are filled with good.

Thou hidest thy face, they are troubled: thou takest away their breath, they die, and return to their dust.

Thou sendest forth thy spirit, they are created: and thou renewest the face of the earth. (Psalm 104: 28-30.)

Who remembered us in our low estate: for his mercy endureth for ever:

And hath redeemed us from our enemies: for his mercy endureth for ever.

Who giveth food to all flesh: for his mercy endureth for ever.

O give thanks unto the God of heaven: for his mercy endureth for ever. (Psalm 136: 23-26.)

The Lord upholdeth all that fall, and raiseth up all those that be bowed down.

The eyes of all wait upon thee; and thou givest them their meat in due season.

Thou openest thine hand, and satisfiest the desire of every living thing.

The Lord is righteous in all his ways, and holy in all his works.

The Lord is nigh unto all them that call upon him, to all that call upon him in truth. (Psalm 145: 14-18.)

Behold the fowls of the air: for they sow not, neither do they reap, nor gather into barns; yet your heavenly Father feedeth them. Are ye not much better than they?

Which of you by taking thought can add one cubit unto his stature?

And why take ye thought for raiment? Consider the lilies of the field, how they grow; they toil not, neither do they spin:

And yet I say unto you, That even Solomon in all his glory was not arrayed like one of these. (Matthew 6: 26-29.)

Are not two sparrows sold for a farthing? and one of them shall not fall on the ground without your Father.

But the very hairs of your head are all numbered.

Fear ye not therefore, ye are of more value than many sparrows. (Matthew 10: 29-31.)

And hath made of one blood all nations of men for to dwell on all the face of the earth, and hath determined the times before appointed, and the bounds of their habitation;

That they should seek the Lord, if haply they might feel after him, and find him, though he be not far from every one of us. (Acts 17: 26, 27.)

PSALMS. (See article on Psalms in Appendix.)

PUBLICAN.

Pub'li-can—under the Roman government of Judea the men who collected the taxes imposed upon the people.

After Judea became a Roman province the imperial government forced the people to pay a sort of tribute tax. This was not collected by the authorities themselves, but was farmed out or leased to wealthy Romans, who paid the government a certain percentage of the whole sum and made a profit off the remainder. These tax-farmers hired and appointed others to do the collecting, and, while both classes were called publicans, the lesser class was the one that was so hated and execrated by the mass of the people. This was because the Jews had never paid any government taxes, and as a matter of fact no taxes at all save what went to the priesthood, and they regarded the payment of such tribute as a violation of their religious belief, conceiving that it was a breach of the law to give any tribute to an earthly ruler, since this giving was an ac-

knowledgment of his sovereignty, whereas they declared they recognized no sovereign but God. As the lesser tax-gatherers were able to collect a small commission, they often were harsh, cruel, and greedy. Such of the Jews who took posts as publicans were regarded as outcasts and practically lost all civil and religious rights. Nevertheless a very large number was so employed. Both Zacchæus and Matthew were publicans, and after the ministry of Jesus began there seems to have been a considerable number of their fellows that embraced the Christian faith. The parable of the Pharisee and the Publican (Luke 18) is an admirable example of the relations of the Jewish classes and the way Jesus showed the true piety of the man who was a social outcast as compared with the hypocrisy of the one who occupied an exalted position in society.

QUARRELING. (See Strife.)

QUICKENING.

Quick'en-ing—literally, the act of giving life, or the state or condition of becoming alive; in a religious sense, the giving of spiritual life to men dead in sin, removing their guilt, and reconciling them with God.

REFERENCES.
General.

Thou, which hast shewed me great and sore troubles, shalt quicken me again, and shalt bring me up again from the depths of the earth. (Psalm 71: 20.)

So will not we go back from thee: quicken us, and we will call upon thy name. (Psalm 80: 18.)

For as the Father raiseth up the dead, and quickeneth them; even so the Son quickeneth whom he will. (John 5: 21.)

It is the spirit that quickeneth; the flesh profiteth nothing: the words that I speak unto you, they are spirit, and they are life. (John 6: 63.)

(As it is written, I have made thee a father of many nations,) before him whom he believed, even God, who quickeneth the dead, and calleth those things which be not as though they were. (Romans 4: 17.)

But if the Spirit of him that raised up Jesus from the dead dwell in you, he that raised up Christ from the dead shall also quicken your mortal bodies by his Spirit that dwelleth in you. (Romans 8: 11.)

And so it is written, The first man Adam was made a living soul; the last Adam was made a quickening spirit. (1 Corinthians 15: 45.)

Who also hath made us able ministers of the new testament; not of the letter, but of the spirit: for the letter killeth, but the spirit giveth life. (2 Corinthians 3: 6.)

And you hath he quickened, who were dead in trespasses and sins. (Ephesians 2: 1.)

For Christ also hath once suffered for sins, the just for the unjust, that he might bring us to God, being put to death in the flesh, but quickened by the Spirit. (1 Peter 3: 18.)

"The Quick and the Dead."

And he commanded us to preach unto the people, and to testify that it is he which was ordained of God to be the Judge of quick and dead. (Acts 10: 42.)

I charge thee therefore before God, and the Lord Jesus Christ, who shall judge the quick and the dead at his appearing and his kingdom. (2 Timothy 4: 1.)

Who shall give account to him that is ready to judge the quick and the dead. (1 Peter 4: 5.)

QUIET. (See Peace, Rest.)

QUI'ET—rest, peace, absence of noise or turmoil.

REFERENCES.

Quiet for the Faithful.

But whoso hearkeneth unto me shall dwell safely, and shall be quiet from fear of evil. (Proverbs 1: 33.)

For thus saith the Lord God, the Holy One of Israel; In returning and rest shall ye be saved; in quietness and in confidence shall be your strength: and ye would not. (Isaiah 30: 15.)

And the work of righteousness shall be peace; and the effect of righteousness, quietness and assurance for ever.

And my people shall dwell in a peaceable habitation, and in sure dwellings, and in quiet resting places. (Isaiah 32: 17, 18.)

Quietness Enjoined.

And that ye study to be quiet, and to do your own business, and to work with your own hands, as we commanded you. (1 Thessalonians 4: 11.)

Now them that are such we command and exhort by our Lord Jesus Christ, that with quietness they work, and eat their own bread. (2 Thessalonians 3: 12.)

I exhort therefore, that, first of all, supplications, prayers, intercessions, and giving of thanks, be made for all men;

For kings, and for all that are in authority; that we may lead a quiet and peaceable life in all godliness and honesty.

For this is good and acceptable in the sight of God our Saviour. (1 Timothy 2: 1-3.)

RABBI AND RABBONI.

RAB'BI, RAB-BO'NI—two Hebrew words meaning "my master." They were only used as marks of the deepest respect toward men of great dignity and learning, especially the teachers of the law. Of the two titles, rabboni was the one least used for the reason that the Jews considered few persons entitled to it. We find it given to Jesus once by Mary Magdalene, when she saw Him after His Resurrection.

References.—Matthew 23: 7, 8; John 1: 38; 3: 2; 20: 16.

RACA.

RA'CA—a Greek form of an Aramaic or Chaldee word meaning "worthless," and used as a term of great reproach and opprobrium. It is used only once in the Bible (Matthew 5: 22).

RACHEL. (See Jacob.)

RA'CHEL—a form of a Hebrew word meaning "a ewe." One of the two daughters of Laban. She became the wife of Jacob and the mother of Joseph and Benjamin. The character of Rachel is not a particularly pleasant one to contemplate. She appears to have been discontented, fretful, and impatient, and to have had more than her share of falsehood and duplicity.

References.—Genesis 29, 30, 31, 34, and 35.

RAIN.

RAIN—the water that falls in drops from the clouds. It is absorbed by the heat of the sun into the atmosphere from rivers, ponds, or the oceans. On encountering currents of cold air it is condensed into clouds and later falls back again to the earth in drops. Being obedient to God's natural laws, it is therefore the gift of God. We find a number of places in Scripture where it is used as a figure of speech.

REFERENCES.

Rain the Gift of God.

And when Pharaoh saw that the rain and the hail and the thunders were ceased, he sinned yet more, and hardened his heart, he and his servants. (Exodus 9: 34.)

Is it not wheat harvest to-day? I will call unto the Lord, and he shall send thunder and rain; that ye may perceive and see that your wickedness is great, which ye have done in the sight of the Lord, in asking you a king. (1 Samuel 12: 17.)

That ye may be the children of your Father which is in heaven: for he maketh his sun to rise on the evil and on the good, and sendeth rain on the just and on the unjust. (Matthew 5: 45.)

Nevertheless he left not himself without witness, in that he did good, and gave us rain from heaven, and fruitful seasons, filling our hearts with food and gladness. (Acts 14: 17.)

Rain Withheld.

And Elijah the Tishbite, who was of the inhabitants of Gilead, said unto Ahab, As the Lord God of Israel liveth, before whom I stand, there shall not be dew nor rain these years, but according to my word. (1 Kings 17: 1.)

And it shall be, that whoso will not come up of all the families of the earth unto Jerusalem to worship the King, the Lord of hosts, even upon them shall be no rain. (Zechariah 14: 17.)

Elias was a man subject to like passions as we are, and he prayed earnestly that it might not rain: and it rained not on the earth by the space of three years and six months. (James 5: 17.)

Rain as an Emblem.

My doctrine shall drop as the rain, my speech shall distil as the dew, as the small rain upon the tender herb, and as the showers upon the grass. (Deuteronomy 32: 2.)

And he shall be as the light of the morning, when the sun riseth, even a morning without clouds; as the tender grass springing out of the earth by clear shining after rain. (2 Samuel 23: 4.)

Thou, O God, didst send a plentiful rain, whereby thou didst confirm thine inheritance, when it was weary. (Psalm 68: 9.)

Sow to yourselves in righteousness, reap in mercy; break up your fallow ground: for it is time to seek the Lord, till he come and rain righteousness upon you. (Hosea 10: 12.)

RAINBOW.

RAIN'BOW—a bow or arch showing the seven basic colors and seen in the heavens. It is formed by the reflection and refraction of the sun's rays in drops of falling rain or moisture. It is seen at its greatest brilliancy when the spectator is between the sun and the raincloud. It is also to be seen in spraying fountains and waterfalls. The Bible alludes to it (Genesis 9: 13) as the promise of God that the earth should not again be destroyed by water.

RAISING FROM THE DEAD. (See Resurrection.)

REAPING.

REAP'ING—the act of cutting down or harvesting a crop of anything, especially grains. The word is often used in the Bible in a figurative sense.

REFERENCES.

Even as I have seen, they that plough iniquity, and sow wickedness, reap the same. (Job 4: 8.)

They that sow in tears shall reap in joy. (Psalm 126: 5.)

He that soweth iniquity shall reap vanity: and the rod of his anger shall fail. (Proverbs 22: 8.)

Let both grow together until the harvest: and in the time of harvest I will say to the reapers, Gather ye together first the tares, and bind them in bundles to burn them: but gather the wheat into my barn. (Matthew 13: 30.)

And he that reapeth receiveth wages, and gathereth fruit unto life eternal: that both he that soweth and he that reapeth may rejoice together.

And herein is that saying true, One soweth, and another reapeth.

I sent you to reap that whereon ye bestowed no labour: other men laboured, and ye are entered into their labours. (John 4: 36-38.)

If we have sown unto you spiritual things, is it a great thing if we shall reap your carnal things? (1 Corinthians 9: 11.)

But this I say, He which soweth sparingly shall reap also sparingly; and he which soweth bountifully shall reap also bountifully. (1 Corinthians 9: 6.)

Be not deceived; God is not mocked: for whatsoever a man soweth, that shall he also reap. (Galatians 6: 7.)

And another angel came out of the temple, crying with a loud voice to him that sat on the cloud, Thrust in thy sickle, and reap: for the time is come for thee to reap; for the harvest of the earth is ripe.

And he that sat on the cloud thrust in his sickle on the earth; and the earth was reaped. (Revelation 14: 15, 16.)

REBEKAH. (See Isaac.)

RE-BEK'AH (also written in the Greek form Rebecca)—a form of a Hebrew word meaning "a noosed cord." Rebekah was the name of a sister of Laban who became the wife of Isaac. Rebekah seems to have had her share of the duplicity which was one of the vices of the house of Laban, as is shown by her plotting for the benefit of Jacob over her firstborn, Esau.

References.—Genesis 22, 24, 27, and 49.

RECONCILIATION.

REC'ON-CIL'I-A'TION—the act or state of being reconciled or brought back into harmony and sympathy with some one or something; the bringing into agreement persons or things at variance. God reconciles the world with Himself; He was the author of the plan to do this, and sent His Son into the world to bring it about through the sacrifice of the cross.

REFERENCES.

But he was wounded for our transgressions, he was bruised for our iniquities: the chastisement of our peace was upon him; and with his stripes we are healed. (Isaiah 53: 5.)

Seventy weeks are determined upon thy people and upon thy holy city, to finish the transgression, and to make an end of sins, and to make reconciliation for iniquity, and to bring in everlasting righteousness, and to seal up the vision and prophecy, and to anoint the Most Holy. (Daniel 9: 24.)

For if, when we were enemies, we were reconciled to God by the death of his Son, much more, being reconciled, we shall be saved by his life. (Romans 5: 10.)

And all things are of God, who hath reconciled us to himself by Jesus Christ, and hath given to us the ministry of reconciliation;

To wit, that God was in Christ, reconciling the world unto himself, not imputing their trespasses unto them; and hath committed unto us the word of reconciliation. (2 Corinthians 5: 18, 19.)

And that he might reconcile both unto God in one body by the cross, having slain the enmity thereby:

And came and preached peace to you which were afar off, and to them that were nigh.

For through him we both have access by one Spirit unto the Father. (Ephesians 2: 16-18.)

And, having made peace through the blood of his cross, by him to reconcile all things unto himself; by him, I say, whether they be things in earth, or things in heaven.

And you, that were sometime alienated and enemies in your mind by wicked works, yet now hath he reconciled

In the body of his flesh through death, to present you holy and unblameable and unreproveable in his sight. (Colossians 1: 20-22.)

Wherefore in all things it behoved him to be made like unto his brethren, that he might be a merciful and faithful high priest in things pertaining to God, to make reconciliation for the sins of the people. (Hebrews 2: 17.)

REDEEMER. (See Christ, Jesus, Salvation.)

RE-DEEM'ER—one who redeems; specifically, the Saviour of the world, Jesus the Christ. We get the use of the word "redeemer" as a name for Christ from the ancient Jewish custom by which a kinsman redeemed the property of one of his family who happened to be in destitute circumstances. As we are destitute of spiritual things Jesus redeemed us, after having become our human kin, by the shedding of His blood. We find this redemption promised in the Old Testament and fulfilled in the death and passion of our Saviour, in the New Testament, with many references to it by His apostles.

REFERENCES.

Redemption Promised.

For I know that my Redeemer liveth, and that he shall stand at the latter day upon the earth. (Job 19: 25.)

Let the words of my mouth, and the meditation of my heart, be acceptable in thy sight, O Lord, my strength, and my redeemer. (Psalm 19: 14.)

And they remembered that God was their Rock, and the high God their Redeemer. (Psalm 78: 35.)

For their Redeemer is mighty; he shall plead their cause with thee. (Proverbs 23: 11.)

Fear not, thou worm Jacob, and ye men of Israel; I will help thee, saith the Lord, and thy Redeemer, the Holy One of Israel. (Isaiah 41: 14.)

As for our Redeemer, the Lord of hosts is his name, the Holy One of Israel. (Isaiah 47: 4.)

And the Redeemer shall come to Zion, and unto them that turn from transgression in Jacob, saith the Lord. (Isaiah 59: 20.)

Doubtless thou art our Father, though Abraham be ignorant of us, and Israel acknowledge us not: thou, O Lord, art our Father, our Redeemer; thy name is from everlasting. (Isaiah 63: 16.)

Their Redeemer is strong; The Lord of hosts is his name: he shall thoroughly plead their cause, that he may give rest to the land, and disquiet the inhabitants of Babylon. (Jeremiah 50: 34.)

I will ransom them from the power of the grave; I will redeem them from death: O death, I will be thy plagues, O grave, I will be thy destruction: repentance shall be hid from mine eyes. (Hosea 13: 14.)

Christ, the Redeemer.

Grace be to you and peace from God the Father, and from our Lord Jesus Christ,

Who gave himself for our sins, that he might deliver us from this present evil world, according to the will of God and our Father. (Galatians 1: 3, 4.)

Christ hath redeemed us from the curse of the law, being made a curse for us: for it is written, Cursed is every one that hangeth on a tree. (Galatians 3: 13.)

But when the fulness of the time was come, God sent forth his Son, made of a woman, made under the law,

To redeem them that were under the law, that we might receive the adoption of sons. (Galatians 4: 4, 5.)

Having predestinated us unto the adoption of children by Jesus Christ to himself, according to the good pleasure of his will,

To the praise of the glory of his grace, wherein he hath made us accepted in the beloved.

In whom we have redemption through his blood, the forgiveness of sins, according to the riches of his grace. (Ephesians 1: 5-7.)

Looking for that blessed hope, and the glorious appearing of the great God and our Saviour Jesus Christ;

Who gave himself for us, that he might redeem us from all iniquity, and purify unto himself a peculiar people, zealous of good works. (Titus 2: 13, 14.)

Forasmuch as ye know that ye were not redeemed with corruptible things, as silver and gold, from your vain conversation received by tradition from your fathers. (1 Peter 1: 18.)

And they sung a new song, saying, Thou art worthy to take the book, and to open the seals thereof: for thou wast slain, and hast redeemed us to God by thy blood out of every kindred, and tongue, and people, and nation. (Revelation 5: 9.)

REFUGE.

REF'UGE—a hiding-place, place of safety, or sanctuary from foes or danger. Under the old law of the Hebrews six cities were set apart as places of refuge for those who had unwittingly become shedders of blood and forced to flee from the kinsmen of the slain person or persons. They were called cities of refuge. The word "refuge" is used figuratively of God as the person to whom sinners may flee for safety and salvation through repentance and belief.

REFERENCES.

Cities of refuge: Numbers 35; Deuteronomy 19: 7-9; Joshua 20: 2, 7, 8.

God as a Refuge.

The eternal God is thy refuge, and underneath are the everlasting arms: and he shall thrust out the enemy from before thee; and shall say, Destroy them. (Deuteronomy 33: 27.)

The God of my rock; in him will I trust: he is my shield, and the horn of my salvation, my high tower, and my refuge, my saviour; thou savest me from violence. (2 Samuel 22: 3.)

The Lord also will be a refuge for the oppressed, a refuge in times of trouble. (Psalm 9: 9.)

God is our refuge and strength, a very present help in trouble. (Psalm 46: 1.)

Wherein God, willing more abundantly to shew unto the heirs of promise the immutability of his counsel, confirmed it by an oath:

That by two immutable things, in which it was impossible for God to lie, we might have a strong consolation, who have fled for refuge to lay hold upon the hope set before us:

Which hope we have as an anchor of the soul, both sure and stedfast, and which entereth into that within the vail. (Hebrews 6: 17-19.)

REGENERATION. (See Conversion.)

RE-GEN'ER-A'TION—in the Scriptural and theological sense, the birth of the new life of the spiritual sort from the old life of the unspiritual sort, thus being made a new creature and a partaker of the Divine Nature through the Holy Spirit. Regeneration is the special work of the Holy Ghost in restoring man to the original image of God.

REFERENCES.

And Jesus said unto them, *Verily I say unto you, That ye which have followed me, in the regeneration when the Son of man shall sit in the throne of his glory, ye also shall sit upon twelve thrones, judging the twelve tribes of Israel.* (Matthew 19: 28.)

But as many as received him, to them gave he power to become the sons of God, even to them that believe on his name:

Which were born, not of blood, nor of the will of the flesh, nor of the will of man, but of God. (John 1: 12, 13.)

Jesus answered and said unto him, *Verily, verily, I say unto thee, Except a man be born again, he cannot see the kingdom of God.*

Nicodemus saith unto him, How can a man be born when he is old? can he enter the second time into his mother's womb, and be born?

Jesus answered, *Verily, verily, I say unto thee, Except a man be born of water and of the Spirit, he cannot enter into the kingdom of God.*

That which is born of the flesh is flesh; and that which is born of the Spirit is spirit.

Marvel not that I said unto thee, Ye must be born again.

The wind bloweth where it listeth, and thou hearest the sound thereof, but canst not tell whence it cometh, and whither it goeth: so is every one that is born of the Spirit. (John 3: 3-5.)

But after that the kindness and love of God our Saviour toward man appeared,

Not by works of righteousness which we have done, but according to his mercy he saved us, by the washing of regeneration, and renewing of the Holy Ghost;

Which he shed on us abundantly through Jesus Christ our Saviour. (Titus 3: 4-6.)

REHOBOAM. (See Solomon.)

RE-HO-BO'AM—a form of a Hebrew word meaning "he enlarges the people." Rehoboam was the son and successor of Solomon and was born about 934 B.C., ascending the throne when he was about forty-one years old. He was of a haughty and foolish disposition, and seems never to have profited by the wisdom which his father had been at pains to teach him. Almost as soon as he became king his unwise acts brought about revivals of old troubles that resulted in the division of the kingdom, a division which finally resulted in the complete overthrow of the Israelites as an independent people. He reigned seventeen years.

References.—1 Kings 11, 12, 14; 2 Chronicles 9, 10, 11, 12.

REJOICING. (See Joy.)

RE-JOI'CING—joy, gladness, delight; an occasion of joy or that which causes joy. We are bidden to rejoice in God and his mercies and goodness.

REFERENCES.

And ye shall rejoice before the Lord your God, ye, and your sons, and your daughters, and your menservants, and your maidservants, and the Levite that is within your gates; forasmuch as he hath no part nor inheritance with you. (Deuteronomy 12: 12.)

Glory ye in his holy name: let the

heart of them rejoice that seek the Lord. (1 Chronicles 16: 10.)

Now therefore arise, O Lord God, into thy resting place, thou, and the ark of thy strength: let thy priests, O Lord God, be clothed with salvation, and let thy saints rejoice in goodness. (2 Chronicles 6: 41.)

But let all those that put their trust in thee rejoice: let them ever shout for joy, because thou defendest them: let them also that love thy name be joyful in thee. (Psalm 5: 11.)

Rejoice in the Lord, O ye righteous: for praise is comely for the upright. (Psalm 33: 1.)

Sing unto God, sing praises to his name: extol him that rideth upon the heavens by his name JAH, and rejoice before him. (Psalm 68: 4.)

In thy name shall they rejoice all the day: and in thy righteousness shall they be exalted. (Psalm 89: 16.)

Rejoice in the Lord, ye righteous; and give thanks at the remembrance of his holiness. (Psalm 97: 12.)

Rejoice with them that do rejoice, and weep with them that weep. (Romans 12: 15.)

Finally, my brethren, rejoice in the Lord. To write the same things to you, to me indeed is not grievous, but for you it is safe. (Philippians 3: 1.)

Rejoice in the Lord alway: and again I say, Rejoice. (Philippians 4: 4.)

Rejoice evermore. (1 Thessalonians 5: 16.)

Therefore rejoice, ye heavens, and ye that dwell in them. Woe to the inhabiters of the earth and of the sea! for the devil is come down unto you, having great wrath, because he knoweth that he hath but a short time. (Revelation 12: 12.)

Rejoice over her, thou heaven, and

ye holy apostles and prophets; for God hath avenged you on her. (Revelation 18: 20.)

REMISSION. (See Forgiveness, Sin.)

Re-mis'sion—discharge from that which is due; relinquishment of a claim or obligation, and, in a special Scriptural sense, pardon for transgression. In the plan of salvation, Christ's blood was shed for the remission of the sins of mankind, and we are specially commanded to observe the Lord's Supper as a perpetual memorial of it.

REFERENCES.

For this is my blood of the new testament, which is shed for many for the remission of sins. (Matthew 26: 28.)

John did baptize in the wilderness, and preach the baptism of repentance for the remission of sins. (Mark 1: 4.)

And said unto them, *Thus it is written, and thus it behoved Christ to suffer, and to rise from the dead the third day:*

And that repentance and remission of sins should be preached in his name among all nations, beginning at Jerusalem. (Luke 24: 46, 47.)

Then Peter said unto them, Repent, and be baptized every one of you in the name of Jesus Christ for the remission of sins, and ye shall receive the gift of the Holy Ghost. (Acts 2: 38.)

And he commanded us to preach unto the people, and to testify that it is he which was ordained of God to be the Judge of quick and dead.

To him give all the prophets witness, that through his name whosoever believeth in him shall receive remission of sins. (Acts 10: 42, 43.)

And almost all things are by the law purged with blood; and without shedding of blood is no remission. (Hebrews 9: 22.)

Now where remission of these is,

there is no more offering for sin. (Hebrews 10: 18.)

REPENTANCE. (See Sin).

Re-pent'ance—literally, a change of mind, coupled with sorrow for something done and the wish that it were undone or had not been done. Theologically and ethically, repentance is that sorrow for sin and contriteness of heart which produces or leads to newness of life. The terms "repentance" and "conversion" must not be confounded. Conversion is the turning of the heart to God or back to God. It is usually the forerunner of repentance, although in some instances repentance may come first, according to the will of the Holy Spirit in its action upon the sinner. As a matter of fact, repentance is one of the daily companions of the Christian, since the Christian is constantly sinning and going to God in contrition for it. True repentance is accompanied by the Divine forgiveness, and the consequent remission of sin, according to the Promise.

REFERENCES.

Nature of Repentance.

The Sense of Guilt:

Have mercy upon me, O God, according to thy lovingkindness: according unto the multitude of thy tender mercies blot out my transgressions.

Wash me throughly from mine iniquity, and cleanse me from my sin.

For I acknowledge my transgressions: and my sin is ever before me.

Against thee, thee only, have I sinned, and done this evil in thy sight: that thou mightest be justified when thou speakest, and be clear when thou judgest.

Behold, I was shapen in iniquity; and in sin did my mother conceive me.

Behold, thou desirest truth in the inward parts: and in the hidden part thou shalt make me to know wisdom.

Purge me with hyssop, and I shall be

clean: wash me, and I shall be whiter than snow. (Psalm 51: 1-7.)

But we are all as an unclean thing, and all our righteousnesses are as filthy rags; and we all do fade as a leaf; and our iniquities, like the wind, have taken us away. (Isaiah 64: 6.)

Now when they heard this, they were pricked in their heart, and said unto Peter and to the rest of the apostles, Men and brethren, what shall we do? (Acts 2: 37.)

And brought them out, and said, Sirs, what must I do to be saved? (Acts 16: 30.)

The Sense of God's Mercy in Christ:

Surely he hath borne our griefs, and carried our sorrows: yet we did esteem him stricken, smitten of God, and afflicted.

But he was wounded for our transgressions, he was bruised for our iniquities: the chastisement of our peace was upon him; and with his stripes we are healed.

All we like sheep have gone astray; we have turned every one to his own way; and the Lord hath laid on him the iniquity of us all. (Isaiah 53: 4-6.)

And thou, child, shalt be called the prophet of the Highest: for thou shalt go before the face of the Lord to prepare his ways;

To give knowledge of salvation unto his people by the remission of their sins,

Through the tender mercy of our God; whereby the dayspring from on high hath visited us,

To give light to them that sit in darkness and in the shadow of death, to guide our feet into the way of peace. (Luke 1: 76-79.)

But God, who is rich in mercy, for his great love wherewith he loved us,

Even when we were dead in sins, hath quickened us together with Christ, (by grace ye are saved;)

And hath raised us up together, and made us sit together in heavenly places in Christ Jesus:

That in the ages to come he might shew the exceeding riches of his grace in his kindness toward us through Christ Jesus. (Ephesians 2: 4-7.)

This is a faithful saying, and worthy of all acceptation, that Christ Jesus came into the world to save sinners; of whom I am chief. (1 Timothy 1: 15.)

But after that the kindness and love of God our Saviour toward man appeared,

Not by works of righteousness which we have done, but according to his mercy he saved us, by the washing of regeneration, and renewing of the Holy Ghost. (Titus 3: 4, 5.)

Sorrow for Sin:

Thou art wearied in the greatness of thy way; yet saidst thou not, There is no hope: thou hast found the life of thine hand; therefore thou wast not grieved. (Isaiah 57: 10.)

I will declare thy righteousness, and thy works; for they shall not profit thee. (Isaiah 57: 12.)

Now I rejoice, not that ye were made sorry, but that ye sorrowed to repentance: for ye were made sorry after a godly manner, that ye might receive damage by us in nothing.

For godly sorrow worketh repentance to salvation not to be repented of: but the sorrow of the world worketh death. (2 Corinthians 7: 9, 10.)

Repentance a Duty.

If iniquity be in thine hand, put it far away, and let not wickedness dwell in thy tabernacles.

For then shalt thou lift up thy face without spot; yea, thou shalt be steadfast, and shalt not fear. (Job 11: 14, 15.)

Thus saith the Lord of hosts, the God of Israel, Amend your ways and your doings, and I will cause you to dwell in this place. (Jeremiah 7: 3.)

Now therefore go to, speak to the men of Judah, and to the inhabitants of Jerusalem, saying, Thus saith the Lord; Behold, I frame evil against you, and devise a device against you: return ye now every one from his evil way, and make your ways and your doings good. (Jeremiah 18: 11.)

Therefore now amend your ways and your doings, and obey the voice of the Lord your God; and the Lord will repent him of the evil that he hath pronounced against you. (Jeremiah 26: 13.)

Therefore I will judge you, O house of Israel, every one according to his ways, saith the Lord God. Repent, and turn yourselves from all your transgressions; so iniquity shall not be your ruin. (Ezekiel 18: 30.)

Wherefore, O king, let my counsel be acceptable unto thee, and break off thy sins by righteousness, and thine iniquities by shewing mercy to the poor; if it may be a lengthening of thy tranquillity. (Daniel 4: 27.)

The Lord hath been sore displeased with your fathers.

Therefore say thou unto them, Thus saith the Lord of hosts; Turn ye unto me, saith the Lord of hosts, and I will turn unto you, saith the Lord of hosts. (Zechariah 1: 2, 3.)

But when he saw many of the Pharisees and Sadducees come to his baptism. he said unto them, O generation of vipers, who hath warned you to flee from the wrath to come?

Bring forth therefore fruits meet for repentance. (Matthew 3: 7, 8.)

Repentance a Divine Call.

From that time Jesus began to preach, and to say, *Repent: for the kingdom of heaven is at hand.* (Matthew 4: 17.)

But go ye and learn what that meaneth, I will have mercy, and not sacrifice: for I am not come to call the righteous, but sinners to repentance. (Matthew 9: 13.)

And saying, *The time is fulfilled, and the kingdom of God is at hand: repent ye, and believe the gospel.* (Mark 1: 15.)

And they went out, and preached that men should repent. (Mark 6: 12.)

Thou hast neither part nor lot in this matter: for thy heart is not right in the sight of God.

Repent therefore of this thy wickedness, and pray God, if perhaps the thought of thine heart may be forgiven thee. (Acts 8: 21, 22.)

Promises to the Penitent.

And it shall come to pass, when all these things are come upon thee, the blessing and the curse, which I have set before thee, and thou shalt call them to mind among all the nations, whither the Lord thy God hath driven thee,

And shalt return unto the Lord thy God, and shalt obey his voice according to all that I command thee this day, thou and thy children, with all thine heart, and with all thy soul;

That then the Lord thy God will turn thy captivity, and have compassion upon thee, and will return and gather thee from all the nations, whither the

Lord thy God hath scattered thee. (Deuteronomy 30: 1-3.)

The Lord is nigh unto them that are of a broken heart; and saveth such as be of a contrite spirit. (Psalm 34: 18.)

He healeth the broken in heart, and bindeth up their wounds. (Psalm 147: 3.)

If thou wilt return, O Israel, saith the Lord, return unto me: and if thou wilt put away thine abominations out of my sight, then shalt thou not remove. (Jeremiah 4: 1.)

But if the wicked will turn from all his sins that he hath committed, and keep all my statutes, and do that which is lawful and right, he shall surely live, he shall not die.

All his transgressions that he hath committed, they shall not be mentioned unto him: in his righteousness that he hath done he shall live. (Ezekiel 18: 21, 22.)

Again, when the wicked man turneth away from his wickedness that he hath committed, and doeth that which is lawful and right, he shall save his soul alive.

Because he considereth, and turneth away from all his transgressions that he hath committed, he shall surely live, he shall not die. (Ezekiel 18: 27, 28.)

Therefore, O thou son of man, speak unto the house of Israel; Thus ye speak, saying, If our transgressions and our sins be upon us, and we pine away in them, how should we then live?

Say unto them, As I live, saith the Lord God, I have no pleasure in the death of the wicked; but that the wicked turn from his way and live: turn ye, turn ye from your evil ways; for why will ye die, O house of Israel?

Therefore, thou son of man, say unto the children of thy people, The right-eousness of the righteous shall not deliver him in the day of his transgression: as for the wickedness of the wicked, he shall not fall thereby in the day that he turneth from his wickedness; neither shall the righteous be able to live for his righteousness in the day that he sinneth. (Ezekiel 33: 10-12.)

Again, when I say unto the wicked, Thou shalt surely die; if he turn from his sin, and do that which is lawful and right;

If the wicked restore the pledge, give again that he had robbed, walk in the statutes of life, without committing iniquity; he shall surely live, he shall not die.

None of his sins that he hath committed shall be mentioned unto him: he hath done that which is lawful and right; he shall surely live.

Yet the children of thy people say, The way of the Lord is not equal: but as for them, their way is not equal.

When the righteous turneth from his righteousness, and committeth iniquity, he shall even die thereby.

But if the wicked turn from his wickedness, and do that which is lawful and right, he shall live thereby.

Yet ye say, The way of the Lord is not equal, O ye house of Israel, I will judge you every one after his ways. (Ezekiel 33: 14-20.)

Blessed are the poor in spirit: for theirs is the kingdom of heaven.

Blessed are they that mourn: for they shall be comforted. (Matthew 5: 3, 4.)

(For he saith, I have heard thee in a time accepted, and in the day of salvation have I succoured thee: behold, now is the accepted time; behold, now is the day of salvation.) (2 Corinthians 6: 2.)

The Impenitent.

A wicked man hardeneth his face: but as for the upright, he directeth his way. (Proverbs 21: 29.)

Then began he to upbraid the cities wherein most of his mighty works were done, because they repented not:

Woe unto thee, Chorazin! woe unto thee, Bethsaida! for if the mighty works, which were done in you, had been done in Tyre and Sidon, they would have repented long ago in sackcloth and ashes.

But I say unto you, It shall be more tolerable for Tyre and Sidon at the day of judgment, than for you. (Matthew 11: 20-22.)

There were present at that season some that told him of the Galileans, whose blood Pilate had mingled with their sacrifices.

And Jesus answering said unto them, *Suppose ye that these Galileans were sinners above all the Galileans, because they suffered such things?*

I tell you, Nay: but, except ye repent, ye shall all likewise perish.

Or those eighteen, upon whom the tower in Siloam fell, and slew them, think ye that they were sinners above all men that dwelt in Jerusalem?

I tell you, Nay: but, except ye repent, ye shall all likewise perish. (Luke 13: 1-5.)

But, after thy hardness and impenitent heart, treasurest up unto thyself wrath against the day of wrath and revelation of the righteous judgment of God. (Romans 2: 5.)

And lest, when I come again, my God will humble me among you, and that I shall bewail many which have sinned already, and have not repented of the uncleanness and fornication and lasciviousness which they have committed. (2 Corinthians 12: 21.)

For ye know how that afterward, when he would have inherited the blessing, he was rejected: for he found no place of repentance, though he sought it carefully with tears. (Hebrews 12: 17.)

And I gave her space to repent of her fornication; and she repented not. (Revelation 2: 21.)

Neither repented they of their murders, nor of their sorceries, nor of their fornication, nor of their thefts. (Revelation 9: 21.)

REPROBATE AND REPROBATION.

REP'RO-BATE—one morally abandoned or lost; also to condemn as unworthy.

REP'RO-BA'TION—in a theological sense, the predestination of a certain part of the human race as reprobates or objects of eternal damnation and punishment. This dogma is laid down by the Calvinistic system of theology.

REFERENCES.

Stay yourselves, and wonder; cry ye out, and cry: they are drunken, but not with wine; they stagger, but not with strong drink.

For the Lord hath poured out upon you the spirit of deep sleep, and hath closed your eyes: the prophets and your rulers, the seers hath he covered.

And the vision of all is become unto you as the words of a book that is sealed, which men deliver to one that is learned, saying, Read this, I pray thee: and he saith, I cannot; for it is sealed:

And the book is delivered to him that is not learned, saying, Read this, I pray thee: and he saith, I am not learned. (Isaiah 29: 9-12.)

Reprobate silver shall men call them,

because the Lord hath rejected them. (Jeremiah 6: 30.)

But ye believe not, because ye are not of my sheep, as I said unto you. (John 10: 26.)

While I was with them in the world, I kept them in thy name: those that thou gavest me I have kept, and none of them is lost, but the son of perdition; that the Scripture might be fulfilled. (John 17: 12.)

What if God, willing to shew his wrath, and to make his power known, endured with much longsuffering the vessels of wrath fitted to destruction. (Romans 9: 22.)

What then? Israel hath not obtained that which he seeketh for; but the election hath obtained it, and the rest were blinded

(According as it is written, God hath given them the spirit of slumber, eyes that they should not see, and ears that they should not hear;) unto this day. (Romans 11: 7, 8.)

Examine yourselves, whether ye be in the faith; prove your own selves. Know ye not your own selves, how that Jesus Christ is in you, except ye be reprobates?

But I trust that ye shall know that we are not reprobates.

Now I pray to God that ye do no evil; not that we should appear approved, but that ye should do that which is honest, though we be as reprobates. (2 Corinthians 13: 5-7.)

And for this cause God shall send them strong delusion, that they should believe a lie:

That they all might be damned who believed not the truth, but had pleasure in unrighteousness. (2 Thessalonians 2: 11, 12.)

Now as Jannes and Jambres withstood Moses, so do these also resist the truth: men of corrupt minds, reprobate concerning the faith.

But they shall proceed no further: for their folly shall be manifest unto all men, as theirs also was. (2 Timothy 3: 8, 9.)

For there are certain men crept in unawares, who were before of old ordained to this condemnation, ungodly men, turning the grace of our God into lasciviousness, and denying the only Lord God, and our Lord Jesus Christ. (Jude 1: 4.)

REPROOF.

RE-PROOF'—generally speaking, rebuke or reprehension spoken to one's face; reprimand. The Bible tells us that reproof spoken to an erring one in the proper spirit is good and acceptable. We should not be forward in reproving our elders. The young should take reproof from their elders. The reproof from a minister of God is by special commission from God. Care should be taken in all reproof that it not go beyond the bounds of decency.

REFERENCES.

Let the righteous smite me; it shall be a kindness: and let him reprove me; it shall be an excellent oil, which shall not break my head: for yet my prayer also shall be in their calamities.

When their judges are overthrown in stony places, they shall hear my words; for they are sweet. (Psalm 141: 5, 6.)

He that reproveth a scorner getteth to himself shame: and he that rebuketh a wicked man getteth himself a blot.

Reprove not a scorner, lest he hate thee: rebuke a wise man, and he will love thee.

Give instruction to a wise man, and he will be yet wiser: teach a just man, and he will increase in learning. (Proverbs 9: 7-9.)

He is in the way of life that keepeth instruction: but he that refuseth reproof erreth. (Proverbs 10: 17.)

Poverty and shame shall be to him that refuseth instruction: but he that regardeth reproof shall be honoured. (Proverbs 13: 18.)

Correction is grievous unto him that forsaketh the way: and he that hateth reproof shall die. (Proverbs 15: 10.)

A scorner loveth not one that reproveth him: neither will he go unto the wise. (Proverbs 15: 12.)

He that refuseth instruction despiseth his own soul: but he that heareth reproof getteth understanding. (Proverbs 15: 32.)

A reproof entereth more into a wise man than a hundred stripes into a fool. (Proverbs 17: 10.)

But to them that rebuke him shall be delight, and a good blessing shall come upon them. (Proverbs 24: 25.)

As an earring of gold, and an ornament of fine gold, so is a wise reprover upon an obedient ear. (Proverbs 25: 12.)

And if any man obey not our word by this epistle, note that man, and have no company with him, that he may be ashamed.

Yet count him not as an enemy, but admonish him as a brother. (2 Thessalonians 3: 14, 15.)

Rebuke not an elder, but entreat him as a father; and the younger men as brethren. (1 Timothy 6: 1.)

REST. (See Quiet, Peace, etc.)

REST—repose; freedom from anything that disturbs; peace or security; sleep or slumber, and thence, figuratively, death. God promises rest to those who come to Him weary, as well as rest to the faithful after death.

REFERENCES.

And in that day there shall be a root of Jesse, which shall stand for an ensign of the people; to it shall the Gentiles seek: and his rest shall be glorious. (Isaiah 11: 10.)

And it shall come to pass in the day that the Lord shall give thee rest from thy sorrow, and from thy fear, and from the hard bondage wherein thou wast made to serve. (Isaiah 14: 3.)

For thus saith the Lord God, the Holy One of Israel; In returning and rest shall ye be saved; in quietness and in confidence shall be your strength: and ye would not. (Isaiah 30: 15.)

Thus saith the Lord, Stand ye in the ways, and see, and ask for the old paths, where is the good way, and walk therein, and ye shall find rest for your souls. But they said, We will not walk therein. (Jeremiah 6: 16.)

Come unto me, all ye that labour and are heavy laden, and I will give you rest. (Matthew 11: 28.)

So I sware in my wrath, They shall not enter into my rest. (Hebrews 3: 11.)

Let us therefore fear, lest, a promise being left us of entering into his rest, any of you should seem to come short of it.

For unto us was the gospel preached, as well as unto them: but the word preached did not profit them, not being mixed with faith in them that heard it.

For we which have believed do enter into rest, as he said, As I have sworn in my wrath, if they shall enter into my rest: although the works were finished from the foundation of the world.

For he spake in a certain place of the seventh day on this wise, And God did rest the seventh day from all his works.

And in this place again, If they shall enter into my rest.

Seeing therefore it remaineth that some must enter therein, and they to whom it was first preached entered not in because of unbelief:

Again, he limiteth a certain day, saying in David, To day, after so long a time; as it is said, To day if ye will hear his voice, harden not your hearts.

For if Jesus had given them rest, then would he not afterward have spoken of another day.

There remaineth therefore a rest to the people of God.

For he that is entered into his rest, he also hath ceased from his own works, as God did from his.

Let us labour therefore to enter into that rest, lest any man fall after the same example of unbelief. (Hebrews 4: 1-11.)

RESURRECTION. (See Body, Christ, Death, Life.)

RES'UR-REC'TION—literally, a rising again; specifically, the resurrection of Jesus Christ as recorded in the Bible, as well as the general resurrection of the dead at the Day of Judgment.

The doctrine of the resurrection is one of the fundamentals of the Christian religion and one of its vital points, for without resurrection there can be no hope beyond this life. The Old Testament prefigures it in sundry cases of persons raised from the dead by prophets divinely led, while of all the prophets Daniel gives the clearest view of the plan (see Daniel 12: 1-3).

The New Testament, however, gives the complete revelation of the divine economy. Jesus died and rose again, and taught the doctrine with directness and simplicity, his disciples and the apostles elaborating the teaching in many different ways and upon many different occasions.

REFERENCES.

Resurrection of the Body Foretold.

And though after my skin worms destroy this body, yet in my flesh shall I see God:

Whom I shall see for myself, and mine eyes shall behold, and not another; though my reins be consumed within me. (Job 19: 26, 27.)

As for me, I will behold thy face in righteousness: I shall be satisfied, when I awake, with thy likeness. (Psalm 17: 15.)

Thy dead men shall live, together with my dead body shall they arise. Awake and sing, ye that dwell in dust: for thy dew is as the dew of herbs, and the earth shall cast out the dead. (Isaiah 26: 19.)

The hand of the Lord was upon me, and carried me out in the Spirit of the Lord, and set me down in the midst of the valley which was full of bones,

And caused me to pass by them round about: and, behold, there were very many in the open valley; and, lo, they were very dry.

And he said unto me, Son of man, can these bones live? And I answered, O Lord God, thou knowest.

Again he said unto me, Prophesy upon these bones, and say unto them, O ye dry bones, hear the word of the Lord.

Thus saith the Lord God unto these bones: Behold, I will cause breath to enter into you, and ye shall live:

And I will lay sinews upon you, and will bring up flesh upon you, and cover you with skin, and put breath in you, and ye shall live; and ye shall know that I am the Lord.

So I prophesied as I was commanded: and as I prophesied, there was a noise, and behold a shaking, and the bones came together, bone to his bone.

And when I beheld, lo, the sinews and the flesh came up upon them, and the skin covered them above: but there was no breath in them.

Then said he unto me, Prophesy unto the wind, prophesy, son of man, and say to the wind, Thus saith the Lord God; Come from the four winds, O breath, and breathe upon these slain, that they may live.

So I prophesied as he commanded me, and the breath came into them, and they lived, and stood up upon their feet, an exceeding great army.

Then he said unto me, Son of man, these bones are the whole house of Israel: behold, they say, Our bones are dried, and our hope is lost: we are cut off for our parts.

Therefore prophesy and say unto them, Thus saith the Lord God; Behold, O my people, I will open your graves, and cause you to come up out of your graves, and bring you into the land of Israel.

And ye shall know that I am the Lord, when I have opened your graves, O my people, and brought you up out of your graves,

And shall put my Spirit in you, and ye shall live, and I shall place you in your own land: then shall ye know that I the Lord have spoken it, and performed it, saith the Lord. (Ezekiel 37: 1-14.)

And at that time shall Michael stand up, the great prince which standeth for the children of thy people: and there shall be a time of trouble, such as never was since there was a nation even to that same time: and at that time thy people shall be delivered, every one that shall be found written in the book.

And many of them that sleep in the dust of the earth shall awake, some to everlasting life, and some to shame and everlasting contempt.

And they that be wise, shall shine as the brightness of the firmament; and they that turn many to righteousness, as the stars for ever and ever. (Daniel 12: 1-3.)

Resurrection Proclaimed by Christ.

The same day came to him the Sadducees, which say that there is no resurrection, and asked him,

Saying, Master, Moses said, If a man die, having no children, his brother shall marry his wife, and raise up seed unto his brother.

Now there were with us seven brethren: and the first, when he had married a wife, deceased, and, having no issue, left his wife unto his brother:

Likewise the second also, and the third, unto the seventh.

And last of all the woman died also.

Therefore in the resurrection whose wife shall she be of the seven? for they all had her.

Jesus answered and said unto them, *Ye do err, not knowing the scriptures, nor the power of God.*

For in the resurrection they neither marry, nor are given in marriage, but are as the angels of God in heaven.

But as touching the resurrection of the dead, have ye not read that which was spoken unto you by God, saying,

I am the God of Abraham, and the God of Isaac, and the God of Jacob? God is not the God of the dead, but of the living. (Matthew 22: 23-32.)

Marvel not at this: for the hour is coming, in the which all that are in the graves shall hear his voice,

And shall come forth; they that have

done good, unto the resurrection of life; and they that have done evil, unto the resurrection of damnation. (John 5: 28, 29.)

Then said Martha unto Jesus, Lord, if thou hadst been here, my brother had not died.

But I know, that even now, whatsoever thou wilt ask of God, God will give it thee.

Jesus saith unto her, *Thy brother shall rise again.*

Martha saith unto him, I know that he shall rise again in the resurrection at the last day.

Jesus said unto her, *I am the resurrection, and the life: he that believeth in me, though he were dead, yet shall he live:*

And whosoever liveth and believeth in me shall never die. Believest thou this? (John 11: 21-26.)

Resurrection Preached by the Apostles.

And as they spake unto the people, the priests, and the captain of the temple, and the Sadducees, came upon them,

Being grieved that they taught the people, and preached through Jesus the resurrection from the dead. (Acts 4: 1, 2.)

Then certain philosophers of the Epicureans, and of the Stoicks, encountered him. And some said, What will this babbler say? other some, He seemeth to be a setter forth of strange gods: because he preached unto them Jesus, and the resurrection. (Acts 17: 18.)

And have hope toward God, which they themselves also allow, that there shall be a resurrection of the dead, both of the just and unjust. (Acts 24: 15.)

Why should it be thought a thing in-credible with you, that God should raise the dead? (Acts 26: 8.)

For if we have been planted together in the likeness of his death, we shall be also in the likeness of his resurrection:

Knowing this, that our old man is crucified with him, that the body of sin might be destroyed, that henceforth we should not serve sin.

For he that is dead is freed from sin.

Now if we be dead with Christ, we believe that we shall also live with him:

Knowing that Christ being raised from the dead dieth no more; death hath no more dominion over him.

For in that he died, he died unto sin once: but in that he liveth, he liveth unto God.

Likewise reckon ye also yourselves to be dead indeed unto sin, but alive unto God through Jesus Christ our Lord. (Romans 6: 5-11.)

Now if Christ be preached that he rose from the dead, how say some among you that there is no resurrection of the dead?

But if there be no resurrection of the dead, then is Christ not risen:

And if Christ be not risen, then is our preaching vain, and your faith is also vain.

Yea, and we are found false witnesses of God; because we have testified of God that he raised up Christ: whom he raised not up, if so be that the dead rise not.

For if the dead rise not, then is not Christ raised.

And if Christ be not raised, your faith is vain; ye are yet in your sins.

Then they also which are fallen asleep in Christ are perished. (1 Corinthians 15: 12-18.)

Else what shall they do which are

baptized for the dead, if the dead rise not at all? why are they then baptized for the dead?

And why stand we in jeopardy every hour?

I protest by your rejoicing which I have in Christ Jesus our Lord, I die daily.

If after the manner of men I have fought with beasts at Ephesus, what advantageth it me, if the dead rise not? let us eat and drink; for to morrow we die. (1 Corinthians 12: 29-32.)

Order of the Resurrection.

Dead to Be Raised First:

But I would not have you to be ignorant, brethren, concerning them which are asleep, that ye sorrow not, even as others, which have no hope.

For if we believe that Jesus died and rose again, even so them also which sleep in Jesus will God bring with him.

For this we say unto you by the word of the Lord, that we which are alive and remain unto the coming of the Lord shall not prevent them which are asleep.

For the Lord himself shall descend from heaven with a shout, with the voice of the archangel, and with the trump of God: and the dead in Christ shall rise first. (1 Thessalonians 4: 13-16.)

Living Saints Next:

Then we which are alive and remain shall be caught up together with them in the clouds, to meet the Lord in the air: and so shall we ever be with the Lord.

Wherefore comfort one another with these words. (1 Thessalonians 4: 17, 18.)

Nature of the Resurrected.

The Same as Before:

Jesus saith unto her, *Thy brother shall rise again.*

Martha saith unto him, I know that he shall rise again in the resurrection at the last day. (John 11: 23, 24.)

Yet Not the Same:

But some man will say, How are the dead raised up? and with what body do they come?

Thou fool, that which thou sowest is not quickened, except it die:

And that which thou sowest, thou sowest not that body which shall be, but bare grain, it may chance of wheat, or of some other grain:

But God giveth it a body as it hath pleased him, and to every seed his own body. (1 Corinthians 15: 35-38.)

The Resurrection Spiritual:

So also is the resurrection of the dead. It is sown in corruption, it is raised in corruption:

It is sown in dishonour, it is raised in glory: it is sown in weakness, it is raised in power:

It is sown a natural body, it is raised a spiritual body. There is a natural body, and there is a spiritual body.

And so it is written, The first man Adam was made a living soul; the last Adam was made a quickening spirit.

Howbeit that was not first which is spiritual, but that which is natural; and afterward that which is spiritual. (1 Corinthians 15: 42-46.)

Now this I say, brethren, that flesh and blood cannot inherit the kingdom of God; neither doth corruption inherit incorruption. (1 Corinthians 15: 50.)

For we know that, if our earthly house of this tabernacle were dissolved, we have a building of God, a house not made with hands, eternal in the heavens.

For in this we groan, earnestly desiring to be clothed upon with our house which is from heaven:

If so be that being clothed we shall not be found naked.

For we that are in this tabernacle do groan, being burdened: not for that we would be unclothed, but clothed upon, that mortality might be swallowed up of life. (2 Corinthians 6: 1-4.)

The Glory of the Resurrection:

Behold, I shew you a mystery; We shall not all sleep, but we shall all be changed,

In a moment, in the twinkling of an eye, at the last trump: for the trumpet shall sound, and the dead shall be raised incorruptible, and we shall be changed.

For this corruptible must put on incorruption, and this mortal must put on immortality.

So when this corruptible shall have put on incorruption, and this mortal shall have put on immortality, then shall be brought to pass the saying that is written, Death is swallowed up in victory.

O death, where is thy sting? O grave, where is thy victory?

The sting of death is sin; and the strength of sin is the law. (1 Corinthians 15: 51-56.)

The Believers' Hope.

And not only they, but ourselves also, which have the firstfruits of the Spirit, even we ourselves groan within ourselves, waiting for the adoption, to wit, the redemption of our body. (Romans 8: 23.)

That I may know him, and the power of his resurrection, and the fellowship of his sufferings, being made conformable unto his death;

If by any means I might attain unto the resurrection of the dead. (Philippians 3: 10, 11.)

REUBEN.

Reu'ben—a form of a Hebrew word meaning "behold a son." Reuben was the eldest son of Jacob. His mother was Leah. His name was given to one of the tribes of the Israelites. For an offense which his father could never forgive, he was deprived of his birthright. The tribe of Reuben was never one of the leading tribes. He was hasty and impetuous, but not crafty or cruel.

REVELATION. (See Books of the Bible in Appendix.)

Rev'e-la'tion—in a religious sense, the act of revealing divine truths, and also that which is revealed as divine truth; also the book known historically as the Apocalypse and commonly as Revelation (for the history and description of which see article on Books of the Bible in the Appendix).

God, in His wisdom and providence, from time to time gives to his human creations knowledge of His plans for them. He has been doing this from the beginning and doubtless will continue to do so until we have arrived at a state of religious perfection, so far as our finite minds can reach such a state. The greatest of all these gifts of knowledge was the knowledge of the plan of salvation, as contained in the life, death, and teachings of Jesus. These unfoldings of God to man are called revelations.

REFERENCES.

The secret things belong unto the Lord our God: but those things which are revealed belong unto us, and to our children for ever, that we may do all the words of this law. (Deuteronomy 29: 29.)

Then he openeth the ears of men,

and sealeth their instruction. (Job 33: 16.)

And the glory of the Lord shall be revealed, and all flesh shall see it together: for the mouth of the Lord hath spoken it. (Isaiah 40: 5.)

Behold, I will bring it health and cure, and I will cure them, and will reveal unto them the abundance of peace and truth. (Jeremiah 33: 6.)

He revealeth the deep and secret things: he knoweth what is in the darkness, and the light dwelleth with him. (Daniel 2: 22.)

Surely the Lord God will do nothing, but he revealeth his secret unto his servants the prophets. (Amos 3: 7.)

Fear them not therefore: for there is nothing covered, that shall not be revealed; and hid, that shall not be known. (Matthew 10: 26.)

At that time Jesus answered and said, *I thank thee, O Father, Lord of heaven and earth, because thou hast hid these things from the wise and prudent, and hast revealed them unto babes.*

Even so, Father: for so it seemed good in thy sight.

All things are delivered unto me of my Father: and no man knoweth the Son, but the Father; neither knoweth any man the Father, save the Son, and he to whomsoever the Son will reveal him. (Matthew 11: 25-27.)

And Jesus answered and said unto him, *Blessed art thou, Simon Bar-jona: for flesh and blood hath not revealed it unto thee, but my Father which is in heaven.* (Matthew 16: 17.)

But as it is written, Eye hath not seen, nor ear heard, neither have entered into the heart of man, the things which God hath prepared for them that love him.

But God hath revealed them unto us by his Spirit: for the Spirit searcheth all things, yea, the deep things of God. (1 Corinthians 2: 9, 10.)

For I neither received it of man, neither was I taught it, but by the revelation of Jesus Christ. (Galatians 1: 12.)

Let us therefore, as many as be perfect, be thus minded: and if in any thing ye be otherwise minded, God shall reveal even this unto you. (Philippians 3: 15.)

Who are kept by the power of God through faith unto salvation ready to be revealed in the last time. (1 Peter 1: 5.)

But rejoice, inasmuch as ye are partakers of Christ's sufferings; that, when his glory shall be revealed, ye may be glad also with exceeding joy. (1 Peter 4: 13.)

The Revelation of Jesus Christ, which God gave unto him, to shew unto his servants things which must shortly come to pass; and he sent and signified it by his angel unto his servant John:

Who bare record of the word of God, and of the testimony of Jesus Christ, and of all things that he saw. (Revelation 1: 1, 2.)

REVENGE.

RE-VENGE'—the infliction of harm upon a person for a real or fancied grievance; also the harm itself; the returning of evil for evil. There are two sorts of revenge: God's, which is righteous and inflicted without passion and is the proper punishment of evil-doers; and man's revenge, which is a breach of God's law, which says that revenge (vengeance) belongs to Him. The Bible warns mankind against taking revenge, especially in the New Testament.

REFERENCES.

Thou shalt not avenge, nor bear any grudge against the children of thy people, but thou shalt love thy neighbour as thyself: I am the Lord. (Leviticus 19: 18.)

Say not thou, I will recompense evil; but wait on the Lord, and he shall save thee. (Proverbs 20: 22.)

Say not, I will do so to him as he hath done to me: I will render to the man according to his work. (Proverbs 24: 29.)

Ye have heard that it hath been said, An eye for an eye, and a tooth for a tooth:

But I say unto you, That ye resist not evil: but whosoever shall smite thee on thy right cheek, turn to him the other also.

And if any man will sue thee at the law, and take away thy coat, let him have thy cloke also.

And whosoever shall compel thee to go a mile, go with him twain. (Matthew 5: 38-41.)

Dearly beloved, avenge not yourselves, but rather give place unto wrath: for it is written, Vengeance is mine; I will repay, saith the Lord.

Therefore if thine enemy hunger, feed him; if he thirst, give him drink: for in so doing thou shalt heap coals of fire on his head.

Be not overcome of evil, but overcome evil with good. (Romans 12: 19-21.)

See that none render evil for evil unto any man; but ever follow that which is good, both among yourselves, and to all men. (1 Thessalonians 5: 15.)

Finally, be ye all of one mind, having compassion one of another, love as brethren, be pitiful, be courteous:

Not rendering evil for evil, or railing for railing: but contrariwise blessing; knowing that ye are thereunto called, that ye should inherit a blessing. (1 Peter 3: 8, 9.)

REVERENCE.

REV'ER-ENCE—a respectful and submissive disposition of mind, arising from affection and esteem and a sense of the superiority of the person reverenced. One of the first duties of the Christian toward God is to give Him due and proper reverence, as well as to all the things that are His. One of the places in which our reverence to God should be shown especially is His house.

REFERENCES.

And he said, Draw not nigh hither: put off thy shoes from off thy feet; for the place whereon thou standest is holy ground.

Moreover he said, I am the God of thy father, the God of Abraham, the God of Isaac, and the God of Jacob. And Moses hid his face; for he was afraid to look upon God. (Exodus 3: 5, 6.)

Ye shall keep my sabbaths, and reverence my sanctuary: I am the Lord. (Leviticus 19: 30.)

God is greatly to be feared in the assembly of the saints, and to be had in reverence of all them that are about him. (Psalm 89: 7.)

He sent redemption unto his people: he hath commanded his covenant for ever: holy and reverend is his name.

The fear of the Lord is the beginning of wisdom: a good understanding have all they that do his commandments: his praise endureth for ever. (Psalm 111: 9, 10.)

Wherefore we receiving a kingdom which cannot be moved, let us have grace, whereby we may serve God acceptably with reverence and godly fear:

For our God is a consuming fire. (Hebrews 12: 28, 29.)

REWARD.

RE-WARD'—to requite; to recompense; to repay; to compensate; also that which is given in requital, recompense, repayment, compensation.

God gives rewards to the godly in the shape of the blessings He bestows upon them, especially the reward of eternal life and salvation from sin. Rewards are not through works, but by God's grace. The evil He rewards with eternal damnation.

REFERENCES.

Rewards for the Righteous.

Ye shall walk in all the ways which the Lord your God hath commanded you, that ye may live, and that it may be well with you, and that ye may prolong your days in the land which ye shall possess. (Deuteronomy 5: 33.)

Ye shall diligently keep the commandments of the Lord your God, and his testimonies, and his statutes, which he hath commanded thee.

And thou shalt do that which is right and good in the sight of the Lord; that it may be well with thee, and that thou mayest go in and possess the good land which the Lord sware unto thy fathers,

To cast out all thine enemies from before thee, as the Lord hath spoken. (Deuteronomy 6: 17-19.)

All the commandments which I command thee this day shall ye observe to do, that ye may live, and multiply, and go in and possess the land which the Lord sware unto your fathers. (Deuteronomy 8: 1.)

He brought me forth also into a large place: he delivered me, because he delighted in me.

The Lord rewarded me according to my righteousness; according to the cleanness of my hands hath he recompensed me. (2 Samuel 22: 20, 21.)

Therefore the Lord hath recompensed me according to my righteousness; according to my cleanness in his eyesight. (2 Samuel 22: 25.)

He brought me forth also into a large place; he delivereth me, because he delighted in me.

The Lord rewarded me according to my righteousness; according to the cleanness of my hands hath he recompensed me. (Psalm 18: 19, 20.)

My son, if thou wilt receive my words, and hide my commandments with thee;

So that thou incline thine ear unto wisdom, and apply thine heart to understanding;

Yea, if thou criest after knowledge, and liftest up thy voice for understanding;

If thou seekest her as silver, and searchest for her as for hid treasures;

Then shalt thou understand the fear of the Lord, and find the knowledge of God. (Proverbs 2: 1-5.)

My son, let not them depart from thine eyes: keep sound wisdom and discretion:

So shall they be life unto thy soul, and grace to thy neck. (Proverbs 3: 21, 22.)

That they may walk in my statutes, and keep mine ordinances, and do them: and they shall be my people, and I will be their God. (Ezekiel 11: 20.)

Not every one that saith unto me, Lord, Lord, shall enter into the kingdom of heaven; but he that doeth the will of my Father which is in heaven. (Matthew 7: 21.)

But he that shall endure unto the end, the same shall be saved. (Matthew 24: 13.)

But rather seek ye the kingdom of God; and all these things shall be added unto you. (Luke 12: 31.)

Ye are they which have continued with me in my temptations.

And I appoint unto you a kingdom,

as my Father hath appointed unto me. (Luke 22: 28, 29.)

He that spared not his own Son, but delivered him up for us all, how shall he not with him also freely give us all things? (Romans 8: 32.)

And let us not be weary in well doing: for in due season we shall reap, if we faint not. (Galatians 6: 9.)

For bodily exercise profiteth little: but godliness is profitable unto all things, having promise of the life that now is, and of that which is to come. (1 Timothy 4: 8.)

I have fought a good fight, I have finished my course, I have kept the faith:

Henceforth there is laid up for me a crown of righteousness, which the Lord, the righteous judge, shall give me at that day: and not to me only, but unto all them also that love his appearing. (2 Timothy 4: 7, 8.)

For we are made partakers of Christ, if we hold the beginning of our confidence steadfast unto the end. (Hebrews 3: 14.)

But we are not of them who draw back unto perdition; but of them that believe to the saving of the soul. (Hebrews 10: 39.)

My brethren, count it all joy when ye fall into divers temptations. (James 1: 2.)

Blessed is the man that endureth temptation: for when he is tried, he shall receive the crown of life, which the Lord hath promised to them that love him. (James 1: 12.)

Reward of Faithful Ministry.

The fruit of the righteous is a tree of life; and he that winneth souls is wise. (Proverbs 11: 30.)

And he that reapeth receiveth wages, and gathereth fruit unto life eternal: that both he that soweth and he that reapeth may rejoice together.

And herein is that saying true, One soweth, and another reapeth.

I sent you to reap that whereon ye bestowed no labour: other men laboured, and ye are entered into their labours. (John 4: 36-38.)

For I know that this shall turn to my salvation through your prayer, and the supply of the Spirit of Jesus Christ,

According to my earnest expectation and my hope, that in nothing I shall be ashamed, but that with all boldness, as always, so now also Christ shall be magnified in my body, whether it be by life, or by death.

For to me to live is Christ, and to die is gain. (Philippians 1: 19-21.)

And when the chief Shepherd shall appear, ye shall receive a crown of glory that fadeth not away. (1 Peter 5: 4.)

Reward of the Wicked.

If I whet my glittering sword, and mine hand take hold on judgment; I will render vengeance to mine enemies, and will reward them that hate me. (Deuteronomy 32: 41.)

And I am this day weak, though anointed king; and these men the sons of Zeruiah be too hard for me: the Lord shall reward the doer of evil according to his wickedness. (2 Samuel 3: 39.)

He shall reward evil unto mine enemies; cut them off in thy truth. (Psalm 54: 5.)

And shall receive the reward of unrighteousness, as they that count it pleasure to riot in the day time. Spots they are and blemishes, sporting themselves with their own deceivings while they feast with you. (2 Peter 2: 13.)

And whosoever was not found written in the book of life was cast into the lake of fire. (Revelation 20: 15.)

RICHES. (See Mammon, Money.)

RICH'ES—the things that make one wealthy—money, lands, goods, or other property; also wealth of a spiritual or mental order, such as righteousness, godliness, love, wisdom, knowledge, etc.

The Bible shows very plainly that worldly riches are not the only ones to be desired, and that in fact those that are not of the world are to be wished for in preference. Love of riches is set down as one of the sins to be avoided, since it leads to many kinds of wrongdoing and offenses against our fellowman. The Master Himself said it is easier for a camel to pass through the eye of a needle (that is, one of the narrow side gates alongside the main gate of an ancient city) than it is for a rich man to enter the kingdom of Heaven. By this He sought to show that the amassing of riches is almost always accompanied by the doing of evil, especially against our fellows.

REFERENCES.

Worldly Riches.

Their Vanity:

If I have made gold my hope, or have said to the fine gold, Thou art my confidence;

If I rejoiced because my wealth was great, and because mine hand had gotten much. (Job 31: 24, 25.)

There is that maketh himself rich, yet hath nothing: there is that maketh himself poor, yet hath great riches.

The ransom of a man's life are his riches: but the poor heareth not rebuke. (Proverbs 13: 7, 8.)

Labour not to be rich: cease from thine own wisdom.

Wilt thou set thine eyes upon that which is not? for riches certainly make themselves wings; they fly away as an eagle toward heaven. (Proverbs 23: 4, 5.)

There is one alone, and there is not a second; yea, he hath neither child nor brother: yet is there no end of all his labour; neither is his eye satisfied with riches; neither saith he, For whom do I labour, and bereave my soul of good? This is also vanity, yea, it is a sore travail. (Ecclesiastes 4: 7, 8.)

He that loveth silver shall not be satisfied with silver; nor he that loveth abundance with increase: this is also vanity.

When goods increase, they are increased that eat them: and what good is there to the owners thereof, saving the beholding of them with their eyes? (Ecclesiastes 5: 10, 11.)

There is an evil which I have seen under the sun, and it is common among men:

A man to whom God hath given riches, wealth, and honour, so that he wanteth nothing for his soul of all that he desireth, yet God giveth him not power to eat thereof, but a stranger eateth it: this is vanity, and it is an evil disease. (Ecclesiastes 6: 1, 2.)

Charge them that are rich in this world, that they be not highminded, nor trust in uncertain riches, but in the living God, who giveth us richly all things to enjoy. (1 Timothy 6: 17.)

Their Temptation and Uselessness:

Beware that thou forget not the Lord thy God, in not keeping his commandments, and his judgments, and his statutes, which I command thee this day:

Lest when thou hast eaten and art full, and hast built goodly houses, and dwelt therein;

And when thy herds and thy flocks multiply, and thy silver and thy gold is multiplied, and all that thou hast is multiplied;

Then thine heart be lifted up, and thou forget the Lord thy God, which brought thee forth out of the land of Egypt, from the house of bondage. (Deuteronomy 8: 11-14.)

And thou say in thine heart, My power and the might of mine hand hath gotten me this wealth.

But thou shalt remember the Lord thy God: for it is he that giveth thee power to get wealth, that he may establish his covenant which he sware unto thy fathers, as it is this day. (Deuteronomy 8: 17, 18.)

A faithful man shall abound with blessings: but he that maketh haste to be rich shall not be innocent. (Proverbs 28: 20.)

He that hasteth to be rich hath an evil eye, and considereth not that poverty shall come upon him. (Proverbs 28: 22.)

And he spake a parable unto them, saying, *The ground of a certain rich man brought forth plentifully:*

And he thought within himself, saying, What shall I do, because I have no room where to bestow my fruits?

And he said, This will I do: I will pull down my barns, and build greater; and there will I bestow all my fruits and my goods.

And I will say to my soul, Soul, thou hast much goods laid up for many years; take thine ease, eat, drink, and be merry.

But God said unto him, Thou fool, this night thy soul shall be required of thee: then whose shall those things be, which thou hast provided?

So is he that layeth up treasure for

himself, and is not rich toward God. (Luke 12: 16-21.)

For where your treasure is, there will your heart be also. (Luke 12: 34.)

And when Jesus saw that he was very sorrowful, he said, *How hardly shall they that have riches enter into the kingdom of God!*

For it is easier for a camel to go through a needle's eye, than for a rich man to enter into the kingdom of God. (Luke 18: 24, 25.)

Riches Profitless to the Wicked:

He hath swallowed down riches, and he shall vomit them up again: God shall cast them out of his belly. (Job 20: 15.)

A little that a righteous man hath is better than the riches of many wicked. (Psalm 37: 16.)

Treasures of wickedness profit nothing: but righteousness delivereth from death.

The Lord will not suffer the soul of the righteous to famish: but he casteth away the substance of the wicked. (Proverbs 10: 2, 3.)

Riches profit not in the day of wrath: but righteousness delivereth from death. (Proverbs 11: 4.)

He that trusteth in his riches shall fall: but the righteous shall flourish as a branch. (Proverbs 11: 28.)

In the house of the righteous is much treasure: but in the revenues of the wicked is trouble. (Proverbs 15: 6.)

An inheritance may be gotten hastily at the beginning; but the end thereof shall not be blessed. (Proverbs 20: 21.)

The getting of treasures by a lying tongue is a vanity tossed to and fro of them that seek death. (Proverbs 21: 6.)

There is a sore evil which I have seen under the sun, namely, riches kept for the owners thereof to their hurt.

But those riches perish by evil travail: and he begetteth a son, and there is nothing in his hand. (Ecclesiastes 5: 13, 14.)

They shall cast their silver in the streets, and their gold shall be removed: their silver and their gold shall not be able to deliver them in the day of the wrath of the Lord: they shall not satisfy their souls, neither fill their bowels: because it is the stumblingblock of their iniquity. (Ezekiel 7: 19.)

True Riches.

Again, the kingdom of heaven is like unto treasure hid in a field; the which when a man hath found, he hideth, and for joy thereof goeth and selleth all that he hath, and buyeth that field.

Again, the kingdom of heaven is like unto a merchant man, seeking goodly pearls:

Who, when he had found one pearl of great price, went and sold all that he had, and bought it. (Matthew 13: 44-46.)

If therefore ye have not been faithful in the unrighteous mammon, who will commit to your trust the true riches? (Luke 16: 11.)

Unto me, who am less than the least of all saints, is this grace given, that I should preach among the Gentiles the unsearchable riches of Christ. (Ephesians 3: 8.)

That their hearts might be comforted, being knit together in love, and unto all riches of the full assurance of understanding, to the acknowledgment of the mystery of God, and of the Father, and of Christ;

In whom are hid all the treasures of wisdom and knowledge. (Colossians 2: 2, 3.)

RIGHTEOUSNESS.

RIGHT'EOUS-NESS — holiness, purity, uprightness, rectitude; conformity of life to the divine law and comprehension of the principles of love and virtue laid down by God. The righteousness of God is His complete perfection, and is entirely distinct from the righteousness of man, which cannot reach a state of perfection. The best man can do is to imitate the righteousness of Christ and strive to live as near the Great Example as possible.

REFERENCES.

Righteousness of God.

O Lord God of Israel, thou art righteous; for we remain yet escaped, as it is this day: behold, we are before thee in our trespasses; for we cannot stand before thee because of this. (Ezra 9: 15.)

The Lord is righteous in all his ways, and holy in all his works. (Psalm 145: 17.)

The Righteousness of Christ.

He shall see of the travail of his soul, and shall be satisfied: by his knowledge shall my righteous servant justify many; for he shall bear their iniquities. (Isaiah 53: 11.)

But unto the Son he saith, Thy throne, O God, is for ever and ever: a sceptre of righteousness is the sceptre of thy kingdom.

Thou hast loved righteousness, and hated iniquity; therefore God, even thy God, hath anointed thee with the oil of gladness above thy fellows. (Hebrews 1: 9, 10.)

The Righteousness of Man.

Speak not thou in thine heart, after that the Lord thy God hath cast them out from before thee, saying, For my righteousness the Lord hath brought me in to possess this land: but for the wickedness of these nations the Lord doth drive them out from before thee.

Not for thy righteousness, or for the uprightness of thine heart, dost thou go to possess their land: but for the wickedness of these nations the Lord thy God doth drive them out from before thee, and that he may perform the word which the Lord sware unto thy fathers, Abraham, Isaac, and Jacob. (Deuteronomy 9: 4, 5.)

But we are all as an unclean thing, and all our righteousnesses are as filthy rags; and we all do fade as a leaf; and our iniquities, like the wind, have taken us away. (Isaiah 64: 6.)

And be found in him, not having mine own righteousness, which is of the law, but that which is through the faith of Christ, the righteousness which is of God by faith. (Philippians 3: 9.)

Righteous and Unrighteous: Conditions Compared.

He withdraweth not his eyes from the righteous: but with kings are they on the throne; yea, he doth establish them for ever, and they are exalted. (Job 36: 7.)

Blessed is the man that walketh not in the counsel of the ungodly, nor standeth in the way of sinners, nor sitteth in the seat of the scornful. (Psalm 1: 1.)

Therefore the ungodly shall not stand in the judgment, nor sinners in the congregation of the righteous.

For the Lord knoweth the way of the righteous: but the way of the ungodly shall perish. (Psalm 1: 5, 6.)

Lead me, O Lord, in thy righteous-

ness because of mine enemies; make thy way straight before my face.

For there is no faithfulness in their mouth; their inward part is very wickedness; their throat is an open sepulchre; they flatter with their tongue. (Psalm 5: 8, 9.)

Lord, who shall abide in thy tabernacle? who shall dwell in thy holy hill?

He that walketh uprightly, and worketh righteousness, and speaketh the truth in his heart. (Psalm 15: 1, 2.)

Commit thy way unto the Lord; trust also in him; and he shall bring it to pass.

And he shall bring forth thy righteousness as the light, and thy judgment as the noonday. (Psalm 37: 5, 6.)

A little that a righteous man hath is better than the riches of many wicked. (Psalm 37: 16.)

Cast thy burden upon the Lord, and he shall sustain thee: he shall never suffer the righteous to be moved. (Psalm 55: 2.)

The righteous shall be glad in the Lord, and shall trust in him; and all the upright in heart shall glory. (Psalm 64: 10.)

He layeth up sound wisdom for the righteous: he is a buckler to them that walk uprightly.

He keepeth the paths of judgment, and preserveth the way of his saints.

Then shalt thou understand righteousness, and judgment, and equity; yea, every good path. (Proverbs 2: 7-9.)

For the froward is abomination to the Lord: but his secret is with the righteous. (Proverbs 3: 32.)

The lips of the righteous feed many: but fools die for want of wisdom. (Proverbs 11: 21.)

The hope of the righteous shall be

gladness: but the expectation of the wicked shall perish. (Proverbs 11: 28.)

The righteous shall never be removed: but the wicked shall not inhabit the earth. (Proverbs 11: 30.)

The lips of the righteous know what is acceptable: but the mouth of the wicked speaketh frowardness. (Proverbs 11: 32.)

Riches profit not in the day of wrath: but righteousness delivereth from death.

The righteousness of the perfect shall direct his way: but the wicked shall fall by his own wickedness.

The righteousness of the upright shall deliver them: but transgressors shall be taken in their own naughtiness. (Proverbs 12: 4-6.)

When it goeth well with the righteous, the city rejoiceth: and when the wicked perish, there is shouting.

By the blessing of the upright the city is exalted: but it is overthrown by the mouth of the wicked. (Proverbs 12: 10, 11.)

Say ye to the righteous, that it shall be well with him: for they shall eat the fruit of their doings. (Isaiah 3: 10.)

Open ye the gates, that the righteous nation which keepeth the truth may enter in. (Isaiah 26: 2.)

Then shall the righteous shine forth as the sun in the kingdom of their Father. Who hath ears to hear, let him hear. (Matthew 13: 43.)

But in every nation he that feareth him, and worketh righteousness, is accepted with him. (Acts 10: 35.)

But glory, honour, and peace, to every man that worketh good, to the Jew first, and also to the Gentile. (Romans 2: 10.)

For the eyes of the Lord are over the righteous, and his ears are open unto their prayers: but the face of the Lord is against them that do evil. (1 Peter 3: 12.)

Little children, let no man deceive you: he that doeth righteousness is righteous, even as he is righteous. (1 John 3: 7.)

He that is unjust, let him be unjust still: and he which is filthy, let him be filthy still: and he that is righteous, let him be righteous still: and he that is holy, let him be holy still. (Revelation 22: 11.)

ROMAN EMPIRE AND ROME.

Ro'man Em'pire—the vast monarchy of which the city of Rome was the center.

Rome—the capital of the Roman empire.

The city of Rome was founded about 753 B.C. two or three years before the first captivity of Israel. The founders were a band of tribesmen from Central Italy called Latins. The place flourished and soon gained an ascendency over the surrounding country. The original government was a monarchy, but the kings proved so bad that the people got rid of them and set up a sort of republic. In the course of time the Romans made themselves the masters of Italy and began to acquire territory elsewhere. The nation was about at the height of its power during the lifetime of Christ. Judea was brought under Roman rule by Pompey about the year 63 B.C. A few years later the Roman republic became a monarchy again under Augustus, the heir of Julius Cæsar and the first of a long line of emperors. By this time all Europe, Northern Africa, and Western Asia were under Roman domination, forming the greatest empire that had existed up to that time. Rome, the capital of the empire, was a most magnificent city, full of beautiful buildings, both public and private. The Roman religion was pagan. There were a large number of gods and goddesses, divided into three sorts, gods of heaven, gods of the world, and gods of the underworld or hell. For the most part they were personifications of the sun, moon, light, darkness, and the various forces of nature, and the higher personal, moral, and mental attributes, such as purity, wisdom, beauty, love, etc. Nature worship was the original form of the Roman faith, but as Rome had conquered other nations the gods of the subdued countries had been absorbed gradually by the Romans. About the time of Christ's death or a little after there were places of worship in Rome for pretty nearly every god known to the world. This brought about a condition of confusion and made the time ripe for the introduction of the Christian faith. The higher classes of the people had little or no religion of a set sort and made offering to any or all of the gods as they saw fit. The Christian religion, with its tenets of purity, meekness, the returning of good for evil, brotherly love, and the worship of one God, was quite unintelligible to the Romans for a long time, and for many years after Christ was crucified the Christians were bitterly persecuted. The first Christian Roman emperor was Constantine, who was converted about the year 315 A.D. He built the first Christian Church in Rome about 324 A.D. The ruins of the Coliseum, a vast amphitheater for the celebration of public games and amusements in the shape of combats between men and men and men and beasts, a place which was also the scene of the death of many a Christian martyr, are still standing.

RUTH.

RUTH—a form of a Hebrew word meaning "a female friend." Ruth was a Moabite woman who married a Hebrew, and, after his death, through devotion to her mother-in-law, Naomi, accompanied her to Judea. There she wedded Boaz, and through him became one of the ancestors of Jesus. The story of Ruth and Boaz is one of the most beautiful love-tales in all literature.

Reference.—The book of Ruth.

SABAOTH.

SAB'A-OTH OR SA-BA'OTH—a Greek form of a Hebrew word meaning "armies" or "hosts." Many persons have inferred from the structure of the word that it is synonymous with Sabbath, an inference which is en-

tirely incorrect. It is used only twice in the Bible.

References.—Romans 9: 29; James 5: 4.

SABBATH.

SAB'BATH—a form of a Hebrew word meaning "the rest" and later corrupted into "the day of rest." The institution of the day of rest is as old as the Creation, according to the Bible, since we have it laid down in the Mosaic account of the beginning of things. It was enjoined by Moses and was a part of the Decalogue. The Jews observed the seventh or last day of the week. With the resurrection of Christ Christians altered the observance of it to the first day, and now it is observed by practically all civilized people. Thus the Jews held and still hold Saturday as the true Sabbath, while for the most part the Christian faith regards Sunday as the Sabbath. By the majority it is called the Lord's Day. Some few denominations continue to observe the Jewish Sabbath or Saturday. The use of the first day of the week, or Sunday, unquestionably came from the fact that in the early Church the day was observed because it was upon Sunday (see Matthew 28: 1) that the Lord arose from the dead, and the Church found the observance of the Jewish Sabbath and the Lord's Day encroached upon each other.

SACKCLOTH.

SACK'CLOTH—a material of coarse stuff, very much in use among the ancients as goods for mourning or penitence or for the expression of sadness at some calamity. They made themselves garments of it and sat in their houses or in the roads and public places heaping ashes upon their heads.

SADDUCEES. (See Pharisees.)

SAD'DU-CEES—one of the Jewish sects at the time of Christ. They were an offshoot of the Pharisees and refused to accept the dogma that the oral law to which the latter pinned much faith was the revelation of God and stood for the written law exclusively. They did not believe in the resurrection nor in the system of future rewards and punishments.

This made them very intolerant of Jesus and His doctrine, and they joined the Pharisees in asking for a sign, which was about the only thing in which they did unite with the Pharisees. They were very much more tolerant and much less hypocritical than the Pharisees—a party of reformers, in fact—which may account for the fact that Jesus did not take them to task so bitterly as he did the Pharisees. At the time of his ministry, however, the high-priest was a Sadducee, and he went pretty much with the current of the Jewish thought of the moment regarding Christ.

SAINT.

SAINT—a person sanctified or good and holy; a person well known for virtue and piety; any true Christian redeemed and consecrated by God; also the blessed in Heaven. These are the original and true meanings of the term, as it is used in Scripture. Later it came to be applied to a few persons passed out of the earthly life and held in special veneration by the Roman Church.

REFERENCES.

The Saints of God.

And he said, The Lord came from Sinai, and rose up from Seir unto them; he shined forth from mount Paran, and he came with ten thousands of saints: from his right hand went a fiery law for them. (Deuteronomy 33: 2.)

He will keep the feet of his saints, and the wicked shall be silent in darkness; for by strength shall no man prevail. (1 Samuel 2: 9.)

All thy works shall praise thee, O Lord; and thy saints shall bless thee. (Psalm 145: 10.)

Praise ye the Lord. Sing unto the Lord a new song, and his praise in the congregation of saints. (Psalm 149: 1.)

He keepeth the paths of judgment, and preserveth the way of his saints. (Proverbs 2: 8.)

But the saints of the Most High shall take the kingdom, and possess the kingdom for ever, even for ever and ever. (Daniel 7: 18.)

Believers as Saints.

And he that searcheth the hearts knoweth what is the mind of the Spirit, because he maketh intercession for the saints according to the will of God. (Romans 8: 27.)

Now therefore ye are no more strangers and foreigners, but fellow-citizens with the saints, and of the household of God. (Ephesians 2: 19.)

Giving thanks unto the Father, which hath made us meet to be partakers of the inheritance of the saints in light. (Colossians 1: 12.)

Beloved, when I gave all diligence to write unto you of the common salvation, it was needful for me to write unto you, and exhort you that ye should earnestly contend for the faith which was once delivered unto the saints. (Jude 1: 3.)

And when he had taken the book, the four beasts and four and twenty elders fell down before the Lamb, having every one of them harps, and golden vials full of odours, which are the prayers of saints. (Revelation 5: 8.)

Obligations and Blessings of the Saints.

Now therefore arise, O Lord God, into thy resting place, thou, and the ark of thy strength: let thy priests, O Lord God, be clothed with salvation, and let thy saints rejoice in goodness. (2 Chronicles 6: 41.)

Sing unto the Lord, O ye saints of his, and give thanks at the remembrance of his holiness. (Psalm 30: 4.)

O love the Lord, all ye his saints: for the Lord preserveth the faithful, and plentifully rewardeth the proud doer. (Psalm 31: 23.)

Let thy priests be clothed with righteousness; and let thy saints shout for joy. (Psalm 132: 9.)

That ye receive her in the Lord, as becometh saints, and that ye assist her in whatsoever business she hath need of you: for she hath been a succourer of many, and of myself also. (Romans 16: 2.)

Salute Philologus, and Julia, Nereus, and his sister, and Olympas, and all the saints which are with them. (Romans 16: 15.)

Dare any of you, having a matter against another, go to law before the unjust, and not before the saints?

Do ye not know that the saints shall judge the world? and if the world shall be judged by you, are ye unworthy to judge the smallest matters? (1 Corinthians 6: 1, 2.)

Praying us with much intreaty that we would receive the gift, and take upon us the fellowship of the ministering to the saints. (2 Corinthians 8: 4.)

And he gave some, apostles; and some, prophets; and some, evangelists; and some, pastors and teachers;

For the perfecting of the saints, for the work of the ministry, for the edifying of the body of Christ. (Ephesians 4: 11, 12.)

Praying always with all prayer and supplication in the Spirit, and watching thereunto with all perseverance and supplication for all saints. (Ephesians 6: 18.)

I thank my God, making mention of thee always in my prayers,

Hearing of thy love and faith, which thou hast toward the Lord Jesus, and toward all saints. (Philemon 1: 4, 5.)

For God is not unrighteous to forget your work and labour of love, which ye have shewed toward his name, in that ye have ministered to the saints, and do minister. (Hebrews 6: 10.)

Salute all them, that have the rule over you, and all the saints. They of Italy salute you. (Hebrews 13: 24.)

SALEM. (See Jerusalem.)

SA'LEM—a form of a Hebrew word meaning "peace" or "peaceful." Salem was the original name of Jerusalem and continued to be used in later times in a poetic sense.

References.—Genesis 14: 18; Hebrews 7: 1.

SALOME.

SA-LO'ME—a Greek form of the Hebrew word "Salem," meaning the same and used as a name for a woman. There are two persons of the name mentioned in the Bible—a woman, apparently the mother of the apostles James and John, and that daughter of Herodias which danced before Herod Antipas and secured the decapitation of John the Baptist.

References.—Mark 15: 40, and 16: 1. No reference for daughter of Herodias.

SALT SEA, The.

SALT SEA—the most ancient and the proper name for the Dead Sea, which title is only met with about 200 years before Christ's time. The name of Dead Sea was given to it by the Greeks and Romans. It is a lake in the course of the Jordan, and is about 46 miles long and about 10 miles wide. It is about 1,300 feet below ocean level. It is 1,300 feet deep in its deepest part. Its shores are high, hilly, and barren, save for where a freshwater brook flows in. The waters of the sea are the heaviest known to science, weighing more than 12 pounds to the gallon, as against 9 pounds for distilled water. This is due to the large quantity of mineral salts held in solution by the water, giving the water a peculiar greenish-blue tinge. There is an old tradition that the sea occupies the site of Sodom and Gomorrah and the "cities of the plain," but this is much to be doubted, as there are a thousand and one indications that the sea was in its present location long before the date of the destruction of the places in question.

SALVATION. (See Redemption.)

SAL-VA'TION—a word used in the Bible in three senses: (1) deliverance from temporal dangers and enemies; (2) deliverance from a state of sin and misery and union with Christ, through His blood; (3) eternal happiness and perfect and lasting fellowship with God. The whole scheme of salvation is based upon the vicarious atonement of Jesus for the sins of the world through the shedding of His blood as the Last Great Sacrifice. By faith in Him we receive the benefit of it, and in no other way can we profit by it.

REFERENCES.

Prayer for Salvation.

Save, Lord: let the king hear us when we call. (Psalm 20: 9.)

Save me, O God, by thy name, and judge me by thy strength. (Psalm 54: 1.)

Be thou my strong habitation, whereunto I may continually resort: thou hast given commandment to save me; for thou· art my rock and my fortress. (Psalm 71: 3.)

Shew us thy mercy, O Lord, and grant us thy salvation. (Psalm 85: 7.)

O turn unto me, and have mercy upon me; give thy strength unto thy servant, and save the son of thine handmaid. (Psalm 86: 16.)

Salvation by Christ.

For the Son of man is come to save that which was lost. (Matthew 18: 14.)

And the angel said unto them, Fear not: for, behold, I bring you good tidings of great joy, which shall be to all people.

For unto you is born this day in the city of David a Saviour, which is Christ the Lord. (Luke 2: 10, 11.)

For the Son of man is not come to destroy men's lives, but to save them. And they went to another village. (Luke 9: 56.)

For the Son of man is come to seek and to save that which was lost. (Luke 19: 10.)

For God sent not his Son into the world to condemn the world; but that the world through him might be saved. (John 3: 17.)

Neither is there salvation in any other: for there is none other name under heaven given among men, whereby we must be saved. (Acts 4: 12.)

For God hath not appointed us to wrath, but to obtain salvation by our Lord Jesus Christ. (1 Thessalonians 5: 9.)

This is a faithful saying, and worthy of all acceptation, that Christ Jesus came into the world to save sinners; of whom I am chief. (1 Timothy 1: 15.)

Who is a liar but he that denieth that Jesus is the Christ? He is antichrist, that denieth the Father and the Son. (1 John 2: 22.)

And we have seen and do testify that the Father sent the Son to be the Saviour of the world. (1 John 4: 14.)

All Men May Be Saved.

If so be they will hearken, and turn every man from his evil way, that I may repent me of the evil, which I purpose to do unto them because of the evil of their doings. (Jeremiah 26: 3.)

And it shall come to pass, that whosoever shall call on the name of the Lord shall be delivered: for in mount Zion and in Jerusalem shall be deliverance, as the Lord hath said, and in the remnant whom the Lord shall call. (Joel 2: 32.)

All that the Father giveth me shall come to me; and him that cometh to me I will in no wise cast out. (John 6: 37.)

And it shall come to pass, that whosoever shall call on the name of the Lord shall be saved. (Acts 2: 21.)

But not as the offence, so also is the free gift: for if through the offence of one many be dead, much more the grace of God, and the gift by grace, which is by one man, Jesus Christ, hath abounded unto many.

And not as it was by one that sinned, so is the gift: for the judgment was by one to condemnation, but the free gift is of many offences unto justification.

For if by one man's offence death reigned by one; much more they which receive abundance of grace and of the gift of righteousness shall reign in life by one, Jesus Christ.

Therefore, as by the offence of one judgment came upon all men to condemnation; even so by the righteousness of one the free gift came upon all men unto justification of life.

For as by one man's disobedience many were made sinners, so by the obedience of one shall many be made righteous.

Moreover the law entered, that the offence might abound. But where sin abounded, grace did much more abound. (Romans 5: 15-20.)

For the Scripture saith, Whosoever believeth on him shall not be ashamed. (Romans 10: 11.)

For whosoever shall call upon the name of the Lord shall be saved. (Romans 10: 13.)

For the love of Christ constraineth us; because we thus judge, that if one died for all, then were all dead:

And that he died for all, that they which live should not henceforth live unto themselves, but unto him which died for them, and rose again. (2 Corinthians 5: 14, 15.)

For this is good and acceptable in the sight of God our Saviour;

Who will have all men to be saved, and to come unto the knowledge of the truth. (1 Timothy 2: 3, 4.)

This is a faithful saying, and worthy of all acceptation.

For therefore we both labour and suffer reproach, because we trust in the living God, who is the Saviour of all men, specially of those that believe. (1 Timothy 4: 9, 10.)

If a man therefore purge himself from these, he shall be a vessel unto honour, sanctified, and meet for the master's use, and prepared unto every good work. (2 Timothy 2: 21.)

For the grace of God that bringeth salvation hath appeared to all men. (Titus 2: 11.)

And he is the propitiation for our sins: and not for ours only, but also for the sins of the whole world. (1 John 2: 2.)

And the Spirit and the bride say, Come. And let him that heareth say, Come. And let him that is athirst come. And whosoever will, let him take the water of life freely. (Revelation 22: 17.)

But Few Are Saved.

Enter ye in at the strait gate: for wide is the gate, and broad is the way, that leadeth to destruction, and many there be which go in thereat:

Because strait is the gate, and narrow is the way, which leadeth unto life, and few there be that find it. (Matthew 7: 13, 14.)

Then said one unto him, Lord, are there few that be saved? And he said unto them,

Strive to enter in at the strait gate: for many, I say unto you, will seek to enter in, and shall not be able. (Luke 13: 23, 24.)

The Means of Salvation.

Wherefore, my beloved, as ye have always obeyed, not as in my presence only, but now much more in my absence, work out your own salvation with fear and trembling. (Philippians 2: 12.)

Nevertheless the foundation of God standeth sure, having this seal, The Lord knoweth them that are his. And, Let every one that nameth the name of Christ depart from iniquity. (2 Timothy 2: 19.)

Wherefore the rather, brethren, give diligence to make your calling and election sure: for if ye do these things, ye shall never fall:

For so an entrance shall be ministered unto you abundantly into the everlasting kingdom of our Lord and Saviour Jesus Christ. (2 Peter 1: 10, 11.)

Thanksgiving for Salvation.

Blessed be the Lord God of Israel; for he hath visited and redeemed his people,

And hath raised up a horn of salvation for us in the house of his servant David;

As he spake by the mouth of his holy prophets, which have been since the world began. (Luke 1: 68-70.)

But thanks be to God, which giveth us the victory through our Lord Jesus Christ. (1 Corinthians 15: 57.)

Now thanks be unto God, which always causeth us to triumph in Christ, and maketh manifest the savour of his knowledge by us in every place. (2 Corinthians 2: 14.)

Thanks be unto God for his unspeakable gift. (2 Corinthians 9: 15.)

Blessed be the God and Father of our Lord Jesus Christ, who hath blessed us with all spiritual blessings in heavenly places in Christ. (Ephesians 1: 3.)

Giving thanks unto the Father, which hath made us meet to be partakers of the inheritance of the saints in light:

Who hath delivered us from the power of darkness, and hath translated us into the kingdom of his dear Son. (Colossians 1: 12, 13.)

Blessed be the God and Father of our Lord Jesus Christ, which according to his abundant mercy hath begotten us again unto a lively hope by the resurrection of Jesus Christ from the dead. (1 Peter 1: 3.)

Salvation by Grace.

But none of these things move me, neither count I my life dear unto myself, so that I might finish my course with joy, and the ministry, which I have received of the Lord Jesus, to testify the gospel of the grace of God. (Acts 20: 24.)

Being justified freely by his grace through the redemption that is in Christ Jesus. (Romans 3: 24.)

But not as the offence, so also is the free gift. For if through the offence of one many be dead, much more the grace of God, and the gift by grace, which is by one man, Jesus Christ, hath abounded unto many.

And not as it was by one that sinned,

so is the gift: for the judgment was by one to condemnation, but the free gift is of many offences unto justification.

For if by one man's offence death reigned by one; much more they which receive abundance of grace and of the gift of righteousness shall reign in life by one, Jesus Christ. (Romans 5: 15-17.)

Even so then at this present time also there is a remnant according to the election of grace.

And if by grace, then is it no more of works: otherwise grace is no more grace. But if it be of works, then is it no more grace: otherwise work is no more work. (Romans 11: 5, 6.)

Having predestinated us unto the adoption of children by Jesus Christ to himself, according to the good pleasure of his will,

To the praise of the glory of his grace, wherein he hath made us accepted in the beloved.

In whom we have redemption through his blood, the forgiveness of sins, according to the riches of his grace. (Ephesians 1: 5-7.)

But God who is rich in mercy, for his great love wherewith he loved us,

Even when we were dead in sins, hath quickened us together with Christ, (by grace ye are saved)

And hath raised us up together, and made us sit together in heavenly places in Christ Jesus:

That in the ages to come he might shew the exceeding riches of his grace, in his kindness towards us, through Christ Jesus.

For by grace are ye saved, through faith, and that not of yourselves: it is the gift of God:

Not of works, lest any man should boast.

For we are his workmanship, created in Christ Jesus unto good works, which God hath before ordained, that we should walk in them. (Ephesians 2: 4-10.)

Who hath saved us, and called us with an holy calling, not according to our works, but according to his own purpose and grace, which was given us in Christ Jesus before the world began,

But is now made manifest by the appearing of our Saviour Jesus Christ, who hath abolished death, and hath brought life and immortality to light through the gospel. (2 Timothy 1: 9, 10.)

Not by works of righteousness which we have done, but according to his mercy he saved us, by the washing of regeneration, and renewing of the Holy Ghost. (Titus 3: 5.)

Receiving the end of your faith, even the salvation of your souls.

Of which salvation the prophets have enquired and searched diligently, who prophesied of the grace that should come unto you. (1 Peter 1: 9, 10.)

SAMARIA.

SA-MA'RI-A—a form of a Hebrew word meaning "watch-height." Samaria, in Bible times, was a city situated in the central part of Palestine, and built on a high hill. It was founded about 925 B.C., and for many years was the metropolis and capital of the kingdom of Israel. After the captivity of Israel it fell into desolation and was rebuilt by Herod the Great with much splendor. There is a tradition that John the Baptist suffered martyrdom there. The present town is little more than a heap of ruins.

SAMSON. (See Delilah.)

SAM'SON—a form of a Hebrew word meaning "little sun" or "sun-like." Samson is one of the most remarkable characters in Scripture. He was a champion, deliverer, and judge of Israel. He was noted for his superhuman strength and moral weakness, and the tragic nature of his death. He married a Philistine woman against the wishes of his parents and later left her. Wishing to return to her and finding her given to another, he wreaked his vengeance on the Philistines by destroying their crops. He was surrounded by an army of 3,000 of them and surrendered, afterwards breaking his bonds and defeating them single-handed and with great slaughter. Captured again, he escaped and carried away the gates of the city of Gaza. The secret of his strength—which lay in his great mass of hair—was discovered by a woman with whom he was in love, Delilah, and he was betrayed by her, after he had been shorn of his hair. While his enemies were celebrating their victory he pulled down the house, perishing with them in the ruins.

References.—Judges 13, 14, 15, and 16.

SAMUEL. (See David, Saul, etc.)

Sam'u-el—a form of a Hebrew word meaning "heard of God." Samuel was the last of the judges of Israel. He was the son of Elkanah and his favorite wife, Hannah. Hannah, who had been childless many years, prayed to God to give her a son, vowing to consecrate him to the Lord's service. Her prayer was answered and her child was set apart under the tutelage of Eli at a very early age. When he was quite a child God used him as a means of communicating the doom that was to befall the house of Eli. For the next twenty years we hear little of the young man, but at the end of that time we find him acting as both judge and prophet. In his old age, Samuel found things going badly among the Israelites, and was importuned to give them a king. He disliked to do this, since he saw in it a destruction of the old theocratic government that had been established by Moses. The Lord comforted him in his sorrow, telling that the Jews had not rejected him (Samuel), but Jehovah, their God. Saul was divinely pointed out as the man to be anointed king, since the people had insisted upon one. Saul's reign proved, as a whole, a bad one, for he disobeyed constantly the orders issued to him by the prophet. Finally,

Samuel practically dethroned him in the anointing of David. Samuel wrote a part of two books, which are found in the Bible under his name—probably the first twenty-four chapters. They embrace one of the most interesting parts of Jewish history.

REFERENCES.

Birth and Dedication to God.

Wherefore it came to pass, when the time was come about after Hannah had conceived, that she bare a son, and called his name Samuel, saying, Because I have asked him of the Lord. (1 Samuel 1: 20.)

And she said, O my lord, as thy soul liveth, my lord, I am the woman that stood by thee here, praying unto the Lord.

For this child I prayed; and the Lord hath given me my petition which I asked of him:

Therefore also I have lent him to the Lord; as long as he liveth he shall be lent to the Lord. And he worshipped the Lord there. (1 Samuel 1: 26-28.)

Samuel's Call.

And the Lord called Samuel again the third time. And he arose and went to Eli, and said, Here am I; for thou didst call me. And Eli perceived that the Lord had called the child. (1 Samuel 3: 8.)

And the Lord came, and stood, and called as at other times, Samuel, Samuel. Then Samuel answered, Speak; for thy servant heareth. (1 Samuel 3: 9, 10.)

And Samuel grew, and the Lord was with him, and did let none of his words fall to the ground.

And all Israel, from Dan even to Beersheba, knew that Samuel was established to be a prophet of the Lord. (1 Samuel 3: 19, 20.)

Samuel Judges Israel.

And Samuel judged Israel all the days of his life.

And he went from year to year in circuit to Bethel, and Gilgal, and Mizpeh, and judged Israel in all those places.

And his return was to Ramah; for there was his house; and there he judged Israel; and there he built an altar unto the Lord. (1 Samuel 4: 15-17.)

Samuel Asked to Make a King.

And said unto him, Behold, thou art old, and thy sons walk not in thy ways: now make us a king to judge us like all the nations.

But the thing displeased Samuel, when they said, Give us a king to judge us. And Samuel prayed unto the Lord.

And the Lord said unto Samuel, Hearken unto the voice of the people in all that they say unto thee: for they have not rejected thee, but they have rejected me, that I should not reign over them.

According to all the works which they have done since the day that I brought them up out of Egypt even unto this day, wherewith they have forsaken me, and served other gods, so do they also unto thee.

Now therefore hearken unto their voice: howbeit yet protest solemnly unto them, and shew them the manner of the king that shall reign over them.

And Samuel told all the words of the Lord unto the people that asked of him a king. (1 Samuel 8: 5-10.)

Samuel Makes Saul King.

Now the Lord had told Samuel in his ear a day before Saul came, saying, To-morrow about this time, I will send thee a man out of the land of Benjamin, and thou shalt anoint him to be captain over my people Israel, that he may save my people out of the hand of the Philistines: for I have looked upon my people, because their cry is come unto me.

And when Samuel saw Saul, the Lord said unto him, Behold the man whom I spake to thee of! this same shall reign over my people. (1 Samuel 9: 15-17.)

Then Samuel took a vial of oil, and poured it upon his head, and kissed him, and said, Is it not because the Lord hath anointed thee to be captain over his inheritance? (1 Samuel 10: 1.)

David Anointed by Samuel.

And the Lord said unto Samuel, How long wilt thou mourn for Saul, seeing I have rejected him from reigning over Israel? fill thine horn with oil, and go, I will send thee to Jesse the Bethlehemite: for I have provided me a king among his sons. (1 Samuel 16: 1.)

Then Samuel took the horn of oil, and anointed him in the midst of his brethren: and the Spirit of the Lord came upon David from that day forward. So Samuel rose up, and went to Ramah. (1 Samuel 16: 13.)

Samuel's Death.

And Samuel died: and all the Israelites were gathered together, and lamented him, and buried him in his house at Ramah. And David arose, and went down to the wilderness of Paran. (1 Samuel 25: 1.)

SANCTIFICATION.

SANC'TI-FI-CA'TION—that work of God's grace in the human soul through which and by which we are renewed in the image of God, set apart for God's service, as well as enabled to die to sin and live to righteousness. Modern theology has a number of different views regarding sanctification and its entirety, which views it would be needless to discuss here, since they involve points of doctrinal dispute.

REFERENCES.

Sanctification by Christ.

And for their sakes I sanctify myself, that they also might be sanctified through the truth. (John 17: 19.)

Unto the church of God which is at Corinth, to them that are sanctified in Christ Jesus, called to be saints, with all that in every place call upon the name of Jesus Christ our Lord, both theirs and ours. (1 Corinthians 1: 2.)

But of him are ye in Christ Jesus, who of God is made unto us wisdom, and righteousness, and sanctification, and redemption. (1 Corinthians 1: 30.)

And such were some of you: but ye are washed, but ye are sanctified, but ye are justified in the name of the Lord Jesus, and by the Spirit of our God. (1 Corinthians 6: 11.)

That he might sanctify and cleanse it with the washing of water by the word. (Ephesians 5: 26.)

For both he that sanctifieth and they who are sanctified are all of one: for which cause he is not ashamed to call them brethren. (Hebrews 2: 11.)

By the which will we are sanctified through the offering of the body of Jesus Christ once for all. (Hebrews 10: 10.)

Jude, the servant of Jesus Christ, and brother of James, to them that are sanctified by God the Father, and preserved in Jesus Christ, and called. (Jude 1: 1.)

Sanctification by the Holy Ghost.

That I should be the minister of Jesus Christ to the Gentiles, ministering the gospel of God, that the offering up of the Gentiles might be acceptable, being sanctified by the Holy Ghost. (Romans 15: 16.)

But we are bound to give thanks alway to God for you, brethren beloved of the Lord, because God hath from the beginning chosen you to salvation through sanctification of the Spirit and belief of the truth. (2 Thessalonians 2: 13.)

Elect according to the foreknowledge of God the Father, through sanctification of the Spirit, unto obedience and sprinkling of the blood of Jesus Christ: Grace unto you, and peace, be multiplied. (1 Peter 1: 2.)

SANCTUARY. (See Refuge, Tabernacle, Temple.)

Sanc'tu-a-ry—a sacred spot, a consecrated place; specifically, the Holy of Holies of the Temple; the most sacred part of any religious edifice; a building consecrated to the worship of God; a sacred asylum or place of refuge.

SANHEDRIN.

San'he-drin (also erroneously spelled sanhedrim)—the supreme council of the Jews about the time of Christ, a council especially given to the consideration of religious affairs.

The Sanhedrin was composed of seventy members, chosen from the highest walks of life and elected to life-membership. It interpreted the law and had jurisdiction in many things besides religious matters. It had the power of life and death, but in cases where capital punishment was awarded the verdict had to be approved by the Roman governor. For inflicting death in the case of Stephen without consulting the Roman authority Annas, the high-priest and president of the Sanhedrin, was deposed. The time of the council's origin is unknown, but the Jews insisted that it began with Moses. Both the Bible and history show this to be wrong. It probably began about the time prophecy fell away from Israel.

SARAH. (See Abraham, Hagar, Isaac, Ishmael.)

SA'RAH—a form of a Hebrew word meaning "princess." Sarah was the half-sister and wife of Abraham. The original form of her name was Sarai.

SATAN. (See Devil.)

SA'TAN—the Englished form of a Greek word derived from the Hebrew and meaning "an opponent." Satan is one of the names given to the Devil, the chief of fallen spirits, the prince of evil and the adversary of good.

References.—See references under Devil.

SAUL. (See David, Jonathan, Samuel.)

SAUL—a form of a Hebrew word meaning "asked for." Saul was the name of the first Israelitish king and the original name of the great apostle to the Gentiles, best known under his later name of Paul.

Saul was the son of Kish, a Benjaminite. In the later days of Samuel the people demanded a king, and Samuel was divinely led to the choice of Saul, although God made an effort to show the people their foolishness. Saul began his reign most auspiciously, but soon fell into evil ways. He disobeyed the injunctions of Samuel regarding the Amalekites and the Philistines, and Samuel conveyed to him the information that the Lord had given him up. In the meantime David had been anointed king, which practically amounted to the religious dethronement of Saul. Saul, angry as well as afraid, sought many times to destroy David. His evil course continued and had as its crowning folly the consultation with the witch of Endor. Shortly afterwards Saul, with Jonathan and his other sons and his army, met the Philistines at Gilboa and was defeated. Saul committed suicide.

Saul, despite his wickedness and his bad reign, had some admirable qualities. He was a good soldier and an admirable leader. His accession to the throne found Israel crushed and helpless. Before he died he defeated many of its enemies and gave the nation a certain secure position among the hostile tribes round about. But he was a man who could not resist temptation, notwithstanding his lofty qualities, and this brought about his fall.

REFERENCES.

Parentage and Choice as King.

Now there was a man of Benjamin, whose name was Kish, the son of Abiel, the son of Zeror, the son of Bechorath, the son of Aphiah, a Benjamite, a mighty man of power.

And he had a son, whose name was Saul, a choice young man, and a goodly: and there was not among the children of Israel a goodlier person than he: from his shoulders and upward he was higher than any of the people. (1 Samuel 9: 1, 2.)

And when Samuel saw Saul, the Lord said unto him, Behold the man whom I spake to thee of! this same shall reign over my people. (1 Samuel 9: 17.)

Then Samuel took a vial of oil, and poured it upon his head, and kissed him, and said, Is it not because the Lord hath anointed thee to be captain over his inheritance? (1 Samuel 10: 1.)

And all the people went to Gilgal; and there they made Saul king before the Lord in Gilgal; there they sacrificed sacrifices of peace offerings before the Lord, and there Saul and all the men of Israel rejoiced greatly. (1 Samuel 11: 15.)

His First Offense and Disfavor in God's Sight.

And Saul smote the Amalekites from Havilah until thou comest to Shur, that is over against Egypt.

And he took Agag the king of the

Amalekites alive, and utterly destroyed all the people with the edge of the sword.

But Saul and the people spared Agag, and the best of the sheep, and of the oxen, and of the fatlings, and the lambs, and all that was good, and would not utterly destroy them: but every thing that was vile and refuse, that they destroyed utterly.

Then came the word of the Lord unto Samuel, saying,

It repenteth me that I have set up Saul to be king: for he is turned back from following me, and hath not performed my commandments. And it grieved Samuel; and he cried unto the Lord all night. (1 Samuel 15: 7-11.)

Secures David as Companion.

But the Spirit of the Lord departed from Saul, and an evil spirit from the Lord troubled him.

And Saul's servants said unto him, Behold now, an evil spirit from God troubleth thee.

Let our lord now command thy servants, which are before thee, to seek out a man, who is a cunning player on an harp: and it shall come to pass, when the evil spirit from God is upon thee, that he shall play with his hand, and thou shalt be well.

And Saul said unto his servants, Provide me now a man that can play well, and bring him to me.

Then answered one of the servants, and said, Behold, I have seen a son of Jesse the Bethlehemite, that is cunning in playing, and a mighty valiant man, and a man of war, and prudent in matters, and a comely person, and the Lord is with him.

Wherefore Saul sent messengers unto Jesse, and said, Send me David thy son, which is with the sheep. (1 Samuel 16: 14-19.)

Jealousy and Fear of David.

And the women answered one another as they played, and said, Saul hath slain his thousands, and David his ten thousands.

And Saul was very wroth, and the saying displeased him; and he said, They have ascribed unto David ten thousands, and to me they have ascribed but thousands: and what can he have more but the kingdom?

And Saul eyed David from that day and forward.

And it came to pass on the morrow, that the evil spirit from God came upon Saul, and he prophesied in the midst of the house: and David played with his hand, as at other times: and there was a javelin in Saul's hand.

And Saul cast the javelin; for he said, I will smite David even to the wall with it. And David avoided out of his presence twice.

And Saul was afraid of David, because the Lord was with him, and was departed from Saul. (1 Samuel 18: 7-12.)

Tries to Kill David.

And Saul called all the people together to war, to go down to Keilah, to besiege David and his men. (1 Samuel 23: 8.)

And David abode in the wilderness in strong holds, and remained in a mountain in the wilderness of Ziph. And Saul sought him every day, but God delivered him not into his hand. (1 Samuel 23: 14.)

Life Spared by David.

And it came pass, when Saul was returned from following the Philistines, that it was told him, saying, Behold, David is in the wilderness of Engedi.

Then Saul took three thousand chosen men out of all Israel, and went to seek David and his men upon the rocks of the wild goats.

And he came to the sheepcotes by the way, where was a cave; and Saul went in to cover his feet: and David and his men remained in the sides of the cave.

And the men of David said unto him, Behold the day of which the Lord said unto thee, Behold, I will deliver thine enemy into thine hand, that thou mayest do to him as it shall seem good unto thee. Then David arose, and cut off the skirt of Saul's robe privily. (1 Samuel 24: 1-4.)

So David and Abishai came to the people by night: and, behold, Saul lay sleeping within the trench, and his spear stuck in the ground at his bolster: but Abner and the people lay round about him.

Then said Abishai to David, God hath delivered thine enemy into thine hand this day: now therefore let me smite him, I pray thee, with the spear even to the earth at once, and I will not smite him the second time.

And David said to Abishai, Destroy him not: for who can stretch forth his hand against the Lord's anointed, and be guiltless?

David said furthermore, As the Lord liveth, the Lord shall smite him; or his day shall come to die; or he shall descend into battle, and perish.

The Lord forbid that I should stretch forth mine hand against the Lord's anointed: but, I pray thee, take thou now the spear that is at his bolster, and the cruse of water, and let us go.

So David took the spear and the cruse of water from Saul's bolster; and they gat them away, and no man saw it, nor knew it, neither awaked: for they were all asleep; because a deep sleep from the Lord was fallen upon them. (1 Samuel 26: 7-12.)

Consults Witch and Hears His Doom.

Then said Saul unto his servants, Seek me a woman that hath a familiar spirit, that I may go to her, and inquire of her. And his servants said to him, Behold, there is a woman that hath a familiar spirit at Endor.

And Saul disguised himself, and put on other raiment, and he went, and two men with him, and they came to the woman by night: and he said, I pray thee, divine unto me by the familiar spirit, and bring me him up, whom I shall name unto thee.

And the woman said unto him, Behold, thou knowest what Saul hath done, how he hath cut off those that have familiar spirits, and the wizards, out of the land: wherefore then layest thou a snare for my life, to cause me to die?

And Saul sware to her by the Lord, saying, As the Lord liveth, there shall no punishment happen to thee for this thing.

Then said the woman, Whom shall I bring up unto thee? And he said, Bring me up Samuel. (1 Samuel 28: 7-11.)

Then said Samuel, Wherefore then dost thou ask of me, seeing the Lord is departed from thee, and is become thine enemy?

And the Lord hath done to him, as he spake by me: for the Lord hath rent the kingdom out of thine hand, and given it to thy neighbour, even to David:

Because thou obeyedst not the voice of the Lord, nor executedst his fierce wrath upon Amalek, therefore hath the Lord done this thing unto thee this day.

Moreover the Lord will also deliver Israel with thee into the hand of the Philistines: and to-morrow shalt thou and thy sons be with me: the Lord also shall deliver the host of Israel into the hand of the Philistines.

Then Saul fell straightway all along on the earth, and was sore afraid, because of the words of Samuel: and there was no strength in him; for he had eaten no bread all the day, nor all the night. (1 Samuel 28: 16-20.)

Saul's Defeat and Suicide.

Now the Philistines fought against Israel: and the men of Israel fled from before the Philistines, and fell down slain in mount Gilboa.

And the Philistines followed hard upon Saul and upon his sons: and the Philistines slew Jonathan, and Abinadab, and Melchishua, Saul's sons.

And the battle went sore against Saul, and the archers hit him; and he was sore wounded of the archers.

Then said Saul unto his armourbearer, Draw thy sword, and thrust me through therewith; lest these uncircumcised come and thrust me through, and abuse me. But his armourbearer would not: for he was sore afraid. Therefore Saul took a sword, and fell upon it.

And when his armourbearer saw that Saul was dead, he fell likewise upon his sword, and died with him.

So Saul died, and his three sons, and his armourbearer, and all his men, that same day together. (1 Samuel 31: 1-6.)

SAVIOR. (See Christ, God, Jesus, Redeemer.)

Sav'ior (written also saviour)—one of the titles of Jesus Christ, as the Redeemer of mankind.

SCRIBES. (See Pharisees.)

Scribes—a body of learned men associated with the Pharisees and the Sanhedrin in the religious government of the people of Judea in the time of Christ. They gave the Pharisees very able assistance in the persecution of Christ.

SCRIPTURES. (See Truth, Word, etc. See Appendix for History of the Bible and Bible Books.)

Scrip'tures—written things; specifically the Holy Scripture, or Scriptures or books of the Bible, which originally were in scripture or manuscript. The Holy Scriptures are the inspired word of God. They contain God's laws to mankind, as well as the various revelations of Himself and his plans for man, the gospels of His Son, and various rules and precepts. They are one of the bases of the Christian faith and contain all that is needful for man for the purpose of showing him God and for the conduct of his life and the outlining of his attitude toward God. They are divided into 66 different books, written by some forty men, under the direction and inspiration of God. These 66 books are consolidated into two parts—the Old Testament, containing the divine attitude and will prior to the coming of Christ; and the New Testament, containing the divine will and attitude after the coming of Christ.

REFERENCES.

Characteristics of Scripture.

Divinely Inspired:

Now these be the last words of David. David the son of Jesse said, and the man who was raised up on high, the anointed of the God of Jacob, and the sweet psalmist of Israel, said,

The Spirit of the Lord spake by me

and his word was in my tongue. (2 Samuel 23: 1, 2.)

And the Lord spake by his servants the prophets, saying. (2 Kings 21: 10.)

Thou camest down also upon mount Sinai, and spakest with them from heaven, and gavest them right judgments, and true laws, good statutes and commandments:

And madest known to them thy holy sabbath, and commandedst them precepts, statutes, and laws, by the hand of Moses thy servant. (Nehemiah 9: 13, 14.)

(Which he had promised afore by his prophets in the holy Scriptures.) (Romans 1: 2.)

And I was with you in weakness, and in fear, and in much trembling.

And my speech and my preaching was not with enticing words of man's wisdom, but in demonstration of the Spirit and of power:

That your faith should not stand in the wisdom of men, but in the power of God. (1 Corinthians 2: 3-5.)

Which things also we speak, not in the words which man's wisdom teacheth, but which the Holy Ghost teacheth; comparing spiritual things with spiritual. (1 Corinthians 2: 13.)

But she is happier if she so abide, after my judgment: and I think also that I have the Spirit of God. (1 Corinthians 7: 40.)

What! came the word of God out from you? or came it unto you only?

If any man think himself to be a prophet, or spiritual, let him acknowledge that the things that I write unto you are the commandments of the Lord. (1 Corinthians 14: 36, 37.)

But I certify you, brethren, that the gospel which was preached of me is not after man.

For I neither received it of man, neither was I taught it, but by the revelation of Jesus Christ. (Galatians 1: 11, 12.)

How that by revelation he made known unto me the mystery; (as I wrote afore in few words.) (Ephesians 3: 3.)

For this cause also thank we God without ceasing, because, when ye received the word of God which ye heard of us, ye received it not as the word of men, but, as it is in truth, the word of God, which effectually worketh also in you that believe. (1 Thessalonians 2: 13.)

All Scripture is given by inspiration of God, and is profitable for doctrine, for reproof, for correction, for instruction in righteousness. (2 Timothy 3: 16.)

Of which salvation the prophets have inquired and searched diligently, who prophesied of the grace that should come unto you.

Searching what, or what manner of time the Spirit of Christ which was in them did signify, when it testified beforehand the sufferings of Christ, and the glory that should follow.

Unto whom it was revealed, that not unto themselves, but unto us they did minister the things, which are now reported unto you by them that have preached the gospel unto you with the Holy Ghost sent down from heaven; which things the angels desire to look into. (1 Peter 1: 10-12.)

Knowing this first, that no prophecy of the Scripture is of any private interpretation.

For the prophecy came not in old time by the will of man: but holy men of God spake as they were moved by the Holy Ghost. (2 Peter 1: 20, 21.)

If we receive the witness of men, the witness of God is greater: for this is the witness of God which he has testified of his Son. (1 John 5: 9.)

Are for All Mankind:

The secret things belong unto the Lord our God: but those things which are revealed belong unto us and to our children for ever, that we may do all the words of this law. (Deuteronomy 29: 29.)

For this commandment which I command thee this day, it is not hidden from thee, neither is it far off.

It is not in heaven, that thou shouldest say, Who shall go up for us to heaven, and bring it unto us, that we may hear it, and do it?

Neither is it beyond the sea, that thou shouldest say, Who shall go over the sea for us, and bring it unto us, that we may hear it, and do it?

But the word is very nigh unto thee, in thy mouth, and in thy heart, that thou mayest do it. (Deuteronomy 30: 11-14.)

I write unto you, fathers, because ye have known him that is from the beginning. I write unto you, young men, because ye have overcome the wicked one. I write unto you, little children, because ye have known the Father.

I have written unto you, fathers, because ye have known him that is from the beginning. I have written unto you, young men, because ye are strong, and the word of God abideth in you, and ye have overcome the wicked one. (1 John 2: 13, 14.)

Efficacious:

My doctrine shall drop as the rain, my speech shall distil as the dew, as the small rain upon the tender herb, and as the showers upon the grass. (Deuteronomy 22: 2.)

I will worship toward thy holy temple, and praise thy name for thy lovingkindness and for thy truth: for thou hast magnified thy word above all thy name. (Psalm 138: 2.)

For as the rain cometh down and the snow from heaven, and returneth not thither, but watereth the earth, and maketh it bring forth and bud, that it may give seed to the sower, and bread to the eater:

So shall my word be that goeth forth out of my mouth; it shall not return unto me void, but it shall accomplish that which I please, and it shall prosper in the thing whereto I sent it. (Isaiah 55: 10, 11.)

Is not my word like as a fire? saith the Lord; and like a hammer that breaketh the rock in pieces? (Jeremiah 23: 29.)

For though I made you sorry with a letter, I do not repent, though I did repent; for I perceive that the same epistle hath made you sorry, though it were but for a season.

That I may not seem as if I would terrify you by letters.

For his letters, say they, are weighty and powerful; but his bodily presence is weak, and his speech contemptible.

Let such a one think this, that, such as we are in word by letters when we are absent, such will we be also in deed when we are present. (2 Corinthians 7: 8-11.)

And take the helmet of salvation, and the sword of the Spirit, which is the word of God. (Ephesians 6: 17.)

For the word of God is quick, and powerful, and sharper than any two-edged sword, piercing even to the dividing asunder of soul and spirit, and of the joints and marrow, and is a discerner of the thoughts and intents of the heart. (Hebrews 4: 12.)

Permanent and Fulfilled:

So these things shall be for a statute of judgment unto you throughout your generations in all your dwellings. (Numbers 35: 29.)

And it shall come to pass, when many evils and troubles are befallen them, that this song shall testify against them as a witness; for it shall not be forgotten out of the mouths of their seed: for I know their imagination which they go about, even now, before I have brought them into the land which I sware. (Deuteronomy 31: 21.)

The righteousness of thy testimonies is everlasting: give me understanding, and I shall live. (Psalm 119: 144.)

Concerning thy testimonies, I have known of old that thou hast founded them for ever. (Psalm 119: 152.)

The grass withereth, the flower fadeth: but the word of our God shall stand for ever. (Isaiah 40: 8.)

Think not that I am come to destroy the law, or the prophets: I am not come to destroy, but to fulfil.

For verily I say unto you, Till heaven and earth pass, one jot or one tittle shall in no wise pass from the law, till all be fulfilled. (Matthew 5: 17, 18.)

The law and the prophets were until John: since that time the kingdom of God is preached, and every man presseth into it.

And it is easier for heaven and earth to pass, than one tittle of the law to fall. (Luke 16: 16, 17.)

Heaven and earth shall pass away; but my words shall not pass away. (Luke 21: 33.)

And he said unto them, *These are the words which I spake unto you, while I was yet with you, that all things must be fulfilled, which were written in the law of Moses, and in the prophets, and in the psalms, concerning me.* (Luke 21: 44.)

If he called them gods, unto whom the word of God came, and the Scripture cannot be broken. (John 10: 35.)

But the word of the Lord endureth for ever. And this is the word which by the gospel is preached unto you. (1 Peter 1: 25.)

The Standard of Truth:

To the law and to the testimony: if they speak not according to this word, it is because there is no light in them. (Isaiah 8: 20.)

Then came to Jesus scribes and Pharisees, which were of Jerusalem, saying,

Why do thy disciples transgress the tradition of the elders? for they wash not their hands when they eat bread.

But he answered and said unto them, *Why do ye also transgress the commandment of God by your tradition?* (Matthew 15: 1-3.)

Howbeit in vain do they worship me, teaching for doctrines the commandments of men.

For laying aside the commandment of God, ye hold the tradition of men, as the washing of pots and cups: and many other such like things ye do.

And he said unto them, *Full well ye reject the commandment of God, that ye may keep your own tradition.* (Mark 7: 7-9.)

Making the word of God of none effect through your tradition, which ye have delivered: and many such like things do ye. (Mark 7: 13.)

For had ye believed Moses, ye would have believed me: for he wrote of me.

But if ye believe not his writings, how shall ye believe my words? (John 5: 46, 47.)

For he mightily convinced the Jews, and that publicly, shewing by the Scriptures that Jesus was Christ. (Acts 18: 28.)

Beware lest any man spoil you through philosophy and vain deceit, after the tradition of men, after the rudiments of the world, and not after Christ. (Colossians 2: 8.)

Hard to Understand:

But the word of the Lord was unto them precept upon precept, precept upon precept; line upon line, line upon line; here a little, and there a little; that they might go, and fall backward, and be broken, and snared, and taken. (Isaiah 28: 13.)

And account that the longsuffering of our Lord is salvation; even as our beloved brother Paul also according to the wisdom given unto him hath written unto you;

As also in all his epistles, speaking in them of these things; in which are some things hard to be understood, which they that are unlearned and unstable wrest, as they do also the other Scriptures, unto their own destruction. (2 Peter 3: 15, 16.)

Pure.

The words of the Lord are pure words: as silver tried in a furnace of earth, purified seven times. (Psalm 12: 6.)

Thy word is very pure: therefore thy servant loveth it. (Psalm 119: 140.)

Every word of God is pure: he is a shield unto them that put their trust in him. (Proverbs 30: 5.)

Now ye are clean through the word

which I have spoken unto you. (John 15: 3.)

Wherefore the law is holy, and the commandment holy, and just, and good. (Romans 7: 12.)

Illuminating:

Thy word is a lamp unto my feet, and a light unto my path. (Psalm 119: 105.)

For the commandment is a lamp; and the law is light; and reproofs of instruction are the way of life. (Proverbs 6: 23.)

We have also a more sure word of prophecy; whereunto ye do well that ye take heed, as unto a light that shineth in a dark place, until the day dawn, and the daystar arise in your hearts. (2 Peter 1: 19.)

Again, a new commandment I write unto you, which thing is true in him and in you: because the darkness is past, and the true light now shineth. (1 John 2: 8.)

Full of Wisdom:

Moreover by them is thy servant warned; and in keeping of them there is great reward.

Thou through thy commandments hast made me wiser than mine enemies; for they are ever with me.

I have more understanding than all my teachers: for thy testimonies are my meditation.

I understand more than the ancients, because I keep thy precepts. (Psalm 119: 98-100.)

Through thy precepts I get understanding: therefore I hate every false way. (Psalm 119: 104.)

The entrance of thy words giveth light; it giveth understanding unto the simple. (Psalm 119: 130.)

To know wisdom and instruction; to perceive the words of understanding;

To receive the instruction of wisdom, justice, and judgment, and equity;

To give subtilty to the simple, to the young man knowledge and discretion. (Proverbs 1: 2-4.)

Jesus saith unto them, *Have ye understood all these things?* They say unto him, Yea, Lord.

Then said he unto them, *Therefore every scribe which is instructed unto the kingdom of heaven, is like unto a man that is a householder, which bringeth forth out of his treasure things new and old.* (Matthew 13: 51, 52.)

And when he was alone, they that were about him with the twelve asked of him the parable.

And he said unto them, *Unto you it is given to know the mystery of the kingdom of God: but unto them that are without, all these things are done in parables:*

That seeing they may see, and not perceive; and hearing they may hear, and not understand; lest at any time they should be converted, and their sins should be forgiven them. (Mark 4: 10-12.)

And Jesus answering said unto them, *Do ye not therefore err, because ye know not the Scriptures, neither the power of God?* (Mark 12: 24.)

Now all these things happened unto them for ensamples: and they are written for our admonition upon whom the ends of the world are come. (1 Corinthians 10: 11.)

Whereby, when ye read, ye may understand my knowledge in the mystery of Christ. (Ephesians 3: 4.)

Satisfying:

Neither have I gone back from the

commandment of his lips; I have esteemed the words of his mouth more than my necessary food. (Job 23: 12.)

More to be desired are they than gold, yea, than much fine gold: sweeter also than honey and the honeycomb. (Psalm 19: 10.)

My soul breaketh for the longing that it hath unto thy judgments at all times. (Psalm 119: 20.)

And I will delight myself in thy commandments, which I have loved.

My hands also will I lift up unto thy commandments, which I have loved; and I will meditate in thy statutes. (Psalm 119: 47, 48.)

The law of thy mouth is better unto me than thousands of gold and silver. (Psalm 119: 72.)

Mine eyes fail for thy word, saying, When wilt thou comfort me? (Psalm 119: 82.)

How sweet are thy words unto my taste! yea, sweeter than honey to my mouth. (Psalm 119: 103.)

As newborn babes, desire the sincere milk of the word, that ye may grow thereby. (1 Peter 2: 2.)

Inspire Hope:

My soul fainteth for thy salvation: but I hope in thy word. (Psalm 119: 81.)

I prevented the dawning of the morning, and cried: I hoped in thy word. (Psalm 119: 147.)

For whatsoever things were written aforetime were written for our learning, that we through patience and comfort of the Scriptures might have hope. (Romans 15: 4.)

Inspire Joy:

The statutes of the Lord are right, rejoicing the heart: the commandment of the Lord is pure, enlightening the eyes. (Psalm 19: 8.)

I have rejoiced in the way of thy testimonies, as much' as in all riches. (Psalm 119: 14.)

I will delight myself in thy statutes; I will not forget thy word. (Psalm 119: 16.)

I rejoice at thy word, as one that findeth great spoil. (Psalm 119: 162.)

And these things write we unto you, that your joy may be full. (1 John 1: 4.)

Comforting and Consoling:

This is my comfort in my affliction: for thy word hath quickened me. (Psalm 119: 50.)

Unless thy law had been my delights, I should then have perished in mine affliction.

I will never forget thy precepts: for with them thou hast quickened me. (Psalm 119: 92, 93.)

So when they were dismissed, they came to Antioch: and when they had gathered the multitude together, they delivered the epistle:

Which when they had read, they rejoiced for the consolation. (Acts 15: 30, 31.)

Sanctifying and Saving:

Concerning the works of men, by the word of thy lips I have kept me from the paths of the destroyer. (Psalm 17: 4.)

Wherewithal shall a young man cleanse his way? by taking heed thereto according to thy word. (Psalm 119: 9.)

But these are written, that ye might believe that Jesus is the Christ, the Son of God; and that believing ye might have life through his name. (John 20: 31.)

For I am not ashamed of the gospel of Christ: for it is the power of God unto salvation to every one that believeth; to the Jew first, and also to the Greek. (Romans 1: 16.)

So then faith cometh by hearing, and hearing by the word of God. (Romans 10: 17.)

And that from a child thou hast known the holy Scriptures, which are able to make thee wise unto salvation through faith which is in Christ Jesus. (2 Timothy 3: 15.)

Wherefore lay apart all filthiness and superfluity of naughtiness, and receive with meekness the engrafted word, which is able to save your souls. (James 1: 21.)

Full of Instruction:

And thou shalt teach them diligently unto thy children, and shall talk of them when thou sittest in thine house, and when thou walkest by the way, and when thou liest down, and when thou risest up.

And thou shalt bind them for a sign upon thine hand, and they shall be as frontlets between thine eyes. (Deuteronomy 6: 7, 8.)

And they taught in Judah, and had the book of the law of the Lord with them, and went about throughout all the cities of Judah, and taught the people. (2 Chronicles 12: 9.)

For Ezra had prepared his heart to seek the law of the Lord, and to do it, and to teach in Israel statutes and judgments. (Ezra 7: 10.)

Also Jeshua, and Bani, and Sherebiah, Jamin, Akkub, Shabbethai, Hodijah, Maaseiah, Kelita, Azariah, Jozabad, Hanan, Pelaiah, and the Levites, caused the people to understand the law: and the people stood in their place.

So they read in the book in the law of God distinctly, and gave the sense, and caused them to understand the reading. (Nehemiah 8: 7, 8.)

For precept must be upon precept, precept upon precept; line upon line, line upon line; here a little, and there a little. (Isaiah 28: 10.)

I came near unto one of them that stood by, and asked him the truth of all this. So he told me, and made me know the interpretation of the things. (Daniel 7: 16.)

Then Jesus sent the multitude away, and went into the house, and his disciples came unto him, saying, Declare unto us the parable of the tares of the field. (Matthew 13: 36.)

And he called the multitude, and said unto them, *Hear, and understand.* (Matthew 15: 10.)

And he said unto them, *Know ye not this parable? and how then will ye know all parables?* (Mark 4: 13.)

And when he had called all the people unto him, he said unto them, *Hearken unto me every one of you, and understand.* (Mark 7: 14.)

And beginning at Moses and all the prophets, he expounded unto them in all the Scriptures the things concerning himself. (Luke 24: 27.)

Then opened he their understanding, that they might understand the Scriptures. (Luke 24: 45.)

And he said, How can I, except some man should guide me? And he desired Philip that he would come up and sit with him. (Acts 8: 31.)

And he began to speak boldly in the synagogue: whom when Aquila and Priscilla had heard, they took him unto them, and expounded unto him the way of God more perfectly. (Acts 18: 26.)

A Blessing to Nations.

Keep therefore and do them; for this is your wisdom and your understanding in the sight of the nations, which shall hear all these statutes, and say, Surely this great nation is a wise and understanding people. (Deuteronomy 4: 6.)

And what nation is there so great, that hath statutes and judgments so righteous as all this law, which I set before you this day? (Deuteronomy 4: 8.)

He sheweth his word unto Jacob, his statutes and his judgments unto Israel. (Psalm 147: 9.)

What advantage then hath the Jew? or what profit is there of circumcision?

Much every way: chiefly, because that unto them were committed the oracles of God. (Romans 3: 1, 2.)

Scripture Not to Be Altered.

Ye shall not add unto the word which I command you, neither shall ye diminish aught from it, that ye may keep the commandments of the Lord your God which I command you. (Deuteronomy 4: 2.)

What thing soever I command you, observe to do it; thou shalt not add thereto, nor diminish from it. (Deuteronomy 12: 32.)

Add thou not unto his words, lest he reprove thee, and thou be found a liar. (Proverbs 30: 6.)

For I testify unto every man that heareth the words of the prophecy of this book, If any man shall add unto these things, God shall add unto him the plagues that are written in this book.

And if any man shall take away from the words of the book of this prophecy, God shall take away his part out of the book of life, and out of the holy city, and from the things which are written in this book. (Revelation 22: 18, 19.)

SEARCHER OF HEARTS. (See God.)

Search'er of Hearts—one of the titles and attributes of God.

References.—1 Chronicles 28: 9; 29: 17; Psalm 7: 9; Jeremiah 17: 10.

SECOND COMING OF CHRIST. (See Millennium.)

SECRET.

Se'cret—hidden; concealed; unseen; unknown. This word is used in the Bible to indicate several things, the more important of which are: things that God keeps from the knowledge of man; things that are gradually revealed by Him; all things, no matter how well concealed they are by man, are known to God.

REFERENCES.

Secret Things Belong to God.

The secret things belong unto the Lord our God: but those things which are revealed belong unto us and to our children for ever, that we may do all the words of this law. (Deuteronomy 15: 8.)

Hast thou heard the secret of God? and dost thou restrain wisdom to thyself? (Job 15: 8.)

Secrets Revealed by God.

The secret of the Lord is with them that fear him; and he will shew them his covenant. (Psalm 25: 14.)

For the froward is abomination to the Lord: but his secret is with the righteous. (Proverbs 3: 32.)

Surely the Lord God will do nothing, but he revealeth his secret unto his servants the prophets. (Amos 3: 7.)

At that time Jesus answered and said, *I thank thee, O Father, Lord of heaven and earth, because thou hast hid these things from the wise and prudent, and hast revealed them unto babes.* (Matthew 11: 25.)

That it might be fulfilled which was spoken by the prophet, saying, I will open my mouth in parables; I will utter things which have been kept secret from the foundation of the world. (Matthew 13: 35.)

Now to him that is of power to stablish you according to my gospel, and the preaching of Jesus Christ, according to the revelation of the mystery, which was kept secret since the world began,

But now is made manifest, and by the scriptures of the prophets, according to the commandment of the everlasting God, made known to all nations for the obedience of faith. (Romans 16: 25, 26.)

All Secrets Known to God.

Shall not God search this out? for he knoweth the secrets of the heart. (Psalm 44: 21.)

Thou hast set our iniquities before thee, our secret sins in the light of thy countenance. (Psalm 90: 8.)

For God shall bring every work into judgment, with every secret thing, whether it be good, or whether it be evil. (Ecclesiastes 12: 14.)

That thine alms may be in secret: and thy Father which seeth in secret himself shall reward thee openly. (Matthew 6: 4.)

For there is nothing hid, which shall not be manifested; neither was any thing kept secret, but that it should come abroad. (Mark 4: 22.)

In the day when God shall judge the secrets of men by Jesus Christ according to my gospel. (Romans 2: 16.)

Some Secrets Not to Be Revealed.

Debate thy cause with thy neighbour himself; and discover not a secret to another:

Lest he that heareth it put thee to shame, and thine infamy turn not away. (Proverbs 25: 9, 10.)

Moreover if thy brother shall trespass against thee, go and tell him his fault between thee and him alone: if he shall hear thee, thou hast gained thy brother. (Matthew 18: 15.)

SELF-DENIAL.

Self-De-ni′al—the act of denying one's own self; the act of forbearing to gratify one's desires.

Self-denial is one of the foremost of the Christian graces. The Scriptures teach us to cultivate it as one of the virtues that lead us into the path God would have us tread, and we are given as our Great Example the self-denial of the Master. Nevertheless, with these admonitions and with the model of Jesus mankind finds self-denial one of the most difficult of the graces to attain, for the reason that man is by nature selfish and inclined to seek his own pleasure and comfort before giving a thought to that of his neighbor.

REFERENCES.

General.

When thou sittest to eat with a ruler, consider diligently what is before thee:

And put a knife to thy throat, if thou be a man given to appetite.

Be not desirous of his dainties: for they are deceitful meat.

Labour not to be rich: cease from thine own wisdom.

Wilt thou set thine eyes upon that which is not? for riches certainly make themselves wings; they fly away as an eagle toward heaven. (Proverbs 23: 1-5.)

But they said, We will drink no wine: for Jonadab the son of Rechab our father commanded us, saying, Ye shall drink no wine, neither ye, nor your sons for ever:

Neither shall ye build house, nor sow seed, nor plant vineyard, nor have any: but all your days ye shall dwell in tents; that ye may live many days in the land where ye be strangers.

Thus have we obeyed the voice of Jonadab the son of Rechab our father in all that he hath charged us, to drink no wine all our days, we, our wives, our sons, nor our daughters;

Nor to build houses for us to dwell in; neither have we vineyard, nor field, nor seed:

But we have dwelt in tents, and have obeyed, and done according to all that Jonadab our father commanded us. (Jeremiah 35: 6-10.)

He answereth and saith unto them, He that hath two coats, let him impart to him that hath none; and he that hath meat, let him do likewise. (Luke 3: 11.)

So likewise, whosoever he be of you that forsaketh not all that he hath, he cannot be my disciple. (Luke 14: 33.)

And sold their possessions and goods, and parted them to all men, as every man had need. (Acts 2: 45.)

Let not sin therefore reign in your mortal body, that ye should obey it in the lusts thereof.

Neither yield ye your members as instruments of unrighteousness unto sin: but yield yourselves unto God, as those that are alive from the dead, and your members as instruments of righteousness unto God. (Romans 6: 12, 13.)

For if ye live after the flesh, ye shall die: but if ye through the Spirit do mortify the deeds of the body, ye shall live. (Romans 8: 13.)

For meat destroy not the work of God. All things indeed are pure; but it is evil for that man who eateth with offence.

It is good neither to eat flesh, nor to drink wine, nor any thing whereby thy brother stumbleth, or is offended, or is made weak. (Romans 14: 20, 21.)

We then that are strong ought to bear the infirmities of the weak, and not to please ourselves.

Let every one of us please his neighbour for his good to edification.

For even Christ pleased not himself; but, as it is written, The reproaches of them that reproached thee fell on me. (Romans 15: 1-3.)

All things are lawful for me, but all things are not expedient: all things are lawful for me, but all things edify not. (1 Corinthians 10: 23.)

Teaching us that, denying ungodliness and worldly lusts, we should live soberly, righteously, and godly, in this present world. (Titus 2: 12.)

Christ's Example of Self-Denial.

For even Christ pleased not himself; but, as it is written, The reproaches of them that reproached thee fell on me. (Romans 15: 3.)

But made himself of no reputation, and took upon him the form of a servant, and was made in the likeness of men:

And being found in fashion as a man, he humbled himself, and became obedient unto death, even the death of the cross. (Philippians 2: 7, 8.)

Self-Denial to Be Followed.

And he that taketh not his cross, and followeth after me, is not worthy of me. (Matthew 10: 38.)

Then said Jesus unto his disciples, *If any man will come after me, let him deny himself, and take up his cross, and follow me.* (Matthew 16: 24.)

SELF-EXAMINATION.

SELF-EX-AM'I-NA'TION — an examination into one's own conduct, motives, and state, with particular reference to religious matters. The Bible teaches constant self-examination as a means of attaining the virtues and graces.

REFERENCES.

Stand in awe, and sin not: commune with your own heart upon your bed, and be still. Selah. (Psalm 4: 4.)

Let us search and try our ways, and turn again to the Lord. (Lamentations 3: 40.)

But let a man examine himself, and so let him eat of that bread, and drink of that cup. (1 Corinthians 11: 28.)

Examine yourselves, whether ye be in the faith; prove your own selves. Know ye not your own selves, how that Jesus Christ is in you, except ye be reprobates? (2 Corinthians 13: 5.)

SELFISHNESS. (See Self-Denial.)

SELF'ISH-NESS—exclusive regard for one's own interest or happiness; a supreme sort of self-love or self-interest which leads its possessor to ignore purposely the interests and happiness, rights and privileges of others. The Bible calls attention to selfishness as a very great sin and warns us to beware of it, as a lure and snare of the Evil One.

REFERENCES.

Yea, they are greedy dogs which can never have enough, and they are shepherds that cannot understand: they all look to their own way, every one for his gain, from his quarter. (Isaiah 56: 11.)

We then that are strong ought to bear the infirmities of the weak, and not to please ourselves. (Romans 15: 1.)

Let no man seek his own, but every

man another's wealth. (1 Corinthians 10. 24.)

And that he died for all, that they which live should not henceforth live unto themselves, but unto him which died for them, and rose again. (2 Corinthians 5: 15.)

Look not every man on his own things, but every man also on the things of others. (Philippians 2: 4.)

If ye fulfil the royal law according to the scripture, Thou shalt love thy neighbour as thyself, ye do well. (James 2: 8.)

SELF-WILL.

SELF-WILL—one's own will as opposed to that of others; obstinacy. Another one of the sins of self.

REFERENCES.

Lift not up your horn on high: speak not with a stiff neck.

For promotion cometh neither from the east, nor from the west, nor from the south.

But God is the judge: he putteth down one, and setteth up another. (Psalm 75: 5-7.)

But chiefly them that walk after the flesh in the lust of uncleanness, and despise government. Presumptuous are they, selfwilled, they are not afraid to speak evil of dignities. (2 Peter 2: 10.)

SENNACHERIB.

SEN-NACH'E-RIB—a noted king of Assyria. He ascended the throne about 702 B.C., and one of his first achievements was the reduction of Babylon and the overthrow of the Babylonian empire. Later he transferred his attentions to Palestine, and threatened King Hezekiah of Judah, whereupon the prophet Isaiah told Hezekiah to have no fear, as the Lord would attend to Sennacherib. The result was what seems to have been a sudden pestilence which carried off 185,000 of the Assyrian host in a night. Sennacherib returned to Assyria, and soon after was murdered by his sons.

SERVANTS.

SERV'ANTS—persons that perform tasks or do work for others; commonly, those who perform menial offices, although by no means necessarily so.

REFERENCES.

But the seventh day is the sabbath of the Lord thy God: in it thou shalt not do any work, thou, nor thy son, nor thy daughter, thy manservant, nor thy maidservant, nor thy cattle, nor thy stranger that is within thy gates. (Exodus 20: 10.)

A son honoureth his father, and a servant his master: if then I be a father, where is mine honour? and if I be a master, where is my fear? saith the Lord of hosts unto you, O priests, that despise my name. And ye say, Wherein have we despised thy name? (Malachi 1: 6.)

Servants, be obedient to them that are your masters according to the flesh, with fear and trembling, in singleness of your heart, as unto Christ;

Not with eyeservice, as men-pleasers; but as the servants of Christ, doing the will of God from the heart. (Ephesians 6: 5, 6.)

Servants, obey in all things your masters according to the flesh; not with eyeservice, as men-pleasers; but in singleness of heart, fearing God:

And whatsoever ye do, do it heartily, as to the Lord, and not unto men;

Knowing that of the Lord ye shall receive the reward of the inheritance: for ye serve the Lord Christ. (Colossians 3: 22-24.)

Let as many servants as are under

the yoke count their own masters worthy of all honour, that the name of God and his doctrine be not blasphemed. (1 Timothy 6: 1.)

SHADRACH. (See Abednego.)

SHA'DRACH—a form of a Chaldee word meaning "circuit of the sun." It was the name given by the Babylonians to Hannaniah, one of the children of Israel in captivity in Babylon and cast into the fiery furnace, from which they were divinely protected.

SHALMANESER.

SHAL'MA-NE'SER—a form of a Syro-Chaldee word meaning "Salman is gracious." Shalmaneser was a noted king of Assyria. He reigned only a few years, but in that time gave the Jews great trouble. While besieging Samaria a rebellion broke out in Assyria and Shalmaneser was deposed. He, however, carried the ten tribes of the kingdom of Israel away into captivity.

SHARON, The Rose of.

SHAR'ON—a form of a Hebrew word meaning "a plain." Sharon was a most beautiful tract of country lying between the high hills of Judea and Samaria and the Mediterranean Sea. It was noted for its richness. "A rose of Sharon" was a Hebrew figure for something that was most beautiful. The title has been applied to Christ and His Church.

SHEBA.

SHE'BA. There are a number of persons and places in the Bible called Sheba. The more important probably is the Queen of Sheba who visited Solomon. The exact location of her kingdom is lost. Some commentators think it was in the southern part of Arabia. Still others believe it to have been in Ethiopia, south of Egypt.

SHEEP AND SHEPHERD.

SHEEP. We find a number of references in the Bible to sheep. They were much used by the Jews in the sacrificial age for offerings.

The comparison of the Church to sheep is an easy one to understand by reason of the flock nature of both the Church and the animals in question and the necessity for a shepherd for both. A sheep—or rather a lamb—is also an emblem of Christ—"Behold the Lamb of God that taketh away the sin of the world"—the Jews having been used to the sin-offering of a lamb.

REFERENCES.

The Church Compared to Sheep.

O God, why hast thou cast us off for ever? why doth thine anger smoke against the sheep of thy pasture? (Psalm 74: 1.)

So we thy people and sheep of thy pasture will give thee thanks for ever: we will shew forth thy praise to all generations. (Psalm 79: 13.)

For he is our God; and we are the people of his pasture, and the sheep of his hand. To day if ye will hear his voice. (Psalm 95: 7.)

Know ye that the Lord he is God: it is he that hath made us, and not we ourselves; we are his people, and the sheep of his pasture. (Psalm 100: 3.)

Son of man, prophesy against the shepherds of Israel, prophesy, and say unto them, Thus saith the Lord God unto the shepherds; Woe be to the shepherds of Israel that do feed themselves! should not the shepherds feed the flocks? (Ezekiel 34: 2.)

For thus saith the Lord God; Behold, I, even I, will both search my sheep, and seek them out.

As a shepherd seeketh out his flock in the day that he is among his sheep that are scattered; so will I seek out my sheep, and will deliver them out of all places where they have been scattered in the cloudy and dark day.

And I will bring them out from the people, and gather them from the countries, and will bring them to their own land, and feed them upon the mountains of Israel by the rivers, and in all the inhabited places of the country.

I will feed them in a good pasture, and upon the high mountains of Israel shall their fold be: there shall they lie in a good fold, and in a fat pasture shall they feed upon the mountains of Israel.

I will feed my flock, and I will cause them to lie down, saith the Lord God.

I will seek that which was lost, and bring again that which was driven away, and will bind up that which was broken, and will strengthen that which was sick: but I will destroy the fat and the strong; I will feed them with judgment. (Ezekiel 34: 11-16.)

But he answered and said, *I am not sent but unto the lost sheep of the house of Israel.* (Matthew 15: 24.)

And before him shall be gathered all nations: and he shall separate them one from another, as a shepherd divideth his sheep from the goats. (Matthew 25: 32.)

But he that entereth in by the door is the shepherd of the sheep.

To him the porter openeth; and the sheep hear his voice: and he calleth his own sheep by name, and leadeth them out.

And when he putteth forth his own sheep, he goeth before them, and the sheep follow him: for they know his voice. (John 10: 2-4.)

For ye were as sheep going astray; but are now returned unto the Shepherd and Bishop of your souls. (1 Peter 2: 25.)

Sheep and Lamb as Emblem of Christ.

He was oppressed, and he was afflicted, yet he opened not his mouth: he is brought as a lamb to the slaughter, and as a sheep before her shearers is dumb, so he openeth not his mouth. (Isaiah 53: 7.)

The next day John seeth Jesus coming unto him, and saith, Behold the Lamb of God, which taketh away the sin of the world. (John 1: 29.)

Christ the Good Shepherd.

He shall feed his flock like a shepherd: he shall gather the lambs with his arm, and carry them in his bosom, and shall gently lead those that are with young. (Isaiah 40: 11.)

For, lo, I will raise up a shepherd in the land, which shall not visit those that be cut off, neither shall seek the young one, nor heal that that is broken, nor feed that that standeth still: but he shall eat the flesh of the fat, and tear their claws in pieces. (Zechariah 11: 16.)

I am the good shepherd, and know my sheep, and am known of mine. (John 10: 14.)

Now the God of peace, that brought again from the dead our Lord Jesus, that great shepherd of the sheep, through the blood of the everlasting covenant. (Hebrews 13: 20.)

For ye were as sheep going astray; but are now returned unto the Shepherd and Bishop of your souls. (1 Peter 2: 25.)

And when the chief Shepherd shall appear, ye shall receive a crown of glory that fadeth not away. (1 Peter 5: 4.)

SHIBBOLETH.

Shib'bo-leth—a form of a Hebrew word meaning "a stream." After Jephthah defeated the Ammonites the tribe of Ephraim took offense at Jephthah's conduct of the campaign and made war. The Ephraimites were defeated, and in order to cut them off Jephthah's people took possession of the fords of the

Jordan. They allowed no one to pass unmolested unless they could pronounce the word shibboleth and give the full phonetic value to the first two letters, a thing which the Ephraimites, because of a difference in speech, could not do, pronouncing the word "sibboleth." As a result, all that pronounced the word in this way were put to death.

Reference.—Judges 12: 6.

SIDON. (See Tyre.)

Si′don—a very ancient city of Phœnicia, situated on the shore of the Mediterranean Sea. It was a part of the country assigned to the tribe of Asher when Canaan was divided, but Asher was never able to conquer it, and it retained its independence until the whole of the country fell into the hands of the Eastern conquerors. Sidon was noted for the skill of its workmen, especially in textile fabrics and in the metals. One of its colonies was the city of Tyre, which later overshadowed the mother city in importance and generally is named first.

SILOAM.

Si-lo′am—a form of a Hebrew word meaning "sent." The pool of Siloam is fed by subterranean springs, which have been flowing for centuries and still continue to flow. It is one of the few places mentioned in Scripture actually located in these times, especially those places in and around Jerusalem.

SIMEON.

Sim′e-on—a form of a Hebrew word meaning "favorable hearing" or "hearkening." Simeon was the name of the second son of Jacob and Leah and gave his name to one of the twelve tribes. It was never remarkable for either its people or its deeds. Simeon was also the name of the aged Jew who, when Jesus was presented at the Temple, recognized him as the Messiah and spoke those wonderful words we find in Luke 2: 29-32. By some commentators he is supposed to have been a famous Pharisee teacher—the father of Hillel and the grandfather of Gamaliel; but there is no evidence to warrant such a conclusion.

Reference.—Luke 2: 25-35.

SIMON.

Si′mon—the same name as Simeon, with the same derivations and meaning. We find in the Bible a number of persons bearing the name of Simon, the more important of whom are (1) Simon, the apostle, whom Jesus named Peter; (2) Simon surnamed Zelotes (the Zealot); (3) Simon the son of Mary and Cleophas; (4) Simon the leper; (5) Simon the Cyrenian; (6) Simon the tanner; (7) Simon Magus.

(1) For history of Simon Peter see article on Peter.

(2) Simon Zelotes was one of the apostles, but we know little or nothing about him. By some he has been identified with Simon the son of Cleophas, but of this there is only conjecture.

(3) Simon the son of Cleophas and Mary was a kinsman of Jesus. Tradition says that he was crucified in Palestine about A.D. 100.

(4) Simon the leper seems to have been a relative of Lazarus whom Jesus raised from the dead. After the event he gave a feast at his house. He seems to have been cured of the leprosy, else he could not have mixed publicly with the people.

(5) Simon the Cyrenian was a man who followed Jesus and gave his two sons, Rufus and Alexander, to the cause of the Master. Probably for this reason the Roman soldiery picked him out as a good person to be made to carry the Master's cross, by which act he is best known to readers of the Bible. After the crucifixion he seems to have dwelt in Rome, where he was held in high regard by Christians.

(6) Simon the tanner was a resident of Joppa, and Paul dwelt in his house for some time. He doubtless was a disciple of Paul's.

(7) Simon Magus was a resident of a city of Samaria, who had been practicing incantations and what was then understood to be forms of magic. He doubtless was an adept in the art of hoodwinking and fooling the people, much the same as so-called spiritualists hoodwink and fool them nowadays. He had gained considerable fame, and was regarded as having power coming from God. He was baptized by Philip, and when he saw Peter and John communicating the Holy Ghost by the laying-on of hands, he sought to buy the

power with money and suffered tremendous rebuke from Peter. After this he disappears from Scripture.

SIN. (See Confession, Repentance, Redemption, etc.)

SIN—transgression of the divine law, or want of conformity to the will of God.

Theologically, sin is divided into two sorts—original sin and actual sin. Original sin is that inborn tendency to do wrong things by which our nature is disordered and our inclinations made contrary to the law of God. This is the sin transmitted to his posterity by Adam by reason of the Fall. Actual sin is the direct violation of God's laws and commands in daily evidence in human life. It may be divided as follows: sins of omission—the leaving undone of things that should be done; sins of commission—the doing of things against which there are positive commands of God; sins of infirmity—sins committed through weakness of the flesh, ignorance, etc.; secret sins—those committed in secret, or which we do not see because of spiritual blindness or prejudice; sins of presumption—sins boldly committed and in full knowledge of their character and with full knowledge of their punishment. The sin known as the unpardonable sin has given much thought to theologians and been the subject of much debate and comment as to its nature. The best of opinion identifies it with the sin against the Holy Ghost, or the imputation of the acts, gifts, and influences of the Holy Ghost to Satan. In this connection it might be well to say that those who worry lest they have committed it may regard their anxiety as groundless, since the nature of the sin presupposes a state of the soul where there is no fear of God and no anxiety regarding repentance and no faith in Jesus Christ. It is impossible that such a condition can exist in the breast of any Christian.

REFERENCES.

The Nature of Sin.

Remember, and forget not, how thou provokedst the Lord thy God to wrath in the wilderness: from the day that thou didst depart out of the land of Egypt, until ye came unto this place, ye have been rebellious against the Lord. (Deuteronomy 9: 7.)

Whosoever he be that doth rebel against thy commandment, and will not hearken unto thy words in all that thou commandest him, he shall be put to death: only be strong and of a good courage. (Joshua 1: 18.)

The thought of foolishness is sin: and the scorner is an abomination to men. (Proverbs 24: 9.)

And he that doubteth is damned if he eat, because he eateth not of faith: for whatsoever is not of faith is sin. (Romans 14: 23.)

Therefore to him that knoweth to do good, and doeth it not, to him it is sin. (James 4: 17.)

Whosoever committeth sin transgresseth also the law: for sin is the transgression of the law. (1 John 3: 4.)

All unrighteousness is sin: and there is a sin not unto death. (1 John 5: 17.)

Origin of Sin.

Now the serpent was more subtile than any beast of the field which the Lord God had made. And he said unto the woman, Yea, hath God said, Ye shall not eat of every tree of the garden?

And the woman said unto the serpent, We may eat of the fruit of the trees of the garden:

But of the fruit of the tree which is in the midst of the garden, God hath said, Ye shall not eat of it, neither shall ye touch it, lest ye die.

And the serpent said unto the woman, Ye shall not surely die:

For God doth know that in the day ye eat thereof, then your eyes shall be opened, and ye shall be as gods, knowing good and evil.

And when the woman saw that the tree was good for food, and that it was pleasant to the eyes, and a tree to be desired to make one wise, she took of the fruit thereof, and did eat, and gave also unto her husband with her; and he did eat.

And the eyes of them both were opened, and they knew that they were naked; and they sewed fig leaves together, and made themselves aprons.

And they heard the voice of the Lord God walking in the garden in the cool of the day: and Adam and his wife hid themselves from the presence of the Lord God amongst the trees of the garden. (Genesis 3: 1-8.)

But those things which proceed out of the mouth come forth from the heart; and they defile the man.

For out of the heart proceed evil thoughts, murders, adulteries, fornications, thefts, false witness, blasphemies. (Matthew 15: 18, 19.)

Ye are of your father the devil, and the lusts of your father ye will do. .He was a murderer from the beginning, and abode not in the truth, because there is no truth in him. When he speaketh a lie, he speaketh of his own: for he is a liar, and the father of it. (John 8: 44.)

Wherefore, as by one man sin entered into the world, and death by sin; and so death passed upon all men, for that all have sinned:

For until the law sin was in the world: but sin is not imputed when there is no law.

Nevertheless death reigned from Adam to Moses, even over them that had not sinned after the similitude of Adam's transgression, who is the figure of him that was to come. (Romans 5: 12-14.)

He that committeth sin is of the devil; for the devil sinneth from the beginning. For this purpose the Son of God was manifested, that he might destroy the works of the devil. (1 John 3: 8.)

Sin's Characteristics.

Righteousness exalteth a nation: but sin is a reproach to any people. (Proverbs 14: 34.)

The way of the wicked is an abomination unto the Lord: but he loveth him that followeth after righteousness. (Proverbs 15: 9.)

Come now, and let us reason together, saith the Lord: though your sins be as scarlet, they shall be as white as snow; though they be red like crimson, they shall be as wool. (Isaiah 1: 18.)

But your iniquities have separated between you and your God, and your sins have hid his face from you, that he will not hear.

For your hands are defiled with blood, and your fingers with iniquity; your lips have spoken lies, your tongue hath muttered perverseness. (Isaiah 59: 2, 3.)

Howbeit, I sent unto you all my servants the prophets, rising early and sending them, saying, Oh, do not this abominable thing that I hate.

But they hearkened not, nor inclined their ear to turn from their wickedness, to burn no incense unto other gods. (Jeremiah 44: 4, 5.)

And have no fellowship with the unfruitful works of darkness, but rather reprove them. (Ephesians 5: 11.)

But exhort one another daily, while it is called To day; lest any of you be hardened through the deceitfulness of sin. (Hebrews 3: 13.)

While it is said, To day if ye will hear

his voice, harden not your hearts, as in the provocation. (Hebrews 3: 15.)

How much more shall the blood of Christ, who through the eternal Spirit offered himself without spot to God, purge your conscience from dead works to serve the living God? (Hebrews 9: 14.)

Universality of Sin among Mankind.

What is man, that he should be clean? and he which is born of a woman, that he should be righteous? (Job 15: 14.)

How then can man be justified with God? or how can he be clean that is born of a woman? (Job 25: 4.)

Behold, I was shapen in iniquity; and in sin did my mother conceive me. (Psalm 51: 5.)

What then? are we better than they? No, in no wise: for we have before proved both Jews and Gentiles, that they are all under sin;

As it is written, There is none righteous, no, not one. (Romans 3: 9, 10.)

If we say that we have no sin, we deceive ourselves, and the truth is not in us. (1 John 1: 8.)

If we say that we have not sinned, we make him a liar, and his word is not in us. (1 John 1: 10.)

But the scripture hath concluded all under sin, that the promise by faith of Jesus Christ might be given to them that believe. (Galatians 3: 22.)

Christ Alone Sinless.

For he hath made him to be sin for us, who knew no sin; that we might be made the righteousness of God in him. (2 Corinthians 5: 21.)

For we have not an high priest which cannot be touched with the feeling of our infirmities; but was in all points tempted like as we are, yet without sin. (Hebrews 4: 15.)

For such an high priest became us, who is holy, harmless, undefiled, separate from sinners, and made higher than the heavens;

Who needeth not daily, as those high priests, to offer up sacrifice, first for his own sins, and then for the people's: for this he did once, when he offered up himself. (Hebrews 7: 26, 27.)

And ye know that he was manifested to take away our sins; and in him is no sin. (1 John 3: 5.)

Christ's Blood Redeems from Sin.

The next day John seeth Jesus coming unto him, and saith, Behold the Lamb of God, which taketh away the sin of the world. (John 1: 29.)

In whom we have redemption through his blood, the forgiveness of sins, according to the riches of his grace. (Ephesians 1: 7.)

But if we walk in the light, as he is in the light, we have fellowship one with another, and the blood of Jesus Christ his Son cleanseth us from all sin. (1 John 1: 7.)

And ye know that he was manifested to take away our sins; and in him is no sin. (1 John 3: 5.)

Repentance and Confession of Sin.

For I will declare mine iniquity; I will be sorry for my sin. (Psalm 38: 18.)

He that covereth his sins shall not prosper: but whoso confesseth and forsaketh them shall have mercy. (Proverbs 28: 13.)

A voice was heard upon the high places, weeping and supplications of the children of Israel: for they have perverted their way, and they have forgotten the Lord their God.

Return, ye backsliding children, and I will heal your backslidings. Behold, we come unto thee, for thou art the Lord our God. (Jeremiah 3: 21, 22.)

If we confess our sins, he is faithful and just to forgive us our sins, and to cleanse us from all unrighteousness. (1 John 1: 9.)

The Fight against Sin.

With Prayer:

Keep back thy servant also from presumptuous sins; let them not have dominion over me: then shall I be upright, and I shall be innocent from the great transgression. (Psalm 19: 13.)

I said, I will take heed to my ways, that I sin not with my tongue: I will keep my mouth with a bridle, while the wicked is before me. (Psalm 39: 1.)

Wash me thoroughly from mine iniquity, and cleanse me from my sin.

For I acknowledge my transgressions: and my sin is ever before me.

Against thee, thee only, have I sinned, and done this evil in thy sight: that thou mightest be justified when thou speakest, and be clear when thou judgest. (Psalm 51: 2-4.)

Search me, O God, and know my heart: try me, and know my thoughts:

And see if there be any wicked way in me, and lead me in the way everlasting. (Psalm 139: 23, 24.)

And forgive us our debts, as we forgive our debtors.

And lead us not into temptation, but deliver us from evil: For thine is the kingdom, and the power, and the glory, for ever. Amen. (Matthew 6: 12, 13.)

With Mortifying the Flesh:

For if ye live after the flesh, ye shall die: but if ye through the Spirit do mortify the deeds of the body, ye shall live. (Romans 8: 13.)

Mortify therefore your members which are upon the earth; fornication, uncleanness, inordinate affection, evil concupiscence, and covetousness, which is idolatry. (Colossians 3: 5.)

With Striving:

Ye have not yet resisted unto blood, striving against sin. (Hebrews 12: 4.)

Punishment of Sin.

But of the tree of the knowledge of good and evil, thou shalt not eat of it: for in the day that thou eatest thereof thou shalt surely die. (Genesis 2: 17.)

Behold, all souls are mine; as the soul of the father, so also the soul of the son is mine: the soul that sinneth, it shall die. (Ezekiel 18: 4.)

For the wages of sin is death; but the gift of God is eternal life through Jesus Christ our Lord. (Romans 6: 23.)

Now the works of the flesh are manifest, which are these; Adultery, fornication, uncleanness, lasciviousness,

Idolatry, witchcraft, hatred, variance, emulations, wrath, strife, seditions, heresies,

Envyings, murders, drunkenness, revellings, and such like: of the which I tell you before, as I have also told you in time past, that they which do such things shall not inherit the kingdom of God. (Galatians 5: 19-21.)

For this ye know, that no whoremonger, nor unclean person, nor covetous man, who is an idolater, hath an inheritance in the kingdom of Christ and of God. (Ephesians 5: 5.)

Then when lust hath conceived, it bringeth forth sin: and sin, when it is finished, bringeth forth death. (James 1: 15.)

And there shall in no wise enter into it any thing that defileth, neither whatsoever worketh abomination, or maketh a lie: but they which are written in the Lamb's book of life. (Revelation 21: 27.)

SINAI.

SI'NAI OR SI'NA-I—a word of obscure origin, given as a name to the mountains and desert forming part of the peninsula between the gulfs of Suez and Akabah. The region is barren, mountainous, and uninviting. Here on one of the half dozen great peaks that jut toward heaven the Law was delivered to Moses. Which one of the peaks it was, however, we have no means of knowing.

SLANDER.

SLAN'DER—a false or untruthful report or tale maliciously uttered or told with the intention of doing injury to the peace of mind or reputation of another; also the act of telling or uttering such things. Slander is a direct violation of the commandment: "Thou shalt not bear false witness against thy neighbor." It is a deadly sin, since it often ruins character and reputation. There will always be people who will believe a false report about another, and even a rectification of the original report will never reach all who heard it. The Bible commands us in no uncertain words not to slander our fellows.

REFERENCES.

Warnings against Slander.

Thou shalt not bear false witness against thy neighbour. (Exodus 20: 16.)

Thou shalt not raise a false report: put not thine hand with the wicked to be an unrighteous witness. (Exodus 23: 1.)

Keep thy tongue from evil, and thy lips from speaking guile. (Psalm 34: 13.)

Thou sittest and speakest against thy brother; thou slanderest thine own mother's son.

These things hast thou done, and I kept silence; thou thoughtest that I was altogether such a one as thyself: but I will reprove thee, and set them in order before thine eyes. (Psalm 50: 20, 21.)

Whoso privily slandereth his neighbour, him will I cut off: him that hath a high look and a proud heart will I not suffer. (Psalm 101: 5.)

He that hideth hatred with lying lips, and he that uttereth a slander, is a fool. (Proverbs 10: 18.)

Take ye heed every one of his neighbour, and trust ye not in any brother: for every brother will utterly supplant, and every neighbour will walk with slanders. (Jeremiah 9: 4.)

Let all bitterness, and wrath, and anger, and clamour, and evil speaking, be put away from you, with all malice. (Ephesians 4: 31.)

Even so must their wives be grave, not slanderers, sober, faithful in all things. (1 Timothy 3: 11.)

Effects of and Conduct Under Slander.

He that covereth a transgression seeketh love; but he that repeateth a matter separateth very friends. (Proverbs 17: 9.)

Where no wood is, there the fire goeth out: so where there is no talebearer, the strife ceaseth.

As coals are to burning coals, and wood to fire; so is a contentious man to kindle strife.

The words of a talebearer are as wounds, and they go down into the innermost parts of the belly. (Proverbs 26: 20-22.)

Blessed are ye, when men shall revile you, and persecute you, and shall say all manner of evil against you falsely, for my sake.

Rejoice, and be exceeding glad: for great is your reward in heaven: for so persecuted they the prophets which were before you. (Matthew 5: 11, 12.)

And labour, working with our own hands: being reviled, we bless; being persecuted, we suffer it:

Being defamed, we intreat: we are made as the filth of the world, and are the offscouring of all things unto this day. (1 Corinthians 4: 12, 13.)

SLOTHFULNESS. (See Diligence.)

SLOTH'FUL-NESS—the state or quality of being indolent, inactive, lazy, without diligence. Slothfulness is a sin we are warned against in the Bible.

References.—See references under Diligence.

SOBRIETY. (See Drunkards, Temperance, etc.)

SO-BRI'E-TY—the state or quality of being sober. Sobriety means many other things besides soberness with relation to the use of strong drink. It means temperance of thought and action, calmness, seriousness, gravity, habitual freedom from overmuch enthusiasm, etc.

REFERENCES.

For I say, through the grace given unto me, to every man that is among you, not to think of himself more highly than he ought to think; but to think soberly, according as God hath dealt to every man the measure of faith. (Romans 12: 3.)

Therefore let us not sleep, as do others; but let us watch and be sober. (1 Thessalonians 5: 6.)

In like manner also, that women adorn themselves in modest apparel, with shamefacedness and sobriety; not with broided hair, or gold, or pearls, or costly array. (1 Timothy 2: 9.)

But a lover of hospitality, a lover of good men, sober, just, holy, temperate. (Titus 1: 8.)

Teaching us that, denying ungodliness and worldly lusts, we should live soberly, righteously, and godly, in this present world. (Titus 2: 12.)

Wherefore gird up the loins of your mind, be sober, and hope to the end for the grace that is to be brought unto you at the revelation of Jesus Christ. (1 Peter 1: 13.)

But the end of all things is at hand: be ye therefore sober, and watch unto prayer. (1 Peter 4: 7.)

Be sober, be vigilant; because your adversary the devil, as a roaring lion, walketh about, seeking whom he may devour. (1 Peter 5: 8.)

SODOM AND GOMORRAH.

SOD'OM AND GO-MOR'RAH—two of the famous (or infamous) cities of the plain, destroyed by God with fire because of their wickedness, the only persons escaping being the family of Lot, even his wife meeting death for looking back upon the perishing cities. The two cities were located in what is known as the vale of Siddim, in the upper end of the Jordan valley. There are absolutely no traces of the towns, not even ruins being left.

References.—Genesis 13, 18, and 19.

SOLOMON. (See Bath-sheba, David, Judah, Jews, Temple, etc.)

SOL'O-MON—a form of a Hebrew word meaning "the pacific" or "the peaceful." The name of Solomon is one of the most familiar of all Old Testament names to the Bible reader and student, standing as it does for the height of kingly wisdom and as a symbol of the Hebrew nation at its greatest. Solomon was the youngest son of David and Bathsheba. He was born about 1035 or 1034 B.C. He was given a thorough education under Nathan the prophet, who named him Jedidiah, or "the loved of Jehovah." He became regarded as the heir to the throne only after the revolt of Absalom. This event and its tragic ending resulted in the anointing of Solomon and his solemn acknowledgment as king (about the year 1015 B.C.). Soon after this, David died and Solomon had trouble with another brother, Adonijah, which ended in the execution of the latter.

At this period began Solomon's real career. Vast wealth had been left to him by David, and Solomon added to this in immense ways by trade. By this means the Hebrews came into contact with nations far and near and greatly increased the national prestige. Careful in administration also, Solomon strongly· fortified many of the principal Israelite cities, and also set to work to erect huge and magnificent buildings. The greatest work of this sort was, the construction of the Temple. It is said that at one time he had no less than 153,000 slaves working upon his structures. In this he imitated the example of the Egyptian pharaohs.

The deaths of Nathan and Zadok, who had been his father's earnest and wise counsellors, brought about a change in Solomon. Polygamy having been tolerated for a number of generations, it is no wonder that a man of Solomon's wealth desired many wives. We are told that in his harem at one time there were no less than 700 wives and 300 concubines, or secondary wives. They were gathered from all nations and all shades of religious faith. Many of them were utterly pagan, and to please them Solomon permitted the erection of shrines and temples of their faith in which they could worship. Thus there crept into Israel the very worst phases of idolatry and the causes for the future break-up of the nation.

It must not be imagined that Solomon was given to loitering away his life in his harem. On the other hand, he must have been a most energetic and busy man. We are assured that he constantly gave judgment to his people and we know that his building operations must have consumed much of his time in thought

and planning, while the administration of his trade relations must have been no small task. He also found time to do a great deal of literary· work. We are told that the Song of Solomon (or Canticles), the book of Proverbs, and the book known as Ecclesiastes came from his pen.

Toward the end of his life troubles began to appear through powerful factions, and enemies raised up both within and without the nation. After his death, which occurred about the year 920 B.C., the kingdom split into the dual monarchies of Israel and Judah.

Solomon's character has never been properly estimated, for the reason that it is so complex as it is given to us that we have no means of arriving at the true nature of the man. He was a wise administrator of his own affairs; but he seems to have lacked the wisdom to leave a compact and united kingdom behind him. He was a great builder, but a vast amount of it was built for his own glory or pleasure. He built up a huge magnificence to God in the shape of the Temple, and yet worshiped heathen gods of all sorts for the pleasure of his womankind. He glorified the throne at the cost of his nation and left to his heir only an empty shell of richness and splendor that collapsed when the pressure of trouble came. He uttered words of deepest wisdom, but he was utterly unable—to use a very homely but very descriptive phrase—to practice what he preached.

REFERENCES.

Choice of Solomon as King.

Wherefore Nathan spake unto Bathsheba the mother of Solomon, saying, Hast thou not heard that Adonijah the son of Haggith doth reign, and David our lord knoweth it not?

Now therefore come, let me, I pray thee, give thee counsel, that thou mayest save thine own life, and the life of thy son Solomon.

Go and get thee in unto king David, and say unto him, Didst not thou, my lord, O king, swear unto thine handmaid, saying, Assuredly Solomon thy·

son shall reign after me, and he shall sit upon my throne? why then doth Adonijah reign?

Behold, while thou yet talkest there with the king, I also will come in after thee, and confirm thy words. (1 Kings 1: 11-14.)

And the king sware, and said, As the Lord liveth, that hath redeemed my soul out of all distress,

Even as I sware unto thee by the Lord God of Israel, saying, Assuredly Solomon thy son shall reign after me, and he shall sit upon my throne in my stead; even so will I certainly do this day.

Then Bath-sheba bowed with her face to the earth, and did reverence to the king, and said, Let my lord king David live for ever.

And king David said, Call me Zadok the priest, and Nathan the prophet, and Benaiah the son of Jehoiada. And they came before the king.

The king also said unto them, Take with you the servants of your lord, and cause Solomon my son to ride upon mine own mule, and bring him down to Gihon:

And let Zadok the priest and Nathan the prophet anoint him there king over Israel: and blow ye with the trumpet, and say, God save king Solomon. (1 Kings 1: 29-34.)

Solomon Asks God for Wisdom.

In Gibeon the Lord appeared to Solomon in a dream by night: and God said, Ask what I shall give thee.

And Solomon said, Thou hast shewed unto thy servant David my father great mercy, according as he walked before thee in truth, and in righteousness, and in uprightness of heart with thee; and thou hast kept for him this great kind-

ness, that thou hast given him a son to sit on his throne, as it is this day.

And now, O Lord my God, thou hast made thy servant king instead of David my father: and I am but a little child: I know now how to go out or come in.

And thy servant is in the midst of thy people which thou hast chosen, a great people, that cannot be numbered nor counted for multitude.

Give therefore thy servant an understanding heart to judge thy people, that I may discern between good and bad: for who is able to judge this thy so great a people?

And the speech pleased the Lord, that Solomon had asked this thing.

And God said unto him, Because thou hast asked this thing, and hast not asked for thyself long life; neither hast asked riches for thyself, nor hast asked the life of thine enemies; but hast asked for thyself understanding to discern judgment;

Behold, I have done according to thy word: lo, I have given thee a wise and an understanding heart; so that there was none like thee before thee, neither after thee shall any arise like unto thee.

And I have also given thee that which thou hast not asked, both riches, and honour: so that there shall not be any among the kings like unto thee all thy days.

Builds the Temple.

And it came to pass in the four hundred and eightieth year after the children of Israel were come out of the land of Egypt, in the fourth year of Solomon's reign over Israel, in the month Zif, which is the second month, that he began to build the house of the Lord. (1 Kings 6: 1.)

In the fourth year was the foundation of the house of the Lord laid, in the month Zif:

And in the eleventh year, in the month Bul, which is the eighth month, was the house finished throughout all the parts thereof, and according to all the fashion of it. So was he seven years in building it. (1 Kings 6: 37, 38.)

God Warns Solomon.

And it came to pass, when Solomon had finished the building of the house of the Lord, and the king's house, and all Solomon's desire which he was pleased to do,

That the Lord appeared to Solomon the second time, as he had appeared unto him at Gibeon.

And the Lord said unto him, I have heard thy prayer and thy supplication, that thou hast made before me: I have hallowed this house, which thou hast built, to put my name there for ever; and mine eyes and mine heart shall be there perpetually.

And if thou wilt walk before me, as David thy father walked, in integrity of heart, and in uprightness, to do according to all that I have commanded thee, and wilt keep my statutes and my judgments:

Then I will establish the throne of thy kingdom upon Israel for ever, as I promised to David thy father, saying, There shall not fail thee a man upon the throne of Israel.

But if ye shall at all turn from following me, ye or your children, and will not keep my commandments and my statutes which I have set before you, but go and serve other gods, and worship them:

Then will I cut off Israel out of the land which I have given them; and this house, which I have hallowed for my name, will I cast out of my sight; and Israel shall be a proverb and a byword among all people:

And at this house, which is high, every one that passeth by it shall be astonished, and shall hiss; and they shall say, Why hath the Lord done thus unto this land, and to this house?

And they shall answer, Because they forsook the Lord their God, who brought forth their fathers out of the land of Egypt, and have taken hold upon other gods, and have worshipped them, and served them: therefore hath the Lord brought upon them all this evil. (1 Kings 9: 1-9.)

Solomon's Sins and Death.

But king Solomon loved many strange women, together with the daughter of Pharaoh, women of the Moabites, Ammonites, Edomites, Zidonians, and Hittites;

Of the nations concerning which the Lord said unto the children of Israel, Ye shall not go in to them, neither shall they come in unto you: for surely they will turn away your heart after their gods: Solomon clave unto these in love.

And he had seven hundred wives, princesses, and three hundred concubines: and his wives turned away his heart.

For it came to pass, when Solomon was old, that his wives turned away his heart after other gods: and his heart was not perfect with the Lord his God, as was the heart of David his father.

For Solomon went after Ashtoreth the goddess of the Zidonians, and after Milcom the abomination of the Ammonites.

And Solomon did evil in the sight of

the Lord, and went not fully after the Lord, as did David his father.

Then did Solomon build a high place for Chemosh, the abomination of Moab, in the hill that is before Jerusalem, and for Molech, the abomination of the children of Ammon.

And likewise did he for all his strange wives, which burnt incense and sacrificed unto their gods.

And the Lord was angry with Solomon, because his heart was turned from the Lord God of Israel, which had appeared unto him twice,

And had commanded him concerning this thing, that he should not go after other gods: but he kept not that which the Lord commanded.

Wherefore the Lord said unto Solomon, Forasmuch as this is done of thee, and thou hast not kept my covenant and my statutes, which I have commanded thee, I will surely rend the kingdom from thee, and will give it to thy servant.

Notwithstanding, in thy days I will not do it for David thy father's sake: but I will rend it out of the hand of thy son.

Howbeit I will not rend away all the kingdom; but will give one tribe to thy son for David my servant's sake, and for Jerusalem's sake which I have chosen. (1 Kings 11: 1-13.)

And the rest of the acts of Solomon, and all that he did, and his wisdom, are they not written in the book of the acts of Solomon?

And the time that Solomon reigned in Jerusalem over all Israel was forty years.

And Solomon slept with his fathers, and was buried in the city of David his father: and Rehoboam his son reigned in his stead. (1 Kings 11: 41-43.)

SON OF GOD. (See Christ, Jesus.)

SON OF GOD—one of the titles of Jesus Christ, expressing His eternal relationship with God the Father.

References.—See references under Christ and Jesus.

SON OF MAN. (See Christ, Jesus.)

SON OF MAN—one of the titles of Jesus Christ, assumed by Him to show the human side of His nature as well as His humiliation.

References.—See references under Christ and Jesus.

SORROW. (See Affliction, Repentance.)

SOR'ROW—grief, sadness; pain of mind at the loss or absence or failure of something or some one; unhappiness; mourning.

REFERENCES.

Godly Sorrow.

For godly sorrow worketh repentance to salvation not to be repented of: but the sorrow of the world worketh death. (2 Corinthians 7: 10.)

Earthly Sorrow.

And he said, My son shall not go down with you; for his brother is dead, and he is left alone: if mischief befall him by the way in the which ye go, then shall ye bring down my gray hairs with sorrow to the grave. (Genesis 42: 38.)

Mine eye also is dim by reason of sorrow, and all my members are as a shadow. (Job 17: 7.)

How long shall I take counsel in my soul, having sorrow in my heart daily? how long shall mine enemy be exalted over me? (Psalm 13: 2.)

The days of our years are threescore years and ten; and if by reason of strength they be fourscore years, yet is their strength labour and sorrow; for it is soon cut off, and we fly away. (Psalm 90: 10.)

And the ransomed of the Lord shall return, and come to Zion with songs and everlasting joy upon their heads: they shall obtain joy and gladness, and sorrow and sighing shall flee away. (Isaiah 35: 10.)

And when he rose up from prayer, and was come to his disciples, he found them sleeping for sorrow. (Luke 22: 45.)

That I have great heaviness and continual sorrow in my heart. (Romans 9: 2.)

But I would not have you to be ignorant, brethren, concerning them which are asleep, that ye sorrow not, even as others which have no hope. (1 Thessalonians 4: 13.)

SOUL. (See Spirit.)

Soul—the spiritual and immortal part of man. Philosophers for centuries have given thought to what constitutes the soul of man and where is the seat of it. Never has a definite and concrete answer been given more than that the soul is that part of man which raises him above the level of the beast—the divine breath breathed into man at his creation, the vital, active principle which perceives, remembers, reasons, loves, hopes, fears, aspires, and believes in its immortality. In other words, it is a part of God given to man along with the likeness of his image. Therefore it is immortal. The human body, being only a likeness, is perishable. It is impossible to give its seat. Some have said the heart, but the heart is simply a pump built of muscles. With more reason, others have said the brain, and yet in the case of persons insane it would be ridiculous to believe the soul has become warped or twisted or upset or in decay by reason of disease of the mass of nerve matter we call the brain. The Chinese philosophers contend that the stomach is the true living-place of the soul, and yet we know that the stomach is nothing but a huge cavernous muscle, with juices, glands, and machinery for the digestion of food; in other words, the

furnace of the human engine. It would be far better to believe that the soul permeates every fiber and organ of the body—a principle or an essence rather than a palpable thing.

SPIRIT.

Spir'it—a word meaning about the same thing as soul and with little or no distinction as to attributes. It also has a few other meanings, such as nature, quality, or the expression of a high or low degree of temperament.

SPIRIT, THE HOLY. (See God, Holy Ghost, Trinity.)

Spir'it, The Ho'ly—another name for the Holy Ghost, the third person of the Trinity.

References.—See articles on God, Holy Ghost, and Trinity.

STEADFASTNESS. (See Faith.)

Stead'fast-ness (written in many Bibles "stedfastness")—the quality or state of being steadfast; firmness; constancy; resolution in a good cause; fixedness of purpose.

The Bible contains many exhortations to steadfastness, which it holds up as a bright jewel of the Christian crown. The Book also gives us many instances of the virtue, while history reveals in a thousand different ways the splendid quality of the grace; as, for instance, the steadfastness of the apostles, the steadfastness with which the Christian martyrs met death in the Roman arena or in the other persecutions that have beset the Church in various ages.

REFERENCES.

The Steadfastness of the Apostles.

And they continued stedfastly in the apostles' doctrine and fellowship, and in breaking of bread, and in prayers. (Acts 2: 42.)

For though I be absent in the flesh, yet am I with you in the spirit, joying and beholding your order, and the stedfastness of your faith in Christ. (Colossians 2: 5.)

Steadfastness Urged.

Thou shalt fear the Lord thy God; him shalt thou serve, and to him shalt thou cleave, and swear by his name. (Deuteronomy 10: 20.)

For then shalt thou lift up thy face without spot; yea, thou shalt be steadfast, and shalt not fear. (Job 11: 15.)

Therefore, my beloved brethren, be ye stedfast, unmoveable, always abounding in the work of the Lord, forasmuch as ye know that your labour is not in vain in the Lord. (1 Corinthians 15: 58.)

Prove all things; hold fast that which is good. (1 Thessalonians 5: 21.)

For we are made partakers of Christ, if we hold the beginning of our confidence stedfast unto the end. (Hebrews 3: 14.)

Seeing then that we have a great high priest, that is passed into the heavens, Jesus the Son of God, let us hold fast our profession. (Hebrews 4: 14.)

Let us hold fast the profession of our faith without wavering; (for he is faithful that promised;)

And let us consider one another to provoke unto love and to good works. (Hebrews 10: 23, 24.)

Whom resist stedfast in the faith, knowing that the same afflictions are accomplished in your brethren that are in the world. (1 Peter 5: 9.)

Ye therefore, beloved, seeing ye know these things before, beware lest ye also, being led away with the error of the wicked, fall from your own stedfastness. (2 Peter 3: 17.)

STEALING. (See Thief.)

STEAL'ING—the act of committing a theft; taking without the consent or knowledge the property of some other person. Stealing is one of the chief sins. As such it is given a place in the Ten Commandments, and the words of the Law admit of no extenuation or prevarication. They simply say: "Thou shalt not steal," which covers the ground amply. The Bible also shows the evil and trouble that befalls the thief and his final doom, unless repentant.

REFERENCES.

Commands, Exhortations, etc.

Thou shalt not steal. (Exodus 20: 15.)

And he that stealeth a man, and selleth him, or if he be found in his hand, he shall surely be put to death. (Exodus 21: 16.)

Ye shall not steal, neither deal falsely, neither lie one to another. Leviticus 19: 11.)

If a man be found stealing any of his brethren of the children of Israel, and maketh merchandise of him, or selleth him; then that thief shall die; and thou shalt put evil away from among you. (Deuteronomy 24: 7.)

I will bring it forth, saith the Lord of hosts, and it shall enter into the house of the thief, and into the house of him that sweareth falsely by my name: and it shall remain in the midst of his house, and shall consume it with the timber thereof and the stones thereof. (Zechariah 5: 4.)

He saith unto him, Which? Jesus said, *Thou shalt do no murder, Thou shalt not commit adultery, Thou shalt not steal, Thou shalt not bear false witness.* (Matthew 19: 18.)

And he said, *That which cometh out of the man, that defileth the man.*

For from within, out of the heart of men, proceed evil thoughts, adulteries, fornications, murders,

Thefts, covetousness, wickedness, de-

ceit, lasciviousness, an evil eye, blas-phemy, pride, foolishness:

All these evil things come from within, and defile the man. (Mark 7: 20-23.)

Let him that stole steal no more: but rather let him labour, working with his hands the thing which is good, that he may have to give to him that needeth. (Ephesians 4: 28.)

But let none of you suffer as a murderer, or as a thief, or as an evildoer, or as a busybody in other men's matters. (1 Peter 4: 15.)

STEPHEN.

STE'PHEN (pronounced as though spelled steven)—a form of a Greek word meaning "a crown" or "crowned." Stephen was one of the original seven deacons of the Apostolic Church, and became the first martyr to the cause of Christ. There seems to be no doubt that he was of Greek birth or descent—in other words, a Jew born out of Palestine, or with one or the other of his parents a Greek. The Scriptures distinguish him as a man full of faith and the Holy Ghost. His zeal in teaching and preaching brought down upon him the rage and enmity of the intolerant Jews who would not accept the Christian faith. He was brought to trial before the Sanhedrin and, of course, convicted. His defense before that body (Acts 7) is one of the most eloquent and masterly expositions of the faith in Scripture. The Jews were so enraged against him that they did not wait for the consent of the Roman governor to the sentence of death they passed, but took Stephen out and stoned his life away. In his last minute he showed the sublime nature of his faith in his cry: "Lord, lay not this sin to their charge." The Roman governor was so angry at the Jews for not submitting the case to him for his approval or disapproval that he deposed Annas, the high-priest who presided at Stephen's trial.

References.—Acts 6 and 7.

STRANGERS. (See Hospitality.)

STRIFE.

STRIFE—exertion or contention for superiority; altercation; contentiousness; quarreling; fighting.

The Christian faith, the Christian breast, and the Christian Church are no places for strife. The whole trend of Christ's teachings was against contention and quarreling. Not only did He teach the fallacy and sin of strife, but His apostles and disciples were careful to call the particular attention of the flock to His commands and wishes on the subject. The New Testament is full of exhortations to avoid strife.

REFERENCES.

Exhortations against Strife.

Strive not with a man without cause, if he have done thee no harm. (Proverbs 3: 30.)

The beginning of strife is as when one letteth out water: therefore leave off contention, before it be meddled with. (Proverbs 17: 14.)

Go not forth hastily to strive, lest thou know not what to do in the end thereof, when thy neighbour hath put thee to shame. (Proverbs 25: 8.)

He that passeth by, and meddleth with strife belonging not to him, is like one that taketh a dog by the ears. (Proverbs 26: 17.)

Let us walk honestly, as in the day; not in rioting and drunkenness, not in chambering and wantonness, not in strife and envying. (Romans 13: 13.)

For ye are yet carnal: for whereas there is among you envying, and strife, and divisions, are ye not carnal, and walk as men? (1 Corinthians 3: 3.)

Now the works of the flesh are manifest, which are these; Adultery, fornication, uncleanness, lasciviousness,

Idolatry, witchcraft, hatred, variance, emulations, wrath, strife, seditions, heresies,

Envyings, murders, drunkenness,

revellings, and such like: of the which I tell you before, as I have also told you in time past, that they which do such things shall not inherit the kingdom of God. (Galatians 5: 19-21.)

Let nothing be done through strife or vainglory; but in lowliness of mind let each esteem other better than themselves. (Philippians 2: 3.)

Do all things without murmurings and disputings. (Philippians 2: 14.)

But foolish and unlearned questions avoid, knowing that they do gender strifes. (2 Timothy 2: 23.)

But avoid foolish questions, and genealogies, and contentions, and strivings about the law; for they are unprofitable and vain. (Titus 3: 9.)

But if ye have bitter envying and strife in your hearts, glory not, and lie not against the truth. (James 3: 14.)

The Origin of Strife.

Hatred stirreth up strifes: but love covereth all sins. (Proverbs 10: 12.)

Only by pride cometh contention: but with the well advised is wisdom. (Proverbs 13: 10.)

A wrathful man stirreth up strife: but he that is slow to anger appeaseth strife. (Proverbs 15: 18.)

A froward man soweth strife: and a whisperer separateth chief friends. (Proverbs 16: 28.)

Cast out the scorner, and contention shall go out; yea, strife and reproach shall cease. (Proverbs 22: 10.)

Where no wood is, there the fire goeth out: so where there is no talebearer, the strife ceaseth. (Proverbs 26: 20.)

He that is of a proud heart stirreth up strife: but he that putteth his trust in the Lord shall be made fat. (Proverbs 28: 25.)

Surely the churning of milk bringeth forth butter, and the wringing of the nose bringeth forth blood: so the forcing of wrath bringeth forth strife. (Proverbs 30: 33.)

He is proud, knowing nothing, but doting about questions and strifes of words, whereof cometh envy, strife, railings, evil surmisings,

Perverse disputings of men of corrupt minds, and destitute of the truth, supposing that gain is godliness: from such withdraw thyself. (1 Timothy 6: 4, 5.)

Results of Strife.

But if ye bite and devour one another, take heed that ye be not consumed one of another. (Galatians 5: 15.)

For where envying and strife is, there is confusion and every evil work. (James 3: 16.)

Strife Condemned.

For it hath been declared unto me of you, my brethren, by them which are of the house of Chloe, that there are contentions among you.

Now this I say, that every one of you saith, I am of Paul; and I of Apollos; and I of Cephas; and I of Christ.

Is Christ divided? was Paul crucified for you? or were ye baptized in the name of Paul? (1 Corinthians 1: 11-13.)

For ye are yet carnal: for whereas there is among you envying, and strife, and divisions, are ye not carnal, and walk as men? (1 Corinthians 3: 3.)

Dare any of you, having a matter against another, go to law before the unjust, and not before the saints?

Do ye not know that the saints shall judge the world? and if the world shall be judged by you, are ye unworthy to judge the smallest matters? (1 Corinthians 6: 1, 2.)

STUBBORNNESS.

Stub'born-ness—the state or quality of being unreasonably obstinate in will or opinion; obdurate; headstrong; self-willed. Stubbornness is not a good quality. It shows an unreasoning will, and a limitation of the mental power of accepting argument that is convincing, which in turn betrays the smallness of the mind. Resolution and determination must not be confounded with the mulish characteristic of stubbornness and obstinacy.

REFERENCES.

Punishment for Stubbornness.

Because I have called, and ye refused; I have stretched out my hand, and no man regarded;

But ye have set at nought all my counsel, and would none of my reproof:

I also will laugh at your calamity; I will mock when your fear cometh. (Proverbs 1: 24-26.)

He, that being often reproved hardeneth his neck, shall suddenly be destroyed, and that without remedy. (Proverbs 29: 1.)

Stubbornness Forbidden.

Now be ye not stiffnecked, as your fathers were, but yield yourselves unto the Lord, and enter into his sanctuary, which he hath sanctified for ever: and serve the Lord your God, that the fierceness of his wrath may turn away from you. (2 Chronicles 30: 8.)

Be ye not as the horse, or as the mule, which have no understanding: whose mouth must be held in with bit and bridle, lest they come near unto thee. (Psalm 32: 9.)

SUFFERINGS. (See Affliction.)

SUNDAY. (See Sabbath.)

Sun'day—the first day of the week; also called the Lord's day. As has been told in the article on the Jewish Sabbath, the modern Christian Sunday or Lord's Day is not the Sabbath of the Jews, who clung close to the literal reading of the Mosaic text in making the seventh day of the week the Sabbath or day of rest. The use of Sunday came about through the observance of the early Christian Church of Sunday as a day devoted to the Lord because of the rising of Christ from His grave on that day. Naturally, the observance of two consecutive days gave rise to much confusion and inconvenience, and the Christians, doubtless anxious to break away as far as possible from the customs of the apostate Jews that had put the Master to death, abandoned Saturday, which was the Jewish Sabbath, and gave all their attention to the following day. In the old Roman calendar Sunday had a special significance. Not only was it dedicated to the sun, which the Romans had personified in the form of one of their gods, but it was also the custom to break bread on that day. To the Christian of the time, these two customs appealed, since on Sunday their Sun of Righteousness had risen from the tomb, and they also commemorated it with the breaking of bread, as He had commanded. The new interpretation the apostolic fathers gave to Sunday as a religious occasion and holy day can easily be imagined.

References.—Matthew 28: 1; Mark 16: 2, 9; John 20: 1, 19, 26; Acts 20: 7; 1 Corinthians 16: 2; Revelation 1: 10.

SUPPER, The Lord's. (See Communion.)

SWEARING. (See Blasphemy, Oath, etc.)

SWORD OF THE SPIRIT. (See Scriptures.)

Sword of the Spir'it—one of the titles given to the word of God, the Scriptures (Ephesians 6: 17). A somewhat similar reference is made to it in Hebrews 4: 12.

TABERNACLE. (See Temple.)

Tab'er-na-cle—a form of a Latin word meaning "a hut." Tabernacles, under the

Jews, were portable tents or structures used in the journeyings through the wilderness and afterwards until the building of the first Temple as places of worship, as well as for the transaction of momentous public business. We have in the Old Testament distinct and definite traces of three tabernacles—the ante-Sinaitic, which seems to have been the dwelling-place of Moses from the time he assumed the leadership of the Israelites until about the second year of the wanderings in the desert. Then a new tabernacle—the Sinaitic—was established. This appears to have done service until the erection of the third tabernacle—the Davidic—at Jerusalem, and even until a later day, as the old tabernacle seems to have been retained for a part of the Israelites at Gibeon. It was the most famous of the three.

References.—For descriptions of the tabernacles, especially the Sinaitic, see Exodus chapters 25, 26, 27, 36, 37, 38, 39, 40, and Numbers 9.

TABLE OF THE LORD. (See Communion.)

TABLES OF STONE. (See Commandments, Decalogue.)

TALEBEARERS. (See Busybodies, Strife, etc.)

TEACHERS and TEACHING. (See Doctrine, Ministers, Ministry, etc.)

TEACH'ERS—persons who teach or instruct. TEACH'ING—the act of instructing; also the instruction itself.

The two great Teachers of the Christian are the Lord Jesus Christ and the word of God, the Holy Bible. Their teaching is the way to eternal life. Under them are the hosts of ministers and men and women devoted to the cause of the Master who are constantly placing before the world the thoughts, precepts, and counsel they have given to us. They are gradually but surely leading mankind to a better knowledge of the Great Truth. All this is a part of the Divine Plan for the redemption of the world, which is growing better each day and nearer to the loving heart of the God that beats so warmly for all men.

But Jesus Christ and the Bible and their earthly assistants are engaged in a constant warfare against the powers of evil, for Satan works to-day as he worked thousands of years ago, by means of false teachers and with all the subtlety of argument and specious reasoning of which he is the master. Of these false teachers we are told to beware, lest they lead us astray.

REFERENCES.

God's Appointed Human Teachers.

Now there were in the church that was at Antioch certain prophets and teachers; as Barnabas, and Simeon that was called Niger, and Lucius of Cyrene, and Manaen, which had been brought up with Herod the tetrarch, and Saul.

As they ministered to the Lord, and fasted, the Holy Ghost said, Separate me Barnabas and Saul for the work whereunto I have called them.

And when they had fasted and prayed, and laid their hands on them, they sent them away. (Acts 13: 1-3.)

Having then gifts differing according to the grace that is given to us, whether prophecy, let us prophesy according to the proportion of faith;

Or ministry, let us wait on our ministering: or he that teacheth, on teaching;

Or he that exhorteth, on exhortation: he that giveth, let him do it with simplicity; he that ruleth, with diligence; he that sheweth mercy, with cheerfulness. (Romans 12: 6-8.)

And God hath set some in the church, first apostles, secondarily prophets, thirdly teachers, after that miracles, then gifts of healings, helps, governments, diversities of tongues.

Are all apostles? are all prophets? are all teachers? are all workers of miracles? (1 Corinthians 12: 28, 29.)

And he gave some, apostles; and some, prophets; and some, evangelists; and some, pastors and teachers;

For the perfecting of the saints, for the work of the ministry, for the edifying of the body of Christ:

Till we all come in the unity of the faith, and of the knowledge of the Son of God, unto a perfect man, unto the measure of the stature of the fulness of Christ. (Ephesians 4: 11-13.)

Whom we preach, warning every man, and teaching every man in all wisdom; that we may present every man perfect in Christ Jesus:

Whereunto I also labour, striving according to his working, which worketh in me mightily. (Colossians 1: 28, 29.)

Let the word of Christ dwell in you richly in all wisdom; teaching and admonishing one another in psalms and hymns and spiritual songs, singing with grace in your hearts to the Lord. (Colossians 3: 16.)

False Teachers.

Foretold and Described:

There is a conspiracy of her prophets in the midst thereof, like a roaring lion ravening the prey; they have devoured souls; they have taken the treasure and precious things; they have made her many widows in the midst thereof.

Her priests have violated my law, and have profaned mine holy things: they have put no difference between the holy and profane, neither have they shewed difference between the unclean and the clean, and have hid their eyes from my sabbaths, and I am profaned among them. (Ezekiel 22: 25, 26.)

And Jesus answered and said unto them, *Take heed that no man deceive you.*

For many shall come in my name, saying, I am Christ; and shall deceive many.

And ye shall hear of wars and rumours of wars: see that ye be not troubled: for all these things must come to pass, but the end is not yet.

For nation shall rise against nation, and kingdom against kingdom: and there shall be famines, and pestilences, and earthquakes, in divers places.

All these are the beginning of sorrows.

Then shall they deliver you up to be afflicted, and shall kill you: and ye shall be hated of all nations for my name's sake.

And then shall many be offended, and shall betray one another, and shall hate one another.

And many false prophets shall rise, and shall deceive many.

And because iniquity shall abound, the love of many shall wax cold.

But he that shall endure unto the end, the same shall be saved. (Matthew 24: 4-13.)

For I know this, that after my departing shall grievous wolves enter in among you, not sparing the flock.

Also of your own selves shall men arise, speaking perverse things, to draw away disciples after them. (Acts 20: 29, 30.)

For such are false apostles, deceitful workers, transforming themselves into the apostles of Christ.

And no marvel; for Satan himself is transformed into an angel of light.

Therefore it is no great thing if his ministers also be transformed as the ministers of righteousness; whose end shall be according to their works. (2 Corinthians 11: 13-15.)

From which some having swerved

have turned aside unto vain jangling;

Desiring to be teachers of the law; understanding neither what they say, nor whereof they affirm. (1 Timothy 1: 6, 7.)

Now the Spirit speaketh expressly, that in the latter times some shall depart from the faith, giving heed to seducing spirits, and doctrines of devils;

Speaking lies in hypocrisy; having their conscience seared with a hot iron;

Forbidding to marry, and commanding to abstain from meats, which God hath created to be received with thanksgiving of them which believe and know the truth.

For every creature of God is good, and nothing to be refused, if it be received with thanksgiving. (1 Timothy 4: 1-4.)

This know also, that in the last days perilous times shall come.

For men shall be lovers of their own selves, covetous, boasters, proud, blasphemers, disobedient to parents, unthankful, unholy,

Without natural affection, trucebreakers, false accusers, incontinent, fierce, despisers of those that are good,

Traitors, heady, highminded, lovers of pleasures more than lovers of God;

Having a form of godliness, but denying the power thereof: from such turn away.

For of this sort are they which creep into houses, and lead captive silly women laden with sins, led away with divers lusts,

Ever learning, and never able to come to the knowledge of the truth. (2 Timothy 3: 1-7.)

But there were false prophets also among the people, even as there shall be false teachers among you, who priv-

ily shall bring in damnable heresies, even denying the Lord that brought them, and bring upon themselves swift destruction.

And many shall follow their pernicious ways; by reason of whom the way of truth shall be evil spoken of.

And through covetousness shall they with feigned words make merchandise of you: whose judgment now of a long time lingereth not, and their damnation slumbereth not. (2 Peter 2: 1-3.)

Not to Be Listened to:

If there arise among you a prophet, or a dreamer of dreams, and giveth thee a sign or a wonder,

And the sign or the wonder come to pass, whereof he spake unto thee, saying, Let us go after other gods, which thou hast not known, and let us serve them;

Thou shalt not hearken unto the words of that prophet, or that dreamer of dreams: for the Lord your God proveth you, to know whether ye love the Lord your God with all your heart and with all your soul. (Deuteronomy 13: 1-3.)

Beware lest any man spoil you through philosophy and vain deceit, after the tradition of men, after the rudiments of the world, and not after Christ. (Colossians 2: 8.)

How to Be Tested:

And when they shall say unto you, Seek unto them that have familiar spirits, and unto wizards that peep and that mutter: should not a people seek unto their God? for the living to the dead?

To the law and to the testimony: if they speak not according to this word, it is because there is no light in them. (Isaiah 8: 19, 20.)

Now I beseech you, brethren, mark them which cause divisions and offences contrary to the doctrine which ye have learned; and avoid them.

For they that are such serve not our Lord Jesus Christ, but their own belly; and by good words and fair speeches deceive the hearts of the simple. (Romans 16: 17, 18.)

But avoid foolish questions, and genealogies, and contentions, and strivings about the law; for they are unprofitable and vain.

A man that is an heretick after the first and second admonition reject;

Knowing that he that is such is subverted, and sinneth, being condemned of himself. (Titus 3: 9-11.)

Beloved, believe not every spirit, but try the spirits whether they are of God: because many false prophets are gone out into the world.

Hereby know ye the Spirit of God: Every spirit that confesseth that Jesus Christ is come in the flesh is of God:

And every spirit that confesseth not that Jesus Christ is come in the flesh is not of God: and this is that spirit of antichrist, whereof ye have heard that it should come; and even now already is it in the world. (1 John 4: 1-3.)

True Teaching from God.

O God, thou hast taught me from my youth: and hitherto have I declared thy wondrous works.

Now also when I am old and greyheaded, O God, forsake me not; until I have shewed thy strength unto this generation, and thy power to every one that is to come. (Psalm 7: 17, 18.)

And all thy children shall be taught of the Lord; and great shall be the peace of thy children. (Isaiah 54: 13.)

It is written in the prophets, And they shall be all taught of God. Every man therefore that hath heard, and hath learned of the Father, cometh unto me. (John 6: 45.)

For I neither received it of man, neither was I taught it, but by the revelation of Jesus Christ. (Galatians 1: 12.)

TEMPERANCE. (See Drunkards, Sobriety, etc.)

TEM'PER-ANCE — moderation; restraint, especially in the use of strong or intoxicating liquors. Drunkenness being one of the most serious menaces of modern civilization, the Christian turns instinctively to the Bible for guidance upon the subject. While wine was almost a household beverage in the times of the Saviour and in the ages preceding Him, we nevertheless find many warnings against the too frequent and the too generous use of liquor. Drunkenness, then as now, was a thing to be guarded against as a great evil and a serious sin, since it brought to the surface all the most brutal and most degraded instincts in man. All through Scripture we find evidence of the horror and loathing in which drunkards were held.

REFERENCES.

Intemperance Condemned.

Wine is a mocker, strong drink is raging: and whosoever is deceived thereby is not wise. (Proverbs 20: 1.)

Look not thou upon the wine when it is red, when it giveth his colour in the cup, when it moveth itself aright. (Proverbs 23: 31.)

And be not drunk with wine, wherein is excess; but be filled with the Spirit. (Ephesians 5: 18.)

The aged women likewise, that they be in behaviour as becometh holiness, not false accusers, not given to much wine, teachers of good things. (Titus 2: 3.)

Punishments of Intemperance.

And it come to pass, when he heareth the words of this curse, that he bless himself in his heart, saying, I shall have peace, though I walk in the imagination of mine heart, to add drunkenness to thirst:

The Lord will not spare him, but then the anger of the Lord and his jealousy shall smoke against that man, and all the curses that are written in this book shall lie upon him, and the Lord shall blot out his name from under heaven.

And the Lord shall separate him unto evil out of all the tribes of Israel, according to all the curses of the covenant that are written in this book of the law. (Deuteronomy 29: 19-21.)

Who hath woe? who hath sorrow? who hath contentions? who hath babbling? who hath wounds without cause? who hath redness of eyes?

They that tarry long at the wine; they that go to seek mixed wine. (Proverbs 23: 29, 30.)

At the last it biteth like a serpent, and stingeth like an adder.

Thine eyes shall behold strange women, and thine heart shall utter perverse things.

Yea, thou shalt be as he that lieth down in the midst of the sea, or as he that lieth upon the top of a mast.

They have stricken me, shalt thou say, and I was not sick; they have beaten me, and I felt it not: when shall I awake? I will seek it yet again. (Proverbs 23: 32-35.)

Woe unto them that rise up early in the morning, that they may follow strong drink; that continue until night, till wine inflame them! (Isaiah 5: 11.)

Woe unto them that are mighty to drink wine, and men of strength to mingle strong drink:

Which justify the wicked for reward, and take away the righteousness of the righteous from him! (Isaiah 5: 22, 23.)

They shall not drink wine with a song; strong drink shall be bitter to them that drink it. (Isaiah 24: 9.)

There is a crying for wine in the streets; all joy is darkened, the mirth of the land is gone. (Isaiah 24: 11.)

Woe to the crown of pride, to the drunkards of Ephraim, whose glorious beauty is a fading flower, which are on the head of the fat valleys of them that are overcome with wine! (Isaiah 28: 1.)

The crown of pride the drunkards of Ephraim, shall be trodden under feet. (Isaiah 28: 3.)

But they also have erred through wine, and through strong drink are out of the way; the priest and the prophet have erred through strong drink, they are swallowed up of wine, they are out of the way through strong drink; they err in vision, they stumble in judgment. (Isaiah 28: 7.)

Awake, ye drunkards, and weep; and howl, all ye drinkers of wine, because of the new wine; for it is cut off from your mouth. (Joel 1: 5.)

For while they be folden together as thorns, and while they are drunken as drunkards, they shall be devoured as stubble fully dry. (Nahum 1: 10.)

Temperance in All Things Commended.

When thou sittest to eat with a ruler, consider diligently what is before thee:

And put a knife to thy throat, if thou be a man given to appetite. (Proverbs 23: 1, 2.)

And every man that striveth for the mastery is temperate in all things.

Now they do it to obtain a corruptible crown; but we an incorruptible.

I therefore so run, not as uncertainly; so fight I, not as one that beateth the air:

But I keep under my body, and bring it into subjection: lest that by any means, when I have preached to others, I myself should be a castaway. (1 Corinthians 9: 25-27.)

But the fruit of the Spirit is love, joy, peace, longsuffering, gentleness, goodness, faith,

Meekness, temperance: against such there is no law. (Galatians 5: 22, 23.)

And be not drunk with wine, wherein is excess; but be filled with the Spirit. (Ephesians 5: 18.)

But a lover of hospitality, a lover of good men, sober, just, holy, temperate. (Titus 1: 8.)

TEMPTATION.

Temp-ta'tion—the state, quality, or act of enticing to evil; seduction toward sin; the holding out of allurements pleasant to the eye or the senses but fatal to the welfare of the soul.

Temptation is one of Satan's favorite methods of winning souls to Hell. Snares of this character beset our feet every day of life, and especially is this true of the Christian, with whom the Devil is constantly at work, seeking to lure him from the path that leads to God. All sorts of human weaknesses are seized and used by the Evil One. Temptations come from every quarter, and from points whence we least expect them and toward which we are least prepared for resistance. In business, in social life, in general intercourse with the world, even in our homes and the bosom of our families, indeed within the walls of the church itself, do temptations come to us. But—the Christian always has three weapons with which to fight. They are repentance, faith, and prayer. Besides, we know that Jesus was tempted in all points as we are, and we have His example of re-

sistance. We also have the promise that God will not permit us to be tempted beyond our power to bear. We must always regard temptation as a trial of our faith and life.

REFERENCES.

The Temptation of Jesus.

Then was Jesus led up of the spirit into the wilderness to be tempted of the devil.

And when he had fasted forty days and forty nights, he was afterward an hungred.

And when the tempter came to him, he said, If thou be the Son of God, command that these stones be made bread.

But he answered and said, *It is written, Man shall not live by bread alone, but by every word that proceedeth out of the mouth of God.*

Then the devil taketh him up into the holy city, and setteth him on a pinnacle of the temple,

And saith unto him, If thou be the Son of God, cast thyself down: for it is written, He shall give his angels charge concerning thee: and in their hands they shall bear thee up, lest at any time thou dash thy foot against a stone.

Jesus said unto him, *It is written again, Thou shalt not tempt the Lord thy God.*

Again, the devil taketh him up into an exceeding high mountain, and sheweth him all the kingdoms of the world, and the glory of them;

And saith unto him, All these things will I give thee, if thou wilt fall down and worship me.

Then saith Jesus unto him, *Get thee hence, Satan: for it is written, Thou shalt worship the Lord thy God, and him only shalt thou serve.*

Then the devil leaveth him, and, behold, angels came and ministered unto him. (Matthew 4: 1-11.)

Temptation as a Trial of Faith and Life.

Many shall be purified, and made white, and tried; but the wicked shall do wickedly: and none of the wicked shall understand; but the wise shall understand. (Daniel 12: 10.)

And I will bring the third part through the fire, and will refine them as silver is refined, and will try them as gold is tried: they shall call on my name, and I will hear them: I will say, It is my people: and they shall say, The Lord is my God. (Zechariah 13: 9.)

And the Lord said, *Simon, Simon, behold, Satan hath desired to have you, that he may sift you as wheat:*

But I have prayed for thee, that thy faith fail not: and when thou art converted, strengthen thy brethren. (Luke 22: 31, 32.)

And when he was at the place, he said unto them, *Pray that ye enter not into temptation.* (Luke 22: 40.)

By faith Abraham, when he was tried, offered up Isaac: and he that had received the promises offered up his only begotten son. (Hebrews 11: 17.)

Blessed is the man that endureth temptation: for when he is tried, he shall receive the crown of life, which the Lord hath promised to them that love him. (James 1: 12.)

Wherein ye greatly rejoice, though now for a season, if need be, ye are in heaviness through manifold temptations:

That the trial of your faith, being much more precious than of gold that perisheth, though it be tried with fire, might be found unto praise and honour and glory at the appearing of Jesus Christ. (1 Peter 1: 6, 7.)

Beloved, think it not strange concerning the fiery trial which is to try you, as though some strange thing happened unto you. (1 Peter 4: 12.)

Prayer against Temptation.

And forgive us our sins; for we also forgive every one that is indebted to us. And lead us not into temptation; but deliver us from evil. (Luke 11: 4.)

God Forbids Excessive Temptation.

There hath no temptation taken you but such as is common to man: but God is faithful, who will not suffer you to be tempted above that ye are able; but will with the temptation also make a way to escape, that ye may be able to bear it. (1 Corinthians 10: 13.)

THANKS and THANKSGIVING.

THANKS—grateful acknowledgment of favors or gifts.

THANKS'GIV'ING—the act of giving thanks, especially thanks to God, for blessings spiritual, temporal, and eternal.

The giving of thanks to God for his manifold mercies and blessings should be one of man's daily acts of devotion to his Creator, and especially should we thank Him for our creation, preservation, and the redemption of the world through Jesus. The giving of thanks for our daily food is one of the beauties of the Christian household. The Master Himself, at the last supper, asked a blessing and gave thanks for the bread and the wine. How much more, then, should we do likewise?

REFERENCES.

Exhortations to Give Thanks.

Offer unto God thanksgiving; and pay thy vows unto the most High. (Psalm 50: 14.)

Let us come before his presence with thanksgiving, and make a joyful noise unto him with psalms. (Psalm 95: 2.)

Enter into his gates with thanksgiving, and into his courts with praise: be thankful unto him, and bless his name. (Psalm 100: 4.)

O give thanks unto the Lord, for he is good: for his mercy endureth for ever. (Psalm 107: 1.)

For the administration of this service not only supplieth the want of the saints, but is abundant also by many thanksgivings unto God. (2 Corinthians 9: 12.)

Be careful for nothing; but in every thing by prayer and supplication with thanksgiving let your requests be made known unto God. (Philippians 4: 6.)

Rooted and built up in him, and stablished in the faith, as ye have been taught, abounding therein with thanksgiving. (Colossians 2: 7.)

Continue in prayer, and watch in the same with thanksgiving. (Colossians 4· 2.)

Saying, Amen: Blessing, and glory, and wisdom, and thanksgiving, and honour, and power, and might, be unto our God for ever and ever. Amen. (Revelation 7: 12.)

Giving of Thanks by Jesus.

And as they were eating, Jesus took bread, and blessed it, and brake it, and gave it to the disciples, and said, *Take, eat; this is my body.*

And he took the cup, and gave thanks, and gave it to them, saying, *Drink ye all of it.* (Matthew 26: 26, 27.)

Giving Thanks at Meals.

And he commanded the people to sit down on the ground: and he took the seven loaves, and gave thanks, and brake, and gave to his disciples to set before them; and they did set them before the people. (Mark 8: 6.)

And when he had thus spoken, he took bread, and gave thanks to God in presence of them all: and when he had broken it, he began to eat. (Acts 27: 35.)

He that regardeth the day, regardeth it unto the Lord; and he that regardeth not the day, to the Lord he doth not regard it. He that eateth, eateth to the Lord, for he giveth God thanks; and he that eateth not, to the Lord he eateth not, and giveth God thanks. (Romans 14: 6.)

Giving thanks always for all things unto God and the Father in the name of our Lord Jesus Christ. (Ephesians 5: 20.)

THESSALONICA.

Thes-sa-lo-ni'ca—a city of Macedonia, named after the sister of Alexander the Great. It is still one of the important towns of the East, being now the chief place (after Constantinople) of European Turkey. The church there was doubtless founded by Paul, and in his time it was the chief center for the spread of Christianity westward. The modern name of the place is Saloniki.

THIEF. (See Stealing.)

THOMAS.

Thom'as—a form of a Greek word derived from the Phœnician and meaning "a twin." Thomas was the name of one of the apostles. He was a native of Galilee. Undoubtedly he was a good man, but one who thought slowly and was equally slow to believe anything he did not see or was not thoroughly demonstrated. He also seems to have been rather despondent by nature. He was a man of courage, however, and hesitated not to go into any danger for the sake of the Master. After the resurrection he insisted upon seeing and feeling the wounds in the hands and feet of Jesus. Tradition tells us that he was martyred. He has always been called "the doubting one" because of his peculiar mental characteristics.

THORN. (See Paul; also Appendix.)

THORN—a hard and sharp-pointed projection common to a number of different varieties of plants, inflicting a ragged and painful wound on coming in contact with human flesh. In Scripture we have two remarkable examples of wounding by thorns. The first is found in the crown of thorns woven by the persecutors of Jesus just prior to the crucifixion and laid upon the Master's head as a derisive imitation of a kingly crown. The other example is the "thorn in the flesh" mentioned by Paul (2 Corinthians 12: 7). Paul said this thorn in the flesh was a messenger of Satan sent to buffet him. We have never been able to learn what was the nature of this thorn. But it seems exceedingly likely that it was some constant temptation which beset the great apostle, but whether it was moral, mental, or physical we have no means of knowing to a certainty. It seems most improbable that the allusion could relate to any thing or incident in Paul's life before his conversion, since he must have felt convinced of the divine pardon for his early persecution of the Church. It is equally improbable that it related to religious ambitions, for Paul never shows that he thought of his own glory or power as paramount to that of his Master. In point of fact, the thorn narrows down to some moral, mental, or physical temptation which must have beset him all his life. Some commentators have thought he may have fretted over the physical ugliness that has been credited to him; but such an explanation seems inadequate when we consider the mental strength of the man, to whom physical beauty must have been only as a passing incident.

Late commentators have offered a very reasonable thought that Paul's thorn was a hasty and impetuous temper, which, chain as he would, would sometimes get the better of him when striving to convince doubters or erring ones. He had been the subject of a miraculous conversion, the memory of which never departed from him, and he knew that God had marked him with glory by it. Yet he did not seek to use this as a means of convincing others, for the reason that it may have seemed to him self-glorification, which trait he abhorred as is seen in the context

pertaining to his statement of the thorn. Knowing the power of God that had been exhibited in his own case could well be exhibited in the case of others it would seem only natural that hasty and impetuous anger should arise against doubters and scoffers. This theory, however, is only a theory and there is nothing but speculation and conjecture to warrant it. What the real nature of the "thorn" was will never be known.

TIGRIS. (See Euphrates.)

TI'GRIS—one of the twin rivers of Mesopotamia. It is mentioned in Scripture as the Hiddekel (Genesis 2: 14; Daniel 10: 4).

TIMOTHY.

TIM'O-THY—the Englished form of a Greek name (Timotheus) meaning "honoring God." Timothy was the son of a Jewish woman and a Greek father and was an early convert to the Christian faith. Paul found in him a well-educated and excellent companion and took him upon one or more of the missionary journeys. He also was in Rome during a part of Paul's captivity. Paul was exceedingly fond of him, as is shown in the various Pauline epistles and in the special ones to Timothy himself. After Paul's martyrdom, Timothy was in charge of the church at Ephesus. He, too, suffered martyrdom. He was put to death under either the Roman emperor Domitian or Nerva.

References.—The two epistles to Timothy.

TITUS. (See Jerusalem.)

TI'TUS—a proper name of Greek origin much used by the Romans. The Titus who figures in the Scriptures was a Christian teacher of Greek birth who became one of the companions of Paul, who converted him. Like Timothy, Paul was very fond of him, and he seems to have accompanied the great apostle on his last journey to Rome. After Paul's death he appears to have gone to Crete and became the head of the church there, dying at a very advanced age.

There is another Titus, who, although he does not appear in Scripture, is nevertheless of very great interest to Bible readers, for the reason that it was he who fulfilled the prophecies of Jesus and of Moses that the city should be destroyed and the temple wiped out of existence (Deuteronomy 28: 57 and Matthew 27: 25). Titus was the son of the Roman emperor Vespasian and was born A.D. 40. He showed great ability as a soldier, and at the age of thirty was the commander of a huge Roman army sent to besiege Jerusalem, then in revolt. The siege lasted more than three years and the fighting was constant and bloody. Hunger so reduced the besieged Jews that in a number of cases infants were eaten by their parents. At last Titus took the city by storm and practically demolished it, destroying the temple. Later Titus became emperor of Rome. He reigned only about two years. It always has been suspected that he was poisoned by his brother, Domitian.

TONGUE.

TONGUE—the principal organ of taste. It also aids in the swallowing of food and in the act of speaking. Figuratively, persons who talk too much or are not careful regarding what they say are said to have unruly tongues and are counseled to bridle them. We find a number of references of this character in Scriptures.

The "gift of tongues" was the power to speak freely and without thought as to discourse or language granted by the Holy Ghost.

REFERENCES.

The Tongue an Unruly Member.

How long wilt thou speak these things? and how long shall the words of thy mouth be like a strong wind? (Job 8: 2.)

Should not the multitude of words be answered? and should a man full of talk be justified? (Job 11: 2.)

As God liveth, who hath taken away my judgment; and the Almighty, who hath vexed my soul;

All the while my breath is in me, and the spirit of God is in my nostrils;

My lips shall not speak wickedness, nor my tongue utter deceit. (Job 27: 2-4.)

Therefore doth Job open his mouth in vain; he multiplieth words without knowledge. (Job 35: 16.)

He that backbiteth not with his tongue, nor doeth evil to his neighbour, nor taketh up a reproach against his neighbour. (Psalm 15: 3.)

I said I will· take heed to my ways, that I sin not with my tongue: I will keep my mouth with a bridle, while the wicked is before me.

I was dumb with silence, I held my peace, even from good; and my sorrow was stirred. (Psalm 39: 1, 2.)

If thou hast done foolishly in lifting up thyself, or if thou hast thought evil, lay thine hand upon thy mouth. (Proverbs 30: 32.)

For a dream cometh through the multitude of business; and a fool's voice is known by multitude of words. (Ecclesiastes 5: 3.)

For in the multitude of dreams and many words there are also divers vanities; but fear thou God. (Ecclesiastes 5: 7.)

A fool also is full of words; a man cannot tell what shall be; and what shall be after him, who can tell him? (Ecclesiastes 10: 14.)

Not that which goeth into the mouth defileth a man; but that which cometh out of the mouth, this defileth a man. (Matthew 15: 11.)

There is nothing from without a man, that entering into him can defile him: but the things which come out of him, those are they that defile the man. (Mark 7: 15.)

Let no corrupt communication proceed out of your mouth, but that which is good to the use of edifying, that it may minister grace unto the hearers. (Ephesians 4: 29.)

Let your speech be always with grace, seasoned with salt, that ye may know how ye ought to answer every man. (Colossians 4: 6.)

Wherefore, my beloved brethren, let every man be swift to hear, slow to speak, slow to wrath. (James 1: 19.)

If any man among you seem to be religious, and bridleth not his tongue, but deceiveth his own heart, this man's religion is vain. (James 1: 26.)

For in many things we offend all. If any man offend not in word, the same is a perfect man, and able also to bridle the whole body. (James 3: 2.)

Even so the tongue is a little member, and boasteth great things. Behold, how great a matter a little fire kindleth!

And the tongue is a fire, a world of iniquity: so is the tongue among our members, that it defileth the whole body, and setteth on fire the course of nature; and it is set on fire of hell. (James 3: 5, 6.)

But the tongue can no man tame; it is an unruly evil, full of deadly poison.

Therewith bless we God, even the Father; and therewith curse we men, which are made after the similitude of God.

Out of the same mouth proceedeth blessing and cursing. My brethren, these things ought not so to be. (James 3: 8-10.)

The Gift of Tongues.

An Interpreter Needed:

So likewise ye, except ye utter by the tongue words easy to be understood, how shall it be known what is spoken? for ye shall speak into the air.

There are, it may be, so many kinds of voices in the world, and none of them is without signification.

Therefore if I know not the meaning of the voice, I shall be unto him that speaketh a barbarian, and he that speaketh shall be a barbarian unto me.

Wherefore let him that speaketh in an unknown tongue pray that he may interpret.

For if I pray in an unknown tongue, my spirit prayeth, but my understanding is unfruitful.

What is it then? I will pray with the spirit, and I will pray with the understanding also: I will sing with the spirit, and I will sing with the understanding also.

Else, when thou shalt bless with the spirit, how shall he that occupieth the room of the unlearned say Amen at thy giving of thanks, seeing he understandeth not what thou sayest?

For thou verily givest thanks well, but the other is not edified.

I thank my God, I speak with tongues more than ye all:

Yet in the church I had rather speak five words with my understanding, that by my voice I might teach others also, than ten thousand words in an unknown tongue. (1 Corinthians 14: 9-19.)

A Sign to Unbelievers:

In the law it is written, With men of other tongues and other lips will I speak unto this people; and yet for all that will they not hear me, saith the Lord.

Wherefore tongues are for a sign, not to them that believe, but to them that believe not: but prophesying serveth not for them that believe not, but for them which believe.

If therefore the whole church be

come together into one place, and all speak with tongues, and there come in those that are unlearned, or unbelievers, will they not say that ye are mad?

But if all prophesy, and there come in one that believeth not, or one unlearned, he is convinced of all, he is judged of all:

And thus are the secrets of his heart made manifest; and so falling down on his face, he will worship God, and report that God is in you of a truth. (1 Corinthians 14: 21-25.)

TRANSFIGURATION.

TRANS-FIG-U-RA'TION. The transfiguration will always be to Christians one of the most wonderful events in the life of the Master. It was the glorification of the Son by the Father, and the committing to three human witnesses—Peter, James, and John—of the final and absolute evidence of Jesus' divine majesty. The transfiguration took place on Mount Hermon.

REFERENCES.

Mark's Account.

And after six days Jesus taketh with him Peter, and James, and John, and leadeth them up into a high mountain apart by themselves: and he was transfigured before them.

And his raiment became shining, exceeding white as snow; so as no fuller on earth can white them.

And there appeared unto them Elias with Moses: and they were talking with Jesus.

And Peter answered and said to Jesus, Master, it is good for us to be here: and let us make three tabernacles; one for thee, and one for Moses, and one for Elias.

For he wist not what to say; for they were sore afraid. (Mark 9: 2-6.)

John's Reference to the Transfiguration.

And the Word was made flesh, and dwelt among us, (and we beheld his glory, the glory as of the only begotten of the Father,) full of grace and truth. (John 1: 14.)

Peter's Reference to the Transfiguration.

For we have not followed cunningly devised fables, when we made known unto you the power and coming of our Lord Jesus Christ, but were eyewitnesses of his majesty.

For he received from God the Father honour and glory, when there came such a voice to him from the excellent glory, This is my beloved Son, in whom I am well pleased.

And this voice which came from heaven we heard, when we were with him in the holy mount. (2 Peter 1: 16-18.)

TRIBULATION. (See Affliction, Sorrow.)

TRIB'U-LA'TION—distress, trouble, severe affliction.

REFERENCES.

Yet hath he not root in himself, but dureth for a while: for when tribulation or persecution ariseth because of the word, by and by he is offended. (Matthew 13: 21.)

For then shall be great tribulation, such as was not since the beginning of the world to this time, no, nor ever shall be. (Matthew 24: 21.)

These things I have spoken unto you, that in me ye might have peace. In the world ye shall have tribulation: but be of good cheer; I have overcome the world. (John 16: 33.)

Confirming the souls of the disciples, and exhorting them to continue in the faith, and that we must through much tribulation enter into the kingdom of God. (Acts 14: 22.)

For verily, when we were with you, we told you before that we should suffer tribulation; even as it came to pass, and ye know. (1 Thessalonians 3: 4.)

And I said unto him, Sir, thou knowest. And he said to me, These are they which came out of great tribulation, and have washed their robes, and made them white in the blood of the Lamb. (Revelation 7: 14.)

TRINITY. (See Christ, God, Jesus, Holy Ghost.)

TRIN'I-TY—a union of three things or persons in one; specifically, the Holy Trinity, or union of God the Father, God the Son, and God the Holy Ghost, as three Persons in one Godhead.

The doctrine of the Trinity is one of the fundamentals of Christianity, and without irreverence may be regarded as one of God's revelations of Himself to man since the appearance of Jesus Christ. The Old Testament does not teach it, yet foreshadows it; but in the New Testament it is taught clearly and unmistakably. In effect, the doctrine is that there are in the Godhead three Persons, one in substance, coeternal and equal in power, the Father, Son, and Holy Ghost, although the Scripture does not make use of the word "trinity" in describing them or the union. The doctrine is called in theology a "mystery" because it is incomprehensible to mankind; in other words, man's finite mind is incapable of grasping the inwardness and complete meaning of it.

REFERENCES.

The Holy Trinity Foreshadowed in Old Testament.

And God said, Let us make man in our image, after our likeness: and let them have dominion over the fish of the sea, and over the fowl of the air, and over the cattle, and over all the earth, and over every creeping thing that creepeth upon the earth. (Genesis 1: 26.)

And the Lord God said, Behold, the man is become as one of us, to know good and evil: and now, lest he put forth his hand, and take also of the tree of life, and eat, and live for ever. (Genesis 3: 22.)

And the Lord said, Behold, the people is one, and they have all one language; and this they begin to do: and now nothing will be restrained from them, which they have imagined to do.

Go to, let us go down, and there confound their language, that they may not understand one another's speech. (Genesis 11: 6, 7.)

New Testament Teaching.

Go ye therefore, and teach all nations, baptizing them in the name of the Father, and of the Son, and of the Holy Ghost. (Matthew 28: 19.)

The grace of the Lord Jesus Christ, and the love of God, and the communion of the Holy Ghost, be with you all. Amen. (2 Corinthians 13: 14.)

For through him we both have access by one Spirit unto the Father. (Ephesians 2: 18.)

In whom ye also are builded together for a habitation of God through the Spirit. (Ephesians 2: 22.)

There is one body, and one Spirit, even as ye are called in one hope of your calling;

One Lord, one faith, one baptism,

One God and Father of all, who is above all, and through all, and in you all. (Ephesians 4: 4-6.)

Elect according to the foreknowledge of God the Father, through sanctification of the Spirit, unto obedience and sprinkling of the blood of Jesus

Christ: Grace unto you, and peace, be multiplied. (1 Peter 1: 2.)

TRUST. (See Faith.)

TRUST—the assured resting of the mind of one person on the integrity, honor, justice, love, truth, or any other sound principle in another. The trust which the Christian has in God is an exemplification of his faith. The greater the trust the greater the degree of faith. The Bible tells us to have complete trust, and shows us the blessings of it.

REFERENCES.

Trust in God.

David said moreover, The Lord that delivered me out of the paw of the lion, and out of the paw of the bear, he will deliver me out of the hand of this Philistine. And Saul said unto David, Go, and the Lord be with thee. (1 Samuel 17: 37.)

He trusted in the Lord God of Israel; so that after him was none like him among all the kings of Judah, nor any that were before him.

For he clave to the Lord, and departed not from following him, but kept his commandments, which the Lord commanded Moses.

And the Lord was with him; and he prospered whithersoever he went forth: and he rebelled against the king of Assyria, and served him not. (2 Kings 18: 5-7.)

Offer the sacrifices of righteousness, and put your trust in the Lord. (Psalm 4: 5.)

Thou hast seen it; for thou beholdest mischief and spite, to requite it with thy hand: the poor committeth himself unto thee; thou art the helper of the fatherless. (Psalm 10: 14.)

Into thine hand I commit my spirit; thou hast redeemed me, O Lord God of truth. (Psalm 31: 5.)

By this I know that thou favourest me, because mine enemy doth not triumph over me. (Psalm 41: 11.)

I am as a wonder unto many; but thou art my strong refuge. (Psalm 71: 7.)

He shall not be afraid of evil tidings: his heart is fixed, trusting in the Lord.

His heart is established, he shall not be afraid, until he see his desire upon his enemies. (Psalm 112: 7, 8.)

It is better to trust in the Lord than to put confidence in man.

It is better to trust in the Lord than to put confidence in princes. (Psalm 118: 8, 9.)

He that is of a proud heart stirreth up strife: but he that putteth his trust in the Lord shall be made fat. (Proverbs 28: 25.)

Who is among you that feareth the Lord, that obeyeth the voice of his servant, that walketh in darkness, and hath no light? let him trust in the name of the Lord, and stay upon his God. (Isaiah 50: 10.)

God Must Be Trusted.

Therefore I say unto you, Take no thought for your life, what ye shall eat, or what ye shall drink; nor yet for your body, what ye shall put on. Is not the life more than meat, and the body than raiment? (Matthew 6: 25.)

Therefore take no thought, saying, What shall we eat? or, What shall we drink? or, Wherewithal shall we be clothed?

(For after all these things do the Gentiles seek:) for your heavenly Father knoweth that ye have need of all these things.

But seek ye first the kingdom of God, and his righteousness; and all these things shall be added unto you.

Take therefore no thought for the morrow: for the morrow shall take thought for the things of itself. Sufficient unto the day is the evil thereof. (Matthew 6: 31-34.)

And he said unto his disciples, *Therefore I say unto you, Take no thought for your life, what ye shall eat; neither for the body, what ye shall put on.* (Luke 12: 22.)

And seek not ye what ye shall eat, or what ye shall drink, neither be ye of doubtful mind. (Luke 12: 29.)

Wherefore lift up the hands which hang down, and the feeble knees;

And make straight paths for your feet, lest that which is lame be turned out of the way; but let it rather be healed. (Hebrews 12: 12, 13.)

Casting all your care upon him; for he careth for you. (1 Peter 5: 7.)

Distrust Shamed.

Wherefore, if God so clothe the grass of the field, which to day is, and to morrow is cast into the oven, shall he not much more clothe you, O ye of little faith? (Matthew 6: 30.)

Fear ye not therefore, ye are of more value than many sparrows. (Matthew 10: 31.)

The life is more than meat, and the body is more than raiment.

Consider the ravens: for they neither sow nor reap; which neither have storehouse nor barn; and God feedeth them: how much more are ye better than the fowls?

And which of you with taking thought can add to his stature one cubit?

If ye then be not able to do that thing which is least, why take ye thought for the rest?

Consider the lilies how they grow:

they toil not, they spin not; and yet I say unto you, that Solomon in all his glory was not arrayed like one of these.

If then God so clothe the grass, which is to day in the field, and to morrow is cast into the oven; how much more will he clothe you, O ye of little faith? (Luke 12: 23-28.)

For all these things do the nations of the world seek after: and your Father knoweth that ye have need of these things. (Luke 12: 30.)

TRUTH. (See God, Scriptures, etc.)

TRUTH—conformity to fact or reality; exact accordance with that which is, or has been, or shall be; exactness; also righteousness and true religion. God is truth. His word is truth. We are expected to accept Him and it with faith, nothing doubting and nothing gainsaying. Moreover, we are expected to reflect that truth in our own lives by walking uprightly and by obedience to His laws and commands.

REFERENCES.

God Is Truth.

Know therefore that the Lord thy God, he is God, the faithful God, which keepeth covenant and mercy with them that love him and keep his commandments to a thousand generations. (Deuteronomy 7: 9.)

Who hast kept with thy servant David my father that thou promisedst him: thou spakest also with thy mouth, and hast fulfilled it with thine hand, as it is this day. (1 Kings 8: 24.)

Thou which hast kept with thy servant David my father that which thou hast promised him; and spakest with thy mouth, and hast fulfilled it with thine hand, as it is this day. (2 Chronicles 6: 15.)

For the word of the Lord is right;

and all his works are done in truth. (Psalm 33: 4.)

For thy mercy is great unto the heavens, and thy truth unto the clouds. (Psalm 57: 10.)

My covenant will I not break, nor alter the thing that is gone out of my lips. (Psalm 89: 34.)

For the Lord is good; his mercy is everlasting; and his truth endureth to all generations. (Psalm 100: 5.)

For thy mercy is great above the heavens: and thy truth reacheth unto the clouds. (Psalm 108: 4.)

For his merciful kindness is great toward us: and the truth of the Lord endureth for ever. Praise ye the Lord. (Psalm 117: 2.)

Thou wilt perform the truth to Jacob, and the mercy to Abraham, which thou hast sworn unto our fathers from the days of old. (Micah 7: 20.)

For what if some did not believe? shall their unbelief make the faith of God without effect?

God forbid: yea, let God be true, but every man a liar; as it is written, That thou mightest be justified in thy sayings, and mightest overcome when thou art judged. (Romans 3: 3, 4.)

Now I say that Jesus Christ was a minister of the circumcision for the truth of God, to confirm the promises made unto the fathers. (Romans 15: 8.)

If we believe not, yet he abideth faithful: he cannot deny himself. (2 Timothy 2: 13.)

In hope of eternal life, which God, that cannot lie, promised before the world began. (Titus 1: 2.)

God's Word Is Truth.

As for God, his way is perfect; the word of the Lord is tried: he is a buckler to all them that trust in him. (2 Samuel 22: 31.)

Thy word is true from the beginning: and every one of thy righteous judgments endureth for ever. (Psalm 119: 160.)

Have not I written to thee excellent things in counsels and knowledge,

That I might make thee know the certainty of the words of truth; that thou mightest answer the words of truth to them that send unto thee? (Proverbs 22: 20, 21.)

Sanctify them through thy truth: thy word is truth. (John 17: 17.)

This is the disciple which testifieth of these things, and wrote these things: and we know that his testimony is true. (John 21: 24.)

For we write none other things unto you, than what ye read or acknowledge; and I trust ye shall acknowledge even to the end. (2 Corinthians 1: 13.)

And he saith unto me, Write, Blessed are they which are called unto the marriage supper of the Lamb. And he saith unto me, These are the true sayings of God. (Revelation 19: 9.)

TYRE. (See Sidon.)

TYRE—one of the celebrated cities of the ancient world. It was originally a Sidonian colony, but soon outstripped the mother city in wealth and prestige. It was noted for its dyes and cloths. It carried on an extensive commerce with the whole of the then known world. Nebuchadnezzar took the place after a long siege, and later it was rebuilt upon a large island of the original harbor. Alexander the Great laid siege to it, but was unable to capture it until he had thrown the ruins of the old city into the water and built with them a tongue of land over which his troops could march to storm the walls. Since that time it never has been a great place. It is now a small and obscure port.

UNBELIEF and UNBELIEVERS.

Un'be-lief'—the state or act of not believing; especially, the rejection of divine revelation, divine prophecy, and the divine plan for the salvation of the world.

Un'be-liev'ers—those who do not believe; especially, those who reject the Bible as a divine revelation, or reject Jesus as a divine or a supernatural person, or reject the existence of God, or reject the plan for the salvation of the world; infidels.

Unbelief is one of the most damning sins. Those who persist in it and go to their graves without accepting Jesus as the Christ and Saviour of the world are lost. The Holy Scriptures are exceedingly plain on this point and admit of no argument or interpretation save that eternal damnation awaits such individuals. Such unbelievers are the true infidels. They have existed in all times and doubtless will continue to exist. We must not, however, confound with them such persons as have not had the gospel presented to them. The unbelief of this last class is one of ignorance and not of self-will, and there is a great difference between them, a difference no doubt recognized in some way by God, whose judgment of a man who had heard of Him and His Son and yet rejected Him unquestionably will be totally different from His judgment of the man who knows nothing at all of Jesus Christ.

REFERENCES.

Unbelief Contrasted with Belief.

He that believeth on him is not condemned: but he that believeth not is condemned already, because he hath not believed in the name of the only begotten Son of God. (John 3: 18.)

He that believeth on the Son hath everlasting life: and he that believeth not the Son shall not see life; but the wrath of God abideth on him. (John 3: 36.)

He that believeth on the Son of God hath the witness in himself: he that believeth not God hath made him a liar; because he believeth not the record that God gave of his Son. (1 John 5: 10.)

The Source of Unbelief.

Afterward he appeared unto the eleven as they sat at meat, and upbraided them with their unbelief and hardness of heart, because they believed not them which had seen him after he was risen. (Mark 16: 14.)

Those by the way side are they that hear; then cometh the devil, and taketh away the word out of their hearts, lest they should believe and be saved. (Luke 8: 12.)

Then he said unto them, *O fools, and slow of heart to believe all that the prophets have spoken.* (Luke 24: 25.)

And ye have not his word abiding in you: for whom he hath sent, him ye believe not. (John 5: 38.)

And because I tell you the truth, ye believe me not. (John 8: 45.)

But ye believe not, because ye are not of my sheep, as I said unto you.

My sheep hear my voice, and I know them, and they follow me. (John 10: 26, 27.)

But when divers were hardened, and believed not, but spake evil of that way before the multitude, he departed from them, and separated the disciples, disputing daily in the school of one Tyrannus. (Acts 19: 9.)

But if our gospel be hid, it is hid to them that are lost:

In whom the god of this world hath blinded the minds of them which believe not, lest the light of the glorious gospel of Christ, who is the image of God, should shine unto them. (2 Corinthians 4: 3, 4.)

Wherein in time past ye walked according to the course of this world, according to the prince of the power of the air, the spirit that now worketh in the children of disobedience. (Ephesians 2: 2.)

That they all might be damned who believed not the truth, but had pleasure in unrighteousness. (2 Thessalonians 2: 12.)

Take heed, brethren, lest there be in any of you an evil heart of unbelief, in departing from the living God. (Hebrews 3: 12.)

Mercy for Repentance After Unbelief.

Who was before a blasphemer, and a persecutor, and injurious: but I obtained mercy, because I did it ignorantly in unbelief. (1 Timothy 1: 13.)

Punishment of Unbelievers.

And the Lord spake unto Moses and Aaron, Because ye believed me not, to sanctify me in the eyes of the children of Israel, therefore ye shall not bring this congregation into the land which I have given them. (Numbers 20: 12.)

Therefore the Lord heard this, and was wroth: so a fire was kindled against Jacob, and anger also came up against Israel;

Because they believed not in God, and trusted not in his salvation. (Psalm 78: 21, 22.)

I said therefore unto you, that ye shall die in your sins: for if ye believe not that I am he, ye shall die in your sins. (John 8: 24.)

And to whom sware he that they should not enter into his rest, but to them that believed not?

So we see that they could not enter in because of unbelief. (Hebrews 3: 18, 19.)

Seeing therefore it remaineth that some must enter therein, and they to whom it was first preached entered not in because of unbelief. (Hebrews 4: 6.)

See that ye refuse not him that speaketh: for if they escaped not who refused

him that spake on earth, much more shall not we escape, if we turn away from him that speaketh from heaven. (Hebrews 12: 25.)

UNITY.

U'NI-TY—the union of a number of things; complete oneness of a collection of units or single things. The Bible teaches the unity of the Church and of the brotherhood of Christian men.

REFERENCES.

And other sheep I have, which are not of this fold: them also I must bring, and they shall hear my voice; and there shall be one fold, and one shepherd. (John 10: 16.)

So we, being many, are one body in Christ, and every one members one of another. (Romans 12: 5.)

For we being many are one bread, and one body: for we are all partakers of that one bread. (1 Corinthians 10: 17.)

For by one Spirit are we all baptized into one body, whether we be Jews or Gentiles, whether we be bond or free; and have been all made to drink into one Spirit.

For the body is not one member, but many. (1 Corinthians 12: 13, 14.)

There is neither Jew nor Greek, there is neither bond nor free, there is neither male nor female: for ye are all one in Christ Jesus. (Galatians 3: 28.)

That in the dispensation of the fulness of times he might gather together in one all things in Christ, both which are in heaven, and which are on earth; even in him. (Ephesians 1: 10.)

Now therefore ye are no more strangers and foreigners, but fellow-citizens with the saints, and of the household of God. (Ephesians 2: 19.)

Endeavouring to keep the unity of the Spirit in the bond of peace.

There is one body, and one Spirit, even as ye are called in one hope of your calling;

One Lord, one faith, one baptism,

One God and Father of all, who is above all, and through all, and in you all. (Ephesians 4: 3-6.)

URIAH. (See David, Bath-sheba.)

U-RI'AH—a form of a Hebrew word meaning "flame of Jehovah." Uriah was a Hittite and one of the leading military men of the kingdom of David, as well as the husband of Bath-sheba, for whom David had conceived a great passion. This passion brought about one of David's greatest sins, for, in order to make Bath-sheba his own, he had Uriah sent upon a mission which he thought would bring about his death. The expected occurred, and David then married Bath-sheba. Thus he was practicably a murderer.

References.—2 Samuel 11; 1 Kings 15.

VANITY. (See Pride, Ostentation.)

VAN'I-TY—the quality or state of being vain; unreal; profitless; empty; unsubstantial; also inordinate pride or conceit.

The Bible contains frequent warnings regarding vanity and vanities, pointing out the profitless and useless nature of things that are vain. Of vanities there are all sorts—of the person, of the mind, of riches, of position or social standing.

REFERENCES.

Vanity of vanities, saith the Preacher, vanity of vanities; all is vanity. (Ecclesiastes 1: 2.)

I the Preacher was king over Israel in Jerusalem.

And I gave my heart to seek and search out by wisdom concerning all things that are done under heaven: this sore travail hath God given to the sons of man to be exercised therewith.

I have seen all the works that are done under the sun; and, behold, all is vanity and vexation of spirit. (Ecclesiastes 1: 12-14.)

Yea, I hated all my labour which I had taken under the sun: because I should leave it unto the man that shall be after me.

And who knoweth whether he shall be a wise man or a fool? yet shall he have rule over all my labour wherein I have laboured, and wherein I have shewed myself wise under the sun. This is also vanity.

Therefore I went about to cause my heart to despair of all the labour which I took under the sun.

For there is a man whose labour is in wisdom, and in knowledge, and in equity; yet to a man that hath not laboured therein shall he leave it for his portion. This also is vanity and a great evil. (Ecclesiastes 2: 18-21.)

Vanity of vanities, saith the Preacher; all is vanity. (Ecclesiastes 12: 8.)

VENGEANCE. (See Revenge.)

VENGE'ANCE—revenge. The Bible teaches us that human vengeance is wrong, and that vengeance, if it is to be taken, belongs to God.

REFERENCES.

Is not this laid up in store with me, and sealed up among my treasures?

To me belongeth vengeance, and recompense; their foot shall slide in due time: for the day of their calamity is at hand, and the things that shall come upon them make haste. (Deuteronomy 32: 34, 35.)

If I whet my glittering sword, and mine hand take hold on judgment; I will render vengeance to mine enemies, and will reward them that hate me.

I will make mine arrows drunk with blood, and my sword shall devour flesh; and that with the blood of the slain and of the captives, from the beginning of revenges upon the enemy.

Rejoice, O ye nations, with his people: for he will avenge the blood of his servants, and will render vengeance to his adversaries, and will be merciful unto his land, and to his people. (Deuteronomy 32: 41-43.)

For we know him that hath said, Vengeance belongeth unto me, I will recompense, saith the Lord. And again, The Lord shall judge his people. (Hebrews 10: 30.)

VISIONS. (See Dreams.)

WASHING.

WASH'ING—cleaning with water or some other fluid. The word is often used in Scripture to show the cleansing process of Christ's blood with relation to sinners.

REFERENCES.

General.

If I wash myself with snow water, and make my hands never so clean;

Yet shalt thou plunge me in the ditch, and mine own clothes shall abhor me. (Job 9: 30, 31.)

When the Lord shall have washed away the filth of the daughters of Zion, and shall have purged the blood of Jerusalem from the midst thereof by the spirit of judgment, and by the spirit of burning. (Isaiah 4: 4.)

Not by works of righteousness which we have done, but according to his mercy he saved us, by the washing of regeneration, and renewing of the Holy Ghost. (Titus 3: 5.)

Let us draw near with a true heart in full assurance of faith, having our hearts sprinkled from an evil conscience, and our bodies washed with pure water. (Hebrews 10: 22.)

Washing by Jesus' Blood.

And such were some of you: but ye are washed, but ye are sanctified, but ye are justified in the name of the Lord Jesus, and by the Spirit of our God. (1 Corinthians 6: 11.)

And from Jesus Christ, who is the faithful witness, and the first begotten of the dead, and the prince of the kings of the earth. Unto him that loved us, and washed us from our sins in his own blood. (Revelation 1: 5.)

And I said unto him, Sir, thou knowest. And he said to me, These are they which came out of great tribulation, and have washed their robes, and made them white in the blood of the Lamb. (Revelation 7: 14.)

Jesus Washes the Disciples' Feet.

After that he poureth water into a bason, and began to wash the disciples' feet, and to wipe them with the towel wherewith he was girded.

Then cometh he to Simon Peter: and Peter saith unto him, Lord, dost thou wash my feet?

Jesus answered and said unto him, *What I do thou knowest not now; but thou shalt know hereafter.*

Peter saith unto him, Thou shalt never wash my feet. Jesus answered him, *If I wash thee not, thou hast no part with me.*

Simon Peter saith unto him, Lord, not my feet only, but also my hands and my head.

Jesus saith to him, *He that is washed needeth not save to wash his feet, but is clean every whit: and ye are clean, but not all.*

For he knew who should betray him; therefore said he, *Ye are not all clean.*

So after he had washed their feet, and had taken his garments, and was set down again, he said unto them, *Know ye what I have done to you?*

Ye call me Master and Lord: and ye say well; for so I am.

If I then, your Lord and Master, have washed your feet; ye also ought to wash one another's feet.

For I have given you an example, that ye should do as I have done to you.

Verily, verily, I say unto you, The servant is not greater than his lord; neither he that is sent greater than he that sent him. (John 13: 5-16.)

WATCHFULNESS.

WATCH'FUL-NESS—the state or quality of being watchful; alertness. The Scriptures command us to watchfulness for a number of different reasons—that we do not fall into temptation and sin, that we walk in the ways of God, that we maintain the proper relations between ourselves and our fellow-men, and that especially we be ready for the second coming of Christ. Watchfulness, therefore, is one of the Christian virtues.

REFERENCES.

Watching for Christ's Second Coming.

Watch therefore; for ye know not what hour your Lord doth come. (Matthew 24: 42.)

For the Son of man is as a man taking a far journey, who left his house, and gave authority to his servants, and to every man his work, and commanded the porter to watch.

Watch ye therefore: for ye know not when the master of the house cometh, at even, or at midnight, or at the cockcrowing, or in the morning:

Lest coming suddenly he find you sleeping.

And what I say unto you I say unto all, Watch. (Mark 13: 34-37.)

And take heed to yourselves, lest at any time your hearts be overcharged with surfeiting, and drunkenness, and cares of this life, and so that day come upon you unawares.

For as a snare shall it come on all of them that dwell on the face of the whole earth. (Luke 21: 34, 35.)

And that, knowing the time, that now it is high time to awake out of sleep: for now is our salvation nearer than when we believed. (Romans 13: 11.)

Watchfulness against Sin, Temptation, etc.

Then saith he unto them, *My soul is exceeding sorrowful, even unto death: tarry ye here, and watch with me.*

And he went a little farther, and fell on his face, and prayed, saying, *O my Father, if it be possible, let this cup pass from me: nevertheless not as I will, but as thou wilt.*

And he cometh unto the disciples, and findeth them asleep, and saith unto Peter, *What, could ye not watch with me one hour?*

Watch and pray, that ye enter not into temptation: the spirit indeed is willing, but the flesh is weak. (Matthew 26: 38-41.)

Wherefore let him that thinketh he standeth take heed lest he fall. (1 Corinthians 10: 12.)

Praying always with all prayer and supplication in the Spirit, and watching thereunto with all perseverance and supplication for all saints. (Ephesians 6: 18.)

Continue in prayer, and watch in the same with thanksgiving. (Colossians 4: 2.)

Therefore let us not sleep, as do others; but let us watch and be sober.

For they that sleep sleep in the night; and they that be drunken are drunken in the night. (1 Thessalonians 5: 6, 7.)

But watch thou in all things, endure afflictions, do the work of an evangelist, make full proof of thy ministry. (2 Timothy 4: 5.)

But the end of all things is at hand: be ye therefore sober, and watch unto prayer. (1 Peter 4: 7.)

Be sober, be vigilant; because your adversary the devil, as a roaring lion, walketh about, seeking whom he may devour. (1 Peter 5: 8.)

WATER.

WA'TER—the fluid which descends in rain from the clouds and which forms lakes, rivers, seas, etc. We find a legion of references to water in the Scriptures, both in a literal sense and figuratively. The reason for this is not difficult to find. To the dwellers in Palestine and the surrounding countries water was a most valuable commodity, much more valuable to them than to most of us nowadays. This was because of the fact that the land was hot and dry, and that, generally speaking, the life-giving fluid was scarce, because of the small size of the streams, the uncertain and rare character of the rainfall and the general lack of an abundant water supply. We can easily imagine the very high regard the ancient dwellers in the Holy Land had for water. Being so highly valued, it is also easy to understand how water came to take a place in the figurative language of the people.

REFERENCES.

Thou visitest the earth, and waterest it: thou greatly enrichest it with the river of God, which is full of water: thou preparest them corn, when thou hast so provided for it.

Thou waterest the ridges thereof abundantly: thou settlest the furrows thereof: thou makest it soft with showers: thou blessest the springing thereof. (Psalm 65: 9, 10.)

When the poor and needy seek water, and there is none, and their tongue faileth for thirst, I the Lord will hear them, I the God of Israel will not forsake them.

I will open rivers in high places, and fountains in the midst of the valleys: I will make the wilderness a pool of water, and the dry land springs of water. (Isaiah 41: 17, 18.)

Ho, every one that thirsteth, come ye to the waters, and he that hath no money; come ye, buy, and eat; yea, come, buy wine and milk without money and without price. (Isaiah 55: 1.)

For my people have committed two evils; they have forsaken me the fountain of living waters, and hewed them out cisterns, broken cisterns, that can hold no water. (Jeremiah 2: 13.)

In that day there shall be a fountain opened to the house of David and to the inhabitants of Jerusalem for sin and for uncleanness. (Zechariah 13: 1.)

Jesus answered, *Verily, verily, I say unto thee, Except a man be born of water and of the Spirit, he cannot enter into the kingdom of God.* (John 3: 5.)

Jesus answered and said unto her, *If thou knewest the gift of God, and who it is that saith to thee, Give me to drink; thou wouldest have asked of him, and he would have given thee living water.*

The woman saith unto him, Sir, thou hast nothing to draw with, and the well is deep: from whence then hast thou that living water?

Art thou greater than our father Jacob, which gave us the well, and drank thereof himself, and his children, and his cattle? (John 4: 10-12.)

In the last day, that great day of the feast, Jesus stood and cried, saying, *If any man thirst, let him come unto me, and drink.*

He that believeth on me, as the Scripture hath said, out of his belly shall flow rivers of living water.

(But this spake he of the Spirit, which they that believe on him should receive: for the Holy Ghost was not yet given; because that Jesus was not yet glorified.) (John 7: 37-39.)

And did all drink the same spiritual drink; for they drank of that spiritual Rock that followed them: and that Rock was Christ. (1 Corinthians 10: 4.)

And he said unto me, It is done. I am Alpha and Omega, the beginning and the end. I will give unto him that is athirst of the fountain of the water of life freely. (Revelation 21: 6.)

WEEPING.

WEEP'ING—the shedding of tears. For those who weep, no matter what the cause, the Scriptures are full of comfort.

REFERENCES.

Depart from me, all ye workers of iniquity; for the Lord hath heard the voice of my weeping. (Psalm 6: 8.)

For his anger endureth but a moment; in his favour is life: weeping may endure for a night, but joy cometh in the morning. (Psalm 30: 5.)

She weepeth sore in the night, and her tears are on her cheeks: among all her lovers she hath none to comfort her: all her friends have dealt treacherously with her, they are become her enemies. (Lamentations 1: 2.)

Therefore also now, saith the Lord, turn ye even to me with all your heart, and with fasting, and with weeping, and with mourning. (Joel 2: 12.)

But the children of the kingdom shall be cast out into outer darkness: there shall be weeping and gnashing of teeth. (Matthew 8: 12.)

Then said the king to his servants, Bind him hand and foot, and take him away, and cast him into outer darkness; there shall be weeping and gnashing of teeth. (Matthew 22: 13.)

Blessed are ye that hunger now: for ye shall be filled. Blessed are ye that weep now: for ye shall laugh. (Luke 6: 21.)

And stood at his feet behind him weeping, and began to wash his feet with tears, and did wipe them with the hairs of her head, and kissed his feet, and anointed them with the ointment. (Luke 7: 38.)

Then when Mary was come where Jesus was, and saw him, she fell down at his feet, saying unto him, Lord, if thou hadst been here, my brother had not died.

When Jesus therefore saw her weeping, and the Jews also weeping which came with her, he groaned in the spirit, and was troubled,

And said, *Where have ye laid him?* They said unto him, Lord, come and see.

Jesus wept. (John 11: 32-35.)

Rejoice with them that do rejoice, and weep with them that weep. (Romans 12: 15.)

And they that weep, as though they wept not; and they that rejoice, as though they rejoiced not; and they that buy, as though they possessed not. (1 Corinthians 7: 30.)

And God shall wipe away all tears from their eyes; and there shall be no more death, neither sorrow, nor crying, neither shall there be any more pain: for the former things are passed away. (Revelation 21: 4.)

WICKED. (See Hell, Righteousness, Sin.)

WICK'ED—the state or quality of being sinful; evil in principle or practice; contrary to divine or moral law; addicted to vice or sin; also a name for a person or the persons who are any of these things or in any of these states. The Bible shows us plainly what happens to those who are wicked. Before repentance, conversion and profession of Christ all men are wicked. It is a matter of our own choice whether we remain so, since we have the offer of pardon and salvation through the blood of Christ and His mediatorship with God the Father for us. For those who reject these boons there is eternal damnation.

REFERENCES.

Wicked and Righteous Contrasted.

With the merciful thou wilt shew thyself merciful, and with the upright man thou wilt shew thyself upright.

With the pure thou wilt show thyself pure; and with the froward thou wilt shew thyself unsavoury.

And the afflicted people thou wilt save: but thine eyes are upon the haughty, that thou mayest bring them down. (2 Samuel 22: 26-28.)

And the Spirit of God came upon Azariah the son of Oded:

And he went out to meet Asa, and said unto him, Hear ye me, Asa, and all Judah and Benjamin; The Lord is with you, while ye be with him; and if ye seek him, he will be found of you; but if ye forsake him, he will forsake you. (2 Chronicles 15: 1, 2.)

Behold, God will not cast away a perfect man, neither will he help the evil doers:

Till he fill thy mouth with laughing, and thy lips with rejoicing. (Job 8: 20, 21.)

For the Lord knoweth the way of the righteous: but the way of the ungodly shall perish. (Psalm 1: 6.)

With the merciful thou wilt shew thyself merciful; with an upright man thou wilt shew thyself upright;

Many sorrows shall be to the wicked: but he that trusteth in the Lord, mercy shall compass him about. (Psalm 32: 10.)

For the arms of the wicked shall be broken: but the Lord upholdeth the righteous.

The Lord knoweth the days of the upright: and their inheritance shall be for ever.

They shall not be ashamed in the evil time: and in the days of famine they shall be satisfied.

But the wicked shall perish, and the enemies of the Lord shall be as the fat of lambs: they shall consume; into smoke shall they consume away. (Psalm 37: 17-20.)

He that walketh uprightly walketh surely: but he that perverteth his ways shall be known. (Proverbs 10: 9.)

The fear of the wicked, it shall come upon him: but the desire of the righteous shall be granted.

As the whirlwind passeth, so is the wicked no more: but the righteous is an everlasting foundation. (Proverbs 10: 24, 25.)

The hope of the righteous shall be gladness: but the expectation of the wicked shall perish.

The way of the Lord is strength to the upright: but destruction shall be to the workers of iniquity.

The righteous shall never be removed: but the wicked shall not inhabit the earth. (Proverbs 10: 28-30.)

The wicked shall be a ransom for the righteous, and the transgressor for the upright. (Proverbs 21: 18.)

Thorns and snares are in the way of the froward: he that doth keep his soul shall be far from them. (Proverbs 22: 5.)

Whoso walketh uprightly shall be

saved: but he that is perverse in his ways shall fall at once. (Proverbs 28: 18.)

Therefore thus saith the Lord God, Behold, my servants shall eat, but ye shall be hungry: behold, my servants shall drink, but ye shall be thirsty: behold, my servants shall rejoice, but ye shall be ashamed:

Behold, my servants shall sing for joy of heart, but ye shall cry for sorrow of heart, and shall howl for vexation of spirit. (Isaiah 65: 13, 14.)

Then shall ye return, and discern between the righteous and the wicked, between him that serveth God and him that serveth him not. (Malachi 3: 18.)

The Prosperity of the Wicked.

Complained about:

The earth is given into the hand of the wicked: he covereth the faces of the judges thereof; if not, where, and who is he? (Job 9: 24.)

The tabernacles of robbers prosper, and they that provoke God are secure; into whose hand God bringeth abundantly. (Job 12: 6.)

Even when I remember I am afraid, and trembling taketh hold on my flesh.

Wherefore do the wicked live, become old, yea, are mighty in power?

Their seed is established in their sight with them, and their offspring before their eyes.

Their houses are safe from fear, neither is the rod of God upon them. (Job 21: 6-9.)

They spend their days in wealth, and in a moment go down to the grave. (Job 21: 13.)

Yet he filled their houses with good things: but the counsel of the wicked is far from me. (Job 22: 18.)

Righteous art thou, O Lord, when I plead with thee: yet let me talk with thee of thy judgments: Wherefore doth the way of the wicked prosper? wherefore are all they happy that deal very treacherously?

Thou hast planted them, yea, they have taken root: they grow, yea, they bring forth fruit: thou art near in their mouth, and far from their reins. (Jeremiah 12: 1, 2.)

Ye have wearied the Lord with your words. Yet ye say, Wherein have we wearied him? When ye say, Every one that doeth evil is good in the sight of the Lord, and he delighteth in them; or, Where is the God of judgment? (Malachi 2: 17.)

And now we call the proud happy; yea, they that work wickedness are set up; yea, they that tempt God are even delivered. (Malachi 3: 15.)

The Wicked Shall Cease.

There are the workers of iniquity fallen: they are cast down, and shall not be able to rise. (Psalm 36: 12.)

Wait on the Lord, and keep his way, and he shall exalt thee to inherit the land: when the wicked are cut off, thou shalt see it.

I have seen the wicked in great power, and spreading himself like a green bay tree.

Yet he passed away, and, lo, he was not: yea, I sought him, but he could not be found. (Psalm 37: 34-36.)

The Doom of the Wicked.

Their Terror:

It is a fearful thing to fall into the hands of the living God. (Hebrews 10: 31.)

And the kings of the earth, and the great men, and the rich men, and the chief captains, and the mighty men, and every bond man, and every free man, hid themselves in the dens and in the rocks of the mountains;

And said to the mountains and rocks, Fall on us, and hide us from the face of him that sitteth on the throne, and from the wrath of the Lamb:

For the great day of his wrath is come; and who shall be able to stand? (Revelation 6: 15-17.)

Their Separation:

Again, the kingdom of heaven is like unto a net, that was cast into the sea, and gathered of every kind:

Which, when it was full, they drew to shore, and sat down, and gathered the good into vessels, but cast the bad away.

So shall it be at the end of the world: the angels shall come forth, and sever the wicked from among the just. (Matthew 13: 47-49.)

And before him shall be gathered all nations: and he shall separate them one from another, as a shepherd divideth his sheep from the goats:

And he shall set the sheep on his right hand, but the goats on the left. (Matthew 25: 32, 33.)

He that is unjust, let him be unjust still: and he which is filthy, let him be filthy still: and he that is righteous, let him be righteous still: and he that is holy, let him be holy still. (Revelation 22: 11.)

Given Over to Satan:

Set thou a wicked man over him: and let Satan stand at his right hand. (Psalm 109: 6.)

And ye are puffed up, and have not rather mourned, that he that hath done this deed might be taken away from among you.

For I verily, as absent in body, but present in spirit, have judged already, as though I were present, concerning him that hath so done this deed,

In the name of our Lord Jesus Christ, when ye are gathered together, and my spirit, with the power of our Lord Jesus Christ,

To deliver such a one unto Satan for the destruction of the flesh, that the spirit may be saved in the day of the Lord Jesus. (1 Corinthians 5: 2-5.)

Of whom is Hymeneus and Alexander; whom I have delivered unto Satan, that they may learn not to blaspheme. (1 Timothy 1: 20.)

Damnation of the Wicked:

There is a way that seemeth right unto a man; but the end thereof are the ways of death. (Proverbs 16: 25.)

Another parable put he forth unto them, saying, *The kingdom of heaven is likened unto a man which sowed good seed in his field:*

But while men slept, his enemy came and sowed tares among the wheat, and went his way.

But when the blade was sprung up, and brought forth fruit, then appeared the tares also.

So the servants of the householder came and said unto him, Sir, didst not thou sow good seed in thy field? from whence then hath it tares?

He said unto them, An enemy hath done this. The servants said unto him, Wilt thou then that we go and gather them up?

But he said, Nay; lest while ye gather up the tares, ye root up also the wheat with them.

Let both grow together until the harvest: and in the time of harvest I will say to the reapers, Gather ye to-

gether first the tares, and bind them in bundles to burn them: but gather the wheat into my barn. (Matthew 13: 24-30.)

He answered and said unto them, *He that soweth the good seed is the Son of man;*

The field is the world; the good seed are the children of the kingdom; but the tares are the children of the wicked one;

The enemy that sowed them is the devil; the harvest is the end of the world; and the reapers are the angels.

As therefore the tares are gathered and burned in the fire; so shall it be in the end of this world.

The son of man shall send forth his angels, and they shall gather out of his kingdom all things that offend, and them which do iniquity;

And shall cast them into a furnace of fire: there shall be wailing and gnashing of teeth. (Matthew 13: 37-42.)

For I was a hungered, and ye gave me no meat: I was thirsty, and ye gave me no drink:

I was a stranger, and ye took me not in: naked, and ye clothed me not: sick, and in prison, and ye visited me not.

Then shall they also answer him, saying, Lord, when saw we thee a hungered, or athirst, or a stranger, or naked, or sick, or in prison, and did not minister unto thee?

Then shall he answer them, saying, Verily I say unto you, Inasmuch as ye did it not to one of the least of these, ye did it not to me.

And these shall go away into everlasting punishment: but the righteous into life eternal. (Matthew 25: 42-46.)

Go to now, ye rich men, weep and howl for your miseries that shall come upon you.

Your riches are corrupted, and your garments are motheaten.

Your gold and silver is cankered; and the rust of them shall be a witness against you, and shall eat your flesh as it were fire. Ye have heaped treasure together for the last days. (James 5: 1-3.)

And many shall follow their pernicious ways; by reason of whom the way of truth shall be evil spoken of.

And through covetousness shall they with feigned words make merchandise of you; whose judgment now for a long time lingereth not, and their damnation slumbereth not. (2 Peter 2: 2, 3.)

WILL.

WILL—that faculty or endowment of the soul which makes it capable of choosing; the faculty of the mind which enables us to do or not to do. God's will is the highest form of this sort of power, for the reason that it is the result of perfect wisdom and perfect knowledge, which elements are lacking in the case of man. The Bible teaches us that God's will is irresistible and that we must bow to it with humbleness and faith. Submission to the will of God is one of the highest forms of Christian virtue.

REFERENCES.

The Irresistible Will of God.

This matter is by the decree of the watchers, and the demand by the word of the holy ones: to the intent that the living may know that the Most High ruleth in the kingdom of men, and giveth it to whomsoever he will, and setteth up over it the basest of men. (Daniel 4: 17.)

And all the inhabitants of the earth are reputed nothing: and he doeth according to his will in the army of heaven, and among the inhabitants of the earth: and none can stay his hand, or say unto him, What doest thou? (Daniel 4: 35.)

God's Will Fulfilled by Christ.

He went away again the second time, and prayed, saying, *O my Father, if this cup may not pass away from me, except I drink it, thy will be done.* (Matthew 26: 42.)

And he said, *Abba, Father, all things are possible unto thee; take away this cup from me: nevertheless not what I will, but what thou wilt.* (Mark 14: 36.)

Saying, *Father, if thou be willing, remove this cup from me: nevertheless not my will, but thine, be done.* (Luke 22: 42.)

Jesus saith unto them, *My meat is to do the will of him that sent me, and to finish his work.* (John 4: 34.)

I can of mine own self do nothing: as I hear, I judge: and my judgment is just; because I seek not mine own will, but the will of the Father which hath sent me. (John 5: 30.)

How Will of God Is to Be Performed.

If any man will do his will, he shall know of the doctrine, whether it be of God, or whether I speak of myself.

He that speaketh of himself seeketh his own glory: but he that seeketh his glory that sent him, the same is true, and no unrighteousness is in him. (John 7: 17, 18.)

Not with eyeservice, as men pleasers; but as the servants of Christ, doing the will of God from the heart;

With good will doing service, as to the Lord, and not to men. (Ephesians 6: 6, 7.)

Forasmuch then as Christ hath suffered for us in the flesh, arm yourselves likewise with the same mind: for he that hath suffered in the flesh hath ceased from sin;

That he no longer should live the rest of his time in the flesh to the lusts of men, but to the will of God. (1 Peter 4: 1, 2.)

And this is his commandment, That we should believe on the name of his Son Jesus Christ, and love one another, as he gave us commandment.

And he that keepeth his commandments dwelleth in him, and he in him. And hereby we know that he abideth in us, by the Spirit which he hath given us. (1 John 3: 23, 24.)

Man Must Submit to God's Will.

After this manner therefore pray ye: Our Father which art in heaven, Hallowed be thy name.

Thy kingdom come. Thy will be done in earth, as it is in heaven. (Matthew 6: 10.)

And when he would not be persuaded, we ceased, saying, The will of the Lord be done. (Acts 21: 14.)

Making request, if by any means now at length I might have a prosperous journey by the will of God to come unto you. (Romans 1: 10.)

That I may come unto you with joy by the will of God, and may with you be refreshed. (Romans 15: 32.)

For that ye ought to say, If the Lord will, we shall live, and do this, or that. (James 4: 15.)

The Will of Man.

So then it is not of him that willeth, nor of him that runneth, but of God that sheweth mercy. (Romans 9: 16.)

Among whom also we all had our conversation in times past in the lusts of our flesh, fulfilling the desires of the flesh and of the mind; and were by nature the children of wrath, even as others. (Ephesians 2: 3.)

For the time past of our life may suffice us to have wrought the will of the Gentiles, when we walked in lasciviousness, lusts, excess of wine, revellings, banquetings, and abominable idolatries. (1 Peter 4: 3.)

WISDOM. (See Knowledge.)

WIS'DOM—knowledge, especially of the higher arts and sciences and branches of learning; prudence and discretion to perceive proper courses to pursue; natural intelligence and sagacity; also, in a Scriptural sense, knowledge of God. The Bible points out in various places the benefits of wisdom, since it overcomes the foolish and volatile in the human nature, molds the character upon better lines and improves the capacity of the brain. True wisdom comes of God and leads toward God; therefore, man should seek to achieve it.

REFERENCES.
Fear of God Wisdom's Beginning.

And unto man he said, Behold, the fear of the Lord, that is wisdom: and to depart from evil is understanding. (Job 28: 28.)

The fear of the Lord is the beginning of wisdom: a good understanding have all they that do his commandments: his praise endureth for ever. (Psalm 111: 10.)

The fear of the Lord is the beginning of knowledge: but fools despise wisdom and instruction. (Proverbs 1: 7.)

The fear of the Lord is the beginning of wisdom: and the knowledge of the Holy is understanding. (Proverbs 9: 10.)

Wisdom Comes from God.

But there is a spirit in man: and the inspiration of the Almighty giveth them understanding. (Job 32: 8.)

Who hath put wisdom in the inward parts? or who hath given understanding to the heart? (Job 38: 36.)

I will instruct thee and teach thee in the way which thou shalt go: I will guide thee with mine eye. (Psalm 32: 8.)

For the Lord giveth wisdom: out of his mouth cometh knowledge and understanding.

He layeth up sound wisdom for the righteous: he is a buckler to them that walk uprightly. (Proverbs 2: 6, 7.)

Evil men understand not judgment: but they that seek the Lord understand all things. (Proverbs 28: 5.)

Thus saith the Lord, thy Redeemer, the Holy One of Israel; I am the Lord thy God which teacheth thee to profit, which leadeth thee by the way that thou shouldest go. (Isaiah 48: 17.)

If any of you lack wisdom, let him ask of God, that giveth to all men liberally, and upbraideth not; and it shall be given him. (James 1: 5.)

Wisdom Is to Be Sought.

Understand, ye brutish among the people: and ye fools, when will ye be wise? (Psalm 94: 8.)

How long, ye simple ones, will ye love simplicity? and the scorners delight in their scorning, and fools hate knowledge?

Turn you at my reproof: behold, I will pour out my spirit unto you, I will make known my words unto you. (Proverbs 1: 22, 23.)

Get wisdom, get understanding: forget it not; neither decline from the words of my mouth.

Forsake her not, and she shall preserve thee: love her, and she shall keep thee.

Wisdom is the principal thing; therefore get wisdom: and with all thy getting get understanding. (Proverbs 4: 5-7.)

Hear counsel, and receive instruction, that thou mayest be wise in thy latter end. (Proverbs 19: 20.)

Cease, my son, to hear the instruction that causeth to err from the words of knowledge. (Proverbs 19: 27.)

Apply thine heart unto instruction, and thine ears to the words of knowledge. (Proverbs 23: 12.)

Buy the truth, and sell it not; also wisdom, and instruction, and understanding. (Proverbs 23: 23.)

Brethren, be not children in understanding: howbeit in malice be ye children, but in understanding be men. (1 Corinthians 14: 20.)

See then that ye walk circumspectly, not as fools, but as wise,

Redeeming the time, because the days are evil.

Wherefore be ye not unwise, but understanding what the will of the Lord is. (Ephesians 5: 15-17.)

Walk in wisdom toward them that are without, redeeming the time. (Colossians 4: 5.)

Wisdom Is Attainable.

Wisdom crieth without; she uttereth her voice in the streets:

She crieth in the chief place of concourse, in the openings of the gates: in the city she uttereth her words, saying. (Proverbs 1: 20, 21.)

Doth not wisdom cry? and understanding put forth her voice?

She standeth in the top of high places, by the way in the places of the paths. (Proverbs 8: 1, 2.)

Unto you, O men, I call; and my voice is to the sons of man.

O ye simple, understand wisdom: and, ye fools, be ye of an understanding heart.

Hear; for I will speak of excellent things; and the opening of my lips shall be right things.

For my mouth shall speak truth; and wickedness is an abomination to my lips.

All the words of my mouth are in righteousness; there is nothing froward or perverse in them. (Proverbs 8: 4-8.)

Wisdom hath builded her house, she hath hewn out her seven pillars:

She hath killed her beasts; she hath mingled her wine; she hath also furnished her table.

She hath sent forth her maidens: she crieth upon the highest places of the city,

Whoso is simple, let him turn in hither: as for him that wanteth understanding, she saith to him,

Come, eat of my bread, and drink of the wine which I have mingled.

Forsake the foolish, and live; and go in the way of understanding. (Proverbs 9: 1-6.)

A scorner seeketh wisdom, and findeth it not: but knowledge is easy unto him that understandeth. (Proverbs 14: 6.)

Where Wisdom Is Not.

For vain man would be wise, though man be born like a wild ass's colt. (Job 11: 12.)

Great men are not always wise: neither do the aged understand judgment. (Job 22: 9.)

But where shall wisdom be found? and where is the place of understanding?

Man knoweth not the price thereof;

neither is it found in the land of the living.

The depth saith, It is not in me: and the sea saith, It is not with me. (Job 28: 12-14.)

Whence then cometh wisdom? and where is the place of understanding?

Seeing it is hid from the eyes of all living, and kept close from the fowls of the air.

Destruction and death say, We have heard the fame thereof with our ears. (Job 28: 20-22.)

I communed with mine own heart, saying, Lo, I am come to great estate, and have gotten more wisdom than all they that have been before me in Jerusalem: yea, my heart had great experience of wisdom and knowledge.

And I gave my heart to know wisdom, and to know madness and folly: I perceived that this also is vexation of spirit. (Ecclesiastes 1: 16, 17.)

All this have I proved by wisdom: I said, I will be wise; but it was far from me.

That which is far off, and exceeding deep, who can find it out?

I applied mine heart to know, and to search, and to seek out wisdom, and the reason of things, and to know the wickedness of folly, even of foolishness and madness. (Ecclesiastes 7: 23-25.)

When I applied mine heart to know wisdom, and to see the business that is done upon the earth: (for also there is that neither day nor night seeth sleep with his eyes:)

Then I beheld all the work of God, that a man cannot find out the work that is done under the sun: because though a man labour to seek it out, yet he shall not find it; yea further; though a wise man think to know it, yet shall

he not be able to find it. (Ecclesiastes 8: 16, 17.)

General Remarks and Exhortations on Wisdom.

I will shew thee, hear me; and that which I have seen I will declare;

Which wise men have told from their fathers, and have not hid it:

Unto whom alone the earth was given, and no stranger passed among them. (Job 15: 17-19.)

Thou shalt also decree a thing, and it shall be established unto thee: and the light shall shine upon thy ways. (Job 22: 28.)

It cannot be gotten for gold, neither shall silver be weighed for the price thereof. (Job 28: 15.)

The mouth of the righteous speaketh wisdom, and his tongue talketh of judgment. (Psalm 37: 30.)

Whoso is wise, and will observe these things, even they shall understand the lovingkindness of the Lord. (Psalm 107: 43.)

Then shalt thou understand righteousness, and judgment, and equity; yea, every good path.

When wisdom entereth into thine heart, and knowledge is pleasant unto thy soul;

Discretion shall preserve thee, understanding shall keep thee. (Proverbs 2: 9-11.)

Happy is the man that findeth wisdom, and the man that getteth understanding:

For the merchandise of it is better than the merchandise of silver, and the gain thereof than fine gold.

She is more precious than rubies: and all the things thou canst desire are not to be compared unto her.

Length of days is in her right hand;

and in her left hand riches and honour.

Her ways are ways of pleasantness, and all her paths are peace.

She is a tree of life to them that lay hold upon her: and happy is every one that retaineth her. (Proverbs 3: 13-18.)

Wisdom is good with an inheritance: and by it there is profit to them that see the sun.

For wisdom is a defence, and money is a defence: but the excellency of knowledge is, that wisdom giveth life to them that have it. (Ecclesiastes 7: 11, 12.)

A wise man's heart is at his right hand; but a fool's heart at his left. (Ecclesiastes 10: 2.)

The light of the body is the eye; if therefore thine eye be single, thy whole body shall be full of light.

But if thine eye be evil, thy whole body shall be full of darkness. If therefore the light that is in thee be darkness, how great is that darkness! (Matthew 6: 22, 23.)

Now concerning spiritual gifts, brethren, I would not have you ignorant. (1 Corinthians 12: 1.)

The eyes of your understanding being enlightened; that ye may know what is the hope of his calling, and what the riches of the glory of his inheritance in the saints. (Ephesians 1: 18.)

But the wisdom that is from above is first pure, then peaceable, gentle, and easy to be entreated, full of mercy and good fruits, without partiality and without hypocrisy. (James 3: 17.)

Wisdom to Be Found in Scripture.

Moreover by them is thy servant

warned; and in keeping of them there is great reward. (Psalm 19: 11.)

Thou through thy commandments hast made me wiser than mine enemies; for they are ever with me.

I have more understanding than all my teachers: for thy testimonies are my meditation.

I understand more than the ancients, because I keep thy precepts. (Psalm 119: 98-100.)

To know wisdom and instruction; to perceive the words of understanding;

To receive the instruction of wisdom, justice, and judgment, and equity;

To give subtilty to the simple, to the young man knowledge and discretion. (Proverbs 1: 2-4.)

Jesus saith unto them, *Have ye understood all these things?* They say unto him, Yea, Lord.

Then said he unto them, *Therefore every scribe which is instructed unto the kingdom of heaven, is like unto a man that is a householder, which bringeth forth out of his treasure things new and old.* (Matthew 13: 51, 52.)

And when he was alone, they that were about him with the twelve asked of him the parable.

And he said unto them, *Unto you it is given to know the mystery of the kingdom of God: but unto them that are without, all these things are done in parables:*

That seeing they may see, and not perceive; and hearing they may hear, and not understand; lest at any time they should be converted, and their sins should be forgiven them. (Mark 4: 10-12.)

And Jesus answering said unto them, *Do ye not therefore err, because ye know not the Scriptures, neither the power of God?* (Mark 12: 24.)

Now all these things happened unto them for ensamples: and they are written for our admonition upon whom the ends of the world are come. (1 Corinthians 10: 11.)

Whereby, when ye read, ye may understand my knowledge in the mystery of Christ. (Ephesians 3: 4.)

Worldly Wisdom Foolishness with God.

For it is written, I will destroy the wisdom of the wise, and will bring to nothing the understanding of the prudent.

Where is the wise? where is the scribe? where is the disputer of this world? hath not God made foolish the wisdom of this world?

For after that in the wisdom of God the world by wisdom knew not God, it pleased God by the foolishness of preaching to save them that believe.

For the Jews require a sign, and the Greeks seek after wisdom. (1 Corinthians 1: 19-22.)

Howbeit we speak wisdom among them that are perfect: yet not the wisdom of this world, nor of the princes of this world, that come to nought. (1 Corinthians 2: 6.)

Let no man deceive himself. If any man among you seemeth to be wise in this world, let him become a fool, that he may be wise.

For the wisdom of this world is foolishness with God: for it is written, He taketh the wise in their own craftiness.

And again, The Lord knoweth the thoughts of the wise, that they are vain. (1 Corinthians 3: 18-20.)

WITNESS.

WIT'NESS—a person or thing that furnishes evidence or proof; also to a certain extent the proof itself. The word is a very important one Scripturally, and is found in the Bible used in a number of different ways, but always with the idea as conveyed in the above definition. The chief uses are: (1) a person who deposes to the occurrence of any fact, a witness of an event; (2) in a general sense, a person who is able to certify to something within his cognizance; (3) a person who is able to testify to the world what God has done to or through him or has revealed through him; (4) the constant profession of Christianity and the witness of the truth of the gospel of God.

REFERENCES.

God Invoked as a Witness.

And the elders of Gilead said unto Jephthah, The Lord be witness between us, if we do not so according to thy words. (Judges 11: 10.)

Then they said to Jeremiah, The Lord be a true and faithful witness between us, if we do not even according to all things for the which the Lord thy God shall send thee to us. (Jeremiah 42: 5.)

Hear, all ye people; hearken, O earth, and all that therein is: and let the Lord God be witness against you, the Lord from his holy temple. (Micah 1: 2.)

For God is my witness, whom I serve with my spirit in the gospel of his Son, that without ceasing I make mention of you always in my prayers. (Romans 1: 9.)

For neither at any time used we flattering words, as ye know, nor a cloke of covetousness; God is witness. (1 Thessalonians 2: 5.)

The Father Bears Witness to Christ.

And Jesus, when he was baptized, went up straightway out of the water: and, lo, the heavens were opened unto him, and he saw the Spirit of God descending like a dove, and lighting upon him:

And lo a voice from heaven saying, This is my beloved Son, in whom I am well pleased. (Matthew 3: 16, 17.)

And the Father himself, which hath sent me, hath borne witness of me. Ye have neither heard his voice at any time, nor seen his shape. (John 5: 37.)

Father, glorify thy name. Then came there a voice from heaven, saying, I have both glorified it, and will glorify it again. (John 12: 28.)

God also bearing them witness, both with signs and wonders, and with divers miracles, and gifts of the Holy Ghost, according to his own will? (Hebrews 2: 4.)

For there are three that bear record in heaven, the Father, the Word, and the Holy Ghost: and these three are one. (1 John 5: 7.)

Holy Ghost Witness to Christ.

And I knew him not: but he that sent me to baptize with water, the same said unto me, Upon whom thou shalt see the Spirit descending, and remaining on him, the same is he which baptizeth with the Holy Ghost. (John 1: 33.)

But when the Comforter is come, whom I will send unto you from the Father, even the Spirit of truth, which proceedeth from the Father, he shall testify of me. (John 15: 26.)

And we are his witnesses of these things; and so is also the Holy Ghost, whom God hath given to them that obey him. (Acts 5: 32.)

Save that the Holy Ghost witnesseth in every city, saying that bonds and afflictions abide me. (Acts 20: 23.)

Whereof the Holy Ghost also is a witness to us: for after that he had said before. (Hebrews 10: 15.)

False Witnesses. (See Commandments, Lying, Perjury.)

Thou shalt not raise a false report: put not thine hand with the wicked to be an unrighteous witness. (Exodus 23: 1.)

And ye shall not swear by my name falsely, neither shalt thou profane the name of thy God: I am the Lord. (Leviticus 19: 12.)

Neither shalt thou bear false witness against thy neighbour. (Deuteronomy 5: 20.)

A faithful witness will not lie: but a false witness will utter lies. (Proverbs 14: 5.)

An ungodly witness scorneth judgment: and the mouth of the wicked devoureth iniquity. (Proverbs 19: 28.)

Be not a witness against thy neighbour without cause; and deceive not with thy lips. (Proverbs 24: 28.)

A man that beareth false witness against his neighbour is a maul, a sword, and a sharp arrow. (Proverbs 25: 18.)

And let none of you imagine evil in your hearts against his neighbour; and love no false oath: for all these are things that I hate, saith the Lord. (Zechariah 8: 17.)

WORD. (See Christ, Jesus, Scriptures.)

WORD—one of the names of Christ; especially applied to Him by John; also a name given to the Scriptures.

WORKS.

WORKS—acts; deeds; achievements. The word "works" is used in Scripture in a number of different ways; chiefly, however, to specify the acts and deeds of God, and the acts and deeds of man. The Bible teaches that all man's good works are inspired of God and that of himself man is incapable of them.

REFERENCES.

Works Required for Justification.

And it shall be our righteousness, if we observe to do all these commandments before the Lord our God, as he hath commanded us. (Deuteronomy 6: 25.)

Was not Abraham our father justified by works, when he had offered Isaac his son upon the altar?

Seest thou how faith wrought with his works, and by works was faith made perfect? (James 2: 21, 22.)

Ye see then how that by works a man is justified, and not by faith only.

Likewise also was not Rahab the harlot justified by works, when she had received the messengers, and had sent them out another way? (James 2: 24, 25.)

Works without Faith Insufficient.

I know it is so of a truth: but how should man be just with God?

If he will contend with him, he cannot answer him one of a thousand. (Job 9: 2, 3.)

What shall we say then that Abraham our father, as pertaining to the flesh, hath found?

For if Abraham were justified by works, he hath whereof to glory; but not before God. (Romans 4: 1, 2.)

Now to him that worketh is the reward not reckoned of grace, but of debt. (Romans 4: 4.)

For as many as are of the works of the law are under the curse: for it is written, Cursed is every one that continueth not in all things which are written in the book of the law to do them. (Galatians 3: 10.)

Faith without Works Insufficient.

Do we then make void the law through faith? God forbid: yea, we establish the law. (Romans 3: 31.)

This is a faithful saying, and these things I will that thou affirm constantly, that they which have believed in God might be careful to maintain good works. These things are good and profitable unto men. (Titus 3: 8.)

And let ours also learn to maintain good works for necessary uses, that they be not unfruitful. (Titus 3: 14.)

What doth it profit, my brethren, though a man say he hath faith, and have not works? can faith save him? (James 2: 14.)

Even so faith, if it hath not works, is dead, being alone.

Yea, a man may say, Thou hast faith, and I have works: shew me thy faith without thy works, and I will shew thee my faith by my works. (James 2: 17, 18.)

But wilt thou know, O vain man, that faith without works is dead? (James 2: 20.)

For as the body without the spirit is dead, so faith without works is dead also. (James 2: 26.)

Works the Fruit of Faith.

Ye shall know them by their fruits. Do men gather grapes of thorns, or figs of thistles?

Even so every good tree bringeth forth good fruit; but a corrupt tree bringeth forth evil fruit.

A good tree cannot bring forth evil fruit, neither can a corrupt tree bring forth good fruit.

Every tree that bringeth not forth good fruit is hewn down, and cast into the fire.

Wherefore by their fruits ye shall know them. (Matthew 7: 16-20.)

Either make the tree good, and his fruit good; or else make the tree corrupt, and his fruit corrupt: for the tree is known by his fruit. (Matthew 12: 33.)

And now also the axe is laid unto the root of the trees: every tree therefore which bringeth not forth good fruit is hewn down, and cast into the fire. (Luke 3: 9.)

For a good tree bringeth not forth corrupt fruit; neither doth a corrupt tree bring forth good fruit.

For every tree is known by his own fruit. For of thorns men do not gather figs, nor of a bramble bush gather they grapes. (Luke 6: 43, 44.)

Man to Be Judged by His Works.

Now if any man build upon this foundation gold, silver, precious stones, wood, hay, stubble;

Every man's work shall be made manifest: for the day shall declare it, because it shall be revealed by fire; and the fire shall try every man's work of what sort it is.

If any man's work abide which he hath built thereupon, he shall receive a reward.

If any man's work shall be burned, he shall suffer loss: but he himself shall be saved; yet so as by fire. (1 Corinthians 3: 12-15.)

WORSHIP.

WOR'SHIP—the act of paying divine honors to the Supreme Being; reading His word, religious reverence and homage by the performance of rites, ceremonies, etc.

REFERENCES.

Praise Is Worship.

I will praise thee for ever, because thou hast done it: and I will wait on thy name; for it is good before thy saints. (Psalm 52: 9.)

Kings of the earth, and all people; princes, and all judges of the earth:

Both young men, and maidens; old men, and children:

Let them praise the name of the Lord: for his name alone is excellent; his glory is above the earth and heaven. (Psalm 148: 11-13.)

Hearing God's Word Is Worship.

Keep thy foot when thou goest to the house of God, and be more ready to hear, than to give the sacrifice of fools: for they consider not that they do evil. (Ecclesiastes 5: 1.)

The Church the Place of Worship.

And he came to Nazareth, where he had been brought up: and, as his custom was, he went into the synagogue on the sabbath day, and stood up for to read.

And there was delivered unto him the book of the prophet Esaias. And when he had opened the book, he found the place where it was written,

The Spirit of the Lord is upon me, because he hath anointed me to preach the gospel to the poor; he hath sent me to heal the broken-hearted, to preach deliverance to the captives, and recovering of sight to the blind, to set at liberty them that are bruised,

To preach the acceptable year of the Lord. (Luke 4: 16-19.)

Now Peter and John went up together into the temple at the hour of prayer, being the ninth hour. (Acts 3: 1.)

General Calls to Worship.

This is the day which the Lord hath made; we will rejoice and be glad in it. (Psalm 118: 24.)

I was glad when they said unto me, Let us go into the house of the Lord. (Psalm 122: 1.)

But the Lord is in his holy temple: let all the earth keep silence before him. (Habakkuk 2: 20.)

From the rising of the sun even unto the going down of the same my Name shall be great among the Gentiles; and in every place incense shall be offered unto my Name, and a pure offering: for my Name shall be great among the heathen, saith the Lord of hosts. (Malachi 1: 11.)

I will arise and go to my father, and will say unto him, Father, I have sinned against heaven, and before thee,

And am no more worthy to be called thy son. (Luke 15: 18, 19.)

Let us come boldly unto the throne of grace, that we may obtain mercy, and find grace to help in time of need. (Hebrews 4: 16.)

Worship in Heaven.

And when those beasts give glory and honour and thanks to him that sat on the throne, who liveth for ever and ever,

The four and twenty elders fall down before him that sat on the throne, and worship him that liveth for ever and ever, and cast their crowns before the throne, saying. (Revelation 4: 9, 10.)

And the four beasts said, Amen. And the four and twenty elders fell down and worshipped him that liveth for ever and ever. (Revelation 5: 14.)

ZACCHÆUS.

Zac-chæ'us—a form of a Hebrew word meaning "just." This man was a superintendent of taxes or collector of customs. He came to hear Jesus preach, and Jesus showed him special favor by going to his house as a guest, also showing that he knew Zacchæus to be a good man and one to whom salvation was near.

Reference.—Luke 19.

ZACHARIAS. (See Elizabeth, John the Baptist.)

Zach'a-ri'as—the father of John the Baptist.

Reference.—Luke 1: 5-65.

ZECHARIAH.

Zech'a-ri'ah—a form of a Hebrew word meaning "whom Jehovah remembers." There are a large number of persons of the name of Zechariah in the Bible. The most important of them probably is the prophet of the name, the eleventh in order.

Reference.—The book of Zechariah.

ZION.

Zi'on—a form of a Hebrew word meaning "sunny." Zion was one of the mounts upon which Jerusalem was built. David brought the ark to the place, and therefore made it sacred, the name of "the holy hill" being thereafter given to it. Afterwards it became quite common to call the whole city of Jerusalem Zion, and the name has been largely used as a title for the Church at large.

APPENDIX

46

THE HISTORY OF THE BIBLE

The Nature of the Holy Bible. THE Bible is a collection of sixty-six books written by about forty different men, inspired by God to the work. It represents about fifteen centuries of labor as it stands, having been begun by Moses, about the year 1500 B.C., and ended by John somewhere between 75 and 100 A.D. It is divided into two sections: the Old Testament, containing thirty-nine books and covering the period from the creation to the end of the prophetic period in the history of the Hebrew people, and the New Testament, containing twenty-seven books, covering the period from the birth of Jesus Christ to the extension of the Church under the apostles, about the year 75 A.D. Between the two divisions there is a gap of about 400 years, which in a measure is filled by a number of books called the Apocrypha, which, while not recognized as having the divine authority of the Bible itself, are considered as being excellent for reading and instruction.

The Bible originally was written in three languages: the Old Testament in Hebrew and Aramaic, the latter language being employed for a part of the books of Daniel and Ezra, and one verse of the book of Jeremiah; and the New Testament in an impure form of Greek used by the Hebrews of the time. It has been translated into almost every tongue spoken by the race of man. The name Bible was applied to it somewhere between the second and fifth centuries of our era. Prior to that time the books were known simply as the Scriptures or sacred. The word "bible" is derived from a Greek word meaning "the small books."

Formation of the Bible. It must not be imagined that the Bible as it stands to-day is the original form of it. It took centuries to form what is known as the canon of Scripture. The word "canon" comes from a Greek word meaning "a measuring rod or rule." Hence, when anything became a standard it conformed to the established measure or rule. Since the Scriptures are the standard and rule of faith, they have been called Canonical Scripture, or the Canon of Scripture. The formation of the Old Testament canon was a very gradual process and covered centuries of time in the days before Christ. "The Book of the Law" was the basis of it. This may be described generally as the first five books, known to the Jews latterly as the Pentateuch. To this was added by Ezra and Nehemiah and the Great Council of the Jews the books up to the return from the Captivity. And later still came the later prophets and the minor prophets. The work was undoubtedly complete by the year 400 B.C.

The various books were written in manuscript, the art of printing not having been discovered until many centuries later. But undoubtedly there were many manuscript copies, this being the only way in which the sacred writings could be studied by the priests or doctors of the law, and circulated. The oldest specimen in existence dates from the ninth century of our era, but it is traceable to very, very much older copies, which go back to the official Hebrew sources, which are known as the Talmud and the Targums. The first great translation was made at Alexandria, Egypt, from about 270 B.C. to 150 B.C., and was started by seventy learned men assembled by the king, Ptolemy Philadelphus, for the purpose. This version was called the Septuagint, because of the numbers of workers upon it. It was used to a large extent in the versions which gave rise to what we now know as the Authorized Version. Later, other translations were made, notably that known as the Vulgate, made by Jerome, about 383 A.D.

With regard to the canon of the New Testament, it was much sooner in forming than the Old. Soon after the ascension of Christ began the preparation of the books, in the shape of histories of the Lord, or gospels, the chronicling of the works of the apostles, which we know as Acts, and in various pastoral letters from the apostles to churches founded by them or under their care, the whole being supplemented by the marvelous prophecy of John, which we know as the book of Revelation. At the same time there were written a large number of other books similar in character and circulated for the same purpose. For close upon three centuries after Jesus died these books accumulated and the Church soon saw the necessity for separating the real from the unreal and the inspired from the uninspired. A rigid and searching investigation was begun and carried on by the most learned scholars and holy men of the times. Finally, in 397 A.D., the Council of Carthage, an assembly of the whole Church, issued a decree setting down once and for all the canon of the New Testament as it stands to-day.

English Translations of the Bible. Prior to the fourteenth century there had been a few attempts to translate the Bible from the ancient tongues into a language intelligible to the mass of the English people. These attempts were in Anglo-Saxon and Anglo-Norman. In Germany the great reformer, Martin Luther, had not yet arisen to give to the world the German Bible, but in England another reformer became busy in the latter part of the fourteenth century. This man was Wyclif. He was followed in 1525, 1530, and 1534 by William Tindale. In 1537 Matthew's Bible was published, as an improvement on the work of Tindale. Then followed the Great Bible, the Geneva Bible, and the so-called Bishops' Bible. These were the chief ones, although several others of less importance were issued. All these, however, led up to the great work known as the Authorized Version, or the King James Bible. This had its inception in 1604 and was promoted by the English king, James. Forty-seven men did the work, completing it in 1611.

This work stood practically untouched for nearly three hundred years, and it doubtless will never be completely laid aside for any other version, although newer ones may be used for their more definite scholarship. In the middle of the nineteenth century there came to the surface a demand for a new version because of certain weak points in the King James Bible discovered through better Greek scholarship and the obsolete character of certain phrases and words. In 1870 the English Church selected fifty revisers and a similar body took up the work in coöperation in this country. The task was completed in 1885 and the work known as the Revised Version, and its American edition, the American Standard Edition, came into being.

Curiosities Concerning the Bible. Bible readers have doubtless noticed the chapter and verse subdivisions of the Book, the descriptive headings of chapters and the presence of italics, or sloping letters, in the text. These did not exist in the original. The division into chapters, which was unquestionably for greater ease of reading and quotation, was made in the thirteenth century in the Vulgate Bible by Cardinal Hugo or Archbishop Langton. At a later period, probably 1551, one Robert Stephens made the division into verses. They are very imperfect and sometimes greatly obscure the meaning. The presence of italics is due to the fact that in many instances it was necessary to introduce words to make clear a meaning which could not be translated easily, or to supply deficiences due to differences in language.

The following facts may be interesting:

The number of *books* in the Old Testament is 39; in the New Testament, 27; total, 66.

Of *chapters,* there are, in the Old Testament, 929; in the New Testament, 260; total, 1,189.

Of *verses,* there are, in the Old Testament, 23,214; in the New Testament, 7,959; total, 31,173.

Of *words,* the Old Testament contains 592,-493; and the New Testament, 181,253; total, 773,746.

Of *letters,* there are, in the Old Testament, 2,728,100; in the New Testament, 838,380; total, 3,566,480.

The middle chapter in the Bible, which is also the shortest, is Psalm 117.

The middle verse is Psalm 118: 8.

The middle line is 2 Chronicles 4: 16.

The word "and" occurs, in the Old Testament, 35,535 times; in the New Testament, 10,684 times; total, 46,219 times.

The word "Jehovah" occurs 6,855 times.

Of the Old Testament, the middle book is Proverbs; the middle chapter is Job 29; the middle verse is 2 Chronicles 20: 18; the shortest verse is 1 Chronicles 1: 1.

Of the New Testament, the middle book is 2 Thessalonians; the middle chapter is between Romans 13 and 14; the middle verse is Acts 17: 17; and the shortest verse, which is also the shortest in the whole Bible, is John 11: 35.

Ezra 7: 21 contains all the letters in the alphabet except "j."

Two chapters in the Bible are alike—namely, 2 Kings 19 and Isaiah 37, a very remarkable coincidence.

THE BOOKS OF THE BIBLE

THE OLD TESTAMENT:

Divisions of the books of the Old Testament. MODERN commentators separate the book of the Old Testament into four grand divisions—namely, the Pentateuch, containing the law and the Mosaic history; the historical books, containing such of the history of the children of Israel as is written in the Bible; the poetical books, containing the part of the religious poetry and philosophy of the Hebrews that has been preserved; and the prophetical books, including the writings and utterances of the major and minor prophets.

The books in the Pentateuch are: Genesis, Exodus, Leviticus, Numbers, and Deuteronomy. Total, 5.

The historical books are: Joshua, Judges, Ruth, 1 Samuel, 2 Samuel, 1 Kings, 2 Kings, 1 Chronicles, 2 Chronicles, Ezra, Nehemiah, and Esther. Total, 12.

The poetical books are: Job, the Psalms, Proverbs, Ecclesiastes, and the Song of Solomon, also known as Canticles. Total, 5.

The prophetical books are: Isaiah, Jeremiah, Lamentations, Ezekiel, and Daniel (called the major prophets); and Hosea, Joel, Amos, Obadiah, Jonah, Micah, Nahum, Habakkuk, Zephaniah, Haggai, Zechariah, and Malachi (called the minor prophets). Total, 17. Grand total, 39.

Following is a brief history and outline of the various books:

The books of the PENTATEUCH. The first book of the Pentateuch, as well as the first of the Bible, is called GENESIS, because it tells of the generation or beginning of things. It contains the history of the world from the creation to the call of Abraham, after which it tells of the history of Abraham and three other patriarchs as the founders of the race of Israel, and the history of the Israelites up to the bondage in Egypt. With the chronology it gives we see that it covers a period of almost 2,400 years. Its authorship is ascribed generally to Moses, although some commentators have thought that he wrote only a part of it, and edited or compiled the rest. The date of its writing was probably about 1500 B.C. It contains 50 chapters.

EXODUS receives its name from the fact that it relates in detail the exodus or departure of the Israelites from Egypt and the bondage they suffered there. It also contains an account of the wanderings of the Israelites through the wilderness and the giving of the Law at Sinai, the defection of the children of Israel from the straight path, their return, and the building of the Tabernacle. As regards the history of the Israelitish people it is closely related to the book of Genesis. It was written about 1490 B.C., almost unquestionably by Moses. It contains 40 chapters.

LEVITICUS receives its name because it contains the ceremonial religious law, the performance of which was entrusted to the Levites. It is really a continuation of the book of Exodus, for in that book is begun the statement of the law. Besides the ceremonial law it contains many other regulations to be observed by the children of Israel in daily life. Its author was Moses, and it was written about 1470 B.C. It contains 27 chapters.

NUMBERS gets its name because of the fact that it was the book of the census of the children of Israel. It contains historical matter, including the census figures and the war organization of the people, besides sundry laws and ordinances. Its author was Moses, and it was written about 1460. It contains 36 chapters.

DEUTERONOMY is the last book of the Pentateuch. It receives its name from the fact that it is the second statement of the law. It contains the repetition of the commands and ordinances, with certain explanations and some additions, and a recapitulation of the events since the departure from Egypt, as well as exhortations to the Israelites to behave themselves in God's way. At the end is a description of the death of Moses, which indicates that the hand of God cut short Moses' authorship of it and that it was finished by some one else, probably Joshua. It contains 34 chapters and was written about 1450 B.C.

THE HISTORICAL BOOKS. JOSHUA begins the section of historical books. In it we find a great change to have taken place in the Hebrew nation. They have come under the leadership of Moses' successor, Joshua, crossed the Jordan into the Promised Land and begun the conquest of the region in obedience to the commands of God. Toward the end we find the conquest practically finished, and we are told of the death of Joshua. In this respect it bears something of a resemblance to Deuteronomy, the matter concerning Joshua's demise having been added by some other hand than his, which wrote the larger part of the book. It was written about 1430 B.C., and contains 24 chapters.

JUDGES is named for the fact that it contains the history of Israel from the death of Joshua to the time of Eli, under the rule of something over a dozen leaders who were called "judges." It is highly probable that the larger part of it was written by Samuel, although there is no doubt that his was not the only pen engaged upon the work. It covers a period of at least 300 years. It is impossible to say just when it was written. It contains 21 chapters.

RUTH, while it contains a certain amount of historical matter, is essentially the story of the devotion of two women and the love story of Ruth and Boaz. Its period is about one hundred years prior to the time of David. It contains but 4 chapters. Its authorship is entirely unknown.

1 SAMUEL and 2 SAMUEL get their name from the character of Samuel, who figures extensively in the opening portion of the first book. Both are full of historical matter of the first importance—the careers of the last two judges, Eli and Samuel, and the first two kings, Saul and David. The books are of vast interest, throwing much light on the wickedness of the Israelites, their wars, and on the efforts of God to get them to reform. The authorship of the books is doubtful, but opinion tends to crediting Samuel, Nathan and one or two others with their writing in fragments and final compilation, editing, and revision by Jeremiah many years later. 1 Samuel contains 31 chapters and 2 Samuel 24 chapters.

1 KINGS and 2 KINGS continue the history of the Israelites, from the death of David and the accession of Solomon up to the destruction of Jerusalem, a period of about 426 years. In them is the only record of the independent kingdom of Israel. Both books seem to have been compiled by Jeremiah. 1 Kings contains 22 chapters and 2 Kings 25 chapters.

1 CHRONICLES and 2 CHRONICLES are Jewish national records. They contain many important genealogical tables, and are especially full of the religious history of the Jews. There is also an excellent history of the independent kingdom of Judah. Daniel and Ezra are regarded as the compilers, the latter probably doing the bulk of the work. The first book contains 29 chapters, and the second 36 chapters.

EZRA continues the history of the Jews for a period of about 80 years, beginning with the return of the Jews from the Captivity It tells of the rebuilding of the Temple and the religious reformation which took place among the people. The work was written by Ezra, one of the greatest of the Hebrew historians, and the man to whom we are indebted for a large amount of collecting and restoring of the Scriptures. It is probable that Daniel, Nehemiah, and Haggai made some additions to Ezra and edited it. The book contains ten chapters.

NEHEMIAH was at one time considered a part of Ezra. It covers much of the same sort of ground as Ezra. Its author, Nehemiah, was a man of distinguished talents and position, and a patriot of the highest type. He did a large amount of work upon the Scriptures in the shape of collation and revision. The book contains 13 chapters.

ESTHER receives its name from the principal figure in it. She had nothing to do with the authorship, according to the most modern opinions. The book relates her history and elevation to be queen to Ahasuerus, and the overthrow of the conspiracy for the slaughter of the Jews formed by Haman. It is possible that the author of the work was Mordecai, or some one who wrote from his dictation. Internal evidence shows familiarity with the manners and customs of the Persians, as well as almost first-hand familiarity with the story itself. The book contains 10 chapters.

THE POETICAL BOOKS. JOB begins the poetical books. It is one of the most marvelous pieces of composition in the Bible, and has been the subject of great debate as to its character. Many critics and scholars believe that it is entirely a fictitious narrative, a sort of ancient Pilgrim's Progress; while others contend that Job really lived and the events as described really occurred. There has also been debate as to its authorship and the time when it was written, but absolutely nothing regarding these questions can be settled definitely. Of this, however, there is no doubt: it is a work of the very highest literary and poetical quality, being, in fact, a dramatic poem. Its teachings are in accordance with the very highest authorities, and its canonicity is unquestioned. It contains 42 chapters.

THE PSALMS, or book of praises, commonly called the Psalms of David, because of his large contributions to it. It was compiled (probably) by Ezra. (See article in Appendix on Psalms.)

PROVERBS receives its name because of the fact that it is a collection of wise sayings. Its authorship is credited to Solomon, although it is possible that some of the proverbs were simply collected by him. It contains 31 chapters.

ECCLESIASTES, meaning "the preacher," is a continuous dissertation on the vanity of human things. It was long supposed that Solomon wrote it, but there is evidence to show that such was not the case. It contains 12 chapters.

THE SONG OF SOLOMON, also known as The Song of Songs and Canticles, is another remarkable poem. It is a description of wedded love, and as such has been regarded as an allegory, showing the love between Christ and His Church. The Jews saw in it allegorical allusion to the covenant between God and their race. Its authorship has been ascribed to Solomon, but this is uncertain. It contains 8 chapters.

THE PROPHETICAL BOOKS. ISAIAH receives its name from its author, Isaiah, the greatest of the Hebrew prophets. It is one of the most interesting books of the entire Bible. It is especially rich in prophecy regarding Jesus Christ. It contains 66 chapters and was written about the year 700 B.C.

JEREMIAH gets its name from its chief character and the man supposed to have written it. He was a man of intense patriotism and religion, and complained bitterly of the sins of Israel and the backsliding of the people. The book contains many exhortations to repentance and some prophecies regarding Christ. It contains 52 chapters.

LAMENTATIONS is another work by Jeremiah. The book contains five separate poems, connected by the same general idea. These poems are constructed with great regard for accurate versification. The book contains 5 chapters.

EZEKIEL gets its name from its author, who was the prophet of the Captivity. He foretells the coming of the Messiah. The book contains 48 chapters.

DANIEL receives its title from its author, a prophet of princely blood and one held in high esteem by both Jews and Christians. It is full of history and prophecy. The history relates to the Babylonian and Persian captivities and empires, and is of much value. The book contains 12 chapters.

HOSEA begins the list of minor prophetical books. It gets its name from its author. The book is one constant rebuke to the Jews for their wickedness and idolatry. The book contains 14 chapters.

JOEL gets its title from its author, of whom however very little is known. It is supposed he lived in the time of Joash and Judah, about 830 B.C. He calls the people to repentance. The book contains 3 chapters.

AMOS gets its name from its author. He follows very much the same line as Joel. The book contains 9 chapters.

OBADIAH receives its name from its writer. Little definite is known regarding him. His prophecies are chiefly against the Edomites. The book contains only one chapter.

JONAH is given its title by its author. It is another of the truly remarkable books of the Bible. It contains the history of Jonah, and his experiences when sent to exhort the people of Nineveh, a mission which he tried to evade. It contains 4 chapters.

MICAH gets its name from its author. The book is full of important prophecy, including the birth of the Saviour in Bethlehem. It contains 7 chapters.

NAHUM is given its name from its author's. We know little of the man, but his style is almost as beautiful as Isaiah's, which it greatly resembles. The fall of Nineveh is his theme. The book contains 3 chapters.

HABAKKUK gets its name from its author. It is a very fine work, especially from a literary point of view. It is in the form of a dialogue. It contains 3 chapters.

ZEPHANIAH receives its name from its author, who was of royal lineage. He foretells the great day of wrath particularly. The book contains 3 chapters.

HAGGAI gets its name from its author. It contains 2 chapters.

ZECHARIAH gets its name from its author. The book is of great importance because there are frequent references in its short length to the Messiah. The riding of Christ into Jerusalem upon an ass's colt, the betrayal, and even the sum Judas got for his treason are foretold. The book contains 14 chapters.

MALACHI is the last book of the prophets and the last of the Old Testament. It takes its name from its author. It reproves the Israelites for their wickednesses and makes further prophecies of the coming of the Messiah.

THE NEW TESTAMENT:

Divisions of the New Testament. THE books of the New Testament are separated into four grand divisions, namely: the historical books, including the four gospels and the acts of the apostles; the epistles of Paul; the general epistles; and the one prophetic book of Revelation.

The historical books are: the Gospel according to Matthew, the Gospel according to Mark, the Gospel according to Luke, the Gospel according to John, and the Acts of the Apostles.

The epistles of Paul are: Romans, 1 Corinthians, 2 Corinthians, Galatians, Ephesians, Philippians, Colossians, 1 Thessalonians, 2 Thessalonians, 1 Timothy, 2 Timothy, Philemon, and Hebrews.

The general epistles are: James, 1 Peter, 2 Peter, 1 John, 2 John, 3 John, and Jude.

The prophetic book is Revelation.

THE HISTORICAL BOOKS. The first four books of the historical section of the New Testament are known as the gospels, an appellation which has been variously interpreted as "the good tidings" and "God's spel" or narrative. The first three furnish a general view of the life of Christ and are called "the synoptical gospels," or gospels that give a general view. The fourth is a doctrinal gospel. Scriptural interpretation has assigned each one a symbol based upon Ezekiel 1: 4-10.

MATTHEW takes its name from its author, a Jew, and before his conversion named Levi, a publican and man of humble birth. It places emphasis upon the historical character of Jesus, in fulfilling the promises of the Old Testament. It was written about A.D. 60. Its symbol as a gospel is a man. It contains 28 chapters.

MARK takes its name also from its author, who also bore the name of John, but must not be confounded with the greater John. Evidences show that it was written for Gentile readers. It sets forth particularly the royal dignity of Jesus. It was written about 63 to 66 A.D. Its particular symbol is a lion. It contains 16 chapters.

LUKE takes its name from its author, who seems to have been of Gentile origin, and a native of Antioch. He was a physician. There seems to be evidence that it was written under the influence of Paul for the purpose of setting forth the sacrificial character of Jesus in being the Redeemer and Saviour of all men. It contains a large amount of matter not contained in any of the other gospels, notably with regard to the incidents prior to the birth of Jesus. It also sustains the chronological order of things more carefully than the other gospels. The symbol of it is an ox. It was written probably about A.D. 60. It contains 24 chapters.

JOHN gets its name from its author, John, who has been honored with the additional title of "the disciple whom Jesus loved." He was the youngest of the twelve. His gospel was written some years after the others, and he doubtless had copies of them before him as he wrote. His aim was to supply things they had omitted, to correct erroneous impressions that might arise from what they had said, and to give his personal testimony as to all that had passed. Since he had been the personal companion of the Master in much of that which had been done, and probably was closer to Jesus than any of the others, his gospel has a value that must not be underestimated. It is particularly full with reference to incidents that occurred during Christ's passion. It is also strong with reference to setting forth the divinity of Jesus. Its special symbol is an eagle. It was written somewhere between 78 and 90 A.D. It contains 21 chapters.

ACTS OF THE APOSTLES receives its name from the fact that it is a history of the doings of the more important of the apostles. It appears to have been written by Luke, the author of the gospel of that name. It sets forth the founding of the Church under Peter and its spread under Paul. It is of vast value in showing the teaching of these two great apostles, and it possesses a vast fund of history as well. It was written about A.D. 63, and contains 28 chapters.

THE PAULINE EPISTLES. The epistles of Paul are not arranged in the Bible according to the date of their authorship. To a certain extent the arrangement is one of importance, and by groups as to churches or individuals.

ROMANS takes its name from the fact that it was written to the people of Rome who were in the Church. They were partly Jews and partly Gentiles, wherefore the epistle was composed to bring about a common footing whereon racial differences might be settled. This common footing is the faith of the Lord Jesus Christ. The book is a strong exposition of Christianity. It was written about A.D. 58, while Paul was in Corinth. It contains 16 chapters.

I CORINTHIANS and 2 CORINTHIANS were written to the Church at Corinth, in Greece. The first was written in rebuke of certain abuses and troubles that had crept into the fold, and to allay troubles that had arisen over the old questions of the mixed races.

The second epistle was an outgrowth of the first, Paul finding it necessary to give considerable autobiography and to make a defense of his ministry for the purpose of quelling those who had not conformed after the first epistle and had spoken ill of him. The first was written in Ephesus A.D. 56 or 57; the second in Philippi in 57 or 58. The first contains 16 and the second 13 chapters.

GALATIANS gets its name from the fact that it was written to the people of Galatia, a province of Asia Minor. It specifically proclaims the freedom of the gospel as opposed to the bondage of the law. It was written from Ephesus about A.D. 54. It contains 6 chapters.

EPHESIANS receives its name from the fact that it was written to the people of the Church at Ephesus. It is remarkable for its description of the ideal church and the duty of the individual in the making of it. It was written during the apostle's first imprisonment in Rome in A.D. 62 or 63. It contains 6 chapters.

PHILIPPIANS is named by reason of its having been written to the people of the Church in Philippi. It is largely an acknowledgment of thanks for the goodness of the people to him. At the same time Paul takes the opportunity to give some good advice. It was written from prison in Rome about the same time as Ephesians. It contains 4 chapters.

COLOSSIANS likewise gets its name from the people to whom it was indited. It contains warnings against heresies, with which the church at that time seems to have been having trouble. It is of about the same date as the other prison epistles. It contains 4 chapters.

I THESSALONIANS and 2 THESSALONIANS were written to the church people of Thessalonica, a town in Macedonia. They are probably the earliest of the Pauline letters, and were written for correction and guidance for those who read them. The time of their writing was probably A.D. 52 and 53. The first contains 5 chapters and the second 3 chapters.

I TIMOTHY and 2 TIMOTHY are letters of a personal nature from Paul to his pupil and helper, Timothy. They are full of pastoral admonition, not only for Timothy but others. The second of them tells Timothy that the writer is about to suffer martyrdom and shows Paul's sublime faith and devotion to the cause of the Master. They were written from Macedonia and Rome respectively about A.D. 67 and 68. The first contains 6 and the second 4 chapters.

Titus is named for the man to whom it was written, a person for whom Paul had much love. It is much the same strain as the writings to Timothy. It was written about the same period. It contains 3 chapters.

Philemon was written to a man of that name, and is a personal and special letter. It shows Paul's love of justice and sympathetic nature. It is very beautiful and throws a strong light upon the character of the apostle. It was written from Rome about A.D. 62. It contains but one chapter.

Hebrews is a doctrinal letter, which, though originally intended for the Hebrews, may be accepted by all Christianity. It particularly stresses Christ's priesthood. It was written from Corinth about A.D. 52. Some critics think that Paul himself did not write it, but that it was done under his influence or by his advice or order, and embodied his views. The weight of evidence, however, is to the effect that it is a direct product of his pen. It contains 13 chapters.

THE GENERAL EPISTLES. James is the first of the general epistles, a name given to them because of the sweeping character of their application. James gets its particular name from its author. It is a wonderful exhortation to patience and piety. It was written about 62 A.D. It contains 5 chapters.

1 Peter and 2 Peter were written by the apostle whose name they bear. They are exhortations to faith, perseverance under persecution, and to holiness. They were written between 60 and 67 A.D., and contain 5 and 3 chapters respectively.

1 John, 2 John, and 3 John were written by the author of the Gospel of John. They are full of love and spirituality, and cast a great sidelight upon the character of the apostle. They were probably written between 85 and 95 A.D. They contain 5, 1, and 1 chapters respectively.

Jude is the last of the general epistles, and was written by the disciple and apostle of that name. It is addressed to all Christians, and is an admonition to stand firm in the faith. It was penned about 60-67 A.D. It contains but one chapter.

THE PROPHETIC BOOK. Revelation is the only prophetic book in the New Testament, but it is one of the most wonderful in the whole Bible. It is a book which requires a very great amount of study and hard reading, and even then it is not always comprehensible. This fact in itself is a proof of its prophetic nature. It is full of symbolism and intense spirituality, rare beauty of thought, and equally rare beauty of expression. It contains 22 chapters.

THE APOCRYPHA:

There are a number of books which are not included in the canons of the Old and New Testaments which are often printed in between the two under the name of the Apocrypha. They are of doubtful origin, whence their name, but are regarded as worthy of perusal for the sake of knowledge or instruction and for some of the sentiments expressed in them. They are: 1 Esdras, 2 Esdras, Tobit, Judith, the rest of the chapters of the Book of Esther, The Wisdom of Solomon, The Wisdom of Jesus the Son of Sirach, or Ecclesiasticus, Baruch, The Song of the Three Holy Children, The History of Susanna, The History of the Destruction of Bel and the Dragon, The Prayer of Manasses, 1 Maccabees, and 2 Maccabees.

GREAT PERIODS OF BIBLE HISTORY

Divisions of Bible History. TAKING the accepted Bible chronology as a basis, the Holy Scriptures cover a period of about 5,100 years—from the Creation to the composition of the book of Revelation. Modern scholarship, however, is inclined to believe that in reality a very much longer period is covered, reaching this conclusion by a process of reasoning based upon the premise that all dates and calculations prior to the time of Abraham are unreliable and that other evidences show a far greater lapse of years than is accounted for in the early chapters of Genesis. Upon this subject a very great amount of uncertainty exists, and different schools of thought have different opinions, which it is not meet to discuss here. The entire period, however, may be divided into ten smaller periods, as follows:

I. The Antediluvian Period: from the Creation to the Flood.

II. The Period of the Dispersion: from the Flood to the Promise to Abraham.

III. The Period of the Patriarchs: from the Promise to the Exodus.

IV. The Period of the Wandering: from the Exodus to the Crossing of Jordan.

V. The Period of the Theocracy or Government by God: from Joshua to Samuel.

VI. The First Intermediate Period: from Samuel to David.

VII. The Period of the Monarchy: from David to the Babylonish Captivity.

VIII. The Period of the Captivity and the Restoration: from the Conquest of Judea to the end of the Canon of the Old Testament.

IX. The Second Intermediate Period: from the end of the Canon of the Old Testament to the Beginning of Jesus' Ministry.

X. The Period of the Apostolic Church: from the Beginning of Jesus' Ministry to the End of the New Testament Canon.

The chief incidents of these periods are:

The Antediluvian Period: The Creation; the birth of Cain and Abel; the birth of Seth; the birth of Enos and the beginning of men "to call upon the name of the Lord;" the birth of Cainan; the birth of Mahalaleel; the birth of Jared; the birth of Enoch; the birth of Methuselah; the birth of Lamech; the death of Adam; the translation of Enoch; the death of Seth; the birth of Noah; the death of Enos; the death of Cainan; the death of Mahalaleel; the death of Jared; the beginning of the Ark; the birth of Noah's eldest son; the birth of Shem; the death of Lamech; the death of Methuselah; the Flood.

The Period of the Dispersion: The Issuance of Noah from the Ark; the birth of Arphaxad; the birth of Salah; the birth of Eber; the birth of Peleg and the Confusion of Tongues; the birth of Reu; the birth of Nahor; the birth of Terah; the death of Peleg; the death of Nahor; the death of Noah; the birth of Abraham (about 1996 B.C.); the death of Reu; the death of Serug; the death of Terah and the departure of Abraham to the land of Canaan (about 1920 B.C.); the Promise of God to Abraham (about 1912 B.C.).

The Period of the Patriarchs: Ishmael born (about 1910 B.C.); the Promise renewed; the visit of the three angels and the Destruction of Sodom and Gomorrah (about 1897 B.C.); Isaac born (about 1859 B.C.); Esau and Jacob born (about 1836 B.C.); death of Abraham (about 1821 B.C.); Jacob marries Leah and Rachel and begins to rear his family of sons after whom the tribes of Israel were named (about 1759 to 1743 B.C.); Joseph sold into Egypt (about 1737 B.C.); Joseph in prison in Egypt (about 1716 B.C.); Joseph raised to power (about 1715 B.C.); first descent of the Patriarchs into Egypt (about 1705 B.C.); Jacob dies (about 1689 B.C.); Joseph dies (about 1633 B.C.); Moses born (about 1571 B.C.); Moses flees to Midian (about 1531 B.C.).

The Period of the Wandering: The flight of the Israelites from Egypt commonly called the Exodus (about 1491 B.C.); the passage of the Red Sea (about 1491 B.C.); the giving of the law on Mt. Sinai (about 1490 B.C.); the forty years of wandering (about 1490 to 1450 B.C.).

The Period of the Theocracy: The siege and capture of Jericho; the peace with Gibeon; the defeat of the five kings and the subjugation of the south of the Land of Promise; the defeat of the kings of the north (from about 1450 to 1445 B.C.); the separate wars against the remainder of the Canaanites and the taking of Jerusalem, etc. (1445 B.C.); the gathering at Shiloh and the erection of the Tabernacle; the cities of refuge and the Israelites assigned, etc. (1444 B.C.); the second convocation at Shiloh at which Joshua delivers his parting charge; the covenant renewed; the death of Joshua (about 1443 B.C.); the angel of the Lord rebukes the people; a period of thirty years of righteousness, after which the people fall away from God and are punished by the first servitude of eight years (1443 to 1405 B.C.); the first judge (1405 B.C.); rest for the land for forty years; period in which eleven judges and five servitudes are chronicled (from 1343 to 1116 B.C.); the Ark in captivity and returned to Israel (1116 B.C.).

The First Intermediate Period: The Deliverance of the Israelites; Samuel begins to judge Israel (about 1116 or 1115 B.C.); period of calm; David born (somewhere between 1086 and 1079 B.C.); Saul finally elected king (between 1070 and 1063 B.C.); David anointed (about 1063 B.C.); David at Saul's court, with the troubles consequent upon Saul's jealousy and David's flight; David spares Saul's life, etc. (from 1063 to 1060 B.C.); Samuel's death (1060 B.C.); David flees to Gath (about 1056 B.C.); war with the Philistines and Saul's death (about 1055 B.C.); David king (1055 to 1048 B.C.).

The Period of the Monarchy: David king over all Israel (1048 B.C.); Solomon succeeds to the throne at David's death (about 1017 B.C.); commencement of the Temple (1014 B.C.); completion of the Temple (1004 B.C.); dedication of the Temple (994 B.C.); death of Solomon and the kingdom is divided (about 975 B.C.). Events from this time onward are shown in the following tables:

THE DIVIDED MONARCHY.

YEARS REIGNED.	KINGS OF JUDAH.	BEFORE CHRIST.	KINGS OF ISRAEL.	YEARS REIGNED.
17	Rehoboam	975		
		974	Jeroboam	22
3	Abijam, or Abijah	957		
41	Asa	955		
		954	Nadab	2
		953	Baasha	24
		930	Elah	2
		929	Zimri	7 days
			Omri	12
		918	Ahab	22
25	Jehoshaphat	914		
		897	Ahaziah	2
		896	Jehoram, or Joram (son of Ahab)	12
8	Jehoram, or Joram (Four years jointly with Jehoshaphat, his father, and four years alone.)	889		
1	Ahaziah, or Jehoahaz	885		
6	Athaliah	884	Jehu	28
40	Jehoash, or Joash	878		
		856	Jehoahaz	17
		839	Jehoash, or Joash	16
29	Amaziah	838		
		825	Jeroboam II	41

THE DIVIDED MONARCHY (CONTINUED).

YEARS REIGNED.	KINGS OF JUDAH.	BEFORE CHRIST.		KINGS OF ISRAEL.	YEARS REIGNED.
52	AZARIAH, or Uzziah............	810			
			784	Interregnum for eleven years.	
			773	ZACHARIAH	6 mo.
			772	SHALLUM	1 mo.
			772	MENAHEM	10
			761	PEKAHIAH................................	2
			759	PEKAH	20
16	JOTHAM	758			
16	AHAZ...........................	742			
			739	HOSHEA kills PEKAH	
				Anarchy for some years.	
			730	HOSHEA settled in the kingdom	9
29	HEZEKIAH	726			
			721	The Kingdom of Israel overthrown by the Assyrians. Shalmaneser, king of Assyria, came up against Samaria in the sixth year of the reign of Hoshea (B.C. 724), and after a siege of three years took the city, carried Israel away into Assyria, and having removed them to the cities of Halah and Habor, by the river Gozan, and into the cities of the Medes, he placed Assyrians in the cities of Samaria in their room.	
55	MANASSEH......................	698			
2	AMON	643			
31	JOSIAH........................	641			
3 mo.	JEHOAHAZ, or Shallum	610			
11	JEHOIAKIM	610			
3 mo.	JEHOIACHIN, or Jeconiah, or Coniah.	599			
11	ZEDEKIAH	599			
	Judah carried captive to Babylon.	588			

THE PERIOD OF THE CAPTIVITY AND RESTORATION.

B.C.	PALESTINE.	CONTEMPORARY EVENTS IN BABYLON, PERSIA, GREECE, ROME.
588	Gedaliah made Governor of Jerusalem. He is slain by Ishmael. Many of the people left behind in Judæa flee to Egypt.	
561		Death of Nebuchadnezzar. Accession of his son Evil-Merodach.
	Evil-Merodach alleviates the captivity of Jehoiachin.	
559		Neriglissar murders Evil-Merodach and succeeds him.
555		Laborosoarchad, son of Neriglissar, murdered in the first year of his reign. Nabonidus or Labynetus seizes the throne.
540		Nabonidus associates with himself his son Belshazzar.
539		Cyrus the Persian invades Babylonia.
538		Babylon taken by Cyrus. Belshazzar slain. Darius "the Mede" (?Astyages) appointed ruler of Babylon.
536	Decree of Cyrus permitting the return of the Jews. Zerubbabel, Governor.	
529		Death of Cyrus; Cambyses succeeds.
525		Cambyses conquers Egypt.
521		Darius Hystaspes.
516	Dedication of Second Temple.	
510		Expulsion of the Tarquins from Rome.
490		Battle of Marathon.
485	Xerxes confirms the privileges of the Jews.	
480		Battles of Thermopylæ and Salamis.
476	Era of Esther and Mordecai.	
458	Mission of Ezra to Jerusalem.	
453		Roman Decemvirs.
444	Nehemiah, Governor........................ Walls of Jerusalem rebuilt.	Pericles supreme at Athens.
433	Nehemiah returns to Persia.	
431		Peloponnesian War begins.
428	Nehemiah's second Reformation.	
420	Prophecies of Malachi begin.	
419	Manasseh builds a temple on Mount Gerizim.	
401		Death of Socrates.
397	Close of Old Testament Canon.	

THE SECOND INTERMEDIATE PERIOD.

B.C.	JEWS IN PALESTINE AND EGYPT.	CONTEMPORARY EVENTS.
350	Jaddua, High Priest.	Egypt a Persian Province.
336	....	Darius Codomannus, King of Persia.
334	....	Alexander invades Persia.
		Victory at the Granicus.
333	....	Battle of Issus.
332	Alexander visits Jerusalem.	Foundation of Alexandria.
331	Settlement of Jews at Alexandria................	Battle of Arbela.
330	Onias I, High Priest.	Death of Darius; end of the Persian Empire.
323	....	Death of Alexander.
		The Ptolemies take the Egyptian kingdom.
320	Ptolemy Soter captures Jerusalem.	Colonies of Jews in Egypt and Cyrene.
	Palestine subject to Egypt.	
314	Palestine subject to Syria.	
310	Simon the Just, High Priest.	
301	Palestine reverts to Egypt.	Battle of Ipsus.
284	Beginning of the LXX translation of the Old Testament.	Ptolemy Philadelphus.
264	....	First Punic War.
219	....	Second Punic War.
201	....	Colonies of Jews from Babylon transplanted.
198	Antiochus the Great becomes master of Palestine.	
170	Tyranny of Antiochus Epiphanes.	
168	Revolt of Mattathias.	
167	Rise of the Maccabees.	
166	Judas Maccabæus.	
165	Battles of Beth-horon and Emmaus.	
	Rededication of the Temple.	
161	Judas killed in battle at Eleasa; Jonathan succeeds him.	
149	....	Third Punic War.
146	....	Fall of Carthage and Corinth.
		Greece a Roman Province.
144	Murder of Jonathan Maccabæus.	
141	Simon Maccabæus completes the deliverance of Palestine.	
135	Murder of Simon Maccabæus; John Hyrcanus succeeds him.	
130	Hyrcanus destroys the temple on Mount Gerizim.	
109	First mention of Pharisees and Sadducees.	
107	Accession of Aristobulus, under the title of "king."	
106	Alexander Jannæus.	
	First mention of the Essenes.	
79	Alexandra, queen.	
69	Aristobulus II.	
63	Pompey subjugates Judæa.	Conspiracy of Catiline.
60	....	The first triumvirate.
58	....	Cæsar in Gaul.
54	The temple plundered by Crassus.	
48	....	Battle of Pharsalia; death of Pompey.
	Hyrcanus II restored.	
47	Antipater the Idumæan appointed by Cæsar Procurator of Judæa.	
	Herod made Governor of Galilee.	
44	....	Assassination of Cæsar.
43	Death of Antipater.	
40	Hyrcanus banished; Antigonus succeeds; last of the Asmonæan priestly line.	
	Herod at Rome.	
	Herod appointed King of Judea.	
37	Herod captures Jerusalem.	
31	....	Battle of Actium.
30	....	Egypt conquered by Cæsar.
29	.:..	Temple of Janus closed.
27	..:...	Augustus made emperor.
19	Herod begins to rebuild the temple.	
16	Herod goes to meet Agrippa and invites him to Judæa.	Agrippa sent to settle the affairs of Syria.
15	Agrippa visits Judæa.	
14	He confirms the privileges of the Jews.	
11	The Outer Temple finished.	
4	Herod dies at Jericho soon after the NATIVITY OF	
A.D.	OUR LORD.	
27	Jesus' ministry begins.	

THE PERIOD OF THE APOSTOLIC CHURCH.

Year.	Events in Christian Church.	Events Elsewhere.
28	John the Baptist beheaded.	Tiberius Emperor at Rome.
29	Jesus Christ crucified; rises on the third day.	Tiberius succeeded by Caligula.
	The Great Pentecost, and coming of the Holy Ghost.	
30	Office of deacon created.	Pontius Pilate commits suicide.
31	Stephen, the first martyr, put to death.	
33	Saul of Tarsus converted.	Herod Agrippa king of Judea.
42	The name *Christian* first given to the followers of Christ at Antioch.	
45	Fearful famine foretold by Agabus.	Wholesale executions in Rome by order of Emperor Claudius.
52	Apostolic Council at Jerusalem on admission to Church of the Gentiles.	Jews expelled from Rome.
64	First general persecution of Christians at Rome by order of Emperor Nero.	Nero emperor in Rome.
68	Paul and Peter suffer martyrdom.	Nero assassinated; Galba made emperor.
95	St. John banished to Patmos.	
100	St. John dies at Ephesus, the last of the Apostles.	

THE BOOK OF PSALMS

Nature of the Psalms. AMONG the very wonderful things given to man in the Old Testament the Book of Psalms is entitled to take an exceeding high place. Probably no other book in that section of the Bible is more widely read, and certainly no other is dearer to the heart of the Christian, no matter what his shade of faith. These two things are self-evident facts, known by pretty nearly every Bible reader. But the Psalms have other remarkable features not so generally known, and not only interesting but productive of much of the special character given to them by scholars and those engaged in Bible research. It will be the province of this article to throw as much light on these features as is possible.

For very many years it was the habit to refer to the Book of Psalms as the work of King David. This is unquestionably erroneous, and was due doubtless to the fact that the great poet-king composed many of the most beautiful portions of the collection—half or a little more than half—but it also is true that no stretch of imagination or facts can make him the author of them all. A great many of them were composed long after David had died, and some long before he was born. Moreover, the beautiful and connected shape in which they reach us in the Bible was the work not of David, but very probably of Ezra. It is possible that the germ of the shape was the work of David, who, with his poetic and constructive ability, took such Psalms as he had written or could collect and arranged them in some sort of sequence. But the bulk of the work seems to have been the work of Ezra, a man history and the results of his work show to have possessed remarkable editorial ability.

The results of modern research show that the Psalms, as they stand to-day, are the results of about one thousand years of poetic labor, from which the choicest specimens have been culled to make up the book. They began with the time and pen of Moses and go down through Jewish history to the days of Malachi. Among the authors besides Moses were David, the sons of Korah, who were noted choristers or singers, Solomon, Asaph, Heman, Ethan, Ezra, and probably Nehemiah, and Jeremiah, besides others whose names will never be known.

Divisions of the Psalms. The Psalms are susceptible of many different divisions, running as they do through almost all shades of religious feeling and of Jewish history, and being the work of so many different authors. For all general purposes, however, the two which follow are sufficient.

Division by authorship or compilation:

PART I. Davidic Psalms (or Psalms almost wholly written by David): Psalms 1 to 41 inclusive.

PART II. Davidic Psalms (or Psalms almost wholly written by David): Psalms 42 to 72 inclusive.

PART III. Asaphic Psalms (or Psalms written by Asaph): Psalms 73 to 89 inclusive.

PART IV. Psalms of the Captivity (or Psalms written in prophecy of or during the Captivity): Psalms 90 to 106 inclusive.

PART V. Psalms of Restoration (or Psalms written in prophecy of or during or after the period of Restoration): Psalms 107 to 150.

Division according to subjects:

PART 1. Psalms of supplication:

A—on account of sin, Psalms 6; 25; 32; 38; 51; 102; 130.

B—on account of suffering, Psalms 7; 10; 13; 17; 22; 31; 35; 41; 42; 43; 54; 55; 56; 57; 59; 64; 69; 70; 71; 77; 86; 88; 94; 109; 120; 140; 141; 142; 143.

C—on account of persecution, Psalms 44; 60; 74; 79; 80; 83; 89; 94; 102: 123; 137.

D—on account of public worship, Psalms 26; 27; 42; 43; 63; 65; 84; 92; 95: 96; 97; 98; 99; 100; 118; 122; 132; 144; 145; 146; 147; 148; 149; 150.

E—on account of trust in God, Psalms 3; 4; 5; 11; 12; 16; 20; 23; 27; 28; 31; 42; 43; 52; 54; 56; 57; 59; 61; 62; 63; 64; 71; 77; 86; 108; 115; 118; 121; 125; 131; 138; 141.

F—setting forth the Psalmist's piety, Psalms 7; 17; 26; 35; 101; 119.

PART 2. Psalms of gratitude:

A—from the Psalmist personally, Psalms 9; 18; 30; 32; 34; 40; 61; 62; 63; 75; 103; 108; 116; 138; 144.

B—on account of the Church, Psalms 33; 46; 47; 65; 66; 68; 75; 76; 81; 85; 87; 95; 98; 105; 106; 107; 124; 126; 129; 134; 135; 136; 149.

PART 3. Psalms of adoration:

A—on account of God's goodness and mercy, Psalms 3; 4; 9; 16; 18; 30; 31; 32; 33; 34; 36; 40; 46; 65; 66; 67; 68; 84; 85; 91; 99; 100; 103; 107; 111; 113; 116; 117; 121; 126; 145; 146.

B—on account of God's power, majesty, and glory, Psalms 2; 3; 8; 18; 19; 24; 29; 33; 45; 46; 47; 48; 50; 65; 66; 67; 68; 76; 77; 89; 91; 92; 93; 94; 95; 96; 97; 98; 99; 100; 104; 105; 106; 107; 108; 110; 111; 113; 114; 115; 116; 117; 118; 135; 136; 139; 145; 146; 147; 148; 149; 150.

PART 4. Didactic or instructive Psalms:

A—setting forth God's blessings to His people and the condition of His enemies, Psalms 1; 3; 4; 5; 7; 9; 10; 11; 12; 13; 14; 15; 17; 24; 25; 32; 34; 36; 37; 41; 50; 52; 53; 58; 62; 73; 75; 82; 84; 91; 92; 94; 101; 112; 119; 121; 125; 127; 128; 129; 133; 149.

B—God's law, Psalms 19; 119.

C—the vanity of things, Psalms 14; 39; 49; 53; 73; 90.

PART 5. Prophetical, typical, and historical Psalms:

Psalms 2; 16; 22; 24; 31; 35; 40; 41; 45; 50; 68; 69; 72; 78; 87; 88; 102; 105; 106; 109; 110; 118; 132; 135; 136.

Purposes of the Psalms. There is not a single doubt as to the purposes for which the vast majority of the Psalms were written. It was to give praise to God; in the same way this is now done by means of hymns. And just as modern hymns set forth longings and aspirations, penitence, and sorrow, or recite the majesty, goodness, and glory of God, so did the Psalmists do the same. David seems to have been the first to introduce such musical parts to the Hebrew religious services. After his death they gradually fell into abeyance and disuse as the Israelites fell deeper into sin. Under Ezra they were restored, and he made selections from the vast number that had been written and placed them much in their present form. After his time others were added occasionally until the time of Malachi. And for the purpose of praise they are just as powerful today as they were in the days when the Hebrews used them. In all ages they have been venerated by the Church, no matter what its shade of faith.

ALPHABETICAL TABLE OF THE FIRST LINES OF THE PSALMS.

HOW TO ANSWER SKEPTICS AND INFIDELS

**PART I:
Special
Topics.**
PERSONS who are opposed to the Bible and the teachings of Christianity because of their lack of religious faith or belief, are very prone to pick out certain passages of Scripture and complain that they are beyond human credence, or that they are contradicted by other passages, or that they are not supported by the facts of science, or that they are contrary to the idea of the goodness and mercy of God, or that they are overturned by other arguments. Very often the religious faith of some hitherto good believer is upset by specious reasoning of this character, for the reason that he does not happen to understand the Scriptural difficulty which is the basis of the unbeliever's contention. This is a great misfortune, since there is not a passage of Scripture, no matter how knotty, that cannot be unraveled, and not a disputed statement that cannot be made to agree with reason and judgment. It never must be forgotten that God is capable of performing miracles, that He has done so, and that He still is capable of performing them. And yet it is not necessary to fall back upon the argument that the passage in dispute is based upon a miraculous happening in order to confute the argument of the unbeliever. In the great majority of cases the application of good, hard common sense, or a study of references will untangle the most tangled skein. In the following pages will be given the explanation of some of the most involved and obscure passages of Scripture, as well as those presenting the greatest difficulty of explanation.

The first chapter of Genesis: The average unbeliever delights in attacking the very first chapter of the Bible. He sees in it vast possibilities for battling with the Christian at the very outset of the Holy Book—and therein displays his immense ignorance. In the first place, he says that the statement that the world was made in six days is absolutely disproved by the unquestionable findings of modern science, which show that the world is probably a million years old, at the least. Science is telling the truth—and so is the Bible. The six days were six periods of time of indefinite length—not six terrestrial days of twenty-four hours each. We find in the Bible many examples of the indefinite period of time being called a day (see Joel 3: 18; Zechariah 2: 11; 13: 1, 2; 14: 9), and in our own speech we have the same latitude of expression (see any good dictionary). We also must not forget that men in the time of Moses wrote in an entirely different manner from that of the present, and that a favorite method was that which is now known as allegory—that is, a fact was stated in the form of a story. If the argument is advanced by the unbeliever that this explanation is simply twisting Scripture to accord with modern science, he can be informed that Augustine, away back in the fourth century, long before science had arrived at any conclusion regarding the structure of the earth, said that the six days of the first chapter of Genesis were unquestionably six very long and indeterminate periods of time. Augustine's position as one of the fathers of the Church makes it impossible to cavil at his orthodoxy of faith.

Another favorite passage of the unbelievers is that which tells of the existence of light before the existence of the sun, or rather before the sun was made, according to Genesis. Those who know anything about science know that there is such a thing as nebular light, and that there was cosmic light long ages before the sun had any existence as such. Any work upon cosmology or astronomy will prove this. The same passage is also explicable in other ways.

Still another objection is offered to the statement regarding the progress of creation from "day" to "day," it being said by objectors that this progress is not in accord with the findings of science. Here again is ignorance displayed, since modern science, from its best exponents, admits the marvelous accord of Scripture and scientific fact. (See Creation in body of book.)

Who was Cain's wife? This is a question which the unbeliever considers unanswerable. On the other hand, it is simplicity itself. Adam and Eve had children besides Cain and Abel whose names are not mentioned. We find evidence of this in Genesis 5: 3. One of these other children was the wife of Cain. The objection is at once raised that Cain's wife therefore must be his sister. This is admitted. If the objector will think for a brief space, he will see that unless some such union occurred among the members of the first human family, it would have been impossible to have continued the race, which was to start from a single family. As the race increased such necessities departed, and nature put a fearful punishment upon such things. We find similar conditions existing in modern times in the raising of stock. Incidentally, it may be well to mention that the Bible does not say that Cain got his wife in the land of Nod, but that he went to dwell there and raised children there.

The question of human sacrifice to God as brought out in the case of Abraham and Isaac: Many skeptics insist that the story of Abraham and Isaac as brought out in the 22nd chapter of Genesis justifies the horrible practice which once was in vogue of making human sacrifices, and that God ordered Abraham to sacrifice his son. The statement is unqualifiedly false. The chapter does not justify human sacrifice, nor does any passage in the Bible do so, nor did God command Abraham to put his son to death. God tested Abraham's faith by telling him to "offer" his son. Abraham, unquestioning, believed God to have ordered Isaac's sacrifice and was willing to carry out what he thought was God's command. What God really had said was simply to "offer" the boy, and He had no thought of permitting Abraham to kill Isaac. Having seen that Abraham was full of faith, He spoke and peremptorily commanded Abraham not to kill Isaac, and that there was the proper kind of a sacrificial victim near at hand. Instead of justifying human sacrifices, we find God expressly forbidding them.

Some skeptics and infidels declare also that the sending of Jesus Christ into the world to suffer and die was nothing more or less than a human sacrifice. It is difficult to imagine a statement or a thought more unspeakably sacrilegious or more sinful. Jesus Christ was the Son of God. He is the second Person in the Trinity. Therefore He is God. His mortal or human nature was assumed simply for the sake of coming to earth to live man's life, to be tempted as is man, to teach and instruct mankind in the New Dispensation of God the Father, and to shed His blood for the redemption, under the new plan, of the human race. His mission was a divine one and full of mercy and goodness. His human body was simply the habitat of His divine soul. In other words, it was God, offering Himself for the benefit of His human children.

The story of Jephthah's daughter (Judges 11: 29-40) is quoted similarly. But when it is carefully read we do not find that Jephthah carried out his rash vow of making a burnt offering of the first thing that came out of his house should he return successful from his expedition. Jephthah had expected it to be an animal of some sort, and when he found that it was his daughter he mourned not because she should be a burnt offering, for the laws of the Israelites expressly prohibited human sacrifices of that sort, but because she would be a sacrifice of an entirely different sort. She must vow herself to a state of perpetual virginity. This would entirely preclude the possibility—as the Jews saw it then—of her becoming the mother of the promised Messiah, which was a possibility always in the mind of every Hebrew woman, and for the matter of that, is still so. We are told that the girl went to the mountains with her companions and bewailed her virginity—another way of stating the fact that she mourned the sacrifice she was to make.

God putting sin into man by "hardening his heart," as in the case of Pharaoh: In Exodus we find a number of passages to the effect that God hardened the heart of Pharaoh to retain the people of Israel in bondage. Infidels say that by hardening Pharaoh's heart God made him sin. The statement is one of the adroit ways enemies of God have of twisting the Scriptures to suit their convenience. What God did was to permit Pharaoh to travel his own path—which was to keep the

Israelites so long as they were profitable to him—and not to put it into his heart to allow them to leave. God is constantly putting it into men's hearts to turn to Him, just as putting it into Pharaoh's heart to let the Israelites go would have been putting it into his heart to turn to God. And God often leaves it entirely to man what he shall do, just as He did with Pharaoh, after He has given man warning after warning to do what is right. God will not always have patience. Thus we see that God does not put sin into man's heart, nor did He put it into Pharaoh's. He puts good there, and very often man thrusts the good out and deliberately chooses to keep the bad, just as Pharaoh did.

God not a merciful God because He permits the sins of fathers to be visited upon children to the third and fourth generation: Enemies of God say that He is not a just and merciful God because He permits the sins of fathers to be visited upon children to the third and fourth generation. (Exodus 20: 5.) This is a law of nature made for the benefit of the many rather than the good of the few. When God made man and the universe and the things that are in them He devised a set of laws for their government. These laws, in God's infinite wisdom, were made for the greatest good of the greatest number. They are called laws of nature. When they are infringed things go wrong, and when things go wrong with men it is only a following out of the original law that for a time things must go wrong with men's children, until the effects of the infringement are worn off. Nature cannot throw off the effect of sin at once, although that sin is not necessarily held against the man or his children. He may be pardoned the sin itself, but he must suffer more or less for it, not in his spiritual body but in his physical body. What man would not cut off his right hand to know that he would reach Heaven? If he had sinned and could win pardon and Heaven by cutting off his hand and enduring the pain and trouble of being handless, would he not do so? God, in His wisdom, knows that man must be made to obey the laws of nature, else the world would come to chaos. And, when the effects of a father's sin go down to succeeding generations, it is a warning that such laws must not

be transgressed. The act is one of mercy to all, not injustice to one.

The question of swearing and taking an oath: Deuteronomy 6: 13 says: "And shalt swear by his name." In Matthew 5 we are told not to swear at all. There is a vast deal of difference between these two passages, and neither conflicts with the other. One has reference to taking a judicial oath, in calling God to witness the truth of an assertion; the other has reference to indiscriminate swearing in ordinary conversation or for the purpose of making an ordinary statement seem more plausible. It is the latter that Jesus meant in Matthew and not the former. He Himself saw no objection to the judicial oath, and we find His apostles following His example.

If God is a merciful God, why did he permit or order the slaughter of all the people of Canaan? This is a favorite question of the infidel and enemy of God and the Bible, and they hold up the passages (Deuteronomy 20) as most terrible things. On the other hand, they are full of love and mercy, and had they been obeyed, it is unquestionable that the world would have been closer to God to-day, and the Jews not an outcast nation. The people of Canaan, and indeed the people of the whole region adjacent, were steeped in wickedness of the most terrible sort. They were pagans who worshiped stone and metal gods with the most revolting rites, who made human sacrifices, who lived in unspeakable sin, and had become great cancerous spots upon the bosom of the world. For the benefit of future mankind it were wise and merciful to cut them off. They had had their chance back in Abraham's day to make their peace with God, and they had not taken advantage of it. To have left any of them alive would have been simply to leave a root upon which a future deadly weed should grow. But the Israelites did just this thing—they did not cut them entirely off and they left a root. The result was the springing up in later years of the nameless idolatries and sins which were the causes of the downfall of the Hebrew nation. Thus do we see that God was a merciful God after all, and that if He had been obeyed much sin and suffering would have been avoided.

Why was David a man after God's own

heart if he was as great a sinner as he is shown by Scripture to be, and as he himself confessed (2 Samuel 24: 10)? For two reasons: (1) David, in his early life, was a good man in every sense of the word, obeying God's commands, having plenteous faith, and living an upright life; and it cannot be doubted that this type of manhood is pleasing to God; (2) he did not become a sinful man until after he had been a powerful king for some time and yielded to the temptations his position brought him. But at the same time David was a man who became a prey to the most bitter remorse and repentance after sin, and he threw himself at God's knees and asked pardon. It cannot be doubted that this also is a type of manhood dear to God. He would have all of His sinful children realize their sin as did David and repentantly come to Him for forgiveness. He knows men are weak and that they cannot help sinning, and He also knows that few of them come to Him repentant as David did, and as manfully accept their punishment as did David.

The story of Jonah and the whale: There never was an infidel or a skeptic who did not deride the account of Jonah spending three days and nights in the interior of a monster of the sea and escaping uninjured therefrom. They declare that no whale ever existed that could swallow a man whole—and that is quite true so far as the whales we know are concerned. But as a matter of fact the Bible does not say that it was a whale that swallowed Jonah, but "a great fish" that "the Lord prepared." This is the statement in Jonah 1: 17. In Matthew 12: 40 the fish is called a whale, but the Greek word so translated is much better translated by the word "sea-monster." Now, as a matter of further fact, there existed up to quite recent times in the very sea into which Jonah was cast, huge monsters more than capable of swallowing a man, and records actually exist of their swallowing horses. This is one explanation. Still another—which seems to clinch the whole situation—is that if the fish was one "prepared" by God, there is no reason why it should not have been able to swallow Jonah, since a miracle is but a miracle, no matter how it is viewed. and when God starts in to perform miracles He does not do it in a halfway manner.

Why did Jesus say, "I come not to send peace but a sword" (Matthew 10: 34), and yet preach the doctrine of non-retaliation for injuries? Infidels gloat over this seeming contradiction. There is no contradiction, for the two things are entirely different. In the first part of the supposed problem He referred to the conflicts that He knew must arise over the old order of things under Judaism and Paganism and the new order of His own kingdom, conflicts He knew must result in the old order perishing or being cut off, as by the sword, which becomes therefore not a literal use of the weapon but a figurative one. The second part of the proposition stands.

If with God all things are possible (Matthew 19: 26), why is it impossible for Him to lie (Hebrews 6: 18)? It is not physically impossible for God to lie, but it is morally so. It was not physically impossible for George Washington to betray his country as did Benedict Arnold; but it was morally impossible for him to do so, as is evidenced by the fact that although tempted he did not do it.

Why could Jesus do no mighty work in his own country (Mark 6: 5)? The context shows that the people were faithless, that they jeered at Him, and that He marveled at their unbelief. In a number of instances He required faith as an accompaniment of His miracles.

If no man has seen God at any time (John 1: 18), how is it that many characters in the Old Testament saw Him? John means to say that no man has seen God in his eternal, invisible, glorious essence, which is spirit and not form. He does not mean to say no man has seen God in a physical manifestation, such as Moses and the elders saw, or as was seen in the Temple, or as was seen in a number of other instances, for the reason that John knew better. He simply did not know that a race of infidels was going to grow up to pick his compositions to pieces.

Why, if Jesus said he judged no man, was judgment committed to him (John 5: 22)? This is another adroit twisting of the Scriptures. Jesus judged none on his earthly mission, nor after the manner of the Jews. The final judgment, especially after His glorification, is quite another matter.

Why, if Christ was the Son of God, was he

ignorant (John 11: 34) of some things? Christ was the son of man as well as the son of God. He had two natures—human and divine. If the average skeptic can bring sufficient intelligence to bear upon the question to realize this he will easily see that the intelligence that was a part of His divine nature was denied to His human nature.

Why does Jesus say, "My Father is greater than I," when in the doctrine of the Trinity it is stated elsewhere that Father, Son, and Holy Ghost are of equal power and eternity?

Jesus is not comparing His nature with that of His Father, but His condition. This was a state of humiliation and lowliness, while that of His Father was glory.

If it is true that Jesus was the first to rise from the dead, what about those who rose in the Old Testament or were raised by Jesus Himself? Jesus was the first who rose from the dead to die no more in actual physical death, the first over whom death had no further power. All the others died again at some time subsequent to their miraculous resurrection.

PART II: General Topics. No Christian is a practical one unless he or she is able to show in an instant the basis for any of the tenets of the Christian faith. This necessitates a considerable knowledge of the Bible. Unfortunately there is a large number of good men and good women who are not practical Christians just because they lack the knowledge of God's word sufficient to have at their tongue's end the passage of Scripture necessary to the satisfactory answering of a question. Often these questions come from infidels and non-believers in an argumentative mood, and the failure to have a ready answer is grasped in glee by the unbeliever. Below will be found set out a number of the usual "catch questions" with their proper Scriptural basis, and with Christ's words where they appear set in *italics*:

How do you know Jesus was divine?

And the Word was made flesh, and dwelt among us, (and we beheld his glory, the glory as of the only begotten of the Father,) full of grace and truth. (John 1: 14.)

No man hath seen God at any time; the only begotten Son, which is in the bosom of the Father, he hath declared him. (John 1: 18.)

Jesus saith unto him, *Have I been so long time with you, and yet hast thou not known me, Philip? he that hath seen me hath seen the Father; and how sayest thou then, Shew us the Father?*

Believest thou not that I am in the Father, and the Father in me? the words that I speak unto you I speak not of myself: but the Father that dwelleth in me, he doeth the works.

Believe me that I am in the Father, and the Father in me: or else believe me for the very works' sake.

Verily, verily, I say unto you, He that believeth on me, the works that I do shall he do also; and greater works than these shall he do; because I go unto my Father.

And whatsoever ye shall ask in my name, that will I do, that the Father may be glorified in the Son.

If ye shall ask any thing in my name, I will do it. (John 14: 9-14.)

Jesus saith unto him, *Thomas, because thou hast seen me, thou hast believed: blessed are they that have not seen, and yet have believed.*

And many other signs truly did Jesus in the presence of his disciples, which are not written in this book:

But these are written, that ye might believe that Jesus is the Christ, the Son of God; and that believing ye might have life through his name. (John 20: 29-31.)

How do you know there is such a thing as a God?

In the beginning God created the heaven and the earth. (Genesis 1: 1.)

The heavens declare the glory of God; and the firmament sheweth his handywork. (Psalm 19: 1.)

Let all the nations be gathered together, and let the people be assembled: who among them can declare this, and shew us former things? let them bring forth their witnesses, that they may be justified: or let them hear, and say, It is truth.

Ye are my witnesses, saith the Lord, and my servant whom I have chosen: that ye may know and believe me, and understand that I am he: before me there was no God formed, neither shall there be after me. (Isaiah 43: 9, 10.)

For the children of Israel shall abide many days without a king, and without a prince, and without a sacrifice, and without an image, and without an ephod, and without teraphim:

Afterward shall the children of Israel return, and seek the Lord their God, and David their king; and shall fear the Lord and his goodness in the latter days. (Hosea 3: 4, 5.)

He that is of God heareth God's words: ye therefore hear them not, because ye are not of God. (John 8: 47.)

What makes you think the Bible is true?

Search the scriptures; for in them ye think ye have eternal life: and they are they which testify of me.

And ye will not come to me, that ye might have life. (John 5: 39, 40.)

For this cause also thank we God without ceasing, because, when ye received the word of God ,which ye heard of us, ye received it not as the word of men, but as it is in truth, the word of God, which effectually worketh also in you that believe. (1 Thessalonians 2: 13.)

All scripture is given by inspiration of God, and is profitable for doctrine, for reproof, for correction, for instruction in righteousness. (2 Timothy 3: 16.)

Knowing this first, that no prophecy of the scripture is of any private interpretation.

For the prophecy came not in old time by the will of man: but holy men of God spake as they were moved by the Holy Ghost. (2 Peter 1: 20, 21.)

If you do as well as you can will you not get to Heaven anyway?

He that believeth on him is not condemned: but he that believeth not is condemned already, because he hath not believed in the name of the only begotten Son of God. (John 3: 18.)

Now we know that what things soever the law saith, it saith to them who are under the law: that every mouth may be stopped, and all the world may become guilty before God.

Therefore by the deeds of the law there shall no flesh be justified in his sight: for by the law is the knowledge of sin. (Romans 3: 19, 20.)

For as many as are of the works of the law are under the curse: for it is written, Cursed is every one that continueth not in all things which are written in the book of the law to do them.

But that no man is justified by the law in the sight of God, it is evident: for, The just shall live by faith.

And the law is not of faith: but, The man that doeth them shall live in them. (Galatians 3: 10-12.)

Cannot a man be a Christian without believing in the divinity of Christ?

Jesus saith unto him, *I am the way, the truth, and the life: no man cometh unto the Father, but by me.* (John 14: 6.)

Then saith he to Thomas, *Reach hither thy finger, and behold my hands; and reach hither thy hand, and thrust it into my side: and be not faithless, but believing.*

And Thomas answered and said unto him, My Lord and my God.

Jesus saith unto him, *Thomas, because thou hast seen me, thou hast believed: blessed are they that have not seen, and yet have believed.*

And many other signs truly did Jesus in the presence of his disciples, which are not written in this book:

But these are written, that ye might believe that Jesus is the Christ, the Son of God; and that be-lieving ye might have life through his name. (John 20: 27-31.)

If we receive the witness of men, the witness of God is greater: for this is the witness of God which he hath testified of his Son.

He that believeth on the Son of God hath the witness in himself: he that believeth not God hath made him a liar; because he believeth not the record that God gave of his Son.

And this is the record, that God hath given to us eternal life, and this life is in his Son.

He that hath the Son hath life; and he that hath not the Son of God hath not life.

These things have I written unto you that believe on the name of the Son of God; that ye may know that ye have eternal life, and that ye may believe on the name of the Son of God. (1 John 5: 9-13.)

Why was it necessary for Jesus to die to save men?

For what the law could not do, in that it was weak through the flesh, God sending his own Son in the likeness of sinful flesh, and for sin, condemned sin in the flesh. (Romans 8: 3.)

Wherefore, as by one man sin entered into the world, and death by sin; and so death passed upon all men, for that all have sinned:

(For until the law sin was in the world: but sin is not imputed when there is no law.

Nevertheless death reigned from Adam to Moses, even over them that had not sinned after the similitude of Adam's transgression, who is the figure of him that was to come.

But not as the offence, so also is the free gift. For if through the offence of one many be dead, much more the grace of God, and the gift by grace, which is by one man, Jesus Christ, hath abounded unto many.

And not as it was by one that sinned, so is the gift: for the judgment was by one to condemnation, but the free gift is of many offences unto justification.

For if by one man's offence death reigned by one; much more they which receive abundance of grace and of the gift of righteousness shall reign in life by one, Jesus Christ.)

Therefore as by the offence of one judgment came upon all men to condemnation; even so by the righteousness of one the free gift came upon all men unto justification of life.

For as by one man's disobedience many were made sinners, so by the obedience of one shall many be made righteous. (Romans 5: 12-19.)

How do you know sins are forgiven?

Wherefore I say unto thee, Her sins, which are many, are forgiven; for she loved much: but to whom little is forgiven, the same loveth little.

And he said unto her, *Thy sins are forgiven.*

And they that sat at meat with him began to say

within themselves, Who is this that forgiveth sins also?

And he said to the woman, *Thy faith hath saved thee; go in peace.* (Luke 7: 47-50.)

Be it known unto you therefore, men and brethren, that through this man is preached unto you the forgiveness of sins:

And by him all that believe are justified from all things, from which ye could not be justified by the law of Moses. (Acts 13: 38, 39.)

If we confess our sins, he is faithful and just to forgive us our sins, and to cleanse us from all unrighteousness. (1 John 1: 9.)

Why will not God or Christ show Himself to man now as before?

That the trial of your faith, being much more precious than of gold that perisheth, though it be tried with fire, might be found unto praise and honour and glory at the appearing of Jesus Christ:

Whom having not seen, ye love; in whom, though now ye see him not, yet believing, ye rejoice with joy unspeakable and full of glory. (1 Peter 1: 7, 8.)

Why do church members "go wrong"?

For many walk, of whom I have told you often, and now tell you even weeping, that they are the enemies of the cross of Christ:

Whose end is destruction, whose God is their belly, and whose glory is in their shame, who mind earthly things. (Philippians 3: 18, 19.)

Now the Spirit speaketh expressly, that in the latter times some shall depart from the faith, giving heed to seducing spirits, and doctrines of devils;

Speaking lies in hypocrisy; having their conscience seared with a hot iron. (1 Timothy 4: 1, 2.)

For men shall be lovers of their own selves, covetous, boasters, proud, blasphemers, disobedient to parents, unthankful, unholy,

Without natural affection, trucebreakers, false accusers, incontinent, fierce, despisers of those that are good,

Traitors, heady, highminded, lovers of pleasures more than lovers of God;

Having a form of godliness, but denying the power thereof: from such turn away. (2 Timothy 3: 2-5.)

571

PROPHECIES RELATING TO JESUS CHRIST AND THEIR FULFILLMENT

Theme:	*Prophecy.*	*Fulfillment.*
Son of God.	I will declare the decree: the Lord hath said unto me, Thou art my Son; this day have I begotten thee. (Psalm 2: 7.)	He shall be great, and shall be called the Son of the Highest: and the Lord God shall give unto him the throne of his father David. (Luke 1: 32.) And the angel answered and said unto her, The Holy Ghost shall come upon thee, and the power of the Highest shall overshadow thee: therefore also that holy thing which shall be born of thee shall be called the Son of God. (Luke 1: 35.)
Born of Woman.	And I will put enmity between thee and the woman, and between thy seed and her seed; it shall bruise thy head, and thou shalt bruise his heel. (Genesis 3: 15.)	But when the fulness of the time was come, God sent forth his Son, made of a woman, made under the law. (Galatians 4: 4.)
Of the Seed of Abraham.	And I will establish my covenant between me and thee and thy seed after thee in their generations for an everlasting covenant, to be a God unto thee, and to thy seed after thee. (Genesis 17: 7.) And in thy seed shall all the nations of the earth be blessed; because thou hast obeyed my voice. (Genesis 22: 18.)	Now to Abraham and his seed were the promises made. He saith not, And to seeds, as of many; but as of one, And to thy seed, which is Christ. (Galatians 3: 16.)
And of Isaac.	And God said unto Abraham, Let it not be grievous in thy sight because of the lad, and because of thy bond-woman; in all that Sarah hath said unto thee, hearken unto her voice; for in Isaac shall thy seed be called. (Genesis 21: 12.)	By faith Abraham, when he was tried, offered up Isaac: and he that had received the promises offered up his only begotten son. Of whom it was said, That in Isaac shall thy seed be called: Accounting that God was able to raise him up, even from the dead; from whence also he received him in a figure. (Hebrews 11: 17-19.)
And of David.	The Lord hath sworn in truth unto	Of this man's seed hath God ac-

Theme.	Prophecy.	Fulfillment.
	David; he will not turn from it; Of the fruit of thy body will I set upon thy throne. (Psalm 132: 11.) Behold, the days come, saith the Lord, that I will raise unto David a righteous Branch, and a King shall reign and prosper, and shall execute judgment and justice in the earth. (Jeremiah 23: 5.)	cording to his promise raised unto Israel a Saviour, Jesus. (Acts 13: 23.) Concerning his Son Jesus Christ our Lord, which was made of the seed of David according to the flesh. (Romans 1: 3.)
Born of a Virgin.	Therefore the Lord himself shall give you a sign; Behold, a virgin shall conceive, and bear a son, and shall call his name Immanuel. (Isaiah 7: 14.)	Now the birth of Jesus Christ was on this wise: When as his mother Mary was espoused to Joseph, before they came together, she was found with child of the Holy Ghost. (Matthew 1: 18.) And she brought forth her firstborn son, and wrapped him in swaddling clothes, and laid him in a manger; because there was no room for them in the inn. (Luke 2: 7.) Now all this was done, that it might be fulfilled which was spoken of the Lord by the prophet, saying, Behold, a virgin shall be with child, and shall bring forth a son, and they shall call his name Emmanuel, which being interpreted is, God with us. (Matthew 1: 22, 23.)
Born in Bethlehem.	But thou, Bethlehem Ephratah, though thou be little among the thousands of Judah, yet out of thee shall he come forth unto me that is to be ruler in Israel; whose goings forth have been from of old, from everlasting. (Micah 5: 2.)	Now when Jesus was born in Bethlehem of Judæa in the days of Herod the king, behold, there came wise men from the east to Jerusalem. (Matthew 2: 1.)
Gifts from the East for Him.	The kings of Tarshish and of the isles shall bring presents: the kings of Sheba and Seba shall offer gifts. (Psalm 72: 10.)	And when they were come into the house, they saw the young child with Mary his mother, and fell down, and worshipped him: and when they had opened their treasures, they presented unto him gifts; gold, and frankincense, and myrrh. (Matthew 2: 11.)
Slaughter of the Innocents.	Thus saith the Lord; A voice was heard in Ramah, lamentation, and bitter weeping; Rachel weeping for her children refused to be comforted for	Then was fulfilled that which was spoken by Jeremy the prophet, saying, In Rama was there a voice heard,

Theme.	Prophecy.	Fulfillment.
	her children, because they were not. (Jeremiah 31:15.)	lamentation, and weeping, and great mourning, Rachel weeping for her children, and would not be comforted, because they are not. (Matthew 2:17, 18.)
Taken to Egypt.	When Israel was a child, then I loved him, and called my son out of Egypt. (Hosea 11:1.)	When he arose, he took the young child and his mother by night, and departed into Egypt: And was there until the death of Herod: that it might be fulfilled which was spoken of the Lord by the prophet, saying, Out of Egypt have I called my son. (Matthew 2:14, 15.)
The Forerunner-ship of John.	The voice of him that crieth in the wilderness, Prepare ye the way of the Lord, make straight in the desert a highway for our God. (Isaiah 40:3.) Behold, I will send my messenger, and he shall prepare the way before me: and the Lord, whom ye seek, shall suddenly come to his temple, even the messenger of the covenant, whom ye delight in: behold, he shall come, saith the Lord of hosts. (Malachi 3:1.)	In those days came John the Baptist, preaching in the wilderness of Judæa, And saying, Repent ye: for the kingdom of heaven is at hand. For this is he that was spoken of by the prophet Esaias, saying, The voice of one crying in the wilderness, Prepare ye the way of the Lord, make his paths straight. (Matthew 3:1-3.)
Spirit of God upon Him.	Thou lovest righteousness, and hatest wickedness: therefore God, thy God, hath anointed thee with the oil of gladness above thy fellows. (Psalm 45:7.) And the spirit of the Lord shall rest upon him, the spirit of wisdom and understanding, the spirit of counsel and might, the spirit of knowledge and of the fear of the Lord. (Isaiah 11:2.) The Spirit of the Lord God is upon me; because the Lord hath anointed me to preach good tidings unto the meek; he hath sent me to bind up the brokenhearted, to proclaim liberty to the captives, and the opening of the prison to them that are bound. (Isaiah 61:1.)	And Jesus, when he was baptized, went up straightway out of the water: and, lo, the heavens were opened unto him, and he saw the Spirit of God descending like a dove, and lighting upon him. (Matthew 3:16.) For he whom God hath sent speaketh the words of God: for God giveth not the Spirit by measure unto him. (John 3:34.) How God anointed Jesus of Nazareth with the Holy Ghost and with power: who went about doing good, and healing all that were oppressed of the devil; for God was with him. (Acts 10:38.)

Theme.	Prophecy.	Fulfillment.
His Priesthood.	The Lord hath sworn, and will not repent, Thou art a priest for ever after the order of Melchizedek. (Psalm 110: 4.)	So also Christ glorified not himself to be made an high priest; but he that said unto him, Thou art my Son, to day have I begotten thee. As he saith also in another place, Thou art a priest for ever after the order of Melchisedec. (Hebrews 5: 5, 6.)
His Ministry.	To proclaim the acceptable year of the Lord, and the day of vengeance of our God; to comfort all that mourn. (Isaiah 61: 2.)	And he said unto them, I must preach the kingdom of God to other cities also: for therefore am I sent. (Luke 4: 43.)
His Teachership and Healing.	Nevertheless the dimness shall not be such as was in her vexation, when at the first he lightly afflicted the land of Zebulun and the land of Naphtali, and afterward did more grievously afflict her by the way of the sea, beyond Jordan, in Galilee of the nations. The people that walked in darkness have seen a great light: they that dwell in the land of the shadow of death, upon them hath the light shined. (Isaiah 9: 1, 2.)	And Jesus went about all Galilee, teaching in their synagogues, and preaching the gospel of the kingdom, and healing all manner of sickness and all manner of disease among the people. (Matthew 4: 23.)
Entry into Jerusalem.	Rejoice greatly, O daughter of Zion: shout, O daughter of Jerusalem: behold, thy King cometh unto thee: he is just, and having salvation; lowly, and riding upon an ass, and upon a colt the foal of an ass. (Zechariah 9: 9.)	And when they drew nigh unto Jerusalem, and were come to Bethphage, unto the mount of Olives, then sent Jesus two disciples, Saying unto them, Go into the village over against you, and straightway ye shall find an ass tied, and a colt with her: loose them, and bring them unto me. And if any man say ought unto you, ye shall say, The Lord hath need of them; and straightway he will send them. All this was done, that it might be fulfilled which was spoken by the prophet, saying, Tell ye the daughter of Sion, Behold, thy King cometh unto thee, meek, and sitting upon an ass, and a colt the foal of an ass. (Matthew 21: 1-5.)

Theme.	Prophecy.	Fulfillment.

Cleansing of the Temple.

And I will shake all nations, and the desire of all nations shall come: and I will fill this house with glory, saith the Lord of hosts.

The silver is mine, and the gold is mine, saith the Lord of hosts.

The glory of this latter house shall be greater than of the former, saith the Lord of hosts: and in this place will I give peace, saith the Lord of hosts. (Haggai 2: 7-9.)

And Jesus went into the temple of God, and cast out all them that sold and bought in the temple, and overthrew the tables of the moneychangers, and the seats of them that sold doves. (Matthew 21: 12.)

Wise, but Rejected of Men.

For he shall grow up before him as a tender plant, and as a root out of a dry ground: he hath no form nor comeliness; and when we shall see him, there is no beauty that we should desire him.

He is despised and rejected of men; a man of sorrows, and acquainted with grief: and we hid as it were our faces from him; he was despised, and we esteemed him not. (Isaiah 53: 2, 3.)

And when the sabbath day was come, he began to teach in the synagogue: and many hearing him were astonished, saying, From whence hath this man these things? and what wisdom is this which is given unto him, that even such mighty works are wrought by his hands?

Is not this the carpenter, the son of Mary, the brother of James, and Joses, and of Juda, and Simon? and are not his sisters here with us? And they were offended at him. (Mark 6: 2, 3.)

And Jesus said unto him, Foxes have holes, and birds of the air have nests; but the Son of man hath not where to lay his head. (Luke 9: 58.)

Meekness and Modesty.

Behold my servant, whom I uphold; mine elect, in whom my soul delighteth; I have put my spirit upon him: he shall bring forth judgment to the Gentiles.

He shall not cry, nor lift up, nor cause his voice to be heard in the street.

A bruised reed shall he not break, and the smoking flax shall he not quench: he shall bring forth judgment unto truth.

He shall not fail nor be discouraged, till he have set judgment in the earth: and the isles shall wait for his law. (Isaiah 42: 1-4.)

But when Jesus knew it, he withdrew himself from thence: and great multitudes followed him, and he healed them all;

And charged them that they should not make him known:

That it might be fulfilled which was spoken by Esaias the prophet, saying,

Behold my servant, whom I have chosen; my beloved, in whom my soul is well pleased: I will put my spirit upon him, and he shall shew judgment to the Gentiles.

He shall not strive, nor cry; neither shall any man hear his voice in the streets.

A bruised reed shall he not break,

Theme.	Prophecy.	Fulfillment.
		and smoking flax shall he not quench, till he send forth judgment unto victory. And in his name shall the Gentiles trust. (Matthew 12: 15-21.)
Gentle and Patient.	And he made his grave with the wicked, and with the rich in his death; because he had done no violence, neither was any deceit in his mouth. (Isaiah 53: 9.)	Who did no sin, neither was guile found in his mouth: Who, when he was reviled, reviled not again; when he suffered, he threatened not; but committed himself to him that judgeth righteously. (1 Peter 2: 22, 23.)
His Parables.	Give ear, O my people, to my law: incline your ears to the words of my mouth. I will open my mouth in a parable: I will utter dark sayings of old: Which we have heard and known, and our fathers have told us. (Psalm 78: 1-3.)	All these things spake Jesus unto the multitude in parables; and without a parable spake he not unto them: That it might be fulfilled which was spoken by the prophet, saying, I will open my mouth in parables; I will utter things which have been kept secret from the foundation of the world. (Matthew 13: 34, 35.)
His Miracles.	Then the eyes of the blind shall be opened, and the ears of the deaf shall be unstopped. Then shall the lame man leap as an hart, and the tongue of the dumb sing: for in the wilderness shall waters break out, and streams in the desert. (Isaiah 35: 5, 6.)	Jesus answered and said unto them, Go and shew John again those things which ye do hear and see: The blind receive their sight, and the lame walk, the lepers are cleansed, and the deaf hear, the dead are raised up, and the poor have the gospel preached to them. And blessed is he, whosoever shall not be offended in me. (Matthew 11: 4-6.) Then gathered the chief priests and the Pharisees a council, and said, What do we? for this man doeth many miracles. (John 11: 47.)
Disbelief in Him.	I am become a stranger unto my brethren, and an alien unto my mother's children. (Psalm 69: 8.) I have trodden the winepress alone; and of the people there was none with me: for I will tread them in mine anger, and trample them in my fury; and their blood shall be sprinkled	He was in the world, and the world was made by him, and the world knew him not. He came unto his own, and his own received him not. (John 1: 10, 11.) His brethren therefore said unto him, Depart hence, and go into Ju-

Theme.	Prophecy.	Fulfillment.
	upon my garments, and I will stain all my raiment. (Isaiah 63: 3.)	dæa, that thy disciples also may see the works that thou doest. For there is no man that doeth any thing in secret, and he himself seeketh to be known openly. If thou do these things, shew thyself to the world. For neither did his brethren believe in him. (John 7: 3-5.)
Foe to the Unfaithful.	And he shall be for a sanctuary; but for a stone of stumbling and for a rock of offence to both the houses of Israel, for a gin and for a snare to the inhabitants of Jerusalem. (Isaiah 8: 14.)	Wherefore? Because they sought it not by faith, but as it were by the works of the law. For they stumbled at that stumblingstone; As it is written, Behold, I lay in Sion a stumblingstone and rock of offence: and whosoever believeth on him shall not be ashamed. (Romans 9: 32, 33.)
Hated without Cause.	They that hate me without a cause are more than the hairs of mine head: they that would destroy me, being mine enemies wrongfully, are mighty: then I restored that which I took not away. (Psalm 69: 4.) Thus saith the Lord, the Redeemer of Israel, and his Holy One, to him whom man despiseth, to him whom the nation abhorreth, to a servant of rulers, Kings shall see and arise, princes also shall worship, because of the Lord that is faithful, and the Holy One of Israel, and he shall choose thee. (Isaiah 49: 7.)	If I had not done among them the works which none other man did, they had not had sin: but now have they both seen and hated both me and my Father. But this cometh to pass, that the word might be fulfilled that is written in their law, They hated me without a cause. (John 15: 24, 25.)
To Be Betrayed by a Friend.	Yea, mine own familiar friend, in whom I trusted, which did eat of my bread, hath lifted up his heel against me. (Psalm 41: 9.) For it was not an enemy that reproached me; then I could have borne it: neither was it he that hated me that did magnify himself against me; then I would have hid myself from him: But it was thou, a man mine equal, my guide, and mine acquaintance. We took sweet counsel together, and walked unto the house of God in company. (Psalm 55: 12-14.)	I speak not of you all: I know whom I have chosen: but that the scripture may be fulfilled, He that eateth bread with me hath lifted up his heel against me. (John 13: 18.) When Jesus had thus said, he was troubled in spirit, and testified, and said, Verily, verily, I say unto you, that one of you shall betray me. (John 13: 21.)

Theme.	Prophecy.	Fulfillment.
Disciples Scattered.	Awake, O sword, against my shepherd, and against the man that is my fellow, saith the Lord of hosts: smite the shepherd, and the sheep shall be scattered: and I will turn mine hand upon the little ones. (Zechariah 13: 7.)	Then saith Jesus unto them, All ye shall be offended because of me this night: for it is written, I will smite the shepherd, and the sheep of the flock shall be scattered abroad. (Matthew 26: 31.) But all this was done, that the scriptures of the prophets might be fulfilled. Then all the disciples forsook him, and fled. (Matthew 26: 56.)
Price of His Betrayal.	And I said unto them, If ye think good, give me my price; and if not, forbear. So they weighed for my price thirty pieces of silver. (Zechariah 11: 12.)	Then one of the twelve, called Judas Iscariot, went unto the chief priests, And said unto them, What will ye give me, and I will deliver him unto you? And they covenanted with him for thirty pieces of silver. (Matthew 26: 14, 15.)
Money Buys Potter's Field.	And the Lord said unto me, Cast it unto the potter: a goodly price that I was prised at of them. And I took the thirty pieces of silver, and cast them to the potter in the house of the Lord. (Zechariah 11: 13.)	And the chief priests took the silver pieces, and said, It is not lawful for to put them into the treasury, because it is the price of blood. And they took counsel, and bought with them the potter's field, to bury strangers in. (Matthew 27: 6, 7.)
The Agony Foretold.	I am poured out like water, and all my bones are out of joint: my heart is like wax; it is melted in the midst of my bowels. My strength is dried up like a potsherd; and my tongue cleaveth to my jaws; and thou hast brought me into the dust of death. (Psalm 22: 14, 15.)	Saying, Father, if thou be willing, remove this cup from me: nevertheless not my will, but thine, be done. And there appeared an angel unto him from heaven, strengthening him. And being in an agony he prayed more earnestly: and his sweat was as it were great drops of blood falling down to the ground. (Luke 22: 42-44.)
To Suffer for Many.	Surely he hath borne our griefs, and carried our sorrows: yet we did esteem him stricken, smitten of God, and afflicted. But he was wounded for our transgressions, he was bruised for our iniquities: the chastisement of our peace was upon him; and with his stripes we are healed.	Even as the Son of man came not to be ministered unto, but to minister, and to give his life a ransom for many. (Matthew 20: 28.)

Theme.	Prophecy.	Fulfillment.

All we like sheep have gone astray; we have turned every one to his own way; and the Lord hath laid on him the iniquity of us all.

He was oppressed, and he was afflicted, yet he opened not his mouth: he is brought as a lamb to the slaughter, and as a sheep before her shearers is dumb, so he openeth not his mouth.

He was taken from prison and from judgment: and who shall declare his generation? for he was cut off out of the land of the living: for the transgression of my people was he stricken. (Isaiah 53: 4-8.)

Therefore will I divide him a portion with the great, and he shall divide the spoil with the strong; because he. hath poured out his soul unto death: and he was numbered with the transgressors; and he bare the sin of many, and made intercession for the transgressors. (Isaiah 53: 12.)

And after threescore and two weeks shall Messiah be cut off, but not for himself: and the people of the prince that shall come shall destroy the city and the sanctuary; and the end thereof shall be with a flood, and unto the end of the war desolations are determined. (Daniel 9: 26.)

Silent Under Accusation and Affliction.

He was oppressed, and he was afflicted, yet he opened not his mouth: he is brought as a lamb to the slaughter, and as a sheep before her shearers is dumb, so he openeth not his mouth. (Isaiah 53: 7.)

But Jesus held his peace. And the high priest answered and said unto him, I adjure thee by the living God, that thou tell us whether thou be the Christ, the Son of God. (Matthew 26: 63.)

And when he was accused of the chief priests and elders, he answered nothing.

Then said Pilate unto him, Hearest thou not how many things they witness against thee?

And he answered him to never a word; insomuch that the governor marvelled greatly. (Matthew 27: 12-14.)

Theme.	Prophecy.	Fulfillment.
Smitten with a Rod.	Now gather thyself in troops, O daughter of troops: he hath laid siege against us: they shall smite the judge of Israel with a rod upon the cheek. (Micah 5: 1.)	And they spit upon him, and took the reed, and smote him on the head. (Matthew 27: 30.)
Reviled and Insulted.	I gave my back to the smiters, and my cheeks to them that plucked off the hair: I hid not my face from shame and spitting. (Isaiah 50: 6.)	And some began to spit on him, and to cover his face, and to buffet him, and to say unto him, Prophesy: and the servants did strike him with the palms of their hands. (Mark 14: 65.)
The Crucifixion.	For dogs have compassed me: the assembly of the wicked have inclosed me: they pierced my hands and my feet. I may tell all my bones: they look and stare upon me. They part my garments among them, and cast lots upon my vesture. (Psalm 22: 16-18.)	Where they crucified him, and two other with him, on either side one, and Jesus in the midst. (John 19: 18.) They said therefore among themselves, Let us not rend it, but cast lots for it, whose it shall be: that the scripture might be fulfilled, which saith, They parted my raiment among them, and for my vesture they did cast lots. These things therefore the soldiers did. (John 19: 24.)
The Cry from the Cross.	My God, my God, why hast thou forsaken me? why art thou so far from helping me, and from the words of my roaring? (Psalm 22: 1.)	And about the ninth hour Jesus cried with a loud voice, saying, Eli, Eli, lama sabachthani? that is to say, My God, my God, why hast thou forsaken me? (Matthew 27: 46.)
Jesus Taunted on the Cross.	All they that see me laugh me to scorn: they shoot out the lip, they shake the head, saying, He trusted on the Lord that he would deliver him: let him deliver him, seeing he delighted in him. (Psalm 22: 7, 8.)	And they that passed by reviled him, wagging their heads, And saying, Thou that destroyest the temple, and buildest it in three days, save thyself. If thou be the Son of God, come down from the cross. Likewise also the chief priests mocking him, with the scribes and elders, said, He saved others; himself he cannot save. If he be the King of Israel, let him now come down from the cross, and we will believe him. He trusted in God; let him deliver him now, if he will have him: for he said, I am the Son of God. (Matthew 27: 39-43.)

Theme.	Prophecy.	Fulfillment.
Given Gall and Vinegar.	They gave me also gall for my meat; and in my thirst they gave me vinegar to drink. (Psalm 69: 21.)	They gave him vinegar to drink mingled with gall: and when he had tasted thereof, he would not drink. (Matthew 27: 34.)
None of His Bones to Be Broken.	In one house shall it be eaten; thou shalt not carry forth ought of the flesh abroad out of the house: neither shall ye break a bone thereof. (Exodus 12: 46.) He keepeth all his bones: not one of them is broken. (Psalm 34: 20.) And I will pour upon the house of David, and upon the inhabitants of Jerusalem, the spirit of grace and of supplications: and they shall look upon me whom they have pierced, and they shall mourn for him, as one mourneth for his only son, and shall be in bitterness for him, as one that is in bitterness for his firstborn. (Zechariah 12: 10.)	But when they came to Jesus, and saw that he was dead already, they brake not his legs: But one of the soldiers with a spear pierced his side, and forthwith came there out blood and water. And he that saw it bare record, and his record is true: and he knoweth that he saith true, that ye might believe. For these things were done, that the scripture should be fulfilled, A bone of him shall not be broken. And again another scripture saith, They shall look on him whom they pierced. (John 19: 33-37.)
Burial in Rich Man's Tomb.	And he made his grave with the wicked, and with the rich in his death; because he had done no violence, neither was any deceit in his mouth. (Isaiah 53: 9.)	When the even was come, there came a rich man of Arimathæa, named Joseph, who also himself was Jesus' disciple: He went to Pilate, and begged the body of Jesus. Then Pilate commanded the body to be delivered. And when Joseph had taken the body, he wrapped it in a clean linen cloth, And laid it in his own new tomb, which he had hewn out in the rock: and he rolled a great stone to the door of the sepulchre, and departed. (Matthew 27: 57-60.)
His Body Uncorrupted.	For thou wilt not leave my soul in hell; neither wilt thou suffer thine Holy One to see corruption. (Psalm 16: 10.)	He seeing this before spake of the resurrection of Christ, that his soul was not left in hell, neither his flesh did see corruption. (Acts 2: 31.)
The Resurrection.	Thy dead men shall live, together with my dead body shall they arise. Awake and sing, ye that dwell in dust: for thy dew is as the dew of	And as they were afraid, and bowed down their faces to the earth, they said unto them, Why seek ye the living among the dead?

Theme.	Prophecy.	Fulfillment.
	herbs, and the earth shall cast out the dead. (Isaiah 26: 19.) After two days will he revive us: in the third day he will raise us up, and we shall live in his sight. (Hosea 6: 2.)	He is not here, but is risen: remember how he spake unto you when he was yet in Galilee, Saying, The Son of man must be delivered into the hands of sinful men, and be crucified, and the third day rise again. (Luke 24: 5-7.)
The Ascension and Exaltation.	Lift up your heads, O ye gates; and be ye lift up, ye everlasting doors; and the King of glory shall come in. (Psalm 24: 7.) Thou hast ascended on high, thou hast led captivity captive: thou hast received gifts for men; yea, for the rebellious also, that the Lord God might dwell among them. (Psalm 68: 18.) The Lord said unto my Lord, Sit thou at my right hand, until I make thine enemies thy footstool. (Psalm 110: 1.)	And it came to pass, while he blessed them, he was parted from them, and carried up into heaven. (Luke 24: 51.) And when he had spoken these things, while they beheld, he was taken up; and a cloud received him out of their sight. (Acts 1: 9.) Who being the brightness of his glory, and the express image of his person, and upholding all things by the word of his power, when he had by himself purged our sins, sat down on the right hand of the Majesty on high. (Hebrews 1: 3.)
Makes Intercession for Man.	Even he shall build the temple of the Lord; and he shall bear the glory, and shall sit and rule upon his throne; and he shall be a priest upon his throne: and the counsel of peace shall be between them both. (Zechariah 6: 13.)	Who is he that condemneth? It is Christ that died, yea rather, that is risen again, who is even at the right hand of God, who also maketh intercession for us. (Romans 8: 34.)
The Foundation of the Church.	Therefore thus saith the Lord God, Behold, I lay in Zion for a foundation a stone, a tried stone, a precious corner stone, a sure foundation: he that believeth shall not make haste. (Isaiah 28: 16.)	Ye also, as lively stones, are built up a spiritual house, an holy priesthood, to offer up spiritual sacrifices, acceptable to God by Jesus Christ. Wherefore also it is contained in the scripture, Behold, I lay in Sion a chief corner stone, elect, precious: and he that believeth on him shall not be confounded. Unto you therefore which believe he is precious: but unto them which be disobedient, the stone which the builders disallowed, the same is made the head of the corner. (1 Peter 2: 5-7.)

Theme.   *Prophecy.*   *Fulfillment.*

His Kingdom.

Yet have I set my king upon my holy hill of Zion. (Psalm 2: 6.)

He shall have dominion also from sea to sea, and from the river unto the ends of the earth. (Psalm 72: 8.)

For unto us a child is born, unto us a son is given: and the government shall be upon his shoulder: and his name shall be called Wonderful, Counsellor, The mighty God, The everlasting Father, The Prince of Peace.

Of the increase of his government and peace there shall be no end, upon the throne of David, and upon his kingdom, to order it, and to establish it with judgment and with justice from henceforth even for ever. The zeal of the Lord of hosts will perform this. (Isaiah 9: 6, 7.)

And there was given him dominion, and glory, and a kingdom, that all people, nations, and languages, should serve him: his dominion is an everlasting dominion, which shall not pass away, and his kingdom that which shall not be destroyed. (Daniel 7: 14.)

He shall be great, and shall be called the Son of the Highest: and the Lord God shall give unto him the throne of his father David:

And he shall reign over the house of Jacob for ever; and of his kingdom there shall be no end. (Luke 1: 32, 33.)

Then Pilate entered into the judgment hall again, and called Jesus, and said unto him, Art thou the King of the Jews?

Jesus answered him, Sayest thou this thing of thyself, or did others tell it thee of me?

Pilate answered, Am I a Jew? Thine own nation and the chief priests have delivered thee unto me: what hast thou done?

Jesus answered, My kingdom is not of this world: if my kingdom were of this world, then would my servants fight, that I should not be delivered to the Jews: but now is my kingdom not from hence.

Pilate therefore said unto him, Art thou a king then? Jesus answered, Thou sayest that I am a king. To this end was I born, and for this cause came I into the world, that I should bear witness unto the truth. Every one that is of the truth heareth my voice. (John 18: 33-37.)

584

THE GOSPELS HARMONIZED

	MATTHEW.	MARK.	LUKE.	JOHN.
"The Word"				1: 1–14
Preface to Theophilus			1: 1–4	
Annunciation of the Baptist's birth			1: 5–25	
Annunciation of the birth of Jesus			1: 26–38	
Mary visits Elizabeth			1: 39–56	
Birth of John the Baptist			1: 57–80	
Birth of Jesus Christ	1: 18–25		2: 1–7	
Two Genealogies	1: 1–17		3: 23–38	
The watching Shepherds			2: 8–20	
The Circumcision			2: 21	
Presentation in the Temple			2: 22–38	
The wise men from the East	2: 1–12			
Flight to Egypt	2: 13–23		2: 39	
Disputing with the Doctors			2: 40–52	
Ministry of John the Baptist	3: 1–12	1: 1–8	3: 1–18	1: 15–31
Baptism of Jesus Christ	3: 13–17	1: 9–11	3: 21, 22	1: 32–34
The Temptation	4: 1–11	1: 12, 13	4: 1–13	
Andrew and another see Jesus				1: 35–40
Simon, now Cephas				1: 41, 42
Philip and Nathanael				1: 43–51
The water made wine				2: 1–11
Passover (1st) and cleansing the Temple				2: 12–22
Nicodemus				2: 23–3: 21
Christ and John baptizing				3: 22–36
The woman of Samaria				4: 1–42
John the Baptist in prison	4: 12; 14: 3	1: 14; 6: 17	3: 19, 20	3: 24
Return to Galilee	4: 12	1: 14, 15	4: 14, 15	4: 43–45
The synagogue at Nazareth			4: 16–30	
The Nobleman's Son				4: 46–54
Capernaum. Four Apostles called	4: 13–22	1: 16–20	5: 1–11	
Demoniac healed there		1: 21–28	4: 31–37	
Simon's wife's mother healed	8: 14–17	1: 29–34	4: 38–41	
Circuit round Galilee	4: 23–25	1: 35–39	4: 42–44	
Healing a leper	8: 1–4	1: 40–45	5: 12–16	
Christ stills the storm	8: 18–27	4: 35–41	8: 22–25	
Demoniacs in land of Gadarenes	8: 28–34	5: 1–20	8: 26–39	
Jairus's daughter. Woman healed	9: 18–26	5: 21–43	8: 40–56	
Blind men, and demoniac	9: 27–34			
Healing the paralytic	9: 1–8	2: 1–12	5: 17–26	
Matthew the Publican	9: 9–13	2: 13–17	5: 27–32	
"Thy disciples fast not"	9: 14–17	2: 18–22	5: 33–39	
Journey to Jerusalem to 2d Passover				5: 1
Pool of Bethesda. Power of Christ				5: 2–47
Plucking ears of Corn on Sabbath	12: 1–8	2: 23–28	6: 1–5	
The withered hand. Miracles	12: 9–21	3: 1–12	6: 6–11	
The Twelve Apostles	10: 2–4	3: 13–19	6: 12–16	
The Sermon on the Mount	5: 1–7: 29		6: 17–49	
The centurion's servant	8: 5–13		7: 1–10	4: 46–54
The widow's son at Nain			7: 11–17	
Messengers from John	11: 2–19		7: 18–35	
Woe to the cities of Galilee	11: 20–24			
Call to the meek and suffering	11: 25–30			
Anointing the feet of Jesus			7: 36–50	
Second circuit round Galilee			8: 1–3	
Parable of the Sower	13: 1–23	4: 1–20	8: 4–15	
Parable of the Candle under a Bushel		4: 21–25	8: 16–18	
Parable of the Sower		4: 26–29		
Parable of the Wheat and Tares	13: 24–30			
Parable of the Grain of Mustard Seed	13: 31, 32	4: 30–32	13: 18, 19	
Parable of the Leaven	13: 33		13: 20, 21	
On teaching by parables	13: 34, 35	4: 33, 34		
Wheat and tares explained	13: 36–43			
The treasure, the pearl, the net	13: 44–52			
His mother and His brethren	12: 46–50	3: 31–35	8: 19–21	
Reception at Nazareth	13: 53–58	6: 1–6		
Third circuit round Galilee	9: 35–38; 11: 1	6: 6		

	MATTHEW	MARK.	LUKE.	JOHN.
Sending forth of the Twelve	10	6: 7-13	9: 1-6	
Herod's opinion of Jesus	14: 1, 2	6: 14-16	9: 7-9	
Death of John the Baptist	14: 3-12	6: 17-29		
Approach of Passover (3d)				6: 4
Feeding of the five thousand	14: 13-21	6: 30-44	9: 10-17	6: 1-15
Walking on the sea	14: 22-33	6: 45-52		6: 16-21
Miracles in Gennesaret	14: 34-36	6: 53-56		
The bread of life				6: 22-65
The washen hands	15: 1-20	7: 1-23		
The Syrophœnician woman	15: 21-28	7: 24-30		
Miracles of healing	15: 29-31	7: 31-37		
Feeding of the four thousand	15: 32-39	8: 1-9		
The sign from heaven	16: 1-4	8: 10-13		
The leaven of the Pharisees	16: 5-12	8: 14-21		
Blind man healed		8: 22-26		
Peter's profession of faith	16: 13-19	8: 27-29	9: 18-20	6: 66-71
The Passion foretold	16: 20-28	8: 30-9: 1	9: 21-27	
The Transfiguration	17: 1-9	9: 2-10	9: 28-36	
Elijah	17: 10-13	9: 11-13		
The lunatic healed	17: 14-21	9: 14-29	9: 37-42	
The Passion again foretold	17: 22, 23	9: 30-32	9: 43-45	
Fish caught for the tribute	17: 24-27			
The little child	18: 1-5	9: 33-37	9: 46-48	
One casting out devils		9: 38-41	9: 49, 50	
Offenses	18: 6-9	9: 42-48	17: 2	
The lost sheep	18: 10-14		15: 4-7	
Forgiveness of injuries	18: 15-17			
Binding and loosing	18: 18-20			
Forgiveness. Parable	18: 21-35			
"Salted with fire"		9: 49, 50		
Journey to Jerusalem			9: 51	7: 1-10
Fire from heaven			9: 52-56	
Answers to disciples	8: 19-22		9: 57-62	
The Seventy disciples			10: 1-16	
Discussions at Feast of Tabernacles				7: 11-53
Woman taken in adultery				8: 1-11
Dispute with the Pharisees				8: 12-59
The man born blind				9: 1-41
The good Shepherd				10: 1-21
The return of the Seventy			10: 17-24	
The good Samaritan			10: 25-37	
Mary and Martha			10: 38-42	
The Lord's Prayer	6: 9-13		11: 1-4	
Prayer effectual	7: 7-11		11: 5-13	
"Through Beelzebub"	12: 22-37	3: 20-30	11: 14-23	
The unclean spirit returning	12: 43-45		11: 24-28	
The sign of Jonah	12: 38-42		11: 29-32	
The light of the body	5: 15; 6: 22, 23		11: 33-36	
The Pharisees	23		11: 37-54	
What to fear	10: 26-33		12: 1-12	
"Master, speak to my brother"			12: 13-15	
Covetousness	6: 25-33		12: 16-31	
Watchfulness			12: 32-59	
Galileans that perished			13: 1-9	
Woman healed on Sabbath			13: 10-17	
The grain of mustard seed	13: 31, 32	4: 30-32	13: 18, 19	
The leaven	13: 33		13: 20, 21	
Toward Jerusalem			13: 22	
"Are there few that be saved?"			13: 23-30	
Warning against Herod			13: 31-33	
"O Jerusalem, Jerusalem"	23: 37-39		13: 34, 35	
Dropsy healed on Sabbath day			14: 1-6	
Choosing the chief rooms			14: 7-14	
Parable of the Great Supper	22: 1-14		14: 15-24	
Following Christ with the Cross	10: 37, 38		14: 25-35	
Parables of Lost Sheep, Piece of Money, Prodigal Son, Unjust Steward, Rich Man and Lazarus			15, 16	
Offenses	18: 6-15		17: 1-4	
Faith and merit	17: 20		17: 5-10	
The ten lepers			17: 11-19	
How the kingdom cometh			17: 20-37	
Parable of the Unjust Judge			18: 1-8	
Parable of the Pharisee and Publican			18: 9-14	
Divorce	19: 1-12	10: 1-12		

	MATTHEW.	MARK.	LUKE.	JOHN.
Infants brought to Jesus	19:13–15	10:13–16	18:15–17	
The rich man inquiring	19:16–26	10:17–27	18:18–27	
Promises to the disciples	19:27–30	10:28–31	18:28–30	
Laborers in the vineyard	20:1–16			
Death of Christ foretold	20:17–19	10:32–34	18:31–34	
Request of James and John	20:20–28	10:35–45		
Blind Men at Jericho	20:29–34	10:46–52	18:35–43	
Zaccheus			19:1–10	
Parable of the Ten Talents	25:14–30		19:11–28	
Feast of Dedication				10:22–39
Beyond Jordan				10:40–42
Raising of Lazarus				11:1–44
Meeting of the Sanhedrin				11:45–53
Christ in Ephraim				11:54–57
The anointing by Mary	26:6–13	14:3–9	7:36–50	12:1–11
Christ enters Jerusalem	21:1–11	11:1–10	19:29–44	12:12–19
Cleansing of the Temple (2d)	21:12–16	11:15–18	19:45–48	2:13–22
The barren fig tree	21:17–22	11:11–14, 19–23		
Pray, and forgive	6:14, 15	11:24–26		
"By what authority," etc	21:23–27	11:27–33	20:1–8	
Parable of the Two Sons	21:28–32			
Parable of the Wicked Husbandmen	21:33–46	12:1–12	20:9–19	
Parable of the Wedding Garment	22:1–14		14:16–24	
The tribute money	22:15–22	12:13–17	20:20–26	
The state of the risen	22:23–33	12:18–27	20:27–40	
The great Commandment	22:34–40	12:28–34		
David's Son and David's Lord	22:41–46	12:35–37	20:41–44	
Against the Pharisees	23:1–39	12:38–40	20:45–47	
The widow's mite		12:41–44	21:1–4	
Christ's Second Coming	24:1–51	13:1–37	21:5–38	
Parable of the Ten Virgins	25:1–13			
Parable of the Talents	25:14–30		19:11–28	
The Last Judgment	25:31–46			
Greeks visit Jesus. Voice from Heaven				12:20–36
Reflections of John				12:36–50
Last Passover (4th). Jews conspire	26:1–5	14:1, 2	22:1, 2	
Judas Iscariot	26:14–16	14:10, 11	22:3–6	
Paschal Supper	26:17–29	14:12–25	22:7–23	13:1–35
Contention of the Apostles			22:24–30	
Peter's fall foretold	26:30–35	14:26–31	22:31–39	13:36–38
Last discourse. The departure; the Comforter				14:1–31
The vine and the branches. Abiding in love				15:1–27
Work of the Comforter in Disciples				16:1–33
The prayer of Christ				17:1–26
Gethsemane	26:36–46	14:32–42	22:40–46	18:1
The betrayal	26:47–56	14:43–52	22:47–53	18:2–11
Before Annas (Caiaphas). Peter's denial	26:57, 58, 69–75	14:53, 54, 66–72	22:54–62	18:12–27
Before the Sanhedrin	26:59–68	14:55–65	22:63–71	
Before Pilate	27:1, 2, 11–14	15:1–5	23:1–3	18:28
The traitor's death	27:3–10			
Before Herod			23:4–11	
Accusation and Condemnation	27:15–26	15:6–15	23:13–25	18:29–40; 19:1–16
Treatment by the Soldiers	27:27–31	15:16–20	23:36, 37	19:2, 3
The Crucifixion	27:32–38	15:21–28	23:26–34	19:17–24
The mother of Jesus				19:25–27
Mockings and railings	27:39–44	15:29–32	23:35–39	
The Malefactor			23:40–43	
The death	27:50	15:37	23:46	19:28–30
Darkness and other portents	27:45–53	15:33–38	23:44, 45	
The bystanders	27:54–56	15:39–41	23:47–49	
The side pierced				19:31–37
The burial	27:57–61	15:42–47	23:50–56	19:38–42
The guard of the Sepulcher	{ 27:62–66 / 28:11–15 }			
The Resurrection	28:1–10	16:1–11	24:1–12	20:1–18
Disciples going to Emmaus		16:12, 13	24:13–35	
Appearances in Jerusalem		16:14–18	24:36–49	20:19–29
At the Sea of Tiberias				21:1–23
On the Mount in Galilee	28:16–20			
Unrecorded Works				20:30, 31; 21:24, 25
Ascension		16:19, 20	24:50–53	

HOW TO READ THE BIBLE THROUGH IN A YEAR

THE following tables are included in this book for the sole purpose of satisfying a demand for a method of reading the Bible through in a year. The writer personally does not think the Bible can be read through in a year with good results in the way of either knowledge or studentship, preferring to take chapter by chapter, or, better still, verse by verse, with the aid of first-class reference books and commentaries as the reading proceeds, and extending the reading over a very much longer period. Such a plan or policy, while it consumes much more time, inevitably will result in a better and more finished studentship of the Scriptures than the mechanical reading of a certain number of chapters or pages daily. But there are many persons who have not the time nor the opportunity for such careful reading and study, and yet are desirous of reading the Book in its entirety. To them, therefore, the following tables will be useful. They are based largely upon an old plan of reading three chapters daily and five on Sunday. The selections have been made as nearly even as possible, and for Sunday reading in additional to the regular amount a general review of the previous week's reading suggested.

JANUARY.			FEBRUARY.		
Date.	Morning.	Evening.	Date.	Morning.	Evening.
1	Genesis 1, 2, 3.	Matthew 1.	1	Exodus 27, 28.	Matthew 21: 1–22.
2	Genesis 4, 5, 6.	Matthew 2,	2	Exodus 29, 30.	Matthew 21: 23–46.
3	Genesis 7, 8, 9.	Matthew 3.	3	Exodus 31, 32, 33.	Matthew 22: 1–22.
4	Genesis 10, 11, 12.	Matthew 4.	4	Exodus 34, 35.	Matthew 22: 23–46.
5	Genesis 13, 14, 15.	Matthew 5: 1–30.	5	Exodus 36, 37, 38.	Matthew 23: 1–12.
6	Genesis 16, 17.	Matthew 5: 31–48.	6	Exodus 39, 40.	Matthew 23: 13–39.
7	Genesis 18, 19.	Matthew 6: 1–18.	7	Leviticus 1, 2, 3.	Matthew 24: 1–31.
8	Genesis 20, 21, 22.	Matthew 6: 19–34.	8	Leviticus 4, 5.	Matthew 24: 32–51.
9	Genesis 23, 24.	Matthew 7.	9	Leviticus 6, 7.	Matthew 25: 1–30.
10	Genesis 25, 26.	Matthew 8: 1–17.	10	Leviticus 8, 9, 10.	Matthew 25: 31–46.
11	Genesis 27, 28.	Matthew 8: 18–34.	11	Leviticus 11, 12.	Matthew 26: 1–25.
12	Genesis 29, 30.	Matthew 9: 1–19.	12	Leviticus 13.	Matthew 26: 26–50.
13	Genesis 31, 32.	Matthew 9: 20–38.	13	Leviticus 14.	Matthew 26: 51–75.
14	Genesis 33, 34, 35.	Matthew 10: 1–20.	14	Leviticus 15, 16.	Matthew 27: 1–26.
15	Genesis 36, 37, 38.	Matthew 10: 21–42.	15	Leviticus 17, 18.	Matthew 27: 27–50.
16	Genesis 39, 40.	Matthew 11.	16	Leviticus 19, 20.	Matthew 27: 51–66.
17	Genesis 41, 42.	Matthew 12: 1–37.	17	Leviticus 21, 22.	Matthew 28.
18	Genesis 43, 44, 45.	Matthew 12: 38–50.	18	Leviticus 23, 24.	Mark 1: 1–22.
19	Genesis 46, 47, 48.	Matthew 13: 1–32.	19	Leviticus 25.	Mark 1: 23–45.
20	Genesis 49, 50.	Matthew 13: 33–58.	20	Leviticus 26, 27.	Mark 2.
21	Exodus 1, 2, 3.	Matthew 14: 1–21.	21	Numbers 1, 2.	Mark 3: 1–19.
22	Exodus 4, 5, 6.	Matthew 14: 22–36.	22	Numbers 3, 4.	Mark 3: 20–35.
23	Exodus 7, 8.	Matthew 15: 1–20.	23	Numbers 5, 6.	Mark 4: 1–20.
24	Exodus 9, 10, 11.	Matthew 15: 21–39.	24	Numbers 7, 8.	Mark 4: 21–41.
25	Exodus 12, 13.	Matthew 16.	25	Numbers 9, 10, 11.	Mark 5: 1–20.
26	Exodus 14, 15.	Matthew 17.	26	Numbers 12, 13, 14.	Mark 5: 21–43.
27	Exodus 16, 17, 18.	Matthew 18: 1–20.	27	Numbers 15, 16.	Mark 6: 1–29.
28	Exodus 19, 20.	Matthew 18: 21–35.	28	Numbers 17, 18, 19.	Mark 6: 30–56.
29	Exodus 21, 22.	Matthew 19.	29	Numbers 20, 21, 22.	Mark 7: 1–23.
30	Exodus 23, 24.	Matthew 20: 1–16.			
31	Exodus 25, 26.	Matthew 20: 17–34.			

NOTE.—On Sundays review the reading of the previous week.

MARCH.

Date.	Morning.	Evening.
1	Numbers 23, 24, 25.	Mark 7: 24–37.
2	Numbers 26, 27.	Mark 8: 1–21.
3	Numbers 28, 29, 30.	Mark 8: 22–38.
4	Numbers 31, 32, 33.	Mark 9: 1–29.
5	Numbers 34, 35, 36.	Mark 9: 30–50.
6	Deuteronomy 1, 2.	Mark 10: 1–27.
7	Deuteronomy 3, 4.	Mark 10: 28–52.
8	Deuteronomy 5, 6, 7.	Mark 11: 1–18.
9	Deuteronomy 8, 9, 10.	Mark 11: 19–33.
10	Deuteronomy 11, 12, 13.	Mark 12: 1–27.
11	Deuteronomy 14, 15, 16.	Mark 12: 28–44.
12	Deuteronomy 17, 18, 19.	Mark 13: 1–20.
13	Deuteronomy 20, 21, 22.	Mark 13: 21–37.
14	Deuteronomy 23, 24, 25.	Mark 14: 1–26.
15	Deuteronomy 26, 27.	Mark 14: 27–53.
16	Deuteronomy 28, 29.	Mark 14: 54–72.
17	Deuteronomy 30, 31.	Mark 15: 1–25.
18	Deuteronomy 32, 33, 34.	Mark 15: 26–47.
19	Joshua 1, 2, 3.	Mark 16.
20	Joshua 4, 5, 6.	Luke 1: 1–25.
21	Joshua 7, 8, 9.	Luke 1: 26–38.
22	Joshua 10, 11, 12.	Luke 1: 39–66.
23	Joshua 13, 14, 15.	Luke 1: 67–80.
24	Joshua 16, 17, 18.	Luke 2: 1–24.
25	Joshua 19, 20, 21.	Luke 2: 25–52.
26	Joshua 22, 23, 24.	Luke 3.
27	Judges 1, 2, 3.	Luke 4: 1–30.
28	Judges 4, 5, 6.	Luke 4: 31–44.
29	Judges 7, 8.	Luke 5: 1–16.
30	Judges 9, 10.	Luke 5: 17–39.
31	Judges 11, 12.	Luke 6: 1–26.

APRIL.

Date.	Morning.	Evening.
1	Judges 13, 14, 15.	Luke 6: 27–49.
2	Judges 16, 17, 18.	Luke 7: 1–30.
3	Judges 19, 20, 21.	Luke 7: 31–50.
4	Ruth 1, 2, 3, 4.	Luke 8: 1–25.
5	1 Samuel 1, 2, 3.	Luke 8: 26–56.
6	1 Samuel 4, 5, 6.	Luke 9: 1–17.
7	1 Samuel 7, 8, 9.	Luke 9: 18–36.
8	1 Samuel 10, 11, 12.	Luke 9: 37–62.
9	1 Samuel 13, 14.	Luke 10: 1–24.
10	1 Samuel 15, 16.	Luke 10: 25–42.
11	1 Samuel 17, 18.	Luke 11: 1–28.
12	1 Samuel 19, 20, 21.	Luke 11: 29–54.
13	1 Samuel 22, 23, 24.	Luke 12: 1–34.
14	1 Samuel 25, 26.	Luke 12: 35–59.
15	1 Samuel 27, 28, 29.	Luke 13: 1–22.
16	1 Samnel 30, 31.	Luke 13: 23–35.
17	2 Samuel 1, 2.	Luke 14: 1–24.
18	2 Samuel 3, 4, 5.	Luke 14: 25–35.
19	2 Samuel 6, 7, 8.	Luke 15: 1–10.
20	2 Samuel 9, 10, 11.	Luke 15: 11–32.
21	2 Samuel 12, 13.	Luke 16.
22	2 Samuel 14, 15.	Luke 17: 1–19.
23	2 Samuel 16, 17, 18.	Luke 17: 20–37.
24	2 Samuel 19, 20.	Luke 18: 1–27.
25	2 Samuel 21, 22.	Luke 18: 28–43.
26	2 Samuel 23, 24.	Luke 19: 1–28.
27	1 Kings 1, 2.	Luke 19: 29–48.
28	1 Kings 3, 4, 5.	Luke 20: 1–26.
29	1 Kings 6, 7.	Luke 20: 27–17.
30	1 Kings 8, 9.	Luke 21: 1–19.

NOTE.—On Sundays review the reading of the previous week.

MAY.

Date.	Morning.	Evening.
1	1 Kings 10, 11.	Luke 21: 20–38.
2	1 Kings 12, 13.	Luke 22: 1–20.
3	1 Kings 14, 15.	Luke 22: 21–46.
4	1 Kings 16, 17, 18.	Luke 22: 47–71.
5	1 Kings 19, 20.	Luke 23: 1–25.
6	1 Kings 21, 22.	Luke 23: 26–56.
7	2 Kings 1, 2, 3.	Luke 24: 1–35.
8	2 Kings 4, 5, 6.	Luke 24: 36–53.
9	2 Kings 7, 8, 9.	John 1: 1–28.
10	2 Kings 10, 11, 12.	John 1: 29–51.
11	2 Kings 13, 14.	John 2.
12	2 Kings 15, 16.	John 3: 1–21.
13	2 Kings 17, 18.	John 3: 22–36.
14	2 Kings 19, 20, 21.	John 4: 1–30.
15	2 Kings 22, 23.	John 4: 31–54.
16	2 Kings 24, 25.	John 5: 1–24.
17	1 Chronicles 1, 2, 3.	John 5: 25–47.
18	1 Chronicles 4, 5, 6.	John 6: 1–21.
19	1 Chronicles 7, 8, 9.	John 6: 22–44.
20	1 Chronicles 10, 11, 12.	John 6: 45–71.
21	1 Chronicles 13, 14, 15.	John 7: 1–27.
22	1 Chronicles 16, 17, 18.	John 7: 28–53.
23	1 Chronicles 19, 20, 21.	John 8: 1–27.
24	1 Chronicles 22, 23, 24.	John 8: 28–59.
25	1 Chronicles 25, 26, 27.	John 9: 1–23.
26	1 Chronicles 28, 29.	John 9: 24–41.
27	2 Chronicles 1, 2, 3.	John 10: 1–23.
28	2 Chronicles 4, 5, 6.	John 10: 24–42.
29	2 Chronicles 7, 8, 9.	John 11: 1–29.
30	2 Chronicles 10, 11, 12.	John 11: 30–57.
31	2 Chronicles 13, 14.	John 12: 1–26.

JUNE.

Date.	Morning.	Evening.
1	2 Chronicles 15, 16.	John 12: 27–50.
2	2 Chronicles 17, 18.	John 13: 1–20.
3	2 Chronicles 19, 20.	John 13: 21–38.
4	2 Chronicles 21, 22.	John 14.
5	2 Chronicles 23, 24.	John 15.
6	2 Chronicles 25, 26, 27.	John 16.
7	2 Chronicles 28, 29.	John 17.
8	2 Chronicles 30, 31.	John 18: 1–24.
9	2 Chronicles 32, 33.	John 18: 25–40.
10	2 Chronicles 34, 35, 36.	John 19: 1–22.
11	Ezra 1, 2.	John 19: 23–42.
12	Ezra 3, 4, 5.	John 20.
13	Ezra 6, 7, 8.	John 21.
14	Ezra 9, 10.	Acts 1.
15	Nehemiah 1, 2, 3.	Acts 2: 1–21.
16	Nehemiah 4, 5, 6.	Acts 2: 22–47.
17	Nehemiah 7, 8, 9.	Acts 3.
18	Nehemiah 10, 11.	Acts 4: 1–22.
19	Nehemiah 12, 13.	Acts 4: 23–37.
20	Esther 1, 2.	Acts 5: 1–21.
21	Esther 3, 4, 5.	Acts 5: 22–42.
22	Esther 6, 7, 8.	Acts 6.
23	Esther 9, 10.	Acts 7: 1–21.
24	Job 1, 2.	Acts 7: 22–43.
25	Job 3, 4.	Acts 7: 44–60.
26	Job 5, 6, 7.	Acts 8: 1–25.
27	Job 8, 9, 10.	Acts 8: 26–40.
28	Job 11, 12, 13.	Acts 9: 1–21.
29	Job 14, 15, 16.	Acts 9: 22–43.
30	Job 17, 18, 19.	Acts 10: 1–23.

NOTE.—On Sundays review the reading of the previous week.

JULY.

Date.	Morning.	Evening.
1	Job 20, 21.	Acts 10: 24–48.
2	Job 22, 23, 24.	Acts 11.
3	Job 25, 26, 27.	Acts 12.
4	Job 28, 29.	Acts 13: 1–31.
5	Job 30, 31.	Acts 13: 32–52.
6	Job 32, 33.	Acts 14.
7	Job 34, 35.	Acts 15: 1–21.
8	Job 36, 37.	Acts 15: 22–41.
9	Job 38, 39, 40.	Acts 16: 1–21.
10	Job 41, 42.	Acts 16: 22–40.
11	Psalms 1, 2, 3.	Acts 17: 1–15.
12	Psalms 4, 5, 6.	Acts 17: 16–34.
13	Psalms 7, 8, 9	Acts 18.
14	Psalms 10, 11, 12.	Acts 19: 1–20.
15	Psalms 13, 14, 15.	Acts 19: 21–41.
16	Psalms 16, 17.	Acts 20: 1–16.
17	Psalms 18, 19.	Acts 20: 17–38.
18	Psalms 20, 21, 22.	Acts 21: 1–17.
19	Psalms 23, 24, 25.	Acts 21: 18–40.
20	Psalms 26, 27, 28.	Acts 22.
21	Psalms 29, 30.	Acts 23: 1–15.
22	Psalms 31, 32.	Acts 23: 16–35.
23	Psalms 33, 34.	Acts 24.
24	Psalms 35. 36.	Acts 25.
25	Psalms 37, 38, 39.	Acts 26.
26	Psalms 40, 41, 42.	Acts 27: 1–26.
27	Psalms 43, 44, 45.	Acts 27: 27–44.
28	Psalms 46, 47, 48.	Acts 28.
29	Psalms 49, 50.	Romans 1.
30	Psalms 51, 52, 53.	Romans 2.
31	Psalms 54, 55, 56.	Romans 3.

AUGUST.

Date.	Morning.	Evening.
1	Psalms 57, 58, 59.	Romans 4.
2	Psalms 60, 61, 62.	Romans 5.
3	Psalms 63, 64, 65.	Romans 6.
4	Psalms 66, 67.	Romans 7.
5	Psalms 68, 69.	Romans 8: 1–21.
6	Psalms 70, 71.	Romans 8: 22–39.
7	Psalms 72, 73.	Romans 9: 1–15.
8	Psalms 74, 75, 76.	Romans 9: 16–33.
9	Psalms 77, 78.	Romans 10.
10	Psalms 79, 80.	Romans 11: 1–18.
11	Psalms 81, 82, 83.	Romans 11: 19–36.
12	Psalms 84, 85, 86.	Romans 12.
13	Psalms 87, 88.	Romans 13.
14	Psalms 89, 90.	Romans 14.
15	Psalms 91, 92, 93.	Romans 15: 1–13.
16	Psalms 94, 95, 96.	Romans 15: 14–33.
17	Psalms 97, 98, 99.	Romans 16.
18	Psalms 100, 101, 102.	1 Corinthians 1.
19	Psalms 103, 104.	1 Corinthians 2.
20	Psalms 105, 106.	1 Corinthians 3.
21	Psalms 107, 108, 109.	1 Corinthians 4.
22	Psalms 110, 111, 112.	1 Corinthians 5.
23	Psalms 113, 114, 115.	1 Corinthians 6.
24	Psalms 116, 117, 118.	1 Corinthians 7: 1–19.
25	Psalm 119: 1-88.	1 Corinthians 7: 20–40.
26	Psalm 119: 89–176.	1 Corinthians 8.
27	Psalms 120, 121, 122.	1 Corinthians 9.
28	Psalms 123, 124, 125.	1 Corinthians 10: 1–18.
29	Psalms 126, 127, 128.	1 Corinthians 10: 19–33.
30	Psalms 129, 130, 131.	1 Corinthians 11: 1–16.
31	Psalms 132, 133, 134.	1 Corinthians 11: 17–34.

NOTE.—On Sundays review the reading of the previous week.

SEPTEMBER.

Date.	Morning.	Evening.
1	Psalms 135, 136.	1 Corinthians 12.
2	Psalms 137, 138, 139.	1 Corinthians 13.
3	Psalms 140, 141, 142.	1 Corinthians 14: 1–20.
4	Psalms 143, 144, 145.	1 Corinthians 14: 21–40
5	Psalms 146, 147.	1 Corinthians 15: 1–28.
6	Psalms 148, 149, 150.	1 Corinthians 15: 29–58.
7	Proverbs 1, 2.	1 Corinthians 16.
8	Proverbs 3, 4, 5.	2 Corinthians 1.
9	Proverbs 6, 7.	2 Corinthians 2.
10	Proverbs 8, 9.	2 Corinthians 3.
11	Proverbs 10, 11, 12.	2 Corinthians 4.
12	Proverbs 13, 14, 15.	2 Corinthians 5.
13	Proverbs 16, 17, 18.	2 Corinthians 6.
14	Proverbs 19, 20, 21.	2 Corinthians 7.
15	Proverbs 22, 23, 24.	2 Corinthians 8.
16	Proverbs 25, 26.	2 Corinthians 9.
17	Proverbs 27, 28, 29.	2 Corinthians 10.
18	Proverbs 30, 31.	2 Corinthians 11: 1–15.
19	Ecclesiastes 1, 2, 3.	2 Corinthians 11: 16–33.
20	Ecclesiastes 4, 5, 6.	2 Corinthians 12.
21	Ecclesiastes 7, 8, 9.	2 Corinthians 13.
22	Ecclesiastes 10, 11, 12.	Galatians 1.
23	Song 1, 2, 3.	Galatians 2.
24	Song 4, 5.	Galatians 3.
25	Song 6, 7, 8.	Galatians 4.
26	Isaiah 1, 2.	Galatians 5.
27	Isaiah 3, 4.	Galatians 6.
28	Isaiah 5. 6.	Ephesians 1.
29	Isaiah 7, 8.	Ephesians 2.
30	Isaiah 9, 10.	Ephesians 3.

OCTOBER.

Date.	Morning.	Evening.
1	Isaiah 11, 12, 13.	Ephesians 4.
2	Isaiah 14, 15 16.	Ephesians 5: 1–16.
3	Isaiah 17, 18, 19.	Ephesians 5: 17–33.
4	Isaiah 20, 21, 22.	Ephesians 6.
5	Isaiah 23, 24, 25.	Philippians 1.
6	Isaiah 26, 27.	Philippians 2.
7	Isaiah 28, 29.	Philippians 3.
8	Isaiah 30, 31.	Philippians 4.
9	Isaiah 32, 33.	Colossians 1.
10	Isaiah 34, 35, 36.	Colossians 2.
11	Isaiah 37, 38.	Colossians 3.
12	Isaiah 39, 40.	Colossians 4.
13	Isaiah 41, 42.	1 Thessalonians 1.
14	Isaiah 43, 44.	1 Thessalonians 2.
15	Isaiah 45, 46.	1 Thessalonians 3.
16	Isaiah 47, 48, 49.	1 Thessalonians 4.
17	Isaiah 50, 51, 52.	1 Thessalonians 5.
18	Isaiah 53, 54, 55.	2 Thessalonians 1.
19	Isaiah 56, 57, 58.	2 Thessalonians 2.
20	Isaiah 59, 60, 61.	2 Thessalonians 3.
21	Isaiah 62, 63, 64.	1 Timothy 1.
22	Isaiah 65, 66.	1 Timothy 2.
23	Jeremiah 1, 2.	1 Timothy 3.
24	Jeremiah 3, 4, 5.	1 Timothy 4.
25	Jeremiah 6, 7, 8.	1 Timothy 5.
26	Jeremiah 9, 10, 11.	1 Timothy 6.
27	Jeremiah 12, 13, 14.	2 Timothy 1.
28	Jeremiah 15, 16, 17.	2 Timothy 2.
29	Jeremiah 18, 19.	2 Timothy 3.
30	Jeremiah 20, 21.	2 Timothy 4.
31	Jeremiah 22, 23.	Titus 1.

NOTE.—On Sundays review the reading of the previous week.

	NOVEMBER.			DECEMBER.	
Date.	Morning.	Evening.	Date.	Morning.	Evening.
1	Jeremiah 24, 25, 26.	Titus 2.	1	Ezekiel 40, 41.	2 Peter 3.
2	Jeremiah 27, 28, 29.	Titus 3.	2	Ezekiel 42, 43, 44.	1 John 1,
3	Jeremiah 30, 31.	Philemon.	3	Ezekiel 45, 46.	1 John 2.
4	Jeremiah 32, 33.	Hebrews 1.	4	Ezekiel 47, 48.	1 John 3.
5	Jeremiah 34, 35, 36.	Hebrews 2.	5	Daniel 1, 2.	1 John 4.
6	Jeremiah 37, 38, 39.	Hebrews 3.	6	Daniel 3, 4.	1 John 5.
7	Jeremiah 40, 41, 42.	Hebrews 4.	7	Daniel 5, 6, 7.	2 John.
8	Jeremiah 43, 44, 45.	Hebrews 5.	8	Daniel 8, 9, 10.	3 John.
9	Jeremiah 46, 47.	Hebrews 6.	9	Daniel 11, 12.	Jude.
10	Jeremiah 48, 49.	Hebrews 7.	10	Hosea 1, 2, 3, 4.	Revelation 1.
11	Jeremiah 50.	Hebrews 8.	11	Hosea 5, 6, 7, 8.	Revelation 2.
12	Jeremiah 51, 52.	Hebrews 9.	12	Hosea 9, 10, 11.	Revelation 3.
13	Lamentations 1, 2.	Hebrews 10: 1–18.	13	Hosea 12, 13, 14.	Revelation 4.
14	Lamentations 3, 4, 5.	Hebrews 10: 19–39.	14	Joel 1, 2, 3.	Revelation 5.
15	Ezekiel 1, 2.	Hebrews 11: 1–19.	15	Amos 1, 2, 3.	Revelation 6.
16	Ezekiel 3, 4.	Hebrews 11: 20–40.	16	Amos 4, 5, 6.	Revelation 7.
17	Ezekiel 5, 6, 7.	Hebrews 12.	17	Amos 7, 8, 9.	Revelation 8.
18	Ezekiel 8, 9, 10.	Hebrews 13.	18	Obadiah.	Revelation 9.
19	Ezekiel 11, 12, 13.	James 1.	19	Jonah 1, 2, 3, 4.	Revelation 10.
20	Ezekiel 14, 15.	James 2.	20	Micah 1, 2, 3.	Revelation 11.
21	Ezekiel 16, 17.	James 3.	21	Micah 4, 5.	Revelation 12.
22	Ezekiel 18, 19.	James 4.	22	Micah 6, 7.	Revelation 13.
23	Ezekiel 20, 21.	James 5.	23	Nahum 1, 2, 3.	Revelation 14.
24	Ezekiel 22, 23.	1 Peter 1.	24	Habakkuk 1, 2, 3.	Revelation 15.
25	Ezekiel 24, 25, 26.	1 Peter 2.	25	Zephaniah 1, 2, 3.	Revelation 16.
26	Ezekiel 27, 28, 29.	1 Peter 3.	26	Haggai 1, 2.	Revelation 17.
27	Ezekiel 30, 31, 32.	1 Peter 4.	27	Zechariah 1, 2, 3, 4.	Revelation 18.
28	Ezekiel 33, 34.	1 Peter 5.	28	Zechariah 5, 6, 7, 8.	Revelation 19.
29	Ezeki 1 35, 36.	2 Peter 1.	29	Zechariah 9, 10, 11, 12.	Revelation 20.
30	Ezekiel 37, 38, 39.	2 Peter 2.	30	Zechariah 13, 14.	Revelation 21.
			31	Malachi 1, 2, 3, 4.	Revelation 22.

NOTE.—On Sundays review the reading of the previous week.

591

THE PARABLES OF JESUS CHRIST

SUBJECT.	MATTHEW	MARK.	LUKE.	THE LESSON.
IN ONE GOSPEL.				
The Tares..........................	13:24-30			Good and evil in life and judgment.
The Treasure Hid in the Field........	13:44			Value of the Gospel.
The Pearl of Great Price.............	13:45,46			Christian seeking salvation.
The Draw-net	13:47,48			Visible Church of Christ.
The Wicked Servant..................	18:23-34			Danger of ingratitude.
The Laborers in the Vineyard........	20:1-16			Call at various epochs.
The Two Sons.......................	21:28-30			Insincerity and repentance.
The Man Without a Wedding Garment.	22:2-14			Need of righteousness.
The Wise and Foolish Virgins........	25:1-13			Watchful and careless profession.
The Talents	25:14-30			Use of advantages.
The Judgment.......................	25:31-46			Final separation of good and bad.
The Secret Growth of Seed..........		4:26-29		Gradual growth of religion.
The Porter Commanded to Watch.....		13:34		Watchfulness.
The Two Debtors....................			7:41,42	Gratitude for pardon.
The Good Samaritan.................			10:30-35	Compassion to suffering.
The Persistent Friend................			11:5-8	Perseverance in prayer.
The Foolish Rich Man...............			12:16-21	Worldly-mindedness.
The Servants Watching..............			12:35-40	Vigilance toward Second Advent.
The Faithful and Wise Steward.......			12:42-48	Conscientiousness in trust.
The Barren Fig Tree.................			13:6-9	Unprofitableness under grace.
The Great Supper, and Excuses.......			14:16-24	Universality of the Divine call.
To Illustrate Counting the Cost.......			14:28-33	
The Lost Coin			15:8-10	Joy over penitence.
The Prodigal Son....................			15:11-32	Fatherly love to penitent son.
The Unjust Steward.................			16:1-8	Preparation for eternity.
The Rich Man and Lazarus...........			16:19-31	Recompense of future life.
Unprofitable Servants...............			17:7-10	God's claim to all our services.
The Persevering Woman and the Unjust Judge			18:2-5	Advantage of persevering prayer.
The Pharisee and the Publican.......			18:10-14	Self-righteousness and humility.
The Ten Pounds.....................			19:12-27	Diligence rewarded, sloth punished.
IN TWO GOSPELS.				
Houses Built upon a Rock and Upon the Sand...........................	7:24-27		6:47-49	Consistent and false profession.
Leaven in the Meal..................	13:33		13:20,21	Pervading influence of religion.
The Lost Sheep.....................	18:12-14		15:4-6	Joy over penitent.
IN THREE GOSPELS.				
The Light under a Bushel............	5:15	4:21	{ 8:16 { 11:33	New doctrine on old prejudices.
New Cloth on an Old Garment........	9:16	2:21	5:36	New spirit in unregenerate heart.
New Wine in Old Bottles.............	9:17	2:22	5:37,38	Hearers divided into classes.
The Sower.........................	13:3-8	4:3-8	8:5-8	Spread of Gospel.
The Mustard Seed	13:31,32	4:30-32	13:18,19	Rejection of Christ by the Jews.
The Wicked Husbandmen.............	21:33-41	12:1-9	20:9-16	Indications of Second Advent.
Fig Tree the Sign of Spring..........	24:32,33	13:28,29	21:29-32	

SYMBOLIC WORDS EXPLAINED

Texts.	Symbols.	Meanings.
Jeremiah 3 : 8, 9; 5 : 7.	Adultery.	Idolatry.
Revelation 1 : 20; 2 : 1, etc.	Angel.	Messenger, hence minister.
Psalm 10 : 15.	Arm.	Power.
Ezra 30 : 21, etc.		
Job 6 : 4.	Arrows.	Judgments.
Revelation 17 : 18.	Babylon.	Rome.
Daniel 7 : 17.	Beast.	A tyrannical heathen monarch.
Job 30 : 30.	Black.	Affliction—anguish.
Joel 2 : 6.		
Isaiah 29 : 18.	Blindness.	Ignorance.
Romans 11 : 25.		
Isaiah 34 : 3.	Blood.	Slaughter—depth.
Ezekiel 32 : 6.		
Job 18 : 15.	Brimstone.	Desolation—torments.
Revelation 14 : 10.		
Revelation 21 : 9.	Bride.	The church of God.
John 3 : 29.	Bridegroom.	Christ, wedded to his church.
Psalm 22 : 12, etc.	Bulls.	Violent enemies.
Revelation 2 : 10.	Candlesticks.	Church.
Psalm 68 : 18, etc.	Chariots.	Heavenly hosts.
James 1 : 12.	Crown.	Victory—reward.
Revelation 2 : 10.		
Psalm 23 : 5.	Cup.	Divine blessings.
Isaiah 51 : 17.		Divine judgments.
Jeremiah 23 : 1.	Darkness.	Misery—adversity—ignorance.
Amos 4 : 13.		
Romans 13 : 12.		
Isaiah 34 : 8, etc.	Day.	An indefinite time—a prophetic year —gospel period.
Revelation 2 : 10, etc.		
1 Thessalonians 5 : 5, etc.		
Matthew 15 : 26.	Dogs.	Gentiles — impure persons — perse-cutors.
Revelation 21 : 8.		
Psalm 22 : 16.		
1 Corinthians 16 : 9.	Door.	An opening.
Revelation 12 : 9.	Dragon.	Satan.
Isaiah 29 : 9.	Drunkenness.	Effects of divine judgments.
Revelation 6 : 12, etc.	Earthquakes.	Revolutions.
Proverbs 15 : 3, etc.	Eyes.	Knowledge.
Psalm 36 : 16, etc.	Face.	The Divine favor.
Jeremiah 5 : 28.	Fat.	Abundance.
Isaiah 42 : 25, etc.	Fire.	Judgments.
Revelation 7 : 3, etc.	Forehead.	A public profession.
Jeremiah 11 : 4.	Furnace.	Affliction.
Revelation 3 : 4, etc.	Garments.	Outward appearance.
Psalm 147 : 13.	Gates.	Power—security.
Job 12 : 18.	Girdles.	Strength.
Matthew 25 : 33.	Goats.	Wicked persons.
Ezekiel 38 : 2; 39 : 11.	Gog and Magog.	God's enemies.
Revelation 20 : 8.		
Revelation 8 : 7.	Grass.	The lower orders, opposed to trees, the higher orders.
Revelation 11 : 19.	Hail.	Divine vengeance.
Psalm 18 : 35; 73 : 23.	Hand, right.	Protection—support.

Texts.	Symbols.	Meanings.
Ezekiel 8:1.	Hand of the Lord.	Divine influence.
Joel 3:13, etc.	Harvest.	A time of destruction.
Ephesians 1:23, etc.	Head.	Rule or ruler.
Isaiah 13:33. Haggai 2:2, 21.	Heavens.	Political or ecclesiastical governments.
Zechariah 10:23.	Horse.	War and conquest.
Matthew 5:6.	Hunger and thirst.	Spiritual desires.
Revelation 5:8.	Incense.	Prayer.
Psalm 120:6. Hebrews 12:22, etc.	Jerusalem.	Church of God. The heavenly state.
Revelation 1:18.	Keys.	Power and authority.
1 Kings 15:4. Psalm 132:17.	Lamp.	A successor or offspring.
Esther 8:16. Isaiah 8:20. Ephesians 5:8, etc.	Light.	Joy—prosperity. Knowledge—bitterness.
	Moon (see Sun)	
Zechariah 4:7. Isaiah 2:2.	Mountains.	A state—Christ's church.
Romans 16:25, etc.	Mystery.	Not a thing unintelligible, but never before made plain.
Revelation 3:17.	Naked.	In the sinful state of nature.
Isaiah 21:12. Revelation 21:25.	Night.	Adversity—affliction—ignorance.
Isaiah 2:13.	Oaks.	Men of rank and power.
Psalm 23:5; 92:11, etc.	Oil.	Abundance—fertility—joy.
Revelation 7:5.	Palms.	Victory.
Luke 23:43. Revelation 2:7.	Paradise.	Heaven.
Psalm 18:2.	Rock.	A secure refuge.
Psalm 2:9, etc. Job 9:34, etc.	Rod.	Authority—correction.
Colossians 4:6, etc. Deuteronomy 29:23.	Salt.	Purity—barrenness.
Isaiah 51:42.	Sea in commotion.	An army.
Song of Solomon 4:12. Isaiah 29:11.	Seal.	Security—secrecy.
Genesis 3:1, etc. 2 Corinthians 11:3. Revelation 12:9.	Serpent.	The devil.
John 10:11, 16, etc.	Sheep.	Christ's disciples.
Nahum 3:18. Ezekiel 34:2, etc.	Shepherds.	Rulers, civil or ecclesiastical.
Psalm 84:9. Ephesians 6:16.	Shield.	Defence—protection.
1 Thessalonians 4:14.	Sleep.	Death.
Isaiah 1:6, etc.	Sores.	Spiritual maladies.
Numbers 24:17, etc.	Star.	A prince or ruler.
Joel 2:31, etc.	Sun, moon, and stars.	The various governors in a state.
Isaiah 34:5. Ezekiel 21:3, etc.	Sword.	War and slaughter.
Deuteronomy 28:13.	Tail.	Subjection—degradation.
Proverbs 30:14.	Teeth.	Cruelty.
Genesis 12:4, etc.	Throne.	Kingdom or government.
Jeremiah 4:31. Galatians 4:19.	Travail.	Anguish—anxiety.
Zechariah 2:1, 2.	Trees.	The great noble.
Psalm 80:8, etc.	Vine.	The Church of God.

TEXTS.	SMYBOLS.	MEANINGS.
Isaiah 5 : 1, etc.	Vineyard.	The Church of God.
Ezekiel 3 : 17.	Watchtower.	The prophets.
Psalm 69 : 1.	Waters.	Afflictions —multitudes—ordinances.
Isaiah 8 : 7, etc.; 55 : 1.		
Daniel 9 : 24.	Week.	Seven years.
Revelation 12 : 6.	Wilderness.	Afflicted state.
Isaiah 28 : 8.	Wind.	Judgments—destructive war.
Jeremiah 51 : 1.		
Isaiah 25 : 6; 55 : 1, etc.	Wine.	Spiritual blessings—Divine judgments.
Psalm 10 : 3, etc.		
Isaiah 58 : 3.	Winepress.	Slaughter.
Revelation 14 : 19.		
Psalm 17 : 8, etc.	Wings.	Protection.
Isaiah 11 : 6; 65 : 25.	Wolves.	Furious, ungodly persons.
Ezekiel 26 : 2, 3.	Woman.	City, or body politic.
Revelation 12 : 1.		The Church of Christ.
Deuteronomy 28 : 48.	Yoke.	Labor—restraint.
Matthew 10 : 29, 30.		
Lamentations 3 : 27.		

PROPHETS AND PROPHETIC UTTERANCES

THE PROPHETIC BOOKS

NAMES.	DATE.	KINGS OF JUDAH.	KINGS OF ISRAEL.	THEME.
I. Prophets of Israel:				
Jonah	783–742 B.C.	Uzziah (Azariah)	Jeroboam II	Fall of Nineveh.
Amos	760–746	Uzziah (Azariah)	Jeroboam II	Sins of Israel.
Hosea	748(?)–734	Uzziah, Jotham, Ahaz, Hezekiah	Jeroboam II. to Hoshea	Sins of Israel.
Joel	756(?)	Uzziah	Jeroboam II	Plagues upon Judah.
Isaiah	735–713	Uzziah, Jotham, Ahaz, Hezekiah	Zachariah to Hoshea	Coming of Christ—Kingdom of God.
Micah	730–	Jotham, Ahaz, Hezekiah	Hoshea	Captivity and Christ.
II. Judah:				
Nahum	664–667	Josiah		Fall of Nineveh.
Zephaniah	639–590	Josiah		Captivity of Judah.
Jeremiah	628–583	Josiah, Jehoahaz, Jehoiakim		Captivity of Judah.
Habakkuk	600–590	Jehoiachin		Chaldæan Invasion.
III. Prophets of the Captivity:		*Kings of Babylon.*		
Daniel	605–536	Nebuchadnezzar to Cyrus		Great Empires.
Ezekiel	592–570	Nebuchadnezzar		Captivity and Return.
Obadiah	586	Nebuchadnezzar		Destruction of Edom.
IV. Post-Exile prophets:				
Haggai	520	Darius I		Rebuilding of the Temple.
Zechariah	520	Darius I		New Israel.
Malachi	432 about	Artaxerxes I		Reformation and the Messiah.

Passage.	Common Version.	Modern Meaning.
Genesis 41:2.	Kine.	Heifers.
Exodus 3:5.	Shoes.	Sandals.
Exodus 3:22.	Borrow.	Ask.
Exodus 4:24.	Inn.	Lodging Place.
Exodus 5:24.	Let.	Hinder.
Exodus 5:8.	Tale.	Number.
Exodus 13:18.	Harnessed.	In ranks.
Exodus 28:40.	Bonnets.	Turbans.
Exodus 34:15.	Whoring.	Astray.
Exodus 34:26.	Seethe.	Boil.
Exodus 34:29.	Wish.	Knew.
Exodus 35:11.	Taches.	Clasps.
Exodus 37:29.	Apothecary.	Perfumer.
Exodus 39:23.	Habergeon.	Coat of mail.
Leviticus 2:1.	Meat offerings.	Wheat offerings.
Numbers 1:2.	Polls.	One by one.
Deuteronomy 11:30.	Champaign.	Plain.
Deuteronomy 16:1-4.	Coast.	Districts.
Joshua 6:9.	Rereward.	Rear.
Joshua 13:25.	Children of Ammon.	Ammonites.
Joshua 20:3.	Unwittingly.	Unintentionally.
Joshua 23:1.	Stricken in age.	Advanced in years.
Judges 3:24.	Covereth his feet.	Reposeth.
Judges 7:10.	Host.	Camp army.
Judges 7:13.	Fellow.	Comrade.
Judges 14:13.	Shirts.	Sheets.
Judges 15:4.	Foxes.	Jackals.
Judges 18:2.	Children of Dan.	Danites.
1 Samuel 1:15.	Daughter of Belial.	Worthless woman.
1 Samuel 2:5.	Seven.	Many.
1 Samuel 2:12.	Sons of Belial.	Worthless men.
1 Samuel 2:29.	Kick.	Spurn.
1 Samuel 3:18.	Every whit.	Everything.
1 Samuel 5:9.	Secret parts.	Inwardly.
1 Samuel 8:12.	Ear.	Till.
1 Samuel 13:17.	Spoilers.	Foragers.
1 Samuel 13:20.	Coultery.	Spade.
1 Samuel 17:24.	Carriage.	Baggage.
1 Samuel 17:24.	Sore.	Exceedingly.
1 Samuel 17:39.	Assayed.	Attempted.
1 Samuel 22:17.	Footman.	Guard.
1 Samuel 26:5.	Pitched.	Encamped.
1 Samuel 26:12.	Cruse.	Jug.
1 Samuel 30:13.	Agone.	Ago.
2 Samuel 3:12.	League.	Covenant.
2 Samuel 17:10.	Utterly melt.	Be dismayed.
2 Samuel 22:6.	Prevented.	Surrounded.
1 Kings 2:8.	Cursed.	Reviled.
1 Kings 3:7.	Go out or come in.	Conduct affairs.
1 Kings 4:2.	Princes.	Chief officers.
1 Kings 6:18.	Knops.	Knobs.
1 Kings 7:16.	Chapiters.	Capitals.
1 Kings 9:22.	Rulers of chariots.	Charioteers.
1 Kings 10:26.	Bestowed.	Stationed.
1 Kings 11:22.	Howbeit.	Nevertheless.
1 Kings 11:28.	Charge.	Imposts.
1 Kings 14:3.	Cracknels.	Cakes.
1 Kings 20:12, 16.	Pavilions.	Booths.
2 Kings 4:43.	Servitor.	Servant.
2 Kings 5:24.	Tower.	Secret place.
2 Kings 24:16.	Craftsmen.	Carpenters.
1 Chronicles 30:1.	Provoked.	Proved.
1 Chronicles 22:5.	Magnifical.	Magnificent.
2 Chronicles 26:14.	Habergeons.	Breastplates.
Job 1:1.	Perfect.	Sincere.
Job 1:1.	Eschewed.	Avoided.
Job 3:12.	Prevent.	Receive.
Job 9:33.	Daysman.	Umpire.
Job 41:26.	Habergeon.	Javelin.
Psalm 4:2.	Leasing.	Falsehood.
Psalm 7:10.	Pate.	Crown.
Psalm 16:10.	Soul in hell.	Body in the grave.
Psalm 44:19.	Dragons.	Serpents.
Psalm 59:10.	Prevent.	Come before, i.e., give timely aid.
Psalm 79:8.	Prevent.	Succor.
Psalm 107:3.	Minished.	Diminished.
Psalm 119:148.	Prevent.	Anticipate.
Ecclesiastes 4:4.	Travail.	Labor.
Isaiah 3:22.	Wimples.	Shawls.
Isaiah 3:22.	Crispingpins.	Purses.
Isaiah 7:23.	Silverlings.	Pieces of silver.
Isaiah 30:24.	Ear.	Till.
Isaiah 31:3.	Holpen.	Helped.
Isaiah 44:9.	Delectable.	Delightful.
Jeremiah 4:30.	Rentest thy face.	Distend thine eyes.
Jeremiah 7:33.	Fray.	Scare.
Jeremiah 10:22.	Bruit.	Rumor.
Ezekiel 13:18.	Scrupillons.	Apply cushions.
Daniel 3:21.	Hosen.	Turbans.
Zechariah 13:6.	My fellows.	United to me.
Matthew 3:12.	Fan.	Winnowing shovel.
Matthew 5:46.	Publicans.	Taxgatherers.
Matthew 6:24.	Mammon.	Riches.
Matthew 12:29.	Garnished.	Set in order.
Matthew 12:20.	Anon.	Immediately.
Matthew 13:12.	Listed.	Chose.
Mark 11:13.	Haply.	Perhaps.
Luke 2:49.	Wist.	Knew.
Luke 7:1.	Audience.	Hearing.
Luke 12:58.	Hale.	Drag.
Luke 17:9.	Trow.	Think.
Acts 1:2.	Passion.	Suffering.
Acts 7:45.	Jesus.	Joshua.
Acts 9:5.	Pricks.	Goads.
Acts 9:26.	Assayed.	Attempted.
Acts 10:42.	Quick.	Living.
Romans 1:13.	Let.	Hindered.
Romans 7:8.	Concupiscence.	Evil desires.
Romans 8:13.	Mortify.	To kill.
Romans 15:11.	Laud.	Celebrate.
1 Corinthians 10:11.	Ensamples.	Examples.
1 Corinthians 11:29.	Unworthy.	Irreverently.
1 Corinthians 11:29.	Damnation.	Condemnation.
1 Corinthians 13:1.	Charity.	Love.
2 Corinthians 1:12.	Conversation.	Behavior.
2 Corinthians 5:21.	Sin.	Sin offering.
2 Corinthians 8:1.	Do you to wit.	Make known to you.
1 Thessalonians 4:15.	Prevent.	Go up before.
Hebrews 1:1.	Divers.	Various.
Hebrews 1:3.	Person.	Substance.
Hebrews 2:11.	Sanctifieth.	Expiateth.
Hebrews 4:8.	Jesus.	Joshua.
James 3:4.	Governor listeth.	Pilot chooseth.
James 3:13.	Good conversation.	Consistent conduct.
1 Peter 2:2.	Sincere.	Unadulterated.
1 Peter 3:11.	Eschew.	Avoid.
1 Peter 3:11.	Ensue.	Pursue.
2 Peter 3:9.	Slack.	Slow.
2 Peter 3:12.	Hasting unto.	Earnestly desiring.
1 John 2:17.	Lust.	Desire.
1 John 2:20.	Unction.	Anointing.
1 John 5:6, 8, 9.	Witness.	Testimony.
Revelation 1:13.	Candlestick.	Lamps.
Revelation 21:19.	Garnished.	Adorned.

SCRIPTURAL HELPS FOR PRAYER

FOR PUBLIC PRAYER.

SUPPLICATION.

God be merciful unto us, and bless us; and cause his face to shine upon us. (Psalm 67: 1.)

Wilt thou not revive us again, that thy people may rejoice in thee? (Psalm 85: 6.)

Show us thy mercy, O Lord, and grant us thy salvation. (Psalm 85: 7.)

INTERCESSION.

Let the people praise thee, O God; let all the people praise thee. (Psalm 67: 3.)

O let the wickedness of the wicked come to an end; but establish the just. (Psalm 7: 9.)

THANKSGIVING.

O that men would praise the Lord for his goodness, and for his wonderful works to the children of men! (Psalm 107: 15.)

For thy mercy is great above the heavens, and thy truth reacheth unto the clouds. (Psalm 108: 4.)

Blessed be the name of the Lord from this time forth and for evermore. (Psalm 113: 2.)

From the rising of the sun unto the going down of the same, the Lord's name is to be praised. (Psalm 113: 3.)

Who is like unto the Lord our God, who dwelleth on high, who humbleth himself to behold the things that are in heaven and in the earth. (Psalm 113: 5, 6.)

Thanks be unto God for his unspeakable gift. (2 Corinthians 9: 15.)

In whom we have redemption through his blood, the forgiveness of sins according to the riches of his grace. (Ephesians 1: 7.)

Blessed be the God and Father of our Lord Jesus Christ, which according to his abundant mercy hath begotten us again unto a lively hope by the resurrection of Jesus Christ from the dead,

To an inheritance incorruptible, and undefiled, and that fadeth not away. (1 Peter 1: 3, 4.)

Blessed be the God and Father of our Lord Jesus Christ, who hath blessed us with all spiritual blessings in Christ. (Ephesians 1: 3.)

DEDICATION.

O Lord our God, other lords besides thee have had dominion over us; but by thee only will we make mention of thy name. (Isaiah 26: 13.)

We are thine. (Isaiah 63: 19.)

DOXOLOGY.

Now unto God and our Father be glory for ever and ever. Amen. (Philippians 4: 20.)

Salvation to our God which sitteth on the throne, and unto the Lamb. (Revelation 7: 10.)

Blessing, and glory, and wisdom, and thanksgiving, and honour, and power, and might, be unto our God for ever and ever. Amen. (Revelation 7: 12.)

FOR PRIVATE PRAYER.

ADORATION.

I will love thee, O Lord, my strength. (Psalm 18: 1.)

The Lord is my rock, and my fortress, and my deliverer; my God, my strength, in whom I will trust; my buckler, and the horn of my salvation, and my high tower. (Psalm 18: 2.)

Truly my soul waiteth upon God; from him cometh my salvation. (Psalm 62: 1.)

He only is my rock and my salvation; he is my defence, I shall not be greatly moved. (Psalm 62: 2.)

CONFESSION.

I acknowledge my transgression, and my sin is ever before me. (Psalm 51: 3.)

For I know that in me, that is in my flesh, dwelleth no good thing: for to will is present with me; but how to perform that which is good I find not. (Romans 7: 18.)

O wretched man that I am, who shall deliver me from the body of this death? (Romans 7: 24.)

Behold, I am vile; what shall I answer thee? I will lay my hand upon my mouth. (Job 40: 4.)

SUPPLICATION.

God be merciful to me, a sinner. (Luke 18: 13.)

Create in me a clean heart, O God; and renew a right spirit within me. (Psalm 51: 10.)

Have mercy upon me, O God, according to thy loving kindness: according unto the multitude of thy tender mercies, blot out my transgressions. (Psalm 51: 1.)

Remember not the sins of my youth, nor my transgressions: according to thy mercy remember thou me for thy goodness' sake, O Lord. (Psalm 25: 7.)

Cast me not away from thy presence; and take not thy holy spirit from me. (Psalm 51: 11.)

Restore unto me the joy of thy salvation; and uphold me with thy free spirit. (Psalm 51: 12.)

O Lord, open thou my lips; and my mouth shall show forth thy praise. (Psalm 51: 15.)

The sacrifices of God are a broken spirit; a broken and a contrite heart, O God, thou wilt not despise. (Psalm 51: 17.)

Hear my voice according unto thy loving kindness: O Lord, quicken me according to thy judgment. (Psalm 119: 149.)

Let my soul live, and it shall praise thee; and let thy judgments help me. (Psalm 119: 175.)

I have gone astray like a lost sheep; seek thy servant; for I do not forget thy commandments. (Psalm 119: 176.)

Search me, O God, and know my heart; try me, and know my thoughts. (Psalm 139: 23.)

Lead me in thy truth and teach me: for thou art the God of my salvation; on thee do I wait all the day. (Psalm 25: 5.)

O that thou wouldst bless me indeed, and enlarge my coast, and that thine hand might be with me, and that thou wouldst keep me from evil, that it may not grieve me! (1 Chronicles 4: 10.)

Remove far from me vanity and lies; give me neither poverty nor riches; feed me with food convenient for me. (Proverbs 30: 8.)

Lest I be full, and deny thee, and say, Who is the Lord? or lest I be poor and steal, and take the name of my God in vain. (Proverbs 30: 9.)

When a few years are come, then I shall go the way whence I shall not return. (Job 16: 22.)

Lord, make me to know mine end, and the measure of my days, what it is; that I may know how frail I am. (Psalm 39: 4.)

INTERCESSION.

Grace be with all them that love our Lord Jesus Christ in sincerity. (Ephesians 6: 24.)

Do good, O Lord, unto those that be good, and to them that are upright in their hearts. (Psalm 125: 4.)

Be thou exalted, O God, above the heavens; let thy glory be above all the earth. (Psalm 57: 11.)

THANKSGIVING.

Many, O Lord my God, are thy wonderful works which thou hast done, and thy thoughts which are to us-ward; they cannot be reckoned up in order unto thee: if I would declare and speak of them, they are more than can be numbered. (Psalm 40: 5.)

Bless the Lord, O my soul, and all that is within me, bless his holy name. (Psalm 103: 1.)

Bless the Lord, O my soul, and forget not all his benefits. (Psalm 103: 2.)

Who forgiveth all thine iniquities, who healeth all thy diseases. (Psalm 103: 3.)

Who redeemeth thy life from destruction: who crowneth thee with loving kindness and tender mercies. (Psalm 103: 4.)

All thy works shall praise thee, O Lord, and thy saints shall bless thee. (Psalm 145: 10.)

DEDICATION.

O Lord, truly I am thy servant; I am thy servant and the son of thine handmaid: thou hast loosed my bonds. (Psalm 116: 16.)

DOXOLOGY.

Now unto the King eternal, immortal, invisible, the only wise God, be honor and glory for ever and ever. Amen. (1 Timothy 1: 17.)

To God, only wise, be glory, through Jesus Christ, for ever. Amen. (Romans 16: 27.)

MIRACLES RECORDED IN THE SCRIPTURES

IN THE OLD TESTAMENT

IN EGYPT.
Aaron's rod turned to serpent. Exodus 7:10-12.
The plagues:
  Water made blood......... Exodus 7:20-25.
  Frogs.................... Exodus 8:5-14.
  Lice..................... Exodus 8:16-18.
  Flies.................... Exodus 8:20-24.
  Murrain.................. Exodus 9:3-6.
  Boils and Blains......... Exodus 9:8-11.
  Thunder and hail........ Exodus 9:22-26.
  Locusts.................. Exodus 10:12-19.
  Darkness................ Exodus 10:21-23.
  Slaying of firstborn...... Exodus 12:29-30.
Parting of Red Sea......... Exodus 14:21-31.

IN THE WILDERNESS.
Curing of waters of Marah... Exodus 15:23-25.
Sending of manna.......... Exodus 16:14-35.
Water from the rock...... Exodus 17:5-7.
Death of Nadab and Abihu.. Leviticus 10:1-2.
Burning of the congregation. Numbers 11:1-3.
Death of Korah, etc......... Numbers 16:31-35.
Budding of Aaron's rod..... Numbers 17:8.
Water at Meribah.......... Numbers 20:7-11.
The brazen serpent........ Numbers 21:8,9.
Stoppage of Jordan......... Joshua 3:14-17.

IN CANAAN.
Fall of Jericho............. Joshua 6:6-25.
Staying of sun and moon.... Joshua 10:12-14.

UNDER THE KINGS.
Death of Uzzah............. 2 Samuel 6:7.
Withering of Jeroboam's hand 1 Kings 13:4-6.

BY ELIJAH.
Staying of oil and meal...... 1 Kings 17:14-16.
Raising of widow's son...... 1 Kings 17:17-24.
Burning of the sacrifice at
  Carmel.................. 1 Kings 18:30-38.
Burning of the captains..... 2 Kings 1:10-12.
Dividing of Jordan......... 2 Kings 2:7,8.

BY ELISHA.
Dividing of Jordan......... 2 Kings 2:14.
Cure of Jericho waters...... 2 Kings 2:21,22.
Destruction of mocking chil-
  dren .... 2 Kings 2:23,24.
Supply of waters to armies.. 2 Kings 3:16-20.
Increase of widow's oil...... 2 Kings 4:2-7.
Raising Shunammite's son.. 2 Kings 4:32-37.
Healing the poison pottage.. 2 Kings 4:38-41.
Twenty loaves for 100 men... 2 Kings 4:42-44.
Cure of Naaman's leprosy... 2 Kings 5:10-27.
Making the axe swim........ 2 Kings 6:5-7.
Smiting the Syrian army.... 2 Kings 6:18-20.
Revival of the dead......... 2 Kings 13:21.

MENTIONED BY ISAIAH.
Destruction of Assyrians.... 2 Kings 19:35.
Return of sun on dial........ 2 Kings 20:9-11.

DURING THE CAPTIVITY.
Deliverance from fiery
  furnace.................. Daniel 3:19-27.
Deliverance from lions' den. Daniel 6:16-23.

MISCELLANEOUS.
Smiting of Philistines....... 1 Samuel 5:3-12.
Leprosy of Uzziah .... 2 Chronicles 26:16-21.
Deliverance of Jonah........ Jonah 2:1-10.

IN THE NEW TESTAMENT

The Miracles of Jesus

NATURE OF THE MIRACLE.	MATTHEW.	MARK.	LUKE.	JOHN.
CONTAINED IN ONE GOSPEL ONLY.				
Two blind men restored.................	9:27-31			
Healing of the Dumb Demoniac..........	9:32,33			
Tribute Money in the Mouth of a Fish....	17:24-27			
Deaf and Dumb Man Cured.............		7:31-37		
Blind Man Healed.....................		8:22-26		
Jesus Escapes Unseen from His Pursuers.			4:30	
First Miraculous Draught of Fishes......			5:1-11	
Widow of Nain's Son Raised............			7:11-17	
Woman with an Infirmity Healed........			13:10-17	
Man with Dropsy Cured................			14:1-6	
Lepers Cleansed			17:11-19	
Ear of the High Priest's Servant Restored			22:50,51	
Water Turned into Wine................				2:1-11
Nobleman's Son Healed of Fever........				4:46-54
Impotent Man at the Pool of Bethesda....				5:1-16
Man Blind from Birth Healed...........				9:1-41
Raising of Lazarus....................				11:1-46
Second Draught of Fishes..............				21:1-11

NATURE OF THE MIRACLE.	MATTHEW.	MARK.	LUKE.	JOHN.
IN TWO GOSPELS.				
Unclean Spirit Cast Out...............		1 : 23–26	4 : 33–37	
Centurion's Servant Healed.............	8 : 5–13		7 : 1–10	
Blind and Dumb Demoniac............	12 : 22		11 : 14	
Daughter of Syrophenician Woman Cured	15 : 21–28	7 : 24–30		
Four Thousand Fed....................	15 : 32–39	8 : 1–9		
Fig Tree Cursed......................	21 : 18–22	11 : 12–14		
IN THREE GOSPELS.				
Cleansing a Leper.....................	8 : 1–4	1 : 40–45	5 : 12–15	
Peter's Wife's Mother Cured...........	8 : 14, 15	1 : 30, 31	4 : 38, 39	
Tempest Stilled......................	8 : 23–27	4 : 36–41	8 : 22–25	
Devils Cast into Swine................	8 : 28–34	5 : 1–20	8 : 26–40	
Palsied Man Cured...................	9 : 1–8	2 : 3–12	5 : 18–26	
Healing Woman with the Issue of Blood..	9 : 20–22	5 : 25–34	8 : 43–48	
Jairus' Daughter Raised...............	9 : 23–25	{ 5 : 22–24 5 : 35–43	{ 8 : 41, 42 8 : 49–56	
Withered Hand Restored on the Sabbath..	12 : 10–13	3 : 1–5	6 : 6–10	
Jesus Walks on the Sea...............	14 : 22–32	6 : 47–51		6 : 16–21
Lunatic Child Healed.................	17 : 14–18	9 : 17–29	9 : 37–42	
Blind Bartimeus......................	20 : 30–34	10 : 46–52	18 : 35–43	
IN ALL GOSPELS.				
Feeding the Five Thousand.............	14 : 15–21	6 : 34–44	9 : 12–17	6 : 5–13

By or for the Apostles After the Death of Jesus.

Lame man at Temple gate healed.....	Acts 3 : 1–11	Dorcas restored to life................	Acts 9 : 36–40
Death of Ananias....................	Acts 5 : 5–11	Peter delivered from prison..........	Acts 12 : 6–11
Death of Sapphira...................	Acts 5 : 5–11	Elymas blinded......................	Acts 13 : 11
Many sick healed....................	Acts 5 : 12–16	Cripple healed at Lystra.............	Acts 14 : 8–10
Apostles delivered from prison........	Acts 5 : 19	Damsel with spirit of divination	Acts 16 : 16–19
Miracles of Stephen	Acts 6 : 8	Miracles by Paul	Acts 19 : 11
Miracles of Philip...................	Acts 8 : 6	Eutychus raised..........	Acts 20 : 8–10
Saul's blindness	Acts 9 : 3–9	Viper's bite harmless................	Acts 28 : 3–6
Ananias recovers Saul................	Acts 9 : 17	Publius' father healed................	Acts 28 : 8, 9
Peter heals Æneas...................	Acts 9 : 33–35		